Venezuela

a Lonely Planet travel survival kit

Krzysztof Dydyński

Venezuela

1st edition

Published by
Lonely Planet Publications
Head Office: PO Box 617, Hawthorn, Vic 3122, Australia
Branches: 155 Filbert St, Suite 251, Oakland, CA 94607, USA
               10 Barley Mow Passage, Chiswick, London W4 4PH, UK
               71 bis rue du Cardinal Lemoine, 75005 Paris, France

Printed by
Colorcraft Ltd, Hong Kong

Photographs by
Krzysztof Dydyński

Front cover: Juan Félix Sanchez chapel, San Rafael
Title page: Kukenán tepui, from photograph by Krzysztof Dydyński

Published
October 1994

Although the authors and publisher have tried to make the information as
accurate as possible, they accept no responsibility for any loss, injury or
inconvenience sustained by any person using this book.

National Library of Australia Cataloguing in Publication Data

Dydyński, Krzysztof.
    Venezuela – a travel survival kit.

    1st ed.
    Includes index.
    ISBN 0 86442 229 6.

    1. Venezuela – Guidebooks.
    I. Title. (Series: Lonely Planet travel survival kit)

918.704633

text & maps © Lonely Planet 1994
photos © photographers as indicated 1994
climate charts compiled from information supplied by Patrick J Tyson, © Patrick J Tyson, 1994

Krzysztof Dydyński

Krzysztof Dydyński was born and raised in Warsaw, Poland. Though he graduated in electronic engineering and became an assistant professor in the subject, he soon realised that there's more to life than microchips. In the mid-1970s he took off to Afghanistan and India and has been back to Asia several times since. In the 1980s a newly discovered passion for Latin America took him to Colombia, where he lived for over four years and travelled throughout the continent. In search of a new incarnation, he has made Australia his home and worked for Lonely Planet as an artist and designer. Apart from this guide he is the author of travel survival kits for *Poland* and *Colombia* and has contributed to other Lonely Planet books.

From the Author

Many friends, colleagues and travellers – both Venezuelans and foreigners – have kindly contributed to this book and deserve the highest praise. I would like to thank all those people for their advice, information, hospitality and much else.

Warmest thanks to Nico de Greiff, Mati Aristeguieta, Santi Pina, Juan Carlos 'El Chino' González, Raquel & Tom Evenou, Leonor & Alvaro Blanco, Kevin Healey and Danka & Tadek Sokołowski.

Special appreciation goes to Angela Melendro who not only was a great companion on the road but also provided invaluable assistance and help throughout all stages of the project.

From the Publisher

This book was edited by Steve Womersley, designed and illustrated by Ann Jeffree and proofread by Caroline Williamson, who also supervised the editorial work. Many thanks go to Jane Hart who designed the cover and to Rob Flynn, Dan Levin and Rick Barker who between them managed to tame the editor's cranky computer.

Warning & Request

Things change – prices go up, schedules change, good places go bad and bad places go bankrupt – nothing stays the same. So if you find things better or worse, recently opened or long since closed, please write and tell us and help make the next edition better.

Your letters will be used to help update future editions and, where possible, important changes will also be included in a Stop Press section in reprints.

We greatly appreciate all information that is sent to us by travellers. Back at Lonely Planet we employ a hard-working readers' letters team to sort through the many letters we receive. The best ones will be rewarded with a free copy of the next edition or another Lonely Planet guide if you prefer. We give away lots of books, but, unfortunately, not every letter/postcard receives one.

Contents

Map Legend

BOUNDARIES

International Boundary
State Boundary
Marine Park Boundary

ROUTES

Freeway
Highway
Major Road
Unsealed Road or Track
City Road
City Street
Railway
Underground Railway
Walking Track
Walking Tour
Ferry Route
Cable Car or Chairlift

AREA FEATURES

Park, Gardens
National Park
Built-Up Area
Pedestrian Mall
Market
Cemetery
Reef
Beach or Desert
Rocks

HYDROGRAPHIC FEATURES

Coastline
River, Creek
Intermittent River or Creek
Lake, Intermittent Lake
Canal
Swamp

SYMBOLS

✪ CAPITAL		National Capital
◉ Capital		State Capital
◍ CITY		Major City
● City		City
● Town		Town
● Village		Village
■		Place to Stay
▼		Place to Eat
�		Pub, Bar
✉	☎	Post Office, Telephone
❶	⊝	Tourist Information, Bank
◒	℗	Transport, Parking
⛫	⌂	Museum, Youth Hostel
⊞	⚲	Caravan Park, Camping Ground
† ➡ †		Church, Cathedral
⚹	✡	Mosque, Synagogue
⊥	⚏	Buddhist Temple, Hindu Temple

✚	★	Hospital, Police Station
✈	✝	Airport, Airfield
▣	✿	Swimming Pool, Gardens
❖	🐘	Shopping Centre, Zoo
←	⛽	One Way Street, Petrol Station
	∴	Archaeological Site or Ruins
🏛	▲	Casa, Monument
▤	⌒	Castle, Cave
▲	※	Mountain or Hill, Lookout
🛆	✕	Lighthouse, Shipwreck
)(	♂	Pass, Spring
🦩		Hato (ranch)
		Ancient or City Wall
		Rapids, Waterfalls
		Cliff or Escarpment, Tunnel
	Ⓜ	Metro Station
		Railway Station

Note: not all symbols displayed above appear in this book

Introduction

Venezuela's modern history has been strongly influenced by oil money which has turned the country into one of the most industrialised and wealthy nations on the continent. As a result, today Venezuela has perhaps the best road network in South America, spectacular 21st-century architecture (of which New York or Sydney wouldn't be ashamed), and a good Western-standard travel infrastructure.

Yet deep in the countryside, people continue to live the traditional way of life as if the 20th century only existed somewhere farther down the road. There are a number of Indian groups still unconquered by encroaching civilisation, the most mysterious of which is the Yanomami, a tribe lost in time along the Venezuela-Brazil border, some of whom have never had contact with the outside world.

The variety of landscapes in Venezuela won't disappoint even the most demanding visitor. The country boasts snow-capped Andes peaks, and there's more mountain territory along the coast, where the Cordillera de la Costa rises up from the beaches to over 2500 metres. The southern part of the country is taken up by the Amazon with its legendary wilderness, but if you prefer beach life, there is some 3000 km of Caribbean coastline.

Venezuela's most unusual natural feature is the *tepuis*, the flat-topped mountains with vertical flanks which loom a thousand metres above rolling savannas. There are about a hundred tepuis scattered around south-eastern Venezuela. Noted for their moonscape and peculiar endemic plantlife, they continue to fascinate explorers and botanists. From one of these tepuis spills the Salto Angel (Angel Falls), the highest waterfall in the world and possibly the most famous tourist sight in the country.

To sum up, Venezuela is a curious hybrid of a Western-style civilisation – it's the most Yankeefied country in South America – and a very traditional world contained within a beautiful natural setting. You can travel smoothly, enjoying Western comfort, yet experience a kaleidoscope of sceneries and traditional cultures.

In practical terms, it's a relatively safe and friendly country, with fairly inexpensive domestic bus and air transport. Venezuela also has the cheapest air links with both Europe and the USA, thus being a natural gateway to the continent. Don't treat it, however, as a bridge only; give yourself some time to discover this land – it's worth it.

Facts about the Country

HISTORY

The Pre-Columbian Period

Radiocarbon dating of archaeological samples has shown that the first people arrived in what is now Venezuela somewhere around the 14th millennium BC. The oldest examples have been excavated in El Jobo.

Primitive nomadic groups' cultures evolved from that time on, using rough stone for tools and weapons for hunting. Around the 5th millennium BC, bone and marine shells also came into use. Pottery only began to appear in the 1st millennium BC. Around the same time agriculture began, and this slowly led to the establishment of sedentary settlements. From this stage on, separate groups began to evolve into distinctive cultures.

Another effect of this more settled way of life was an increase in population growth. It's estimated that by the time of the Spanish Conquest about half a million Indians inhabited the region which is now Venezuela. There were isolated tribes of various ethnic backgrounds, belonging to three main linguistic families: Carib, Arawak and Chibcha.

The warlike Carib tribes inhabited the central and eastern coast, living off fishing and shifting agriculture. Various Arawak groups were scattered over a large area of western Llanos and north up to the coast. They lived off hunting and food-gathering, and only occasionally practised farming.

The Timote-Cuica, members of the Chibcha linguistic family (the same family to which the Muisca and Tayrona of Colombia belonged) were the most advanced of Venezuela's pre-Hispanic societies. They chose the Andes as their home, where they founded settlements linked by a maze of trails. They practised fairly advanced agricultural techniques, including irrigation and terracing.

Venezuela's pre-Hispanic cultures didn't reach the level of architectural or artistic development of the great civilisations of, say, the Maya or Inca. They didn't leave behind any significant artefacts, save for some pottery and other simple objects found during excavations.

Petroglyphs (drawings or carvings on rock), which have been discovered throughout the country, are possibly the most remarkable testimony to the culture of the indigenous people. However, when exactly they were done and by whom remains a mystery.

Las Amazonas, by Levinus Hulsius

The Spanish Conquest

Christopher Columbus was the first European to set foot on Venezuelan soil. This was the only part of the South American mainland Columbus landed on.

In 1498, on his third trip to the New World, he landed at the eastern tip of Península de Paria opposite Trinidad. At first he thought he had discovered yet another island, but continuing along the coast he found the wide mouth of the voluminous Río Orinoco (the Orinoco River) – sufficient proof that he had found something much more than an island. Astonished with his discovery, he wrote in his diary: 'Never have I read or heard of so

10

much sweet water within a salt ocean', and named the gulf 'El Mar Dulce', or the Sweet Sea. Today it is called the Golfo de Paria.

A year later another explorer, Alonso de Ojeda, most likely accompanied by the Italian Amerigo Vespucci, sailed up to the Península de la Guajira, at the western extremity of present-day Venezuela. After entering Lago Maracaibo the Spaniards saw the local Indians living in rustic, thatched houses on stilts above the water. Sarcastically, they called the land 'Venezuela' (literally 'Little Venice'), as the settlement was obviously far from the opulence of the Italian city they knew.

The first Spanish settlement on Venezuelan soil, Nueva Cádiz, was established on the small island of Cubagua just south of Isla de Margarita in about 1500 (although it was not until 1519 that it was granted a formal act of foundation). The town swiftly developed into a busy port engaged in pearl harvesting. However, in 1541, it was completely destroyed by an earthquake and tidal wave. The earliest town still in existence, Cumaná, on the north-east coast, dates from 1521.

Officially, Venezuela was ruled by Spain from Santo Domingo (Hispaniola, today the Dominican Republic) until 1717, when it fell under the administration of the newly created Viceroyalty of Nueva Granada with its capital in Bogotá. It remained so until independence. In practice, however, the region was allowed a large degree of autonomy. It was, after all, such an unimportant, sparsely populated backwater, with an uninviting steamy climate, that the Spaniards gave it low priority, focusing instead on Colombia, Peru and Bolivia, which were abundant in gold and silver. In many ways, Venezuela remained a backwater until the oil boom.

The early European settlers went panning for gold, but soon abandoned their fruitless search in favour of agriculture (which relied on Indian slave labour) along the coast and in the central highlands. It was another 150 years before they began to spread out and settle Los Llanos and the area around Lago Maracaibo in the north-west.

Colombus discovers the New World,
by anonymous Italian (1493)

Independence Wars

Apart from three brief rebellions against colonial rule between 1749 and 1797, Venezuela had a relatively uneventful history for 300 years after the arrival of the Europeans.

All this changed at the beginning of the 19th century when Venezuela gave to Latin America its greatest ever hero, Simón Bolívar. 'El Libertador', as he is commonly known, together with his most able lieutenant, Antonio José de Sucre, was responsible for ending colonial rule all the way to the Argentinian border. Every Spanish American town has at least one plaza or street named after one or the other of these generals, and there are innumerable museums containing memorabilia of both. In Venezuela itself, statues of Bolívar are everywhere, even more so than were Lenin busts in the Soviet Union under communism.

The revolutionary flame was lit by Francisco de Miranda in 1806, but his efforts at setting up an independent administration at Caracas came to an end when he was handed over to the Spanish by his fellow conspirators. The Spanish shipped him to Spain and he died shortly afterwards in a Cádiz jail.

Leadership of the revolution was taken over by Bolívar. After unsuccessful attempts

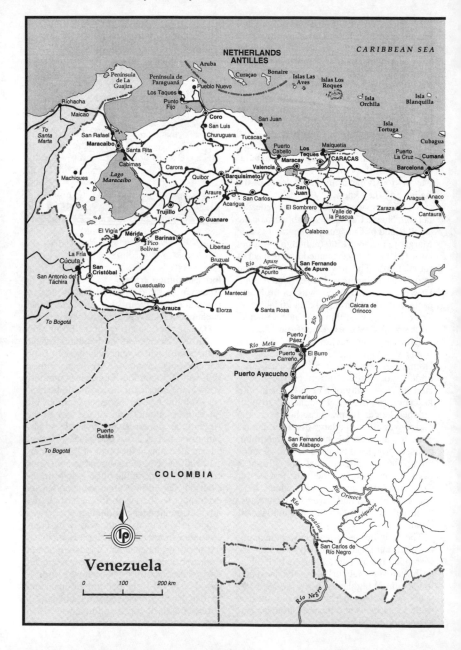

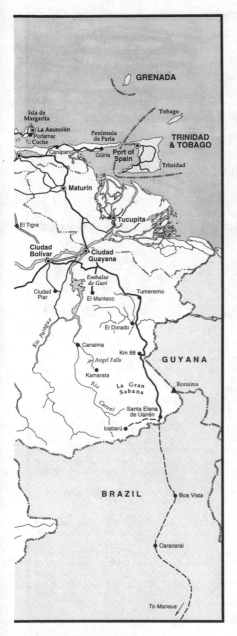

to defeat the Spaniards at home, he withdrew to Colombia, then to Jamaica until the opportune moment came in 1817.

At the time, events in Europe were in Bolívar's favour. The Napoleonic Wars had ended and Bolívar's agent in London was able to raise money and arms and to recruit over 5000 British veterans of the Peninsular War who were being demobbed from the armies which had been raised to fight Napoleon. With this force of British mercenaries and an army of horsemen from Los Llanos, Bolívar marched over the Andes and defeated the Spanish at the battles of Pantano de Vargas and Boyacá, thus bringing independence to Colombia in August 1819.

Four months later in Angostura (present-day Ciudad Bolívar), a congress was held which proclaimed Gran Colombia, a new state unifying Colombia, Venezuela and Ecuador (though the last two were still under Spanish rule).

The liberation of Venezuela was completed with Bolívar's victory over the Spanish forces at Carabobo in 1821, though the Spanish royalists continued to put up a desultory rearguard fight from Puerto Cabello for another two years. With these victories under their belts, Bolívar and Sucre went on to liberate Ecuador, Peru and Bolivia, which they accomplished by the end of 1824.

Although both economically and demographically Venezuela was the least important of the areas which made up Gran Colombia, it bore the brunt of the fighting. Not only did Venezuelan patriots fight on their own territory, they also fought in the armies which Bolívar led into Colombia and down the Pacific coast. It is estimated that over a quarter of the population died in these wars.

Gran Colombia managed to exist for only 10 years before it split into three separate countries. Bolívar's dream of a unified republic fell apart even before he died in 1830.

The Post-Independence Period

Venezuela's post-independence period was

Simón Bolívar

'There have been three great fools in history: Jesus, Don Quixote and I' – this is how Bolívar summed up his life shortly before he died. The man who brought independence from Spain to the whole north-west of South America – today's Venezuela, Colombia, Panama, Ecuador, Peru and Bolivia – died abandoned, lonely and poor.

Ironically, the house in which he died had been offered to him by a Spaniard, Joaquín de Mier. It was de Mier, too, who donated one of his shirts to dress the dead body, as there had been none among Bolívar's possessions. The funeral, the coffin and the tomb were financed by a collection taken up by local citizens.

The Bolívar family came to the New World from Spain in 1557. They first settled in Santo Domingo, but in 1589 moved to Venezuela, where they were granted a hacienda in San Mateo, near Caracas. The family was well off and steadily extended its possessions. One of the descendants, Juan Vicente Bolívar, acquired a town house in Caracas. He was 47 years old when, in 1773, he married 15-year-old María de la Concepción Palacios y Blanco. They had four children; the second child, born on 24 July 1783, was named Simón.

Juan Vicente died in 1786 and María six years later. The boy was brought up by his uncle, Carlos, and was given a tutor, Simón Rodríguez, an open-minded teacher who – as it turned out – had a strong influence on his pupil.

In 1799 Bolívar left for Spain and France to continue his education. After having mastered French, he turned to that country's literature. The political views of Voltaire and Rousseau – his favourite authors – were influential.

In 1802, he married his Spanish bride, María Teresa Rodríguez de Toro, and not long after the young couple sailed to Caracas. The marriage lasted only eight months; María Teresa died of yellow fever. This marked a drastic shift in Bolívar's destiny. He returned to France, where he met with revolutionary political leaders, and then travelled to the USA to get a closer look at the North-American experiences. By the time he returned to Caracas (1807) he was full of revolutionary theories based on these two successful examples.

At the time, disillusion with Spanish rule was on the point of breaking out into open revolt. Francisco de Miranda, the first patriot seriously involved in the independence movement, recruited volunteers in the USA, but this operation proved to be a failure. On 19 April 1810, the Junta Suprema was installed in Caracas and on 5 July 1811 the Congress declared independence. This was only the beginning; the declaration triggered a long, bitter war, most of which was to be orchestrated by Bolívar.

His military career began under Francisco de Miranda, in Valencia in 1811. After Miranda was captured by the Spaniards in 1812, his post was taken over by Bolívar. Over the next decade, he hardly had a moment to rest; battles followed each other with astonishing frequency until 1824. Of the battles personally directed by Bolívar, 35 were won. Of these, the major strategic masterpieces were the Battle of Boyacá (7 August 1819, which secured the independence of Colombia) and the Battle of Carabobo (24 June 1821, which brought freedom to Venezuela).

Bolívar's long-awaited dream materialised: Gran Colombia, the unified state comprising Venezuela, Colombia and Ecuador came into being. He was elected president and Francisco de Paula Santander became vice-president. However, the task of putting the new-born country on its feet proved to be even more difficult than winning battles. Bolívar's glory slowly began to fade.

The main bone of contention was differences over the political organisation of Gran Colombia. Bolívar strongly supported a centralised republic, while Santander favoured a federal union of sovereign states. It soon became apparent that a central regime was incapable of governing such a vast territory, consisting as it did of three economically and socially different countries. Furthermore, Bolívar was off fighting for the independence of Peru and Bolivia, which meant that a large degree of power was left in the hands of Santander. The young state began to disintegrate from the moment of its inception.

Bolívar insisted on holding the weak union together, but matters began to slip out of his hands. His impassioned and vehement speeches – for which he was widely known – no longer swayed the growing opposition. As the dangerous separatist tendencies increased, Bolívar removed Santander from office by decree, and on 27 August 1828 he assumed dictatorship. This step did more harm than good. His popularity waned, as did his circle of personal friends and supporters. Shortly after, he miraculously escaped an assassination attempt in Bogotá. Disillusioned and in bad health, he resigned the presidency in early 1830 and decided to travel to Europe. The formal disintegration of Gran Colombia was just months ahead.

After Venezuela separated from Gran Colombia, the Venezuelan Congress approved a new constitution and – irony of ironies – banned Bolívar from his homeland. A month later, Antonio José de Sucre, the closest of Bolívar's friends, was assassinated in southern Colombia. These two pieces of news reached Bolívar shortly before he was to board a ship bound for France. Depressed and ill, he accepted the invitation of Joaquín de Mier to stay at his house, Quinta de San Pedro Alejandrino, in Santa Marta. He died on 17 December 1830 of pulmonary tuberculosis. A priest, a doctor and a few officers were by his bed, but none of his close friends.

It took the Venezuelan nation 12 years to realise its debt to the man to whom it owed its freedom. In 1842, Bolívar's remains were brought from Santa Marta to Venezuela and deposited in Caracas' cathedral. In 1876, the remains were solemnly transferred to the National Pantheon, where they rest now.

El Libertador – as he was named at the beginning of the liberation campaign and is still commonly called today – was no ordinary man. An idealist with a poetic mind and visionary ideas, his goal was not only to topple Spanish rule but to create a unified America. This, of course, was impossible, nonetheless the military conquest of some five million sq km is an extraordinary accomplishment. This amateur strategist of genius won battles which still puzzle experts today. The campaign over the Andean Cordillera in the rainy season was, 100 years later, described as 'the most magnificent episode in the history of war'.

Like any other great person, Bolívar has attracted the interest of numerous scholars, politicians, writers and artists. Innumerable works detailing various aspects of Bolívar's life and battles have been written and recorded on canvas. If one could gather together all the paintings of Bolívar, the collection would easily fill any of the world's largest museums.

The first account of Bolívar was written by his friend and companion on numerous campaigns, Daniel O'Leary. The most recent important contribution to Bolívar's bibliography is Gabriel García Márquez's *The General in his Labyrinth (El General en su Laberinto)*, published in 1989. This novel, solidly based on fact, features the final months of Bolívar's life comprising his voyage from Bogotá to Santa Marta. ■

marked by serious governmental problems which continued for over a century. With a few short interludes, these were times of despotism and anarchy, with the country being ruled by a series of military dictators known as *caudillos*. It took until 1947 for the first democratic government to be elected.

The first of the caudillos, General José Antonio Páez, represented the conservative oligarchy and was in control of the country for 18 years (1830-1848). Despite his tough rule, he succeeded in establishing a certain political stability and put the weak economy on its feet. He is perhaps the most warmly remembered of the caudillos.

The period which followed was an almost uninterrupted series of civil wars resulting in political strife, only stopped by another long-lived dictator, General Guzmán Blanco. He came to power in 1870 and kept it, with few breaks, until 1888. A conservative with liberal leanings, he launched a broad programme of reforms, including a new constitution, compulsory primary education, religious freedom and a package of regulations designed to improve the economy.

Administrative Divisions

There is no doubt he resolved some of the country's crucial domestic questions and assured temporary stability. However, his despotic rule triggered wide popular opposition, and when he stepped down, the country plunged again into civil war.

Things were not going much better on the international front. In the 1840s Venezuela raised the question of its eastern border with British Guiana (modern Guyana). Based on the pre-independence borders, the Venezuelan government laid claim to as much as two-thirds of Guiana, up to the Río Essequibo. The issue required lengthy diplomatic negotiations and led to severe strains in international relations in the 1890s. It was finally settled in 1899 by an arbitration tri-

bunal which found in favour of Great Britain. Despite this, Venezuela still claims it owns the territory. To this day, all Venezuelan-produced maps have this chunk of Guyana included within their national boundaries and labelled 'Zona en Reclamación'.

Another conflict which led to serious tensions in international relations was Venezuela's failure to repay loans from Great Britain, Italy and Germany; these debts were accumulated during the irresponsible government of yet another caudillo, General Cipriano Castro (1899-1908). In response, the three countries sent their navies to blockade Venezuelan seaports in 1902.

Modern Times

The first half of the 20th century was dominated by five successive military rulers from the Andean state of Táchira, the first of whom was the incompetent Cipriano Castro. The longest-lasting of the caudillos and the most despotic was General Juan Vicente Gómez, who seized power in 1908 and didn't relinquish it until his death in 1935. Gómez phased out the parliament, crushed the opposition and, with the support of a strong army, an extensive police force and a well-developed network of spies, he monopolised power. Thanks to the discovery of oil in the 1910s, the Gómez regime was able to stabilise the country and in some ways helped make it prosperous. By the late 1920s, Venezuela became the world's largest exporter of oil. This not only contributed enormously to the recovery of the economy but also allowed it to pay off the country's entire foreign debt. Needless to say, Gómez creamed off his share of the profits and in the process amassed a personal fortune which made him one of the richest men in the country.

Little of the oil wealth filtered down to people on the street. The vast majority continued to live in poverty with little or no educational or health facilities, let alone reasonable housing. Oil money also resulted in the neglect of agriculture. Food had to be imported in increasing amounts and prices rose rapidly. When Gómez died in 1935, the people of Caracas went on a rampage,

Administrative Divisions

State	Area (sq km)	Capital
Distrito Federal	1,930	Caracas
Dependencias Federales	120	–
Estado Amazonas	177,617	Puerto Ayacucho
Estado Anzoátegui	43,300	Barcelona
Estado Apure	76,500	San Fernando
Estado Aragua	7,014	Maracay
Estado Barinas	35,200	Barinas
Estado Bolívar	240,528	Ciudad Bolívar
Estado Carabobo	4,650	Valencia
Estado Cojedes	14,800	San Carlos
Estado Delta Amacuro	40,200	Tucupita
Estado Falcón	24,800	Coro
Estado Guárico	64,986	San Juan de los Morros
Estado Lara	19,800	Barquisimeto
Estado Mérida	11,300	Mérida
Estado Miranda	7,950	Los Teques
Estado Monagas	28,900	Maturín
Estado Nueva Esparta	1,150	La Asunción
Estado Portuguesa	15,200	Guanare
Estado Sucre	11,800	Cumaná
Estado Táchira	11,100	San Cristóbal
Estado Trujillo	7,400	Trujillo
Estado Yaracuy	7,100	San Felipe
Estado Zulia	63,100	Maracaibo

burning down the houses of his relatives and supporters and even threatening to set fire to the oil installations on Lago Maracaibo.

Gómez was succeeded by his own war minister, Eleázar López Contreras, and six years later by yet another Táchiran general, Isaías Medina Angarita. Meanwhile, popular tensions rose dangerously, and exploded in 1945. Rómulo Betancourt, the founder and leader of the left-wing Acción Democrática party, took control of the government. He was supported by the majority of the people, including some junior army officers. A new constitution was adopted in 1947, and a noted novelist, Rómulo Gallegos, became president after the first democratic election in the country's history.

The pace of reforms was too fast for the old military forces. The inevitable coup took place only eight months later, and Colonel Marcos Pérez Jiménez took power. Once in control, Jiménez began ruthlessly crushing the opposition. At the same time he ploughed the oil money back into public works, industries which would help diversify the economy and, particularly, into modernising Caracas.

The spectacular buildings which mushroomed in Caracas were a poor substitute for a better standard of living and access to political power for the mass of the population. Opposition to Jiménez's rule grew, and in 1958 he was overthrown by a coalition of soldiers, sailors and civilians. Yet he retained the fortune he had built up during his rule and, like Gómez before him, ended up as one of the wealthiest citizens in the country.

Shortly after his fall, the country returned to democratic rule and an election was held in which the left-wing Betancourt was elected president. He put an end to the former dictator's accommodating policy towards foreign big business but he was careful this time not to act impetuously.

Despite opposition from both communists and right-wing factions, Betancourt enjoyed widespread popular support and succeeded in completing the constitutional five-year term in office – the first democratically elected Venezuelan president to do so. He stepped down voluntarily in 1963.

Over the next 25 years there were six changes of president and all were constitutionally elected. They were: Raúl Leoni of the Acción Democrática (1964-69); Rafael Caldera of the Copei or Christian Democrat Party (1969-74); Carlos Andrés Pérez of the Acción Democrática (1974-79); Luis Herrera Campins of the Copei (1979-84); Jaime Lusinchi of the Acción Democrática (1984-89); and Pérez, elected for the second time in December 1988.

Presidents are elected every five years in December and take office in February of the subsequent year. The years given in brackets refer to the actual presidency periods.

Oil has been the most influential factor in Venezuela's politics. Presidents Leoni and Caldera had relatively easy terms, since oil money flowed into the country and this was

Presidents of Venezuela in the 20th Century

Cipriano Castro	1899-1908	Wolfgang Larrazábal	1958
Juan Vicente Gómez	1908-29	Rómulo Betancourt	1959-64
Juan Bautista Pérez	1929-31	Raúl Leoni	1964-69
Juan Vicente Gómez	1931-35	Rafael Caldera	1969-74
Eleázar López Contreras	1935-41	Carlos Andrés Pérez	1974-79
Isaías Medina Angarita	1941-45	Luis Herrera Campins	1979-84
Rómulo Betancourt	1945-47	Jaime Lusinchi	1984-89
Rómulo Gallegos	1947-48	Carlos Andrés Pérez	1989-93
Carlos Delgado Chalbaud	1948-50	Ramón J Velásquez	1993-94
Germán Suárez Flamerich	1950-52	Rafael Caldera	1994-
Marcos Pérez Jiménez	1952-58		

generally enough to quell social unrest. Yet not much was done during that period to solve the problems of the less affluent.

During his first term in office, President Pérez witnessed the oil bonanza. Not only did the production of oil rise but, more importantly, the price quadrupled overnight following the Arab-Israeli war. Pérez nationalised the iron ore and oil industries and went on a spending spree. Imported luxury goods crammed the shops and the nation believed El Dorado had materialised.

In the late 1970s the growing international recession and oil glut undermined Venezuela's economic stability. Oil revenue declined. Unemployment and inflation rose and popular discontent increased.

Presidents Herrera and Lusinchi managed to sneak unscathed through their terms, but Pérez was not so lucky. The 1988 drop in world oil prices cut the country's revenue in half, and put into serious doubt Venezuela's ability to pay off its foreign debt.

A package of austerity measures introduced by the government in February 1989 triggered a wave of protests, culminating in three days of riots known as the 'Caracazo' and costing over 300 lives.

This violent confrontation arose just three weeks after Pérez took office and his popularity thus began to decline right from the start of his term. Further measures (basically consisting of price increases) immediately spurred protests, mostly beginning in the universities and frequently escalating into riots. Disturbances continued intermittently over the next three years.

On 4 February 1992, a faction of mid-rank military officers led by Hugo Chávez Frías attempted a coup d'état. This was a shock to most Venezuelans. The president escaped from the Palacio de Miraflores (Presidential Palace) minutes before the rebel tanks broke in. There was shooting throughout Caracas, and over 20 lives were lost. Eventually the government regained control. Chávez was sentenced to a long term in prison.

On 27 November 1992 came another attempt to seize power, led by junior officers of the air force. The air battle over Caracas,

with war planes flying between the skyscrapers, gave the attempted coup a cinematic, if not apocalyptic, dimension. The Palacio de Miraflores was bombed, and partially destroyed. The army was called on again to defend the president, which it dutifully did. This time over 100 people lost their lives. About a hundred of those involved in the coup were judged by a War Council created by the president himself. They were sentenced to 15 to 25 years in prison; however, the Supreme Court objected on the grounds that the trial had been unconstitutional.

Both coups were launched under grandiloquent patriotic slogans: 'rescuing the country', 'continuation of Bolívar's ideals' and the like. Both failed as the army leadership gave their support to the president. But will they be so loyal next time? The army is increasingly divided and disillusioned with the economic stalemate and the consequent reduction of its income. The two attempts have left a clear message: despite 35 years of democracy, the army is ready to take centre stage at any time.

Bolívar once referred to Quito as a monastery, Bogotá as a university and Caracas as a barracks. Some 170 years on, this remark is still relevant.

In 1992 a noted journalist revealed that the president had been involved in shady financial operations in 1989. According to the allegations, Pérez had taken 250 million bolívares from a secret defence account, changed the money to US dollars at a favourable government rate and then sold the dollars at the market price – making some US$11 million in the process.

The Supreme Court was requested to examine the issue, and on 20 May 1993 it declared there was enough evidence to charge the president. Pérez was suspended from his duties and Ramón J Velásquez was appointed to serve as the interim president for the last eight months of the statutory Pérez term.

Meanwhile, another corruption scandal emerged concerning another ex-president, Jaime Lusinchi; the inquiry into this matter was, at the time of writing, still under way.

These two investigations show that Venezuela is still a democratic country. On a continent where the political trial of a president was until recently a rare occurrence, this is an optimistic sign. Nevertheless, the country is in its deepest political crisis since 1958.

Recent Developments

The 1993 elections were held in a nervous and uncertain atmosphere. The neck-and-neck race was eventually won by Rafael Caldera, the former president (1969-74), who captured 28% of the vote. Caldera, now 77 years of age, no longer represents the Copei, the party he founded almost 50 years ago. He ran as an independent backed by a coalition of 16 small parties, known as the Convergencia Nacional.

Andrés Velásquez, of the union-based Causa R, the Radical Cause Party, came second by a narrow margin, winning 26% of the vote. Interestingly, the candidates put forward by the two traditional parties came third and fourth: Oswaldo Álvarez Paz of Copei won 22% of the vote, and Claudio Fermín of the Acción Democrática took only 20% of the vote. This is a significant change in the country's politics.

Meanwhile, the economy continues to suffer severe difficulties. In mid-January 1994, Venezuela's second largest bank, Banco Latino, collapsed and had to be rescued by a government takeover at a cost of some US$2 billion. Half a dozen other banks asked for financial assistance from the government. Panic-stricken depositors rushed to withdraw their money so that they could locate it more securely, in many cases overseas. Inflation is growing and foreign-currency reserves are melting.

In the hope of rescuing the economy, President Caldera suspended economic rights by decree only three weeks after taking office. The state of emergency gave the government the power (normally reserved for Congress) to intervene in any area of economic activity, including price controls.

In an attempt to pacify the armed forces, Caldera pardoned Hugo Chávez and other leaders of the 1992 military uprisings in March 1994, while the sentences of the other officers involved in the attempted coups were shortened. However, on his release, Chávez stated that he would be seeking to gain political power, and hasn't ruled out the possibility of another coup d'état.

Venezuela's economic and political prospects are uncertain and likely to remain so for some time.

GOVERNMENT & ADMINISTRATION

Venezuela is a federal republic. The president is elected by direct vote for a five-year term and cannot be re-elected for two consecutive terms. The president is the head of state and of the armed forces.

The National Congress is made up of two houses, the 47-seat Senate and the 199-seat Chamber of Deputies. The members of Congress are elected at federal and state elections, simultaneously with the presidential elections, and also for periods of five years. Voting is compulsory for citizens over 18 years of age.

There are a number of political parties. Until recently, the core was formed by the two traditional movements, the Acción Democrática (AD) and Partido Social Cristiano (Copei). For 30 years, up to the 1993 elections, Venezuelan presidents were always members of one of these two parties.

Venezuela is a member of the United Nations (UN), Organisation of American States (OAS), Latin American Integration Association (LAIA), Organisation of Petro-

leum Exporting Countries (OPEC), the Andean Group and the Grupo de los Tres (G3).

The Venezuelan flag, adopted in 1811, has three horizontal stripes of equal width: from top to bottom, yellow, blue, and red. There's an arc of seven white stars on the blue portion, representing the seven original provinces of Venezuela in 1811.

The country is divided into 22 states and the federal district of Caracas. The islands of Isla de Margarita, Coche and Cubagua collectively form a state on their own, Nueva Esparta; the remaining 72 islands are all federal dependencies.

GEOGRAPHY

With an area of 916,445 sq km, Venezuela is South America's sixth largest country. It's bigger than the UK and France combined, or much the same as Texas and Oklahoma put together. About eight Venezuelas would fit on the Australian continent. Stretching some 1500 km east to west and 1300 km north to south, it occupies the northernmost extremity of South America. Its neighbours are Colombia to the west, Brazil to the south and Guyana to the east.

In the north, Venezuela is bordered by some 3000 km of coastline, of which about

Geographical Regions

RÍO ORINOCO

The Río Orinoco, at about 2150 km in length, is South America's third longest river (after the Amazon and La Plata), and drains an area of roughly one million sq km of Venezuela and Colombia. Its entire course, from the source to the mouth, lies in Venezuela. Its major left-bank tributaries are Río Apure, Río Arauca, Río Meta, and Río Vichada, while the main right bank tributaries include Río Caroní and Río Caura.

The Orinoco is also the third most voluminous river on the continent. Its flow and discharge largely depends on the season. The difference between the low and high water levels (in March and August, respectively) can exceed 15 metres.

The river carries about 50 billion tons of sediments annually and, consequently, its delta spreads out into the Atlantic. The delta consists of a maze of natural channels which cut through a predominantly marshy land. The Orinoco Delta covers an area of about 25,000 sq km, which is not much less than the total size of Belgium. There are more than 50 river mouths, distributed along 400 km of the Atlantic coast.

One of these mouths, the outlet of Caño Mánamo, was found by Christopher Columbus in 1498, shortly after he landed at the tip of the Paria Peninsula, opposite Trinidad. Accordingly, the Orinoco was the first major river discovered in the New World by a European. From that moment on, the river began to draw in adventurers and explorers, mostly because they supposed it was the gateway to the unspecified but legendary wealth of El Dorado.

Diego de Ordaz launched an expedition in 1531, and sailed upstream as far as the Raudales de Atures (near present-day Puerto Ayacucho), but the rapids effectively defended the river's upper course from penetration.

Alexander von Humboldt managed to explore some of the upper reaches of the Orinoco in 1800. His major goal was the intriguing Brazo Casiquiare, discovered earlier by missionaries. The Casiquiare is a 220-km-long natural channel which links the Orinoco with the Río Negro. It thus spans the two vast fluvial systems, of the Orinoco and the Amazon, and is possibly the only phenomenon of its kind in the world. Even more unusual is the apparently paradoxical fact that the Casiquiare generously sends a portion of the Orinoco waters (roughly between 20% and 35%, depending on the season) down the Río Negro and down to the Amazon; the point is that the way via the Orinoco is less than half as far as the roundabout route through the Amazon.

The uppermost reaches of the Orinoco were rarely seen by explorers. This has always been an inaccessible land, and a home to the mysterious Yanomami tribe, who have not been particularly open to outsiders. Actually, it wasn't until 1951 that the exact source of the Orinoco was determined, when a joint French-Venezuelan expedition found the 70-metre-high cliff of the Cerro Delgado Chalbaud (at an altitude of 1047 metres), close to the Brazilian border, where the river originates. ■

Viviendas de los aborigines del Delta del Orinoco (Indian dwellings of the Orinoco Delta), Segun Grabado del Viaje de Raleigh de Levinus Hulsius, Nuremberg (1599)

half is beaches. Just south of the coast looms a 500-km-long mountain chain, the Cordillera de la Costa, with a number of peaks exceeding 2000 metres. This is a structural continuation of the Andes, separated from the main Andean range by wide lowlands. The coastal mountain chain rolls southward into a vast area of plains known as Los Llanos, which stretches as far as the Río Orinoco and the Río Meta. Los Llanos occupies a third of the national territory.

The land south of the Orinoco, known as Guayana (which is roughly half of the country's area) can be broadly divided into two regions. To the south-west is a chunk of the Amazon, thick tropical forest, partly inaccessible. To the north-east lies an extensive plateau of open savanna, the Guayana Highlands. It's here that the majority of tepuis are located. These gigantic mesas (table mountains), with vertical walls and flat tops, are all that's left of the upper layer of a plateau which gradually eroded over millions of years. They rise up to 1000 metres above the surrounding countryside, but reach nearly 3000 metres above sea level.

The north-western part of Venezuela is another area of geographical contrasts. Here lies the Sierra Nevada de Mérida, the northern end of the Andean chain. The Sierra is Venezuela's highest mountain range, and its highest point, at 5007 metres, is the snow-capped Pico Bolívar. North of the Andes is the marshy lowland basin around the shallow and muddy Lago Maracaibo. At 13,500 sq km (160 km long and 120 km wide) it's the largest lake in South America and is linked to the Caribbean Sea by a narrow strait. The lake is the main oil-producing area of the country. North-east of the lake, near the town of Coro, is Venezuela's sole desert, the Médanos de Coro.

The 2150-km-long Río Orinoco is by far the longest river in the country. The second longest is the Río Caroní (640 km), a tributary of the Orinoco.

Venezuela possesses a number of islands scattered around the Caribbean Sea (off the country's northern coast). The largest of these is Isla de Margarita. Other islands and archipelagos of importance include Las Aves, Los Roques, La Orchila, La Tortuga and Blanquilla.

CLIMATE

Temperatures are fairly constant throughout the year. They do, however, vary with altitude, dropping about 6°C with every 1000-metre increase in altitude. Since over 90% of Venezuela lies below 1000 metres, you'll experience average temperatures of about 23°C in most places. The Andean and coastal mountain ranges, though, will require warmer clothing and if you plan on

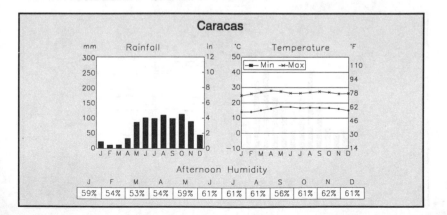

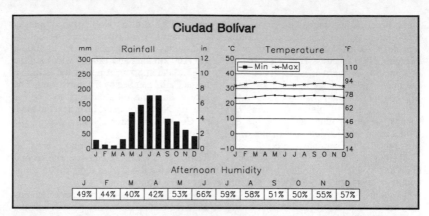

Ciudad Bolívar

Rainfall / Temperature (Min — Max)

Afternoon Humidity

J	F	M	A	M	J	J	A	S	O	N	D
49%	44%	40%	42%	53%	66%	59%	58%	51%	50%	55%	57%

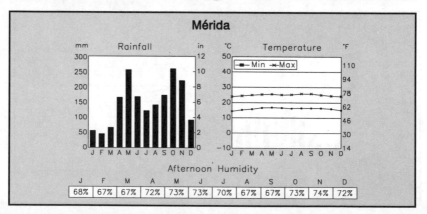

Maracaibo

Rainfall / Temperature (Min — Max)

Afternoon Humidity

J	F	M	A	M	J	J	A	S	O	N	D
58%	58%	58%	61%	64%	61%	60%	59%	61%	65%	65%	62%

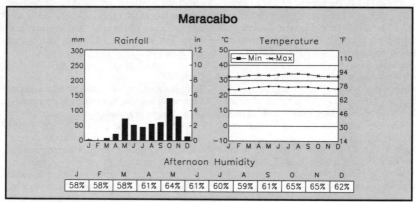

Mérida

Rainfall / Temperature (Min — Max)

Afternoon Humidity

J	F	M	A	M	J	J	A	S	O	N	D
68%	67%	67%	72%	73%	73%	70%	67%	67%	73%	74%	72%

climbing the highest peaks of the Sierra, a good jacket won't be out of place.

Venezuela has dry and wet seasons, rather than summer and winter. Broadly speaking, the dry season (known as the *verano*) goes from December to April or May while the wet season (known as the *invierno*) lasts the remaining part of the year. There are many regional variations in the amount of rain and the length of the seasons. For example, the upper reaches of the mountains receive more rainfall than the coast and can be relatively wet for most of the year, while you can visit the Coro desert on almost any day of the year and not need an umbrella. The Amazon has no distinct dry season, with annual rainfall exceeding 2000 mm distributed evenly throughout the year. See preceding page for climate charts.

FLORA & FAUNA

As a tropical country with a diverse geography, Venezuela's has a varied and abundant flora and fauna. Distinctive biohabitats have evolved in different regions, each with its own peculiar wildlife.

Other factors, common to the whole of South America, are significant. The continent never experienced the ice ages which affected North America and Western Eurasia and consequently numerous species were spared. Furthermore, a variety of species came over the Bering Strait from Eastern Asia, down through North America and across the Isthmus of Panama, which rose from the sea some 3 million years ago.

Humboldt and Bompland were among the first serious explorers dedicated to studying and recording local species, and their work was continued by subsequent expeditions. Although the frequency of these scientific explorations has increased, particularly in recent decades, the picture is still incomplete.

Birds

There are some 1250 species of birds in Venezuela (which is more than recorded in Europe and North America combined). Birds are plentiful and many are spectacular and easy to see. There are a number of regions famous for bird-watching. The largest and possibly the best is Los Llanos. Parts of the coast, especially those with a developed mangrove ecosystem (eg in Parque Nacional Morrocoy), and cloudforests (eg in Parque Nacional Henri Pittier) are also good territories for bird-watchers.

The bird world ranges from the species commonly associated with tropical forests, such as macaws (*guacamayo*), parrots (*loro*), and toucans (*tucán*), to a variety of water birds including ibis (*ibis*), herons (*garza*), pelicans (*pelícano*) and flamingos (*flamenco*). [20](The names in italics given above – in the singular – as well as in the remaining part of this section are the common local names.)

The hummingbird (*colibrí*) is one of the most fascinating birds. This colourful little 'helicopter' beats its wings up to 80 times a second as it hovers, producing a characteristic hum, which is where its name comes from.

The famous Andean condor (*cóndor*) was almost wiped out in Venezuela, but recently some specimens were brought from abroad and released in the Mérida region.

The oilbird (*guácharo*), a species of nocturnal, fruit-eating bird, is the only one of its kind in the world. It inhabits dozens of Venezuelan caves. See the Cueva del Guácharo section for details.

The *turpial*, noted for its magnificent yellow, white and black plumage, is the national bird.

Mammals

With some 250 species recorded in Venezuela, mammals are pretty well represented. One of the most intriguing, due to both its mythological importance in various pre-Columbian civilisations and its peculiar beauty, is the jaguar (*tigre*), the largest cat in the New World. Today it's almost extinct and hard to spot. What does abound is the capybara (*chigüire*), the world's largest rodent, weighing up to 60 kg. If you are touring the outback country tracks of Los Llanos you may have to stop your car to let a family of capybara cross.

Sloths *(pereza)* invariably hang motionless from tree limbs, and can even be seen in the city parks. The specimen inhabiting Plaza Bolívar in Caracas is one of the square's main attractions; however it seems that it moved recently in search of greener pastures. Watching sloths brings to mind a video played at an extremely low speed. They're possibly even slower than turtles or koalas.

Monkeys *(mono)* are faster. There's a variety of species and they, too, sometimes seem quite comfortable in city parks (eg Parque Loefling in Ciudad Guayana).

Other mammals include the armadillo *(armadillo)*, the anteater *(oso hormiguero)*, the tapir *(danta)*, the puma *(puma)*, the ocelot *(ocelote)* and the peccary *(báquiro)*, to name just a few.

Reptiles

There are numerous species of reptile in Venezuela. Possibly the most characteristic Venezuelan reptile is the cayman *(caimán)*, or American crocodile. There are five species of cayman. They range from the common, modest-sized *baba*, to the huge *caimán del Orinoco*. The latter inhabits the rivers of the Orinoco basin and can sometimes exceed five metres in length. Its favourite diet is fish, but birds, other reptiles and mammals are a frequent diversion. Watch out: it wouldn't turn its nose up at a tourist. Unfortunately, it has been extensively hunted since the 1920s for its leather, highly valued on local and international markets, and this has put its existence in jeopardy. At present, its population is estimated at between 500 and 1000 specimens.

Another giant, the *caimán de la costa*, lives, as its name suggest, along the coast, principally in the lower reaches of the rivers emptying into the Caribbean Sea and Lago Maracaibo. It, too, can reach five to six metres from head to tail, and has an uncommon ability to live in both salt and fresh water.

As well as cayman there are snakes. These include the famous anaconda (the world's longest snake) and the boa, but perhaps the most typical and dangerous is the venomous *mapanare*, most of which inhabit Lara state. Rattlesnakes *(cascabel)* are not a welcome sight either. It's much safer to encounter the iguana *(iguana)* which, despite its alarming size, is only a large herbivorous lizard.

Insects

This is certainly the most populous wildlife group, albeit the least known and recorded. Of some 30,000 species so far discovered, the ones that are most spectacular are the butterflies. There's a great variety of them but the *morphos* are probably the highlight, both for their size (up to 15 cm wingspan), and for their electric-blue wings.

The *jején* is less attractive. It's a small gnat which infests the Gran Sabana. Its bites are desperately itchy for days.

Plants

The flora of Venezuela is every bit as varied and interesting as the fauna. Tropical forest – which still covers a quarter of the country's total area – is quite different from the temperate woodlands to which Europeans and North American are accustomed. It abounds in plant species, so one can appreciate a wide range of plant life in any particular spot.

There are also some botanical surprises above the forest, in the upper reaches of the Andes. Probably most unusual of these are the *páramos*, or the boggy highland meadows which rise from about 3300 to 4400 metres, and sometimes even higher. Páramos can only be found in limited mountainous areas of Venezuela and Ecuador and, to a larger extent, in Colombia where they are more numerous and diversified. A typical feature of the páramos is the *frailejón*, or espeletia, an amazing plant which has large, down-covered, cream-green leaves arranged in a rosette pattern. It blooms in November and December.

Still more fascinating is the flora on the tops of the tepuis, in the south-east corner of the country. Isolated from the savanna below and from other tepuis for millions of years, the plant life on top of each of these plateaus developed independently. In effect, these

Tepui plant life

biological islands have a totally distinctive flora, half of which is considered endemic and typical to only one or a group of tepuis.

The *flor de mayo*, one of several thousand species of orchid *(orquídea)*, is Venezuela's national flower. The *araguaney*, known in English as the trumpet tree, is the national tree, and is particularly spectacular at the end of the dry season when it is covered with bright yellow blossoms.

Underwater Life

Venezuela has some 3000 km of coastline sprinkled with a maze of small islands and their coral reefs, and the submarine flora and fauna is enormously rich. As soon as you dive beneath the water, you'll see multi-coloured fish, starfish, sea urchins, sea anemones, corals etc. There are many good areas for snorkellers and scuba divers. Parque Nacional Mochima and Parque Nacional Morrocoy are probably the most accessible of these.

National Parks

The growing awareness of the need for conservation of wildlife and for ecosystems as a whole has led to the formation of the national park system in Venezuela. The first nature reserve, Parque Nacional Henri Pittier, was established in 1937. It took another 15 years for the next park to be established, but after this things went more smoothly and today Venezuela has 42 national parks. Between 1989-93 alone 11 new parks appeared on the map, and several more are expected to be declared in the near future.

National parks aside, Venezuela also has an array of other nature reserves called *monumentos naturales*. These are usually smaller than the parks and are intended to protect a particular natural feature such as a lake, a mountain peak, or a cave.

The whole system of parks and other reserves covers about 15% of the country's territory. You'll find the parks' names, area and location on the National Parks map and key. The parks are listed in order of their creation.

The Instituto Nacional de Parques, commonly referred to as Inparques, is the governmental body created to run and take care of national parks and other nature reserves. Unfortunately, it seems they only have nominal control over their parks. Deforestation, contamination, hunting and fishing aren't eliminated by simply declaring an area a national park, and there's not sufficient funds or personnel to enforce the parks' laws.

Only a handful of parks have any Inparques-built tourist facilities, or *guardaparques*, the Inparques-nominated rangers. Most other parks are either wilderness or have been swiftly taken over by local private operators, who have built their own tourist facilities and charge for them what they wish.

You need a permit to visit national parks and you can get this from the central or regional Inparques offices. However, except for a few parks, you'll probably never be asked for the permit.

NATIONAL PARKS

	Parque Nacional	State	Area (sq km)*	Foundation (year)
1	Henri Pittier	Aragua/Carabobo	1078	1937
2	Sierra Nevada	Mérida/Barinas	2764	1952
3	Guatopo	Miranda/Guárico	1224	1958
4	El Ávila	Distrito Federal/Miranda	818	1958
5	Yurubí	Yaracuy	236	1960
6	Canaima	Bolívar	30,000	1962
7	Yacambú	Lara	145	1962
8	Cueva de la Quebrada El Toro	Falcón	48	1969
9	Archipiélago Los Roques	Dependencia Federal	2211	1972
10	Macarao	Distrito Federal/Miranda	150	1973
11	Mochima	Sucre/Anzoátegui	949	1973
12	Laguna de La Restinga	Nueva Esparta	188	1974
13	Médanos de Coro	Falcón	912	1974
14	Laguna de Tacarigua	Miranda	391	1974
15	Cerro El Copey	Nueva Esparta	71	1974
16	Aguaro-Guariquito	Guárico	5857	1974
17	Morrocoy	Falcón	320	1974
18	El Guácharo	Monagas	627	1975
19	Terepaima	Lara	186	1976
20	Jaua Sarisariñama	Bolívar	3300	1978
21	Serranía La Neblina	Amazonas	13,600	1978
22	Yapacana	Amazonas	3200	1978
23	Duida Marahuaca	Amazonas	2100	1978
24	Península de Paria	Sucre	375	1978
25	Perijá	Zulia	2952	1978
26	El Tamá	Táchira	1091	1978
27	San Esteban	Carabobo	435	1987
28	Sierra de San Luis	Falcón	200	1987
29	Cinaruco-Capanaparo	Apure	5843	1988
30	Guaramacal	Trujillo	210	1988
31	Dinira	Lara/Trujillo/Portuguesa	420	1988
32	Páramos Batallón-La Negra	Mérida/Táchira	952	1989
33	Chorro El Indio	Táchira	108	1989
34	Sierra La Culata	Mérida	2004	1989
35	Cerro Saroche	Lara	322	1989
36	Turuépano	Sucre	700	1991
37	Mariusa-Delta del Orinoco	Delta Amacuro	3310	1991
38	Ciénaga del Catatumbo	Zulia	2500	1991
39	Parima-Tapirapecó	Amazonas	34,200	1991
40	Tirgua	Cojedes/Yaracuy	910	1992
41	El Guache	Portuguesa/Lara	122	1992
42	Tapo-Caparo	Táchira/Mérida	1250	1993

	Monumento Natural	State	Area (sq km)*	Foundation (year)
I	Cueva del Guácharo	Monagas	2	1949
II	Morros de San Juan	Guárico	28	1949
III	María Lionza	Yaracuy	117	1960
IV	Cerro Santa Ana	Falcón	19	1972
V	Laguna de los Marites	Nueva Esparta	37	1974
VI	Las Tetas de María Guevara	Nueva Esparta	17	1974
VII	Cerros Matasiete & Guayamurí	Nueva Esparta	17	1974
VIII	Piedra del Cocuy	Amazonas	1	1978

Monumento Natural *(cont)*		State	Area (sq km)*	Foundation (year)
IX	Cerro Autana	Amazonas	1	1978
X	Morros de Macaira	Guárico	1	1978
XI	Cueva Alfredo John	Miranda	1	1978
XII	Laguna de Urao	Mérida	1	1979
XIII	La Chorrera de las González	Mérida	1	1980
XIV	Platillón	Guárico	80	1987
XV	Loma El León	Lara	73	1989
XVI	Formaciones de Tepuyes	Bolívar/Amazonas	10,698	1990
XVII	Pico Codazzi	Distrito Federal/Aragua	118	1991
XVIII	Abra Río Frío	Táchira	123	1992
XIX	Piedra La Tortuga	Amazonas	5	1992
XX	Piedra Pintada	Amazonas	8	1992

* Figures showing area are approximate

1 Henri Pittier
2 Sierra Nevada
3 Guatopo
4 El Ávila
5 Yurubí
6 Canaima
7 Yacambú
8 Cueva de la Quebrada El Toro
9 Archipiélago Los Roques
10 Macarao
11 Mochima
12 Laguna de La Restinga
13 Médanos de Coro
14 Laguna de Tacarigua
15 Cerro El Copey
16 Aguaro-Guariquito
17 Morrocoy
18 El Guácharo
19 Terepaima
20 Jaua Sarisariñama
21 Serranía La Neblina
22 Yapacana
23 Duida Marahuaca
24 Península de Paria

25 Perijá
26 El Tamá
27 San Esteban
28 Sierra de San Luis
29 Cinaruco-Capanaparo
30 Guaramacal

31 Dinira
32 Páramos Batallón-La Negra
33 Chorro El Indio
34 Sierra La Culata
35 Cerro Saroche
36 Turuépano

37 Mariusa-Delta del Orinoco
38 Ciénaga del Catatumbo
39 Parima-Tapirapecó
40 Tirgua
41 El Guache
42 Tapo-Caparo

National Parks

ECONOMY

Oil is Venezuela's main natural resource and the heart of the economy. Since its discovery in 1914, it turned Venezuela – at that stage a poor debtor nation – into just about the richest country in South America. Until 1970 Venezuela was the world's largest exporter of oil and though it was later overtaken by the Middle-Eastern oil-producing countries, its oil income expanded year after year.

As co-founder of OPEC, Venezuela was influential in the fourfold rise in oil prices introduced in 1973-74. This quadrupled Venezuela's revenue. Oil revenues peaked in 1981 with export earnings of US$19.3 billion, representing about 96% of the country's exports.

On the strength of this, Venezuela borrowed heavily from foreign banks to import almost everything other than petroleum. However, the early 1980s saw the global recession and the decline of world oil prices. Export earnings from oil fell drastically to a low of US$7.2 billion in 1986. This left the country with an unsustainable foreign debt, and forced a 1987 agreement with creditor banks to 'reschedule' some US$20 billion in repayments.

In 1988 the foreign debt was some US$35 billion, with annual interest payments equal to about 22% of annual export income. By 1993 the debt reached US$40 billion, requiring annual interest payments of US$4 billion.

The main oil deposits are in the Maracaibo basin, but other important oil reserves have been discovered and exploited on the eastern outskirts of Los Llanos (in Anzoátegui and Monagas states) and in the Orinoco Delta.

Predictably, oil has overshadowed other sectors of the economy. Agriculture, which had never been strong, was largely neglected and only a small portion of the country's territory is under cultivation. The major crops include bananas, sugarcane, maize, coffee, cacao, cotton and tobacco. Despite its long coastline, Venezuela hasn't realised the potential of the fishing industry and it accounts for only 4% of the total catch of South America. Shrimp, sardine and tuna are the most important fish, and it's only recently that technological advances in the industry have been employed in order to increase the harvest from the sea.

Oil apart, Venezuela is rich in natural resources, and though most of them are still largely underexplored and underexploited, there has been significant progress over the few past decades. Iron ore, with huge deposits found south of Ciudad Bolívar, is the most important mineral after oil. It gave birth to the creation and the subsequent expansion of Ciudad Guayana, the centre of this industry.

Other major subsoil riches are bauxite (from which aluminium ore is extracted), gold and diamonds, all in Guayana, and coal near the border with Colombia, north of Maracaibo.

Manufacturing industries have also progressed as a result of the government's policy of diversifying the economy. The motor vehicle assembly industry and the chemical, textile, footwear, paper and food industries are already well established.

Hydroelectric potential is considerable: the Guri Dam, south of Ciudad Guayana, is the second largest hydroelectric plant in the world, with a potential of 10 million kilowatts.

POPULATION & PEOPLE

The total population is estimated at 21 million people of which about one-fifth live in Caracas. The rate of population growth stands at around 2.4% which is one of the highest figures in Latin America. Venezuela is a young nation, with over half of its inhabitants under 18 years of age. Yet, at nearly 70 years, life expectancy is remarkably high. The literacy of the population over 10 years of age is about 88%.

The mean population density, at about 23 people per sq km, is low, although it varies a great deal from place to place. The central coastal region, including the cities of Valencia, Maracay and Caracas, is the most densely populated, while Los Llanos and Guayana are sparsely populated. More than 75% of Venezuelans live in towns and cities.

Venezuela is a country of mixed blood.

About 70% of the population is a blend of European, Indian and African ancestry, or any two of the three. The rest are Whites (about 21%), Blacks (8%) and Indians (1%). Indians don't belong to a single ethnic or linguistic family, but form different independent groups scattered throughout the country. There are about two dozen indigenous groups comprising some 200,000 people. The main Indian communities include the Guajiro north of Maracaibo; the Piaroa, Guajibo, Yekuana and Yanomami in the Amazon; the Warao in the Orinoco Delta; and the Pemón in south-eastern Guayana.

Venezuela has experienced significant post-war immigration from Europe (estimated at about a million), mostly from Spain, Italy and Portugal. It nearly stopped in the 1960s, and many migrants returned home. From the 1950s on, there has been a stream of immigrants from other South American countries, particularly from Colombia. According to official statistics, about 600,000 foreigners live in the country today but unofficial estimates put the number of Colombians alone at some 2 million. Caracas is the country's most cosmopolitan city.

Major Indian Groups Living Today

By and large, Venezuelans are friendly, lively and hospitable. However, the oil crisis has meant life is tougher and consequently some people's enthusiasm and hospitality has diminished. This is particularly the case in the large urban centres.

EDUCATION

The education system has been expanded and modernised over the past few decades to meet the needs of the country's developing economy. There's compulsory six-year primary education for children who have reached seven years of age. Then comes the optional four-year secondary school, followed by a one-year preparatory course for the university. There are 31 universities in the country, of which the Universidad Central de Venezuela in Caracas is the largest and oldest (70,000 students, founded in 1725) followed by the Universidad de los Andes in Mérida (35,000 students, founded in 1785). Primary education is run by the state and is free, as are some secondary schools and a few government-sponsored universities.

ARTS
Music

There was music in pre-Hispanic times but almost nothing is known about its early forms, functions and instruments. The arrival of the Spanish, and with them the Blacks, introduced new rhythms and instruments and brought diversity to the colony's musical world. The European and African traditions gradually merged with one another and with the indigenous music, eventually producing what is now Venezuela's musical identity. It's not uniform as different forms have evolved in different regions of the country.

If there's a characteristic Venezuelan rhythm, it is the *joropo*, which developed in Los Llanos and gradually conquered the country. The joropo is usually sung and accompanied by harp, *cuatro* (small, four-stringed guitar) and *maracas*. There's a dance form of joropo as well. There are also plenty of regional beats, which haven't been dominated by the joropo.

In the eastern part of the country you'll hear, depending on the particular region, the *estribillo*, *polo margariteño*, *malagueñas*, *fulías*, and *jotas*. In the west, on the other hand, the *gaita zuliana* is typical for Maracaibo while the *bambuco* is one of the popular rhythms of the Andes. The central coast echoes with African drumbeats, a visible mark of the sizeable Black population. Caracas has absorbed all the influences, both local and international, and blasts as much with joropo and merengue as with salsa and Western rock.

As for classical music, it only emerged in the 19th century. The first composers of note include José Angel Lamas (1775-1814) and Cayetano Carreño Rodríguez (1774-1836), both of whom wrote religious music. The beginnings of concert music are accredited to Felipe Larrazábal (1818-73), a piano composer and the founder of the Caracas Conservatory. The most prominent figure in Venezuela's classical music of that century was Teresa Carreño (1853-1917), a pianist and composer. Born in Caracas, she had her first concert at the Irving Hall in New York at the age of nine. She lived most of her life in Germany, visiting her native country only twice.

The first half of the 20th century hasn't seen any outstanding musical talents, except perhaps for Reynaldo Hahn (1874-1947), another pianist, who lived and composed in Paris, and Juan Bautista Plaza (1898-1965) whose career was also established overseas (in Rome).

During the last few decades, Venezuelan musical culture has developed more swiftly. This has been due to both the opening of musical schools and the building of new concert halls. In 1930, the Symphony Orchestra of Venezuela was founded in Caracas, and followed by three other orchestras. Contemporary composers of note include Alfredo del Mónaco, Alfredo Rugeles, Federico Ruiz and Juan Carlos Núñez.

Visual Arts

Like music, the visual arts existed long before the Spaniards arrived. The most obvious surviving early works are the petroglyphs, predominantly carvings on rock, which have been found at about 200 locations throughout the country. The majority of the petroglyphs are in the central coastal region between Barquisimeto and Caracas, and along the Río Orinoco and the Río Caroní.

One of the best examples is on the Cerro Pintado, a 50-metre-high cliff near Puerto Ayacucho. A number of cave paintings have also been discovered, almost all of them in Bolívar and Amazonas states. The most common colours used by these unknown artists from pre-Columbian tribes were black, white and various tones of ochre.

The painting and sculpture of the colonial period had an almost exclusively religious character. Although mostly executed by local artisans, the style was largely influenced by the Spanish art of the day. Much of that production, consisting mainly of paintings of saints, carved wooden statues and retables (ornamental altar screens), can be seen in old churches and museums.

With independence, painting departed from strictly religious themes and began to immortalise important historical events. The first artist to do so was Juan Lovera (1778-1843), whose two most famous paintings, *19 April 1810* and *5 July 1811* can be seen in the Capilla de Santa Rosa de Lima in Caracas.

The most outstanding figure of historical painting was Martín Tovar y Tovar (1827-1902), particularly remembered for his monumental works in Caracas' National Capitol. Other artists who contributed to 19th-century Venezuelan painting include Cristóbal Rojas (1857-90) and Arturo Michelena (1863-98). The latter received wide international recognition during his short life. He lived in Paris and his works were exhibited at important salons of what was then the world's art capital. Also living in France, Emilio Boggio (1857-1920) also acquired an international reputation. Influenced by his French colleagues, and by Van

Gogh in particular, he became Venezuela's first impressionist.

The epic historical tradition of the painter Tovar y Tovar was continued by Tito Salas (1888-1974) who dedicated himself to commemorating Bolívar's life and achievements and produced a number of paintings on the subject. His best-known works are the wall-paintings in the National Pantheon in Caracas.

Modern painting began with Armando Reverón (1889-1954), who made his home in Macuto near Caracas where he executed most of his expressionist works. Another artist who made his mark in the transition from the traditional to modern painting was Carlos Otero (1886-1977). Other artists working in the same period include Rafael Monasterios (1884-1961), Federico Brandt (1879-1932), Marcos Castillo (1897-1966) and Manuel Cabré (1890-1984).

Francisco Narváez (1905-82) is commonly acclaimed as the first modern sculptor Venezuela produced. The art museum in Porlamar (Isla de Margarita), where he was born, has the largest single collection of his works, but there are also a number of his sculptures distributed around Caracas.

The recent period has been characterised by a proliferation of artists representing a wide variety of schools, trends and techniques. Possibly the most remarkable of them is the painter Héctor Poleo (1918-1989), who expressed himself in a variety of styles, easily switching from realism to surrealism, with some metaphysics in between. Equally captivating is the expressionist painting of Jacobo Borges (born 1931) who by deforming human figures turns them into caricatures.

Other leading contemporary figures in painting and sculpture include Oswaldo Vigas (born 1926), Alejandro Otero (1921-90), Mateo Manaure (born 1926), Alirio Palacios (born 1938), Manuel Quintana Castillo (born 1928) and Marisol Escobar (born 1930).

The No 1 internationally renowned Venezuelan artist of the last decades is Jesús Soto (born 1923), the leading representative of kinetic art (art, particularly sculpture, which contains moving parts). Born in Ciudad Bolívar (where a museum with a collection of his works has been established), he has adorned many public buildings and plazas, not only in Venezuela, but beyond (eg in Paris, Toronto and New York). Carlos Cruz Díez (born 1923), somewhat overshadowed by Soto's fame, is also noted for his kinetic art.

Architecture

Pre-Hispanic dwellings were built from perishable materials such as adobe, wood and vegetable fibres and, obviously, no examples have survived to this day. However, the homes of some remote tribes, whose traditions have continued almost unchanged for centuries, do approximate the form and design of the early Indian homes.

With the arrival of the Spanish, brick and tile made their way into the colony. Following rigid rules established by the Crown, the newly founded towns were laid out on a square grid with the streets running at right angles to each other. The Plaza Mayor, the cathedral and the government house habitually formed the centre from which all the towns spread outwards. All buildings, religious, civil and military, were direct reflections of the Spanish style, with only a touch of local colour showing through.

Since the Province of Venezuela was a backwater of the Crown, local architecture never reached the grandeur that marked its wealthier neighbours, such as, say, Colombia, Ecuador and Peru. The churches were unpretentious. The houses followed the modest Andalusian style. They were usually straightforward one-storey constructions, without much external decoration or internal splendour. Only in the last half-century of the colonial era, when there was noticeable economic growth, did a class of wealthier merchants emerge who built residences which reflected their new social position. Nonetheless, these were few and far between, and only a few notable examples survive, mainly in Coro.

The first 50 years of independence didn't affect Venezuelan architecture much, until a thorough modernisation programme for Caracas was launched in the 1870s by Guzmán Blanco. It resulted in a number of public buildings, in a hotch-potch of styles, from neogothic to neoclassical, depending on the whim of the particular architect in charge. Strolling about the centre of Caracas today, you can admire the results of this modernisation.

The second rush towards modernity came with the oil money and culminated in the 1960s and 1970s. The pace of urban change has slowed down considerably over the last decade.

This period was characterised by the rather indiscriminate demolition of the old urban fabric and its replacement by modern architecture. Predictably, many colonial buildings, dilapidated by time and use, fell prey to progressive urban planners. Accordingly, Venezuela's colonial legacy can be disappointing when compared to that of other Andean countries. On the other hand, Venezuela has some of the best ultra-modern architecture on the continent.

Plenty of international and local architects took part in the transformation of Caracas and other major cities. Amongst international city planners, Maurice Rotival has probably left the biggest mark on the new face of Caracas. Carlos Raúl Villanueva is by far the most outstanding Venezuelan architect and has left behind a large number of projects in Caracas and other cities. He began in the 1930s with fairly classical designs, such as the Galería de Arte Nacional, but soon developed his individual modern style. The Universidad Central de Venezuela, the complex of the university buildings in Caracas, is regarded as one of his best and most coherent designs.

Literature

There was no written language on the continent before the Spanish Conquest, apart from a variety of petroglyphs, the meaning of which is still largely undeciphered. Accordingly, there wasn't, in the strict sense of the word, a pre-Hispanic Indian literature.

Yet there must have been a rich world of tales, legends and stories created, conserved and passed orally from generation to generation. This 'literature' provided invaluable information on the pre-Columbian culture for the first Spanish chroniclers.

The first chronicles narrating the early history of Venezuela include *Brevísima Relación de la Destrucción de las Indias Occidentales* by Fray Bartolomé de las Casas, *Noticias Historiales* (1627) by Fray Pedro Simón, and *Elegías de Varones Ilustres de Indias* (1589) by Juan de Castellanos. Far more analytical and comprehensive is one of the later and perhaps the best chronicles, *Historia de la Conquista y Población de la Provincia de Venezuela* (1723) by José de Oviedo y Baños.

Almost all literature during the colonial period was written by the Spanish, who obviously imposed not only the Spanish language but also the cultural perspective which accompanied it, reflecting particular views on religion, law, art etc. A more independent approach emerged with the dawn of the 19th century, with the birth and crystallisation of revolutionary trends. The first 30 years of that century were dominated by political literature.

The first work of that period of significant historical value was the autobiography of Francisco de Miranda (1750-1816). Simón Bolívar (1783-1830) has left the most extensive literary heritage, including letters, proclamations, discourses and dissertations, and also some more literary achievements such as *Mi Delirio sobre El Chimborazo*. As literature, it has strong merits, notably for its expression of ideals and ambitions for the nation as it fought for independence, as well as for its prophetic visions.

Bolívar was influenced by his close friend Andrés Bello (1781-1865), the first important Venezuelan poet. Bello was also a noted philologist, essayist, historian, journalist, literary critic, jurist and translator.

With Independence achieved, political writing was put to one side, giving way to other literary manifestations. However, it was only during the rule of Guzmán Blanco

Andrés Bello

that literature began to develop more swiftly. In the 1920s, Andrés Eloy Blanco (1896-1955) appeared on the scene, becoming the best poet Venezuela has ever produced. This Cumaná-born poet went into exile in Mexico, escaping the persecution of the dictator Pérez Jiménez, and tragically died in a car accident in 1955. *Angelitos Negros* is probably the most popular of his numerous poems.

At the same time, several notable novelists emerged, amongst whom Rómulo Gallegos (1884-1969) was the most outstanding talent and is still, perhaps, internationally the best-known writer in the country's literary history. *Doña Bárbara*, his most famous novel, was first published in Spain in 1929 and since then translated into a dozen languages. Other important novels by this writer, who was also the first democratically elected president in Venezuela's history (in 1947), include *Canaima* and *Cantaclaro*.

Somewhat in the shade of Gallegos, Miguel Otero Silva (1908-85) was also a remarkable novelist of the period. A great admirer of the visual arts, he managed to assemble quite a collection of Venezuelan paintings, which was donated to the museums of Caracas and Barcelona after his death. As for his literary work, he's best remembered for *Casas Muertas*, a best-seller published in 1957.

Mariano Picón Salas (1901-65) was yet another important writer of the time, noted for his work in a variety of literary forms, of which essays were possibly his favourite means of expression. A professor, minister and ambassador, he frequently touched on historical and political issues. His extensive literary output includes *El Último Inca* and *Preguntas a Europa*.

Arturo Uslar Pietri (born 1906) stands out as an authority in the field of literature. A novelist, essayist, historian, literary critic and journalist, he has been also a prominent figure in politics, having been a minister on various occasions and even a presidential candidate. He's not only the most versatile writer in the country, but also the man with the longest involvement in literature. Since his first important novel, *Lanzas Coloradas*, published in the 1930s, he has written a great deal, and is still active on the literary scene.

Other modern Venezuelan writers of note include Denzil Romero (historical novels); Salvador Garmendia (short forms); Aquiles Nazoa (humour); and Francisco Herrrera Luque (historical novels). There's a lot of literary activity among the younger generation, both in poetry and in prose.

Theatre

The first theatre, Teatro del Conde, was founded in Caracas in 1784. Since then the theatre tradition has slowly developed. Several theatres opened at the end of the 19th century, in Caracas (Teatro Nacional and Teatro Municipal), Maracaibo (Teatro Baralt), Valencia (Teatro Municipal) and Barcelona (Teatro Cajigal). However, mostly European fare was presented; infrequent local productions mimicked the style and contents of the Old World.

The national theatre was only born a few decades ago, with its major centre in Caracas. Today, there are several groups, most of them in Caracas. *Rajatabla*, tied to the Ateneo de Caracas, is probably Venezuela's most innovative theatre.

Cinema

The first films screened in Venezuela appeared in Maracaibo in January 1897, only 13 months after the famous show by the Lumière brothers took place in Paris. Venezuela's first short film was shot in 1909, and the first feature film, *La Dama de las Cayenas*, was made in 1913.

Venezuela is not renowned for its cinema. It doesn't produce very many films for a start. Only during the past few decades have Venezuelan films made their way onto international screens, but so far they haven't received any significant praise, or secured any important international festival awards. One of the few film directors whose name is known beyond Venezuela is Román Chalbaud. His film, *El Pez que Fuma* (The Fish that Smokes), made in 1977, has received some critical acclaim abroad.

Programmes designed to subsidise and promote national film production were largely unsuccessful. Public demand for Venezuelan films is low and as a consequence profits are small. The film distributors prefer foreign films, and only occasionally does a locally made film appear. Over 60% of the Venezuelan film industry's profit is made in Caracas.

In contrast to cinema, TV production is booming. Venezuelans are fans of *telenovelas*, or soap operas, and producers and directors do everything they can to meet the demand. Over the last two decades Venezuela has become one of the major Latin American producers of that fare, catching up with the two traditional telenovela-powers, Mexico and Brazil.

RELIGION

Most Venezuelans are Roman Catholics. Many Indian tribes, too, adopted Catholicism and only a few, primarily those living in isolation, still practice their ancient beliefs. There are various Protestant churches in Venezuela and lately they have been gaining in importance, taking adherents away from the Roman Catholic Church. There are only small populations of Jews and Muslims practising their beliefs.

One religious curiosity is the cult of María Lionza, today widespread throughout the country (see the Chivacoa section for details).

LANGUAGE

Spanish is Venezuela's official language and, except for some remote Indian tribes, all of the population speaks it. There are over 25 Indian languages spoken in the country.

Some people, mostly in large urban centres, speak English, but it's certainly not a commonly understood or spoken language, even though it's taught as a mandatory second language in the public school system. What can be said, however, is that it's easier to find somebody speaking English in Venezuela than in, say, Colombia, Ecuador or Peru.

Most of the time you will be in an exclusively Spanish-speaking world. You can travel around without knowing a word of Spanish, but you will miss out on a good part of the pleasure of meeting people and your experience of the country will be limited.

Spanish is quite an easy language to learn and it's useful in most other Latin American countries as well. It's well worth making some effort to learn at least the essentials before setting off. Take a Spanish course, buy or borrow books, cassettes or records. Even if you learn only a little, it will be a good basis upon which to start practising during your trip. Venezuelans will encourage your Spanish, so there is no need to feel self-conscious about vocabulary, grammar or pronunciation.

A Spanish-English/English-Spanish dictionary and a phrasebook are worthwhile additions to your backpack. See the Book section in the Facts for the Visitor chapter for suggestions.

Venezuelan Spanish

Venezuelan Spanish is not the clearest or easiest to understand on the continent. Venezuelans speak rather more rapidly than most other South Americans (except for people from the Andes, who speak slower and more clearly) and tend to drop some endings, especially plurals.

The use of the forms *tu* and *usted* is very flexible in Venezuela. Both forms are used but with regional variations. Any form you use is OK, though the best way is to answer in the same form in which you are addressed. Use the *usted* form for the police and the guardia nacional.

Note, that in Venezuela, as in all Latin American countries, *vosotros* (the plural of *tu*) has almost disappeared and *ustedes* is commonly used in both informal and formal situations.

Vocabulary

There are many differences in vocabulary between European and American Spanish, and among Spanish-speaking countries in the Americas. There are also considerable regional differences within these countries not attributable to accent alone; the locals have created a number of typical words, reflecting peculiar features of the region. The Indian tongues have also influenced Spanish vocabulary, and some words from Indian languages are today a part of Venezuelan Spanish. Check the Glossary for some of these terms.

Venezuelans and other South Americans normally refer to the Spanish language as *castellano* rather than *español*.

Pronunciation

Spanish pronunciation is, in general, consistently phonetic. Once you are aware of the basic rules, it should cause little difficulty. Speak slowly to avoid getting tongue-tied until you become confident of your ability.

Pronunciation of the letters **f, k, l, n, p, q, s** and **t** is virtually identical to English, as is **y** when used as a consonant; **ll** is a separate letter, pronounced like the Spanish 'y' when it's used as a consonant. It comes after 'l' in the alphabet. **Ch** and **ñ** are also separate letters; in the alphabet they come after 'c' and 'n' respectively.

Vowels The pronunciation of Spanish vowels is uniform and they all have easy

English equivalents. For example the Spanish 'a' has one pronunciation rather than the numerous pronunciations we find in English, such as the 'a's in 'cake', 'art' and 'all'.

a is like 'a' in 'father'
e is like the 'e' in 'met'
i is like 'ee' in 'feet'
o is like 'o' in 'for'
u is like 'oo' in 'boot'
y is a consonant except when it stands alone or appears at the end of a word, in which case its pronunciation is identical to the Spanish 'i'

Consonants Spanish consonants generally resemble their English counterparts, but there are some major exceptions:

b resembles its English equivalent, and is not distinguished from 'v'; for clarification, refer to the former as 'b larga', and the latter as 'b corta' (the word for the letter itself is pronounced like English 'bay')
c is like 's' in 'see' before 'e' and 'i', otherwise like English 'k'
ch is like 'ch' in 'chair'
d in an initial position and after 'l' and 'n', is like 'd' in 'dog'; elsewhere as 'th' in 'though'
g before 'e' and 'i', is similar to 'h' in 'hell'; otherwise like 'g' in 'go'
h is never pronounced
j is similar to 'h' in 'hell' (the same as the Spanish 'g' before 'e' and 'i')
ll is similar to 'y' in 'yellow'
ñ is similar to 'ni' in 'onion'
q is like 'k' in 'key'; 'q' is always followed by a silent 'u' and is only combined with 'e' as in *que* and 'i' as in *qui*
r is strongly rolled at the beginning of the word, or after 'n', 'l' and 's'; in other positions it is pronounced with one trill
rr is always strongly rolled
v see 'b', above
x is like 'x' in 'taxi'
z is like 's' in 'sun'

Diphthongs Diphthongs are combinations of two vowels which form a single syllable. In Spanish, the formation of a diphthong depends on combinations of 'weak' vowels (i and u) and strong ones (a, e, and o). Two weak vowels or a strong and a weak vowel make a diphthong, but two strong ones are separate syllables.

A good example of two weak vowels forming a diphthong is the word *diurno* (during the day). The final syllable of *obligatorio* (obligatory) is a combination of weak and strong vowels.

Stress There are two general rules regarding stress. For words ending in a vowel, or the letters 'n' or 's', the stress goes on the second-to-last syllable. For example: *amigo* (friend) – the stress is on the 'mi'.

For words ending in a consonant other than 'n' or 's' the stress is on the last syllable. For example: *amor* (love) – the stress is on 'mor'.

Any deviation from these rules is indicated by a visible accent. For example: *sótano* (basement) the stress is on the 'só'. Accents over capital letters are often not shown, but they still affect the pronunciation.

Basic Grammar

Nouns in Spanish are masculine or feminine. The definite article ('the' in English) agrees with the noun in gender and number; for example, the Spanish word for 'train' is masculine, so 'the train' is *el tren*, and the plural is *los trenes*. The word for 'house' is feminine, so 'the house' is *la casa*, and the plural is *las casas*.

The indefinite articles (a, an, some) work in the same way: *un libro* (a book) is masculine singular, while *una carta* (a letter) is feminine singular. Their plurals are, respectively: *unos libros* (some books), *unas cartas* (some letters). Most nouns ending in 'o' are masculine and those ending in 'a' are generally feminine. Normally, nouns ending in a vowel add 's' to form the plural, while those ending in a consonant add 'es'.

Adjectives also agree with the noun in gender and number, and usually come after the noun they describe. Possessive adjectives *mi* (my), *tu* (your) *su* (his/her) etc come before the noun and agree with the thing possessed, not with the possessor. For example 'his suitcase' is *su maleta*, while 'his suitcases' is *sus maletas*. A simple way to indicate possession is to use the preposition *de* (of). 'Juan's room', for instance, would be *la habitación de Juan* (literally, 'the room of Juan').

Personal pronouns are usually not used with verbs. There are three main categories of verbs: those which end in 'ar' such as *hablar* (to speak), those which end in 'er' such as *comer* (to eat), and those which end in 'ir' such as *reir* (to laugh); there are many irregular verbs, such as *ir* (to go) and *venir* (to come).

To form a comparative, add *más ... que* (more ... than) or *menos ... que* (less ... than) with the adjective in the middle. For example, *alto* is 'high', *más alto que* is 'higher than' and *menos alto que* is 'lower than'.

A characteristic feature of South American Spanish is the very common use of diminutives. They tend to either convey the meaning of small or, more often, express affection. They are formed by adding suffixes *-ito/a*, *-cito/a*, *-illo/a* and *-cillo/a* to nouns and adjectives. For example, *cafecito* is the diminutive form of *café* (coffee), meaning 'small coffee', and *amorcito* is a tender version of *amor* (love).

Greetings & Civilities

hello	*hola*
good morning	*buenos días*
good afternoon	*buenas tardes*
good evening	*buenas noches*
good night	*buenas noches*
goodbye	*adiós, chao*
please	*por favor*
thank you	*gracias*
excuse me	*disculpe*
I'm sorry	*disculpe, lo siento*
you're welcome	*de nada*

Useful Words & Phrases

yes	*sí*
no	*no*
and	*y*

to/at	*a*
for	*por, para*
of/from	*de, desde*
in	*en*
with	*con*
without	*sin*
here	*aquí*
there	*allí*

Where?	*¿Dónde?*
Where is ...?	*¿Dónde está/ queda ...?*
When?	*¿Cuándo?*
How?	*¿Cómo?*
I would like ...	*Me gustaría ...*
How much?	*¿Cuánto?*
How many?	*¿Cuántos?*

People & Personal Pronouns

Madam/Mrs	*Señora*
Sir/Mr	*Señor*
Miss	*Señorita*
man	*hombre*
woman	*mujer*
husband	*marido, esposo*
wife	*mujer, esposa*
boy	*chico, chamo*
girl	*chica, chama*
child	*niño/a*
father	*padre, papá*
mother	*madre, mamá*
son	*hijo*
daughter	*hija*
grandfather	*abuelo*
grandmother	*abuela*
family	*familia*
friend	*amigo/a*

I	*yo*
you (singular)	*tú* (informal), *usted* (formal)
you (plural)	*ustedes*
he	*él*
she	*ella*
we	*nosotros/as*
they	*ellos/ellas*

Emergencies

| accident | *accidente* |
| ambulance | *ambulancia* |

clinic	*clínica*
dentist	*dentista*
doctor	*doctor, médico*
help	*auxilio, ayuda*
hospital	*hospital*
medicine	*medicina*
pharmacy	*farmacia*
police	*policía*

I feel bad.
  Me siento mal.
I have a fever.
  Tengo fiebre/temperatura.
Please call a doctor/the police.
  Por favor llame a un doctor/la policía.
Where is the nearest hospital?
  ¿Dónde queda el hospital más cercano?
Could you help me, please?
  ¿Me podría ayudar, por favor?
Could I use your telephone?
  ¿Podría usar su teléfono?
I want to call my embassy.
  Quiero llamar a mi embajada.

Language Problems
Do you speak English?
  ¿Habla inglés?
Does anyone here speak English?
  ¿Alguien habla inglés aquí?
I don't speak Spanish.
  No hablo castellano.
I understand.
  Entiendo.
I don't understand.
  No entiendo.
Please speak more slowly.
  Por favor hable más despacio.
Could you repeat that please?
  ¿Puede repetirlo, por favor?
What does it mean?
  ¿Qué significa?/¿Qué quiere decir?
Please write that down.
  Por favor escríbalo.

Accommodation
hotel	*hotel, pensión, residencia, posada*
room	*habitación*
single room	*habitación sencilla*
double room	*habitación doble*

toilet, bath	*baño*
shared bath	*baño compartido*
private bath	*baño privado*
shower	*ducha*
towel	*paño, toalla*
soap	*jabón*
toilet paper	*papel higiénico*
bed	*cama*
double bed	*cama matrimonial*
bed sheets	*sábanas*
pillow	*almohada*
blanket	*manta*
fan	*ventilador, abanico*
air-conditioning	*aire acondicionado*
key	*llave*
padlock	*candado*

cheap	*barato/a*
expensive	*caro/a*
clean	*limpio/a*
dirty	*sucio/a*
good	*bueno/a*
poor	*malo/a*
noisy	*ruidoso/a*
quiet	*tranquilo/a*
hot	*caliente*
cold	*frío/a*

Do you have rooms available?
  ¿Hay habitaciones?
May I see the room?
  ¿Puedo ver la habitación?
What does it cost?
  ¿Cuánto cuesta?
Does it include breakfast?
  ¿Incluye el desayuno?

Toilets
The most common word for 'toilet' is *baño*, but *servicios sanitarios*, or just *servicios* (services) is a frequent alternative. Men's toilets will usually bear a descriptive term such as *hombres* or *caballeros*. Women's toilets will say *señoras* or *damas*.

Food
Only some basic words are given here. See the Food & Drink section in the Facts for the Visitor chapter for more terms.

the bill	la cuenta
cup	taza
dish	plato
fork	trinche, tenedor
glass	vaso
knife	cuchillo
menu	menú, carta
plate	plato
spoon	cuchara
teaspoon	cucharita

bread	pan
butter	mantequilla
egg	huevo
fish	pescado
fruit	fruta
ham	jamón
meat	carne
milk	leche
pepper	pimienta
potatoes	papas
rice	arroz
salad	ensalada
salt	sal
sandwich	sánduche
sugar	azúcar
vegetables	verduras
water	agua

Getting Around

plane	avión
train	tren
bus	bus
small bus	por puesto, colectivo, micro, buseta, carrito
ship	barco, buque
boat	bongo, lancha, bote
car	auto, carro
taxi	libre, taxi
truck	camión
pickup truck	camioneta
bicycle	bicicleta
motorbike	motocicleta
hitchhike	pedir cola

airport	aeropuerto
train station	estación del tren
bus terminal	terminal de pasajeros
bus stop	parada
port	puerto
wharf, pier	muelle

city	ciudad
town	pueblo
village	pueblo, caserío
road	carretera
freeway	autopista
street	calle
street corner	esquina
bridge	puente
downtown	centro
tourist office	oficina de turismo
petrol station	bomba de gasolina
police station	estación de policía
embassy	embajada
consulate	consulado
bank	banco
public toilet	baño público

castle	castillo
cathedral	catedral
church	iglesia
market	mercado
monument	monumento
monastery	monasterio
museum	museo
palace	palacio
park	parque
square	plaza
university	universidad

entrance	entrada
exit	salida
open	abierto/a
closed	cerrado/a

ticket	boleto, pasaje
ticket office	taquilla
first/last/next	primero/último/próximo
1st/2nd class	primera/segunda clase
one-way/return	ida/ida y vuelta
left luggage	guardaequipaje

Where is...?
   ¿Dónde queda/está...?
How can I get to ...?
   ¿Cómo llegar a ...?
I would like a ticket to ...
   Quiero un boleto/pasaje a ...
What's the fare to ...?
   ¿Cuánto cuesta a ...?
When does the next bus leave for ...?
   ¿Cuándo sale el próximo bus para ....?

Post & Telecommunications

post office	*correo*
letter	*carta*
parcel	*paquete*
postcard	*postal*
airmail	*correo aéreo*
registered mail	*correo certificado*
stamps	*estampillas*
letter box	*buzón*
public telephone	*teléfono público*
telephone card	*tarjeta CANTV*
long-distance call	*llamada de larga distancia*
international call	*llamada internacional*
person to person	*persona a persona*
collect call	*cobro revertido*

Geographical Terms

The expressions below are among the most common you will encounter in this book and in Spanish language maps and guides.

archipelago	*archipiélago*
bay	*bahía*
beach	*playa*
cave	*cueva*
coast	*costa*
gulf	*golfo*
hill	*cerro*
island	*isla*
lake	*lago*
lagoon	*laguna*
mount	*pico*
mountain	*montaña*
mountain range	*cordillera, serranía, sierra*
national park	*parque nacional*
pass	*paso*
peninsula	*península*
rapids	*raudal*
river	*río*
sea	*mar*
valley	*valle*
waterfall	*cascada, salto*

Shopping

shop	*almacén, abasto*
shopping centre	*centro comercial*
supermarket	*supermercado*

price	*precio*
change	*vuelta*
money	*dinero, plata*
coin	*moneda*
banknote	*billete*
cash	*efectivo*
cheque	*cheque*
credit card	*tarjeta de crédito*
expensive	*caro*
cheap	*barato*
big	*grande*
small	*pequeño*
many/much	*muchos/mucho*
few	*pocos*
a little	*un poco*
a pair	*un par*
a dozen	*una docena*
enough	*suficiente*
more	*más*
less	*menos*

How much is it?
  ¿Cuánto cuesta/vale?
I (don't) like it.
  (No) me gusta.
Do you have...?/Are there....?
  ¿Hay...?

Countries

The list below includes only countries whose spelling differs in English and Spanish.

Brazil	*Brasil*
Canada	*Canadá*
Denmark	*Dinamarca*
England	*Inglaterra*
France	*Francia*
Germany	*Alemania*
Great Britain	*Gran Bretaña*
Ireland	*Irlanda*
Italy	*Italia*
Japan	*Japón*
Netherlands	*Holanda*
New Zealand	*Nueva Zelanda*
Peru	*Perú*
Scotland	*Escocia*
Spain	*España*
Sweden	*Suecia*
Switzerland	*Suiza*

United States	*Estados Unidos*
Wales	*Gales*

Time

time	*hora, tiempo*
today	*hoy*
tonight	*esta noche*
this week	*esta semana*
now	*ahora*
yesterday	*ayer*
day before yesterday	*anteayer, antier*
last week	*la semana pasada*
tomorrow	*mañana*
day after tomorrow	*pasado mañana*
next week	*la semana entrante*

early	*temprano*
late	*tarde*
often	*con frecuencia*
seldom	*de vez en cuando, pocas veces*
before	*antes*
after	*después*
soon	*pronto*
already	*ya*
right away	*en seguida*

sunrise	*amanecer*
morning	*mañana*
noon	*mediodía*
afternoon	*tarde*
sunset	*atardecer*
evening	*tarde*
night	*noche*
midnight	*medianoche*

second	*segundo*
minute	*minuto*
hour	*hora*
day	*día*
week	*semana*
month	*mes*
year	*año*
century	*siglo*

The Clock

Eight o'clock (8.00) is *las ocho*, while 8.30 is *las ocho y treinta* (literally, 'eight and thirty') or *las ocho y media* (eight and a half). Quarter to eight (7.45) can be *las ocho menos quince* (literally, 'eight minus fifteen'), *las ocho menos cuarto* (eight minus one quarter), *un cuarto para las ocho* (one quarter to eight) or *quince para las ocho* (fifteen to eight).

A 24-hour clock is often used for official purposes, especially with transportation schedules. In everyday conversations, however, people commonly use the 2 x 12 hour system and, if necessary, add *de la mañana* (in the morning), *de la tarde* (in the afternoon) or *de la noche* (at night).

What time is it?
   ¿Qué horas son? ¿Qué hora es?
It's 7 am.
   Son las siete de la mañana.
It's 7.15.
   Son las siete y cuarto.
It's late.
   Es tarde.
It's early.
   Es temprano.

Days of the Week

Monday	*lunes*
Tuesday	*martes*
Wednesday	*miércoles*
Thursday	*jueves*
Friday	*viernes*
Saturday	*sábado*
Sunday	*domingo*

Months

January	*enero*
February	*febrero*
March	*marzo*
April	*abril*
May	*mayo*
June	*junio*
July	*julio*
August	*agosto*
September	*septiembre*
October	*octubre*
November	*noviembre*
December	*diciembre*

Seasons

rainy season/winter	*invierno*
dry season/summer	*verano*
spring	*primavera*
autumn	*otoño*

Cardinal Numbers

0	*cero*
1	*uno*
2	*dos*
3	*tres*
4	*cuatro*
5	*cinco*
6	*seis*
7	*siete*
8	*ocho*
9	*nueve*
10	*diez*
11	*once*
12	*doce*
13	*trece*
14	*catorce*
15	*quince*
16	*dieciseis*
17	*diecisiete*
18	*dieciocho*
19	*diecinueve*
20	*veinte*
21	*veintiuno*
22	*veintidós*
23	*veintitrés*
24	*veinticuatro*
30	*treinta*
31	*treinta y uno*
32	*treinta y dos*
33	*treinta y tres*
40	*cuarenta*
41	*cuarenta y uno*
42	*cuarenta y dos*
50	*cincuenta*
60	*sesenta*
70	*setenta*
80	*ochenta*
90	*noventa*
100	*ciento*
	(*cien* when a noun directly follows the number)

101	*ciento uno*
102	*ciento dos*
110	*ciento diez*
120	*ciento veinte*
130	*ciento treinta*
200	*doscientos*
300	*trescientos*
400	*cuatrocientos*
500	*quinientos*
600	*seiscientos*
700	*setecientos*
800	*ochocientos*
900	*novecientos*
1000	*mil*
1100	*mil cien*
1200	*mil doscientos*
2000	*dos mil*
5000	*cinco mil*
10,000	*diez mil*
50,000	*cincuenta mil*
100,000	*cien mil*
1,000,000	*un millón*
2,000,000	*dos millones*

Ordinal Numbers

1st	*primero/a*
2nd	*segundo/a*
3rd	*tercero/a*
4th	*cuarto/a*
5th	*quinto/a*
6th	*sexto/a*
7th	*séptimo/a*
8th	*octavo/a*
9th	*noveno/a*
10th	*décimo/a*
11th	*undécimo/a*
12th	*duodécimo/a*
20th	*vigésimo*

Fractions

¼	*un cuarto*
⅓	*un tercio*
½	*medio/a*
¾	*tres cuartos*

Facts for the Visitor

VISAS & EMBASSIES

Nationals of the USA, Canada, Australia, New Zealand, the UK and most Western and Scandinavian European countries don't need visas if they fly into Venezuela; a Tourist Card (Tarjeta de Ingreso) will be issued by the airline at no cost. The Tourist Card is valid for 90 days and can be extended for another 60 days. A tourist visa valid for one year is available at a cost of US $30.

All foreign nationals who enter Venezuela by land from any neighbouring country (Colombia, Brazil or Guyana) need a visa. However, Venezuelan consulates in South America are difficult places to arrange visas. In Colombia, for example, possibly the only consulate which gives tourist visas to non-Colombians is the one in Cúcuta, on the Venezuelan frontier. Even the consulate in Bogotá is likely to refuse to issue you with such a visa, regardless of how strong your finances are. The same applies to the consulate in Boa Vista, Brazil, which is on the only road linking these two countries.

What the Venezuelan consulates in both Colombia and Brazil (and probably other countries on the continent) can do is give you a 72-hour transit visa. These visas cannot be extended in Venezuela, whatever the consulate tells you.

The only viable alternative to this situation is to fly into Venezuela, in which case you will be automatically be granted a 60-day Tourist Card. Flying in is pretty cheap if you're coming from Colombia, but not so from Brazil (read the Getting There & Away chapter).

If you plan on travelling overland it's best to get the visa in your country of residence before you leave. Venezuelan authorities have introduced multiple-entry tourist visas which are valid for one year from the date of issue. Consulates in most Western countries, including the USA, the UK and Australia, now issue this type of visa. The official requirements for this visa are: your passport must be valid for at least one more year; you must have a letter from your bank declaring your funds; a letter from your employer stating your wages, an onward ticket and one photo. The visa may take a couple of days before it's issued and its cost varies according to the country in which you applied (up to US$30).

On entering the country your passport will be stamped (make sure this happens) by the Dirección de Identificación y Extranjería (DIEX) border officials. You may be asked to present an onward ticket, though it's no longer the rule: it varies from one border crossing to another and from one official to another.

Visa & Tourist Card Extensions

Visa extensions are handled by the Caracas office of DIEX. Visas and Tourist Cards can be extended for a maximum of two months. Each month's extension costs US$12.50. Plan ahead and don't leave it to the last minute. See the Caracas chapter for further details.

Venezuelan Embassies & Consulates

Venezuelan embassies and consulates include:

Australia
    MLC Tower, Phillip, ACT 2606 (☎ (06) 282-4828)
Belgium
    6 Rue Paul Emile Janson, 1050 Brussels (☎ (2) 647-5212, 647-8745)
Canada
    32 Range Rd, Ottawa, Ontario K1N 8J4 (☎ (613) 235-5151)
Denmark
    Holbergsgade 14, 1057 Copenhagen (☎ 936-311, 936-476)
France
    11 Rue Copernie, 75116 Paris (☎ (1) 4553-2998)
Germany
    Im Rheingarten 7, 5300 Bonn 3 (☎ (0228) 400-920)
Italy
    Via Nicolo Tartaglia 11, 00197 Rome (☎ (06) 807-9845, 807-9850)

Japan
38 Kowa Bdg 703, 12-24 Nishi Azabu 4 Chrome,
Min, Tokyo 106 (☎ (3) 3409-1501)
Netherlands
Nassaulaan 2, 2514 JS The Hague
Portugal
Avda Duque de Loule 47-4, 1000 Lisbon (☎ (1)
573-803, 573-865)
Russian Federation
Ulitsa Ermolovoy 13/15, 103051 Moscow
(☎ (095) 299-9621, 299-4042)
Spain
Calle Francisco Gervas 11, Piso 4-B, Distrito
Postal 20, Madrid (☎ (1) 555-8452)
Sweden
Engelbrekdshadan 35B, 11432 Stockholm (☎ (8)
110-996)
Switzerland
Morellonstrasse 9, Bern (☎ (31) 371-3282)
UK
1 Cromwell Rd, London SW7 2HW (☎ (071)
581-2776, 581-2777)
USA
1099 30th St, NW, Washington DC 20007
(☎ (202) 342-2214)

In the USA, Venezuela has consulates in Baltimore, Boston, Chicago, Houston, Miami, New Orleans, New York, Philadelphia and San Francisco. In Canada, there are consulates in Montreal and Toronto. There's no Venezuelan embassy in New Zealand.

In Colombia, there are Venezuelan embassy and consulate in Bogotá, and consulates in Arauca, Barranquilla, Bucaramanga, Cartagena, Cúcuta, Medellín, Puerto Carreño and Riohacha. In Brazil, Venezuela has its embassy and consulate in Brasilia, and consulates in Belém, Boa Vista, Manaus, Porto Alegre, Rio de Janeiro and São Paulo.

Other Venezuelan representatives in the region include embassies and consulates in Argentina (Buenos Aires), Barbados (Bridgetown), Bolivia (La Paz), Chile (Santiago), Costa Rica (San José), Cuba (Havana), Dominican Republic (Santo Domingo), Ecuador (Quito), El Salvador (San Salvador), Grenada (St Georges), Guatemala (Guatemala City), Guyana (Georgetown), Haiti (Port-au-Prince), Jamaica (Kingston), Mexico (Mexico City), Nicaragua (Managua), Panama (Panama City), Paraguay (Asunción), Peru (Lima), Puerto Rico (San Juan), St Lucia (Castries), St Vincent (Kingstown), Suriname (Paramaribo), Trinidad & Tobago (Port of Spain), Uruguay (Montevideo) and Aruba, Bonaire and Curaçao (Netherlands Antilles).

Foreign Embassies in Venezuela

All foreign embassies are in Caracas (refer to that section for addresses).

DOCUMENTS

A valid passport is your most essential document and it must be stamped with a visa if you need one. Once in Venezuela, you must carry your passport with you at all times. Identity document checks are not uncommon on country roads and city streets. Your passport is the first document the police will ask for. Some police officers may be satisfied with a certified photocopy of your passport but most won't accept it as a valid document.

If you come from an area infected with yellow fever or cholera, you may be asked for an International Health Certificate proving you have been inoculated against these diseases.

A student card isn't much use in Venezuela. You'll save a few bolívares at museums but that's about it. Except for Aeropostal airlines who will occasionally give you a student discount, there are no student fares on domestic flights or buses. An International Youth Hostel card is useless as there are no youth hostels in Venezuela.

If you bring your own vehicle or plan on hiring a car, make sure you have your driver's licence. According to Venezuelan law, drivers' licences which are valid in other countries are also valid in Venezuela for a period of one year from the date of your arrival, provided the licence is not used to drive vehicles for profit. Despite this, some police and rental company staff may be unfamiliar with foreign drivers' licences, so it's best to bring along an International Driver's Permit as well. The minimum driving age in Venezuela is 18 years of age but in order to rent a car you must be at least 21 years of age and have a credit card.

Don't forget about an insurance policy for

both your luggage and health. Even if you don't need to use it, it will help you to sleep more peacefully.

Credit cards are relatively handy in Venezuela, for both safety and convenience, so bring one or two (see the Money section for details).

Officially, at least, you must have an onward ticket on entering the country, though you won't often be asked to actually present it. You'll probably be obliged to have it anyway to get a visa or Tourist Card.

Have several extra passport photos with you for any visas or documents you might need to organise in Venezuela. For your security, it's worth having a photocopy of your passport, airline tickets and travellers' cheque numbers. Needless to say, keep them somewhere different from where you keep the originals.

CUSTOMS

Customs regulations don't differ much from other countries on the continent. You are allowed to bring in personal belongings and presents you intend to give to Venezuelan residents. The quantity, kind and value of these items shouldn't arouse suspicions that they may have been imported with a commercial purpose in mind. You can bring with you cameras (still, video and movie), a typewriter, a tape recorder, a radio, camping equipment, sports accessories, a personal computer and the like without any problems.

The entry of products derived from milk or pork is prohibited. It's also forbidden to introduce seeds, flowers, fruit or plants of any kind. According to Venezuelan law, the possession, trafficking or consumption of drugs is a serious offence and subject to heavy penalties. You would be crazy to try smuggling them across the border.

When leaving the country, you can take souvenirs and handicrafts with you, but not in quantities that could be suspected of being commercial.

Customs formalities are usually not much more than that: formalities. However, you may encounter a thorough check. If you're coming overland from Colombia your baggage is likely to be searched at the border and/or at *alcabalas* (police road checkpoints). This is because of the considerable drug traffic that passes this way.

MONEY
Venezuelan Currency

The unit of currency is – not surprisingly – the bolívar (abbreviated to Bs), which is divided into 100 céntimos. There are ½, 1, 2 and 5 bolívar coins and 10, 20, 50, 100, 500 and 1000 bolívar notes.

Changing Money

You can change money at a bank or at a *casa de cambio* (an authorised money exchange office). Banks change cash and travellers' cheques and give cash advances to credit card holders. Casas de cambio change cash but seldom change travellers' cheques. US dollars and American Express travellers' cheques are by far the most popular in Venezuela. Visa, MasterCard and American Express are the most widely accepted credit cards in Venezuela. They are accepted by banks and many other establishments such as hotels, restaurants, airlines and shops.

Banks are plentiful in Venezuela but not all of them handle foreign exchange operations. The availability of this service seems to differ from bank to bank, branch to branch and city to city, and changes from day to day. In other words, it's likely to take some walking around before you find a helpful bank. Fortunately, at least, most of the major banks are concentrated in the city centres. As a general rule, the banks to look for are:

Banco Consolidado (who almost always change American Express travellers' cheques and credit cards and sometimes cash)
Banco Unión (who usually change cash, Visa and MasterCard but rarely travellers' cheques)
Banco de Venezuela (who irregularly change cash, travellers' cheques or credit cards, ie you never know what a particular branch will change)
Banco Mercantil (who really only deal with MasterCard)

Banco Latino, Banco Construcción, Banco Provincial, Banco Italo Venezolano and some regional banks may, sometimes, also be useful.

The opening hours of banks are the same throughout the country: Monday to Friday from 8.30 to 11.30 am and 2 to 4.30 pm. Banks are closed on Saturdays, Sundays and public holidays. Banks are also closed on the first Monday after 6 January (Epiphany), 19 March (St Joseph's Day), Ascension Day, 29 June (St Peter's & St Paul's Day), 15 August (Assumption), 1 November (All Soul's Day) and 8 December (Immaculate Conception).

The frustrating thing about Venezuelan banks, especially those in smaller provincial cities, is that often you can only change money during limited hours. These hours are not fixed and depend upon a number of factors.

After opening, the bank calls its central branch and asks for the day's exchange rates. Sometimes they can't get a connection for an hour or two, and sometimes they can't get through at all, in which case they don't change money.

Some banks set limits on the number of foreign exchange operations they do per day (or the total amount of money they can change daily) so if you arrive too late they may refuse to change your money. The best time to try is somewhere between 9 and 10 am. Remember, it's always wise to change enough money to last you through to the next large city.

Another annoying feature of Venezuelan banks is that they are painfully slow. It can take half an hour or more changing money or travellers' cheques.

Your passport is essential if you want to change either cash or travellers' cheques. When it comes to changing cheques, some banks may also require you to produce a customer copy of your purchase record. This is the form you would have been given when you bought the cheques. Make sure to carry this copy with you.

If you are in a provincial bank always ask more than one teller whether or not the bank changes money. Not all tellers are sure of what the bank can and can't do. They have been known to take the safest (and easiest) line and say that no exchange is possible, when this is not actually the case.

Casas de cambio in large cities change cash at a rate which is marginally lower than that of the banks. However, the advantage is that the whole operation only takes a minute. Casas de cambio also sell foreign currency; mostly, or exclusively, US dollars. Only some casas de cambio change travellers' cheques and you may find the exchange rate is pretty poor.

The place to report the loss or theft of American Express travellers' cheques and apply for a replacement or refund is at Turisol. Its head office is in Caracas and it has branches in Barquisimeto, Maracay, Valencia, Maracaibo, Mérida, Puerto La Cruz and Porlamar. See the sections on those places for addresses and phone numbers. If you lose Thomas Cook travellers' cheques, the refund assistance office is in Caracas (see that chapter).

Keep in mind that you may be asked for details of the place where you bought the cheques and the date of purchase.

There's no black market in Venezuela and you'll probably never get a better rate than in the banks.

Exchange Rates

The exchange rates for cash and travellers' cheques are more or less the same, though some banks will charge a commission on cheques. The rate varies only marginally between the banks, so it's usually not worth shopping around. The approximate exchange rates are:

A$1	=	124 Bs
Can$1	=	124 Bs
DM1	=	102 Bs
FF1	=	30 Bs
UK£1	=	257 Bs
US$1	=	169 Bs

The depreciation of the bolívar against hard currencies stood at around 35% per year in 1993, and the authorities expect (maybe too optimistically) that it won't exceed this figure in 1994.

Credit Cards

Credit cards come in handy in Venezuela. Their use is not as universal as it is in Western countries, but they have become quite popular over the last decade. A number of banks accept credit cards and will pay cash advances in bolívares. On the whole, it's easier to find a bank which will service your credit card than it is to find a bank which will accept your US dollars or travellers' cheques.

It may be difficult or impossible to get cash advances with any credit card other than American Express, Visa or MasterCard. Banco Consolidado is the bank which services American Express credit card holders. Visa and MasterCard are accepted by various banks, but not by Banco Consolidado.

Credit cards can also be used for payments at the more up-market hotels, restaurants, travel agencies and stores. If you plan on renting a car, they are essential.

Costs

Venezuela is no longer one of the most expensive countries on the continent, as it was during the oil bonanza of the late 1970s and early '80s when the prices of goods and services soared almost to the level of US prices. With the end of the oil boom and the devaluation of the local currency, costs dropped to levels which are more attractive to foreign visitors. Generally speaking, Venezuela is now somewhere in the middle-price bracket when compared to other South American countries. It is more expensive than Ecuador, Peru and Colombia, but cheaper than Brazil, Chile and Argentina.

How much you spend in Venezuela largely depends, of course, on what degree of comfort you require, what kind of food you eat, where you go, how fast you travel and the means of transport you use. If, for instance, you are used to rental cars and plush hotels, you will probably spend just as much as you would if you were in the West. If you're a budget traveller, though, prepared for basic conditions and willing to endure some discomfort on the road, you should find that you get by on US$20 to US$25 per day. This would cover accommodation in budget hotels, food in low to middle-range restaurants, and transport by bus. If you want to leave a comfortable margin for beers, taxis, movies and other extras, add US$5 per day to this average.

If you economise, it's possible to cut the average daily cost down to US$15, but this limits your experience of the country and can turn your trip into more of an endurance test than a holiday. After all, you don't set off on a trip to put yourself through hell.

Accommodation, food and transport are the three major expenses. If you are prepared for basic conditions, you shouldn't have to spend more than US$6 a night (on average) for a budget hotel. The cost will be lower (or the standard better) if you travel in a group or, better still, in a couple.

If budget dining is what you're used to, you shouldn't have to spend more than US$10 a day on food. Because Venezuela's average temperature is fairly hot you'll drink a lot. Fortunately soft drinks and mineral water are inexpensive.

Buses are the main means of transport and they're pretty cheap, considerably cheaper than in neighbouring Colombia and Brazil. City buses cost next to nothing. Taxis, particularly when you're in a group, aren't expensive. They are definitely worth considering if you're carrying all your gear with you and you're on your way to or from the airport or bus terminal.

Most museums don't charge an admission fee – a welcome custom – and those which do keep the fee well under a dollar. Cultural events (cinema, theatre, music etc) are all fairly inexpensive. On the other hand, the combination of nightclubs and alcohol can deplete your funds quickly, especially if you drink at the same rate Venezuelans do.

Tours, however, can really eat into your budget. They cost between US$60 and US$100 per day and rarely are they just one-day trips. A tour to Salto Angel (Angel Falls), a must for almost every tourist, is a considerable expense, even if you do it on your own.

Broadly speaking, travel in the countryside is cheaper than in the cities. Caracas is the most expensive Venezuelan city. There's a hell of a difference in cost between camping on the beach for a week, and exploring Caracas nightclubs for the same length of time.

WHEN TO GO

The tourist season in Venezuela runs year-round so, theoretically, any time you visit is OK. There are two factors, however, which you might like to consider before you finalise your travel plans.

The first is the climate. Venezuela has one dry season (roughly November or December to April or May) and one wet season (the rest of the year). The dry season is certainly more pleasant for travelling. This is particularly true if you plan on hiking. In the wet season, paths are muddy and views obscured. It's not much fun trudging in rain all day anyway. If you plan on mountaineering, the rainy (or, more correctly, snowy) season is not only unpleasant but can be dangerous. Conventional sightseeing, either in the cities or the countryside, won't be greatly disturbed by rain.

Keep in mind, too, that the weather pattern is not uniform throughout the country. Some regions (eg parts of Lara, Falcón, Anzoátegui and Sucre states as well as Isla de Margarita) are relatively dry for most of the year, so the season doesn't really matter much. On the other hand the upper Amazonas is wet more or less year-round.

In some regions, the season doesn't determine which time is best for visiting. For example, wildlife trips to Los Llanos can be just as fascinating during the dry season as in the wet season, though you'll encounter completely different landscapes and plant and animal life. Salto Angel, the tourist's 'must see', is easier to see in the dry season, but certainly more impressive in the wet season.

The second consideration to keep in mind when planning your trip are the periods when Venezuelans take their holidays. They are mad about travelling to visit friends and family over Christmas and Holy Week (Easter), and during Carnaval.

In these three peak periods, you'll just have to plan ahead and do a little more legwork before you find a place to stay. On the other hand, these periods are colourful and alive with a host of festivities. Schools break for annual vacations in August but this doesn't affect public transport or accommodation.

WHAT TO BRING

The first and most important rule of travel is to bring with you the minimum possible – a large, heavy backpack may become a nightmare. At times you may even be driven to the desperate thought that travel would be easier if it was stolen.

Almost everything you might need can easily be bought in Venezuela. Clothes, footwear, toiletries, stationery, etc are readily available in Venezuelan shops, supermarkets and markets, and they are usually cheaper than they would be if you bought them at home. There's absolutely no need to bring in large stocks of envelopes, spare batteries, T-shirts and shampoo enough to last the whole trip. *Zapaterías*, or shoestores, are ubiquitous (Venezuelans seem to be shoe-crazy) and the shoes are cheap and come in a large variety of styles.

The overwhelming majority of the country is lowland, so you don't need much in the way of warm clothing. If you stick to hotels, you don't need bedsheets or blankets, as even the most down-to-earth *residencias* provide them.

When preparing for your trip, concentrate on the more important items such as a strong, comfortable backpack. Photographers will find that their photographic gear will probably be the heaviest and bulkiest part of their luggage (see the Film & Photography section).

Some essentials which might be worth packing include: a travel alarm clock (for those early morning buses); a small torch (for dodgy electricity supplies); sunglasses and a hat; a Spanish/English dictionary; flip-flops or thongs (to protect feet against fungus infections in shabby hotel bathrooms); and a small pocketknife.

Make sure to bring with you any prescription medications you would normally take, and a spare pair of glasses or contact lenses if applicable. A small medical kit is recommended if you plan on leaving the beaten track – refer to the Health section for specifics.

Rain gear will come in handy if you're visiting the country during the wet season. Swimming gear is essential if you're heading to one or more of the hundreds of beaches on the coast. Bring a mask and snorkel (to save on rental fees), and old running shoes to protect your feet against the coral. Have one set of nice clothes for dining out in fancy restaurants and for other special occasions. Bookworms might want to bring along some paperbacks as the choice offered by local bookshops may not be what they are used to back home.

If you plan to go mountain hiking or on a jungle trip you should include in your luggage all the necessary equipment: tent, sleeping bag, warm clothes etc. If you are bringing a cooking stove (Gaz Bluet is the most common brand) you can stock up on gas canisters in Caracas.

Camping equipment is available in Venezuela (mostly in Caracas and Mérida), but it can be quite expensive and the choice is limited. The Roraima trip alone probably justifies bringing your camping gear with you (read that section). You will also save money at Salto Angel by camping (see the Salto Angel section).

TOURIST OFFICES

Corporación de Turismo, or Corpoturismo, is the government agency promoting tourism and providing tourist information. Their head office is in Caracas (see that chapter for details). They publish material on the country's attractions but it's not always available.

Outside Caracas, the provision of tourist information has been taken over by regional tourist bodies which have their offices in the respective state capitals and in some other cities. Some are better than others but, on the whole, they lack city maps and brochures. They are usually friendly but the staff don't always speak English, and sometimes they only have a vague idea about what attractions they have in their state.

The practical information they provide also leaves something to be desired, especially if you are a budget traveller. They seldom know which banks currently change money and which is the cheapest hotel in town.

Outside Venezuela there aren't many tourist information agencies. One of the few is the Venezuelan Tourist Association (VTA) (☎ (415) 332-2720) PO Box 3010, Sausalito, CA 94966, USA, which provides general information and maps.

Venezuelan consulates and embassies can provide limited tourist information, and Viasa airline's overseas offices occasionally have a brochure or two.

USEFUL ORGANISATIONS

Only international organisations are listed in this section. For information about useful organisations within Venezuela, see the Caracas chapter.

South American Explorers Club

One of the most useful resources for visitors to South America is the South American Explorers Club (☎ (607) 277-0488), 126 Indian Creek Road, Ithaca, NY 14850, USA. This club provides services, information and support to travellers, scientific researchers, mountaineers and explorers. It sells a wide range of books, guides and maps of South America, and as well as publishing a quarterly journal it runs a mail order catalogue. The club maintains clubhouses in Ecuador and Peru. Membership is US$30 a year per individual, US$40 per couple.

Information for Disabled Travellers

Disabled travellers from the USA might like to contact the Society for the Advancement of Travel for the Handicapped (☎ (718) 858-5483), 26 Court St, Brooklyn, New York, NY 11242. In the UK, a useful contact is the Royal Association for Disability & Rehabilitation (☎ (071) 242-3882), 25 Mortimer St, London W1N 8AB.

Environmental Organisations

Many organisations are promoting the preservation of rainforests and other endangered environments. For more details contact any of the following groups:

Australia
> Friends of the Earth, 312 Smith St, Collingwood, Vic 3066 (☎ (03) 419-8700)
> Greenpeace Australia Ltd, 24/26 Johnston St, Fitzroy, Vic 3065 (☎ (03) 670-1633)

UK
> Friends of the Earth, 26/28 Underwood St, London N17JU
> Survival International, 310 Edgeware Rd, London W2 1DY (☎ (071) 723-5535)

USA
> Rainforest Action Network (RAN), 301 Broadway, Suite A, San Francisco, CA 94133 (☎ (415) 398-4404)
> Conservation International, 1015 18th St, NW, Suite 1000, Washington, DC 20036 (☎ (202) 429-5660)
> Cultural Survival, 215 First St, Cambridge, MA 02142 (☎ (617) 621-3818)
> Nature Conservancy, 1815 N Lynn St, Arlington, VA 22209 (☎ (703) 841-5300)
> Survival International USA, 2121 Decatur Place, NW, Washington, DC 20006
> Friends of the Earth, 218 D St, SE, Washington, DC 20003 (☎ (202) 544-2600)
> Greenpeace, 1436 U St, NW, Washington, DC 20009 (☎ (202) 462-8817)
> Earthwatch, 680 Mt Auburn St, Box 403, Watertown, MA 02272 (☎ (617) 926-8200)
> The Chico Mendes Fund, Environmental Defence Fund, 257 Park Ave South, New York, NY 10010
> Rainforest Alliance, 270 Lafayette St, Suite 512, New York, NY 10012
> Rainforest Foundation Inc, 1776 Broadway, 14th floor, New York, NY 10019

BUSINESS HOURS & HOLIDAYS

The office working day is theoretically eight hours long, from 8 am to noon and 2 to 6 pm, Monday to Friday. The public opening hours of government offices are usually shorter; they close at 4 or 5 pm. All banks in Venezuela have the same business hours and keep pretty close to them (see the Money section). Almost all firms and offices, including most of the tourist offices, are closed on Saturdays and Sundays.

The usual shopping hours are from 9 am to 6 or 7 pm, Monday to Saturday. Many shops close for lunch but some work the *horario corrido*, ie without a lunch time break. Large stores and supermarkets in the cities usually stay open until 8, 9 or sometimes even 10 pm.

Take this as a rough guide only; the hours vary considerably, from shop to shop and office to office, and from cities to countryside. In remote places, opening hours are often shorter and are usually taken less seriously.

Pharmacies alternate Sunday and all-night opening. Check local newspapers for the list of pharmacies on 24-hour duty. You can recognise them by a board or a neon sign declaring 'TURNO' (on duty).

Most of the better restaurants in the larger cities, particularly in Caracas, tend to stay open until 11 pm or midnight (some stay open even longer) whereas restaurants in smaller towns often close by 9 pm or earlier. Many restaurants don't open at all on Sundays.

The opening hours of museums and other tourist sights vary greatly. Most museums are closed on Mondays but are open on Sundays. The opening hours of churches are even more difficult to pin down. Some are open all day, while others only open for certain hours, and still others remain locked except during Mass.

Public Holidays

Official public holidays include 1 January (New Year's Day), Monday and Tuesday before Ash Wednesday (Carnaval), Maundy Thursday and Good Friday (Easter), 19 April (Declaration of Independence), 1 May (Labour Day), 24 June (Battle of Carabobo), 5 July (Independence Day), 24 July (Bolívar's Birthday), 12 October (Discovery of America) and 25 December (Christmas Day).

CULTURAL EVENTS

Given the strong Catholic character of Venezuela, a good number of the feasts and celebrations follow the Church calendar. Accordingly, Christmas, Easter, Corpus

Christi and the like are often enthusiastically celebrated, particularly so in more traditional rural communities. The religious calendar is dotted with saints' days, and every village and town has its own patron saint – you can take it for granted the locals will be holding a celebratory feast that day. In many cases, the once strictly church ceremonies have been enriched with a more genuinely popular flavour.

Possibly the biggest event celebrated throughout the country is Carnaval, or Carnival, which takes place on the Monday and Tuesday prior to Ash Wednesday. Feasting usually breaks out by the end of the preceding week. The festival is characterised by music, dancing, parades and masquerades and lots of gaiety and amusement in general. Carnaval varies from region to region in terms of its length, intensity and character. In Santa Elena de Uairén, for example, there is a Brazilian feel, an obvious reflection of the town's proximity to that border. Carúpano is known nationwide for its elaborate Carnaval, as is, to a lesser extent, El Callao.

Venezuela's most colourful event is perhaps Los Diablos Danzantes, or the Devil Dancers. It's held on Corpus Christi in San Francisco de Yare, some 60 km south of Caracas. The ceremony consists of a spectacular parade and the dance of devils, performed by dancers disguised in elaborate, if grotesque, masks and costumes.

Cultural events such as festivals of theatre, film or classical music, are almost exclusively confined to Caracas.

Venezuela's main religious and cultural events are:

Paradura del Niño – Mérida state; January.
Danceros de la Candelaria – Mérida state; beginning of February.
Carnaval – throughout the country, particularly in Carúpano; February or March.
Fiesta del Joropo – Elorza (Apure state) and, on a smaller scale, in the other towns of Los Llanos; 19 March.
Semana Santa – processions on Maundy Thursday and Good Friday in many towns, but perhaps most elaborate in Mérida, Caripito and Tostos; March or April.

Festival Internacional de Teatro – Caracas; April of even years.
Velorio de la Cruz de Mayo – throughout the country; May.
Los Diablos Danzantes – San Francisco de Yare; Corpus Christi, May or June.
Fiesta de San Juan – Curiepe and neighbouring villages (Miranda state), dances to drum music, with an African flavour (the region is the centre of Black culture); 23 June, but usually extending till 28 June.
Fiestas de la Virgen – La Asunción (Isla de Margarita); 15 August.
Fiesta de la Virgen de Coromoto – Guanare; 8 September.
Fiesta de Nuestra Señora del Valle – Valle del Espíritu Santo (Isla de Margarita); 8-15 September.
Feria de la Chinita – Maracaibo; 18 November.

POST & TELECOMMUNICATIONS
Post
The postal service is run by Ipostel which has post offices throughout the country. There are a score of Ipostel offices in Caracas, a few in each of the other big cities but only one post office in the smaller cities and towns. The Ipostel offices in the major cities are open during normal office hours (8 am to noon and 2 to 6 pm, Monday to Friday), but elsewhere they tend to open later and close earlier.

Ipostel service is slow, inefficient and unreliable. Air mail to the USA or Europe can take up to a month to arrive; that's assuming it arrives at all. Internal mail is also painfully slow.

Aerogrammes are more likely to arrive safely, although, perhaps, no quicker than stamped letters. The most secure way to send letters, although its delivery rate is not perfect, is by certified mail *(correo certificado)*. Bear this in mind before sending an important letter or a valuable parcel through Ipostel. Avoid problems by using telephones, faxes, or courier services. If you are on your way to Colombia or Brazil, wait and post items from there as both these countries have more reliable postal services.

Ipostel is not only inefficient, it's expensive. Airmailing a postcard or a letter (up to 20 grams) to anywhere in the Americas costs US$0.80. If you were to send a postcard or a letter (up to 20 grams) to somewhere outside the Americas it would cost you US$1. Letters between 20 and 50 grams cost US$1.50 sent within the Americas and US$1.70 to elsewhere.

It costs US$11 to send a one-kg parcel airmail to the Americas, US$15 if you are sending it to Europe or Africa and US$19 if you are sending it to Asia, Australia or New Zealand. A 10-kg parcel will cost US$49/74/114 and a 20-kg parcel (the maximum weight allowed) will cost US$96/144/186. Ipostel staff will promise you it only takes eight days for a parcel to reach its destination, but you shouldn't take this claim too seriously.

It is cheaper to send parcels by surface mail. A one-kg parcel costs US$23/27/30 and a 20-kg parcel costs US$36/48/56. You will be told that it will take approximately 20 days for delivery but this is rather wishful thinking on Ipostal's part.

There are also problems when it comes to sending letters and parcels to Venezuela from abroad. They take a long time to be delivered and sometimes they simply never make it. The confusing Venezuelan system of addresses only exacerbates the problems.

As might be expected, Ipostel's inefficiency has prompted a growth in both national and international courier services. DHL and other big companies are already well established in Caracas and other big cities.

Telegram

The telegram service is handled by some Ipostel offices, but this also leaves a bit to be desired. What can be said about the service is that it seems to be more reliable and telegrams usually arrive before letters. Still, international telegrams have been known to take a few weeks getting to their destination.

Telephone

The telephone system is largely automated for both domestic and international connections. Public telephones exist in the larger cities but many are out of order. Coins are used for local calls, although newly installed telephones only operate on phone cards (*tarjeta CANTV*, also known as *tarjeta inteligente*). It's worth buying one if you think you might be using public phones frequently. You can buy cards to the value of 250, 500, 1000 or 2000 Bs (a standard local call costs approximately 5 Bs for three minutes). They are convenient for local and intercity calls. You can also use the tarjeta for international calls, or you can go to the nearest CANTV office and make the call through an operator. The cards can be bought at CANTV offices and at other establishments such as stationers and pharmacies. If you can't find an operable public telephone try the nearest CANTV office, which should have at least one that is working.

Area codes for major Venezuelan cities and towns detailed in this book are listed in the table on the following page.

The international telephone service is expensive. When dialling direct, either from a public phone booth or from a private telephone, the call will be charged according to the length of time you were talking. If you place the call through the international operator, either at a CANTV office or from a private phone, the minimum charge is the same as for a three-minute call. This will cost about US$8 if you're calling the USA and US$12 if you're calling somewhere outside the Americas. Every extra minute costs a third more. For a person-to-person call (*persona a persona*), add an extra minute's charge. Waiting time for a connection doesn't usually exceed 15 minutes, but sometimes it can take an hour or more to get through.

Collect or reverse-charge phone calls are possible to a number of countries including the USA, the UK, Canada, New Zealand and France. They cannot be made to Germany, Spain or Australia. The list of countries this service applies to changes from year to year so check with a CANTV office to be sure. If you want to place a collect call from a private telephone, call ☎ 112 and ask for *llamada de cobro a destino* or *llamada de cobro revertido*.

The country code for Venezuela is 58. To

Area codes for major Venezuelan cities

Araure	055	Chivacoa	051	Puerto Cabello	042
Barcelona	081	El Callao	088	Puerto La Cruz	081
Barinas	073	El Tocuyo	053	Puerto Ordaz	086
Barquisimeto	051	Güiria	094	Punto Fijo	069
Caraballeda	031	Juangriego	095	San Antonio	
Caracas	02	La Asunción	095	del Táchira	076
Carúpano	094	La Guaira	031	San Cristóbal	076
Caripe	092	Macuto	031	San Félix	086
Carora	052	Maiquetía	031	San Fernando	
Ciudad Bolívar	085	Maracaibo	061	de Apure	047
Ciudad Guayana	086	Maracay	043	Santa Elena de Uairén	088
Ciudad Piar	085	Maturín	091	Trujillo	072
Colonia Tovar	033	Mérida	074	Tucacas	042
Coro	068	Pampatar	095	Tucupita	087
Cumaná	093	Porlamar	095	Valencia	041
Chichiriviche	042	Puerto Ayacucho	048	Valera	071

call a number in Venezuela from abroad, dial the international access code of the country you're calling from, the country code (58), the area code (they are given above, but drop the initial '0') and the local phone number.

Fax

Faxes can be sent from the major branches of CANTV offices. There's also a growing number of private companies in the larger cities offering fax services. The best hotels, too, will send and receive faxes for you, but will charge heavily for this already expensive service.

TIME

All of Venezuela lies within the same time zone, four hours behind Greenwich Mean Time, and there's no daylight saving. See table below for times in other cities when it is noon in Caracas.

ELECTRICITY

Electricity is 110 volts, 60 cycles AC all over the country. US-type flat two-pin plugs are used.

LAUNDRY

There are dry cleaners in the larger cities and it usually takes a couple of days to get your clothes cleaned. Top-class hotels offer laundry facilities and they are faster. Self-service laundrettes are scarce but there are some which offer service washes.

WEIGHTS & MEASURES

Venezuela uses the metric system. There's a conversion table at the back of this book.

Times in other cities when it is noon in Caracas

Auckland	4 am next day
Berlin	5 pm
Bogotá	11 am
Buenos Aires	1 pm
Frankfurt	5 pm
Hong Kong	midnight
Lima	11 am
London	4 pm
Los Angeles	8 am
Melbourne	2 am next day
Mexico	10 am
Montreal	11 am
New York	11 am
Paris	5 pm
Quito	11 am
Rio de Janeiro	1 pm
San Francisco	8 am
Sydney	2 am next day
Tokyo	1 am next day
Toronto	11 am
Vancouver	8 am

BOOKS

You will get far more out of your visit if you read up on the country before you go. There are plenty of books in English which cover various aspects of Venezuela, some of which are recommended below. If you want to study a particular aspect of the country in detail, have a look at *Venezuela: World Bibliographic Series* by D A G Waddell (Clio Press, Oxford and Santa Barbara, California, 1990), which lists over 800 books concerning Venezuela.

If you read Spanish, you'll find invaluable sources of information in Venezuela itself. The country publishes many books and other publications, few of which have been translated into foreign languages.

History & Politics

A good overview of the period of Spanish colonisation is provided by John Hemming's *The Search for El Dorado*. The book is a fascinating insight into the conquest of Venezuela and Colombia. Equally captivating is *The Explorers of South America* by Edward J Goodman (Collier MacMillan, London, 1972) which brings to life some of the more incredible explorations of the continent, from Columbus to Humboldt. You'll read more about explorers and their studies in the following Geography & Wildlife section.

Venezuela: the Search for Order, the Dream of Progress by John V Lombardi (Oxford University Press, New York, Oxford, 1982) provides good general reading on history, politics, geography and people.

There are numerous titles concerning Venezuela's modern history, though most publications focus mainly or exclusively on the oil boom and/or the oil crisis.

For a comprehensive 20th-century history, try *Venezuela, a Century of Change* by Judith Ewell (C Hurst & Co, London, 1984) or *Venezuela* by David Eugene Blank (Praeger Publishers, New York, 1984).

Paper Tigers and Minotaurs by Moisés Naim (The Carnegie Endowment for International Peace, Washington, 1993) provides good information on economic policies over the past decade.

Geography & Wildlife

Venezuela's unique geological phenomenon, tepuis, has captivated explorers, scientists and writers for ages. One of the first authors attracted by the tepuis was the eminent Sir Arthur Conan Doyle who – although he had never been to Venezuela – was inspired by the fabulous stories of Colonel Fawcett's explorations of the plateaux. Conan Doyle gave play to his imagination in *The Lost World* (Buccaneer Books, 1977, originally published 1912), which is a rollicking science-fiction tale set in a prehistoric world.

For something less fanciful, try reading 'Venezuela's Islands in Time', an article by Uwe George, published in *National Geographic* (May 1989). It has good general information about the tepuis and how they emerged. It is also illustrated with spectacular photos of these unique formations.

The Lost World of Venezuela and its Vegetation by Charles Brewer-Carías (Caracas, 1987) looks at the mysterious and endemic plant life of the tepuis. The book contains a photographic record of the plants and describes the research carried out by the author on the top of several tepuis. This book also has a Spanish edition. Unfortunately both editions are hard to find, especially outside Venezuela.

Another explorer's account of the tepuis is *Churún Merú, the Tallest Angel* by Ruth Robertson (Whitmore Publishing, Pennsylvania, 1975). This is the report of the expedition to Auyantepui. It was on this expedition that the height of Salto Angel was measured for the first time, confirming its status as the world's highest waterfall.

The famous German geographer and botanist Alexander von Humboldt didn't make it to the tepuis, but he explored and studied other regions of Venezuela (as well as regions in Colombia, Ecuador and Peru). He describes it all in amazing detail in his three-volume *Personal Narrative of Travels to the Equinoctial Regions of America, 1799-1801*. Volume No 2 covers the Venezuelan section of his journey.

Travellers with a serious interest in South

American wildlife have quite a choice when it comes to background reading and practical guides. *World of Wildlife – Animals of South America* by F R de la Fuente (Orbis Publishing, 1975) is a good basic reference work. *Neotropical Rainforest Mammals – A Field Guide* by Louise H Emmons (University of Chicago Press, Chicago, 1990) is a practical guide containing descriptions and illustrations of several hundred species, many of which can be found in Venezuela.

If birds are what interest you most, you could start with *A Guide to the Birds of South America* (Academy of Natural Science, Philadelphia). Alternatively, try the valuable reference work, *The Birds of South America* by R S Ridgley & G Tudor (University of Texas Press, 1989). It comes in several volumes; amateurs will find it extremely detailed and technical. Then, for the trip itself, get a copy of *A Guide to the Birds of Venezuela* by Rodolphe Meyer de Schauensee & William H Phelps (Princeton University Press, New Jersey, 1978) which is a good, illustrated field-guide. *South American Birds – A Photographic Aid to Identification* by John S Dunning (1987) would be another good companion on your trip. A number of the bird species featured in the book are found in Venezuela.

A recommended rainforest guide is *Rainforests – A Guide to Research and Tourist Facilities at Selected Tropical Forest Sites in Central and South America* by James L Castner (Feline Press, Florida, 1990). This book has useful background information and has descriptions of 40 rainforests in half a dozen countries.

Society & Culture

What is probably most intriguing for foreign travellers to Venezuela is the native Indian population. By far the most complete work on the subject is the three-volume *Los Aborígenes de Venezuela* (Fundación La Salle, Caracas). Volume No 1 (1980) refers to the Indian groups of the past, whereas volume Nos 2 and 3 (1983 and 1988, respectively) feature all the major communities (15 groups) currently living in Venezuela. The

work was researched and written by an international group of anthropologists and ethnologists and gives a thorough insight into the social organisation, religion and culture of each group. It is well illustrated with maps and photos. There is only a Spanish edition and it's hard to get a hold of outside Venezuela; for those who read Spanish it's a treasure trove of information.

Internationally, the most widely publicised Indian group is the Yanomami. The tribe was considered to have an essentially stone-age culture when it was first discovered in modern times. Perhaps the best authority on the matter is Jacques Lizot, who published a score of research studies on the group, including *Le Cercle des Feux: Faits et Dits des Indiens Yanomami* (Recherches Anthropologiques, Editions du Seuil, Paris, 1976). The work has been translated into English.

Another noted investigator of Yanomami culture is Napoleon Chagnon, whose doctoral dissertation emphasised the Indians' warrior culture. He was later criticised for this. Read 'Yanomamo, the True People', his article in the *National Geographic* (August 1976). Also, have a look into *Aborigines of the Amazon Rain Forest: The Yanomami* by Robin Hanbury-Tenison (Time Life Books, 1982).

Travel Guides

There are not many guidebooks covering Venezuela. Among the best is *Venezuela* by Hilary Dunsterville Branch (Bradt Publications, Bucks, UK, 1993) which focuses on outdoor activities, predominantly hiking in national parks. Cities and their cultural sights are described in much less detail.

Guide to Venezuela by Janice Bauman & Leni Young (Ernesto Armitano Editor, Caracas, 1987) covers just about every sight and town and has a wealth of practical information, though not much of it is relevant to the budget traveller. Unfortunately, it's almost impossible to find this guide outside Venezuela. See the Information section in the Caracas chapter for further details.

Venezuela Alive by Arnold Greenberg

(Alive Publications, New York, 1989) covers only the places that are of major interest to tourists (Caracas, Margarita, Puerto La Cruz, Cumaná, Mérida, Salto Angel, and Maracaibo) and its practical information only applies to the up-market bracket. It is distributed in Venezuela by Distribuidora Santiago, Caracas.

Insight Guides – Venezuela (APA Publications, Hong Kong, 1992) provides interesting reading, fascinating photography, but sparse practical information.

Hiking in the Venezuelan Andes by Forest Leighty (Venezuelan Andes Press, Miami, 1992) is a useful guide for those planning on walks in the Andes.

The *South American Handbook* (Trade & Travel Publications, Bath, UK) covers everything between Tierra del Fuego and the Darien Gap and has a 90-page chapter on Venezuela. The guide is suitable for everyone from backpackers to business people. Unfortunately, this means a lot of the information contained in it is relevant to only a small number of readers.

South America on a Shoestring (Lonely Planet, Melbourne, 1994) is geared more towards the independent budget traveller and has twice as many maps as the *South American Handbook*.

There are a number of travel guides in German. Unfortunately none of them offer much practical information for budget travellers.

Reise Know-How: Venezuela von den Anden zum Orinoco by Diethelm Kaiser & Olivia Gordones (Därr-Reisebuch Verlags, Hohenthann, 1991) has 220 pages of general information and it's packed with sketch maps.

Just as comprehensive is *Venezuela mit Isla Margarita – Das Praktische Reisehandbuch für Erlebnisurlaub* by Linda O'Bryan & Hans Zaglitsch (Peter Meyer Reiseführer, Katzenelnbogen, Frankfurt am Main, 1992).

Another well-researched guide is *Preiswert Reisen – Venezuela* by Beatrix Diel (Hayit Verlag, Cologne, 1992), although it doesn't have many maps.

Goldstadt – Reiseführer Venezuela by Friedrich Schmithüsen (Goldstadtverlag Pforzheim, München, 1991) doesn't have any practical information at all, but it does have some interesting information of a more general nature.

Finally, there is the compact *Richtig Reisen: Venezuela, Kolumbien und Ecuador* by Karl-Arnulf Rädecke (DuMont Buchverlag, Cologne, 1991), which may be useful if you plan on visiting all three of these countries. For French-speaking travellers, *Venezuela* by Anne et Jean Maille de Trevanges (Guide Arthaud, Paris, 1990) appears to be the only French-language travel guide worth mentioning.

Useful Local Publications

Venezuela doesn't really publish many travel guides as such, but it does produce a lot of material of a more descriptive nature, most of which is in Spanish.

Coffee-table books dealing with Venezuelan nature, architecture and art are often beautiful and make great souvenirs. They can also help you to decide where to go and what to see. For example, if you were mad about colonial churches, reading *Templos Coloniales de Venezuela* by Graziano Gasparini (Ernesto Armitano, Caracas), which features 100 photos of important old churches, would ensure you included the best in your itinerary.

Corpoven and Lagoven, two major oil companies, publish a wealth of material, and it's not all necessarily about oil. Corpoven's *Tierra Mágica* covers a variety of local issues such as ethnography, architecture, popular feasts and religion. Lagoven's publications tend more towards geography and natural history. It has a series of brochures dealing with national parks and wildlife. These are not commercial publications and you won't find them in bookshops. If you're particularly interested, just visit either company's Caracas or Maracaibo offices to see what they have in stock.

Venezuelan Literature

Over the last 50 years or so there's been an enormous boom in Latin American literature.

Authors such as Gabriel García Márquez (Colombia), Isabel Allende (Chile), Jorge Amado (Brazil), Mario Vargas Llosa (Peru), Carlos Fuentes (Mexico) and Julio Cortázar (Argentina) have been translated into most of the major languages and their books have become worldwide bestsellers.

Venezuela has remained somewhat in the shade as it hasn't yet produced a writer of the stature of these other South Americans. Its best-known writers are Rómulo Gallegos and Arturo Uslar Pietri. See the Arts section in the Facts about the Country chapter for more information concerning these and other local authors.

Phrasebooks & Dictionaries

Lonely Planet's *Latin American Spanish Phrasebook* (Lonely Planet, Melbourne, 1991) is a worthwhile addition to your backpack. A good alternative is the *Latin-American Spanish for Travellers* published by Berlitz. The latter is also available with a cassette.

Because Spanish is one of the world's major languages there are loads of Spanish-English dictionaries available all over the world. The *University of Chicago Spanish-English, English-Spanish Dictionary*, is small, lightweight and perfect for overseas travel.

For something more comprehensive, look for the *Pequeño Larousse Español-Inglés, English-Spanish* dictionary. This detailed yet compact reference is one of the most helpful dictionaries you'll ever come across. It's published as either a single volume or as two separate volumes but contains the same amount of information in each edition.

MAPS

You'll probably find it difficult to buy anything other than general maps of Venezuela outside the country itself. Check with good travel bookshops and map shops to see what is available. In the USA, Maplink (☎ (805) 965-4402), 25 E Mason St, Dept G, Santa Barbara, CA 93101, has an excellent supply of maps. A similarly extensive selection of maps is available in the UK from Stanfords (☎ (071) 836-1321), 12-14 Long Acre, London WC2E 9LP.

For general maps of South America with excellent topographical detail, it's hard to beat the sectional maps published by International Travel Maps (Canada). Coverage of Venezuela is provided in *South America – North West* (1993, 2nd edition). At the time of writing International Travel Maps was in the process of finalising a map of Venezuela. It should be available from Bradt Publications in the UK (who are one of a number of distributors), or from Stanfords. If not, International Travel Maps' address is 345 West Broadway, Vancouver, BC, Canada V5Y 1P8.

Within Venezuela, folded road maps of the country are produced by Lagoven, Corpoven and several publishers. Although they are almost out of print, Lagoven's maps may still be available at some Lagoven petrol stations. Corpoven's maps, which are drawn to a larger scale but which aren't as accurate, can be bought at Corpoven petrol stations. A few other publishers distribute maps through bookshops. *Mapas de Carreteras y Ciudades para el Turismo en Venezuela*, the book-format road atlas, published by Seguros Progreso, Caracas, is probably the most detailed. It can be bought in some of the better bookshops.

Dirección de Cartografía Nacional is the government mapping body. Its head office is in Caracas. They produce and sell a variety of maps – see the Map section in the Caracas chapter for further details.

MEDIA
Newspapers & Magazines

All the main cities have their own daily newspapers. The two leading Caracas papers, *El Universal* and *El Nacional*, have country-wide distribution. Both have good coverage of national and international affairs, sports, economics and culture. Both cost US$0.30 except on Sundays when they cost US$0.40. Caracas has several other newspapers and periodicals, including *Economía Hoy*, *El Mundo* and *El Globo*.

The major newspaper in Maracaibo is *Panorama*, in Valencia it's *El Carabobeño*, and in Barquisimeto they have *El Inform-ador* and *El Impulso*.

The Daily Journal is the main English-language newspaper published in Venezuela. It has good coverage of national politics and economics, social and cultural events, sports, TV programmes etc. It's available at major newsstands and at selected bookshops in Caracas. Elsewhere, it can be difficult to come by.

The Guardian Weekly (Latin American Edition), is a 24-page UK paper focusing on South American issues. It is circulated on Sundays and comes as a supplement of *Domingo Hoy* newspaper, which can be easily recognised by the cream-orange colour of the paper on which it's printed.

International dailies and periodicals, such as the *International Herald Tribune*, *The Times*, *Der Spiegel*, *Le Monde*, *Time* and *Newsweek*, can be bought in Caracas from selected newsstands and bookshops. The best place to look for them is at the news-stands in five-star hotels.

Radio

There are over a hundred radio stations in Venezuela broadcasting on either AM or FM. Every fair-sized town has its own local radio station. In Caracas, there are some 15 stations broadcasting on FM stereo alone.

Most of the programming is dominated by imported pop, rock, disco and the like. Jazz and classical music are less popular but some stations do grant them air-time. Radio Nacional is one of the best of these stations and it broadcasts on 630 kHz (AM). In Caracas, La Emisora Cultural broadcasts a balanced menu of classical music, jazz and spoken programmes on 97.7 mHz (FM).

Almost all programmes are transmitted in Spanish. If you need English-language news, tune into the BBC World Service which can be picked up on various short wave AM frequencies.

TV

One government and three private TV stations operate out of Caracas and reach most of the country. The government-owned

Venezolana de Televisión broadcasts on Channel 8, while the three commercial networks, Radio Caracas La Televisión, Venevisión and Televén, broadcast on Channels 2, 4 and 10, respectively. All four have morning and evening news programmes and some of them also offer midday news. They all offer the usual fare, ranging from music to feature films to sports to cultural programmes. Prime-time is dominated by *telenovelas*, or soap operas, Venezuelans' favourite TV entertainment. Almost all programming is in Spanish, including foreign films which are dubbed.

A second government-owned station, Televisora Nacional (Channel 5), closed down in 1993, but there are efforts to reopen it. It featured educational and cultural programmes, news and some of the more mentally stimulating films.

Apart from the above-mentioned stations, there's Omnivisión, a pay-TV station, which offers a mixed Spanish/English package of feature films, sports, music, soap operas and CNN news.

Satellite TV has boomed in Caracas and, to a lesser extent, in the other major cities. The *parabólica* (satellite dish) has become the ultimate status-symbol, and a new feature of the Caracas skyline. They are conspicuous in the wealthier suburbs and are spreading like wildfire in other districts.

Caracas' major papers (including *The Daily Journal*) list the programmes of all TV channels and a score of satellite stations which can be picked up in the city.

FILM & PHOTOGRAPHY

Given the country's spectacular and varied geography, wildlife, colonial and modern architecture, and its ethnic mosaic, there's plenty to capture on film or video. How you go about it is up to you. Some travellers are happy with a small automatic camera, while others travel with their backpacks almost brimming over with photographic gear.

Except for the usual restrictions on photographing military installations and some other strategic facilities (eg oil refineries) you can take pictures almost anywhere and of just about anything. Taking photos is permitted in virtually every church and in many museums (though some don't allow flash).

Photo Equipment

Bring all necessary equipment from home. Cameras and accessories can be bought in Venezuela but the choice is limited, unpredictable and the prices hardly welcoming. It's difficult to get cameras repaired in Venezuela, so make sure your gear is reliable.

The first thing to consider before you leave home is what camera and accessories you will need. An automatic 35-mm reflex with a zoom lens is universally considered appropriate for general purposes, including landscapes, portraits and architecture. The choice between a zoom and a set of straight lenses is a matter of individual preference. Zooms are definitely more convenient, as you can frame your shot easily and work out the optimum composition. The problem is that they absorb a lot of light and require higher ASA film if you're taking shots in anything but bright daylight.

A straight lens – that is, a lens with a fixed focal length – will yield better results and greater clarity than a zoom, but you then have to carry several different lenses and change them according to the particular shot.

Serious wildlife photography requires a long telephoto lens. A reasonable length would be somewhere between 200 and 300 mm. Of course, a 500-mm lens will bring the action up still closer, but it is heavier, requires higher ASA films and/or a tripod.

Long telelenses are also useful for taking photos of people, but do it discreetly and be sensitive. If necessary, ask for permission to photograph and don't insist or snap a photo if permission is denied.

A wide-angle lens can be useful, sometimes indispensable, for photographing architecture or tight interiors. The macro, which comes as a standard in most zooms, is handy for photographing insects, tiny flowers and the like. A UV filter is essential when photographing at high altitudes to minimise the effects of ultraviolet rays.

A tripod is an important but heavy and bulky piece of equipment. It is particularly useful in dim interiors (eg in churches) and may also be necessary when using telephotos. If you decide to take one, don't forget to also take a cable release.

A flash is another useful piece of photo equipment, and fortunately it is fairly light. Other useful accessories include a spare set of batteries to your camera, a lens cleaning kit, and plenty of silica-gel packs and plastic bags to protect your gear from the humidity, dust, sand and water. Whatever combination of lenses and accessories you decide to bring, make sure they are carried in a sturdy bag which will protect them from the elements and the hard knocks they're sure to receive. Don't take a flashy camera bag which is likely to attract the attention of thieves. Needless to say, make sure your equipment is insured.

Film

Films are easy to come by and there's quite a choice in Caracas and a few of the other big cities. Elsewhere, particularly in the country, it may be difficult to get the film type and speed you require. The price of film is comparable to what you would spend in the USA.

Kodak, Fuji and, to a lesser extent, Agfa are the most popular brands. Negative films are found almost everywhere. Slide films, especially high-speed and professional ones are harder to find. Prints can be processed in any number of laboratories, often within an hour or two, and the quality is usually OK, but E6 slide processing is not as common and the quality is not always good.

If you're taking slides, it's best to bring films with you and have them processed back home. Don't be caught out without a healthy supply of films.

Bring a variety of film stock: rainforests are surprisingly dark and may require very fast films (400 ASA and upwards) whereas the snowy peaks of the Sierra Nevada de Mérida and the sunny white beaches along the coast usually don't need anything faster than 50 ASA film.

Heat and humidity can ruin films, so remember to keep them in the coolest, driest place available, both before and after exposure. Films should be processed soon after exposure, but don't panic about it: you might get a better result by waiting for two months to have them developed in a professional laboratory at home rather than processing them immediately in an unknown local venue.

Use a lead film bag to protect films from airport X-ray machines. This is important for the sensitive high-ASA films; 100 ASA film and below comes through unharmed.

Video
Venezuela is sufficiently safe (except perhaps for Caracas) and attractive enough to justify carrying a video camera. If you decide to bring a camera, don't forget to bring along a conversion plug to fit electric sockets (US flat two-pin type) if you have a different system. Remember that Venezuela's electricity is 110 volts, 60 cycles.

VHS is the standard format for recording from TV and viewing rented films at home. Betamax does exist but it is less popular. Most amateurs shooting their own videos opt for a Video 8 mm system. The equipment, cassettes and accessories for all systems are available, but the variety is limited and it's expensive.

HEALTH
Venezuela has a fairly well-developed health service. There are numerous well-stocked *farmacias* (pharmacies), private clinics and hospitals. Its sanitary conditions are better than the South American average, though the current economic decline is putting this standard at risk.

It is safe to drink water straight from the tap in Caracas and several of the larger cities, but if you'd prefer to avoid it, bottled waters and other drinks are readily available in supermarkets and shops.

No vaccinations are required for entry to Venezuela, unless you come from an area infected with cholera or yellow fever.

Your health while travelling depends on your predeparture preparations, your day-to-day health care and how you handle any medical problem or emergency that does arise. The list of potential dangers included in this section may seem frightening, but don't panic: with some basic precautions and adequate information few travellers should experience anything more than an upset stomach.

This section has information on preventative measures, symptoms and suggestions about what to do if there is a problem. It isn't meant to replace professional diagnosis or prescription, and visitors to South America should discuss with their physician the most up-to-date methods used to prevent and treat the threats to health which may be encountered.

If a serious medical problem arises during the trip, seek qualified help wherever possible, as self-diagnosis and treatment can be risky. Medical advice should be sought before administering any drugs. Your embassy or consulate can usually recommend a good place to go for such advice. So can five-star hotels, although they often recommend doctors with five-star prices – this is when the medical insurance really comes in useful.

Predeparture Preparations
Health Insurance A travel insurance policy to cover medical problems is a wise idea. However fit and healthy you are, do take out medical insurance. Even if you don't get sick, you might be involved in a accident.

There are a wide variety of policies and your travel agent will have recommendations. The international student travel policies handled by STA and other student travel organisations are usually good value. When buying a policy, it's important to check the small print:

- Some policies specifically exclude 'dangerous activities' which can include scuba diving, motorcycling or even trekking. If these activities are on your agenda, such a policy would be of limited value.
- You may prefer a policy which pays doctors or hospitals directly rather than you having to pay them on the spot and claim later. If you have to claim later, make sure you keep all documentation. Some policies ask you to call back (reverse charges) to a centre in your home country where an immediate assessment of your problem is made.
- Check if the policy covers ambulances or an emergency flight home – someone has to pay if you have to stretch out across a few airline seats.

Travel Health Information In the USA, you can contact the Overseas Citizens Emergency Center and request a health and safety information bulletin on Venezuela by writing to the Bureau of Consular Affairs Office, State Department, Washington, DC 20520. This office also has a special telephone number for emergencies while abroad: ☎ (202) 632-5525.

The International Association for Medical Assistance to Travelers (IAMAT), 417 Center St, Lewiston, New York, NY 14092, can provide travellers with a list of English-speaking physicians in Venezuela.

In the UK, contact Medical Advisory Services for Travellers Abroad (MASTA) (☎ (071) 631-4408), Keppel St, London WC1E 7HT. MASTA provides a variety of services, including a choice of concise or comprehensive 'Health Briefs' and a range of medical supplies. Another source of medical information and supplies is the British Airways Travel Clinic (☎ (071) 831-5333).

In Australia, make an appointment with the Traveller's Medical and Vaccination Centre in Sydney (☎ (02) 221-7133) or Melbourne (☎ (03) 650-7600) for general health information pertaining to Venezuela and the requisite vaccinations for travel in South America.

There are a number of books on travel health. *Staying Healthy in Asia, Africa & Latin America* (Volunteers in Asia) is probably the best all-round guide to carry, as it's compact, detailed and well organised. *Travellers' Health* by Richard Dawood (Oxford University Press) is comprehensive, easy to read and authoritative although it's rather large to lug around.

The Center for Disease Control's (CDC's) *Health Information for International Travel* (which is a supplement of the *Morbidity & Mortality Weekly Report*) and the World Health Organisation's (WHO's) *Vaccination Certificate Requirements for International Travel & Health Advice to Travellers* are useful references.

Medical Kit Give some thought to a medical kit for your trip. The size and contents of your first-aid kit depends on your knowledge of first-aid procedures, where and how far off the beaten track you are going, how long you will need the kit for, and how many people will be sharing it.

It's not necessary to take every remedy for every illness you might contract during your trip. Venezuelan pharmacies stock all kinds of drugs which are cheaper than in the West. There are few restricted medications, so almost everything is sold over the counter. In the past, foreign pharmaceutical companies sold drugs which had exceeded their shelf life to South American firms. Fortunately this practice has been abandoned. Many drugs are manufactured locally under foreign licence. When buying drugs anywhere in South America, be sure to check their expiry dates.

Travellers should be aware of any drug allergies they may have, and avoid using such drugs or their derivatives. Since common names of prescription medicines in South America may be different from the ones you're used to, ask a pharmacist before taking anything you're not sure about.

A possible kit may include:

- The prescription medications you normally take
- Aspirin or Panadol – for pain or fever
- Antihistamine (such as Benadryl) – useful as decongestants, to ease the itching from insect bites, or to help prevent motion sickness
- Antibiotics – useful if you're travelling well off the beaten track; unlike in the West, many antibiotics are available in Venezuela without a prescription
- Kaolin and pectin preparation such as Pepto-Bismol for stomach upsets, and Imodium or Lomotil in case of diarrhoea during long-distance travel
- Rehydration mixture – for treatment of severe diarrhoea; this is particularly important if travelling with children
- Antiseptic liquid or cream and antibiotic powder – for cuts and grazes
- Calamine lotion – to ease irritation from bites or stings
- Ear and eye drops
- Foot and groin (antifungal) powder
- Bandages and Band-aids
- Scissors, tweezers and a thermometer (note that mercury thermometers are prohibited by airlines)
- Insect repellent, sunscreen, suntan lotion, chap stick and water purification tablets
- Sterile syringes; be sure you have at least one large enough for a blood test – those normally used for injections are too small

- Plastic container with a sealable lid, to pack your medical kit in
- Contraceptives, including condoms – even if you're not expecting to have sex while you are travelling

Ideally, antibiotics should be administered only under medical supervision and should never be taken indiscriminately. Overuse of antibiotics can weaken your body's ability to deal with infections naturally, and can reduce the drug's efficacy on a future occasion. Take only the recommended dose at the prescribed intervals and continue using the antibiotic for the prescribed period, even if the illness seems to have been cured. Antibiotics are infection specific, so if there are any serious, unexpected reactions, discontinue use immediately. If you are not sure whether or not you have the correct antibiotic, don't use it at all.

Health Preparations Make sure you're healthy before you start travelling. If you are embarking on a long trip have your teeth checked and make sure they are OK.

If you wear glasses or contacts, bring a spare pair and your optical prescription. Losing your glasses can be a real problem, although in many Venezuelan cities you can get new spectacles made up quickly, cheaply and competently.

At least one pair of good-quality sunglasses is essential, as the glare is terrific and dust and sand can get into the corners of your eyes. A hat, sunscreen lotion and lip protection are also important.

If you require a particular medication take an adequate supply with you, as it may not be available locally. Take the original prescription with you, specifying the generic rather than the brand name (which may not be locally available). It's also wise to have the prescription with you to prove you're using the medication legally. Customs and immigration officers may become excited at the sight of syringes or mysterious powdery preparations. The organisations listed under Travel Health Information can provide medical supplies and multilingual customs documentation.

Immunisations No immunisations are necessary for Venezuela, unless you are coming from an infected area, but the further off the beaten track you go the more necessary it is to take precautions. All vaccinations should be recorded on an International Health Certificate, which is available from your physician or government health department.

Plan your vaccinations ahead of time: some of them require an initial shot followed by a booster, while some vaccinations should not be given together. Most travellers from Western countries will have been immunised against various diseases during childhood but your doctor may still recommend booster shots. The period of protection offered by vaccinations differs widely and some are not advisable for pregnant women.

A yellow fever vaccination is highly recommended for every traveller in Venezuela; furthermore, if you're continuing on to Brazil, Brazilian authorities may not grant entrance without it. Other commonly recommended vaccinations for travel in South America are typhoid, tetanus and polio vaccines as well as gamma globulin as protection against hepatitis A. Smallpox has now been wiped out worldwide, so immunisation against this disease is no longer necessary.

The list of possible vaccinations includes:

Yellow Fever Protection lasts 10 years and it is recommended for all travel in South America. You usually have to go to a special yellow fever vaccination centre. Vaccination isn't recommended during pregnancy, but if you must travel to a high-risk area, it is probably better to take the vaccine.

Cholera Venezuela may require a cholera vaccination if you are coming from an infected area, particularly from Colombia where there was an outbreak in 1993. Protection is not very effective, it lasts for a maximum of six months and is contraindicated if you are pregnant.

Tetanus Most people in developed countries are vaccinated against this disease at school age. Boosters are necessary every 10 years and are recommended as a matter of course.

Polio Polio has been wiped out in Venezuela, but is endemic in Brazil, where recent outbreaks have been reported in the southern states. You probably had the oral polio vaccine while you were at school, but a complete immunisation series should be boosted if more than 10 years have elapsed since the last course.

Typhoid Protection lasts for three years and is useful if you are travelling for longer periods in rural tropical areas. The vaccination consists of two injections taken four weeks apart, so you have to think well ahead, more so if you plan on having a gamma globulin shot (read below). You may have some side effects such as pain at the injection site, fever, headache and a general feeling of being unwell.

Hepatitis Gamma globulin is the common protection; this is not a vaccination but a ready-made antibody which has proven successful in reducing the chances of contracting infectious hepatitis (hepatitis A). Because it may interfere with the development of other immunities, it should not be given until at least 10 days after administration of the last vaccine. It should be given as close as possible to departure because of its relatively short protection period – normally about six months.

Basic Rules

Paying attention to what you eat and drink is the most important health rule. Stomach upsets are the most common travel health problem but most of these upsets will be relatively minor. However, don't be paranoid about trying local food – it's part of the travel experience and you shouldn't miss it.

Drinks The tap water in Caracas and several other key cities is safe to drink, although it doesn't taste great. If you'd prefer to avoid it, bottled water and soft drinks are easily available in countless restaurants, shops and supermarkets. Outside the big cities, tap water isn't always drinkable. If you don't know for certain whether or not the water is safe, don't drink it. This goes for ice as well. Fortunately bottled drinks are almost always at hand.

In rural areas, take care with fruit juice, particularly if water may have been added. Milk should be treated with suspicion, as it is often unpasteurised. Boiled milk is fine if it is kept hygienically, and yoghurt is always good. Tea or coffee should also be OK, since the water will probably have been boiled.

The problems begin, though, when you go further afield into wilderness areas where there are no Coca Cola stands. One solution is to bring water from civilisation; the other

is to purify the local water. The simplest way of purifying water is to boil it thoroughly: this means boiling it for 10 minutes. Remember that at higher altitudes water boils at lower temperatures, so germs are less likely to be killed.

Simple filtering will not remove all dangerous organisms, so if you cannot boil suspect water, it should be treated chemically. Chlorine tablets (Puritabs, Steritabs or other brand names) will kill many but not all pathogens. Iodine is an effective water purifier and is available in tablet form (such as Potable Aqua), but follow the directions carefully and remember that too much iodine is harmful. If you can't find tablets, tincture of iodine (2%) or iodine crystals can be used.

Food Theoretically at least, salads and fruit should be washed with purified water or peeled where possible. Ice cream is usually OK, but beware of street vendors selling ice cream that has melted and been refrozen. Thoroughly cooked food is safe but not if it has been left to cool or if it has been reheated. Take great care with shellfish or fish and avoid undercooked meat. If a place looks clean and well run and if the vendor also looks clean and healthy, then the food is probably all right. In general, places that are packed with locals will be fine, while empty restaurants are questionable.

Nutrition If your diet is poor or you're travelling hard and fast and missing meals you can soon start to lose weight and place your health at risk.

Make sure your diet is well balanced. Eggs, beans, lentils and nuts are all safe sources of protein. Fruit you can peel (eg bananas, oranges or mandarins) is always safe and a good source of vitamins. Eat sufficient rice and bread. Remember that although food is generally safer if it is well cooked, overcooked food loses much of its nutritional value. If your diet isn't well balanced or if your food intake is insufficient, it's a good idea to take vitamin and iron supplements.

Most of Venezuela is lowland, so you'll

enjoy, or suffer, the heat. Make sure you drink enough – don't rely on thirst alone to tell you when to drink. Not needing to urinate or dark-yellow urine are signs of dehydration. Always carry a water bottle with you on off-the-beaten-track trips.

On the other hand, excessive drinking causes excessive sweating, and this can lead to a loss of salt and muscle cramping. If you find that your sweat is not salty enough, add more salt than usual to your food.

Everyday Health A normal body temperature is 98.6°F or 37°C; more than 2°C higher is a 'high' fever. A normal adult pulse rate is 60 to 80 beats per minute (children 80 to 100, babies 100 to 140). You should know how to take a temperature and a pulse rate. As a general rule, the pulse increases about 20 beats per minute for each °C rise in fever.

Respiration rates can also indicate health or illness. Count the number of breaths per minute: between 12 and 20 is normal for adults and older children (up to 30 for younger children, 40 for babies). People with a high fever or serious respiratory illness (like pneumonia) breathe more quickly than normal. More than 40 shallow breaths a minute usually means pneumonia.

Many health problems can be avoided by taking care of yourself. Wash your hands frequently – it's quite easy to contaminate your own food. Clean your teeth with purified water rather than water which has come straight from the river. Avoid extremes of temperature: keep out of the sun when it's hot, dress warmly when it's cold.

Some diseases can be avoided by dressing sensibly. Worm infections can be caught through walking barefoot and dangerous cuts are likely if you walk over coral without shoes. Avoid insect bites by covering bare skin and/or by using insect repellents and a mosquito net at night. Seek local advice: if you're told the water is unsafe due to crocodiles or piranha, don't go in.

Diseases of Insanitation
Diarrhoea Diarrhoea is probably the most common problem among travellers and

sooner or later it makes its appearance, usually at the most inconvenient moment. In general, it is not a serious problem but a reaction to a change of diet and a lack of resistance to local strains of bacteria.

Moderate diarrhoea – half a dozen loose movements in a day – is a nuisance but not a reason for loading up on antibiotics, as they can do more harm than good. If the bacteria in your body are able to build up an immunity to them, the antibiotics may not work when you really need them.

Dehydration is the main danger with diarrhoea and children are even more at risk. Fluid replenishment is the main treatment. Weak black tea with a little sugar, soda water, or soft drinks allowed to go flat and diluted with water are all good. If possible, don't eat, rest and avoid travelling. If you can't stand starving, keep to a light diet of dry toast, biscuits and plain rice. Once you're headed toward recovery, try some yoghurt, but stay away from sweets, fruit, and dairy products.

Lomotil or Imodium can relieve the symptoms, but they won't actually cure the problem. Use these drugs only if absolutely necessary – for example, if you must travel – but don't take them if you have a high fever or if you are severely dehydrated.

If you're not feeling better after several days, and the symptoms persist or become worse, it's probably time for antibiotics. These can be useful in treating severe diarrhoea, especially if it is accompanied by nausea, vomiting, stomach cramps or mild fever. Ampicillin, a broad spectrum penicillin, is usually recommended. However, before you start using it, see a doctor to be tested because the diarrhoea may be the beginning of other problems such as giardia, dysentery, cholera and so on.

Giardia This intestinal parasite is present in contaminated water. The symptoms are stomach cramps, nausea, a bloated stomach, headache, foul-smelling diarrhoea and frequent gas. Giardia can appear weeks after you have been first exposed to the parasite. The symptoms may disappear for a few days and then return; this can go on for several weeks. Metronidazole, sometimes known by its brand name, Flagyl, is the recommended drug, but it should only be taken under medical supervision. Antibiotics are of no use.

Dysentery This serious illness is caused by contaminated food or water and it usually presents as severe diarrhoea, often with blood or mucus in the stool, and painful gut cramps. There are two kinds of dysentery: bacillary and amoebic.

Bacillary dysentery is characterised by rapid development; its typical symptoms are a high fever, acute diarrhoea, headache, vomiting and stomach pains. It is highly contagious. Since it's caused by bacteria it responds well to antibiotics and it generally doesn't last longer than a few days. Even if not treated by antibiotics, it will disappear pretty fast without any further complications.

Amoebic dysentery is, as its name suggests, caused by amoebas (a parasite, not a bacteria). It takes longer to develop, usually has no fever or vomiting, but is a more serious illness. It is not a self-limiting disease: if left untreated, it will persist and can recur and cause long-term damage.

A stool test is necessary to determine which kind of dysentery you have, so you should seek medical help. In the case of an emergency, Tetracycline is the prescribed treatment for bacillary dysentery, whereas Metronidazole is normally used for amoebic dysentery.

Hepatitis This disease, which has five strains named with consecutive letters of the alphabet, is caused by a virus which attacks the liver. Hepatitis A is the most common form and it is spread by contaminated food or water. The symptoms appear from two to six weeks after contraction and include fever, chills, headache, fatigue, weakness, lack of appetite, and aches and pains. The most characteristic symptoms are dark urine, light-coloured faeces and conspicuously yellowish eyes. An infected person will also experience tenderness in the right side of the abdomen (where the liver is located).

You should seek medical advice but, in general, there is not much you can do apart from rest and a low-fat diet. Stop smoking and drinking immediately. As soon as you discover you have the disease, you should be extremely careful not to give it to your travelling companion or any other people. Maintain strict personal hygiene and don't share any eating or drinking utensils.

If you contract hepatitis A during a short trip to South America, the best thing to do is probably to make arrangements to return home. If you can afford the time, however, the best cure is to stay in bed in a quiet place and only get up to go to the toilet. Arrange for somebody to bring you food and drinks if you're not travelling with a reliable travelling companion who can do this for you. Keep to a diet rich in proteins and vitamins.

After two or three weeks you should feel like living again. This is the time to start thinking about continuing your trip. Take it easy at first: no strenuous exercise, no extensive walks, no rides on bumpy roads, and keep to your diet until your health returns to normal. This should take another two or three weeks. Forget alcohol and cigarettes for the next six months; your liver needs this long to recover.

The best preventative measure available for hepatitis A is an immune serum globulin shot (commonly called gamma globulin). It is not 100% effective but it may reduce the severity of an infection. The shot should be taken just before departure and if your trip is to take longer booster shots are recommended every three or four months while you're away (beware of insanitary needles).

A gamma globulin shot is also in order if you come in contact with an infected person. If you come down with hepatitis, anyone who has been in recent contact with you should take the shot too.

Hepatitis B, which used to be called serum hepatitis, is spread through contact with infected bodily fluids which may be transmitted through sexual contact, unsterilised needles or blood transfusions. Avoid having your ears pierced, tattoos done or injections in establishments where you have reason to doubt their sanitary standards. The incubation period of hepatitis B is between four and 24 weeks. The symptoms are much the same as those of hepatitis A except that they are more severe and may lead to irreparable liver damage or liver cancer.

Although there is no treatment for hepatitis B, an effective prophylactic vaccine is available in most countries. However, it's very expensive. The immunisation schedule requires two injections at least a month apart, followed by a third dose five months after the second. Gamma globulin is not effective against hepatitis B.

Hepatitis C is similar to B but is less common. Hepatitis D is also similar to B and always occurs in conjunction with it; its occurrence is currently limited to drug users. Hepatitis E is similar to A and is spread in the same manner, by water or food contamination. Tests are available for these strands (except Hepatitis E) but they are very expensive. Travellers shouldn't be too paranoid about the proliferation of hepatitis strains; they are fairly rare (so far), and by following the same precautions as for A and B you should avoid them.

Cholera Cholera is transmitted orally through the ingestion of contaminated food or water. The symptoms, which appear one to three days after infection, consist of a sudden onset of acute diarrhoea with 'rice water' stools, vomiting, muscular cramps, and extreme weakness. You need medical attention but your first concern should be rehydration. Drink as much water as you can – if it refuses to stay down, keep drinking anyway. If there is likely to be a considerable delay in reaching medical treatment, begin a course of Tetracycline, but it should not be administered to children or pregnant women.

The cholera vaccination is not very effective, to say the least: protection is estimated (depending on the authority) at between 20% and 80% efficiency. It only lasts for a maximum of six months and it can have side effects. It's probably worth getting vacci-

nated anyway, as there have been outbreaks of cholera over the last three years in various South American countries, including Peru, Colombia, Brazil and Venezuela itself (in the Orinoco Delta). Fortunately, they haven't reached epidemic dimensions.

Typhoid Typhoid fever is another gut infection that travels via contaminated water and food. Vaccination against typhoid is not 100% effective and since it is one of the most dangerous infections, medical attention is necessary.

Early symptoms are like those of many other travellers' illnesses – you may feel as though you have a bad cold or the flu combined with a headache, a sore throat and a fever. The fever rises a little each day until it exceeds 40°C, while the pulse slowly drops – unlike a normal fever where the pulse increases. These symptoms may be accompanied by vomiting, diarrhoea or constipation.

In the second week the high fever and slow pulse continue and a few pink spots may appear on the body. Trembling, delirium, weakness, weight loss and dehydration set in. If there are no further complications, the fever and other symptoms will slowly fade during the third week. Medical attention is essential, however, since typhoid is extremely infectious and possible complications include pneumonia or peritonitis (burst appendix).

When feverish, the patient should be kept cool. Watch for dehydration. The recommended antibiotic is Chloramphenicol, but Ampicillin causes fewer side effects.

Viral Gastroenteritis This is caused not by bacteria but, as the name implies, by a virus. It is characterised by stomach cramps, diarrhoea, and sometimes by vomiting and a slight fever. All you can do is rest and drink lots of fluids.

Insect-Borne Diseases
Malaria This serious disease is spread by mosquito bites.

If you are travelling in endemic areas it is

extremely important to take malarial prophylactics. Symptoms include headaches, fever, chills and sweating which may subside and recur. Without treatment malaria can develop more serious, potentially fatal effects.

Antimalarial drugs do not prevent you from being infected but kill the parasites during a stage in their development.

There are a number of different types of malaria. The one of most concern is falciparum malaria. This is responsible for the very serious cerebral malaria. Falciparum is the predominant form in many malaria prone areas of the world, including Africa, South-East Asia and Papua New Guinea. Contrary to popular belief cerebral malaria is not a new strain.

The problem in recent years has been the emergence of increasing resistance to commonly used antimalarials like chloroquine, maloprim and proguanil. Newer drugs such as mefloquine (Lariam) and doxycycline (Vibramycin, Doryx) are often recommended for chloroquine and multidrug resistant areas. Expert advice should be sought, as there are many factors to consider when deciding on the type of antimalarial medication, including the area to be visited, the risk of exposure to malaria-carrying mosquitoes, your current medical condition, and your age and pregnancy status. It is also important to discuss the side-effect profile of the medication, so you can work out some level of risk versus benefit ratio.

It is also very important to be sure of the correct dosage of the medication prescribed to you. Some people inadvertently have taken weekly medication (chloroquine) on a daily basis, with disastrous effects. While discussing dosages for prevention of malaria, it is often advisable to include the dosages required for treatment, especially if your trip is through a high-risk area that would isolate you from medical care.

The main messages are:

Primary prevention This must always be in the form of mosquito avoidance measures. The mosquitoes that transmit malaria bite from dusk to dawn and during this period travellers are advised to:

- wear light coloured clothing
- wear long pants and long sleeved shirts
- use mosquito repellents containing the compound DEET on exposed areas
- avoid highly scented perfumes or aftershave
- use a mosquito net - it may be worth taking your own

Drugs While no antimalarial is 100% effective, taking the most appropriate drug significantly reduces the risk of contracting the disease.

Diagnosis No one should ever die from malaria. It can be diagnosed by a simple blood test. Symptoms range from fever, chills and sweating, headache and abdominal pains to a vague feeling of ill-health, so seek examination immediately if there is any suggestion of malaria.

Contrary to popular belief, once a traveller contracts malaria he/she does not have it for life. One of the parasites may lie dormant in the liver but this can also be eradicated using a specific medication. Malaria is curable, as long as the traveller seeks medical help when symptoms occur.

Since mosquitoes live in tropical regions up to about 2000 metres above sea level, most of Venezuela is in a malaria-risk area. The risk of infection is highest in steamy lowlands during the wet season. The areas of greatest risk include the Amazonas, Los Llanos and the Orinoco Delta. Use common sense and take precautions if necessary.

As the symptoms of malaria only appear several weeks after contraction of the disease, this may lead to a certain confusion with diagnosis. By that time you may be home in your temperate country and local doctors may not suspect such an exotic disease. Make sure to give your doctor details of your trip.

Yellow Fever Yellow fever is found in much of South America except for the Andean highlands and the southern part of the continent. This viral disease, which is transmitted by mosquitoes, first manifests itself as a fever, with headaches, abdominal pain and vomiting. There may appear to be a brief recovery before it progresses into its more severe stages, including possible liver failure. There is no treatment apart from keeping the fever as low as possible and avoiding dehydration. The yellow fever vaccination gives good protection for 10 years, and is highly recommended for every person travelling on the continent.

Worms Worms are common in most humid tropical areas. They can be present on unwashed vegetables or in undercooked meat, or you can pick them up by walking barefoot. Infestations may not show up for some time and although they are generally not serious, they can cause further health problems if left untreated. A stool test on your return home is not a bad idea. Once the test pinpoints the problem, medication is usually available over the counter and the treatment is easy and short.

The most common form you're likely to contract are hookworms. They are usually caught by walking barefoot on infected soil. The worms bore through the skin, attach themselves to the inner wall of the intestine and proceed to suck your blood, resulting in abdominal pain and sometimes anaemia.

Typhus Typhus is spread by ticks, mites and lice. It begins as a severe cold and is followed by a fever, chills, headache, muscle pains and a body rash. There is often a large and painful sore at the site of the bite, and nearby lymph nodes become swollen and painful.

Trekkers may be at risk from cattle or wild game ticks. Seek local advice about whether or not ticks are present in the area and check yourself carefully after walking in suspect areas. A strong insect repellent can help, and serious walkers should consider treating their boots and trousers with repellent.

Diseases Spread by People & Animals

Tetanus This potentially fatal disease is found in underdeveloped tropical areas. It is difficult to treat but it is easily prevented by immunisation. Tetanus occurs when a wound becomes infected by a germ which lives in human and animal faeces. Clean all cuts, punctures and animal bites. Tetanus is also known as lockjaw as the first symptom may be a difficulty in swallowing or a stiffening of the jaw and neck; this can be followed by painful convulsions of the jaw and whole body.

Rabies Rabies is present in most of South America. It is caused by a bite or scratch by an infected animal. Bats and dogs are the most notorious carriers. Any bite, scratch or lick from a mammal should be cleaned immediately and thoroughly. Scrub the site with soap and running water and then clean it with an alcohol solution. If there is any possibility that the animal is infected, medical help should be sought. Even if the animal is not rabid, all bites should be treated seriously as they can become infected or result in tetanus. Avoid any animal that appears to be foaming at the mouth or acting strangely.

If you are bitten, try to capture the offending animal so that it can be tested. If that's impossible, you must assume the animal is rabid. Rabies is almost always fatal if untreated, so don't take the risk. The rabies virus incubates slowly in its victim, so while medical attention isn't urgent, it shouldn't be delayed.

The treatment consists of a series of seven injections taken for seven subsequent days. A rabies vaccination is now available and should be considered if you intend to spend a lot of time around animals.

Fungal Infections Hot-weather fungal infections are most likely to occur between the toes or fingers, around the groin and sometimes on other parts of the body as well. The infection is spread by infected animals or humans. You may contract it walking barefoot in damp areas.

To prevent fungal infections wear loose, comfortable clothes, avoid artificial fibres, wash frequently and dry thoroughly. Use thongs (flip-flops) in the showers of cheap hotels.

If you do become infected, wash the infected area daily with a disinfectant or medicated soap, and rinse and dry well. Apply an antifungal powder like the widely available Tinaderm. Try to expose the infected area to air or sunlight as much as possible and wash all towels and underwear in hot water and change them often.

Syphilis & Gonorrhoea Sexual contact with an infected partner can result in you contracting a number of diseases. Abstinence is 100% effective but the use of a condom lessens the risk of infection considerably.

The most common sexually transmitted diseases are gonorrhoea and syphilis, which in men first appear as sores, blisters or rashes around the genitals and discharge or pain when urinating. Symptoms may be less marked in women and they may not present at all. Syphilis symptoms eventually disappear but the disease continues and may cause severe problems in later years. Gonorrhoea and syphilis are treated by antibiotics.

HIV & AIDS Human Immunodeficiency Virus (HIV) was identified in the early 1980s, by which stage the disease had been spreading rapidly throughout the world without anybody realising it. By 1994, about 20 to 25 million people worldwide were HIV-positive. It's predicted that by the year 2000 this figure could triple. It's estimated that over 100,000 people in Venezuela are HIV-positive.

The virus is likely to develop into AIDS (Acquired Immunodeficiency Deficiency Syndrome). It is impossible to detect the HIV-status of an otherwise healthy-looking person without a blood test. Although in the West the disease is most commonly spread through contaminated intravenous needles and male homosexual activity, in South America it is transmitted primarily through heterosexual activity. HIV/AIDS can also be contracted through infected blood transfusions; most developing countries cannot afford to screen blood for transfusions. The virus can also be picked up via unsterilised acupuncture and tattoo needles and via ear and nose piercing implements.

As yet, there is no cure for AIDS, and there probably won't be for a while. Never have sex without using a condom, unless you are sure about the HIV status of your partner and yourself.

Climate & Altitude-Related Illnesses
Sunburn Most of Venezuela lies in humid lowland tropics, where the sun's rays are more direct and concentrated than in the temperate zones. In highland areas, particularly in the Andes, you are susceptible to hazardous UV rays and can be sunburnt surprisingly quickly, even through cloud. Use a sunscreen and take extra care to cover areas which don't normally see sun – for example, your feet. A hat provides added protection, and sunglasses will prevent eye irritation (especially if you wear contact lenses). Fair-skinned people should be particularly careful to prevent sunburn.

Prickly Heat Prickly heat is an itchy rash caused by excessive perspiration trapped under the skin. It usually strikes people who have just arrived in a hot climate and whose pores have not yet opened sufficiently to cope with the increased sweating. Frequent baths and application of talcum powder will help relieve the itch.

Heat Exhaustion Serious dehydration or salt deficiency can lead to heat exhaustion. Salt deficiency, which can be brought on by diarrhoea or vomiting, is characterised by fatigue, lethargy, headaches, giddiness and muscle cramps. Salt tablets may help. However, the best way to avoid heat exhaustion is by preventing it: drink lots of liquids and eat salty foods.

Anhydrotic heat exhaustion, caused by an inability to sweat, is quite rare. Unlike the other forms of heat exhaustion, it is likely to strike people who have been in a hot climate for some time, rather than newcomers.

Heatstroke This serious, sometimes fatal, condition can occur if the body's heat-regulating mechanism breaks down and the body temperature rises to dangerous levels. Long, continuous periods of exposure to high temperatures can leave you vulnerable to heatstroke. Alcohol intake and strenuous activity can increase chances of heatstroke, especially amongst those who've recently arrived in a hot climate.

Symptoms include minimal sweating, a high body temperature (39°C to 40°C), and a general feeling of being unwell. The skin may become flushed and red. Severe, throbbing headaches, decreased coordination, and aggressive or confused behaviour may be signs of heatstroke. Eventually, the victim may become delirious and go into convulsions. Get the victim out of the sun, if possible, remove clothing, cover with a wet towel and fan continually. Seek medical help as soon as possible.

Cold Too much cold is just as dangerous as too much heat, and may lead to hypothermia. Fortunately, in Venezuela, hypothermia is probably only a threat in the highest reaches of the Andes and, occasionally, on the top of Roraima.

Hypothermia occurs when the body loses heat faster than it can produce it. It is caused by exhaustion and exposure to cold, wet or windy weather. It is surprisingly easy to progress from being very cold to dangerously cold due to a combination of wind, wet clothing, fatigue and hunger, even if the air temperature is well above freezing.

It is best to dress in layers; silk, wool and some of the new artificial fibres are all good insulating materials. A hat is important, as a lot of heat is lost through the head. A strong, waterproof outer layer is essential, and keeping dry is vital. Carry food containing simple sugars to generate heat quickly, and lots of fluid to drink.

Symptoms of hypothermia include exhaustion, numb skin (particularly toes and fingers), shivering, slurred speech, irrational or violent behaviour, lethargy, stumbling, dizzy spells, muscle cramps and violent bursts of energy.

To treat hypothermia, first get the patient out of the wind and/or rain, remove their clothing if it's wet and replace it with dry, warm garments. Give them hot liquids – not alcohol – and easily digestible food. This should be enough for the early stages of hypothermia, but if it has gone further, it may be necessary to place victims in a sleeping bag and get in with them in order to provide as much warmth as possible. If no improvement is noticed within a few minutes, seek help but don't leave the victim alone while doing so. The body heat of another person is more important than medical attention.

Altitude Sickness Altitude sickness, and its more serious stage known as Acute Mountain Sickness (AMS), occurs at high altitudes and in extreme cases can be fatal. They are caused by a too rapid ascent to a high altitude, which does not allow the body time to adapt to the lower oxygen concentration in the atmosphere. Light symptoms can appear at altitudes as low as 2500 metres. They become increasingly severe the higher up you go. Most people are affected to some extent at altitudes between 3500 and 4500 metres. You may reach these altitudes if trekking in the Sierra Nevada de Mérida.

The best ways to minimise the risk of altitude sickness are to ascend slowly, to increase liquid intake and to eat meals which are rich in energy-rich carbohydrates. Most importantly, do not trek alone.

Even with acclimatisation, however, you may still have trouble if you push on. Headaches, nausea, dizziness, a dry cough, breathlessness and loss of appetite are the most frequent symptoms. As long as they remain mild there's no reason to panic, but the ascent should be halted and the victim watched closely and given plenty of fluids and rest. If there is no improvement after a few hours, descend to a lower altitude. This becomes particularly important if the symptoms become more serious.

Descend immediately, helping the victim to avoid undue exertion by carrying their backpack or, if necessary, taking them on your back. Often a few hundred metres drop is sufficient for considerable relief. Descend further and rest for a day or two. Don't take risks with altitude sickness; many people have died because they have ignored the early symptoms and pressed on to higher altitudes.

Altitude sickness is completely unpredictable – there is no rule as to who is susceptible. Youth and fitness are no advantage. Furthermore, those who've had no problems at high altitudes before may suddenly come down with altitude sickness at considerably lower altitudes.

Cuts, Bites & Stings

Cuts & Scratches In the warm, moist tropical lowlands skin punctures can easily become infected and may have difficulty healing. Even a small cut or scratch can become painfully infected and this can lead to more serious problems.

The best treatment for cuts is to frequently cleanse the affected area with soap and water and to apply Mercurochrome or an antiseptic cream. Where possible, avoid using bandages, which keep wounds moist and encourage the growth of bacteria. If, despite this, the wound becomes tender and inflamed, then use a mild, broad-spectrum antibiotic. Remember that bacterial immunity to certain antibiotics may build up, so it's not wise to take these medicines indiscriminately or as a preventative measure.

Coral cuts are notoriously slow to heal, as the coral injects a weak venom into the wound. Avoid coral cuts by wearing shoes when walking on reefs and clean any cut thoroughly.

Bites & Stings A constellation of ants, gnats, mosquitoes, bees, spiders, flies and other exotic creatures exist in Venezuela and you may experience a variety of bites and stings. Some are more dangerous or annoying than others but it's best to protect yourself from bites anyway. The problem is more serious in the countryside than in the cities, and dense, humid forests are probably the worst place for bites and stings. Protect your skin, especially from dusk to dawn when many insects, including malaria-transmitting mosquitoes, like to feed.

Cover yourself well with clothing. Wear long-sleeved shirts and long trousers instead of T-shirts and shorts, and shoes or runners instead of sandals or thongs.

Use insect repellent on exposed skin and, if necessary, apply it to your clothes. Sleep under a mosquito net if you are outdoors or if your hotel room doesn't have a fan or if the fan doesn't produce enough of a breeze. Burning incense also lowers the risk. Good repellents, mosquito nets and incenses are available in Venezuela.

Avoid scratching bites as this may cause them to become infected. There are creams and lotions which will alleviate itching and deal with infections. They are sold in local pharmacies.

Bee and wasp stings are usually more painful than dangerous. Calamine lotion will provide some relief and ice packs will reduce the pain and swelling.

Body lice and scabies mites are common but shampoos and creams are available to eliminate them. In addition to hair and skin, clothing and bedding should be washed thoroughly to prevent further infestation.

Bedbugs love to live in dirty mattresses and in the bedding of seedy hotels. Spots of blood on bedclothes or on the wall around the bed might suggest it's worth looking for another hotel. Bedbugs leave itchy bites; calamine lotion may help alleviate them.

Leeches may be present in damp rainforests. They attach themselves to your skin and suck your blood. Trekkers often get them on their legs or in their boots. Salt or a lighted cigarette end will make them fall off. Do not pull them off, as the bite is then more likely to become infected. An insect repellent may keep them away.

Vaseline, alcohol or oil will persuade a tick to let go. You should always check your body if you have been walking through a tick-infested area, as they can spread typhus.

It's rather unlikely that you'll be stung by a scorpion or a spider, but if you are it may be severely painful (though rarely fatal). They tend to shelter in shoes and clothing, so check them before putting them on. Also, check your bedding or sleeping bag before going to sleep.

Snakebite Even though there's only a small chance of snakebite in Venezuela, you should take precautions, particularly in Amazonas and Lara states. The most dangerous snake is the mapanare. It's an extremely venomous, aggressive snake and many live in Lara state. It's the largest poisonous snake in South America and is distinguished by its rhomboid markings, similar to those of the rattlesnake (which is the next in line in terms of danger).

Wear boots, socks and long trousers when walking through undergrowth. A good pair of canvas gaiters will protect your legs. Don't put your hands into holes and crevices, and be careful when collecting firewood. Check shoes, clothing and sleeping bags before use.

Snakebites do not cause instantaneous death and antivenins are available. It is vital that you positively identify the snake in question or, at the very least, be able to describe it.

If someone is bitten by a snake, keep the victim calm and still, wrap the bitten limb tightly, as you would for a sprain, then attach a splint to immobilise it. Seek medical help immediately and, if possible, bring the dead snake along for identification. Don't attempt to catch the snake if there is a chance of being bitten again. Tourniquets and trying to suck out the poison are now comprehensively discredited as treatments.

If you plan on trekking in the wilderness, antivenins for some local snakes can be bought at the Universidad Central de Venezuela in Caracas. Antivenins must be kept at a low temperature, otherwise their efficiency quickly decreases. It's a good idea to carry a field guide with photos and detailed descriptions of the possible perpetrators.

Motion Sickness
If you are prone to motion sickness sit somewhere with minimal disturbance – near the wing on an aircraft, midships on a boat or front and in the middle of a bus. Eating lightly before and during a trip will reduce the chances of motion sickness. Fresh air almost always helps, but reading and cigarettes make matters worse.

Commercial motion sickness preparations, which can cause drowsiness, have to be taken before the trip; if you're already feeling sick, it's too late. Dramamine tablets, one of the most popular medications, should

be taken three hours before departure. Ginger can be used as a natural preventative and it is available in capsule form.

Women's Health
Gynaecological Problems Poor diet, lowered infection resistance (due to the use of antibiotics) and even contraceptive pills can lead to vaginal infections when travelling in hot climates. Keeping the genital area clean, and wearing skirts or loose-fitting trousers and cotton underwear, will help to prevent infections.

Yeast infections, characterised by an itchy rash and discharge, can be treated with a vinegar or lemon-juice douche or with yoghurt. Nystatin suppositories are the usual medical prescription. Trichomonas is a more serious infection; symptoms include a discharge and a burning sensation when urinating. Male sexual partners must also be treated, and if a vinegar-water douche is not effective, medical attention should be sought. Metronidazole (Flagyl) is the most frequently prescribed drug.

Pregnancy Most miscarriages occur during the first three months of pregnancy, so this is the most risky time to travel as far as your own health is concerned. Miscarriage is not uncommon, and can occasionally lead to severe bleeding. The last three months should also be spent within reasonable distance of good medical care. A baby born as early as 24 weeks stands a chance of survival, but only in a good modern hospital. Pregnant women should avoid all unnecessary medication, but vaccinations and malarial prophylactics should still be taken where possible. Additional care should be taken to prevent illness and particular attention should be paid to diet and nutrition. Alcohol and nicotine, for example, should be avoided.

Women travellers often find that their periods become irregular or even cease while they're on the road. Remember that a missed period in these circumstances doesn't necessarily indicate pregnancy. There are health posts or Family Planning clinics in many small and large urban centres in developing countries, where you can seek advice and have a urine test to determine whether you are pregnant or not.

Back Home

Be aware of illness after you return home; take note of odd or persistent symptoms of any kind, get a check-up and remember to give your physician a complete travel history. Most doctors in temperate climates will not suspect unusual tropical diseases. If you have been travelling in malarial areas, have yourself tested for the disease.

Health Glossary

This basic glossary of illnesses and other health-related terms may be useful. See the Language section in the Facts about the Country chapter for emergency terms and phrases.

AIDS	*SIDA (síndrome de inmunodeficiencia adquirida)*
allergy	*alergia*
antibiotic	*antibiótico*
bite	*picadura* (insect, snake) *mordedura* (dog)
blood	*sangre*
blood test	*examen de sangre*
cold or flu	*gripe*
cholera	*cólera*
condom	*condón*
cough	*tos*
cut	*cortadura*
diarrhoea	*diarrea*
disease	*enfermedad*
dizziness	*mareo*
dysentery	*disentería*
earache	*otitis, dolor de oido*
fatigue	*fatiga, cansancio*
fever	*fiebre*
headache	*dolor de cabeza*
heart attack	*ataque cardíco, infarto*
hepatitis	*hepatitis*
health	*salud*
heatstroke	*insolación*
HIV	*VIH (virus de inmunodeficiencia humana)*
injection	*inyección*
insurance	*seguro*
itching	*ardor*
malaria	*malaria*
medicament	*droga, medicamento*
miscarriage	*aborto*
nausea	*náusea*
pain	*dolor*
penicillin	*penicilina*
contraceptive pills	*píldoras/pastillas anticonceptivas*
pneumonia	*pulmonía*
polio	*polio*
pregnancy	*embarazo*
prescription	*receta*
rabies	*rabia*
rash	*erupción cutánea, escozor, rasquiña*
stomach	*estómago*
symptom	*síntoma*
syringe	*jeringa*
sore throat	*dolor de garganta*
sunburn	*quemadura de sol*
tablets	*pastillas*
tetanus	*tétano*
toothache	*dolor de muelas*
typhoid	*fiebre tifoidea*
vaccination	*vacuna*
vomiting	*vómito*
weakness	*debilidad*
wound	*herida*
yellow fever	*fiebre amarilla*

WOMEN TRAVELLERS

Like most of South America, Venezuela is very much a 'man's country'. Machismo and sexism are palpable throughout society: from the level of the family right up to the highest levels of government. The dominant Catholic Church with its conservative attitude towards women doesn't help matters. In this context, it's not difficult to imagine how an unmarried gringa travelling by herself is regarded.

If you are a woman, you'll find you attract more curiosity and attention from Venezuelan men than you would from men in the West. Venezuelan men often sing flirtatiously and make passes at women. Gringas are seen as more exotic and challenging conquests. Local males will pick you out in the crowd and do their best to capture your attention. These advances are often light-hearted but can sometimes be more direct and rude. Men in the larger cities, especially in Caracas, will display more bravado and be more insistent than those in obscure villages.

The best way to deal with this is to simply ignore their advances. Look away and act as if there was nobody around. Dressing modestly will obviously lessen the chances of you being the object of macho interest. Watch what Venezuelan women are wearing and try to wear similar fashions.

Travelling with a companion will make things easier and you will have each other for support.

Unfortunately, a woman travelling alone faces more risks than does a man. Women should avoid shabby barrios, solitary streets and beaches and all places considered male territory such as bars, sports matches, mines and the like. Don't hitch alone, especially if you are off the beaten track.

DANGERS & ANNOYANCES

Venezuela is a relatively safe country to travel in, although robbery is becoming more common. Crime is on the increase in the larger cities. Caracas is the most dangerous place in the country and you should take care while strolling about the streets, particularly at night.

Elsewhere, you can travel more peacefully but you should always observe basic precautions and use common sense. Leaving your backpack unattended while buying your coffee, for example, is just asking for trouble.

This section, detailing quite a variety of potential dangers, may look alarming. Don't panic, however; Venezuela is still safe, even though it has for its neighbours two of the most violent nations on the continent, Colombia and Brazil. The intention of this section is not to frighten you with how many things you can lose but to demonstrate how many things you can do to prevent loss.

Predeparture Precautions

The most important precaution is to take with you only those items which you are prepared to lose. Accordingly, only take used or cheap items, or if they are expensive (for example a camera), it's best if they're standard models which are easy to replace. As far as replacement goes, the best guarantee is travel insurance – make sure to buy some. A good policy is essential for two reasons: it gives you the psychological comfort of knowing that a loss won't ruin you or the trip; and it gives you the actual security of replacement if something is lost (touch wood). Violent or petty theft is always a stressful experience, but, if you keep to the above-mentioned advice, you'll get through it with less trauma.

Don't bring jewellery, chains, expensive watches or anything flashy – this will only increase the chances of robbery. Don't bring anything of sentimental value, the loss of which would cause significant grief. And, above all, take as little as possible: the less you carry with you, the less you have to lose.

Keep money and documents as secure as possible (see Security Accessories). Take photocopies of all your important documents and their details: your passport; travellers' cheques; credit cards; airline tickets, contact addresses etc. Keep one copy with you, one with your belongings and another with a travelling companion.

Don't take your original address/phone book with you: make a copy. Take a note of your camera's serial number and do the same with the lenses, your camcorder and any other pieces of high-tech gear you'll be taking with you.

Take most of your money in travellers' cheques and credit cards, leaving only an emergency amount in cash (preferably US dollars). Keep a record of the place and date of the purchase of your cheques – this information may be necessary if you need to report their loss or theft. Make sure you know the number to call if you lose your credit card, and be quick to cancel it if it's lost or stolen.

Cabling money is time-consuming, difficult and expensive. You must know the name and address of both the bank sending (record this and keep this with your documents) and the bank receiving the money.

Security Accessories

It's best if your backpack is fitted with double zippers, which can be secured with small combination locks. Padlocks are also good, but are easier to pick. A thick backpack cover or modified canvas sack improves protection against pilfering, the planting of drugs, and general wear and tear. Double zippers on your daypack can be secured with safety pins which will make it harder for petty thieves to get at your belongings. Some travellers deter razor-thieves by lining the inside of their daypacks (and even their backpacks) with lightweight wire mesh. A spare combination lock or padlock is useful for replacing the padlocks on your hotel door.

A swanky camera bag is not a good idea: take something less conspicuous. Many travellers carry their photo equipment in daypacks. Bring a plain, sober daypack rather than one which is fluorescent orange or an outrageous shade of purple.

Various types of money belts are available. These can be worn around the waist, neck or shoulder. Those made of leather or cotton are more comfortable than the synthetic variety. Money belts are only useful if worn under clothing – pouches worn outside clothing attract attention and are easy prey. Determined thieves are wise to conventional money belts. Some travellers also sew cloth pouches into their trousers or other items of clothing. Other methods include belts with a concealed zipper compartment and bandages or pouches worn around the leg.

If you wear glasses, secure them with an elastic strap to avoid them falling off and breaking and to deter petty theft. Better still, wear contact lenses.

Precautions in Venezuela

For a starter, don't put all your eggs into one basket: distribute your valuables about your person and luggage to avoid the risk of losing everything in one fell swoop. It's a good idea to have a small emergency packet containing the important details of your passport, cheques, credit cards, tickets etc as well as a US$100 bill. Keep the packet separately in a safe place, for example sewn into your trousers. Keep in mind that expensive clothes are also appreciated by robbers.

Your dress is an important piece of information for thieves. The rule 'the shabbier you look, the better' works well in risky areas but use common sense and wear more decent clothes in less dangerous places. Your dress should be casual and inexpensive; it's best to follow local fashion.

If you carry a daypack, it's safer to wear it strapped to your front rather than on your back. Many local youth now carry their packs that way, particularly in Caracas.

If you're in a bus terminal, restaurant, shop or somewhere public and you have to put your daypack down, put your foot through the strap. If you have a camera, don't wander around with it dangling over your shoulder or around your neck – keep it out of sight as much as possible. Your camera bag – if you've opted to bring one and carry it with you – will entice thieves and robbers. In genuinely risky areas, you shouldn't carry your camera at all. If you have to, for whatever reason, camouflage it as best you can – an ordinary plastic bag from a local supermarket is one way of disguising it.

Get used to keeping small amounts of money, say, your expected daily expenditure, in a pocket or another easily accessible place, so you can pay your expenses without extracting a bundle of notes and attracting attention. This money is also useful in case you are assailed: muggers can become annoyed if you don't have anything for them and they may react unpredictably. The rest of your money should be well hidden, in a body pouch, money belt etc. Leave your wallet at home as it's an easy mark for pickpockets.

Don't look lost. Don't stand with a blank expression in the middle of the street or in front of the bus terminal. Helpless-looking tourists are the favourite victims of thieves and robbers.

Before arriving in a new place, make sure you have a map or at least a rough idea of orientation. Try to plan your schedule so you don't arrive at night, and use a taxi if this seems the appropriate way to avoid walking through high-risk areas. Remain vigilant and learn to move like a street-smart local.

Thieves often work in pairs or groups, and while one or more of them distracts you, the accomplice does the deed. There are hundreds, if not thousands, of ways of distracting you and new scams are dreamt up every day. Someone 'accidentally' bumps into you, throwing you off balance; a group of strangers appears in front of you and greets you as if you were lifelong friends; a elderly woman drops her shopping bag at your feet; a character spills something on your clothes or your daypack; several kids start a fight around you. Try not to get distracted although, of course, it's easier said than done.

Keep your eyes open when you're leaving your hotel, bank, casa de cambio etc. Look for anyone who appears to be watching you, and if you think you're being followed or closely observed, let them know that you are aware of them and alert.

If you happen to be in a crowded place keep a close eye on your pockets and daypack. Even if you have a cheap watch, it's better to keep it in your pocket than on your wrist – it attracts attention.

On intercity bus journeys, put your backpack in the luggage compartment, where it will be relatively safe. As for your daypack or handbag, don't put it down on the floor or up on the luggage rack – keep it under your arm next to you or, if you are with a companion, tight between the two of you.

Muggings are rare in Venezuela except in Caracas, where they have become more common over the last few years. The most usual weapon is a knife but pistols are not unheard of. The attack usually goes something like this: you are stopped on the street by a man or, more often, a group of men who show you a knife (even if they don't, you can take it for granted that they have one) and ask you for your money and valuables, or set

about searching for themselves. It is best to give them what they are after. Don't try to escape or struggle – your chances are slim. The favourite places for robbery are slum areas, but some Caracas gangs have been known to 'work' in the central districts during daylight hours. Don't count on any help from passers-by.

There are also purse-snatchers in Caracas, operating from motorbikes, so carry your handbag on the side away from the street.

Police

If you do lose your passport and other valuables go to the police station and make a *denuncia* (report). They will give you a copy which serves as a temporary identity document, and if you have insurance, you will need to present it in order to make a claim. Don't expect your things to be found as the police are unlikely even to look for them.

There are plenty of *alcabalas* (police road checkposts) on the country roads, which stop and control the traffic passing through, mostly trucks and public buses. They sometimes check the identity documents of passengers but seldom check their luggage. In the cities, ID checks by the police are not common but they do occur, so always have your passport with you. If you don't you may end up at the police station.

By law you must carry your passport with you at all times. A certified photocopy of the passport is not a legal identity document. Although some police officers may be satisfied with it, others won't accept it.

If you happen to get involved with the police, be polite but not overly friendly. Don't get nervous or angry – this only works against you.

Be wary of false plain-clothes police. Although they are comparatively rare in Venezuela they are well known in some other South American countries, such as Colombia and the problem may spread over the borders.

Drugs

The presence of Colombian cocaine in Venezuela is on the rise. Drugs pass through

Venezuela en route to US and European destinations. The number of locals involved in drug trafficking is increasing and so is corruption and the other crimes that accompany this illicit business. Fortunately, planting drugs on tourists in order to extort bribes hasn't, as yet, been reported.

Keep well away from drugs, don't carry even the smallest quantity, and watch carefully while police officers search your luggage. Politely refuse any request from a stranger at the airport to take a piece of their luggage with you on to the plane.

Annoyances

Plumbing and toilets in down-to-earth hotels might not be what you are accustomed to in the West. Since the tubes are narrow and the water pressure is weak, toilets usually don't cope with toilet paper. A wastebasket is normally provided; if there is no receptacle or if it's already full, toss the used toilet paper on the floor and someone may get around to cleaning it up.

If you ask for information or directions, don't always expect a correct answer, especially in the countryside. The campesinos have different notions of time and space, and often, even if they have no idea, they will tell you anything just to appear helpful and knowledgeable. Ask several people the same question and if one answer seems to pop up more frequently than the others it may be the correct one. Avoid 'yes' or 'no' questions; instead of 'is this the way to...?' ask 'which is the way to ...?'.

Never show any disrespect for Bolívar – he is a saint to Venezuelans. For instance, sitting on a bench in Plaza Bolívar with your feet on the bench, or crossing the plaza carrying bulky parcels (or a backpack) may be considered disrespectful and police may hassle you for it.

ACTIVITIES

Venezuela has much to offer those who love the great outdoors. Its 40-odd national parks provide a good choice of walks ranging from easy, well-signposted trails to jungle paths where a machete might be a useful tool. If you arrive in Venezuela at Caracas, try Parque Nacional El Ávila first before heading for the less developed trails in Guatopo, Terepaima, San Esteban, and Canaima national parks.

Sierra Nevada de Mérida is the best region in Venezuela for high-mountain trekking and, if you're up to it, you can try mountaineering and rock climbing there; guides and equipment are available. Incidentally, Mérida state is also the best area for mountain bike riding which has become quite popular; bikes and guides can be hired.

Mérida is also the best place to go hanggliding. Paragliding is relatively new but it is becoming more widespread in Caracas and Mérida. Double gliders are available, so even greenhorns can try this breathtaking experience.

Some of the national parks, including Morrocoy, Henri Pittier and Yacambú, are excellent for wildlife watchers, and particularly for bird-watchers. You can go on your own, combining hiking and bird-watching or if you'd prefer a more comfortable way to observe the flora and fauna, it's best to go to one of the hatos in Los Llanos, where a boat or a jeep will take you on a guided safari through an amazing animal world.

With 3000 km of coastline, beach fanatics can sunbathe to their hearts' content (although I'm not exactly sure this qualifies as an 'activity'). Fans of snorkelling and scuba diving will be in their element. Submatur in Tucacas is the best specialist on dive matters. They sell and rent equipment, fill tanks, organise courses and diving trips. Sailing is another attractive possibility but unless you come with your own yacht you'll need a fat wallet to hire one.

Fishing enthusiasts can try their luck on the coast or they can go fishing in rivers; the Orinoco and some of its tributaries are good places for this. Before you go fishing, inquire about seasonal permits: the Inparques offices if you plan on fishing in national parks; and the Ministerio de Agricultura y Cría in Caracas for fishing in rivers and lakes outside the parks.

Speleologists can explore some of

Venezuela's several hundred caves. The longest and possibly the most spectacular is the Cueva del Guácharo. If you want to visit its galleries which are closed to the general public, you need a special permit from Caracas. Inquire at the Inparques office.

ACCOMMODATION

In this book the accommodation listed in the Places to Stay sections is almost invariably ordered according to price (going from the least expensive to the most expensive). Accordingly, budget travellers should read these sections from the beginning, whilst more affluent visitors will probably go straight to the closing paragraphs.

Where the hotels are broken down into price categories, the bottom-end accommodation includes anything costing less than around US$12 for a double, the middle-range hotels run from approximately US$12 to US$25 per double, and anything over US$25 for a double is considered top end.

Venezuela doesn't belong to Hostelling International and has no youth hostels.

Hotels

There are heaps of hotels for every budget and it's usually easy enough to find a room, except perhaps on major feast days. The cheapies tend to be grouped together in certain areas, which are, by and large, around the market and/or in the city centre. Top-class hotels, on the other hand, are usually scattered around the wealthier districts, which aren't necessarily close to the centre. You can expect to find at least one mid-priced hotel on the Plaza Bolívar or in its immediate vicinity.

Budget Hotels On the whole, low-budget hotels are uninteresting, shabby places – just bare walls, a bed and perhaps a few other bits of furniture. Most of the cheapies have private baths which are usually separated from the main room by a half-hearted partition (often just a section of wall which doesn't even reach the ceiling) and there is hardly ever a door between the two areas. Note that toilets in bottom-end hotels can't

cope with toilet paper, so throw your refuse into the wastebasket which is normally provided.

Budget accommodation appears under a variety of names such as a *hotel, residencia, hospedaje, posada* or *pensión*. The last two tend to be small, family-run guesthouses. They often have more character and are friendlier than the rest (although sometimes they may be even worse).

As most of the country lies in the lowland tropics, a fan is a staple in cheap hotel rooms and you may find the room has air-conditioning. Understandably, there's no hot water.

Air-conditioning in these hotels is not always an advantage. The equipment often dates from the oil-rich years and, after a decade or more of use, it may be in a desperate state of disrepair and as noisy as a tank. There's usually only the on/off alternative, and it's not always clear which is better. Sometimes they're too efficient and they turn the room into a freezer, at other times they don't cool the room at all.

In the cheapies, always have a look at the room before booking in and paying. While inspecting the room, check that the toilet flushes and that the water runs in the shower (and that it is in fact hot water if they have assured you they have it). Make sure the fan (or air-conditioning) works and check the lock on the door to see if it's sufficiently secure. If you're not satisfied with the room you're shown, ask to see another. After deciding and checking in, you should be given a towel, a small piece of soap and a roll of toilet paper.

Brothels and 'love hotels' (places which rent rooms by the hour) are not uncommon in Venezuela. Many cheap hotels double as love hotels, and it's often impossible to recognise them and to avoid staying in one from time to time. However, it's probably not worth avoiding them as they are often just as safe as other places (after all the guests have other things on their minds) and the staff normally separate the sex section from the rest.

The price of cheap hotels is roughly similar throughout the country (except in

Caracas) and doesn't seem to depend much on whether you're in a big city or a small town, or whether the place is touristy or not. Count on roughly US$5 to US$7 for a single room *(habitación sencilla)* and US$7 to US$9 for a double *(habitación doble)*. Some hotels don't have singles and the cheapest is the so-called *habitación matrimonial*. This is the room with one wide double bed intended for couples. It often costs the same for one as for two, so travelling as a couple considerably reduces the cost of accommodation.

By and large, hotels are safe places, but certain precautions and common sense are advisable. Most budget places lock their doors at night and some even lock them during the day, opening them for the guests only.

The biggest threat to the security of your belongings is most likely to come from the other guests. The thief's 'work' is made easier by the partial hardboard partitions between the rooms and the flimsy catches with easily-picked padlocks on the doors. Even if your hotel provides a padlock, it's recommended that you use your own combination lock (or padlock) instead. A hotel padlock obviously increases the number of people with access to your room. As a rule, the bigger hotels aren't as safe as the smaller ones as the atmosphere is less personal and a thief won't stand out in a crowd.

Most budget hotels offer a deposit facility which usually means that the management can put your gear into their own room as there are no other safe places. This reduces the risk but doesn't eliminate it completely. In most cheapies, the staff probably won't want to give you any receipt, and if you insist on one, they may simply refuse to guard your valuables. Decide for yourself which is safer.

Mid-Range & Top End Hotels Mid-range hotels provide more facilities although they often lack character. Some of these hotels are very reasonably priced for what they offer, and you may sometimes find an excellent place for, say, US$20 per double room. Others are outrageously overpriced. It's a good idea to inspect the room in these hotels before you commit yourself.

In top-end hotels, you can be more sure about the standard, though the prices vary greatly and don't always reflect the actual value. Except for Caracas, where the prices seem to be somewhat inflated, you can normally grab a quite posh double with all facilities for somewhere between US$50 and US$80.

Only Caracas and Isla de Margarita, and to a lesser extent Puerto La Cruz and Maracaibo, have a reasonable choice of five-star hotels. Be prepared to pay about US$100 upwards for a single and US$120 upwards for a double.

Hotels charge foreigners a 10% tax on top of the room price, though not all budget places do it. The prices listed in this book have included this tax already.

These hotels have the reception desk open round the clock with proper facilities to safeguard guests' valuables.

Camping

Campgrounds, as you might think of them in the West, are few and far between in Venezuela. You can camp rough outside the urban centres and camping on the beach is popular. Be careful though, and don't leave your tent unattended.

If you camp in wilderness or other fragile areas, try to minimise your impact on the environment. Biodegradable items may be buried but food scraps and cigarette butts should be carried out, lest they be dug up and scattered by animals. If there are no toilet facilities, select a site at least 50 metres from water sources, and bury waste. If possible, burn the used toilet paper or bury it well. Use biodegradable soap products. Wash dishes and brush your teeth well away from watercourses. Make sure you have a sufficient stock of sturdy bags to take your garbage out of the area when you leave.

FOOD & DRINK

Venezuela is a good place to eat. On the whole, the food is good and relatively inexpensive, though dearer than, say, in Colombia or Ecuador. Apart from a variety of typical local dishes, there are plenty of

Western cuisines available. Given that Venezuela is the most Americanised country on the continent, there's any number of gringo fast-food outlets including the ubiquitous McDonald's. Spanish and Italian restaurants are particularly well represented thanks to the sizeable migration from these two countries. There are also some good Chinese and Middle Eastern restaurants, mostly in the main cities.

Gourmets will enjoy their stay in Caracas which offers the widest range of international delicacies, but at a price. On the other hand, non-demanding, rock-bottom travellers should look for restaurants which serve the so-called *menú del día*, a set meal consisting of soup and a main course, which is cheaper than any à la carte dish. There's a good supply of barbecued chicken joints; half a chicken with arepa, potatoes, yuca or other side dish can be found for about US$3. The market is, as in most of South America, a good cheap option, offering typical food which is usually tasty and fresh.

In virtually every dining or drinking establishment, a 10% service charge will automatically be added to the bill. In budget eateries, tipping is uncommon, but in up-market restaurants, a small tip is customary.

Venezuelan Cuisine

The following list includes some typical snacks and dishes, collectively referred to as *comida criolla*:

Arepa – a maize pancake, which in itself is plain and comes as accompaniment to some dishes. More often it's served as a snack stuffed with a variety of fillings. There are plenty of snack bars, commonly called *areperas*, which serve arepas stuffed with cheese, beef, ham, octopus, shrimps, sausage, eggs, salad, avocado and just about anything you might think of. It's a good snack for about US$1.

Cachapa – a round pancake made of fresh corn, often served with cheese and/or jam.

Cachito – a sort of croissant filled with chopped ham and served hot.

Casabe – a very large, dry flat bread made from yuca amarga; common in the Gran Sabana.

Empanada – a deep-fried cornmeal turnover stuffed with ground meat, cheese, beans or baby shark; a ubiquitous snack found throughout the continent, with numerous local varieties.

Hallaca – chopped pork, beef and/or chicken with vegetables and olives, all folded in a maize dough, wrapped in banana leaves and steamed; particularly popular during Christmas.

Hervido – a hearty soup made of beef (*hervido de res*) or chicken (*hervido de gallina*) with potatoes, carrots and a variety of local root vegetables.

Lechón – a whole suckling pig stuffed with pork and rice, and roasted on a spit.

Mondongo – a seasoned tripe cooked in bouillon with maize, potatoes and other vegetables.

Muchacho – roast loin of beef served in sauce.

Pabellón criollo – a main course consisting of shredded beef, rice, black beans, cheese and fried ripe plantain (*tajada*); it's Venezuela's national dish.

Parrillada – also called *parrilla*, barbecue of different kinds of meat; originally an Argentine speciality but now widespread in Venezuela.

Sancocho – a vegetable stew with fish, beef or chicken.

Tequeño – white cheese strips wrapped in pastry and deep-fried.

Drinks

Expresso coffee is strong and excellent in Venezuela. It's served in *panaderías*, coffee shop-cum-bakeries, which are plentiful. Ask for *café negro* if you want it black; for *café marrón* if you prefer half coffee half milk; or *café con leche* if you like very milky coffee.

Fruit juices are popular and readily available in restaurants, *fuentes de soda*, *fruterías*, *refresquerías* and other eating outlets. Given the variety of fruit in the country, you have quite a choice. Juices come pure or watered-down (*batidos*), or as milk shakes (*merengadas*).

The favourite alcoholic drink is beer, particularly Polar beer which is the dominant brand. It is sold everywhere in either cans (about 0.3 litre) or bottles (0.22 litre) and costs from US$0.40 in down-to-earth eateries (more in other places). Other local beer brands include: Regional, Cardenal and Nacional.

The local production of wine is small and the quality poor. There are plenty of imported wines available from other South American countries, Europe and the USA. Chilean and Argentine wines are not bad and come at affordable prices, but European wines are expensive, especially so in restaurants.

Among spirits, *ron* (rum) heads the list and it comes in numerous varieties and different qualities. The Ron Añejo Aniversario Pampero is, without a doubt, the best dark rum Venezuela produces. The 0.75-litre bottle, elegantly packed in a leather pouch, will cost about US$7.50 in a bottle shop.

Food & Drink Terms

Here is a glossary of food and drink terms you are likely to come across in Venezuela:

aceite – oil
aceituna – olive
agua – water
aguacate – avocado
ají – red chilli pepper
ajo – garlic
ajoporro – leek
alcaparra – caper
aliño – combination of spices
almeja – clam
almendra – almond
almuerzo – lunch
apio – root vegetable
arepera – snack bar that serves arepas
arroz – rice
arveja – green peas
atún – tuna
auyama – pumpkin
avellanas – hazelnuts
azúcar – sugar

bagre – catfish
batata – sweet potato
batido – fresh fruit juice
bebida – drink, beverage
berenjena – eggplant
bienmesabe – sponge cake with coconut flavour
brócoli – broccoli

calabacín – zucchini, courgette
calabaza – squash
calamar – squid
calentado – typical hot drink in the Andean highlands, made from miche (anise-flavoured sugarcane liqueur) and warm milk
camarón – small shrimp
cambur – banana
canela – cinnamon
cangrejo – crab
carabina – Mérida version of hallaca
caracol – snail
caraota – black bean
carite – cero mackerel, king fish
carne – meat
carne de cochino – pork
carne de res – beef
carne molida – mince meat
carne guisada – stewed beef
carne mechada – shredded beef
cazón – baby shark
cebolla – onion
cebollín – scallion, spring onion
céleri – celery
cerdo – pork
cereza – cherry
cerveza – beer
cilantro – coriander
ciruela – plum
cocada – blended drink made from coconut milk
coco – coconut
coctel – cocktail
cocuy – a kind of liqueur made from sugar cane
cochino – pork
codorniz – quail
coliflor – cauliflower
contorno – accompaniment
cordero – lamb

corocoro – grunt (fish)
corvina – blue fish
costilla – rib
cotufa – popcorn
crema agria – sour cream

champiñón – mushroom
charcutería – pork butcher's, a shop selling hams, sausages, salamis etc
chayote – christophene, chayote. A light green pear shaped vegetable
chicha – corn or rice low-alcohol (sometimes not so low) drink
chicharrón – pork crackling
chimbombo – okra, ladies fingers, gumbo
chivo – goat
chocolate – chocolate
chorizo – seasoned sausage
chuleta – chop, rib steak
churro – fried pastry tubes sprinkled with sugar; often sold on the street

dátil – date
desayuno – breakfast
dorado – dolphin fish
dulce – small cake
durazno – apricot

ensalada – salad
espárrago – asparagus
espinaca – spinach

falda – flank
frambuesa – raspberry
fresa – strawberry
frijoles – red beans

galleta – biscuit, cracker
gallina – hen
garbanzo – chickpea
grasa – fat
guacuco – clam
guanábana – soursop
guarapita – drink made from a sugar cane spirit and fruit juice
guasacaca – a sauce often served with chicken or parrillas, made of capsycum, onions and seasoning
guayaba – guava
guayoyo – weak black coffee

guisante – pea

haba – large lima bean common in the Andes
helado – ice cream
hielo – ice
hígado – liver
higo – fig
hongo – mushroom, fungus
huevo – egg
huevos fritos – fried eggs
huevos revueltos – scrambled eggs

jamón – ham
jamón serrano – cured ham
jojoto – kernel corn, fresh corn
jugo – juice
jurel – jurel, saurel, scad

langosta – lobster
langostino – large shrimp, large prawn
lebranche – black mullet
leche – milk
leche de burra – alcoholic beverage made of egg and miche (anise-flavoured sugarcane liqueur), common in the Andes
leche descremada – skimmed milk
lechosa – papaya, pawpaw
lechuga – lettuce
lenguado – sole, flounder
lenteja – lentil
lima – lime
limón – lemon
limonada – lemonade
lisa – silver mullet, grey mullet
lomito – tenderloin
lunchería – restaurant serving staple food and snacks

maíz – corn, maize
maíz pelado – unleavened cornflour
mamón – grape-sized fruit, with green skin and reddish edible flesh you suck until you get to the core
mandarina – mandarin, tangerine
mango – mango
maní – peanuts
mantecado – vanilla or dairy ice cream
mantequilla – butter
manzana – apple
marisco – shellfish, seafood

margarina margarine
masa – dough
mayonesa – mayonnaise
mejillones – mussels
melón – cantaloupe, rockmelon
melocotón – peach
merengada – fruit milk shake
merey – cashew
mero – grouper (groper) or sea bass
milanesa – thin steak
miche – anise-flavoured liqueur made from sugar cane
mora – blackberry
mostaza – mustard
muchacho – roast beef

nabo – turnip
naranja – orange
nata – thick sweat cream
natilla – sour-milk butter
níspero – fruit of the medlar tree
nuez – nut, walnut

ñame – a type of yam, edible tuber

ocumo – root vegetable with dark skin and white meat; basic food for many Indian groups
ostra – oyster

paella – Spanish dish of rice, pork, chicken and seafood.
pámpano – pompano (fish)
pan – bread
papa – potato
papas fritas – chips, French fried
papelón – crude brown sugar, sold in solid blocks in cubic or pyramid shape
parchita – passion fruit
pargo – red snapper
pasapalo – hors d' oeuvres, snack
pastel – pastry
pasticho – lasagne
paticas – pig's feet
patilla – watermelon
pato – duck
pavo – turkey
pavón – peacock bass, a tasty freshwater fish, common in the Los Llanos

payara – a type of peacock bass, common in the Orinoco River and its tributaries
pechuga – breast (poultry)
pepino – cucumber
pepitona – ark-shell clam
pera – pear
perejil – parsley
pernil – leg of pork
perro caliente – hot dog
pescado – fish that has been caught, considered as food
pez – a live fish
pimentón – capsicum
pimienta – pepper
piña – pineapple
plátano – plantain (green banana)
pollo – chicken
pulpo – octopus
punta trasera – top rump

quesillo – caramel custard
queso – cheese

rábano – radish
raspao – snowcone, ice ball made by scraping a block of ice and adding artificial flavours; sold only on the street
refresco – soft drink
reina pepiada – chicken with avocado, a tasty stuffing for arepas
remolacha – beetroot
repollo – cabbage
riñones – kidneys
róbalo – snook, bass
ron – rum
rosbif – roast beef
rueda – fish steak

sal – salt
salchicha – sausage
salmón – salmon
salsa – sauce
salsa de tomate – tomato sauce, ketchup
sangría – red wine diluted with soda water with chunks of fruit
sardina – sardine
sierra – king mackerel, sawfish
solomo – sirloin
sopa – soup

tajada – fried ripe plantain
tamarindo – tamarind
té – tea
teta – iced fruit juice in a plastic wrap, which is eaten by sucking
tizana – a variety of chopped fruit in fruit juice; it usually includes pieces of pawpaw, banana, watermelon, cantaloupe, pineapple and orange
tocineta – bacon
tomate – tomato
toronja – grapefruit
torta – cake
tortilla – omelette
tostón – fried plantain
trago – alcoholic drink
trigo – wheat
trucha – trout

uva – grape
uva pasa – raisin

vieira – scallop
vinagre – vinegar
vino blanco – white wine
vino espumoso – sparkling wine
vino rosado – rosé
vino tinto – red wine

yuca – yucca (edible root)

zanahoria – carrot

This information on the preparation of food may be of help:

ahumado/a – smoked
a la parrilla – broiled, grilled
al horno – baked
asado/a – roasted
cocido/a – boiled
estofado/a – braised, stewed
frito/a – fried
guisado/a – stewed

bien cocido/a – well-done
poco cocido/a – rare
término medio – medium
tres cuartos – medium well-done

ENTERTAINMENT
Cinemas
Movies are popular and there are cinemas in almost every town. In Caracas alone, there are more than 50 cinemas. Most movies are the regular US commercial fare. If you need something more mentally stimulating, try the *cinematecas* (art cinemas) in Caracas.

Most movies are screened in their original language with Spanish subtitles. A cinema ticket costs between US$1 and US$2. Cinemas in the lowlands are air-conditioned and may sometimes be cool; come prepared.

Theatre & Classical Music
Most theatre activity is confined to Caracas, where there are about 20 theatres. Other large cities have their theatres but the choice, and usually the quality of the productions, doesn't match up to that of Caracas. Much the same can be said about other areas of artistic expression such as the ballet, opera and classical music. Refer to the Entertainment section in the Caracas chapter for further information.

Spectator Sports
As far as Western imports go, baseball, soccer and basketball are probably the most popular spectator sports. Horse races have always been run in Los Llanos but they are now run on racetracks built according to international rules with betting included. La Rinconada in Caracas is the best racetrack in the country but other large cities such as Maracaibo and Valencia have their own tracks.

The *corrida* or bullfighting is a more local passion. Brought from Spain, it has found fertile soil in Venezuela. Most major cities have their own bullrings. The *plaza de toros* (bullring) in Valencia is capable of seating 27,000 people and is the largest in the country, followed by the bullring of San Cristóbal. The Plaza de Toros Maestranza in Maracay and the Nuevo Circo in Caracas are among the country's most stylish bullrings. The bullfighting season peaks during the Carnaval, when top-ranking matadors are invited from Spain and Latin America (especially Mexico and Colombia).

Another cruel and breathtaking spectator sport is cockfighting. Like most countries on the continent, it's popular in Venezuela and *galleras*, or cockfight rings, can be found in most cities.

Also thrilling but bloodless is the *toros coleados*, a sort of rodeo which is popular in Los Llanos. Two teams of riders compete to bring down a bull. The aim is to overthrow the bull by grabbing it by the tail from a galloping horse.

Another popular game – and an easier one to participate in – is the so-called *bolas criollas*. Two teams, each consisting of two players, throw eight wooden balls, aiming to place them as close as possible to the smaller ball known as *mingo*.

Chess and dominos have plenty of addicts throughout the country and they are played as much in the villages as they are in the malls of Caracas.

Things to Buy

Given the number of Indian groups living in the country, there is a variety of crafts to buy. Perhaps the most interesting are the crafts of the Guajiro and those of several groups of Amazonas. Although there are plenty of handicraft shops in Caracas and most major cities, the best and the cheapest places to buy crafts are the regions where they are made. Shop around local markets rather than shops.

If you are interested in typical music, comb Caracas's music shops which have the best selection. Some of the music is now recorded on CDs.

Venezuela is noted for gold and diamonds, but don't expect to find a bargain. Possibly the best place to buy gold jewellery is Ciudad Bolívar.

Getting There & Away

AIR

Being at the northern extremity of South America, Venezuela has the cheapest air links with Europe and North America and is the most convenient northern gateway to the continent. North Americans and Europeans who plan an overland trip around South America will find the information contained in this chapter useful.

Most travellers fly into Caracas, which is Venezuela's major international airport. A small number of visitors fly into Punto Fijo, Maracaibo or Porlamar (Isla de Margarita).

Venezuela requires visitors to have an onward ticket before they're allowed into the country. This is quite strictly enforced by airlines and travel agents: it's probable that none of them will sell you a one-way ticket unless you can show them an onward ticket.

Upon arrival in Venezuela, the immigration official probably won't ask you to present your onward ticket, but it will be necessary if you want to extend your visa.

It's worth remembering that round-trip fares are always cheaper than two one-way tickets. Similarly, a single air ticket which includes a number of stopovers will be cheaper than a number of tickets for the same route which have been bought separately.

Air tickets bought from travel agents are generally cheaper than those bought directly from an airline, even if they cover the same route and have similar conditions and restrictions. How much you save largely depends on where you buy. In some countries and cities there is an active trade in budget tickets, in others it is limited, and the prices not very competitive. Unfortunately, Venezuela belongs to the latter category. Tickets to Europe or Australia are expensive. Only flights to Miami can be bought for a good price, comparable to what you would pay if you were flying from there to Venezuela.

Have the whole route covered by a ticket bought at home so you can return at short notice if necessary.

If you plan on travelling by air within Venezuela, note that Avensa, one of the local carriers, offers a domestic air pass (see the Air section in the Getting Around chapter).

Buying the ticket can be a time-consuming and annoying operation – the following section will give you some tips.

Buying the Ticket

Your plane ticket will probably be the single most expensive item in your budget, and buying it can be an intimidating business. There is likely to be a multitude of airlines and travel agents hoping to separate you from your money, and it is always worth putting aside a few hours to research the current state of the market. Start early: some of the cheapest tickets have to be bought months in advance, and some popular flights sell out early. Talk to other recent travellers – they may be able to stop you making some of the same old mistakes. Look at the ads in newspapers and magazines, consult reference books and watch for special offers. Read the attached Air Travel Glossary to get some basics about the business and the relevant terms. Then phone round travel agents for bargains. Find out the fare, the route, the duration of the journey and any restrictions on the ticket. Then sit back and decide which is best for you.

Airlines can supply information about routes, timetables and their fares (usually full fares); except during airline price-wars, they don't offer the cheapest tickets. It's worth calling them anyway so that at least you'll know the full fare.

Agents may tell you that all their cheap flights are 'fully booked, but we have another one that only costs a bit more...' You might find that the cheapest flight is on an airline which is notorious for its poor safety standards and for leaving passengers stranded in undesirable airports mid-journey. They may claim that they only have two seats left but, if you hurry, they will hold them for you for two hours. Don't be pushed – keep ringing around.

Use the fares in this book as a guide only. Quoted airfares do not necessarily constitute a recommendation for the carrier.

If you are travelling from the UK or the USA, you will probably find that the cheapest flights are being advertised by obscure bucket shops (known as consolidators in the USA) whose names haven't yet reached the telephone directory. Many such firms are honest and solvent, but there are a few rogues who will take your money and disappear, to reopen elsewhere a month or two later under a new name. If you feel suspicious about a firm, don't give them all the money at once – leave a small deposit and pay the balance when you get the ticket.

Before putting down a deposit, clarify all details of the ticket including conditions, restrictions and the total fare. Otherwise it may sometimes happen that when it comes to picking up your ticket, you'll discover some unmentioned extras on top of the previously agreed price which makes the ticket substantially more expensive; if you don't want it, your deposit is lost. If they insist on full cash in advance, go somewhere else. And once you have the ticket, ring the airline to make sure that you are actually booked onto the flight you thought you were.

You may decide to pay more than the rock-bottom fare by opting for the safety of a better-known travel agent. Firms such as STA, who have offices worldwide, Council Travel in the USA or Travel CUTS in Canada are not going to disappear overnight, leaving you clutching a receipt for a nonexistent ticket, and they, too, do offer good prices.

Once you have your ticket, write its number down, together with the flight number and other details (or make a photocopy of it), and keep the copy somewhere separate. If the ticket is lost or stolen, this will help you get a replacement.

It's sensible to buy travel insurance as early as possible. If you buy it the week before you fly, you may find, for example, that you're not covered for delays to your flight caused by industrial action.

Air Travellers with Special Needs
If you have special needs of any sort – you're asthmatic, you've broken a leg, you're vegetarian, you're travelling in a wheelchair, you're taking the baby, you're terrified of flying – you should let the airline know as soon as possible so that they can make appropriate arrangements. You should remind them of your needs when you reconfirm your booking (at least 72 hours before departure) and again when you check in at the airport. It may also be worth ringing around the airlines before you make your booking to see how they can handle your particular needs.

Airports and airlines can be surprisingly helpful, but they do need advance warning. Most international airports will provide escorts to assist you from the check-in desk to the plane if this is necessary. Most airports have ramps, lifts, and accessible toilets and telephones. Aircraft toilets, on the other hand, are likely to present a problem if your mobility is limited; travellers should discuss this with the airline at an early stage and, if necessary, with their doctor.

Guide dogs for the blind will often have to travel in a specially pressurised baggage compartment with other animals, away from their owner, although smaller guide dogs may be admitted to the cabin. Guide dogs are subject to the same quarantine laws (six months in isolation etc) as any other animal when entering or returning to countries currently free of rabies such as the UK or Australia.

Deaf travellers can ask for airport and in-flight announcements to be written down for them.

Children under two years of age travel for 10% of the standard fare (or free, on some airlines), as long as they don't occupy a seat. They don't get a baggage allowance either. 'Skycots' should be provided by the airline if requested in advance; these will take a child weighing up to about 10 kg. Children between two and 12 years of age can usually occupy a seat for half to two-thirds of the full fare, and do get a baggage allowance. Pushchairs (strollers) can often be taken aboard as hand luggage.

Air Travel Glossary

Apex Tickets Apex stands for Advance Purchase Excursion fare. These tickets are usually between 30% and 40% cheaper than the full economy fare, but there are restrictions. You must purchase the ticket at least 21 days in advance (sometimes more) and you must be away for a minimum period (normally 14 days) and intending to return within a maximum period (90 or 180 days). Stopovers are not allowed and if you have to change your dates or destination, there will be extra charges. If you have to cancel altogether, the refund is often considerably less than what you originally paid for the ticket. Take out travel insurance to cover yourself should you have to cancel your trip unexpectedly – for example, due to illness.

Baggage Allowance This will be written on your ticket. You are usually allowed one 20 kg piece of baggage which will be placed in the hold, and one item of hand luggage. Some airlines which fly transpacific and transatlantic routes allow for two pieces of luggage (although there are limits on their dimensions and weight).

Bucket Shops At certain times of the year and in certain parts of the world many airlines fly with empty seats. This isn't profitable: it's more cost-effective for them to fly full even if that means having to sell a certain number of drastically discounted tickets. They do this by off-loading them onto bucket shops (UK) or consolidators (USA), travel agents who specialise in discounted fares. The agents, in turn, sell them to the public at reduced prices. These tickets are often the cheapest you'll find. Availability varies so you'll not only have to be flexible about your travel plans but you'll also have to be quick off the mark.

Most of the bucket shops are reputable organisations, but there will always be the odd fly-by-night operator who sets up shop, takes your money and then either disappears or issues an invalid ticket. Be sure to check what you're buying before handing over the dough.

Bucket shop agents advertise in many newspapers and magazines and there's a lot of competition – especially in places like Bangkok, Amsterdam and London which are crawling with them – so it's a good idea to telephone first to ascertain availability before you start rushing from shop to shop. Naturally, they'll advertise the cheapest available tickets, but by the time you get there, these may be sold out and you may be looking at something slightly more expensive.

Bumped Just because you have a confirmed seat doesn't mean you're definitely going to get on the plane – see Overbooking.

Cancellation Penalties If you have to cancel or change an Apex or other discount ticket there may be a heavy penalty involved; insurance can sometimes be taken out to cover these penalties. Some airlines impose cancellation penalties on regular tickets as well, particularly if you are a 'no show' passenger.

Check In Airlines ask you to check in ahead of the flight departure (usually 1½ to two hours on international flights). If you fail to check in on time and the flight is overbooked the airline can cancel your booking and give your seat to somebody else.

Confirmation Having a ticket with the flight and date you want doesn't mean that you have a seat. The agent has to confirm with the airline that your status is 'OK'. Prior to this confirmation your status is 'on request'.

Discounted Tickets There are two types of discounted fares – officially discounted (see Promotional Fares) and unofficially discounted. The lowest prices often impose drawbacks like flying with unpopular airlines, inconvenient schedules, or unpleasant routes and connections. A discounted ticket can save you more than just money – you may be able to pay Apex prices without the associated Apex advance booking and other requirements.

Economy-Class Tickets Economy-class tickets are usually not the cheapest way to go, although they do give you maximum flexibility and the tickets are valid for 12 months. Most are fully refundable if you don't use them, as are unused sectors of a multiple ticket.

Full Fares Airlines traditionally offer first class (coded F), business class (coded J) and economy class (coded Y) tickets. These days there are so many promotional and discounted fares available that few passengers pay full fare.

Lost Tickets If you lose your airline ticket an airline will usually treat it like a travellers' cheque and, after inquiries, issue you with a replacement. Legally, however, an airline is entitled to treat it like cash and if you lose it then it's gone forever. Take good care of your tickets.

MCO MCO (Miscellaneous Charges Order) is a type of voucher (to the value of a given amount) which resembles a plane ticket and can be used to pay for a specific flight with any IATA (International Air Transport Association) airline. MCOs, which are more flexible than a regular ticket, may satisfy the irritating onward ticket requirement, but some countries are now reluctant to accept them. MCOs are fully refundable if unused.

No Shows No shows are passengers who fail to show up for their flight for whatever reason. Full-fare no shows are sometimes entitled to travel on a later flight. The rest of us are penalised (see Cancellation Penalties).

On Request An unconfirmed booking for a flight; see Confirmation.

Open Jaws A return ticket where you fly to one place but return from another. If available, this can save you backtracking to your arrival point.

Overbooking Airlines hate to fly with empty seats and since every flight has some passengers who fail to show up (see No Shows), there are often more passengers booked on any given flight than there are seats. Usually the excess passengers balance those who fail to show up, but occasionally somebody gets bumped. If this happens, guess who's the most likely candidate? – the passenger who checks in late.

Promotional Fares Officially discounted fares like Apex fares which are available from travel agents or direct from the airline.

Reconfirmation At least 72 hours prior to departure time you must contact the airline and 'reconfirm' that you intend to be on the flight. If you don't do this, the airline can delete your name from the passenger list and you could lose your seat. In Venezuela it's best to reconfirm more than once, and preferably in person not by phone.

Restrictions Discounted tickets often have various restrictions on them such as the necessity of advance purchase, limitations on the minimum and maximum period you must be away, restrictions on breaking the journey or changing the booking or route etc.

Round-the-World Fares Round-the-World (RTW) tickets have become all the rage in the past few years. Basically, there are two types of airline tickets and agent tickets.

An airline RTW ticket is issued by two or more airlines that have joined together to market a ticket which takes you around the world on their combined routes. It permits you to fly pretty well anywhere you choose using their combined routes as long as you don't backtrack, ie keep moving in approximately the same direction east or west. Other restrictions are that you (usually) must book the first sector in advance and cancellation penalties then apply. There may be restrictions on how many stops you are permitted. Usually, the RTW tickets are valid for 90 days up to a year.

The other type of RTW ticket, the agent ticket, is a combination of cheap fares strung together by an enterprising travel agent. These may be cheaper than an airline RTW ticket but the choice of routes will be limited.

Standby A discounted ticket where you only fly if there is a seat free at the last moment. Standby fares are usually only available on domestic routes.

Student Discounts Some airlines offer student-card holders 15% to 25% discounts on their tickets. The same often applies to anyone under the age of 26. These discounts are generally only available on ordinary economy-class fares. You wouldn't get one, for instance, on an Apex or a RTW ticket, since these are already discounted.

Tickets Out An entry requirement for many countries is that you have an onward or return ticket, in other words, a ticket out of the country. If you're not sure what you intend to do next, the easiest solution is to buy the cheapest available onward ticket to a neighbouring country or a ticket from a reliable airline which can later be refunded if you do not use it.

Transferred Tickets Airline tickets cannot be transferred from one person to another. Travellers sometimes try to sell the return half of their ticket, but officials can ask you to prove that you are the person named on the ticket. This is not often checked on domestic flights, but international flight tickets are usually compared with passports.

Travel Agencies Some travel agencies simply handle tours, while full-service agencies handle everything from tours and tickets to car rentals and hotel bookings. A good agency will do all these things, but if all you want is a ticket at the lowest possible price, then you really need an agency specialising in discounted tickets.

Travel Periods Some officially discounted fares, Apex fares in particular, vary with the time of year. There is often a low (off-peak) season and a high (peak) season. Sometimes there's an intermediate or shoulder season as well. At peak times, when everyone wants to fly, both officially and unofficially discounted fares will be higher, or there may simply be no discounted tickets available. Usually the fare depends on your outward flight – if you depart in the high season and return in the low season, you pay the high-season fare. ■

To/From the USA

North America is a relative newcomer to the bucket shop traditions of Europe and Asia, so bargain tickets cannot be bought on every corner and are usually not as cheap. Due to the aggressive competition between carriers and governmental red tape, flights originating in the USA are subject to numerous restrictions and regulations. This is especially true of bargain tickets; anything cheaper than the standard economy fare must be purchased at least 14 days, and sometimes as many as 30 days, prior to departure.

In addition, you'll often have to book departure and return dates in advance and these tickets will be subject to minimum and maximum stay requirements: usually seven days and six months respectively. It's often cheaper to purchase a return ticket and trash the return portion rather than paying the one-way fare. From the USA, open tickets which allow an open return date within a 12-month period are generally not available, and penalties of up to 50% are imposed if you make changes to the return booking.

Don't worry too much, however. There are always options in the country which claims to be the world's No 1 air power. After all, Venezuela is just a stone's throw from Miami, so even the full economy fare is not astronomically high.

Check the weekend travel sections in major newspapers (the *Los Angeles Times*, the *San Francisco Examiner* and the *Chronicle* on the west coast and the *New York Times* on the east coast). The student travel bureaux may have some interesting offers. They have offices in most major cities nationwide, including:

Whole World Travel
　　Suite 400, 17 East 45th St, New York, NY 10017
　　(☎ (212) 986-9470)
Council Travel
　　205 East 42nd St, New York, NY 10017
STA
　　166 Geary St, San Francisco, CA 94108 (☎ (415) 391-8407)
　　Suite 507, 2500 Wilshire Blvd, Los Angeles, CA 90057 (☎ (213) 380-2184)

STA has a toll-free number (☎ 1-800-777-0112) and has offices (apart from those listed above) in Santa Monica, San Diego, Berkeley, Boston, Cambridge and New York.

A recommended publication is the newsletter *Travel Unlimited* (PO Box 1058, Allston, MA 02134) which gives details of the cheapest airfares and courier possibilities for destinations all over the world from the USA. Send US$5 for their latest edition.

Courier flights are a relatively new system. Businesses use them to ensure the arrival of urgent freight and to avoid excessive customs hassles. The system is operated by courier companies. They hire couriers who commit themselves to delivering packages to any of the companies' destinations all over the world. In return, the companies provide a discount air ticket which is sometimes a phenomenal bargain. In effect, what the courier companies do is to ship their freight as your luggage on regular commercial flights. This is a legitimate operation – all freight that you are to deliver is completely legal.

There are two drawbacks, however: the short turnaround time of the ticket, usually no longer than a month; and your luggage allowance, usually restricted to hand luggage only.

New York and Miami are the only places to look for courier flights to South America. For the widest selection of destinations, try Now Voyager (☎ (212) 431-1616), Air Facility (☎ (718) 712-0630) or Travel Courier (☎ (718) 738-9000) in New York, and Linehaul Services (☎ (305) 477-0651) or Discount Travel International (☎ (305) 538-1616) in Miami.

As an example only, a two-week courier fare on the Miami to Caracas to Miami flight will cost around US$200, and the New York to Caracas to New York route will cost around US$400.

The major US gateway to Venezuela is Miami. Plenty of airlines fly from there to Caracas and a few other Venezuelan cities. They include several major international carriers and various minor South and Central American airlines. Three Venezuelan carriers alone fly this route.

Given the tough competition, airfares tend to fluctuate and there are, from time to time, some great deals. For example, in 1993 Viasa, Avensa and some other airlines cut the Caracas to Miami airfare down to US$99 one way and kept it there for a few months. The offer was valid from either end and the tickets were to be bought directly from the airline offices.

At the time of writing, the Zuliana de Aviación, a little-known Venezuelan carrier based in Maracaibo, was offering what were probably the cheapest fares to both Venezuela and Colombia. Their routes and prices (in US$) from Miami were:

To	One-Way	Return
Caracas	196	366*
Maracaibo	155	285*
Medellín	205	385
Bogotá	205	385

* The return airfares marked with the asterisk are maximum 60-day fares; the others are valid for 12 months.

The flights run daily on Boeing 727s. If these routes and prices stay much the same you can assume they are popular, so advance booking is recommended, although they don't have any advance purchase restrictions.

For details, contact their Miami office (☎ (305) 579-8780 or toll-free ☎ 1-800-223-8780) Suite 200, 7001 NW 25th Street, Miami, Florida 33122. Other airlines may have some good deals as well. For example, Aeropostal (☎ 1-800-468-9419) has flights to Caracas from Atlanta, Orlando and San Juan de Puerto Rico and is worth a call. Viasa (☎ 1-800-468-4272) does the Miami to Caracas run.

Another important gateway to Venezuela is New York. Several carriers fly to Caracas (including two Venezuelan airlines, Viasa and Avensa), and almost all of them stop over in Miami. A one-way full economy fare to Caracas is likely to be around US$480, and the 30-day Apex ticket will cost around US$540.

On the west coast, the major departure points are Los Angeles and San Francisco, but flights to Caracas from there tend to be expensive. The cheapest return ticket (off-peak for a stay of up to 21 days) will cost around US$700, whereas a 60-day peak round-trip fare will cost more than US$1100. Contact American Airlines (☎ 1-800-624-6262), United Airlines (☎ 1-800-538-2929) or Aeropostal (☎ 1-800-468-9419). Aeropostal doesn't cover the whole route but cooperates with the US carriers.

It will probably work out cheaper to go on a cheap domestic flight to Miami and fly to Caracas from there, but check beforehand to see what discount fares are available from Miami.

To/From Canada

Although Viasa flies from Toronto to Caracas, these flights are not cheap (about C$800 one way and C$1200 return). Agents can discount these prices but the fares will remain unattractive. If you're prepared for some effort and inconvenience, the cheapest way of getting to Venezuela is to get a bus to the USA, and then to catch an internal US flight to Miami, and from there a cheap flight to Venezuela (see From the USA).

There may be charter flights (mostly during the winter) from Toronto and Montreal to Venezuela and they may be an interesting alternative to consider. If you wait until the last minute, assuming your schedule is flexible, the prices can drop considerably. The Last Minute Club and Marlin Travel are two of the agencies specialising in last minute package discounting. They advertise on Saturdays in the travel sections of the *Toronto Star* and the *Montreal Gazette*. Also contact Andes Travel, one of the travel agents specialising in flights to South America. Call them in Toronto on ☎ (416) 537-3447, or in Montreal on ☎ (514) 274-5565.

Don't forget to check out Travel CUTS, Canada's national student travel agency (you needn't to be a student to use their services). Their head office is in Toronto (☎ (416) 977-3703, fax (416) 977-4796), 171 College St, Toronto, Ontario M5T 1P7, and they have branch offices in Vancouver, Victoria, Edmonton, Saskatoon, Ottawa, Montreal and Halifax.

Adventure Centre is also useful and they have offices in Vancouver, Edmonton, Calgary and Toronto.

To/From Europe

A number of airlines (Viasa, British Airways, Air France, KLM, Lufthansa, Alitalia, Swissair, Iberia and Avianca) link Caracas with European cities.

London, where bucket shops are ten to the dozen, is the cheapest jumping-off point for Venezuela. Other cities with a reputation for ticket discounting include Amsterdam, Brussels, Frankfurt and Paris. Elsewhere, special deals come and go, but the range is smaller and the airfares are generally higher. This is particularly true in Scandinavia where budget tickets are difficult to find. For this reason, many European budget travellers buy their tickets from London bucket shops. Some London travel agents will make arrangements over the phone, so you don't actually have to go to London to shop around for a good deal. However, you may be obliged to come to London to pick up your ticket in person, as not many British agencies will want to send the ticket outside the UK.

To/From the UK In London, several magazines advertise bucket shops. You'll find discounted fares to Caracas and all the other major destinations in South America. A word of warning, however: don't take the advertised fares as gospel truth. To comply with advertising laws in the UK, companies must offer some tickets at their cheapest quoted price, but they may only have one or two of them per week. If you're not one of the lucky ones, you'll be looking at higher priced tickets.

One of the best sources of information about cheap fares around the world is the monthly *Business Traveller*, available at newsstands in many countries, or direct from 60/61 Fleet St, London EC4. See also the London weekly entertainment guide *Time Out*, available from newsstands in London, and *LAM*, a free London weekly magazine

for entertainment, travel and jobs, available at underground stations. *News & Travel Magazine* is another free weekly with advertisements for cheap airfares.

The Globetrotters Club (BCM Roving, London WC1N 3XX) publishes a newsletter called *Globe* which covers obscure destinations and helps people to find travelling companions.

When the time comes to start calling agents, contact Journey Latin America (JLA) (☎ (081) 747-3108), fax (081) 742-1312), 14-16 Devonshire Rd, Chiswick, London W4 2HD, which specialises in flights to Latin America. They will make arrangements over the phone. Ask for *Papagaio*, their free magazine. They are well informed on South American destinations, have a good range of South American air passes, and they can issue tickets from South America to London and deliver them to any of the main South American cities, which is cheaper than buying the same ticket in South America.

Another reputable agency is Trailfinders (☎ 071) 938-3366, 938-3939), 42-50 Earls Court Rd, London W8 6EJ. Their useful travel newspaper, *Trailfinder*, is free. They offer cheap flights to a wide variety of destinations. Ask about RTW tickets.

South American Experience (☎ (071) 379-0344) is also worth checking out. In Manchester, contact Travel Bug (☎ (061) 721-4000). STA, another useful agency, has offices in London, Manchester, Bristol, Leeds, Oxford and Cambridge.

Venezuela is the cheapest and one of the most popular destinations in South America, and the London to Caracas route is a staple of many travel agents. Prices for discounted flights between London and Caracas start at around UK£200 one way and UK£380 return. Bargain hunters should have little trouble finding even lower prices, but be sure to use a travel agent which is 'bonded' by ABTA (Association of British Travel Agents). If an ABTA-registered agent goes out of business, ABTA will guarantee to refund your ticket or offer you an alternative. Unregistered bucket shops are riskier but also sometimes cheaper.

To/From France The Paris-Caracas route is serviced by several airlines, including Air France, Iberia and Avianca. However, travel agents often use indirect routes serviced by other carriers (which can go via Amsterdam, London, Frankfurt or even Rome) as they can work out to be cheaper.

Following is the list of the Paris offices of some recommended agencies. Many have branch offices in other major French cities.

Access Voyages
   6 Rue Pierre Lescot, 75001 Paris (☎ 40-13-02-02, 42-21-46-94)
Counci l Travel
   22 Rue des Pyramides, 75001 Paris (☎ 44-55-55-44, 40-75-95-10)
   31 Rue St Augustin, 75002 Paris (☎ 42-66-20-87)
Forum Voyages
   67 Av Raymond Poincaré, 75016 Paris (☎ 47-27-89-89)
   140 Rue du Faubourg Saint Honoré, 75008 Paris (☎ 42-89-07-07)
Fuaj (Fédération Unie des Auberges de Jeunesse)
   27 Rue Pajol, 75018 Paris (☎ 44-89-87-27)
   9 Rue Brantôme, 75003 Paris (☎ 48-04-70-40)
Jumbo
   38 Av de l'Opéra, 75002 Paris (☎ 47-42-06-92)
   62 Rue Monsieur le Prince, 75006 Paris (☎ 46-34-19-79)
Nouvelles Frontières
   87 Bd de Grenelle, 75015 Paris (☎ 41-41-58-58)
Nouveau Monde
   8 Rue Mabillon, 75006 Paris (☎ 43-29-40-40)
OTU (Office de Tourisme Universitaire)
   39 Av Georges Bernanos, 75005 Paris (☎ 44-41-38-50, 43-29-90-78)
STA Travel
   c/o Voyages Découvertes, 21 Rue Cambon, 75001 Paris (☎ 42-61-00-01)
Uniclam
   11 Rue du 4 Septembre, 75002 Paris (☎ 40-15-07-07)
   46 Rue Monge, 75005 Paris (☎ 43-25-21-18)
   63 Rue Monsieur le Prince, 75006 Paris (☎ 43-29-12-36)

The cheapest Paris-Caracas return tickets can be bought for about FF5000. Many of the listed agencies specialise in student travel and may offer even cheaper fares for students. Most discounted return tickets have a maximum stay period of two or three months, rarely longer, but student fares usually allow for a up to six-month stay.

To/From Australia & New Zealand
Travel between Australasia and Venezuela has certain drawbacks, to say the least. Firstly, it's a long flight and far from cheap. Secondly, there are several routes of which none is clearly better or cheaper than the others. Thirdly, there is not much to be found in Australia or New Zealand in the way of budget tickets to South America. There are discounts on the popular routes, say, to London or Los Angeles, but mention Caracas to an agent and their eyes are likely to roll back in their heads. Few agents in Australasia have a clear idea about flying to South America.

In theory, there are four air routes to South America. Perhaps the most popular is the route through Los Angeles, but getting to Venezuela from there can be expensive (see From the USA). Moreover, even a couple of days in the USA would eat up all the savings in airfares, so it's only good value if you want to visit the USA anyway or if you go through without stopping. Try to arrange the ticket for the whole route in Australia. A return ticket is likely to cost somewhere between A$2200 and A$2800, depending on the season, length of stay etc.

The route through Europe is the longest but not as absurd as it sounds. Given the relatively cheap airfares to London, and the attractive fares from London to Caracas, the total fare may be cheaper than travelling via Los Angeles. It's best to arrange the ticket for the whole route in Australia or have the London to Caracas leg prepared for you by a London agent.

The shortest route to South America goes over the South Pole. Aerolíneas Argentinas, the only Latin American carrier landing in Australia, flies once weekly from Sydney to Buenos Aires with a stopover in Auckland. However, if you're interested in Venezuela in particular, note that Buenos Aires is at the opposite end of the continent. The cost of the Sydney to Buenos Aires return flight depends on the length of stay: around A$2200 with a maximum stay of 21 days; A$2350 for 45 days; and about A$2500 for six months. Up to six stopovers are permitted. New Zealanders can join the flight in Auckland, but the fares from there are only marginally lower.

Finally, you can fly right across the southern Pacific to Santiago de Chile. Lan Chile flies from Papeete (Tahiti) via Easter Island to Santiago. Associated carriers take passengers to and from Australia and New Zealand. The Sydney to Santiago return fares are roughly comparable to those for the Sydney to Buenos Aires route. Unfortunately, you'll have the same problem as with the previous route: you end up quite a long way from Venezuela, even if Lan Chile can bring you closer by providing you with an onward ticket to Rio de Janeiro at little or no extra cost.

Unless you are particularly interested in any of the four above-mentioned routes, it's worth thinking about a RTW ticket. RTW tickets with various stopovers can still be found for as little as A$2100, but these tend to include only northern hemisphere stopovers; RTWs which include Latin America or the South Pacific will automatically cost about A$1000 more. One of the most interesting options may be a one-year RTW with Aerolíneas Argentinas and KLM on the route from Sydney to Auckland to Buenos Aires to (here you can chose a few South American stopovers) Caracas to Amsterdam to Singapore to Sydney.

Alternatively, look for a cheap northern hemisphere RTW which includes Miami, from where you can make a side trip to Venezuela for a few hundred US$ (see From the USA).

The Saturday issues of the major newspapers the *Sydney Morning Herald* and *The Age* in Melbourne – carry travel sections containing numerous ads for discount airfare agents, but very few of them include South American destinations. It's better to get a copy of *El Español*, the Spanish-language newspaper, published in Australia, which details travel agents specialising in South America.

STA has its Australian offices in Adelaide, Brisbane, Cairns, Canberra, Darwin, Melbourne, Perth, Sydney and Townsville. In New Zealand, it has offices in Auckland, Christchurch, Dunedin and Wellington. Flight Centres International, which have offices in most major cities in both Australia and New Zealand, may also be of use.

To/From Central America

Bucket shops are thin on the ground in Central America. Furthermore, direct flights from Central America to Venezuela are scarce and the fares are high. You'll probably have to travel via Colombia. Most travellers use San Andrés Island (a Colombian sovereignty) as a bridge, flying there from either Guatemala City (US$125) or Tegucigalpa (US$117), and then continuing on to Cartagena on the Colombian mainland on a domestic flight (US$90). For information on how to get from Colombia to Venezuela see From Colombia.

To/From Brazil

A number of airlines, including Viasa and Varig, fly between Brazil and Venezuela but they are painfully expensive. For example, the flight from Sao Paulo or Rio de Janeiro to Caracas costs around US$750 (US$850 return). Apparently the cheapest air route from Brazil to Venezuela is the Manaus to Caracas flight which costs about US$400. There are no flights between Boa Vista and Santa Elena de Uairén.

To/From Colombia

Several carriers, including Avianca, Avensa and Viasa, operate flights between Bogotá and Caracas. The one-way fare offered by the airlines is US$194 and the one-year return ticket costs US$250. Zuliana de Aviación, however, will fly you from Bogotá to Caracas (via Medellín and Maracaibo) for US$122 (US$244 return).

Other possible routes from Colombia to Venezuela include: Cartagena to Caracas with Viasa (US$172, US$199 one-year return); Barranquilla to Caracas with Lacsa (US$161, US$193 for a 30-day return); Bogotá to Valencia with Valenciana de Aviación (US$120, US$200 for a 60-day return); Bogotá or Medellín to Maracaibo

Colonial face of Caracas

Left & Right: Modern face of Caracas
  Bottom: Kinetic work by Jesús Soto, Cubo Negro, Caracas

with Zuliana de Aviación (US$81, US$162 one-year return); and Bogotá to Santo Domingo (near San Cristóbal) with Avensa (US$50, US$100 one-year return).

All international tickets bought in Colombia attract a 19% tax (9.5% on return flights) on top of the listed fares.

To/From Netherlands Antilles

There are regular flights by Avensa and Aeropostal from Aruba, Curaçao and Bonaire to Caracas (U$84, US$85 and US$91). There are also chartered flights on light planes from Aruba, Curaçao and Bonaire to Coro. See the Coro section for information.

To/From Trinidad

Flights between Port of Spain (Trinidad) and Caracas are operated by United Airlines and Aeropostal and the one-way fare is US$114. There are no longer flights between Port of Spain and Maturín.

To/From Guyana

There are no direct flights between Venezuela and Guyana. The shortest roundabout route is via Trinidad.

LAND

Venezuela has road connections with Colombia and Brazil only. There is no road link with Guyana; you must go via Brazil.

To/From Brazil

There's only one road connecting Brazil and Venezuela. It leads from Manaus to Boa Vista (Brazil) to Santa Elena de Uairén (Venezuela) and then continues on via El Dorado to Ciudad Guayana. See the Santa Elena de Uairén section for details.

You may also enter Venezuela through the Amazon at San Simón de Cocuy. This is an adventurous river/road route seldom used by travellers. See the Puerto Ayacucho section for information.

To/From Colombia

You can enter Venezuela from Colombia at four border crossings. There's a coastal

smuggling route between Maicao and Maracaibo (see the Maracaibo section for details). Further south is the most popular border crossing, between Cúcuta and San Antonio del Táchira (see the San Antonio del Táchira section for information). Next comes an unpopular, dangerous (because of guerilla activity on the Colombian side) and inconvenient crossing from Arauca to El Amparo de Apure. Finally, there's an unusual but interesting overland route from Puerto Carreño in Colombia to either Puerto Páez or Puerto Ayacucho in Venezuela. The Puerto Ayacucho section will give you details.

SEA
To/From the USA

CAVN Venezuelan lines (☎ (713) 461-2286), 820 Gessner, Houston, TX 77024, have monthly cargo ships from US ports on the Gulf of Mexico to several Venezuelan ports. Passengers must disembark at the first stop, which is usually Maracaibo. The ships can take seven to 12 passengers and cost US$190 one way. They usually need a month's notice and berths are almost unobtainable in July, August and September. Remember that for entry to Venezuela by sea, you need a visa, and in order to get one a return or onward ticket is required.

To/From Lesser Antilles

There's a ferry service between the Lesser Antilles (St Lucia, Barbados, St Vincent and Trinidad) and Pampatar (Isla de Margarita) and Güiria in Venezuela. Refer to the Güiria section for details.

To/From Netherlands Antilles

There's no ferry service between Curaçao and La Vela de Coro (the port of Coro), nor between Aruba and Punto Fijo on the Paraguaná Peninsula. Both services were closed down in 1992 and may or may not reopen somewhere in the future. There are plans to open a new ferry route from the Netherlands Antilles to Puerto Cabello.

TOURS
Overland Companies
Overland trips have become popular, especially with UK and Australasian travellers. Contact one of the following South America overland operators, all of which are based in the UK (Exodus and Encounter also have offices in Australia, New Zealand, the USA and Canada):

Dragoman
    Camp Green, Kenton Rd, Debenham, Suffolk IP14 6LA (☎ (0728) 861-133, fax (0728) 861-127)
Encounter Overland
    267 Old Brompton Rd, London SW5 9JA (☎ (071) 370-6845)
Exodus Expeditions
    9 Weir Rd, London SW12 0LT (☎ (081) 673-0859, fax (081) 673-0779)
Geodyssey
    29 Harberton Rd, London N19 3JS (☎ (071) 281-7788, fax (071) 281-7878)
Guerba Expeditions
    101 Eden Vale Rd, Westbury, Wiltshire BA13 3QX (☎ (0373) 826-611, fax (0373) 838-351)
Hann Overland
    201/203 Vauxhall Bridge Rd, London SW1V 1ER (☎ (071) 834-7337, fax (071) 828-7745)
Top Deck
    Top Deck House, 131/135 Earls Court Rd, London SW5 9RH (☎ (071) 244-8641, fax (071) 373-6201)

Geodyssey specialises in Venezuela and offers a variety of tours to almost every corner of the country, including some adventurous expeditions. Most of their tours commence in Caracas and last 19 days.

Environmental Tours
UK The worldwide boom in ecotourism has prompted a number of groups and organisations to monitor the effects of tourism and provide assessments and recommendation for those involved. For more information on ecotours, contact the Centre for the Advancement of Responsible Travel (☎ (0732) 352-757); Tourism Concern (☎ (081) 878-9053); and Green Flag International (☎ (0223) 893-587).

USA Assessments and information about ecological and other types of tours can be obtained from the following organisations: North American Coordinating Center for Responsible Tourism, 2 Kensington Rd, San Anselmo, CA 94960; One World Family Travel Network, PO Box 4317, Berkeley, CA 94703; and Travel Links, Co-op America, 2100 M St NW, Suite 310, Washington DC 20036.

Earthwatch organises trips for volunteers to work overseas on scientific and cultural projects with a strong emphasis on the protection and preservation of ecology and the environment.

Other organisations which provide tours with a similar emphasis include Conservation International and The Nature Conservancy. For the addresses of these and other environmental organisations, see the Useful Organisations section in the Facts for the Visitor chapter.

LEAVING VENEZUELA
On departing Venezuela, the airport tax on international flights is US$10, payable either in dollars or bolívares at the exchange rate of the day.

Recently a traveller reported that Venezuela had introduced an exit fee of US$8 for anyone leaving the country overland via San Antonio del Táchira. The payment has to be made at the bank, so plan to arrive on weekdays during bank business hours. It's not known whether the new regulation refers to other land border crossings.

Getting Around

AIR

Venezuela has a number of airlines and an extensive network of air routes. Caracas (or, more precisely, Maiquetía, which is where Caracas's airport is located) is the country's aviation hub. There are several departures daily to each of the other major cities and a few flights to the smaller cities. Unfortunately, these flights don't necessarily depart according to schedule.

Airlines

Viasa is Venezuela's main international carrier. It doesn't, however, service domestic routes. Aeropostal and Avensa are the major Venezuelan domestic airlines. These two airlines and Servivensa, a young offspring of Avensa, also service international routes.

There are half a dozen smaller carriers which cover regional routes. A few of them, such as Zuliana de Aviación and Valenciana de Aviación, fly abroad as well. More than a dozen applications to open new airlines are currently being processed by the Ministry of Transport and Communications. The applicants plan to service both domestic and international routes. Venezuela's major airlines are:

Viasa – flies to Amsterdam, Frankfurt, Lisbon, London, Madrid, Milan, Oporto, Paris, Roma, Santiago de Compostela, Tenerife, Zürich, Miami, Houston, New York, Toronto, Havana, Santo Domingo, Bogotá, Cartagena, Quito, Lima, Santiago de Chile, Buenos Aires, São Paulo and Rio de Janeiro.

Avensa – the most important carrier after Viasa, operates both domestic and international routes. It flies to Miami, New York, Mexico City, Panama, Bogotá, and Aruba, Bonaire and Curaçao (the Netherlands Antilles). It has the widest network of domestic routes, linking 24 Venezuelan cities.

Aeropostal – services 22 major Venezuelan cities. It also flies to Atlanta, Orlando, San Juan (Puerto Rico), Havana, Santo Domingo, Fort de France (Martinique), Barbados, Port of Spain (Trinidad), and Curaçao and Aruba (the Netherlands Antilles).

Zuliana de Aviación – a relative newcomer, operates out of Maracaibo (Zulia state). It has international flights to Miami, Bogotá and Medellín, and internal connections to Caracas, Santa Bárbara and Porlamar (Isla de Margarita). At the time of writing, it had some attractive international and domestic airfares.

Airfares

Domestic air-travel in Venezuela is cheap when compared to neighbouring Colombia or Brazil, but no longer the bargain it used to be. Airfares have doubled (and in some cases, tripled) over the past few years.

Aeropostal's fares are usually cheaper than Avensa's. Furthermore, Aeropostal is the only Venezuelan airline which offers 15% student and 50% senior citizen discounts. Normally, the student discount only applies to Venezuelan students, but some offices have been known to sell discounted tickets to foreign students with an international student card. The senior citizen discount (for passengers 65 years of age and over) generally applies to both nationals and foreigners. For details on routes and fares see the Caracas chapter.

Make sure to reconfirm your flight at least 72 hours before departure (preferably in person rather than by phone). Remember, not all flights depart when they're scheduled to, so be patient. There's an airport tax of around US$0.50 on all domestic flights.

Avensa Air Pass

Avensa is the only Venezuelan airline which offers an air pass. It permits 14 days' travel around the country with Avensa between any of their 24 domestic airports including Canaima. The pass also allows you to travel to Aruba, Curaçao and Bonaire (the Netherlands Antilles). The pass is like a round ticket: you start and end at the same point, which is meant to be your point of entry into Venezuela (most likely Caracas), but this is not always enforced. The pass doesn't allow you to visit the same destination twice. The

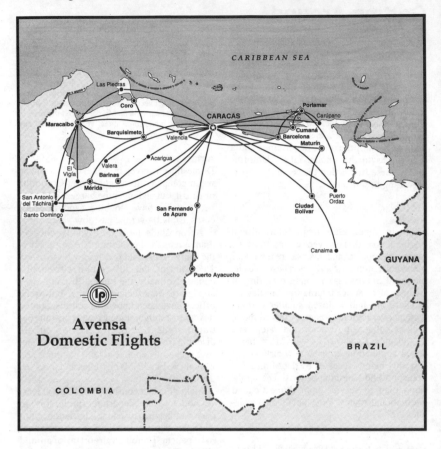

CARIBBEAN SEA

Las Piedras

Coro

Portamar

Carúpano

CARACAS

Maracaibo

Barquisimeto

Valencia

Cumaná
Barcelona
Maturín

El
Vigía

Valera

Acarigua

Barinas

San Antonio
del Táchira

Mérida

San Fernando
de Apure

Puerto
Ordaz

Ciudad
Bolívar

Santo Domingo

Canaima

GUYANA

Avensa
Domestic Flights

Puerto Ayacucho

BRAZIL

COLOMBIA

pass costs US$333 and can be bought both outside and inside the country; only non-residents of Venezuela are allowed to use it.

BUS

As there are no railways of any importance in Venezuela, most travelling is done by bus or *por puesto* (see below).

Buses are generally fast and efficient, especially on the main roads, which are all surfaced. There are frequent daily buses between all the major population centres.

All intercity buses depart from and arrive at a *terminal de pasajeros* or bus terminal.

Every city has such a terminal, usually nowhere near the city centre, but always linked to it by local transport. The terminal is home to the various bus companies' offices. Caracas has the busiest bus terminal, from which buses run to just about every corner of the country.

Bus companies run a plethora of buses which range from archaic pieces of junk to the latest models. The former tend to ply the regional secondary roads, while the latter cover the main long-distance routes. If there is more than one company servicing the same route, you shouldn't find much difference in their fares. The standard, however, may differ from one company to another: you'll soon get to know which companies are better than others.

Many major companies have introduced the so-called *servicio ejecutivo* in modern air-conditioned buses, which provide better standards and shorter travelling time for about 10% to 15% more than the ordinary service. See the Caracas chapter for the bus fares on main routes.

In general, there's no need to buy tickets in advance for the major routes on which there are plenty of buses. This rule, however, doesn't apply during Christmas, Carnaval and Easter, when Venezuelans are mad about travelling.

Another widespread means of transport is the por puesto (literally 'by the seat'). It is a cross between a bus and a taxi – like the *colectivo* in Colombia or Peru. They are usually taxis (less often, minibuses), which ply fixed routes (both long and short distances) and depart when all seats are filled. They cost about 50% to 80% more than buses but they are faster and usually more comfortable. On some routes they are the dominant or exclusive means of transport.

TRAIN

The only railway which operates a passenger service is the 173-km Barquisimeto-Puerto Cabello line. See the sections on these cities for details.

CAR & MOTORBIKE

Travelling independently by car or motorbike (either owned or rented) is a great way of getting around Venezuela. The advantages are flexibility, access to remote areas, and the ability to seize fleeting photographic opportunities.

The country is relatively safe, the road network is extensive and usually in good repair, and local driving manners seem to be better than in the neighbouring countries. Petrol stations are everywhere and petrol costs next to nothing: US$0.05 to US$0.10 per litre, depending on the octane level (reputedly the cheapest petrol in the world).

The government is planning to double or triple the price, but even if it does, petrol will still be a bargain.

According to Venezuelan law, your home country's driver's licence is a valid legal document which allows you to drive in Venezuela for a period of one year from your date of arrival in the country (provided the licence is not used to drive vehicles for profit). However, some police officers and rental company staff may be unfamiliar with some drivers' licences (especially if they are from less well-known countries and/or not in the Latin alphabet). Hence, it's always a good idea to bring along an International Driver's Permit which can usually be obtained fairly easily from the automobile club in your home country.

Venezuelan Road Rules

Traffic in Venezuela, especially in Caracas, is probably not what you're used to. It's wild, chaotic, noisy, polluting and anarchic. If you're coming from, say, Italy or Spain you may not notice any big difference, but if you're fresh from Australia, Germany or Canada you're in for a shock. It's not that road rules don't exist; it's just that nobody respects them and they're not enforced.

Watching the crazy traffic, reminiscent of Formula I racing, you'd never suspect, for example, that there are any speed limits, but they do legally exist. Unless traffic signs say otherwise, the maximum speed limit in urban areas is 40 km/h and outside built-up areas it's 80 km/h.

Officially, traffic coming from the right has priority, unless indicated otherwise by signposts. In practice, however, it seems that the right of way depends more on the size of the vehicle than any regulations. Accordingly, trucks usually have priority over cars, cars over motorbikes, and motorbikes over pedestrians.

Cars must be equipped with seat belts for front seats, and they must have a spare tyre, wheel block, jack and a special reflector triangle which, in case of accident or breakdown, has to be placed 50 metres behind the car. Motorcyclists have to wear a crash helmet and motorbikes cannot be ridden at night. However, once again, this is entirely theoretical.

The minimum driving age in Venezuela is 18 years. Although there are limits on maximum blood alcohol level, driving drunk is not unusual; the rules relating to it are seldom enforced.

Car Rental

There are several international and a number of local car rental companies in Venezuela, including Hertz, Avis, Budget and National. They have offices at major airports throughout the country and in city centres. Their addresses are not always included here, but any top-class hotel, tourist office or travel agent will be able to steer you in the right direction.

Car rental is not cheap in Venezuela – the prices are comparable to full-price rental in Europe or the USA – and there are seldom any discounts. The small local companies are cheaper than the international operators, but their cars and rental conditions may leave something to be desired.

Rental agencies will require you to produce your driver's licence and to pay by credit card (Visa, MasterCard and American Express are the most common and universally accepted). You need to be at least 21 years of age to rent a vehicle, although some cars (particularly luxury models and 4WDs) may require you to be at least 23 or 25 years of age. Some companies also have an age ceiling of, usually, 65 years of age.

National Car Rental is the major local company; they have the widest choice of vehicles and the largest number of offices (about 100) distributed throughout the country. You can pick up the car in one place and return it to either the same place or to any of the others; this is convenient and flexible. National is marginally cheaper than Avis and Hertz.

When you get rental quotes, make sure they include insurance in the price. Otherwise, you'll have to pay for it on top of the quoted price as it's compulsory. Some com-

panies allow a set number of free km per day or week, but others don't, and will apply a per km rate from the moment you take the car.

As a rough guide only, a small car will cost around US$50 to US$60 per day, while the discount rate for a full week will be about US$300 to US$350. A per km rate is around US$0.25. A 4WD vehicle is considerably more expensive and harder to obtain.

Isla de Margarita is the cheapest place to rent a car, mainly because of the large number of rental companies which have set up business there and the strong competition between them.

When renting a car, read the contract carefully before signing it. Pay close attention to any theft clause, as it may load a large percentage of any loss onto the hirer. Look at the car carefully and insist on making a note of any defects (including scratches) on the rental form. Check the spare tyre to make sure it's not flat and take a note of whether or not there is a jack and a wheelbrace.

Bringing your own Vehicle

Bringing a car into the country is expensive. Since there is no road through the Darien Gap it's impossible to drive all the way from Central or North America; any vehicle has to be shipped or flown in.

From the USA or Canada you can continue by road as far as Panama, from where the only way to move your vehicle any further south is by sea or air.

The cheapest way will probably be the Colón (Panama) to Barranquilla (Colombia) route, but expect to pay some US$600 to US$1000 for the shipping of a medium-sized car. The procedure is time-consuming as there's a lot of paperwork involved at both ends.

Security while shipping is minimal so take every possible precaution and get the best insurance you can. It's probably not far from the truth to say that everything that can be stolen, will be stolen: mirrors, radio/cassette player, wipers, tools, personal belongings, you name it. The only sure way of avoiding theft is to travel in your car but, unfortunately, this is difficult to arrange.

Motorcyclists should consider having their motorbike flown over: it's safer, easier and faster than shipping it by boat although it's more expensive. Start by asking the cargo departments of the airlines that fly to Colombia (like Copa), or at the cargo terminal at Tocumen International Airport in Panama City. Travel agents can sometimes help.

Another possibility is shipping your vehicle directly from the USA to Venezuela. You thus avoid any corrupt Panamanian and Colombian shipping companies and arrive straight in one of Venezuela's ports, most probably in La Guaira, Puerto Cabello or Maracaibo. The cheapest point of departure from the USA will probably be Miami. Prices are variable, so call several places before committing yourself; look in the Yellow Pages under 'Automobile Transporters' for toll-free 800 numbers. You usually need to give the shipping company one or two weeks' notice. Expect it to take a month or more from the date of sailing. The cost of shipping a car is likely to be somewhere between US$1200 and US$2000.

Shipping a car from Europe is even more expensive (roughly US$2500 to US$5000) and probably only makes sense if it's a specially prepared vehicle (eg for an overland expedition across South America).

Car and motorbike owners will need the vehicle's registration papers, liability insurance and an International Driver's Permit in addition to their domestic licence. You may also need a *Carnet de passage en douane* (this is like a passport for the vehicle and it acts as a temporary waiver of import duty). The carnet may also need to have listed any expensive spares you're planning to carry with you, such as a gearbox. This is necessary when travelling in some countries in Central and South America, and is designed to prevent car import rackets. Contact your local automobile association and relevant consulates for details about all documentation.

Liability insurance is not available in advance for many out-of-the-way countries, but has to be bought when crossing the border. The cost and quality of such local insurance varies widely, and you will find in some countries that you are effectively travelling uninsured.

Anyone who is planning to take their own vehicle with them needs to check in advance to see what spares and petrol are likely to be available. Lead-free petrol is not universally available, and neither is every little part for your car.

Venezuela has quite a developed automobile industry. Various US, European and Japanese makes are assembled locally: Chrysler (Wrangler, Comanche, Cherokee), Fiat (Uno, Premio, Florino, Tempra), Ford (Shapire), General Motors (Chevette, Swift, Blazer), Honda (Civic, Integra, Accord, Prelude, Legend), Mitsubishi, Renault (R11, Gala, R19, R21) and Toyota (Corolla, Sky, Samurai). Most spare parts for these models are available locally. However, spare parts for cars other than those assembled in Venezuela are almost impossible to obtain, so bring along a good supply.

An alternative to bringing your own car from overseas is to purchase a vehicle in South America. Unfortunately, yet again, the price and paperwork are major drawbacks. Cars (both new and used) are expensive in Venezuela, even those which are assembled locally. Furthermore, you can't buy a car in Venezuela unless you have a Venezuelan *cédula*, or the national identity card, which you can only get if you come to study or work in Venezuela, or if you are a resident of the country. The best place on the continent to buy a vehicle, be it motorbike or car, new or second-hand, is apparently Santiago de Chile.

Driving in Venezuela

Whether you bring your own vehicle or hire one from a rental company, drive carefully and defensively. Don't expect local drivers to obey the rules. Don't assume, for example, that a vehicle will stop at a red light or stop sign. Indicating before making a turn is rare.

When you drive in Caracas and other big cities, it's best to have the doors locked and windows closed (or almost closed), to prevent unexpected theft at red lights or in traffic jams. If you can't stand windows closed, don't have handbags and packets lying around on the seats, and wear your watch on the hand away from the window.

Never run out of petrol. It's forbidden by law and, unlike other rules, strictly enforced. Note that petrol can only be dispensed at petrol stations directly into a car's tank; you can't fill containers or jerry cans. However, there are so many petrol stations that you shouldn't have any problems if you plan ahead.

Car security is a problem: avoid leaving valuables in the vehicle and lock it securely. If possible, always leave the vehicle in a guarded car park *(estacionamiento vigilado)*. If your car is stolen, report the theft immediately to the police. You'll then have to fill in a *denuncia*, or a report, which is essential if you are going to claim on your insurance. If it is a rental car, the company you rented it from will also require a denuncia as proof that it was stolen.

If you are involved in a road accident, don't move your car – regardless of how badly traffic is blocked – until the transit police arrive. They should be called as soon as possible on ☎ 167. If you move your vehicle before the transit police make a report, you can't claim the insurance. If you have an accident resulting in injuries or death, you'll be detained as a matter of routine, and your vehicle impounded temporarily, even if you're not at fault.

Touring y Automóvil Club de Venezuela is a useful organisation for travellers with their own vehicles. They provide general driving information and can help you with information on the regulations that apply to shipping your vehicle into or out of Venezuela. They also offer various services (towing, car maintenance, documentation etc), which are usually discounted for members. Their Caracas office (☎ 910-639, 914-448, 914-879, 916-373) is in Centro Integral Santa Rosa de Lima, Planta Baja, Local 11 and 12, Avenida Principal Santa Rosa de Lima, corner of Calle A.

BICYCLE

Cycling is a cheap, convenient, healthy, environmentally sound and above all fun way of travelling. All this sounds terrific, but the problem is that Venezuela is not the best place on earth for cyclists. There are almost no bike tracks, bike rentals or any other facilities. Drivers don't show much courtesy to cyclists either. Cycling is not popular among locals, and foreign travellers with their own bikes are a rarity. Mérida is the only area where mountain bike riding has started to become popular and bikes can be hired.

This doesn't mean that cycling is impossible or not worth the bother. The roads are usually in good shape and most of the country is flat. Except for the cities (particularly Caracas) where cycling can be annoying and dangerous, there are no major problems for independent cyclists. Cycling will let you cover a fair amount of ground without going too fast to enjoy the scenery. Locals will certainly be curious if you are travelling by bike and it's a good way to get talking.

Before you leave home, go over your bike with a fine-toothed comb and fill your repair kit with every imaginable spare. As with cars and motorbikes, you won't necessarily be able to buy that crucial gizmo for your machine when it breaks down somewhere in the back of beyond just as the sun sets. Bring along a solid lock to protect your bike.

Bicycles can be taken with you on the plane. You can take them to pieces and put them in a bike bag or box, but it's much easier to simply wheel your bike up to the check-in desk, where it should be treated as a piece of baggage. You may have to remove the pedals and turn the handlebars sideways so that it takes up less space in the aircraft's hold; check all this with the airline well in advance, preferably before you pay for your ticket.

HITCHING

Hitching is never entirely safe in any country in the world, and we don't recommend it. Travellers who decide to hitch should understand that they are taking a small but potentially serious risk. However, many people do choose to hitch, and the advice that follows should help to make their journeys as fast and safe as possible.

Hitching in Venezuela is not as good as it used to be a decade or so ago. Still, it can be an alternative way of getting around, particularly as there's an extensive array of roads and many people have cars. A considerable proportion of vehicles are open pick-up trucks, and drivers don't mind putting you in the back, regardless of how bulky your backpack is.

Hitchhiking on secondary roads, where buses are infrequent, is easier than on the main highways. I've had some success hitchhiking in the Gran Sabana and on Paraguaná Peninsula. Los Llanos seems to be another region good for hitching.

Needless to say, it's easier to get a ride from a place where cars are stationary than to wave down a vehicle on the open road. Petrol stations and roadside restaurants are good points to hunt for a lift. The alcabalas (police road check posts) may also be good but this is a bit of a lottery: some police are friendly and might even ask a driver to take you with them; others are suspicious and will check your documents first, and may want to search your luggage as well.

BOAT

Venezuela has a number of islands off its Caribbean coast, the main one being Isla de Margarita. See the sections on Puerto La Cruz, Cumaná and Isla de Margarita for details about boats and ferries going to and from the latter. There are no regular boat services to Venezuela's other islands.

The Río Orinoco is the country's major waterway, and it is navigable from its mouth up to Puerto Ayacucho. However, there's no passenger service operating along the river. You can try getting a ride on either a cargo or fishing boat, or you can book yourself on a tour.

TOURS

Tours are quite a popular way of visiting some parts of Venezuela, and many travellers take advantage of them, despite their ele-

vated prices. This is largely because vast areas of the country are either hardly accessible by public transport (eg the Amazon), or because a visit on one's own to scattered sights over a large territory (eg the Gran Sabana) may be considerably more time-consuming and eventually more expensive than a tour.

Some general advice: try to arrange the tour from the regional centre closest to the area you are going to visit. Otherwise, you will pay for mileage to get to the area and back (at the tour operator's price, of course) and, furthermore, you may find that nationwide tour operators are less knowledgeable about distant places than the agents within the region.

Accordingly, for hikes in the Andes there's no better place to look for a guide than Mérida; for excursions around the Gran Sabana, the cheapest organised trips are to be found in Santa Elena de Uairén; for the Amazon, the obvious place is Puerto Ayacucho; for the Orinoco Delta, Tucupita is the right address; and for tours to Salto Angel (Angel Falls), Ciudad Bolívar is the place to shop around, as most flights to Canaima (the base for Salto Angel) depart from there. You'll find details in the respective sections.

LOCAL TRANSPORT
Bus

Almost all city transport (as well as many short-distance regional routes) is serviced by small buses called, depending on the region, *buseta, carro, carrito, micro, camioneta* or *camionetica*, or por puestos.

The buses are usually slow and crowded, but cost next to nothing: the fare in most cities and towns is about US$0.15. The fare is a flat rate, so you pay the same to go one block as to go right across the city.

In most cities you can easily recognise bus stops by the sign 'parada'. If you can't find one, ask a local where to catch the bus.

You get in and off by the front door which is usually the only one. You pay the driver or their assistant directly on entering or, more often, when you get off. You never get a ticket. To let the driver know that you intend to get off, you simply shout 'parada' or clap your hands twice, and he will stop at the next bus stop.

In many cities, you can also use por puestos (shared taxis). The fare is somewhere between 20% and 80% higher than on buses, but it's still a bargain.

Metro

Caracas is the only Venezuelan city that has an underground railway system, referred to as the metro. See the Caracas chapter for details.

Taxi

Taxis are a relatively inexpensive and convenient means of getting around, especially if you are travelling with a few companions. The price will usually be the same regardless of the number of passengers, though some drivers may demand more if you have a lot of luggage.

Taxis are particularly useful when you arrive at an unfamiliar city and want to get from the bus terminal or the airport to the city centre to look for a cheap room. A bonus is that taxi drivers often have a much better idea of where to find cheap accommodation than do the tourist offices.

A taxi may also be chartered for longer distances. This method is convenient if you want to visit places near major cities which are outside local transport areas but too near to be covered by long-distance bus networks.

Taxis are identifiable by a sign reading 'taxi' or 'libre'. In major cities they have meters, although drivers are not always eager to switch them on, preferring to charge tourists arbitrarily according to how wealthy they look and their proficiency in Spanish. It's always advisable to ask a few people (shopkeepers and locals) what the usual taxi fare to your destination would be. Then, if the first taxi driver you talk to quotes you a significantly more expensive fare, bargain. If you can't agree on a price, try another taxi.

Caracas

Founded in 1567, Caracas was for a long time a small and unhurried place. Its rapid growth only really began after WWII. Today it's a metropolis of between four and five million inhabitants and, like most of the large cities on the continent, it's a striking mixture of all things Latin American. What is perhaps most characteristic of the city is its spectacular setting, pleasant climate and modern architecture. Very Yankeefied and almost denuded of its colonial character, it's a vibrant, fast, progressive and cosmopolitan city – attractive, impressive and captivating in many aspects, though also depressing and disappointing in others. You just have to go there and see for yourself.

Caracas now has some of the best modern architecture on the continent. It also has a web of motorways, unknown in other South American capitals. However, the estimated half a million vehicles circulating in the city cause serious environmental problems, and there are frequent traffic jams.

Another consequence of this unbalanced expansion is the vast expanse of *ranchos*, the slum suburbs in the hills surrounding the city centre. These are the result of huge post-war migration, spurred on by the illusory dream of wealth. The inhabitants have never managed to get their share of the city's prosperity and lead a hand-to-mouth existence in tin shacks. Caracas' spectacular setting in a valley amidst rolling hills only highlights the contrast between wealth and poverty.

Caracas is the centre of political, scientific, cultural and educational life in Venezuela. Nowhere else will you find as much to choose from in the way of good food, plush hotels, theatre, museums or shopping.

Set at an altitude of about 900 metres, Caracas enjoys an agreeable, relatively dry and sunny climate with a mean temperature of about 22°C. The rainy season goes from June to October.

On a less enticing note, Caracas is the least

secure of all Venezuelan cities. Petty crime in general, and robbery and armed assaults in particular, are increasing daily.

HISTORY

Caracas had its precarious beginning in 1560. It was then that Francisco Fajardo of Isla de Margarita discovered the green valley (today entirely taken up by the city) that was inhabited by the warlike Toromaima Indian tribe. He founded a settlement named San Francisco. However, he was soon driven out by the natives. A year later, Juan Rodríguez Suárez, the founder of Mérida, arrived and resurrected the Villa de San Francisco, which had been razed by the Indians.

The years that followed witnessed the struggle of the village to survive from repeated Indian attacks, in which many of the small population were killed, including Rodríguez himself.

In 1567 a complete conquest of the valley was ordered by the then governor of the province, Pedro Ponce de León. An expedition of 136 men under the command of Captain Diego de Losada was sent from El Tocuyo. They defeated a fierce Indian resistance and re-established the settlement yet again on 25 July. The new village was named

Santiago de León de Caracas: Santiago after the patron saint of Spain, León after the governor, and Caracas after the Indian group which inhabited the coastal cordillera and which was apparently less troublesome and hostile than the other tribes in the region.

In 1577, Juan de Pimentel, the governor of the day, elected the newly born town as the administrative seat of the Province of Venezuela. Thus Caracas became the third and final capital of the province (Coro was the first, in 1527-46, followed by El Tocuyo in 1547-77).

The earliest map of Caracas, drawn in 1578, clearly shows the extension of the 'city': it stretched two blocks each way from the Plaza Mayor, and consisted altogether of 25 blocks. Caracas at that time was inhabited by 60 families.

From the beginning, the town's development was hindered by constant setbacks: pirates, plagues and natural disasters. The first pirate attack came in 1595, and the town was sacked and burnt to the ground. Reconstructed and revived, Caracas went on to be destroyed by a violent earthquake in 1641, only four years after the bishops had moved the archdiocese here from Coro. Some 500 inhabitants died.

The 18th century proved to be more fortunate for the city. In 1725 the Universidad Real y Pontificia de Caracas (today Universidad Central de Venezuela) was founded and this became the province's first university. Three years later, the Real Compañía Guipuzcoana was created. This trading company, comprised of 700 captains and merchants from the Basque province (in Spain), was given the monopoly over trade between Spain and the colony. In Venezuela, the company had its headquarters in the port of La Guaira and a branch in Puerto Cabello. The company contributed greatly to Caracas' progress, though later on its aggressive practices and corruption aroused widespread discontent amongst the colonists. In 1749 Juan Francisco de León marched on Caracas with 800 men to protest against the company's abusive tactics. In the opinion of many historians, this riot is considered to be

Caracas coat-of-arms

the first open protest of importance and it sowed the seeds that eventually became the independence movement. The company was eventually dissolved in 1785.

On 28 March 1750 Caracas witnessed the birth of Francisco Miranda and on 24 July 1783 that of Simón Bolívar; the former was to pave the way to independence, the latter was to make it fact.

On 19 April 1810, a group of councillors, supported by some notable Caraqueños, denounced the authority of the Spanish governor and formed a Supreme Junta to take over the government. The political struggle continued for over a year until 5 July 1811, when the congress convened in Caracas and solemnly declared the independence of Venezuela. The document was signed by all but one delegate.

On Maundy Thursday (the Thursday before Easter) of 1812, an earthquake almost completely wrecked the town and killed some 10,000 people. The conservative clergy seized the opportunity to declare that it was a punishment from Heaven for the rebellion against the Spanish Crown. Independence, however, was only nine years away, and was eventually sealed by Bolívar's victory at the Battle of Carabobo on 24 June 1821. It wasn't until 1845 that

Spain finally recognised the sovereignty of Venezuela.

Despite its political achievements, Caracas continued to grow at a very modest pace. The first person to launch an extensive modernising programme was General Guzmán Blanco, known as El Modernizador, who erected a number of monumental buildings, among them the Capitol Building and the National Pantheon. Unfortunately, in 1900 yet another serious earthquake ruined many buildings and reconstruction work had to begin all over again.

Then came the oil boom. Over the last 50 years, the city's population has expanded from some 350,000 to over four million people. Oil money has been pumped into modernisation, successfully transforming the somewhat bucolic colonial town into a vast concrete sprawl. In the name of progress, most colonial buildings were demolished and their place taken by futuristic complexes and steel-and-glass towers. The last important urban planning achievement was the metro which opened in the 1980s.

Old Caracas

ORIENTATION

The city spreads for at least 20 km along a valley from east to west. To the north looms the massive green wall of Parque Nacional El Ávila, an area which is uninhabited. To the south, in contrast, the city is expanding up the hillsides, with modern *urbanizaciones* and shabby *ranchitos* invading and occupying every possible piece of land.

The valley itself consists of forests of skyscrapers rising above a mass of low-rise buildings. The area from El Silencio to Chacao is packed with commercial centres, banks, offices, shops, restaurants and public buildings. The main line of the metro (No 1) goes right along the axis of the city.

The historic quarter is at the western end of the centre, and it is clearly recognisable on the map by the original chessboard layout of the streets. To the east stretches the district of Los Caobos which has several good museums. Next comes the Sabana Grande centred on an attractive pedestrian mall lined

with shops and restaurants. Proceeding east, one comes to Chacaíto and Chacao, two commercial districts which are unlikely to be interesting for tourists. El Rosal and Las Mercedes to the south boast a number of trendy restaurants. The Caracas Country Club and Altamira to the north are predominantly elegant and wealthy residential zones.

Addresses in the historic quarter may be difficult for newcomers to follow. It's not the streets which bear names but the street intersections, or *esquinas*. A place is identified by the corners on either side. If the address is, for instance, Piñango a Conde, you know that the place is between these two street corners. If the place is right on the corner, its address is Esquina Conde. In modern times, the authorities, supposedly in effort to modernise the 'ridiculous' traditional system, have named the streets with the cardinal points ('Este', 'Oeste', 'Norte' and 'Sur'), followed by numbers. Nonetheless, locals continue to stick to the esquinas. Other than

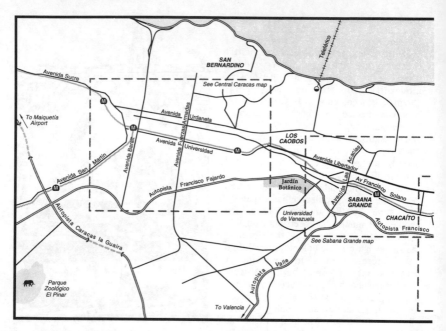

in the old town, a conventional system is applied in which the streets, and not the corners are named. Major streets are commonly named Avenidas. Street numbers are seldom used and you'll rarely find one on façades or entrance doors.

INFORMATION
Tourist Offices

The Corpoturismo tourist office (☎ 507-8815, 507-8829) is on the 37th floor of the Torre Oeste (West Tower), Parque Central (metro Bellas Artes). The office is open Monday to Friday from 8 am to noon and 2 to 5 pm. Don't expect much in the way of leaflets on Caracas, or city maps.

There's also a tourist office at the Maiquetía Airport (international terminal, arrival hall) but travellers describe it as 'useless'.

Local brochures proudly state that a 24-hour phone service, *Ayuda Permanente al Turista* (Permanent Help for Tourists), has been created, offering bilingual English/Spanish information, which can be reached on ☎ 573-8983 and 507-8829. Take it easy though; these are actually the Corpoturismo phone numbers, only available during their normal office hours (given above), and not all the staff speak English.

Useful Organisations

Fairmont International (782-8433, 781-7091, 782-8688), at Plaza Venezuela (metro Plaza Venezuela) in Sabana Grande, can book a room in any of some 250 hotels throughout the country (obviously not the budget ones). They also sell air tickets and arrange car rentals. The office is open Monday to Friday from 8 am to 6 pm, Saturday 9 am to 3 pm.

The Dirección General de Parques Nacionales, commonly known as Inparques (☎ 285-4106, 285-4360, 285-4859), is the office where you get national parks permits. In theory, you have to have a permit to visit

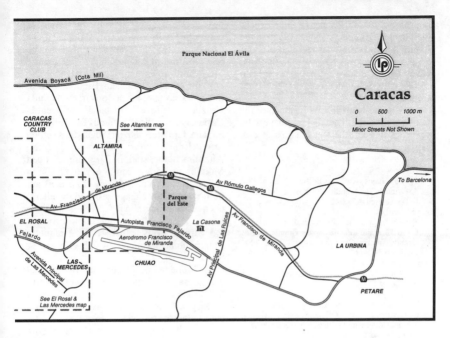

each park except for El Ávila where you just pay the US$0.10 fee at the entrance to the park. In practice, though, you'll rarely be asked for the permit in any of the parks, though it's always better to have one, just in case. The permit costs nothing and it is issued on the spot. Get permits to all parks you plan to visit. Specify 'camping' if that's what you intend doing.

The Inparques office is just east of the Parque del Este metro station and it is open Monday to Friday from 8.30 am to 12.30 pm and 1.30 to 5 pm. The office doesn't provide much information about the parks and it has virtually no maps or brochures. They are now organising their library which may improve the situation. It's planned to open to the public on Wednesdays and Fridays from 1 to 5 pm.

Centro Excursionista de Caracas is an association of outdoor activities enthusiasts who organise weekend hikes to the country-side. These are essentially one or two-day excursions around Caracas and the central states, but longer hikes to other regions are also organised for long weekends and holiday periods. Foreign travellers are warmly welcomed. Some members are for-eigners living in the city or Caraqueños who speak foreign languages, so you may find a companion for some English/French/German/etc conversation.

The club meetings are on Saturday, between 2 and 5 pm, in a house in the Zona Verde (green area) of Urbanización San Román, Calle Chivacoa, corner of Calle Yare. Otherwise, call Vicente Arlán (president) ☎ 261-9626 (home); Fritz Werner (vice-president, speaks German) ☎ 930-385 (home), ☎ 939-053 (work); Enrique Herrera ☎ 292-3747 (home, best between 9 and 11 am); or Nelly ☎ 242-0475.

Tours

There are umpteen travel agents who can send you to virtually any corner of the country, but these trips can be quite expensive. See the comments under 'Tours' in the Getting Around chapter. If you plan on a tour to Salto Angel, check the Avensa offer first, as they fly to Canaima and have packages on offer (see the Salto Angel section for further information).

Tours to the hatos in Los Llanos (see the Hatos section for full details) may have to be organised through their agents in Caracas. They include:

Hato El Frío
    Epsilon Viajes y Turismo, Edificio Belmont, Piso 3, Oficina 32, Avenida Beethoven, Colinas de Bello Monte (☎ 752-4592)
Hato El Cedral
    Turven Tropical Travel Services, Edificio Unión, Local 13, Calle Real de Sabana Grande, Sabana Grande (metro Chacaíto) (☎ 951-1032, 951-1787, fax 951-1176)
Hato La Trinidad de Arauca
    Edificio 3-H, Oficina 62, Boulevard de Sabana Grande (☎ 271-8644)
Hato Macanillal
    Francisco Freites, Torre Lincoln (opposite Torre La Previsora), Piso 8, Oficina 8G, Gran Avenida, Sabana Grande (metro Plaza Venezuela) (☎ 782-1546, 782-4831, fax 781-7421)
Hato Piñero
    Edificio General de Seguros, Piso 6, Oficina 6B, Avenida La Estancia, Chuao (☎ 912-011)

Money

There's a constellation of banks in Caracas but only a few of them will change cash or travellers' cheques. Those that do include the Banco Consolidado, which deals with American Express cheques, and Banco Unión, which handles cash exchanges (though not all branches of these banks do). Banco do Brasil, which has recently moved to Centro Lido, Avenida Francisco de Miranda (metro Chacaíto or Chacao), changes cash at the best rate in town. However, the difference is so small that it's only worth a special trip if you intend to change a large amount.

It's easier to find a bank that gives cash advances to MasterCard and Visa credit card holders. The Banco de Venezuela, Banco Unión, Banco Mercantil and Banco Provincial, among others, can do this.

If you can't find a bank to change cash and

travellers' cheques, or you don't want to waste time with lengthy transactions, go to a casa de cambio; there are plenty of them. The one with the best reputation is Italcambio. They have several offices throughout the city: on Avenida Urdaneta, Esquina Veroes, one block north of Plaza Bolívar; on Avenida Urdaneta, Ánimas a Platanal; on Avenida Casanova, one block south of Boulevard de Sabana Grande; and on Segunda Avenida Sur Altamira, one block south of the Altamira metro station. They are all open Monday to Friday from 8 am to 12.30 pm and 1.30 to 5 pm, Saturday from 8.30 am until noon. They change cash and travellers' cheques and pay about 0.5% less than the banks. There's also an Italcambio office at the Simón Bolívar Airport in Maiquetía (international terminal), which is open 24 hours.

La Moneda and Profesional, two convenient casas de cambio near the western end of the Boulevard de Sabana Grande, also give a good rate for cash dollars (La Moneda pays better for travellers' cheques).

Casas de cambio also sell foreign currency; the rate difference is about 1% for US dollars but much higher (up to 5%) for other currencies.

American Express travellers' cheques can be bought in Turisol in Centro Ciudad Comercial Tamanaco (CCCT), Nivel PB. Turisol is also the place to report the loss or theft of American Express cheques and to apply for a refund. The office where you do this is also in CCCT, but on Nivel C2 (☎ 959-1011, 959-2115, 959-1648, fax 959-2867), and is open Monday to Friday from 8 am to noon and 2 to 6 pm. Turisol has a 24-hour phone information service, (☎ 206-0000, 208-4999).

The refund assistance point for the holders of Thomas Cook travellers' cheques is in Edificio Cavendes, Oficina 706, Avenida Francisco de Miranda, Los Palos Grandes (☎ 284-3866, 284-3255).

Post

The main post office is on Avenida Urdaneta, Esquina Carmelitas, close to Plaza Bolívar.

Have a look at the building itself – it was one of the most sumptuous, palatial residences in 18th-century Caracas. Another conveniently located, central post office is on Plaza La Candelaria, next to the church. There are plenty of other offices scattered throughout the city, including one in Sabana Grande (Avenida Casanova), in Chacao (Avenida Francisco de Miranda) and in Altamira (Plaza Sur Altamira).

Amongst the several international courier services, probably the cheapest is UPS, or United Parcel Service (☎ 203-1444), Edificio Transvalcar, Avenida Principal de La Urbina, corner of Calle 10, La Urbina (metro Petare). Their office is open Monday to Friday from 8 am to noon and 1 to 6 pm. The postage for a parcel weighing up to 500 grams will cost about US$18 to Florida, US$22 to the rest of the USA and US$28 elsewhere. They can send your parcels to almost anywhere in the world.

DHL, which has its head office (☎ 263-2122, 263-0211) in Torre Credival, Planta Baja, Segunda Avenida de Campo Alegre (metro Chacaíto or Chacao), will charge about twice as much as UPS.

Telephone

The main CANTV office is at Plaza Caracas in the Centro Simón Bolívar. It's open 24 hours. The only other CANTV office open round the clock is at the Simón Bolívar Airport in Maiquetía.

The Caracas telephone system is unreliable. There are both six and seven digit numbers – the result of several stages of modernisation. The recent privatisation of the telephone company is adding to this chaos, with many phone numbers changing.

Foreign Embassies & Consulates

The embassies and consulates of selected countries are listed below. See the phone directory at a CANTV office, any travel agency or decent hotel for a full list.

Australia
    Quinta Yolanda, Avenida Luis Roche between Transversales 6 and 7, Altamira (☎ 261-4313)

Austria
    Torre Las Mercedes, Piso 4, Oficina 408, Avenida La Estancia, Chuao (☎ 913-863)
Barbados
    Centro Profesional Santa Paula, Torre B, Piso 12, Oficina 1204, Avenida Circunvalación del Sol, Santa Paula (☎ 987-6490)
Belgium
    Quinta La Azulita, Avenida 11 between Transversales 6 and 7, Altamira (☎ 261-9397)
Bolivia
    Quinta Embajada de Bolivia, Avenida Principal Luis Roche, corner of Transversal 6, Altamira (☎ 261-4563)
Brazil
    Centro Gerencial Mohedano, Piso 6, Calle Los Chaguaramos, corner of Avenida Mohedano, La Castellana (metro Altamira or Chacao) (☎ 261-7553, 261-4481)
Canada
    Torre Europa, Piso 7, Avenida Francisco de Miranda, Campo Alegre (metro Chacaíto) (☎ 951-6174)
Colombia
    Embassy: Torre Credival, Piso 11, Segunda Avenida de Campo Alegre, corner of Avenida Francisco de Miranda, Campo Alegre (☎ 261-8358)
    Consulate: Edificio Consulado de Colombia, Calle Guaicaipuro, Chacaíto (☎ 951-3631)
Costa Rica
    Edificio For You, Pent House, Avenida San Juan Bosco between Transversales 1 and 2, Altamira (☎ 327889)
Denmark
    Edificio Easo, Piso 17, Avenida Francisco de Miranda, Chacaíto (☎ 951-6618)
Ecuador
    Centro Andrés Bello, Torre Oeste, Piso 13, Avenida Andrés Bello (☎ 781-6090)
Finland
    Edificio Atrium, Piso 1, Calle Sorotaima between Avenidas Tamanaco and Venezuela, El Rosal (☎ 952-4111)
France
    Edificio Los Frailes, Piso 5, Calle La Guairita (opposite the Eurobuilding Hotel), Chuao, (☎ 910-324)
Germany
    Edificio Panaven, Piso 12, Avenida San Juan Bosco, corner of Transversal 3, Altamira Norte (☎ 261-1205)
Grenada
    Edificio Los Frailes, Piso 3, Calle La Guairita, Chuao (☎ 911-237)
Guyana
    Quinta Roraima, Avenida del Paseo, Prados del Este (☎ 771-158)

PLACES TO STAY

8 Hotel Terepaima
9 Hotel Metropol
10 Hotel Inter
22 Hotel El Conde
28 Plaza Catedral Hotel
31 Hotel Mara
33 Hotel Hollywood
52 Hotel Peral
53 Hotel Caracol
61 Hospedaje Mari Tere
63 Hotel Center Park
64 Hotel Curamichate
68 Hotel San Roque
69 Pensión Española
93 Hotel Caracas Hilton

PLACES TO EAT

6 Restaurant Dama Antañona
26 Restaurant El Atrio
42 Restaurant La Atarraya
72 Restaurant El Coyuco
73 Tasca Segoviana
74 Tasca Don Quijote
77 Tasca La Carabela
79 Tasca La Tertulia
80 Tasca La Cita
81 Tasca Guernica
82 Tasca Bar Basque
83 Tasca Dena Ona

OTHER

1 Panteón Nacional
2 Iglesia Las Mercedes
3 Iglesia Altagracia
4 Librería Mundial
5 Italcambio (Money Exchange)
7 Banco Unión
11 Italcambio (Money Exchange)
12 Banco de Venezuela
13 Banco Unión
14 Banco Unión
15 Banco Consolidado
16 Museo de Arte Colonial
17 Palacio de Miraflores
18 Ipostel Central Post Office
19 Aeropostal Office
20 Librería Kuai-Mare
21 Biblioteca Metropolitana
23 Casa Amarilla
24 Librería Historia
25 Santa Capilla
27 Palacio de Gobernación
29 Catedral
30 Banco Consolidado
32 Second-hand Book Stalls
34 Metro Capitolio & El Silencio
35 Capitolio Nacional
36 Palacio Municipal,
   Museo Criollo & Capilla
   de Santa Rosa de Lima
37 Banco Provincial
38 Banco de Venezuela
39 Museo Bolivariano
40 Casa Natal de Bolívar
41 Plaza El Venezolano
43 Former Supreme Court
44 Palacio de las Academias
45 Iglesia de San Francisco
46 Banco Mercantil
47 Dirección de Cartografía
   Nacional
48 Museo Fundación
   John Boulton
49 Banco Unión
50 Banco Latino
51 Metro La Hoyada
54 Plaza Caracas
55 CANTV Office
56 DIEX Office
57 Teatro Municipal
58 Banco Consolidado
59 Basílica de Santa Teresa
60 Teatro Nacional
62 Cuadra Bolívar
65 Carritos to La Guaira
66 Carritos to Los Teques
67 Nuevo Circo Bus Terminal
70 Carritos to Junquito
71 Nuevo Circo Bullring
75 Plaza La Candelaria
76 Ipostel Post Office
78 Iglesia de la Candelaria
84 Metro Parque Carabobo
85 Paseo Anauco
   (Second-hand Book Stalls)
86 Metro Bellas Artes
87 Galería de Arte (Future Seat)
88 Carritos to the Airport
89 Museo de los Niños
90 Torre Oeste (West Tower) &
   Tourist Office
91 Torre Este (East Tower)
92 Museo de Arte Contemporáneo
94 Complejo Cultural
   Teresa Carreño
95 Ateneo de Caracas
96 Museo de Ciencias Naturales
97 Galería de Arte Nacional &
   Museo de Bellas Artes
98 Mosque

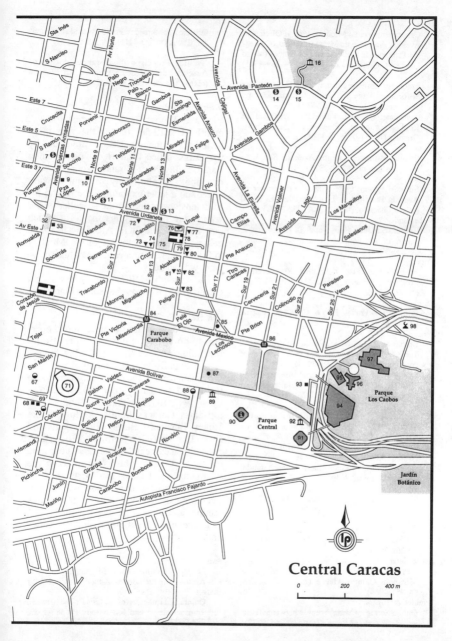

Central Caracas

0   200   400 m

Israel
     Centro Empresarial Miranda, Piso 4, Oficina D,
     Avenida Francisco de Miranda, corner of Aven-
     ida Principal de Los Ruices, Los Ruices (metro
     Los Dos Caminos or Los Cortijos) (☎ 239-4511)
Italy
     Embassy: Edificio Atrium, Pent House, Calle
     Sorocaima between Avenidas Zamanaco and
     Venezuela, El Rosal (☎ 952-7311)
     Consulate: Quinta Las Imeldas, Avenida Luis
     Roche, corner of Transversal 7, Los Palos
     Grandes (☎ 261-0755, 261-2803)
Japan
     Quinta Miton or Sacura, Avenida San Juan
     Bosco, Altamira (☎ 261-8333)
Mexico
     Edificio Forum, Calle Guaicaipuro, corner of
     Avenida Principal de Las Mercedes, El Rosal
     (metro Chacaíto) (☎ 952-2408, 952-5777)
Netherlands
     Edificio San Juan, Pisos 9 and 10, Transversal 2,
     corner of Avenida San Juan Bosco, Altamira
     (☎ 263-3076)
Norway
     Edificio Exa, Piso 9, Oficina 905, Avenida
     Libertador, corner of Calle Alameda, El Rosal
     (☎ 262-1506)
Panama
     Edificio Los Frailes, Piso 6, Calle La Guairita,
     Chuao (☎ 929-093, 929-182)
Peru
     Embassy: Centro Empresarial Andrés Bello,
     Torre Oeste, Avenida Andrés Bello, corner of
     Avenida Maripérez (☎ 793-7974)
     Consulate: Centro Empresarial Andrés Bello,
     Torre Este, Avenida Andrés Bello, corner of
     Avenida Maripérez (☎ 793-0726)
Spain
     Embassy: Quinta Marmolejo, Avenida
     Mohedano between Transversales 1 and 2, La
     Castellana (☎ 263-1956)
     Consulate: Edificio Banco Unión, Piso 2,
     Avenida Abraham Lincoln (Boulevard de Sabana
     Grande), Sabana Grande (metro Sabana Grande)
     (☎ 762-0421, 762-7449)
Suriname
     Quinta Los Milagros, Avenida 4 between Trans-
     versales 7 and 8, Altamira (☎ 261-2095)
Sweden
     Torre Europa, Piso 8, Avenida Francisco de
     Miranda, Campo Alegre (metro Chacaíto)
     (☎ 261-7906)
Switzerland
     Torre Europa, Piso 6, Avenida Francisco de
     Miranda, Campo Alegre (metro Chacaíto)
     (☎ 951-4064)
Trinidad & Tobago
     Quinta Serrana, Cuarta Avenida between Trans-
     versales 7 and 8, Altamira Norte (☎ 261-4772)

UK
     Edificio Las Mercedes, Piso 3, Avenida La Estan-
     cia, Chuao (☎ 993-4111)
USA
     Avenida Francisco de Miranda, corner of
     Avenida Principal de la Floresta, La Floresta
     (metro Altamira) (☎ 285-2222)

Visa Extensions

Visa and Tourist Card extensions for one
month (US$12.50) or for the maximum
period of two months (US$25) are issued by
the DIEX office (2nd floor) on Avenida
Baralt, facing Plaza Miranda. Your passport,
one photo, a photocopy of your onward
ticket and a letter explaining the reason for
an extension written on the so-called *papel
sellado* are required, plus the form which
they'll give you to fill in. All of this has to be
delivered between 8 am and 11 am, Monday
to Friday, and the procedure may take up to
eight working days.
     The only other DIEX office which might
extend your visa is on the Isla de Margarita.

Car Rental

There are more than a dozen car rental operators, both national and international
(including most of the world's big boys –
Avis, Hertz, Dollar, Budget etc). Apart from
their main offices, the major companies also
maintain desks at the Simón Bolívar International Airport in Maiquetía, and in the
top-class Caracas hotels, including the
Hilton, Tamanaco, Eurobuilding, Ávila and
Paseo Las Mercedes. National is the principal national car rental agency and it has nine
offices in Caracas plus desks in both the
international and domestic airport terminals.
Car may also be hired through Fairmont
International (see the Useful Organisations
section) and some other travel agents.
     The central offices of the major companies
are:

Avis
     Edificio Centro Altamira, Mezzanine, Local 5,
     Avenida San Juan Bosco, Altamira (☎ 322-805)
Budget
     Quinta Los Irunes, Avenida Luis Roche between
     Transversales 5 and 6, Altamira (☎ 283-4333,
     284-0023)

Hertz
  Edificio Pichincha, Piso 5, Avenida Principal El Bosque, corner of Avenida Francisco Solano, Chacaíto (☎ 952-1603, 952-1396)
National
  Edificio Nacional, Local 5, Centro Los Ruices, Avenida Diego Cisneros, Los Ruices (☎ 239-3791, 239-2486)

For more information about rental conditions, prices and driving in general, see the Car & Motorbike section in the Getting Around chapter.

Maps

Some of the better bookshops sell folded city maps of Caracas which have a map of the whole country on the reverse. The best Caracas/country map has been published by the Lagoven Oil Company, but it's not distributed through bookshops. It's still available at some Lagoven petrol stations but they're running out of stock.

If you can't get either of these, there's a reasonable Caracas city map on the back of the local phone directory – just photocopy it.

For large-scale regional maps, go to the Dirección de Cartografía Nacional (☎ 408-1710), (1st floor, oficina 111) Calle Este 6, Esquina Colón, off Plaza Diego Ibarra. The office is open Monday to Friday from 8.30 to 11.30 am and 2 to 4 pm. They produce and sell 1:100,000 and 1:25,000 maps. So far, only the northern part of the country is well covered; there is only a handful of maps of Amazonas and Guayana. They also have some major city maps. Unfortunately, many of these maps are out of date; some go back 20 or 30 years.

If they run out of the colour originals (which is usually the case), they will make a black and white copy for you on the spot. Maps featuring strategic installations such as airports, military zones, oil refineries etc require a special permit from military authorities, which takes several days to be issued, but it is usually granted without any problems.

Maps cost somewhere between US$3.50 and US$6 per sheet, depending on their size.

Guidebooks

There are several locally published guidebooks to Caracas, some of them in English. The content of most of them is unimpressive, and their practical information, especially for budget travellers, is insignificant.

Two guides are useful, especially if you are going to stay in Caracas for a long while.

Living in Venezuela 1991-92, published by the Venezuelan-American Chamber of Commerce and Industry, is theoretically a guide to the whole country but most of it is dedicated to the capital. This English-language book is packed with practical information and describes plenty of the city sights. The 1993-94 edition is in preparation and should be available by the time you read this. The book can be bought in the Chamber of Commerce's office (☎ 263-0833), Torre Credival, Piso 10, Segunda Avenida de Campo Alegre, near the corner of Avenida Francisco de Miranda, Campo Alegre (midway between metro Chacaíto and Chacao).

Guía de Venezuela by Janice Bauman and Leni Young, was published by Ernesto Armitano as a single volume and was last updated in 1987. The book was then taken under the wing of Corpoven, whose editors decided to split it into several volumes. So far three updated volumes have been published. Volume No 1 refers entirely to Caracas and covers places of tourist interest in detail. Unlike the Armitano editions, which issued both Spanish and English versions, Corpoven only publishes a Spanish edition. They can be bought directly from the Corpoven office (☎ 208-6111), Edificio Sucre, Avenida Francisco de Miranda, corner of Avenida Principal de la Floresta (opposite the US Embassy), La Floresta (metro Altamira).

Press

El Nacional and *El Universal* are the two leading Caracas papers and both give good coverage of local and international politics, economy, culture and sport. Other local papers include *El Diario* and *El Globo*.

Economía Hoy is the business newspaper. On Sunday, it appears under the title of

Domingo Hoy and has a good 'what's on' section (Guía del buen vivir y del buen gusto) for the forthcoming week. The Sunday edition also contains the English-language *Guardian Weekly* (Latin American Edition) as a supplement, but there's not much about Venezuela in it.

If you want to keep a track of Venezuelan politics, buy the *Daily Journal* which is the best source of information about the country for English-speaking readers. All the above-mentioned papers are available from countless newsstands.

Mira!, possibly the best Venezuelan travellers' paper (published monthly in Porlamar on Isla de Margarita), can sometimes be bought at central Caracas newsstands (for example on Boulevard de Sabana Grande, amongst others) and from some of the top-class hotels.

Major foreign papers such as the *New York Times*, the *International Herald Tribune*, the *Times*, *Le Monde*, *Der Spiegel* etc are sold by some of the better central newsstands and bookshops. *Time* and *Newsweek* are the most widely distributed foreign weekly magazines.

Bookshops

There are plenty of bookshops throughout the city which deal in locally published Spanish-language books. Librería Kuai-Mare focuses on Venezuelan politics, ethnology, ethnography, nature and the like. There's a chain of Kuai-Mare bookshops: in Centro Simón Bolívar, Torre Norte, Pasaje Río Orinoco; on Calle Norte 4, El Conde a Carmelitas; on Boulevard de Sabana Grande near the Chacaíto metro station, and at the Altamira and Plaza Venezuela metro stations.

Somewhat hidden from the street, the Librería Mundial (☎ 862-0337), Calle Norte 2, Santa Capilla a Mijares, offers a large selection of books, as does Librería Historia, Calle Oeste 2, Monjas a Pepe Sierra, just off Plaza Bolívar.

An even more extensive choice of both new and second-hand books can be found at La Gran Pulpería de Libros Venezolanos (☎ 541-0046), in Pasaje Zingg, Local 9,

between Avenida Universidad and Plaza Diego Ibarra. There's also a good Librería La Crónica near the western end of Boulevard de Sabana Grande. At the opposite end of the Boulevard, try the Librería Lectura (☎ 952-0586) in the Centro Comercial Chacaíto, Local 16, on Plaza Luis Brion (commonly referred to as Plaza Chacaíto), which also has some English-language paperbacks. Tamanaco Libros Técnicos in the Centro Comercial Ciudad Tamanaco (CCCT), Nivel C2, is also worth checking out.

The above-mentioned bookshops boast a variety of lavishly illustrated coffee table books on Venezuela's art, architecture and nature – they make tempting souvenirs. They also stock some dictionaries and, occasionally, maps and locally produced guidebooks.

Books are not cheap in Venezuela. If you want to save some bolívares, first check the second-hand book markets. The cheapest place to buy books is at the street stalls on Avenida Fuerzas Armadas, between Romualda and Plaza López (metro La Hoyada). They have a haphazard range of new and second-hand books, including some rare old editions which are virtually unobtainable elsewhere. A similar street market, but smaller and not so cheap, is on Paseo Anauco just off Avenida México (metro Bellas Artes). There's are also a dozen or so bookstalls on the campus of Universidad Central de Venezuela. They sell new books but at about 20% below normal bookshop prices.

The American Book Shop, Avenida San Juan Bosco, one long block north of Altamira metro station, has possibly the best selection of English-language books, whereas Librería Rizzoli, Transversal 1 between Primera Avenida and Avenida Andrés Bello (metro Altamira), offers the largest choice of Italian-language publications.

Dangers & Annoyances

Since the late 1980s, Caracas has become increasingly unsafe, more so than any other city in the country. One obvious reason for this is the city's large and rapidly growing population, many of whom live below the poverty level in ranchos. The other reason is the declining standard of living, the result of the precarious economy and the political instability; social programmes for the poor are the last thing the government has in mind. Predictably, the poor barrios are where the majority of violent crimes are reported but, they have spread to the more affluent districts.

One needs to be on one's guard. See the Dangers & Annoyances section in the Facts for the Visitor chapter for general tips. Don't venture into shantytowns at any time of the day, let alone at night. Central districts are OK during the day, but armed robberies occasionally occur. Expensive jewellery, watches and cameras, will definitely multiply your chances of being mugged.

The historic centre becomes unsafe for strolling around after 8 pm or so, as does the area around the Nuevo Circo bus terminal. The Sabana Grande is going the same way, though so far it only becomes unpleasant late at night.

Caracas' traffic is heavy, fast and wild – be careful! Drivers don't obey traffic rules and they may run red lights or crawl against the flow up a one-way street, if that's what they feel like doing. Crossing the street may involve some risk; take it for granted that no driver will stop to give you right of way.

Air pollution is largely a by-product of the busy traffic and the poor mechanical condition of many of the vehicles, which often trail clouds of fumes. The pollution may be appalling to visitors from 'clean' countries, especially when there is no wind to disperse it.

There are no self-contained public toilets in Caracas. The easiest alternative is to take advantage of the toilets of restaurants, though not all basic establishments have them (or if they do, they may be in a disastrous state). If you feel uncomfortable about sneaking in just to use the toilet, order a soft drink, a beer, a coffee or whatever. Museums usually have toilets as do some of the large shopping centres. You'll never see toilet paper in public toilets, so make sure to carry it with you at all times.

Emergency

Below is a selected list of important phone numbers you might need (hopefully not!).

THINGS TO SEE

Despite the city's size, most of the tourist sights are grouped in a few areas. The excellent metro system helps enormously in moving from one district to another.

Plaza Bolívar

The historic sector has lost much of its identity. In a rush towards modernisation many of the colonial houses were replaced with 20th-century buildings, from nondescript through to modern tinted-glass cubes.

The nucleus of this part of the city is Plaza Bolívar with the inevitable monument to the hero in the middle. The equestrian statue was cast in Europe, shipped in pieces, assembled and unveiled in 1874, later than planned as the ship carrying it foundered on the Archipiélago de Los Roques. Pigeons and squirrels are ubiquitous in the trees, and sloths and iguanas can occasionally be seen as well. Plaza Bolívar is a favourite playground for local orators who speak on religion, politics etc. They mainly gather on the corner next to the cathedral.

The **Catedral**, on the eastern side of the plaza, was built in 1665-1713 after the 1641

Service	Phone Nos	When to Call Them
Police	☎ 169	general emergency
Traffic Police	☎ 167	car accident
Ambulance	☎ 545-4545	ambulance needed urgently
Medical Emergency	☎ 483-7021, 483-6092	doctor needed urgently

All the above-mentioned services operate 24 hours a day. You also may want to seek help or advice from your embassy (see the Foreign Embassies & Consulates section for phone numbers).

earthquake had destroyed the previous church. A wide five-nave interior supported on 32 columns was largely remodelled in the late 19th century. The Bolívar family chapel is in the middle of the right-hand aisle and can be easily recognised by a modern sculpture of El Libertador mourning his parents and wife.

The **Palacio de Gobernación**, on the northern side of the square, was built in the 1930s and holds temporary exhibitions on the ground floor. Half of the western side of the plaza is occupied by the 17th-century **Casa Amarilla**, much altered over the years. It once housed the royal prison. In Republican times it served as the Government House, and today it is the seat of the Ministry of Foreign Affairs.

The southern side of the square is lined by the **Palacio Municipal** which was constructed by the Caracas bishops in 1640-96 as the home of the Colegio Seminario de Santa Rosa de Lima. This was the first seat of the Universidad de Caracas, established in 1725. Today, the **Museo Criollo** on the ground floor features items related to the town's history and a collection of dioramas depicting the life of the turn-of-the-century Caracas. These were created by a local artist, Raúl Santana. Don't miss the amazing models of central Caracas in the 1810s and 1930s. The museum is open Tuesday to Friday from 9 to 11.30 am and 2.30 to 4.30 pm, Saturday and Sunday from 10.30 am to 4 pm.

On the 1st floor is a collection of 80 paintings by Emilio Boggio (1857-1920), a Venezuelan artist who lived in Paris. It's normally closed to the general public, but if you are interested in seeing it, talk to the tourist attendants by the main entrance, and they'll most likely show you around.

The western side of the palace houses the **Capilla de Santa Rosa de Lima**, where on 5 July 1811 the Congress declared Venezuela's independence, though it was another 10 years before this became a reality. The chapel has been restored with the decoration and furniture of the time. While visiting the palace, have a look at the famous Caracas map of 1578; an enlarged reproduction is displayed in the courtyard's cloister.

South of Plaza Bolívar

The entire block south-west of Plaza Bolívar is taken up by the neoclassical **Capitolio Nacional**, a complex of two buildings commissioned in the 1870s by Guzmán Blanco, on the site of a convent. The nuns had been expelled by the dictator not long before.

In the central part of the northern building is the famous **Salón Elíptico**, the oval hall with a large mural on its domed ceiling. The painting, depicting the Battle of Carabobo, was executed in 1888 by perhaps the most notable Venezuelan artist of the day, Martín Tovar y Tovar. The southern wall of the hall is crammed with portraits of distinguished leaders of the independence wars. Underneath the central painting of Bolívar is a marble pedestal with his bust on top; the Act of Independence of 1811 is kept inside the pedestal.

Tovar y Tovar left behind more military works of art in two adjoining halls: the Salón Amarillo has on its ceiling the Battle of Junín while the Salón Rojo has been embellished with the Battle of Boyacá. The Capitolio is open for visits daily from 9 am to 12.30 pm and 3 to 5 pm.

Just south of the Capitolio is the **Iglesia de San Francisco**, which originated in the

Guzmán Blanco

1570s but was remodelled on several occasions during the 17th and 18th centuries. Guzmán Blanco couldn't resist his passion for modernising and placed a new neoclassical façade on the church, probably to harmonise with the just built Capitol building. Fortunately, the interior of the church didn't undergo such an extensive alteration and it still preserves its colonial character and much of its old decoration. Have a look at the richly gilded Baroque altarpieces.

Of particular interest is the chapel of the Tertiary Order, to the left of the high altar. Dating from the mid-17th century, this is the oldest surviving chapel of all Caracas' churches, and its retable is acclaimed as possibly the best piece of Venezuela's colonial art. While you're looking around the interior, stop at San Onofre, in the right-hand aisle. He is the most venerated saint in the church due to his miraculous powers of bringing health, happiness and a good job.

It was in this church in 1813 that Bolívar was proclaimed El Libertador, and also here that his much-celebrated funeral was held in 1842, after his remains had been brought over from Santa Marta in Colombia, 12 years after his death.

Two blocks east is the **Casa Natal de Bolívar**, the house where, on 24 July 1783, this great man was born. Its reconstructed interior (which has lost almost all its colonial features) has been decorated with a score of large paintings by Tito Salas, depicting Bolívar's heroic battles and other scenes from his life.

A few paces north, the **Museo Bolivariano**, in another colonial house (which has preserved a bit more of its original style), displays a variety of independence memorabilia, documents, period weapons and banners plus a number of Bolívar's portraits. Among the exhibits is the coffin in which the remains of Bolívar were brought from Santa Marta to Caracas in 1842. The ashes were then kept in the cathedral from where they were moved in 1876 in the *arca cineraria* (a funeral ark, also exhibited in the museum) to their eventual resting place, the National Pantheon. Both museums are open Monday

Simón Bolívar

to Friday from 9 am to noon and 2 to 5 pm, Saturday and Sunday from 10 am to 1 pm and 2 to 5 pm.

In the same area, in the Torre El Chorro (Piso 11), Esquina El Chorro, is the **Museo Fundación John Boulton**. The museum features a collection of historic and artistic objects that have been accumulated by the family over the generations. Among the exhibits are paintings by Arturo Michelena, colonial furniture, Bolívar's memorabilia and an extensive collection of ceramics from all over the world. The museum is open Monday to Friday from 9 am to noon and 2 to 5 pm.

A complex of buildings topped by twin towers, one block south of the Capitolio Nacional, is the **Centro Simón Bolívar**, packed with a number of government offices and shops. This is where the large-scale, indiscriminate demolition of the old town began in the 1950s, in the name of modernity. The Centro was for a long time the symbol and favourite postcard image of the new Caracas, until more modern towers sprung up in the Parque Central.

Just south of the Centro is the handsome oval building of the **Teatro Municipal**, commissioned by Guzmán Blanco and inaugurated with great pomp in 1881. One block east, the neoclassical **Basílica de Santa Teresa** is yet another achievement of Guzmán Blanco. There are actually two churches in the building, Santa Ana to the west and Santa Teresa to the east.

Just to the south of the church is the **Teatro Nacional**, which is noted for the allegorical ceiling paintings by Herrera Toro, representing the Dance, Music, Comedy and Drama. The theatre was opened in 1905 and continues to be one of the main city performance spaces.

Four blocks south is the **Cuadra Bolívar**, a Bolívar family summer house where he spent much of his childhood and youth. Restored to its original appearance and full of period furniture, the house is today a museum, open Monday to Friday from 9 am to noon and 2 to 5 pm, Saturday and Sunday from 10 am to 1 pm and 2 to 4 pm.

North of Plaza Bolívar

One block north of Plaza Bolívar is the neo-Gothic **Santa Capilla**, ordered by Guzmán Blanco in 1883. The church, modelled on the Sainte Chapelle of Paris, was constructed on the site of the rustic Iglesia de San Mauricio where the first mass was celebrated after the foundation of the town. Illuminated by the warm light passing through a number of large stained-glass windows, the decorative interior boasts a hotch-potch of artwork including the painting *Multiplication of the Bread* by Arturo Michelena (in the right-hand aisle).

Three blocks west along Avenida Urdaneta, you'll find the monumental **Palacio de Miraflores**. It was commissioned as a private residence by General Joaquín Crespo, the caudillo who seized power in 1892 and kept it for six years. At the time, it was considered to be the largest, most magnificent and expensive private residence built in the country. Crespo didn't

enjoy the pleasure of living in the palace: he was overthrown before the building was completed, and General Cipriano Castro, who seized the presidency in 1899, was its first resident. Later the palace became the office of the president, as it is today.

Four blocks north, on Esquina Urapal, is the **Museo Arturo Michelena**, installed in what was once the home and studio of the artist, which now displays a modest collection of his works.

The **Panteón Nacional**, five blocks due north of Plaza Bolívar, is just about the most sacred building in the city. There was once a church on the site but it was destroyed in the 1812 earthquake. It was reconstructed and continued as a place of worship until 1874, when, by decree, Guzmán Blanco turned it into the pantheon. Since then it has been the last resting place for eminent Venezuelans.

The whole central nave is dedicated to Bolívar – his bronze sarcophagus placed in the presbytery instead of the high altar – while the 163 tombs of other distinguished figures (including only three women) were pushed out to the aisles. Two tombs are empty, awaiting the remains of Francisco de Miranda, who died in a Spanish jail in 1816 and who was buried in a mass grave, and Antonio José de Sucre whose ashes are in the Quito Cathedral, as he is considered by the Ecuadorians as the liberator of Ecuador. The vault of the pantheon is covered by paintings depicting scenes from Bolívar's life, all done by Tito Salas in the 1930s. Note the huge crystal chandelier donated in 1883 on the centenary of Bolívar's birth. It consists of 4000 pieces and 230 lights. The pantheon is open Monday to Friday from 9 am to noon and 2.30 to 5 pm, Saturday and Sunday from 10 am to noon and 3 to 5 pm.

La Candelaria

La Candelaria, the district centred around Plaza La Candelaria, one km east of Plaza Bolívar, is the home of many Spanish migrants. Architecturally, the area is pretty undistinguished. Perhaps the most interesting sight is the **Iglesia de la Candelaria**, even though its interior isn't outstanding, apart from the gilded retables in the presbytery. The main attraction is the tomb of José Gregorio Hernández, in the first chapel off the right-hand aisle, which is invariably packed with the faithful. Though not canonised, José Gregorio is considered one of the most important saints by many Venezuelans, more so than many genuine saints whose images adorn the altars of this and other churches.

Hernández (1864-1919) graduated as a doctor in Caracas and later studied in France and the USA. He was one of the founders of experimental medicine in Venezuela and he distinguished himself by treating the poor without charging a fee. Soon after his death in a car accident, a cult emerged around him and it has become widespread throughout the country. Countless miracles are attributed to him, including numerous healings. Meanwhile, the Vatican has a hard nut to crack trying to decide how to separate the religion from the magic, and so far it hasn't authorised his canonisation.

Quinta de Anauco

Way off the tourist routes, in the undistinguished suburb of San Bernardino, is a beautiful colonial country mansion from 1797, known as Quinta de Anauco, laid out around a charming patio and surrounded by gardens. Inside the main house is the **Museo de Arte Colonial**, the most pleasant of all the museums listed so far. You'll be guided around the meticulously restored interiors which are filled with carefully selected works of art, furniture and household implements. The museum is open Tuesday to Saturday from 8.30 to 11.30 am and 2 to 4.30 pm, Sunday from 10 am to 5 pm. The ticket costs US$0.40 and covers the guide service. English-language guides are available at no additional cost. On Sunday at 11 am free concerts are held.

Teleférico

The famous Teleférico, a cable car to the top of El Ávila which provided breathtaking views over the city, closed several years ago. There have been murmurs about privatising

Candle-wrapper with a portrait of José Gregorio Hernández

it, which might speed up its reopening, but so far its future is unclear.

The cable car was built by a German company in 1956-57, during the dictatorship of Marcos Pérez Jiménez. It consists of two lines: the one-stage, four-km run from Caracas up to El Ávila; and the three-stage, 7.5-km run from El Ávila down to Macuto on the coast. Both lines are currently closed. Pérez Jiménez also commissioned the teleférico in Mérida, which fortunately does operate (see the Mérida section for details).

Parque Central

A good place to go for a taste of modern Caracas is Parque Central, 1.5 km south-east of Plaza Bolívar. The parque is not a green area, but a concrete complex consisting of several high-rise residential slabs of apocalyptic appearance, plus two 53-storey octagonal towers, the tallest in the country. Even if you are not impressed by the architecture, there are some important sights in the area, especially if you are keen on art, music and theatre.

The **Museo de Arte Contemporáneo** occupying the eastern end of the complex is by far the best of its kind in the country and possibly the best on the continent. In 16 halls on five levels you'll find works by nearly all the prominent Venezuelan artists, including Armando Reverón, Francisco Narváez, Jacobo Borges, Alejandro Otero and Jesús Soto, the latter noted for his kinetic pieces. There are also some remarkable paintings by international figures such as Picasso, Chagall, Leger and Miró, and – the pride of the museum – a collection of about 100 engravings by Picasso, created by the artist in 1931-34. Part of the exhibition space is given to changing displays; since its opening in 1974 the museum has presented over 300 temporary exhibitions dedicated to both local and international artists.

The museum is open Tuesday to Sunday from 10 am to 6 pm. You can take pictures (without flash) of the exhibits. There's a good museum bookshop which sells books about art and posters, and there's an art library, the Biblioteca Pública de Arte.

There are three more museums in Parque Central of which the most captivating is the **Museo de los Niños**, or Children's Museum. It's in the western end of the complex and it is open Wednesday to Sunday from 9 am to noon and 2 to 5 pm. It stops selling tickets one hour before closing but it's best to allow at least two hours anyway. It's an excellent museum where adults have as much (or perhaps more) fun than the kids. Avoid weekends, when the museum is literally besieged by visitors.

The two remaining museums are the **Museo del Teclado**, which has a collection of old musical instruments, and the **Museo Audiovisual**, both a few steps from the Children's Museum.

East of Parque Central

Just to the east, across the street from Parque Central, is the **Complejo Cultural Teresa Carreño**, a modern performing arts centre, opened in 1983, which hosts concerts, ballet, plays, recitals etc in an excellent main hall capable of seating 2500 patrons. Hour-long guided tours around the complex are conducted several times a day and cost US$1.50. Call ☎ 573-0075 before you go if you need an English-speaking guide. At the back of the building is a small museum dedicated to Teresa Carreño (1853-1917), the best pianist Venezuela has ever produced.

Next to the Complejo Cultural Teresa Carreño is another cultural centre, the **Ateneo de Caracas**, which houses a concert hall, theatre, cinema, art gallery, bookshop and café. Behind the Ateneo is the **Museo de Ciencias Naturales**, open Monday to Friday from 9 am to 4.45 pm, Saturday and Sunday from 10 am to 4.45 pm.

Opposite the Museo de Ciencias, the **Galería de Arte Nacional** has a permanent collection of some 4000 works of art embracing four centuries of Venezuela's artistic expression, plus some pre-Hispanic art. The building, which owes much to the neoclassical style, was designed in 1935 by a noted Venezuelan architect, Carlos Raúl Villanueva. Note the three bas-reliefs by Francisco Narváez, Venezuela's first modern sculptor, placed over the doors at the entrance to the building. A new, spacious centre for the gallery is under construction next to Parque Central and it is expected to be completed by 1996.

Adjoining the gallery is the modern six-storey **Museo de Bellas Artes**, also designed by Villanueva, which features mainly temporary exhibitions. Go to the rooftop terrace for fine views over the city and the spectacular, brand-new mosque which is just to the north.

Both art museums are open Tuesday to Friday from 9 am to 5 pm, Saturday and Sunday from 10 am to 5 pm. The latter has a shop which sells good contemporary art.

To the east stretches **Parque Los Caobos**, named after the mahogany tree which is well represented in the park. To the south of the park, across the Autopista Francisco Fajardo, is the **Jardín Botánico**, open daily from 8 am to 5 pm. It is a good place to rest after tramping through the museums. However, its unfortunate location beside the autopista means that it suffers from noise. Occasional exhibitions are held in the Instituto Botánico building on the grounds. The entrance to the gardens is from Avenida Interna UCV, a short walk south of Plaza Venezuela (you can't reach the gardens directly from Parque Los Caobos).

South of the gardens is the **Universidad Central de Venezuela**, Caracas' largest university (about 70,000 students) and the most frequent site of student protests. The campus, built in the early 1950s, is considered to be one of the milestones of architect Carlos Raúl Villanueva's career. Although its architecture looks pretty dull today, the campus is still a pleasant place to look around, thanks to the abstract sculptures and murals adorning its grounds and buildings. There's an excellent concert hall, Aula Magna, on the grounds, with a fairly regular and interesting programme – it's worth checking out what's going on (see the Entertainment section for more details).

Sabana Grande

Sabana Grande is an attractive, busy district east of the Botanical Gardens. It is packed with hotels, restaurants and shops. There are no special tourist sights here, but there's the **Boulevard de Sabana Grande**, the most fashionable mall in the city, vibrant and alive until late – don't miss strolling back and forth along it. It stretches between the metro stations of Plaza Venezuela and Chacaíto.

Parque del Este

The **Parque del Este**, just south of the metro station of the same name, is the largest city park. It's a good place for leisurely walks, and you can visit their snake house, aviary and cactus garden, and (only on Saturday and Sunday afternoons) enjoy a show in the Planetario Humboldt. The park is open daily except Mondays from 5 am to 5 pm.

Whilst in the park, take the opportunity of visiting the **Museo del Transporte** which is just to the east and which can be reached from the park by a pedestrian bridge. The museum has a collection of old steam locomotives, cars and planes and is open Wednesday from 9 am to 2 pm, Saturday and Sunday from 9 am to 5 pm.

La Casona

A short walk south of the Transport Museum is La Casona, the home of Venezuela's presidents. Established at the beginning of the 18th century as a cacao hacienda, it was established as the presidential residence by Rómulo Gallegos, and after remodelling was completed in 1966, Raúl Leoni moved in as its first resident.

The complex consists of several houses – some dating from the colonial period, others from the late 19th century – and seven internal patios and gardens (manicured, as you might expect).

A part of the hacienda (not the area where the president lives, of course) can be visited. You'll be guided around the colonial interiors which are fitted out with Spanish-Criollo furnishings and embellished with a nice collection of paintings (Michelena, Reverón, Poleo and Cabré, among others). You can also walk around some of the gardens.

A visit to La Casona, though, is not

straightforward. First you must call ☎ 284-6322 and ask for permission, giving the names of all potential visitors and their passport numbers. If your party is sufficiently large, a separate tour will be arranged for your group and you can then ask for an English-speaking guide; if not, they will try to put you into one of their already scheduled tours and that will, most likely, be conducted in Spanish. Tours are run on Tuesdays and Wednesdays, but may sometimes be scheduled on other days as well. The waiting time for a visit can be up to two weeks. Plan ahead but do call, as sometimes you may be lucky enough to get onto a tour within two or three days.

Petare

Today, Petare is the eastern suburb of Caracas, easily accessible by metro. It was founded in 1621 and developed side by side with Caracas as a small colonial town. Although it has been swallowed up by the larger metropolis, it hasn't lost its historic character and, as such, it is an oasis of colonial architecture amidst a host of new suburbs.

The town is centred around the well-preserved and restored Plaza Sucre, with an equestrian statue of the Gran Mariscal in the middle. The eastern side of the square is occupied by the large mid-18th-century **Iglesia del Dulce Nombre de Jesús**, which still boasts some of the original retables from the time of the church's construction. In the north-western corner of the plaza is the Galería Tito Salas, which stages temporary exhibitions.

On the corner of Calle Guanche and Calle Lino de Clemente, two blocks south of the plaza, is the **Museo de Arte Popular de Petare** in a beautiful colonial house. The museum presents temporary exhibitions of naive art and is open Tuesday to Sunday from 10 am to 5 pm.

Have a stroll around the town's central streets to have a look at the old houses, some of which have been adorned with paintings by local artists. Take precautions though: the town is not secure, especially after dark.

Zoological Gardens

Caracas has two zoos, both in the south-western part of the city. The **Parque Zoológico El Pinar** is four km south-west of the historic quarter. To get there, take the metro line No 2 to the Artigas station and walk for 15 minutes south down Avenida Washington.

The **Parque Zoológico de Caricuao** is six km further to the south-west but the metro will put you down at the entrance (Zoológico station). This zoo is larger and better. Both zoos are open Tuesday to Sunday from 9 am to 5 pm.

PLACES TO STAY

There are loads of hotels scattered throughout the city and in several areas they are particularly numerous. On the whole, Caracas' low-budget accommodation is poor, ranging from ultra basic to basic, and the hotels tend to be located in shabby, unsafe areas.

The vast majority of bottom-end and mid-priced hotels double as love hotels, and some as brothels; business is particularly brisk on Fridays and Saturdays. Consequently, many places will turn you down on the weekends. If your itinerary is flexible, avoid arriving in Caracas on these days.

Note that staying in a distant district of the city is not a problem, as long as you are close to the metro line.

The Bus Terminal Area

This is a very unattractive district and is not safe at night; even during the day you should be on your guard. On the other hand, this is the cheapest area in which to stay and there's an advantage in being close to the bus terminal if you plan on leaving Caracas by bus.

At the rock-bottom end, there are two primitive shelters on Avenida Lecuna, just south of the bus terminal: the *Hotel San Roque* and, next door, the *Pensión Española*. Both have doubles with bath for US$7, although standards are low. Further south, there are about 10 more basic places, but don't go there: the area becomes increasingly unpleasant the further south you go and, moreover, you won't find anything there that is cheaper than the two above-mentioned places anyway.

The *Hotel Center Park* (☎ 541-8619), Avenida Lecuna, Velásquez a Miseria, two blocks west of the bus terminal, is clean and friendly and has become popular with travellers, but the management, once it realised this, swiftly took advantage of the fact to raise its prices to US$9/12 for a single/double with bath. If this is too much for you, just round the corner is the basic but cheap *Hotel Curamichate* (☎ 541-7563), costing US$4/7 for a single/double with bath.

A few blocks further west, between Teatro Nacional and Cuadra Bolívar, you'll find a host of suspicious-looking hospedajes. For example, in one block alone, Cárcel a Monzón, there are perhaps 10 places to stay (or, more precisely, to make love). This is a shabby district and there's really nothing to recommend it, even though you can find a single/double for less than US$4/7. If you insist on staying there anyway, try *Hospedaje Mari Tere* (☎ 545-1858), Castán a Candilito, where a basic double with bath costs US$7.

If you decide to stay near the bus terminal, it's more convenient and probably safer to be north of Avenida Bolívar. There are two conveniently located hotels on Esquina Peinero, just one block from La Hoyada metro station. They are the *Hotel Peral* (☎ 545-3111) and the *Hotel Caracol* (☎ 451-228), both offering pretty much the same: singles/doubles with air-conditioning and private bath for around US$10/12.

The Colonial Centre

There are no genuine cheapies in the historic centre, except for a few brothels (such as *Hotel Bidasoa*, Ibarras a Maturín, if you want to risk it). The cheapest acceptable place seems to be *Hotel Hollywood* (☎ 561-3536), Avenida Fuerzas Armadas, Esquina Romualda, which charges about US$9/11 for a single/double with bath and fan and about US$2 more for rooms with air-conditioning.

Two blocks north along the same avenida you have the *Hotel Metropol* (☎ 562-8666),

Plaza López a Socorro, and the *Hotel Terepaima* (☎ 562-5184), Socorro a San Ramón. Both are good, if noisy, places with air-conditioned doubles for about US$18. The *Hotel Inter* (☎ 564-0251), one block east on Esquina Calero is quieter and it costs much the same, but is often full.

Perhaps the best value for money is the *Hotel Mara* (☎ 561-5600), Avenida Urdaneta, Esquina Pelota. Spacious doubles with TV, fan, bath and hot water cost US$16. Choose a room on one of the top floors to avoid the noise from busy traffic on the Avenida below.

The *Plaza Catedral Hotel* (☎ 564-2111), overlooking Plaza Bolívar from Esquina La Torre, is the best-located mid-priced hotel in the centre, and it's well worth its price: US$20/25/30 for comfortable singles/doubles/triples with all facilities. There's a pleasant restaurant on the top floor.

The top end in the centre is represented by the *Hotel El Conde* (☎ 262-1016), Esquina El Conde, one block west of Plaza Bolívar, but it costs twice as much as the Plaza Catedral.

Sabana Grande

There are plenty of hotels throughout Sabana Grande, most of which are concentrated around Avenida Las Acacias, Calle San Antonio and Calle El Colegio, three parallel streets 100 metres apart; in effect, within a radius of 200 metres there are perhaps 30 hotels. If you want to stay in Sabana Grande, just go there; either take a taxi or go by metro to Plaza Venezuela station and walk south for five minutes.

The problem with most of these hotels is that they attract not only tourists but loving couples and, not infrequently, prostitutes. The trade is very busy on weekends.

The cheapest in the area are the *Nuestro Hotel* on Calle El Colegio, 50 metres south of the corner of Avenida Casanova, and the *Hotel Capri Casanova* on Calle San Antonio, also close to the south of Avenida Casanova. Both are rather shabby, not exactly innocent places and they cost about US$9/12 for a single/double with bath.

Appreciably better is the *Hotel Alse* (☎ 582-5510) on Avenida Las Acacias, which has singles/doubles with bath and air-conditioning for US$13/16. The *Hotel La Mirage* next door, is a good alternative, with doubles going for US$18. Check other nearby hotels – there's actually an uninterrupted line of them on this street.

The *Hotel Cristal* (☎ 719-193) is not very classy but it is perfectly located on Boulevard de Sabana Grande (corner of Pasaje Asunción). It costs US$16/20 for a single/double with bath and air-conditioning.

For something plusher near the Boulevard, try *Hotel El Cóndor* (☎ 762-9911) on Avenida Las Delicias (metro Chacaíto), for US$30/40 a single/double; *Hotel Coliseo* (☎ 762-7916) on Avenida Casanova near the corner of Calle Coromoto (metro Sabana Grande), for US$40/50; or the *Hotel Tampa* (☎ 762-3771) on Avenida Francisco Solano near the corner of Avenida Los Jabillos (metro Plaza Venezuela), for US$60 a double.

The *Lincoln Suites* (☎ 761-2727, 762-8575) is one of the best up-market yet reasonably priced hotels in Sabana Grande, also on Avenida Francisco Solano near the corner of Avenida Los Jabillos (metro Plaza Venezuela). Double suites with full amenities cost around US$90.

The five-star *Hotel Meliá Caracas*, Avenida Casanova, is currently being refurbished and will probably be the poshest (and certainly the most expensive) option in Sabana Grande. It will add to the collection of half a dozen luxury hotels scattered throughout the inner districts, which include the *Hotel Caracas Hilton* (☎ 574-1122, 574-2122), next to Parque Central; the *Hotel Tamanaco Inter-Continental* (☎ 208-7111) in Las Mercedes; and the *Hotel Eurobuilding Caracas* (☎ 907-1111, 959-1133) in Chuao. They all offer high standards but are probably not worth the money: somewhere between US$150 and US$200 for a single, and US$200 to US$250 for a double. The three and four-star hotels are usually better value for money.

Further East

Eastern Caracas is predominantly residential and there aren't many hotels there. A good area to stay in, though rather up-market, is in the vicinity of the Altamira metro station, which is a pleasant and safe district dotted with a number of good restaurants.

The *Hotel Residencia Monserrat* (☎ 263-3533), on Segunda Avenida Sur Altamira, just south of the station is perhaps the best value for money (US$30 a double) but it is often full. Next door is the slightly more expensive *Hotel La Floresta* (☎ 263-1955).

Should you need something better, there's the modern, high-rise, three-star *Hotel Continental Altamira* (☎ 262-1139) on Avenida San Juan Bosco, a five-minute walk north of the metro station.

PLACES TO EAT

You could easily stay in Caracas a whole year, and eat out three times a day without visiting the same restaurant twice.

There's a number of budget eateries around the bus terminal and in the centre, as well as in the eastern districts, where one can have menú del día for about US$2 to US$3. Places serving chicken are a good alternative and are also numerous. Don't forget about the arepas which are perfect for between-meals snacks. For breakfast, try any of the ubiquitous panaderías, which will invariably offer you a choice of croissants, pasteles, cachitos and fresh bread. Wash it all down with a batido or a café negro, which is perhaps the world's most caffeinated coffee. There are plenty of Spanish tascas (bars-cum-restaurants) for dinner; they dot many of the central corners, particularly near the Iglesia de la Candelaria. They are also numerous in Sabana Grande. If you are addicted to Western fare, McDonald's, Burger King, Pizza Hut and several other big chains are well represented and will do the honours.

The Centre

The centre encompasses the whole area of the Central Caracas map. A number of down-to-earth eating outlets are south of Avenida

Top Left: Guard at Campo Carabobo
Top Right: Restaurant facade, Caracas
Bottom Left: Devil dancer's mask & baskets
Bottom Right: Preparations for a beauty contest, Puerto Cabello

Top Left: Monument to César Girón, Plaza de Toros Maestranza, Maracay
Top Right: Restaurant, Maracay
   Bottom: Ticket office of bullfight ring, Plaza de Toros Maestranza, Maracay

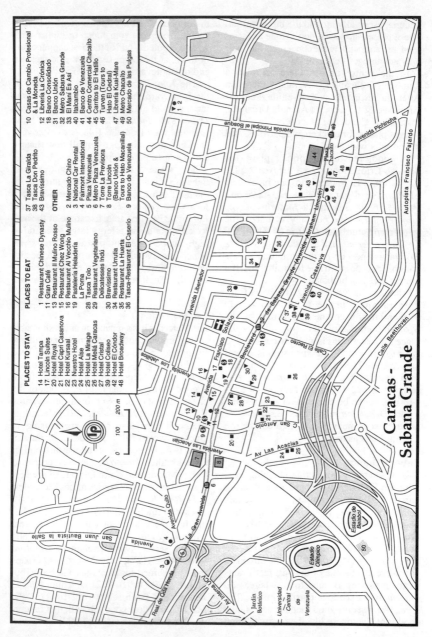

Lecuna, especially around the bus terminal. These places, however, don't shine as far as food and atmosphere are concerned and their only advantage is cheapness.

In the centre proper, there are also a number of cheapies, several of them on Avenida Urdaneta and Avenida Fuerzas Armadas. *El Coyuco*, on Avenida Urdaneta, Platanal a Candilito, is one of the better budget places for chicken and parrillas, and it's popular with locals.

A good, reasonably priced place for Spanish-Criollo food is *La Atarraya* (☎ 545-8235), Plaza El Venezolano, one block east of Plaza Bolívar. The *Dama Antañona* (☎ 563-5639), Jesuitas a Maturín, serves good regional food but only at lunch time (closed on Saturdays). *El Atrio* (☎ 814-062), *La Torre a Veroes*, half a block north of Plaza Bolívar, is a new up-market restaurant (international cuisine) with fine food, although the atmosphere is a bit bland.

The area between the Iglesia de la Candelaria and Parque Carabobo is the residential and commercial centre of the Spanish community and – of course – the place for tascas. This is where to come if you want to enjoy authentic Spanish cuisine and atmosphere. There is a score of tascas packed into several blocks; *La Carabela*, *Bar Basque* (☎ 572-4857) and *La Cita* (☎ 572-8180) have the best reputation amongst the locals. *Dena Ona* serves good Basque food. Other tascas nearby are marked on the Central Caracas map.

Sabana Grande

Sabana Grande is another good dining area, with any number of restaurants and snack bars to suit any budget and taste. Avenida Francisco Solano is flooded with Italian pasta houses (try for example *Al Vecchio Mulino*, ☎ 712-695) and the Spanish tasca bars (*El Caserío* is perhaps the most pleasant). *Urrutia* (☎ 710-448) is unanimously considered to be one of the best restaurants in town serving Basque food, whereas *La Huerta* has excellent parrilla mixta. The *Chez Wong* serves good Sichuan and Hunan food (not Cantonese like the overwhelming

majority of Chinese establishments in Venezuela). Complete your lunch or dinner with what is reputedly one of the best cappuccinos in town, at the *Gran Café* near the western end of Boulevard de Sabana Grande.

The *Tolo*, Pasaje Asunción, just south of the Boulevard, has an inexpensive vegetarian menú del día for lunch, except Sundays. *Delicatesses Indu*, Calle Villa Flor, just a few minutes' walk from the Tolo, is a better vegetarian outlet (although not all that cheap), and it's open until 10 pm.

The western end of the Boulevard de Sabana Grande is filled with a number of open-air cafés, which are popular with both locals and visitors. *Pastelería Heladería La Poma*, in the same area, has some of the best ice cream and also offers a large selection of high-calorie cakes and pastries. *Bravíssimo*, which has several outlets throughout the city including one at the eastern end of the Boulevard, is another place for good ice cream.

Las Mercedes

Las Mercedes has a reputation as a fashionable dining district and it becomes particularly lively late in the evening. Restaurants here are directed at a more affluent clientele, but there are also some which serve cheap food. A good example is the *Real Past*, one of the cheapest pasta houses in town, on Avenida Río de Janeiro. *El Riviera*, Calle Madrid, is another inexpensive place, specialising in chicken and parrillas. Similar in menu and price is *El Tranquero*, at the western end of Calle Londres. *Horno de Leña*, on corner of Calles Madrid and Caroní, is one of the best reasonably priced pizzerias in Las Mercedes.

Le Petit Bistrot de Jacques (☎ 918-108), Avenida Principal de Las Mercedes, probably has the best French food in the area, while *La Petite Suisse* (☎ 922-669), Calle Madrid, serves Swiss specialities. *Hereford Grill* (☎ 925-127), Calle Madrid, is perhaps most acclaimed for its carnes a la brasa, but *Maute Grill* (☎ 910-892), Avenida Río de Janeiro, and *Aranjuez* (☎ 752-1067), Calle Madrid, also do a good job with this favourite. The *Gran China* (☎ 914-023) and *Salón*

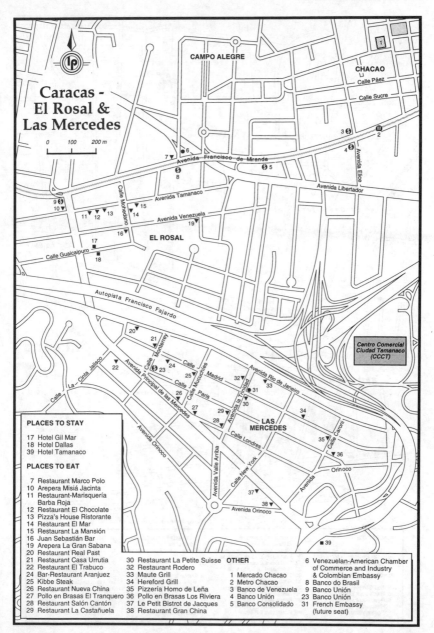

Caracas – El Rosal & Las Mercedes

CAMPO ALEGRE

CHACAO

Calle Páez

Calle Sucre

3 ⑤
Ⓜ 2

4 ⑤

Avenida Francisco de Miranda

Avenida Elice

7 ▼ ● 6

⑤ ● 5

8 ⑤

Avenida Libertador

Avenida Tamanaco

9 ⑤
10 ▼

▼ 15

11 ▼ ▼ 13

14 ▼

12

Calle Mohedano

Avenida Venezuela

19 ▼

16 ▼

EL ROSAL

17 ■

Calle Guaicaipuro

18 ■

Autopista Francisco Fajardo

Centro Comercial
Ciudad Tamanaco
(CCCT)

20 ▼

21 ▼

Calle Monterrey

Avenida Principal de las Mercedes

Calle La Cinta

Calle La - Cinta - Jalisco

22 ▼

⑤ 23

24 ▼

25 ▼

Calle Madrid

32 ▼

Avenida Río de Janeiro

● 31

33 ▼

26 ▼

Calle Paris

27 ▼

28 ▼

29 ▼

30 ▼

34 ▼

LAS MERCEDES

Calle Londres

35 ▼

Calle Caroní

▼ 36

Avenida Orinoco

Avenida Valle Arriba

Calle New York

37 ▼

38 ▼

Avenida Orinoco

Orinoco

Avenida

■ 39

PLACES TO STAY

17 Hotel Gil Mar
18 Hotel Dallas
39 Hotel Tamanaco

PLACES TO EAT

7 Restaurant Marco Polo
10 Arepera Misiá Jacinta
11 Restaurant-Marisquería
Barba Roja
12 Restaurant El Chocolate
13 Pizza's House Ristorante
14 Restaurant El Mar
15 Restaurant La Mansión
16 Juan Sebastián Bar
19 Arepera La Gran Sabana
20 Restaurant Real Past
21 Restaurant Casa Urrutia
22 Restaurant El Trabuco
24 Bar-Restaurant Aranjuez
25 Kibbe Steak
26 Restaurant Nueva China
27 Pollo en Brasas El Tranquero
28 Restaurant Salón Cantón
29 Restaurant La Castañuela

30 Restaurant La Petite Suisse
32 Restaurant Rodero
33 Maute Grill
34 Hereford Grill
35 Pizzería Horno de Leña
36 Pollo en Brasas Los Riviera
37 Le Petit Bistrot de Jacques
38 Restaurant Gran China

OTHER

1 Mercado Chacao
2 Metro Chacao
3 Banco de Venezuela
4 Banco Unión
5 Banco Consolidado

6 Venezuelan-American Chamber
of Commerce and Industry
& Colombian Embassy
8 Banco do Brasil
9 Banco Unión
23 Banco Unión
31 French Embassy
(future seat)

0   100   200 m

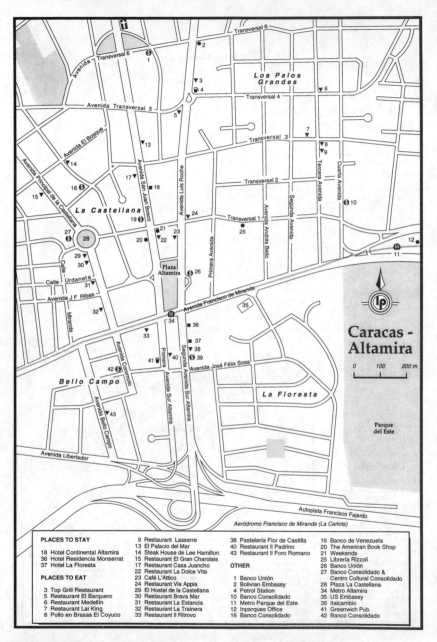

Caracas -
Altamira

0   100   200 m

PLACES TO STAY

18 Hotel Continental Altamira
36 Hotel Residencia Monserrat
37 Hotel La Floresta

PLACES TO EAT

3   Top Grill Restaurant
5   Restaurant El Barquero
6   Restaurant Medellín
7   Restaurant Lai King
8   Pollo en Brasas El Coyuco

9   Restaurant Lasserre
13 El Palacio del Mar
14 Steak House de Lee Hamilton
15 Restaurant El Gran Charolais
17 Restaurant Casa Juancho
22 Restaurant La Dolce Vita
23 Café L'Attico
24 Restaurant Via Appia
29 El Hostal de la Castellana
30 Restaurant Brava Mar
31 Restaurant La Estancia
32 Restaurant La Trainera
33 Restaurant Il Ritrovo

38 Pastelería Flor de Castilla
40 Restaurant Il Padrino
43 Restaurant Il Foro Romano

OTHER

1   Banco Unión
2   Bolivian Embassy
4   Petrol Station
10 Banco Consolidado
11 Metro Parque del Este
12 Inparques Office
16 Banco Consolidado

19 Banco de Venezuela
20 The American Book Shop
21 Weekends
25 Librería Rizzoli
26 Banco Unión
27 Banco Consolidado &
    Centro Cultural Consolidado
28 Plaza La Castellana
34 Metro Altamira
35 US Embassy
39 Italcambio
41 Greenwich Pub
42 Banco Consolidado

Cantón are probably the best Chinese restaurants. *La Castañuela* (☎ 926982) is among the best places when it comes to seafood. You'll find more recommended places marked on the El Rosal & Las Mercedes map.

El Rosal

Low budget places are almost nonexistent in this area but there are several good areperas, some of which are open 24 hours. El Rosal is conveniently accessible by metro (Chacaíto station).

Pizza's House Ristorante, Avenida Tamanaco, has reasonably priced pizzas and other Italian fare. Next door, *El Chocolate* (☎ 951-6130) serves good Spanish food. Next door to it, *Barba Roja* (☎ 951-1062) is good, if not that cheap, for seafood. Probably the most delicious Italian food in the area is to be found at the *Marco Polo* (☎ 261-3225), in Torre La Primera, Avenida Francisco de Miranda.

Altamira

Altamira, which is generally considered to include the smaller districts of La Castellana, Los Palos Grandes, Bello Campo and La Floresta, is an up-market zone. There are plenty of good and posh restaurants here but not that much for budget travellers. *El Coyuco*, on the corner of Transversal 3 and Cuarta Avenida, in Los Palos Grandes, is one of the few that will fill you up nicely for under US$5.

The *Lasserre* (☎ 283-4558), next door to El Coyuco, is one of the classiest French restaurants in town, with prices to match. The *Casa Juancho* (☎ 334-614), Avenida San Juan Bosco, is much the same for the Spanish cuisine.

El Hostal de la Castellana (☎ 334-260), Plaza La Castellana, is an atmospheric Spanish restaurant (open until 1 am) with three separate dining rooms, each with its own ambience. Try their paella – the speciality of the house. One block south is *La Estancia* (☎ 331-937) which is good for parrillas.

The *Café L'Attico* (261-2819), an attractive bar-cum-restaurant on Avenida Luis Roche, is one of the trendiest places thanks to its excellent food (including some North American specialities), its affordable prices and the good atmosphere. However, it's hard to get a table in the evening.

El Gran Charolais (☎ 332-723), Avenida Principal de la Castellana, is well known for its carnes a la brasa, whereas *El Palacio del Mar*, Avenida San Juan Bosco, and *La Trainera*, Avenida Principal de la Castellana, are the best places for seafood. *Il Foro Romano* (☎ 331-164), Avenida Bello Campo, looks impressive from the outside but there are many other Italian restaurants which serve just as good if not better food, such as *Il Padrino* (☎ 327-684), Primera Avenida Sur Altamira, or *Il Ritrovo*, Avenida Francisco de Miranda.

Explore the district by yourself – it's a pleasant area to stroll around anyway – and you'll discover many other well-appointed restaurants. Some of them have been marked on the Altamira map.

MARKETS

Caracas has plenty of markets but most of them have lost the colour and atmosphere which one associates with postcard South American markets full of Indians, their children, fruit, vegetables and animals.

One of the most central is the **Mercado Coche**, just north of the Nuevo Circo bus terminal (metro La Hoyada). **Mercado Guaicaipuro** on Avenida Andrés Bello (metro Bellas Artes) is perhaps more colourful but it is only open on Tuesdays and Thursdays. There's also the **Mercado Chacao**, three short blocks north of Chacao metro station.

Mercado de las Pulgas, or the flea market, is held on Saturdays and Sundays in the car park of the Universidad Central de Venezuela's baseball stadium (metro Plaza Venezuela). However, most of the sellers seem to be the same street vendors you see elsewhere who flock here to sell their new but low-quality merchandise, including clothes, shoes, household appliances, watches etc.

Probably the most unusual market is the **Mercado Chino**, Avenida Gloria near the corner of Avenida Principal El Bosque (metro Chacaíto). It starts at dawn on Sundays and it's all over by 9 am. This very small but authentic market is where Chinese come to sell and buy typical Chinese vegetables and other food which are not easily available elsewhere in the city. If you do happen to visit this market, you can enjoy a genuine Chinese breakfast in the corner *Chinese Dynasty* restaurant.

ENTERTAINMENT
Cinema
Caracas has more than 50 cinemas but the overwhelming majority of films on show are commercial US productions. For something more artistic, check out the two leading *cinematecas* (art cinemas), in the Galería de Arte Nacional and the Ateneo de Caracas.

Theatre
There are a score of theatres in the city to choose from. They are usually open from Wednesday to Sunday but some only perform at weekends. Tickets cost somewhere between US$1 and US$3, and there are student discounts in some theatres. Midweek sessions (usually on Wednesdays) are often cheaper than weekend performances. The Ateneo often has something interesting on in its theatre. It's home to the Rajatabla, directed by Carlos Jiménez, possibly Venezuela's most interesting theatre group.

If you are lucky enough to come during the Caracas International Theatre Festival, held in April every even-numbered year, you'll have a chance to see some of the best theatre on the continent and from beyond. Almost all city theatres are taken over by invited theatre groups.

Classical Music & Ballet
The best place to look for a concert or ballet is the Complejo Cultural Teresa Carreño, which has the widest choice and is the usual venue for invited foreign performers. Check out the programme of the Aula Magna in the Universidad Central de Venezuela. The Aula Magna, an excellent performing arts hall

capable of seating 2700 patrons, was built in the early 1950s and it is thought to have the best acoustics in the country. A US designer, Alexander Calder, largely contributed to this by hanging a set of *platillos volantes* (flying saucers) from the ceiling. Concerts of the Symphony Orchestra of Caracas are usually held on Sundays at 11 am, and other spectacles are staged on weekdays. Tickets for Sunday concerts (US$1, half price for students) can be bought from Aula's ticket office Thursday to Saturday from 2 to 5 pm, and directly before the concerts. The university has a lot in the way of cultural activities so it's worth visiting anyway.

Nightlife
Las Mercedes, El Rosal, La Floresta and La Castellana are the districts to go to for nightlife. *Greenwich Pub* on Primera Avenida Sur Altamira (metro Altamira) is one place for an evening beer. There are also a few discos around. *Weekends* (☎ 261-4863) on Avenida San Juan Bosco, one long block north of the Altamira metro station, is a US-style short-order restaurant open until late, with live music, bingo and other activities.

Juan Sebastián Bar (☎ 951-0595), on Avenida Venezuela in El Rosal (metro Chacaíto), is a bar-cum-restaurant and one of the few real jazz spots in the city. Live jazz, performed by various groups, goes from early afternoon until 2 am. There's no cover charge. People in T-shirts and shorts aren't allowed in.

More informal is *El Maní es Así*, Avenida El Cristo, Sabana Grande, which has taped and live salsa music.

GETTING THERE & AWAY
Air
The Simón Bolívar International Airport is in Maiquetía near the port of La Guaira on the Caribbean coast, about 25 km from Caracas. It's linked to the city by a freeway (built in 1950-53) which cuts through the coastal mountain range with three tunnels, the main being two km long. The airport has two separate terminals, one for international

and one for domestic flights, located 400 metres from each other.

The international terminal has a range of facilities, including the tourist office, car rental desks, three casas de cambio, post and telephone offices, a restaurant, two cafeterias and a couple of travel agencies. It even has a chapel but no left-luggage office. The domestic terminal doesn't have much apart from airline offices.

There's a frequent bus service which runs from 6 am to 11 pm and operates between the airport and the city centre. In the city the buses park next to Parque Central, on the corner of Avenida Sur 17 and Avenida Bolívar. At the airport they leave from the front of the domestic terminal. The trip costs US$1.25 and takes about 50 minutes but traffic jams, particularly on weekends and holidays, can double that time. The drivers may try to charge you extra for any second piece of luggage but they shouldn't charge you for the first one. A taxi to or from the airport to the city will cost about US$18; ask at the taxi desk inside the terminal for the official current price, thus avoiding overcharging.

If you fly into Venezuela via Simón Bolívar International Airport in Maiquetía, change your money upon arrival. The best place for this is at the Italcambio which is open 24 hours and which pays the best rate for travellers' cheques. Ignore any shady individuals who approach you claiming that they are from the tourist office offering help and information (they're not); they'll demand an astronomical fee for almost anything they do for you. The real tourist office is in the arrival hall, but don't expect much. Then, if you want to go by bus to Caracas, make your way through the horde of taxi drivers, who will besiege you swearing on the souls of their mothers that there are no buses, and turn left and walk east for five minutes until you get to the domestic terminal from where you can get the bus.

If all you have is an overnight stop in Maiquetía, there's probably no point in going into Caracas. Instead you can stay the night on the coast for example in Macuto (see

'El Litoral' in the Around Caracas section). To get there, leave the terminal, walk straight ahead, across the car park, cross the main road and wave down the Macuto carrito (a small bus) which should cost about US$0.40. A taxi to Macuto shouldn't cost any more than US$7.

There are plenty of international and domestic flights. For international connections see the Getting There & Away chapter earlier in this book. Some of the major domestic routes and their approximate prices (in US$) with the two main national carriers, Avensa and Aeropostal, include:

To	Avensa	Aeropostal
Barcelona	46	42
Barinas	59	–
Barquisimeto	47	44
Carúpano	49	49
Ciudad Bolívar	58	54
Coro	44	–
Cumaná	47	47
Las Piedras		
(Punto Fijo)	51	47
Maracaibo	62	59
Maturín	51	51
Mérida	65	61
Porlamar	51	47
Puerto Ayacucho	61	61
Puerto Ordaz		
(Ciudad Guayana)	62	59
San Antonio del Táchira	70	66
San Fernando de Apure	47	47
Santo Domingo		
(San Cristóbal)	68	65
Valencia	35	–
Valera	54	50

Avensa has daily flights to Canaima (for Salto Angel) for US$125 return, and CAVE airlines flies to the Archipiélago Los Roques, due north of Caracas, for US$100 return.

On leaving Venezuela, you pay a US$10 airport tax (in dollars or bolívares). If you fly out with Viasa, Iberia or Aerolíneas Argentinas, there's a convenient pre-check-in service in Caracas, in the Centro Ciudad Comercial Tamanaco (CCCT), Nivel C2. If your departure is between 6 am and 5 pm, you check-in the preceding day between 3 and 9 pm; for flights scheduled between 5 pm and 6 am, check-in is on the same day

Nuevo Circo Timetable

To	Distance (km)	Ordinary Fare (US$)	Deluxe Fare (US$)	Time (hours)
Barcelona	310	6.50	7.25	4.5
Barinas	515	9.75	–	8.5
Barquisimeto	351	6.50	–	5.5
Carúpano	521	10.75	12.00	8.5
Ciudad Bolívar	591	11.00	12.25	9.0
Ciudad Guayana	698	13.00	14.50	10.0
Coro	453	8.50	–	7.0
Cumaná	402	8.25	9.25	6.5
Guanare	425	8.00	–	7.0
Güiria	679	13.75	14.75	11.0
Maracaibo	706	13.00	14.25	11.0
Maracay	109	2.50	–	1.5
Maturín	518	10.00	–	8.5
Mérida	682	14.00	15.50	11.0
Puerto Ayacucho	814	18.50	–	16.0
Puerto Cabello	211	4.00	–	3.5
Puerto La Cruz	320	6.50	7.25	5.0
Punto Fijo	530	10.25	–	8.5
San Antonio del Táchira	877	15.00	16.50	14.0
San Cristóbal	841	14.00	15.50	13.0
San Fernando de Apure	404	7.75	–	8.0
Santa Elena de Uairén	1314	–	28.50	16.0
Tucupita	730	13.75	–	11.0
Valencia	158	3.00	–	2.5
Valera	585	10.75	–	9.5

between 7 and 11 am. They take your luggage and give you your boarding pass. There's a charge of US$0.20 for each piece of luggage. This means that you then travel light to the airport.

Bus

The Nuevo Circo bus terminal, right in the city centre, is chaotic, noisy, dirty and unsafe. It will eventually be replaced by two new bus terminals, one at the eastern and one at the western end of the city, but the work is inching along at a snail's pace.

The Nuevo Circo terminal handles all intercity runs to almost every corner of the country. The main destinations, distance, fares for ordinary and deluxe service and the approximate length of time of the journey are given in the table above.

Local carritos to La Guaira, Macuto, Los Teques and El Junquito park around the bus terminal.

Boat

La Guaira, the port of Caracas, is one of the busiest freight ports in the country, but there's no passenger service to any of Venezuela's offshore possessions. The boat to Los Roques is no longer operating. See the Los Roques section (Around Caracas) for information on how to get there.

GETTING AROUND
Metro

The metro is probably all you'll need to use to get around Caracas. It's fast, well organised, clean and cheap. Perhaps the only thing its designers seem to have forgotten are public toilets at the stations.

The underground system has two lines, with a total length of 40 km and 35 stations. Line No 1 goes east-west all the way along the city axis. Line No 2 leads from the centre south-west to the zoo and the distant suburb of Caricuao. Further lines are under construction. The system also includes several bus routes, known as Metrobus, which link some of the southern suburbs to metro stations.

The metro operates daily from 5.30 am to 11 pm. Tickets cost US$0.18 for a ride up to three stations; US$0.23 for a run from four to seven stations; and US$0.25 for any longer route. The transfer ticket *(boleto integrado)* for the combined metro/bus route costs US$0.25. You buy tickets at the ticket counter at the station or from a coin-operated machine. There are always lines at the counters, so you'd be better off having enough coins with you and buying a ticket from the machine. If you plan to use the metro often, it's worth buying the *multiabono*, a multiple ticket costing US$1.80, which is valid for 10 rides of any distance. You not only save money, but you also avoid having to queue each time at the ticket counters. Bulky packages which might get in the way of other passengers are not allowed in the metro.

Bus

The bus network is extensive and covers all suburbs within the metropolitan area as well as all the major neighbouring localities. The main type of vehicle operating city routes is a small bus, commonly called a carrito. They run frequently but move only as fast as the traffic allows, which means that they are often trapped in traffic jams. Use carritos only if you are going to destinations which are otherwise inaccessible by metro, or at night: there are a few main, east-west routes which operate round the clock. It's worth taking a carrito ride anyway just to get a taste of local character: the radio will be blasting and the driver undertaking breathtaking manoeuvres – definitely a different kind of trip to the smooth and silent metro ride.

Taxi

Taxis, identifiable by either the 'Taxi' or 'Libre' sign, are a fairly inexpensive means of transport and you are likely to use them to get to places not reached by the metro. You can either wave one down on the street or you can request one by phone by calling any of the numerous companies that provide a radio service. Several companies such as Teletaxi (☎ 752-9122) or Móvil Enlace (☎ 573-4533) service the entire Caracas area 24 hours a day.

Metro de Caracas

Around Caracas

EL HATILLO
A small, old town 15 km south-east of the city centre, El Hatillo is today a distant suburb of Caracas. Centred around the obligatory Plaza Bolívar, with its statue of the hero looking as though he's on his way home from a heavy drinking session, the town still retains some of its colonial architecture. The parish church on the plaza has preserved its exterior pretty well, but its interior was radically (and rather controversially) modernised.

The town has become a trendy weekend getaway for Caraqueños and it's packed with cars and people, particularly on Saturdays and Sundays. Every next house is either a restaurant, a snack bar, a café or a handicraft shop. The biggest and best craft shop, the Hannsi, is half a block north of the church.

Frequent carritos run to El Hatillo from Avenida Humboldt, just off Boulevard de Sabana Grande, near the Chacaíto metro station.

PARQUE NACIONAL EL ÁVILA
Parque Nacional El Ávila is a steep, green mountain which looms above Caracas just to the north. The park encompasses about 90 km of the coastal range running east-west along the coast and separating the city from the sea. The highest peak of the ridge is Pico Naiguatá, 2765 metres.

The southern slope, overlooking Caracas, is virtually uninhabited, while the northern side, running down to the sea, is dotted with houses and farms which are grouped together into several hamlets, the major one being San José de Galipán. There are a few 4WD tracks which cross the park from south to north, as well as the inoperable teleférico, or cable car.

The teleférico used to go from the Maripérez Station (980 metres), next to Avenida Boyacá in Caracas, up to El Ávila Station (2150 metres), close to Pico El Ávila which is crowned by the modern, circular Hotel Humboldt. The hotel was closed after the cable car stopped running. Today it's just a fantastic landmark overlooking Caracas, visible from just about every point of the city.

The upper station and its vicinity offer breathtaking views of Caracas and the Valle del Tuy beyond, and, towards the north, the beautiful panorama of the coast with the Caribbean Sea on the horizon.

Parque Nacional El Ávila provides the best tourist facilities of any of Venezuela's parks. There are about 200 km of good walking trails, most of them well signposted. Half a dozen camping grounds distributed around the park are equipped with sanitary facilities and there are many more places without facilities which are good for camping.

There are a dozen entrances which lead into the park from Caracas; all originate from Avenida Boyacá, commonly known as Cota Mil, as it runs at an altitude of 1000 metres. Whichever route you choose will require a quite steep ascent, and you will soon come across a guard post where you pay a nominal park entrance fee. The rangers *(guarda-*

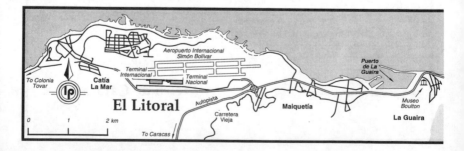

parques) may have a trail map of the park, although it seems to be out of print. In any case, they will give you information about routes, and suggest one if you haven't yet decided.

There are plenty of half and full-day hikes. You can, for example, go up to Pico Ávila; there are at least four routes leading there. If you are prepared to camp, probably the most scenic walk is the two-day hike to Pico Naiguatá. Take good rain gear and warm clothes. Water is scarce, so bring some along. The dry season is from December to April and it often goes well into May.

EL LITORAL

Parque Nacional El Ávila slopes steeply, almost down to the sea, leaving only a narrow flat belt of land between the foothills and the shore, commonly referred to as El Litoral. Still, the area is quite developed and densely populated, with as many as perhaps 400,000 people living in a chain of towns lining the waterfront. From west to east, the most populous urban centres of El Litoral are Catia La Mar, Maiquetía, La Guaira, Macuto, Caraballeda and Naiguatá. The first two towns sit at opposite ends of the airport and have little charm, La Guaira is an important and busy Caracas port, while the three remaining places have developed into popular seaside resorts for Caraqueños, who come here en masse on weekends to enjoy the sea air. Further east, the holiday centres thin out, although the paved road continues for another 20 km up to Los Caracas.

The central coast is dramatic and spectacular (especially the Naiguatá to Los Caracas stretch) but not particularly good for bathing. The shore is mostly rocky all the way from Catia La Mar to Los Caracas, with short stretches of beach (good wild beaches only begin east of Los Caracas). The straight coastline is exposed to ocean surf and strong currents can make swimming dangerous. Most of the holidaying activity is confined to *balnearios*, sections of beach that have been walled in and dotted with facilities, and to private beach clubs. Macuto, Caraballeda and Naiguatá all have balnearios, and there are a few more, such as Camurí Chico, between Macuto and Caraballeda. An array of hotels and restaurants sprung up along the waterfront, providing an adequate choice of comfortable beds and good fried fish.

All in all, this is a pleasant enough area to hang around for a while if you like the beach life and you want to escape from Caracas' rush. If you fly into Venezuela via Maiquetía and you have an overnight stop, it's probably better to stay on the coast than to go to Caracas for the night.

Apart from the beach, you can visit the Museo Reverón in Macuto, established in the former home/studio of a renowned painter, Armando Reverón (1889-1954). La Guaira has a partly preserved and restored old town which is noted for its lovely, narrow streets lined by houses with grilled windows. The largest and most imposing building in town is the Casa Guipuzcoana, the customs house built on the waterfront in 1734 by the infamous trade company of the same name.

Behind it is the Museo Boulton, featuring some of the town's history. Enveloped in ranchos, La Guaira isn't the safest place on earth, so be on your guard and use common sense when visiting.

Places to Stay & Eat

There are virtually no hotels in Maiquetía and La Guaira, but Macuto and Caraballeda have plenty of places to stay in and eat.

In Macuto, several hotels are located near the seafront, including (from west to east) *El Coral, Santiago, Álamo, Riviera, Mar Azul* and *Tijuana*. The Álamo (☎ 461236) and El Coral (☎ 461632) are amongst the cheapest in the area, costing around US$16 for a double. El Coral and Santiago have pleasant open-air restaurants overlooking the sea.

Caraballeda, five km east of Macuto, is a much larger resort and has more accommodation and dining options. It's here that the two best hotels in El Litoral, the *Macuto Sheraton* (☎ 944300) and *Meliá Caribe* (☎ 945555), are located. For somewhere with a more reasonable price, try either the *Litoral Palacios* or *Costa Azul*.

Getting There & Away

There are frequent carritos from Caracas (you catch them one block west of Nuevo Circo bus station) to Macuto and many go all the way up to Caraballeda and even Naiguatá.

ARCHIPIÉLAGO DE LOS ROQUES

Los Roques is an amazing archipelago of small coral islands some 150 km due north of El Litoral. Stretching about 36 km east to west and 27 km north to south, the atoll consists of some 40 islands big enough to deserve a name and perhaps 250 other islets, rocks and cays. There's a large central lagoon, the Laguna Central, and many other small shallow lagoons around the cays. The soft white sandy beaches are clean and lovely, although shadeless, and the coral reefs even better – a paradise for snorkelling and scuba diving.

The islands' vegetation consists mainly of grasses, cactuses, low bushes and mangroves. Bird species dominate the local fauna – as many as 80 species have been recorded as either living permanently or seasonally on the archipelago. There are no native mammals on the islands. However, there are reptiles, including four species of turtle and some small lizards, salamanders and iguanas. As you might expect, the waters abound in fish and lobster, though the latter has been overfished over the past decade. The whole archipelago (2211 sq km) was declared Parque Nacional Archipiélago Los Roques in 1972.

The archipelago was originally inhabited by a group of Indians, who arrived from the mainland about a thousand years ago. During colonial times, the islands were occasionally visited by pirates and explorers, but none of them seemed to be interested in settling there. Later on, fishermen from Isla de Margarita were attracted by the abundance of fish, and gradually settled the main island, El Gran Roque. They make up the majority of the local population (nearly 1000 people); the locals are known as *los roqueños*. Over the past decades, affluent Caraqueños have discovered the archipelago, seeing it as some sort of paradise lost, and they have begun to move in, building their summer beach houses and changing the demographic character of the area.

El Gran Roque, on the northern outskirts of the archipelago, has a small fishing village of about 800 souls and an airstrip. There is also a wharf from which locals can take you in their fishing boats to other islands of the atoll. The village has desalinisation and electricity plants, neither of which is very reliable.

The wealthy have chosen other nearby islands as their vacation homes, and there are already some 50 constructions built, a good number of them on the islands of Rasquí and Madrizquí.

Away from the locals and the rich, on the island of Dos Mosquises Sur, on the southwest edge of the archipelago, is the Marine Biological Station run by the Fundación Científica Los Roques. They have tanks on

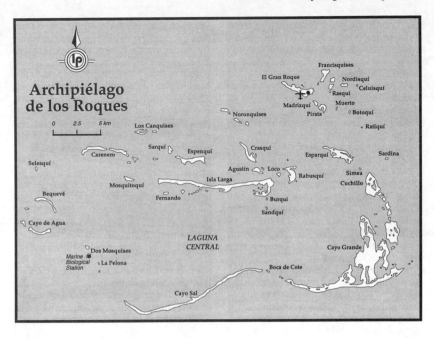

the island, where they raise turtles and other endangered species. The animals are then set free around the archipelago. The station has already reared more than 5000 turtles.

The station can be visited on Saturdays, Sundays and public holidays. Contact the foundation for further information before you set off. Their office is in Caracas (☎ 261-3461), Quinta Machado, Avenida El Estanque, corner of Transversal B, Caracas Country Club. There is a specialised library attached which is open to the public Monday to Friday from 8 am to 12.30 pm. The foundation isn't exactly intending to boost tourism to Los Roques, but it will give you information on the archipelago.

Places to Stay & Eat
Since tourism arrived on the islands, locals have moved swiftly to transform their homes into guest houses. There are already a dozen posadas in Gran Roque, most of them being small and simple places which offer both lodging and dining. Food is expensive and limited, as everything, except fish, has to be shipped in from the mainland. At the bottom end, expect to pay around US$20 per person for a bed plus breakfast and dinner. Prices seem to vary greatly from weekdays to weekends and largely depend on tourist demand. If you come on a tour, food and accommodation will be included in the price of the package.

The cheapest way of staying on the archipelago is to camp. Locals can put you down on the island of your choice (or of their choice, as they know best as to which islands are good for camping and snorkelling), and pick you up and bring you back to Gran Roque at a pre-arranged date. So far, it seems that camping is allowed on the archipelago, but check this out beforehand with Inparques. In any case, take a permit with you as the archipelago is a national park.

If you plan on camping, you have to be entirely self-sufficient in both camping gear and food. Bring along snorkelling or scuba diving gear and good sun protection – there's almost no shade on the islands.

Getting There & Away

Air CAVE flies daily to Los Roques from Simón Bolívar International Airport in Maiquetía, US$100 return for foreigners, US$60 for Venezuelans. Only 10 kg free luggage is permitted; you pay US$1 for every additional kg. Check it out with the CAVE Caracas office (☎ 952-5320).

CAVE also has tours on offer. A one-day tour, including the return flight to Los Roques, a boat excursion around the nearby islands, lunch, soft drinks and snorkelling (equipment provided) costs US$140 (US$90 for Venezuelans). A two-day tour, all inclusive, costs US$200. If you want to stay longer, each additional day will cost US$95.

Aereotuy (☎ 761-6231) offers much the same deal at similar prices. A growing number of travel agencies run tours to Los Roques, but they are more expensive.

If you can't afford a ticket, try hitching a lift on a plane with Caraqueños who own beach houses on the archipelago, and who fly themselves there, mostly on weekends. A good number of them depart from the Aeroclub at the Aeródromo Francisco de Miranda, commonly known as La Carlota. The airport is in the heart of eastern Caracas, just south of Parque del Este. The Aeroclub is on the southern side of the airport, on Avenida Río de Janeiro. A spare seat or two can sometimes be tracked down if you come in the morning and ask around. You can also charter a plane from Aeroclub; call them on ☎ 917-555 or 917-691 and they will put you in contact with a pilot.

Boat There's no regular boat service to Los Roques. To get there, either talk to the fishermen in La Guaira port, or ask around the marinas in Caraballeda and Naiguatá. Los Roques is a popular destination amongst the yachting fraternity; many yachts then sail on to other islands in the area, such as Islas Las Aves and Isla La Orchila.

The Central North

Commonly referred to as El Centro, the central northern region encompasses the states of Carabobo, Aragua, Miranda and Distrito Federal. This is the most developed part of the country, both industrially and agriculturally. It is also the most densely populated: occupying less than 2.5% of the national territory, these four states are home to around 45% of Venezuela's population. Half live in Caracas, while the other half is distributed throughout dozens of fair-sized towns and the two other important cities in the region: Valencia and Maracay.

However, there are still extensive areas of woodland, some of which have been declared national parks. There are six parks in the region; the most popular of them, El Ávila, is detailed in the Caracas chapter (the Around Caracas section), while in this chapter another splendid park, Henri Pittier, is described.

National parks aside, the region boasts a number of other attractions, including the charming town of Colonia Tovar and Venezuela's best hot spring complex at Las Trincheras.

Aragua State

COLONIA TOVAR

Lost amidst the rolling forests of the Cordillera de la Costa, about 60 km west of Caracas, sits the unusual mountain town of Colonia Tovar. It was founded in 1843 by 376 German settlers from Schwarzwald, led by Italian cartographer Agustín Codazzi, the brain behind the whole plan (see the box on next page).

Effectively isolated from the outer world by both the lack of roads and internal rules prohibiting marriage outside the colony, the village followed the mother culture, language and architecture for a century. Only in the 1940s was Spanish introduced as the

official language and the ban on marrying outside the community abandoned. It was not until 1963 that a serviceable road was opened linking Colonia to Caracas. This marked a turning point in the history of the town, which by then had only 1300 souls.

Today Colonia Tovar has perhaps five times as many inhabitants and it is a classic tourist town. On weekends, the central streets are lined with stalls selling crafts and fruits and vegetables, which attract hordes of visitors. They park their cars anywhere they can, and if you arrive late, you have to park outside the town. You can still see the original architecture, enjoy a genuine German lunch or dinner, and buy bread or sausage made according to old German recipes. Taking advantage of the temperate climate (the town lies at an altitude of about 1800 metres), the locals turned to fruit growing, and you can buy delicious strawberries, apples, peaches and blackberries.

Call at the Museo de Historia y Artesanía (open Saturdays and Sundays only, from 9 am to 6 pm) for a taste of the town's history, and don't miss visiting the local church. It's a curious L-shaped building with two perpendicular naves (one for women, the other for men) and the high altar placed in the

Agustín Codazzi

Adventurer, sailor, explorer, corsair, soldier, merchant, but primarily remembered as a cartographer, Agustín Codazzi was born in 1793 in Lugo, a town in northern Italy. At the age of 17, after Napoleon took control of that part of Italy, Codazzi enrolled in the Napoleonic army and for three years was taught mathematics, geometry, topography and the like, in order to train him as a professional artillery officer (which, as it turned out, gave him a solid basis for cartography). Later, he took part in various battles under Napoleon's banners, but then, after Waterloo, there was nothing much for him to do.

He turned his hand to commerce but here, too, the winds were not favourable: his boat, with all his merchandise on board, sank in the Mediterranean and Codazzi – who miraculously survived – was financially ruined. Managing a casino in Constantinople (today Istanbul) was his next endeavour but soon his passion for exploring overcame him and he took to wandering all over Europe, up to Russia and, in 1817, to Baltimore in the USA.

When Codazzi heard that Bolívar was recruiting foreigners for a new Venezuelan army, he was the first to enrol. However, he met the famous French corsair Louis Aury and, on their way south, they landed on Old Providence (today Providencia, a Colombian island). From this island, the two adventurers regularly ransacked Spanish galleons, an activity which was not only profitable but, also, ironically, contributed to the eventual defeat of the Spaniards. Based on the island for three years, Codazzi didn't miss the chance to explore large parts of Nueva Granada (now Colombia). It was on Providence Island that his first maps were drawn.

Once the Spanish were defeated, there was not much left to ransack. Codazzi returned to his native Lugo and dedicated himself to agriculture, not for long though. His adventurous spirit took him back to the New World. Arriving in Cartagena in 1826, he made his way to Bogotá where he met Bolívar and Santander. The Independence heroes appreciated Codazzi's artillery abilities more than his cartographic skills and they sent him to Maracaibo to head the local military post before a possible Spanish return.

Four years later, Gran Colombia split into three separate countries. General José Antonio Páez, the first ruler of independent Venezuela, commissioned Codazzi to draft maps of various regions of the country. The job took the cartographer 10 years. Once completed, Codazzi went to Paris where, in 1841, he published the *Atlas Físico y Político de la República de Venezuela* and the corresponding *Resumen de la Geografía de Venezuela*. His work immediately received wide recognition amongst French scientific circles and Codazzi was appointed as an honorary member of the Académie Royale des Sciences in Paris.

It was about this time that the Venezuelan government began to look for European migrants who could settle and work in Venezuela, to help revive an economy devastated by the Independence War. Having appreciated Codazzi's abilities, the government proposed that he devise a colonisation plan. First he went to Venezuela to select a place which would offer acceptable climatic conditions for European migrants. He then returned to Europe, collected a group of several hundred German peasants (the nationality he thought was the most adaptable to foreign life) and came with them to Venezuela. After an arduous hike up the coastal cordillera, they founded Colonia Tovar, in 1843. By then, the Venezuelan authorities had lost all enthusiasm for continuing the colonisation programme and Codazzi, again, dedicated himself to mapping.

The coup d'état of 1848, launched by Tadeo Monagas, brought Venezuela to the brink of civil war and Codazzi fled to Nueva Granada. After arriving in Bogotá in 1849, he was soon appointed as the head of the Comisión Corográfica. Over the next 10 years, until his death, he drafted detailed maps, region by region, of six of the eight existing departments of Colombia.

At the beginning, the work enjoyed the interest and sponsorship of the government and advanced smoothly. Later on, however, internal political strife pushed cartographic concerns to one side and funds were cut off. It was only due to his personal dedication and enthusiasm that he set off north to complete the two missing coastal provinces. Disillusioned and abandoned, he died of malaria in 1859 in the obscure village of Espíritu Santo (today Agustín Codazzi) in northern Colombia. His name and work sank into obscurity for a century.

The man who created Venezuelan and Colombian cartography was forgotten by these two countries. It has only been over the last few decades that his name has begun to attain its deserved recognition, and his excellent maps have become the pride of national archives in both Colombia and Venezuela. ■

angle where the naves join. From above, the patron saint of the town, San Martín de Tours, overlooks both naves.

Places to Stay & Eat

There are perhaps a dozen hotels and cabañas, and most of them have their own restaurants. Accommodation is expensive in Colonia, with the bottom-end prices starting at about US$16 per double. Some places offer lodging with meals which is convenient but means that you are stuck with the same kitchen for the duration of your stay.

The *Hotel Selva Negra* (☎ 51415) is the oldest and the best known lodge in town. Built in the 1930s, it now has about 40 cabañas of different sizes, for two to six people, costing US$40 for two people plus US$8 for each additional person. The atmospheric restaurant is in the original house.

Cheaper options include *Hotel Edelweiss* (☎ 51260), *Hotel Drei Tannen* (☎ 51246) and *Hotel Bergland* (☎ 51229), the last being noted for its good food.

Getting There & Away

The trip from Caracas to Colonia Tovar includes a change at El Junquito. Carritos from Caracas to El Junquito depart from the corner just south of the Nuevo Circo bus terminal and cost US$0.50. From El Junquito, vans take you the remainder of the journey for US$0.60. The whole trip takes about two hours.

If you don't want to return to Caracas, you can take an exciting ride south down to La Victoria. Over a distance of only 34 km, the road descends about 1250 metres. Vans depart from Colonia Tovar several times a day; the ride takes one hour and costs US$0.70.

LA VICTORIA

Today a busy city of some 100,000 people, La Victoria was for a long time an important commercial centre. It was the capital of Aragua state until 1916, when Juan Vicente Gómez moved the capital to Maracay.

There's not much to do in the city, but you may stop there anyway if you are heading

from Colonia Tovar to San Mateo and Maracay, or vice versa. If this is the case, take a short stroll around the central sector of the city, between Plaza Ribas and Plaza Bolívar. Both plazas boast a church: the large neoclassical Iglesia de la Victoria faces Plaza Ribas, whereas the small Iglesia de la Candelaria adorns Plaza Bolívar.

There's frequent bus transport to both Maracay and Caracas. Por puestos leave for Colonia Tovar a few times a day.

SAN MATEO

San Mateo, a small town 10 km west of La Victoria (87 km west of Caracas), is yet another site with a link to Bolívar. The land was granted to the Bolívar family in 1593, soon after they came to the colony from their homeland, Spain. At the beginning of the 18th century, the *ingenio de caña de azúcar*, or sugarcane mill, was established on the hacienda, and, as was the case throughout the region, African slaves worked the crops.

In 1814, the hacienda was turned into a military camp by Bolívar and it eventually became the scene of a fierce battle. Bolívar's forces, counting some 1800 men, defended the camp against attacks by the royalist troops who were outnumbered four to one. The battle was eventually won by the patriots, thanks to a heroic defence by Antonio Ricaurte, one of Bolívar's lieutenants. Later on, Bolívar passed through San Mateo on various occasions, including a short rest stop after the battle of Carabobo in 1821 (when he freed the local slaves), and once on his return from Peru in 1827.

During the 19th century, the hacienda passed through the hands of various owners, until it was eventually bought by the government of Juan Vicente Gómez in 1924 and turned into a barracks. It was later transformed into a museum. Restored in the 1980s to its original state, the hacienda now houses two museums, both open Tuesday to Sunday from 10 am to 4 pm.

The **Museo de la Caña de Azúcar** has been installed in what was originally the sugarcane mill. Exhibits include the *trapiche* (the sugarcane mill) and a variety of tools,

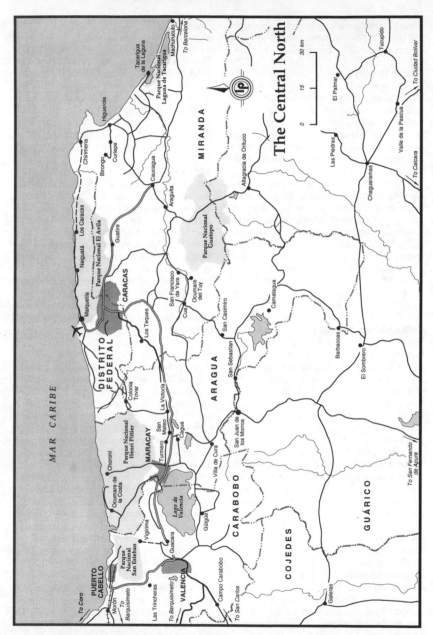

implements and objects related to sugar production.

On the opposite side of the road on the top of a hill, is the **Museo Histórico Militar**. This finely restored house contains a collection of period armour plus the usual Bolivariana, comprising documents and a number of Bolívar's portraits. The outbuildings, which served as the armoury during Bolívar's defence, were intentionally left in a state of ruin, as they have been since 25 March, 1814. It was here that on this day Antonio Ricaurte, a Colombian patriot in the service of Bolívar, sacrificed himself to save the battle being lost to the Spaniards. Closely encircled by the royalists, he led them into the armoury, then set fire to the gunpowder kegs, thus blowing up both the enemies and himself.

Getting There & Away

You can easily get to the museums from either Caracas or Maracay. There are direct buses from Caracas through La Victoria, which will put you down at the entrance to the museums (US$1.25). Ask the driver to drop you off at El Ingenio Bolívar, as the place is commonly known. It's not in San Mateo township itself but a couple of km before. If no bus is due to depart from Caracas for San Mateo, take any bus to La Victoria and change to either a carrito or to a bus to Maracay via the old road (not the autopista) which will pass through the hacienda. If you plan on continuing westwards, you can stop in the town of San Mateo and see the mid-18th-century retable in the local church.

From Maracay, carritos depart frequently for La Victoria, passing through the town of San Mateo, and not far beyond it pass by the museums.

MARACAY

The capital of Aragua state, Maracay is a thriving city of some 450,000 inhabitants. It's quite developed industrially and it is the centre of an important agricultural area. Sitting at an altitude of about 450 metres, Maracay has a pretty hot climate (warmer than Caracas, but far more pleasant than Maracaibo), with the average temperature being 25°C and most of the rain falling between April and October.

There's almost nothing left of the colonial period in this 300-year-old city, and modern architecture is not Maracay's strong point either. What the city does possess, though, are plenty of parks and leafy plazas, including the largest Plaza Bolívar in the country. Justifiably, Maracay's called the Ciudad Jardín, or the Garden City. There are numerous tourist attractions, but none of them is really first-rate. To sum up, the city is an interesting stop if you are passing through, but probably not worth a special journey in itself.

At the time of the Spanish conquest, the valley in which Maracay is set was inhabited by the Aragua Indian group, led by Cacique Maracay; this is where the name of the city and the state comes from. A Spanish settlement was established somewhere around the mid-16th century, but it was not until 1701 that a formal act of foundation was signed, and ever since this has been considered the official birth of Maracay. At that time the town numbered about 750 inhabitants.

Thanks to the valley's fertile soil, agriculture became the basis of the region's development – cacao, indigo, coffee, sugarcane, cotton and tobacco were the major crops. However, the town's growth was pretty slow: by the year 1900 the population had only reached a mere 10,000. Maracay would have probably continued at this unhurried rate if it hadn't been for Juan Vicente Gómez, who first came here in 1899 and fell in love with the town. After he had assumed power in 1908, he settled for good in Maracay in 1912 and four years later moved the Aragua state capital from La Victoria to Maracay. The latter actually became not only the state capital, but virtually the national capital, from which Gómez ruled the country until his death in 1935.

During the Gómez days, Maracay saw a rash of new constructions, including the government house, a bullring, an aviation school, an opera house, a zoo, and the most splendid hotel to be built in the country. Gómez was well aware of threats to his life, and it's said that he never slept in the same bed two nights in a row, and that he built a system of escape tunnels from his office. It is a fact though that he constructed a road from Maracay over the mountains to the coast, in case he was forced to flee the country, and he surrounded himself with a strong military force, for which vast barracks were built. Lastly, he didn't forget to erect a mausoleum for himself.

The city's second wave of development came with the industrialisation of the 1950s. The 1950 population of 65,000 doubled over the next decade, and doubled again during the 1960s. The freeway linking Caracas with Valencia via Maracay, built in the 1950s by another ruthless dictator, Marcos Pérez Jiménez, also contributed to the city's growth. Today, Maracay continues to be an important military (particularly airforce) base. Although Maracay was the cradle of Venezuelan aviation (with Gómez being considered its father), the city has no civilian airport.

Juan Vicente Gómez

Information

Tourist Office The tourist office is in Edificio Fundaragua, in La Soledad district, north of the city centre.

Inparques The Inparques office (☎ 413933) is in Parque Zoológico, in Las Delicias district.

Money Most of the useful banks are either on or nearby Plaza Girardot. Cash can be exchanged in Banco Unión and Banco Consolidado; the latter also handles American Express travellers' cheques and credit card transactions. Banco Unión, Banco de Venezuela and Banco del Caribe provide cash advances on Visa credit cards; Banco del Caribe also accepts MasterCard.

Turisol (☎ 411058, fax 411357) is in Centro Comercial y Residencial La Floresta, Locales 9, 10 and 11, Avenida Las Delicias, La Floresta.

Things to See

The historic heart of Maracay, the **Plaza Girardot**, has no colonial buildings left except for the **Catedral** on its eastern side. This fair-sized, handsome church was completed in 1743 (according to the inscription over the side door), and not much has changed since. Recently white-washed, the exterior is attractive, especially with late afternoon sunlight striking the façade. The interior, however, is pretty dull.

The southern side of the plaza is occupied by an arcaded building which was erected by Gómez as the seat of government. Today, the building houses two museums, neither of which is inspiring. In the eastern side of the building is the **Museo de Historia**, which has one room dedicated to Bolívar and one to Gómez, plus a handful of exhibits loosely related to Venezuelan history. The **Museo de Arqueología**, which occupies the opposite side of the building, features local pre-Hispanic pottery, but the collection is haphazard and captions almost nonexistent. In the basement of this museum is the Sala de Etnología (the ethnological section) displaying crafts from some of the Indian groups living today, including the Samena, Maquiritare, Warao,

Piaroa, Guajibo, Perijá and Guajiro. Both museums are open Tuesday to Friday from 8 am to noon and 2 to 6 pm, Saturday and Sunday from 9 am to 1 pm. The ethnological section may only be open Tuesday to Friday from 8 am to noon.

One block north of Plaza Girardot, on Avenida Santos Michelena, is a fine house built in 1927-29 by Gómez for his favourite lover, and known locally by her name as **Casa de Dolores Amelia**. The house has been restored and is now occupied by an insurance company, Grupo Asegurador La Venezolana. It is not a tourist sight, but if you turn up during office hours, someone may let you in and show you around the patio and adjoining parts of the building, clad with *azulejos* (ornamental tiles) and reminiscent of the Alhambra in Granada, Spain. It's said that the house was linked by an underground tunnel with the Gómez office in the Plaza Girardot.

One block, east along Avenida Santos Michelena, you come across the **Teatro Ateneo de Maracay**, the city's old theatre, currently being restored. Just north-east of it is the large, Spanish/Moorish **Plaza de Toros Maestranza**. The bullring was modelled on the one in Seville and built in 1933; it's possibly the most stylish and beautiful bullring in the country. It's dedicated to César Girón, Venezuela's most famous matador, who died in a traffic accident. The monument to him, which depicts him fighting with a bull, stands in front of the bullring. If you want to see the bullring from the inside, try getting in through the back door on the eastern side.

Bullfights are held irregularly on Sundays during the year, but mostly between Christmas and Easter; the major corrida is celebrated during the Fiesta de San José, the city's most important event which takes place over several days around 19 March, the city's patron saint's day.

If you head east from the bullring, along Avenida 19 de Abril, you'll pass by the modern **Casa de la Cultura**, which runs a variety of cultural activities. Keep going and you'll arrive at the main entrance to the

Museo Aeronáutico, one block further east. This is the only aeronautical museum in the country. There are about 30 aircraft displayed, most of which are war planes from the 1920s through to the 1950s which once served in the Venezuelan Air Force. Some have already been restored, whilst others are yet to be tackled. The collection's gem is a French plane from the 1910s, which is beautifully finished and is reputedly in perfect working order. The museum also has a replica of the famous Jimmie Angel's plane; the engine is original.

The museum has been closed for years but optimistic plans schedule reopening for 1994. If you turn up on a weekday between 8 and 11.30 am or between 1.30 and 3 pm, at the side gate at the end of Avenida Santos Michelena and ask for the *sargento* (sergeant), he will probably show you around.

A hundred metres north of the aeronautical museum is the **Museo de Arte** which stages temporary exhibitions of modern art. For more in the way of visual arts, keep going north for five minutes until you reach the modern Edificio Consejo Municipal, which houses the **Galería Municipal de Arte**. Here, too, you'll find changing exhibitions of contemporary art. The Salón Municipal de Pintura is an annual event, and the selected paintings from that competition are exhibited in the gallery from March through to May.

Three blocks long and shady, **Plaza Bolívar** is the largest in the country and its indispensable monument to El Libertador is in the middle; this one is an exact replica of the Caracas statue. The two large buildings on the northern border of the plaza are the barracks – don't approach them dangling a camera.

To the south of the plaza is another large edifice, the **Palacio de Gobierno**. This was originally the splendid Hotel Jardín, built by Gómez in 1924, and overshadowing all other Venezuelan hotels of the day. Much has changed since the time of its construction, but you can still feel the charm of the cloisters and interior gardens. You can have a look around the place during office hours, though

it's not a regular tourist sight. You'll probably have to argue with police security guards
who may or may not let you in. If they refuse
you entry at the front door, try the back
(south) gate, from Avenida Páez.

Next to the government house stands the
Teatro de la Ópera. Commissioned by
Gómez in 1932, the theatre was intended to
be the best in the country, to match the capital
status of the city. This monumental edifice
was designed by Luis Malausena, and a huge
budget of 2,000,000 bolívares was allotted
for the structure alone. Planned to be opened
in 1936, the work progressed swiftly and by
December 1935 (the month Gómez died) the
theatre was almost ready; only the ceiling,
imported from the USA, had to be fixed and
the interior furnished. Nonetheless, the work
was stopped by the new government of
General López Contreras and a part of the
already imported decoration was moved to
Caracas for theatres there. For more than 30
years, no government assumed responsibility for completing the theatre, which in the
meantime served as a storage room and
offices. It wasn't until 1973 that the theatre
was opened.

The theatre can seat 860 and presents a
variety of forms including opera, ballet,
theatre, folkloric dance etc (performed
mostly by visiting groups). During the International Theatre Festival in Caracas (in April
of even years) the Maracay theatre invites
some groups taking part in the Caracas Festival to perform here.

On the south-western outskirts of the city
centre is the cemetery. Just south of it, separated by a wall from the cemetery, and with
its own entrance, is the **Mausoleo de
Gómez**, also referred to as the Panteón de
Gómez. A rather pretentious structure topped
with a white Moorish dome, the pantheon
houses the tomb of the general and members
of his family. There are thanksgiving plaques
placed on the interior walls. All have an
almost identical inscription which reads,
'thanks for the favours', but none is signed
with a full name, only with initial letters.
Fresh flowers and lit candles are a frequent
sight on the tomb, evidence that he is not

forgotten. On the contrary, respect for
Gómez seems to have been revived in
Maracay over the past several years, partly
as a result of the recent economic and political crisis. The mausoleum is open from 6 am
to 3 pm except Mondays.

Outside the town centre, at the northern
city limits, is the **Jardín Zoológico**, yet
another Gómez achievement, established by
him on one of his own estates. The zoo is well
laid out with plenty of cage space for most
of the animals, many of which are typical of
Venezuela. It's open Tuesday to Sunday
from 9 am to 5 pm. To get there from the city
centre, take the Castaño/Zoológico buseta,
which goes all the way along Avenida Las
Delicias, and which will deposit you right at
the entrance to the zoo.

Places to Stay

There are several budget hotels right in the
city centre. The best of the lot are two cheapies on Avenida Santos Michelena: *Hotel
Central* (☎ 452834) and, 20 metres further
down the street, *Hotel María Isabel*. Both
have rooms with private baths and fans, and
cost US$7 for a single or matrimonial and
US$8 for a double. Just around the corner,
opposite the Teatro Ateneo, is *Hotel Venezia*.
It costs much the same as the two above-
mentioned places, but it is more basic.
Another option, for a similar price, is the
nondescript *Hotel Guayana* on Avenida
Bolívar. Alternatively, you can try the *Hotel
La Hormiga* (☎ 453815), Calle Sánchez
Carrero, just off Avenida Bolívar, three
blocks west of Plaza Girardot. All these
hotels may witness the odd loving couple
passing through, but this shouldn't really
bother you much.

Hotel Mar de Plata, Calle Santos
Michelena, is the cheapest option for those
who need air-conditioning. A double room
with private bath will cost US$9. Marginally
better is *Hotel Canaima* (☎ 338278),
Avenida Bolívar Este No 53, one block west
of Plaza Bolívar. It costs US$9/13 for air-
conditioned singles/doubles with their own
baths. Appreciably better, for the same price,
is *Hotel Bolívar* (☎ 450253) on Avenida

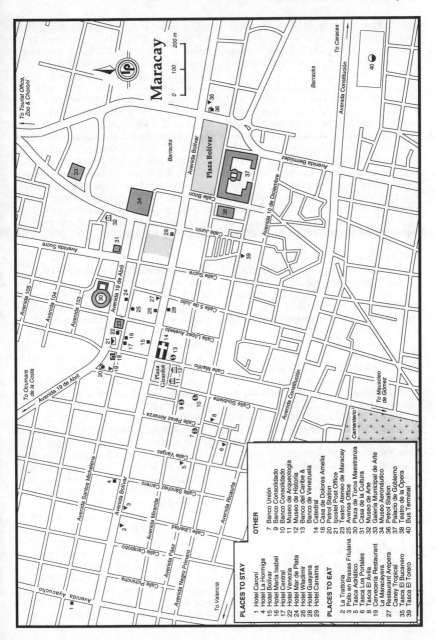

Maracay

0   100   200 m

To Tourist Office,
Zoo & Choroní

To Ocumare
de la Costa

To Valencia

To Caracas

To Mausoleo
de Gómez

Plaza Bolívar

Plaza
Girardot

Barracks

Barracks

Cementerio

Avenida Ayacucho · **Calle Pichincha** · **Avenida Santos Michelena** · **Avenida Bolívar** · **Calle Carabobo** · **Avenida Miranda** · **Avenida Páez** · **Calle Libertad** · **Avenida Negro Primero** · **Calle Ricaurte**

Avenida 105 · **Avenida 104** · **Avenida 103** · **Avenida 19 de Abril** · **Avenida Sucre** · **Avenida 19 de Abril**

Calle Sánchez Carrero · **Calle Vargas** · **Calle Pérez Almarza** · **Calle Soublette** · **Avenida Constitución** · **Calle Mariño** · **Calle López Aveledo** · **Calle 5 de Julio** · **Calle Sucre** · **Calle Junín** · **Calle Brión** · **Avenida Bolívar** · **Avenida 10 de Diciembre** · **Avenida Bermúdez** · **Avenida Constitución**

PLACES TO STAY
1 Hotel Caroní
4 Hotel La Hormiga
15 Hotel Bolívar
16 Hotel María Isabel
17 Hotel Central
22 Hotel Venezia
24 Hotel Mar de Plata
26 Hotel Wladimir
28 Hotel Guayana
29 Hotel Canaima

PLACES TO EAT
2 La Trattoria
3 Pollo en Brasas Friulana
5 Tasca Adriático
6 Tasca Los Portales
8 Tasca El Ávila
19 Cervecería Restaurant
     La Maracay
27 Restaurant Arepera
     Caney Tropical
35 Tasca El Bucanero
39 Tasca El Torero

OTHER
7 Banco Unión
9 Banco Consolidado
10 Banco Consolidado
11 Museo de Arqueología
12 Museo de Historia
13 Banco del Caribe &
     Banco de Venezuela
14 Catedral
18 Casa de Dolores Amelia
20 Petrol Station
21 Ipostel Post Office
23 Teatro Ateneo de Maracay
25 Avensa Office
30 Plaza de Toros Maestranza
31 Casa de la Cultura
32 Museo de Arte
33 Galería Municipal de Arte
34 Museo Aeronáutico
36 Petrol Station
37 Palacio de Gobierno
38 Teatro de la Ópera
40 Bus Terminal

Bolívar Este No 9, opposite the cathedral. Finally, the best central choice is *Hotel Wladimir* (☎ 22566, 24988), Avenida Bolívar Este No 27. Air-conditioned singles/doubles go for US$16/20.

If you don't mind staying a bit out of the city centre, the *Hotel Caroní* (☎ 541817, 547855) on Avenida Ayacucho, seven blocks west of Plaza Girardot, is perhaps the best value for money. Spotlessly clean air-conditioned singles/doubles with private baths and constant hot water cost US$12/16.

There are no top-end hotels in the city centre. They opted for more respectable locations amidst the residential districts, mostly along Avenida Las Delicias, north of the centre. They include the three-star *Hotel Byblos* (☎ 415111), *Hotel Maracay* (☎ 410544) and *Hotel Italo* (☎ 20195, 22897). The Italo, in Urbanización La Soledad, is the closest to the city centre. Further north, on Avenida Principal El Castaño (the road to Choroní), is the four-star *Hotel Pipo Internacional* (☎ 412022), the latest (and the poshest) addition to the city's up-market accommodation.

Places to Eat

There are plenty of reasonably priced places to eat scattered throughout the centre. To name a few: *La Maracayera* serves inexpensive set meals; *Caney Tropical* is good for arepas; *La Trattoria* has cheap pizzas and Italian-influenced local food; and *Pollo en Brasas Friulana* is the place for chicken. All these places are marked on the city map.

Should you need a fine dinner in an atmospheric place, walk north along Avenida Las Delicias where there are plenty of up-market, well-appointed restaurants; *El Bodegón de Sevilla* is a good example, serving excellent Spanish food.

Getting There & Away

Bus The bus terminal is on the south-eastern outskirts of the city centre. It's within walking distance of Plaza Bolívar, but it's quicker to take any of the frequent busetas.

Maracay's terminal is vast and busy, and there's frequent transport to most major cities. Buses to Caracas depart every 10 or 15 minutes (US$2.50, 1½ hours), as do buses to Valencia (US$0.60, one hour). There are at least 10 departures a day to Barquisimeto (US$4.50, four hours), Maracaibo (US$10.75, nine hours) and San Cristóbal (US$13.25, 11½ hours). Half a dozen buses run to San Antonio del Táchira (US$14.25, 12½ hours) and Coro (US$6.50, 5½ hours). Three or four buses per day go to Mérida (US$13.25, 10 hours). There are also several buses to San Fernando de Apure (US$6, five hours); a couple of these buses continue on to Puerto Ayacucho (US$13, 12 hours), but in the dry season only.

For transportation to Ocumare de la Costa and Puerto Colombia, see the Parque Nacional Henri Pittier section.

PARQUE NACIONAL HENRI PITTIER

As Venezuela's oldest national park, created in 1937, Parque Nacional Henri Pittier occupies most of the north of Aragua state; it stretches from the Caribbean coast in the north, south almost as far as the Valencia-Caracas autopista and the city of Maracay. The park was originally named Rancho Grande, but in 1953, three years after Henri Pittier's death, it was renamed in honour of the park's actual creator (see the box on following page).

With an area of 1078 sq km, the park covers Aragua's portion of the Cordillera de la Costa, the coastal mountain range which is considered the northern part of the great Andean system. The Cordillera (also known as Serranía de la Costa) is not a single range, but rather a chain of coastal outcrops separated by lowlands, stretching from the region of Puerto Cabello in the west nearly to the eastern tip of the Península de Paria, opposite Trinidad. Cordillera's highest peak, Pico Naiguatá (2765 metres), is just north of Caracas in the Parque Nacional El Ávila.

In the Parque Nacional Henri Pittier, the ridge in some areas exceeds 2000 metres, and the highest point within the park's boundaries lies at an elevation of 2436 metres. From its ridge, the Cordillera rolls dramatically down to the seashore to the north, and south to the Aragua valley.

Given the wide range in elevation, there's a variety of thermal zones within the park and a diversity of habitats. Going from Maracay northwards (ie upwards), one passes through semi-dry deciduous woods, to ascend to humid evergreen tropical forest and, further up, to dense, exuberantly rich cloudforest. All this can be found over a surprisingly short distance; it takes an hour to cover it in a bus or car. Over the crest and descending northwards towards the sea, you get the same sequence in reverse, with the difference being that, as you approach the seashore, you also encounter arid coastal scrub, before you finally reach the beaches, mangroves and coconut groves. And this only takes another hour or so.

The animal world is also rich and diverse, including tapirs, deer, pumas, agoutis, peccaries, ocelots, opossums, armadillos, monkeys, snakes, frogs and bats. However, the park is most famous for its birds.

About 520 species of bird have been identified in the park, which represents some 42% of the bird species found in Venezuela, and nearly 7% of all the birds known in the world. Given the small area of the park, it's not a bad total, and hardly any other park of that size in the world can match it.

This diversity is the combined result of the variety of habitats (produced by a staircase of microclimates) and the unspoiled condi-
tion of these habitats. Additionally, the Portachuelo pass in the park's ridge is on a natural migratory route for birds and insects flying inland from the sea, and vice versa, from such distant places as Argentina and Canada. Migratory birds mainly gather in the park from September to October.

There are two roads, both paved, which cross the park north-south. Both originate in Maracay and go as far as the coast. The western road, the one built by Gómez as an escape route, leads from Maracay to Ocumare de la Costa, and continues on to Cata; it ascends to 1128 metres at Paso Portachuelo. The eastern road heads from Maracay due north to Choroní, and reaches the seashore two km further on at Puerto Colombia. It's a narrower, poorer and more twisting route, but it climbs much higher, to 1830 metres, and it is more spectacular. Both routes are about 55 km long and both are occasionally blocked by landslides. There's no road connection between the coastal ends of these roads; a rented boat is the only way to get from one end to the other if you want to complete the loop.

The coast is rocky cliffs in some parts, as the Cordillera drops sharply to the sea; in other parts, particularly where there are bays, there are flat belts of land beside the shore, usually filled with coconut groves and bordered by beaches. These are another big attraction of the park, particularly for Venezuelan holidaymakers. A few seaside resorts

---

Henri Pittier

Henri François Pittier Dormond was born in Bex, Switzerland, in 1857, and graduated with a doctorate in Sciences and Civil Engineering. Eventually botany became his real passion. Attracted by tropical nature, he explored Costa Rica and Panama before settling in Venezuela in 1917. His extensive travels throughout the country resulted in the collection and classification of more than 30,000 specimens of local plant, the basis for the creation of Herbario Nacional, or national herbariums.

The author of about 160 studies on forests, herbs, fruit and other aspects of botany, he soon realised the necessity for the protection of Venezuela's ecosystems, and proposed the creation of the national parks system to the government. The struggle took several years until, in 1937, President Eleázar López Contreras eventually decreed the Parque Nacional Rancho Grande as Venezuela's first national park. The park was later renamed to honour the memory of the father of Venezuela's national park system. It took another 15 years, until 1952, before the government woke up and declared a second protected area, Parque Nacional Sierra Nevada. ■

have already sprung up, the main ones being Cata and Puerto Colombia. Both offer a wide choice of hotels and restaurants, and boat-hire facilities.

Things to See & Do

Parque Nacional Henri Pittier has something for nearly everyone. Most Venezuelan tourists go principally for the park's beaches; they drive straight to the waterfront (Cata and, to a lesser extent, Puerto Colombia are the main destinations, and both have their own beach) and then run to the beach to enjoy hot sun and cold beer. There are other attractive things to see and do in the park, however. Probably the most fascinating opportunity the park provides is the bird-watching, but hikers, architecture buffs and fiesta lovers will all find something to enjoy.

The park is good for both day trips and longer stays. The one-day trip from Maracay to the coast and back again, passing through the cloudforest twice, is more than enough to justify the trip. Take the eastern road to Puerto Colombia, as the scenery is more spectacular and you will have the chance to visit Choroní, the finest colonial town in the park.

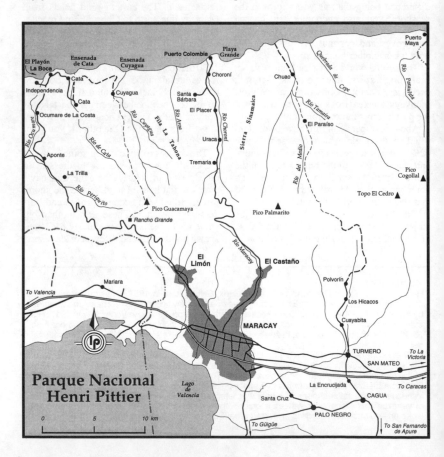

Colonial Towns The coast has been inhabited for centuries, and the few colonial towns that have survived in the park are the best proof of that. It's interesting to note that all these old settlements are set back from the waterfront; Cuyagua, Cata, Choroní and Chuao have all been founded several km inland, back from the sea. This was to provide the towns with some protection against the pirates who roamed the coast and sometimes raided inland.

Choroní is a tiny 300-year-old town. Most of its narrow streets are lined with old pastel-coloured houses. The well-shaded Plaza Bolívar boasts a lovely parish church, which is worth entering. There's a finely decorated ceiling, and the wall over the high altar has been painted to look like a carved retable. The carved wooden Virgin Mary and Child (in the right aisle) look charming with wigs on their heads. The feast of Santa Clara, the patron saint of the town, is celebrated in August.

Several km east of Choroní is the village of **Chuao**, well known as a centre of cacao plantations. Chuao has a very simple, fine colonial church and lives in almost complete isolation: it has no roads other than a rough five-km track which leads to the sea. The village is widely known for its Diablos Danzantes (Devil Dancers) celebrations. Access to Chuao is by boat from Puerto Colombia followed by a one-hour walk from the shore to the town.

Other old towns noted for their Diablos Danzantes tradition are **Cata** and **Cuyagua**, located in the western, coastal section of the park. They are connected to one another and to Maracay by road. Before setting off, check the celebration dates, as they vary from town to town and from one year to the next.

There's a significant Black population in these towns, especially in Chuao, so drum beats are an integral part of life, and can be heard all year round – particularly on weekends and during holidays.

Bird-watching Although birds live throughout the park (and outside it), the best area for bird-watchers is the cloudforest in the upper reaches of the Cordillera. Without a doubt, the best point is the Paso Portachuelo area, which not only abounds in endemic birds (ie birds living there permanently), but is also a natural corridor for migratory birds, as this is the lowest point in the ridge.

A few hundred metres from the pass is the Estación Biológica Rancho Grande, the biological station proposed by Pittier after the park was founded. The station is an intriguing question-mark-shaped building. This was yet another project of dictator Gómez; it was originally destined to be a posh country hotel. The building was only half-completed by the time Gómez died, and was left by the workers in the state it was when they heard the news of the dictator's death. A decade later it was eventually converted into the research station. The station is run by the Escuela de Agronomía (School of Agronomy) of Universidad Central de Venezuela. They have their base (π 450153) in El Limón, on the north-western outskirts of Maracay.

There are several paths leading from the station off into the forest, which provide fabulous opportunities for bird-watching. The best conditions are to be found early in the morning. September and October are the best months for viewing migratory birds. You may also see agoutis, peccaries, snakes (wear good, calf-length boots) and butterflies.

The station does grant permission to stay on the premises to those who are seriously interested, but you have to arrange this beforehand. Contact the director of the Escuela de Agronomía, Professor Alberto Fernández Badillo (π 450153). Alternatively, call the Sociedad de Amigos Parque Nacional Henri Pittier (π 544454), and talk to its director, Ernesto Fernández Badillo, Alberto's brother.

Conditions in the station are simple; they include beds and kitchen facilities, but no food is provided. It's recommended that you bring a sleeping bag as it gets pretty cold at night, and obviously your own food and provisions. Camping is also possible if you have your own tent. Remember that it rains quite a lot in the area, so bring along reliable rain gear.

The station lies just off the Maracay-Ocumare road, 28 km from Maracay. Any Ocumare bus will put you down near the entrance.

Hiking There are not many routes in the park for inexperienced hikers, except for short walks around the biological station. Longer trails are few and far between; they are not well marked. Reclaimed by the lush vegetation, they become faint and hard to follow in the rainy season. Well-prepared, experienced hikers may want to face the challenge anyway, as the flora and fauna on these tracks are spectacular. Remember that northern slopes of the Cordillera receive more rain than the southern ones and the upper parts are pretty wet most of the year. The driest months are January to March.

One of the beautiful longer trails begins at the biological station at Paso Portachuelo and winds its way north-east, up to Pico Guacamaya (1828 metres). It then turns north and you head down along a ridge to the village of Cuyagua. From Cuyagua, there's a road out to Cata and from there back to the biological station and Maracay. Ask at the station for information and news on the condition of the trail. It's much better to undertake this hike in the dry season. Count on two days of walking, but keep a third day up your sleeve, as you may lose the trail from time to time.

Another marvellous trail traverses the Cordillera from Chuao to Turmero, 14 km east of Maracay. Again, it's unmarked, not clear in parts and its upper reaches may be very wet and muddy in the rainy season. This hike also can be done in two days but it may run to three. The trail goes from Chuao southward and uphill to the hamlet of El Paraíso. It then continues, rising to Hacienda La Azucena, the last point where you can get information about the rest of the route. The trail (in parts faint) climbs to about 1950 metres and then descends gradually over the southern slope to Hacienda Portapán at around 1500 metres (where you are likely to see a human being again). From the hacienda, a 4WD track slants all the way down to Turmero's outskirts, where it eventually becomes a paved road. The trail can also be done in reverse, from Tumero to Chuao.

Beaches There are some good beaches on the park's coast. Since the bays are relatively small, the beaches are not long, but they are pretty wide and are often shaded by coconut palms.

Before you go, decide which road to take as you have to choose between beaches of either the Cata or Puerto Colombia areas. Boats can take you to any other isolated beach you wish, but they are not cheap, especially if the boatman cannot assemble six passengers, the boat's usual capacity. Boats can transfer you from one end to the other (Cata to Puerto Colombia, or vice versa) but this trip costs somewhere between US$60 and US$80 per boat. Because the competition between boat operators is fierce, prices are negotiable, and you should always try to bargain. Keep in mind that popular beaches tend to be covered with rubbish.

In the Cata area, going from west to east, the first easily accessible beach is **El Playón**, a wide beach with facilities at the northern end of the town of Independencia. Five km eastward is the most famous beach in the park, **Cata**, a fine crescent of sand bordering the Bahía de Cata. It's developed (or overdeveloped, some would say), and a few tower blocks have already sprung up. Boats from Cata take tourists to the smaller but quieter beach, **Catita**, on the eastern side of the same bay. It takes 10 minutes to get there, and the ride costs US$0.60 per person.

Further east is the unspoilt and usually deserted **Cuyagua** beach. You can get there by road by going to the town of Cuyagua and then taking a 2.5-km sand track. Alternatively, boats can be rented from Cata for about US$25 return.

In the Puerto Colombia area, the most popular beach is **Playa Grande**, a five-minute walk on a dirt road east of town. It's some half a km long and shaded by coconuts, but suffers from litter during weekends. There are several rustic shack restaurants at the entrance to the beach, serving good fried fish for US$3 to U$$5. You can camp on the beach, but don't leave your tent unattended.

If this one is too crowded or littered for you, go to the wild **Playa Escondida**, on the opposite (western) side of the town. It's not that easy to find, as its name –'hidden' – suggests. To get there you take a dirt track which branches off the Choroní-Puerto Colombia road roughly halfway along it, next to a bridge. The track soon becomes just a path leading through the woods, then descends by a rocky cliff. Ask for directions if in doubt.

Other beaches are accessible only by boat. Boats crowd around the river mouth in the heart of Puerto Colombia, and they are eager to take passengers to isolated beaches like **Aroa** (US$25 return), **Chuao** (US$25 return) or **Cepe** (US$30 return).

Places to Stay & Eat

Predictably, the best range is to be found at the most popular beaches, ie in Cata (beach, not town) and Puerto Colombia.

Puerto Colombia & Around There are perhaps a dozen hotels in the tiny Puerto Colombia, and locals also rent out their rooms if there's the demand. The prices usually rise at weekends. Restaurants, too, are in good supply, so starving is improbable; a fried fish is the local staple.

One of the cheapest places to stay in Puerto Colombia is the family-run *Habitaciones La Abuela*, facing the Plaza San Juan, near the bus stop. Rooms have fans but no private baths, and cost US$6/8/11 for a single/double/triple. *Hotel Bahía*, 20 metres from the pedestrian bridge leading to Playa Grande, offers doubles with bath and fan for US$11. Marginally better are *Hotel Don Miguel*, next to the alcabala at the entrance to the town, and *Hospedaje La Montañita*, on the main street near the waterfront, but their doubles cost US$16. *Hostel Costa Brava* has raised their prices to US$20 a double, which is too much for what they offer.

Hotel Alemania at the entrance to the town has clean, simple rooms with fan and bath,

for US$15/28 a single/double, breakfast is included.

Hotel Club Cotoperix, installed in an old colonial house on the main street, is about the best place to stay in town. A double room will cost about US$35, breakfast included. The hotel has its own restaurant, which is not bad but not all that cheap. Boat trips to beaches can be organised with the manager.

Budget eating is provided by a few simple restaurants gathered next to each other by the bridge. Restaurants at Playa Grande are also good (probably even better) for inexpensive meals, mostly fried fish. *Tasca Bahía* is the best restaurant in town.

Choroní, two km inland, has only one hotel, *Posada Gran Sabana*. Owned and run by a friendly North American from Arizona, this charming 1816 house has only three rooms for guests and costs US$15 per person, breakfast included. If this is too much for you, or if the rooms are occupied, the owner can put you up in another house nearby, for US$6 per head (but without breakfast). He also offers boat trips to any beach you want. The Posada can be booked in Caracas via Costa Tours (☎ 323336).

Choroní's sole restaurant, *Santa Clara*, on Plaza Bolívar, opens on weekends only.

Cata & Around Here, too, hotels and restaurants tend to stick close to the beaches and adjust their prices according to demand. Try *Hotel Playa Azul* or *Hotel Montemar*, one block back from El Playón beach. Both offer doubles with bath and air-conditioning for around US$25.

In the Bahía de Cata, there are a dozen basic cabañas (each for four people) beside the beach, and a string of restaurants.

Getting There & Away

The departure point for the park is the Maracay bus terminal. Buses to Ocumare de la Costa depart every hour, from 7 am to 5 pm (US$1.25, two hours). In Ocumare, you catch a carrito to Cata beach (US$0.60, 15 minutes). To Puerto Colombia, buses leave every two hours from (US$1.25, two hours). The last bus from both Ocumare and Puerto

Colombia back to Maracay departs at 5 pm (later on weekends).

Note that these schedules are not always respected in practice. Some buses may be cancelled due to an insufficient number of passengers (the driver is, of course, the judge of what number is 'sufficient'), and the last buses are not very reliable, especially on weekdays.

Carabobo State

VALENCIA

Founded in 1555 and named after its Spanish mother town, Valencia has had a tumultuous and chequered history. It had not yet reached its seventh anniversary, when Lope de Aguirre, the infamous adventurer obsessed with finding El Dorado, sacked the town and burnt it almost to the ground. Twenty years later and not yet fully recovered, the town experienced an attack by Carib Indians who did much the same as Aguirre. A century later the town was seized and destroyed again, this time by French pirates.

The town's proximity to the Lago de Valencia didn't contribute to development either. The disease-breeding marshes brought about smallpox epidemics which decimated the population. Survivors were scared away and new settlers were few and far between. By the year 1800, ie after 250 years of existence, Valencia had barely 6000 inhabitants.

In 1812, a devastating earthquake shook the Andean shell, all the way from Mérida to Caracas, and left Valencia – as well as several other cities including Barquisimeto, Trujillo, San Felipe, Mérida and Caracas – in ruins yet again. Only two years later the town was besieged by royalist troops under the command of José Tomás Boves (known as the Butcher) and taken 17 days later. The slaughter which followed left 500 people dead, including many innocent inhabitants.

For the next seven years, more than a score of battles were fought around the town, until 24 June 1821 when Bolívar's decisive victory at the Battle of Carabobo eventually sealed Venezuela's independence.

The victory seems to have been a turning point in the town's fortunes. In 1826, Valencia was the first town to oppose Bolívar's sacred union, Gran Colombia, and called for Venezuela to be declared a sovereign state. Four years later, in 1830, this became fact after the Congress convened in Valencia and decreed the formal secession from Gran Colombia. At the same time Congress made Valencia the new-born country's capital, rather than Caracas. A year later, however, General Páez was elected president and the government moved back to Caracas.

Valencia experienced particularly rapid growth after WWII. It was then that Venezuela's industrial development accelerated, and Valencia caught the new economic winds in its sails. The Caracas authorities, concerned about over-industrialisation of the capital, pushed some industries out of the city, and Valencia, which already had a good transport infrastructure and other facilities, was one of the most blessed recipients.

Today, Valencia is Venezuela's most industrialised city (except for heavy industry which has gathered in Ciudad Guayana). It is also the centre of the most developed agricultural region, endowed with fertile soil and favourable climate. Incidentally, like its Spanish mother city, Valencia is famous nationwide for its oranges.

Home to some 950,000 people, Valencia is Venezuela's third largest city, after Caracas and Maracaibo, and the capital of Carabobo state. Set at an altitude of 480 metres, the annual average temperature is about 25°C, and the climate is much the same as that of Maracay – pretty hot and humid.

Valencia is a pleasant enough place, but won't come on the top of the average traveller's list of places to visit. The two major local events, Semana de Valencia, in late March, and Ferias de Valencia, in mid-November.

Information

Tourist Office There's no tourist office in Valencia; it has moved to Puerto Cabello.

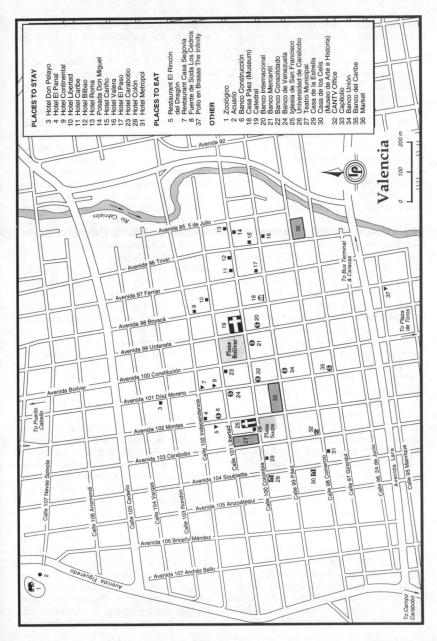

PLACES TO STAY
3   Hotel Don Pelayo
4   Hotel El Panal
9   Hotel Continental
10 Hotel Libertad
11 Hotel Caribe
12 Hotel Bilbao
13 Hotel Roma
14 Posada Don Miguel
15 Hotel Cariño
16 Hotel Valera
17 Hotel El Paso
23 Hotel Carabobo
28 Hotel Colón
31 Hotel Metropol

PLACES TO EAT
5   Restaurant El Rincón
    del Dragón
6   Restaurant Casa Segovia
7   Fuente de Soda Los Cedros
8   Fuente de Soda Los Cedros
37 Pollo en Brasas The Infinity

OTHER
1   Zoológico
2   Acuario
6   Banco Construcción
18 Casa Páez (Museum)
19 Catedral
20 Banco Internacional
21 Banco Mercantil
22 Banco Consolidado
24 Banco de Venezuela
25 Iglesia de San Francisco
26 Universidad de Carabobo
27 Teatro Municipal
29 Casa de la Estrella
30 Casa de los Celis
    (Museo de Arte e Historia)
32 CANTV Office
33 Capitolio
34 Banco Unión
35 Banco del Caribe
36 Market

Valencia

Money Banco Unión and Banco Con-solidado change cash; the latter also handles American Express travellers' cheques and credit card operations. Visa and MasterCard advances can be dealt with by Banco de Venezuela, Banco Mercantil and Banco Unión. Other banks, which may be useful in future (at present they're not), have also been marked on the map.

Turisol (☎ 227057, 222135, fax 229259) is in Edificio Exterior, Local 3, Avenida Bolívar, Sector las Acacias.

Things to See

The heart of the historic town, **Plaza Bolívar**, boasts, as always, the monument to the Liberator in its middle. Unlike the dozens of equestrian statues (usually replicas of the Caracas monument) which you've probably already inspected whilst travelling through the country, this one comes as a certain novelty. The bronze figure of Bolívar stands on a 15-metre-high white marble column which was brought from Italy.

The **Catedral**, on the eastern side of the plaza, is reputedly 400 years old, but it has experienced so many alterations in its history – the last ones as recently as the 1950s – that today it's an eclectic hotch-potch of styles. For the city's 400th anniversary, for example, the ceiling was changed to look like a wedding cake.

The most revered treasure in the cathedral, the figure of Nuestra Señora del Socorro, is kept in the chapel in the left transept. Carved in the late 16th century, the sorrowful Virgin in black was the first statue in Venezuela to be crowned (in 1910) by Rome. The gold crown encrusted with innumerable precious stones is kept in a safe place, however, and it's only taken out for very special celebrations, among them 1 August, the Virgin's holy day.

The two large paintings, *The Last Supper* and *The Entry into Jerusalem*, which hang opposite one another on the side walls of the chapel, are the work of Antonio Herrera Toro, a noted Valencia-born artist, who left behind a number of murals and paintings in local churches and public buildings. Having studied in Rome, his art is strongly influenced by the great masters of the Italian Renaissance.

A short walk from the Cathedral, on the corner of Calle Páez and Avenida Boyacá, is the **Casa Páez**, home of Venezuela's first president. General José Antonio Páez first distinguished himself by forging a formidable army of llaneros which fought under Bolívar on numerous fronts and largely contributed to the eventual triumph in the War of Independence. In 1830, on the day when Venezuela split from Gran Colombia, Páez became the first acting president of the newborn sovereign country. It was then that Valencia became Venezuela's capital, and Casa Páez was turned into the general's home. A year later Páez was elected president of the republic and moved with the government to Caracas.

Today the Casa is a museum, open Tuesday to Friday from 9 am to noon and 3 to 5.30 pm, Saturday and Sunday from 9 am to 2 pm. This fine colonial house, restored and furnished with period fittings, has a lovely central patio. The walls of the cloister lining the patio are embellished with a series of murals depicting the nine battles the general fought. The work was done by Pedro Castillo, and supposedly directed by Páez himself.

Three blocks west, along Calle Páez, is the **Capitolio**, a large building occupying half of the entire block. Built in 1772 as a convent, it became the government house a century later, after Guzmán Blanco expelled the former occupants, as he did with many other religious institutions throughout the country. The only reason for visiting the building is to see the famous portrait by Arturo Michelena of Bolívar mounted on his horse. The painting is displayed in the Salón Bolívar, the central room serving as the assembly hall. Enter the main entrance (from Calle Páez) during office hours, inquire at the desk, and someone will open the hall for you.

West, across the street from the Capitolio, is **Plaza Sucre**. On its northern side stands the 16th-century Iglesia de San Francisco, much altered in the mid-19th century and

Top Left: Local church nave, Choroní
Top Right: Old town, Puerto Cabello
Bottom: Colonial architecture, Coro

Facades of Coro

next door, the building of the Universidad de Valencia, created in 1892 and later renamed the Universidad de Carabobo. To the west of this is the **Teatro Municipal**, modelled on the Paris Opera House and inaugurated in 1894. The theatre was renovated in the 1970s; instead of a few months, as expected, the work took a decade to be completed. The highlight here is the ceiling decoration painted by Antonio Herrera Toro in 1892, depicting famous men of music and literature, including Rossini, Goethe, Shakespeare and Beethoven. The guards may let you in during the day or before an evening performance.

One block west of the theatre is the **Casa de la Estrella**, a large casona where, on 6 May 1830, the sovereign state of Venezuela was born, after Congress convened here and decreed secession from Gran Colombia. Supposedly built around 1660 as a hospital, the house was later remodelled as a college and today it is the seat of the Instituto de la Historia. You can enter the casa if you wish, if only to stand in the birthplace of the country; there's nothing special to see here.

There's more to see in the **Casa de los Celis**, 1½ blocks south, possibly the most beautiful colonial mansion in the city. Built in the 1760s and named after one of its owners, Colonel Pedro Celis, the casa now houses the **Museo de Arte e Historia**. There's a small collection of colonial religious art in one of the rooms, while the other rooms are dedicated to Antonio Herrera Toro (1857-1914) and Andrés Pérez Mujica (1873-1920), both of whom were artists born in Valencia. The museum is open Tuesday to Friday from 8 am to 2 pm, Saturday and Sunday from 9.30 am to 12.30 pm.

The **Acuario**, nine blocks north of the museum, on the opposite side of Avenida Figueredo, is the favourite drawcard for the *caraboveños*, or Valencia's inhabitants. The star attractions are the *tonimas*, or freshwater dolphins. They are kept in a large central pool and are fed at 10.30 am, and 1.30, 3 and 5 pm. The feeding is accompanied by dolphin shows. The stairs at the far end of the pool lead down to windows which enable

you to watch dolphins underwater (but not during the shows).

At the back of the same building is the aquarium-terrarium, which has the best collection of Venezuelan freshwater fish and some typical snakes – highly worth visiting. Electric eels, piranhas and anacondas – they're all here.

Beyond the acuario is the small **Zoológico**, featuring some of Venezuela's typical animal species, including jaguar, tapir, caimán del Orinoco, turtles and a variety of birds. A certain curiosity is the *manatí*, or manatee, an aquatic mammal vaguely resembling a small whale. This one is eight years of age, three metres long and weighs 300 kg. It lives in the pond at the entrance to the zoo, and it is fed at 9 am, noon and 4 pm, which are the only times to see it.

Both the acuario and zoológico are open Tuesday to Sunday from 9 am to 6 pm (they may also be open on Mondays in August), and the entrance to either of them costs US$0.60.

The **Plaza de Toros Monumental** is the pride of Valencia. It is indeed monumental, the second largest in the Americas after the one in Mexico City. Built in 1967, it is capable of seating 27,000 spectators. Architecturally, however, it's not an outstanding design. The main corridas are held during the city's two major events, Semana de Valencia and Ferias de Valencia, while other minor bullfights take place irregularly throughout the year. Behind the plaza, in the Parque Sur, is the **Museo Antropológico**, which features a small collection of artefacts related to pre-Hispanic cultures of the region.

The bullring is on the southern edge of the city, at the end of Avenida Las Ferias, a southern extension of Avenida Construcción. Take the city bus (locally called *camionetica*) from the corner of Avenida Construcción and Avenida Lara, which will set you down a five-minute walk from the plaza.

Places to Stay

There are plenty of budget hotels in the city centre, including *Metropol, Continental, Libertad, Caribe, Bilbao, Don Miguel,*

Roma, *Cariño*, *Valera* and *El Paso*. Unfortunately, they all range from ultra basic to basic, and they apparently all double as love hotels. Accordingly, almost all have only rooms with one double bed, fan and private bath, and prefer couples passing through for an hour or two to guests who stay for 24 hours. Consequently, some managers may tell you that the hotel is full if you arrive in the morning, but will accept you if you turn up in the evening. The price is about US$7 per single or couple. Rooms with two beds are infrequent, but if there are any, they cost only marginally more or the same as matrimoniales. The Metropol and Cariño are the cheapest of the lot, US$5 per couple, but they are very basic. The Libertad and Continental are slightly better than the rest. The area west of Plaza Bolívar is safer than the sector east of the square (where most of these hotels are located, unfortunately).

Hotel El Panal offers marginally better standards than the above-mentioned lot, for US$8/10 a double with fan/air-conditioning, but it is noisy.

For something appreciably better, go to *Hotel Colón* (☎ 577105) at Calle Colombia 103-37, which has singles/doubles/triples with air-conditioning, TV, private bath and hot water for US$15/15/18. The *Hotel Carabobo* (☎ 89666), at Calle Libertad 100-37, on the corner of Plaza Bolívar, offers much the same. It costs US$18/22/25, and also has quadruples for US$30.

Top-end accommodation in the city centre is represented by *Hotel Don Pelayo* (☎ 579378), at the corner of Avenida Díaz Moreno and Calle Rondón. Singles/doubles/triples with all facilities cost US$35/40/45.

Other mid-priced and top-range hotels are stranded out from the city centre. Some of them, such as *Hotel Le Paris* (☎ 215555), *Hotel 400* (☎ 210533) and *Hotel Excelsior* (☎ 214055), are on Avenida Bolívar. They all have air-conditioned rooms costing, at most, the same as the rooms of the Don Pelayo.

The best hotel in town is the expensive five-star *Hotel Intercontinental Valencia* (☎ 211033), Calle Juan Uslar, Urbanización La Viña, about four km north of the city centre.

Places to Eat

The centre is OK for cheap eating but not for quality dining. Restaurants tend to close by 8 pm, except for tascas which at that time turn into heavy drinking venues. However, at lunch time some of them offer an inexpensive menu ejecutivo (eg the tasca in *Hotel Colón*), which is usually good value for money.

A number of fuentes de soda (eg *Los Cedros* on Avenida Díaz Moreno) offer a reasonably priced range of typical dishes. *Pollo en Brasas The Infinity* is possibly the best central chicken outlet and it also has pizzas, parrillas and churrasco. One of the best restaurants in the centre is in the *Hotel Don Pelayo*.

A better area for dining out is outside the centre. There are plenty of good places on Avenida Bolívar, including *El Toro Rojo* (parrillas), *Braman Grill* (parrillas), *Marisquería El Marchica* (fish and seafood), *La Trattoria Romana* (Italian), *Germania Grill* (German), *El Regio* (Italian) and *La Hostería del Rey* (French).

Getting There & Away

Air The airport is several km east of the city centre. There are direct flights to Caracas (US$35), Barcelona (US$59), Maracaibo (US$59) and Porlamar (US$53); other destinations are reached via one of the above-mentioned, principally Caracas.

Valencia is the home town of Valenciana de Aviación, Carabobo's state airline. They have flights to Bogotá, Colombia, for US$120. Contact their office (☎ 670856, 670256) for details.

Bus The bus terminal is about four km east of the city centre, and it is easily accessible by frequent local buses. The terminal is large, relatively well organised and has a lot of facilities, including restaurants and snack bars.

Buses run regularly to all major cities. To Caracas, they depart every 10 minutes or so (US$3, 2½ hours) and pass through Maracay (US$0.60, one hour). Frequent buses run to Puerto Cabello (US$1, 50 minutes), Tucacas

(US$2, two hours), and Chichiriviche (US$2.50, 2½ hours). Hourly buses run to Barquisimeto (US$3.50, three hours) and most of them continue on to Maracaibo (US$10, eight hours). There are about 10 buses a day to San Cristóbal (US$12.50, 10½ hours) and several of them go on to San Antonio del Táchira (US$13.25, 11½ hours). Four buses a day depart for Mérida (US$12.50, nine hours), and at least half a dozen buses go to Coro (US$5.50, 5½ hours).

CAMPO CARABOBO

Campo Carabobo, or the Carabobo Battlefield, is the site where, on 24 June 1821, the battle which sealed Venezuela's independence was fought between the Spanish royalist army and Bolívar's troops. Bolívar's regiments were strengthened by the lancers of Páez and the British legionnaires, and thanks to these two assisting forces El Libertador was able to win the battle. He commanded the battle from the nearby hill. The whole operation continues to fascinate scholars as they see it as a masterpiece. To commemorate the event, a complex of monuments has been erected on the site where the battle took place.

The approach is a wide entrance road, which turns into a formal walkway lined with bronze busts of the heroes of the battle. The walkway leads to the huge **Triumphal Arch** and the **Tomb of the Unknown Soldier** beneath it. Two soldiers keep guard of the tomb; their gala uniforms from the period seem more suitable for a Siberian winter than for the baking sun of Carabobo. Fortunately for them, the changing of the guard takes place every two hours.

A hundred metres beyond the arch is the **Monument**, no doubt the largest in Venezuela. It was designed by Manuel Rodríguez del Villar and erected in 1930. The monument depicts the main heroes and allegoric figures, all made in stone and bronze. On the top of this realistic-symbolic composition is, as might be expected, an equestrian statue of Bolívar.

About one km to the west is the **Mirador**,

from which Bolívar commanded the battle. It houses a large model of the battlefield, and provides a panoramic view over the whole site. The Diorama cubicle, to the right of the access road, seems to have closed down.

Campo Carabobo is 32 km south-west of Valencia, on the road to San Carlos. Frequent suburban buses (marked Campo Carabobo) go from Valencia to the battlefield. In Valencia, they go east along Calle Comercio and turn south into Avenida Carabobo; catch them on either of these streets. They will leave you in Carabobo at the end of the entrance road. The ride takes an hour and costs US$0.20.

CERRO PINTADO

There are a number of groups of petroglyphs in Carabobo state, the most important of which is the site known as Cerro Pintado. Also called Parque Piedras Pintadas (though it's not a park), the site lies 22 km north-east of Valencia, near the village of Tronconero. This is one of the largest groups so far found, consisting of dozens of weathered rocks and slabs scattered over a grassy slope. Many of the stones bear shallow engravings of mysterious designs and figures. Further on, there's a group of upright megalithic stones.

To get to the Cerro from Valencia, take the bus to Vigirima. It goes regularly and the ride costs US$0.50. The bus passes through Guacara, 13 km east of Valencia, then turns north for the 12-km trek to Vigirima. You should get off midway along this stretch, by the Bodega Los Tres Samanes. Ask the driver to let you down at the Cruce de Tronconero, or the Cerro Pintado turnoff. A dirt road which branches off to the left (west) will bring you to the Río Tronconero, about 1.5 km from the turnoff. Shortly past the bridge, take a 4WD track which branches off to the north. This track passes a rural school (soon after the turnoff, on your right), and continues north for another 1.5 km, eventually getting to the foothills of the Cerro. You can camp at the site if you wish. Bring food and water, as there is no water around.

Other interesting groups of petroglyphs in Carabobo state include the sites in the

Montaña de Mataburro, several km north of Vigirima; along the Río Chirgua, near the town of Chirgua, west of Valencia; in the area of Montalbán, still further west; and in the region of the town of Güigüe, near the southern shore of Lago de Valencia.

LAS TRINCHERAS

The village of Las Trincheras, 18 km north of Valencia, is noted for its hot springs. At about 92°C, the springs are amongst the hottest in the world. They are also widely acclaimed for their curative properties. A large bath complex, Centro Termal Las Trincheras, has been built on the site of the springs, and includes a hotel, a restaurant, baths, mud bath and sauna, and is the best centre of its kind in the country.

The springs have been known for centuries and have attracted a number of explorers and naturalists, among them Alexander von Humboldt, who successfully boiled eggs in the hot water. In 1889, thermal baths were built that included a hotel and pools. In 1980, the old hotel was restored, a new one was constructed beside it, and the pools were largely reconstructed. There are three pools with water of different temperature from warm to very hot, and a mud bath with a temperature of about 42°C.

The springs are renowned for their therapeutic properties, recommended in the treatment of a variety of diseases, including rheumatic, digestive, respiratory and allergic problems. They are also useful in helping you to lose weight, make the skin feel fresh and smooth, and help with general relaxation.

You can either come to the baths for the day (open from 7 am to 10 pm, mud bath until 6 pm only, entrance fee US$2), or you can stay in their hotel, using the baths and other facilities at the complex at no additional cost. The hotel has its own pool, for the exclusive use of guests.

Places to Stay & Eat.

Centro Termal Las Trincheras offers comfortable lodging in its hotel. Singles/doubles/triples cost US$13/18/22, and there

are also suites for US$25 to US$40. The price of the hotel includes the use of the baths, sauna and other facilities. The restaurant offers breakfast, lunch and dinner for both hotel guests and day visitors.

It's usually easy to get a room during the working week but at weekends the hotel tends to fill up. Advance booking is available through either their Valencia office (☎ (041) 669795), Autopista Valencia-Puerto Cabello, or the Caracas office (☎ (02) 661-3626, 661-3724, fax 661-3502), Edificio Carini, Local 1, Avenida Alma Mater, Los Chaguaramos.

Right opposite the entrance to the baths complex is the *Hotel Turístico Da Ilona* (☎ 669437), which has doubles/triples for US$12/17. It runs its own restaurant specialising in German cuisine. The price doesn't include entrance to the baths.

Getting There & Away

There are city buses from Valencia to Las Trincheras; you catch them in the city centre on Avenida Bolívar. They go by the old Valencia-Puerto Cabello road and deposit you at the entrance to the baths. The trip takes half an hour to one hour and costs US$0.20. You can also get to the baths from the Valencia bus terminal by catching any of the frequent buses to Puerto Cabello. These buses go via the autopista (freeway) and charge the full fare to Puerto Cabello (US$1), and they take 20 minutes to get to Las Trincheras. They will put you down on the autopista, which is a 10-minute walk from the baths.

If you want to continue on from Las Trincheras north to Puerto Cabello, Tucacas or Chichiriviche, wave down the appropriate bus on the autopista.

PUERTO CABELLO

Puerto Cabello, 55 km north of Valencia on the autopista, is Venezuela's second most important port after La Guaira, but often it surpasses Caracas' port in freight volume. The port has a shipyard with a dry dock, and a large harbour, part of which is occupied by the naval base. Puerto Cabello has grown considerably over recent decades, stretching towards the west for some seven km along the freeway up to the airport, and today has nearly 150,000 people. Sitting on the seaside, the city has a hot climate with an average temperature of 28°C.

Puerto Cabello was born somewhere in the mid-16th century around a perfect natural anchorage. There was hardly a better place for a port on the whole Caribbean coast; the ample coatal lagoon provided excellent protection from winds and waves and was connected with the open sea by a convenient strait. Since then, the town's development has been closely linked to that of the port.

During the 17th century the small port had a more Dutch than Spanish flavour, as it was involved in a busy contraband trade (mostly dealing in cacao) with Curaçao. Predictably, the port was frequently prey to pirates and corsairs marauding the Caribbean coast. It wasn't until 1730 that the Spanish finally brought the port under their full control and developed it, after the Real Compañía Guipuzcoana had moved in. The company built warehouses and wharves, and two forts to protect the port.

During the War of Independence, Puerto Cabello became an important royalist stronghold, from which attacks were launched against Bolívar's troops. After having lost the battle of Carabobo, the Spanish retreated to Puerto Cabello and kept it until 7 November 1823; only then did they surrender the town to Páez. Puerto Cabello was the last place in Venezuela to be freed from Spanish rule.

During the 19th century Puerto Cabello was Venezuela's busiest port, through which a good deal of cacao, coffee, indigo and cotton was shipped abroad. The port was modernised during the dictatorships of Gómez and Pérez Jiménez, and again over recent decades.

While the attention of governors was concentrated on the port and its infrastructure, the colonial part of the city was gradually falling into ruins. Only recently has the government realised the value of the town's historic architecture, and launched an extensive restoration programme. A few streets have already been restored – with quite good results – and the work on others is in progress, though it seems to have slowed down in the past few years.

There are several beaches to the east of Puerto Cabello, which have become an attraction among carabobeños. However, they are not the best beaches in the country.

Information

Tourist Office The tourist office (☎ 614622, 613255, 612814) is in the Edificio Gobierno de Carabobo, Calle Ricaurte, facing Plaza Bolívar. The office is open Monday to Friday from 8 am to noon and 2 to 6 pm.

Money The main banks are scattered around the city centre and the colonial sector. As elsewhere, the most reliable are the Banco Consolidado for American Express travellers' cheques and the Banco Unión for cash. Banco de Venezuela handles Visa and MasterCard. The location of these and other banks which may be useful are given on the map.

Things to See

The **Plaza Bolívar**, north of the city centre, at the southern edge of the colonial sector, boasts yet another copy of the Caracas statue of Bolívar. A massive, odd edifice built from coral rock, occupying the eastern edge of the plaza, is the **Iglesia de San José**. It was begun in the mid-19th century and only completed some 100 years later; yet even today it looks unfinished. The bell tower was added in the 1950s, which makes the church look still more ridiculous. The interior is almost void of decoration – not worth the effort of going to mass, the only time the church is open.

Two streets run north of the plaza, **Calle de los Lanceros** and **Calle Bolívar**; both have been fully restored and are the most pleasant areas to stroll about. Note the overhanging balconies and massive doorways which adorn some of the houses lining these streets. The house of the **Museo de Historia**

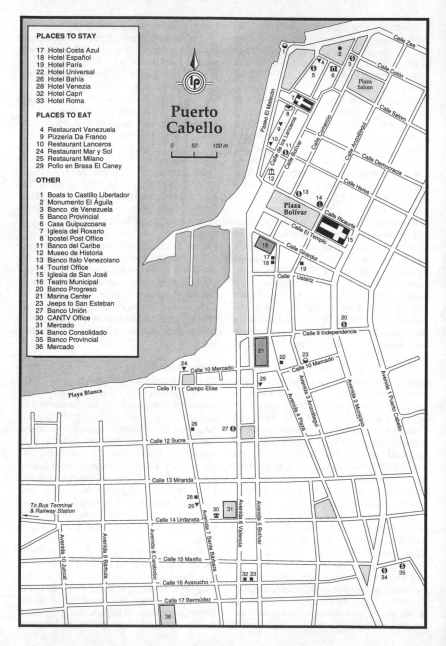

PLACES TO STAY

17 Hotel Costa Azul
18 Hotel Español
19 Hotel París
22 Hotel Universal
26 Hotel Bahía
28 Hotel Venezia
32 Hotel Capri
33 Hotel Roma

PLACES TO EAT

4 Restaurant Venezuela
9 Pizzería Da Franco
10 Restaurant Lanceros
24 Restaurant Mar y Sol
25 Restaurant Milano
29 Pollo en Brasa El Caney

OTHER

1 Boats to Castillo Libertador
2 Monumento El Águila
3 Banco de Venezuela
5 Banco Provincial
6 Casa Guipuzcoana
7 Iglesia del Rosario
8 Ipostel Post Office
11 Banco del Caribe
12 Museo de Historia
13 Banco Italo Venezolano
14 Tourist Office
15 Iglesia de San José
16 Teatro Municipal
20 Banco Progreso
21 Marina Center
23 Jeeps to San Esteban
27 Banco Unión
30 CANTV Office
31 Mercado
34 Banco Consolidado
35 Banco Provincial
36 Mercado

Puerto
Cabello

0   50   100 m

is possibly the finest of all. Built in 1790 as a residence, it is a large building with a gracious internal patio and façades over both streets. The balcony facing Calle Bolívar is particularly impressive, one of the best in the country. The museum itself, which houses a collection related to the town's history, was at the time of writing closed for refurbishing.

At the northern end of the two streets is the **Iglesia del Rosario**, a handsome white-washed church built in 1780. It's unused and apparently permanently locked.

One block north of the church is the **Casa Guipuzcoana**, built in 1730 as the office for the Compañia Guipuzcoana. Today it's a public library which you can enter.

The casa faces a triangular square with the **Monumento El Águila** in the middle. The monument, a tall column topped by an eagle, was erected to the memory of the North Americans who lost their lives in the struggle for the independence of Venezuela. They were recruited by Francisco de Miranda and sailed in 1806 from New York to Ocumare de la Costa, north of Maracay. Upon dropping anchor, however, two boats with Americans aboard were surprised and captured by Spanish guard boats. Ten officers were hung and the remaining 50-odd recruits were sent to prison. Miranda arrived in Coro a few months later with new recruits, but this expedition proved to be a failure as well.

Further north, separated from the old town by the entrance channel to the harbour, is the **Castillo Libertador**, also referred to as Fortín San Felipe. The fort was constructed in the 1730s by the Compañía Guipuzcoana to protect the port and warehouses. The fort was for a time in the patriots' hands, serving as the ammunition depot, but it was lost, along with the arsenal, to the royalists in 1812. Miranda was jailed here before the Spanish sent him to prison in Spain. The fort was recovered in 1823 after the eventual surrender of the Royalists, and it served the Venezuelan army. General Gómez used the fort as a jail, mostly for political prisoners. Only in 1935, at the end of Gómez' rule, was the prison finally closed down, and 14 tons of chains and leg irons were thrown into the sea.

The fort is within the naval base, but can be visited by the general public. The base operates a free boat across the channel, taking tourists there and back.

Return to the city centre by taking the waterfront boulevard, the **Paseo Malecón**. Many old buildings lining it have been restored, and now house restaurants and snack bars. You'll then skirt the Plaza Bolívar and, one block further south, pass by the **Teatro Municipal**, a massive neoclassical building erected in the 1880s, now used irregularly by visiting orchestras and theatre groups. Two blocks south you'll get to the Marina Center, the Disneyland-looking food centre.

The **Playa Blanca**, which stretches westward for about one km along the Golfo Triste (Sad Gulf), is the city beach, popular with locals though pretty polluted. Avoid it – it's notorious for the armed robbery of tourists, especially north of the bus terminal.

On the 100-metre-high hill just south of the city sits the **Fortín Solano**, another fort built (during the 1760s) by the Guipuzcoana Company to provide security for its commercial operations. The fort is in ruins, but commands excellent views of the city and the harbour. The road to the fort branches off from the road to San Esteban on the outskirts of Puerto Cabello. It's a good idea to combine a visit to the fort with that of San Esteban.

Places to Stay

Puerto Cabello's accommodation doesn't impress. There's not a single really decent hotel in the city centre. Of the dozen central budget hotels, most double as sex hotels and some allow prostitutes as well.

Probably the best bottom-end choice is the *Hotel París* (☎ 616648), Calle Anzoátegui 7-11, which is clean, quiet and friendly, and apparently one of the very few that doesn't rent rooms by the hour. A single or double with fan and bath costs US$7.

Possibly the cheapest place to stay is the *Hotel Universal*, facing the Marina Center. Matrimoniales (rooms with a double bed) with fan and bath cost US$6. The hotel also offers air-conditioned doubles/triples/quadruples for US$9/12/16.

Hotel Roma and, next door, *Hotel Capri*, Calle Ayacucho, are both acceptable. The former has air-conditioned doubles for US$9, the latter has matrimoniales with fan without/with bath for US$7/9, and air-conditioned rooms for US$11.

Hotel Costa Azul and *Hotel Español*, next to each other, near Teatro Municipal, cost much the same as the above-mentioned but are not recommended – use them as a last resort.

Hotel Venezia (☎ 614380), Calle Santa Bárbara 13-36, is run by a friendly Italian and costs US$10/14 for a double with fan/air-conditioning. On the same street, the *Hotel Bahía* offers air-conditioned doubles for US$15.

Better hotels are west of the city centre. *Hotel Cumboto* (☎ 69362), on the beach, about 2.5 km to the west, is perhaps the most pleasant option. It is an old house that once belonged to the Hacienda Cumboto, and has a salt water pool and an open-air restaurant.

Hotel Suite Caribe (☎ 615556), on the autopista, five km west of the city centre (two km east of the airport) offers possibly better standards, but not much in the way of style. It has air-conditioned rooms with bath and TV, plus its own restaurant and a swimming pool.

Places to Eat

In the city centre, there are several eating establishments in the Marina Center. The cheapest is the *Marina Center*, which has acceptable food, though the tablecloths seem not to have been changed for months. *El Mezón del Puerto* is cleaner and serves larger portions, but the prices are higher. *El Emperador* and *El Dorado* are still more expensive. There's also a good *Arepera La Mina*.

A few paces south of the Center, on Calle Bolívar, is the good and pleasant *Restaurant Milano*, which specialises in pasta and seafood. The best in the area is *Restaurant Mar y Sol*, overlooking the bay from the western end of Calle Mercado. Mariscos are delicious here, but not cheap.

Three blocks south along Calle Santa Bárbara, next door to Hotel Venezia, is *Pollo en Brasa El Caney*, a cheap and good chicken outlet.

In the colonial sector, north of the city centre, most restaurants have gathered on Paseo Malecón. *Pizzería Da Franco* is a pleasant, inexpensive place which puts tables outside, and stays open until 11 pm. Further north, near the Monumento El Águila, is *Restaurant Venezuela*.

Getting There & Away

Air The airport is seven km west of Puerto Cabello, next to the autopista.

Bus The bus terminal is about one km west of the city centre, on the corner of Calle Urdaneta and Calle Ayacucho. Frequent carritos run between the terminal and the centre, or you can walk the distance in 10 minutes. Never go via the beach.

Buses to Valencia depart every 10 or 15 minutes (US$1, 50 minutes). There are also regular buses to Tucacas (US$1, one hour), Chichiriviche (US$1.50, 1½ hours), San Felipe (US$1.25, 1½ hours), Barquisimeto (US$3, 2½ hours) and Caracas (US$4, 3½ hours).

For transport to the nearby beaches and San Esteban, see the Around Puerto Cabello section.

Train Puerto Cabello is the terminus of the only passenger railway line in Venezuela, which heads 173 km west to Barquisimeto. The railway station is 200 metres past the bus terminal, on Avenida La Paz (western extension of Calle Urdaneta). There are two trains daily on weekdays (6 am and 4 pm) and three trains on weekends and public holidays (6 and 10 am and 4 pm). The ride takes about 3½ hours with several stops and, as yet, costs only US$0.30, but this ridiculous price will probably be changed to match the bus fare.

Boat Puerto Cabello plans on opening a ferry service to Curaçao, Aruba and Bonaire (the Netherlands Antilles). Contact the tourist office for current information.

AROUND PUERTO CABELLO
Beaches

There are several beaches to the east of Puerto Cabello, off the road to Patanemo. First comes **Playa Quizandal** which is about five km from the city and a couple of km down a side road which branches off to the left. This beach is quite developed, with a car park, showers, restaurants and a drive-in cinema.

From the beach, boats can take you to **Isla Larga**, an island popular with beachgoers, swimmers and snorkellers. There are two wrecks near the island, an additional attraction for snorkellers. Food stalls are open on the weekends (and sometimes on weekdays as well) and they can stuff you with fish. Take good sun protection, as there is no shade on the island. On weekends, when there are many holidaymakers, the boat ride will cost US$2.50 return, but during the week you'll probably have to pay the fare for the whole boat, US$20 return (negotiable).

The next exit off the Patanemo road, one km beyond that to Playa Quizandal, leads to the small **Playa Huequito**. In the same place another road branches off to the right and heads to the town of Borburata. About 1½ km further on from the junction, the Patanemo road passes by the village known as **Rincón del Pirata**. This is the only place where the road runs close to the seashore, but the village is unpleasant and the beach is poor – not worth coming here.

From this point, the road winds up a coastal hill, then descends and you get to yet another turnoff (six km beyond the Rincón), which leads 1.5 km to the **Bahía de Patanemo**. This is the best beach in the area, wide and shaded by coconut palms. Fish stalls open on the weekends, but on weekdays the beach is fairly solitary. You can pitch your tent amidst the palms; bring your own food and water.

At the turnoff is a pleasant hotel, *La Churuata*, with its own restaurant, but it's overpriced at US$30/45 for a double without/with bath. The road continues half a km to the village of Los Caneyes, and 2.5 km further on it eventually reaches the village of Patanemo.

Frequent carritos run between the Puerto Cabello bus terminal and Patanemo, and will put you down at any turnoff of your choice,

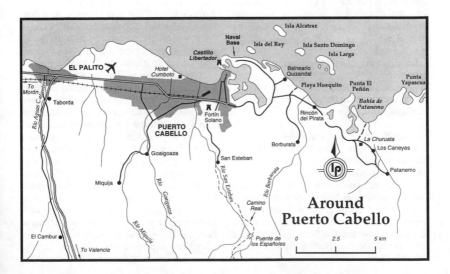

Around Puerto Cabello

within reasonable walking distance of the beach. The ride to Patanemo village takes half an hour and costs US$0.25.

San Esteban

San Esteban is a pleasant village seven km south of Puerto Cabello. It's surrounded by lush vegetation, has a more enjoyable climate than the port and boasts a couple of attractions. It's also the starting point for the Camino Real, the old Spanish trail leading south to Valencia (see the following Parque Nacional San Esteban section). Carritos to San Esteban depart regularly from the corner of Calle Mercado and Calle Anzoátegui in Puerto Cabello. They get to the bridge in San Esteban, where the road ends.

Walk south (600 metres from the bridge) along a path on the same side of the river, and you'll get to a large rock known as the Piedra del Indio, covered with petroglyphs. The rock is just next to the path, on your left.

San Esteban was the birthplace of Bartolomé Salom, one of the heroes of the War of Independence, who accompanied Bolívar all the way to Ayacucho. The house where he was born is 800 metres back along the road from the point where the carritos terminate. It has been left half-ruined, and is open for visitors from 9 am to 4 pm. Inside the main room is a life-sized statue of the general sitting in a hammock – quite an unusual sight.

Bar Club Popular near the bridge is, as it may be concluded from its name, the place to get some of the local folklore, while trying the leche de burra or the guarapita, both local alcoholic drinks.

Parque Nacional San Esteban

This national park, the western extension of Parque Nacional Henri Pittier, stretches from San Esteban southward almost to Naguanagua, on the northern outskirts of Valencia. Like its eastern neighbour, the park protects a part of the Cordillera de la Costa, but the mountains are not so high as in Carabobo state, and therefore the flora and fauna are not as diverse as they are in Parque Nacional Henri Pittier.

There's a popular trail in the park, known as the Camino Real. In colonial times, it was the main route linking Puerto Cabello with Valencia, along which goods were transported. The trail leads north-south, passing over the ridge at an altitude of about 1400 metres. You can still see traces of the cobbled Spanish road and even encounter the original Spanish bridge, the Puente de los Españoles from 1808. The trail is relatively easy, though side paths joining it may be confusing. Although the walking time between San Esteban and Naguanagua is about eight hours, count on two days to take it at a leisurely pace. There are some problems at the southern end, as the northern suburb of Naguanagua, Bárbula, is noted for armed robbery.

Many walkers departing from the northern end (San Esteban) make it just a one-day return trip by only going as far as the Spanish bridge. It's about a three-hour walk up and a two-hour walk back down. If you want to do the whole route, Bradt's *Venezuela* has all the details.

MORÓN

An undistinguished town of 60,000 people, sitting at the busy Y-junction of the roads to/from Puerto Cabello, Tucacas and San Felipe, Morón is for passing through rather than stopping. However, you may find yourself stuck here for the night if, for example, you are coming from the north and want to continue by train to Barquisimeto. If this is the case, the cheapest place to stay in town (US$7 for a matrimonial) is *Hotel Capri*, right in the centre, where all the buses stop. There are several inexpensive restaurants around. If you stop here, have a look at a unique Monument to the Mosquito, diagonally opposite the hotel. The monument, which depicts a large dead mosquito, commemorates Venezuela's achievements in the fight against malaria.

The railway station is about one km west of the mosquito, by the main road. Trains to Barquisimeto come through half an hour after their departure from Puerto Cabello. Buses run frequently in all three directions.

The North-West

Venezuela's north-west is a land of contrasts. Here you'll find such diverse natural features as coral islands and beaches (the best supposedly in Parque Nacional Morrocoy), the country's only desert (near Coro), and the largest lake in South America, Lago Maracaibo. The region combines the traditional with the contemporary, from living Indian cultures such as the Guajiros, to well-preserved colonial remains (the best are found in Coro), to the modern city of Maracaibo. Administratively, the north-west, as described in this chapter, covers the states of Lara, Yaracuy, Falcón and Zulia.

Falcón State

PARQUE NACIONAL MORROCOY

Morrocoy National Park, comprising a coastal strip and a number of cays and their coral reefs, is located some 250 km west of Caracas by road. The islands, with their white sandy beaches surrounded by turquoise sea and coral reefs, are indeed beautiful. Sadly, they have become increasingly littered. The park is also noted for its variety of water birds, including ibis, herons, cormorants, ducks, pelicans and flamingos. They inhabit, either permanently or intermittently, some of the islands, the Golfete de Cuare, coastal mangroves and lagoons. The park lies between Tucacas and Chichiriviche, these towns being its main gateways.

Tucacas is a hot town on the Valencia-Coro road with nothing to keep you here for long. Yet, with the park just a stone's throw away, the town is steadily developing into a holiday centre, and has an array of hotels and other tourist facilities. The nearest island that is a part of the park is reached over the bridge from the town's waterfront. If you want to go further into the park, go to the *embarcadero* (wharf), close to the west of the bridge, from where boats can take you for a trip along

caños (channels) through mangroves, or put you down on one of the many small islands. The most popular of these is Cayo Sombrero, which has coral reefs and some of the best beaches. Boats take up to eight people and charge the same for one as for eight. The return fare to Cayo Sombrero is around US$25. On weekdays during the off-season, you can usually beat the price down, sometimes considerably. Snorkelling gear can be rented from some boat operators and hotel owners (about US$6 per day) or from the Submatur diving shop near the wharf (see the Information section).

Another popular gateway to the park is Chichiriviche, which provides access to half a dozen neighbouring cays. The town is smaller than Tucacas but equally undistinguished and unpleasant. If you have a tent or a hammock, it's best to stay on the islands; if not, you'll be limited to one-day trips, treating the town as a dormitory. When camping on the islands, take food, water, snorkelling gear and a good insect repellent.

Boats depart from the wharf, which is at the end of Avenida Principal, the main street. Just as in Tucacas, the boat takes a maximum of eight passengers and the fare is per boat, regardless of the number of people aboard.

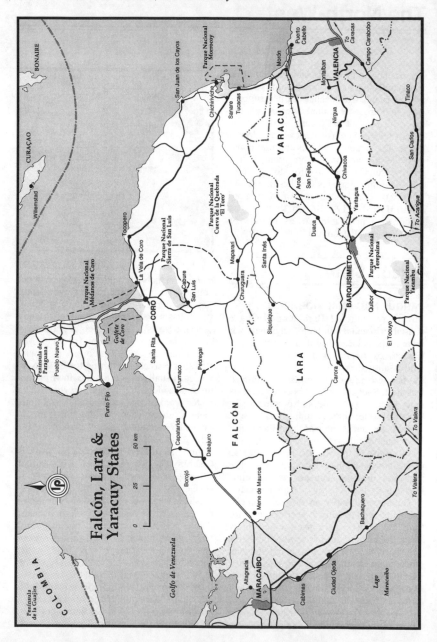

Falcón, Lara &
Yaracuy States

The return fare to the closest cays, such as Cayo Muerto, Cayo Sal or Cayo Pelón is about US$8, whereas the return fare to the furthest cays, such as Cayo Borracho, Cayo Sombrero or Cayo Pescadores, is about US$25. Haggling over the price is also possible here. You can arrange with the boatman to pick you up from the island in the afternoon or at a later date. Only pay after they have returned you to the mainland.

Information

Money There are no banks in Chichiriviche, and the only useful bank in Tucacas is Banco Unión, on Avenida Libertador, just off the Coro-Morón highway. Some up-market establishments will change your dollars at a poor rate, so it's best to come with enough bolívares.

Activities Submatur (☎ 84082, fax 831051), at Calle Ayacucho No 6 in Tucacas, between Plaza Bolívar and the wharf, is a diving centre and shop owned by Mike Osborn. The shop is well equipped with everything you could need for snorkelling or diving. Some of the equipment can be rented. The centre is run by professional, licensed diving instructors and offers a variety of services. The first day of diving includes a course and one half-hour dive, and costs US$60. Each following day (US$55) includes two dives. They also offer a five-day, intensive diving course which consists of theory (in English or French on request) and eight dives, for US$300. In both cases the equipment and boat trips are included in the price (but not accommodation or food).

Submatur also organises three-hour trips along the Río Yaracuy (US$14 per person), bird-watching excursions, yachting trips and may design a programme to suit your needs. Boat excursions to Los Roques and Las Aves are organised from time to time (US$130 per person a day, all inclusive). You can pay for their services in US dollars. Submatur is about to open an outlet in Chichiriviche, which should be operating by the time you read this.

Flamingo

Places to Stay & Eat

Tucacas The most popular place to stay among travellers is *Hotel Las Palmas* (☎ 84065), Avenida Libertador No 5, opposite Tasca La Esperanza. There's no name on the door; the place is recognisable by the 'si hay habitaciones' inscription. If you can't track it down, just ask for Carlos, the owner. You pay US$10 for a good double room with bath, and you can use the kitchen and fridge at no additional cost.

Across Avenida Libertador, Carlos' brother runs *Hotel Otidalimar*, with rooms costing much the same. Yet another place in the same area is *Hotel La Suerte*, at similar prices.

André Nahon, one of the Submatur instructors, rents out two rooms in his home (US$10 each) and also has a few hammocks (but no mosquito net) for US$3. Here, too, you can use the kitchen.

There's a choice of mid-priced and top-end hotels in Tucacas. One of these is the centrally located *Hotel Gaeta* (☎ 84414), Avenida Libertador No 34. Air-conditioned doubles/triples with bath and TV cost US$35/45.

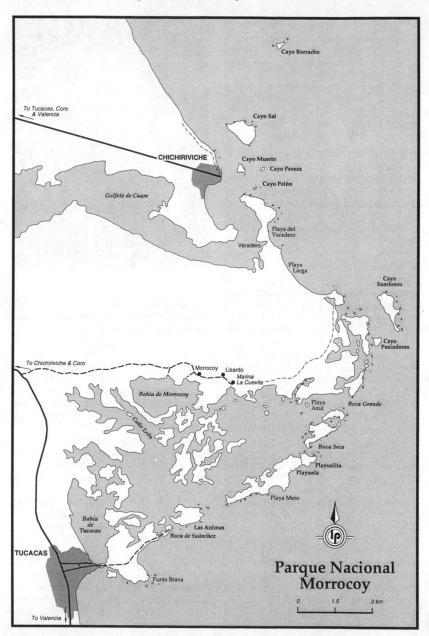

Parque Nacional Morrocoy

0   1.5   3 km

Chichiriviche There are about ten places to stay in Chichiriviche, but you probably won't find anything for less than US$12 per double. At this price, the best options seem to be the two small houses which rent out rooms and which are locally known by the names of their owners, *Delia* and *Gregoria*. They are 30 metres from each other, on Calle Mariño, the second street north of Avenida Principal.

On the Avenida itself, 100 metres from the waterfront, is the *Hotel Capri* but it's probably not worth the price of US$15/22 for a double with fan/air-conditioning. The *Panadería El Centro*, opposite the Capri, rents doubles/quadruples for US$13/18. For something better, try the pleasant *Hotel Náutico* on the seaside in the southern part of town.

The *Hotel La Garza* (☎ 86048) on Avenida Principal at the inland entrance to the town and the *Hotel Mario* (☎ 86115), just across the road, are the town's top-end accommodation options.

Some locals rent out rooms; these can be recognised by boards at the entrance that read 'se alquilan habitaciones'.

There are several unpretentious restaurants serving good fish though they are not as cheap as you might expect.

Getting There & Away
Bus Tucacas lies on the main road and there are regular buses between Valencia and Coro passing through the town.

Chichiriviche is about 22 km off the main road and there are no direct buses from either Caracas or Coro. The cheapest way of getting there from Caracas is to take any of the frequent buses to Valencia (US$2.50, 2½ hours) and change there for the equally frequent busetas to Chichiriviche (US$2.50, 2½ hours).

An alternative is to take a bus to Coro (there are about six daily), get off in Sanare where the road to Chichiriviche branches off, and catch the above-mentioned Valencia-Chichiriviche buseta (US$0.60, 20 minutes). The problem is that the bus companies serving the Caracas-Coro route charge the full fare to Coro (US$8.50) regardless of whether you go to the end of the line or only as far as Sanare, 180 km before Coro. If your Spanish is good enough, try bargaining with the driver.

If you start from Coro, take any bus to Valencia, get off in Sanare (US$2.50, three hours) and catch the Valencia-Chichiriviche buseta just as above.

The last 12-km stretch of the road to Chichiriviche runs along a causeway through mangrove swamps. This is a favourite feeding ground for flamingos, which gather here mostly between November and February, but can occasionally be spotted at other times of the year as well.

CORO
Set at the base of the curiously shaped Península de Paraguaná, Coro is the capital of Falcón state and a pleasant, peaceful town, today home to some 130,000 people. Thanks to a large university it has a noticeably cultured air. More importantly, Coro has some of the best colonial architecture to be found in the country.

Founded in 1527, it was one of the earliest towns on the continent and the first capital of the newly created Province of Venezuela. In the same year it was leased, together with the entire province, to the Welsers of Germany to conquer, settle and exploit it. The contract was made by King Carlos I of Spain who was heavily in debt to German banking firms for loans he had used to buy the title of Holy Roman Emperor, Karl V (Charles V) in 1519. The Germans were eager to share in the reputedly fabulous riches of the just discovered continent.

The Church was quick to follow and in 1531 it established the Episcopal See in Coro, the first archdiocese to be founded in the New World.

Despite this early and promising start, Coro's development bogged down right from the beginning. The town became not much more than a jumping-off point for repetitive expeditions in search of treasure, but El Dorado never materialised. In 1546 the contract with the Welsers was cancelled and the administrative seat of the province moved to El Tocuyo, 200 km to the south. The Church was more patient but finally relocated the archdiocese to Caracas in 1637.

The town almost died and was only revived by contraband trade with Curaçao and Bonaire in the 18th century. Most of the historic buildings date from that time, and are influenced by the Dutch Baroque in their architectural details.

Information

Tourist Office The main tourist office (☎ 511116) is on the pedestrian mall just north of Plaza Bolívar, but the place for information is the office a bit further north, on the opposite side of the same mall. Helpful and knowledgeable, the staff have free brochures on the town and region. The office is open Monday to Friday from 8 am to 8 pm, and on Saturday from 8 am to noon.

Inparques The Inparques office (☎ 518765) is at Calle Cabure No 5, Urbanización Urupagua. It's about two km east of the city centre, off Avenida Independencia. They can give you information on the two national parks in the state not detailed in this book: Sierra de San Luis and Cueva de la Quebrada El Toro.

Money The Banco de Venezuela will most likely exchange your dollars, and Banco Unión and Banco Consolidado will do it occasionally. The Banco Consolidado, as elsewhere, changes American Express travellers' cheques while Banco Unión services MasterCard and Visa credit cards.

Things to See

Since Coro's historic centre was declared a national monument in the 1950s, a number of old buildings have been restored and work on others is advancing slowly. The cobblestoned Calle Zamora, where most of the restoration work has been done, is the loveliest colonial-style street, and it's there that the majority of spectacular, old mansions are located.

The oldest building in town, though, is the **Catedral**. This massive, fortress-like structure was begun in the 1580s and concluded half a century later, making it just about the oldest church in Venezuela, competing for this title with the cathedral in La Asunción on the Isla de Margarita. There are no reminders of its early history inside, though the 1770 Baroque main retable is a good example of late colonial art.

One block east, the **Museo de Arte Coro**, established in a beautiful colonial house, is a branch of the Caracas Museum of Contemporary Art and, like its parent, does a good job. Exhibitions are changed regularly. The museum is open Tuesday to Saturday from 9 am to 12.30 pm and 3 to 7.30 pm, Sunday from 9 am to 4 pm.

For an insight into the colonial past, go two blocks north to the **Museo de Coro Lucas Guillermo Castillo** which has been installed in an old convent. An extensive collection of both religious and secular art from the region and beyond, including some extraordinary pieces, is displayed in 22 rooms. It's one of the best collections of its kind in the country. The museum is open Tuesday to Saturday from 9 am to noon and 3 to 6 pm, Sunday from 9 am to 1 pm; all visits are guided (in Spanish only) and the tour takes about an hour (hence, turn up at the museum at least one hour before the scheduled closing time). Next to the museum is the 18th-century **Iglesia de San Francisco**, currently under restoration after decades of neglect.

Across the street, in a barred pavilion on a small plaza, stands the **Cruz de San Clemente**. This is said to be the cross used in the first mass celebrated after the town's foundation. The cross is made from the wood of the *cují* tree, a xerophytic (adapted to dry surroundings), slow-growing species of acacia which grows in this arid region. The 18th-century **Iglesia de San Clemente**, on the western side of the plaza, was laid out on a Latin cross floor plan; it's one of only a few examples of its kind in the country. Note the anchor hanging from the middle of the ceiling, commemorating St Clement's martyrdom.

West, across the street stands the **Casa de**

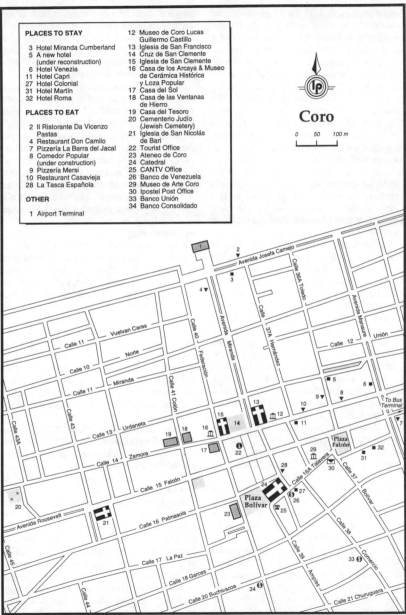

PLACES TO STAY

3 Hotel Miranda Cumberland
5 A new hotel
   (under reconstruction)
6 Hotel Venezia
11 Hotel Capri
27 Hotel Colonial
31 Hotel Martín
32 Hotel Roma

PLACES TO EAT

2 Il Ristorante Da Vicenzo
   Pastas
4 Restaurant Don Camilo
7 Pizzería La Barra del Jacal
8 Comedor Popular
   (under construction)
9 Pizzería Mersi
10 Restaurant Casavieja
28 La Tasca Española

OTHER

1 Airport Terminal

12 Museo de Coro Lucas
   Guillermo Castillo
13 Iglesia de San Francisco
14 Cruz de San Clemente
15 Iglesia de San Clemente
16 Casa de los Arcaya & Museo
   de Cerámica Histórica
   y Loza Popular
17 Casa del Sol
18 Casa de las Ventanas
   de Hierro
19 Casa del Tesoro
20 Cementerio Judío
   (Jewish Cemetery)
21 Iglesia de San Nicolás
   de Bari
22 Tourist Office
23 Ateneo de Coro
24 Catedral
25 CANTV Office
26 Banco de Venezuela
29 Museo de Arte Coro
30 Ipostel Post Office
33 Banco Unión
34 Banco Consolidado

Coro

0   50   100 m

los **Arcaya**, noted for its long, tile-roofed balconies. The mansion houses the **Museo de Cerámica Histórica y Loza Popular**, a small but interesting museum of pottery and ceramics, open during the same hours as the Museo de Coro Lucas Guillermo Castillo. At the back of the house is a cactus-filled garden, and you can also see a cují tree, the species from which Cruz de San Clemente was made. The tree is thought to be 260 years old. Opposite the house is the **Casa del Sol**, so named for the decorative sun motif over its doorway. One block west are two more carefully restored houses: the **Casa de las Ventanas de Hierro**, noted for a splendid doorway and the wrought-iron grilles (imported from Spain) across the windows, and the **Casa del Tesoro**. Both are privately owned and cannot be visited.

The **Cementerio Judío**, three blocks west along Calle Zamora, was established in the 1830s and is the oldest Jewish cemetery still in use on the continent. Jews came to Coro from Curaçao in the early 19th century, a period of intensive trade with the Dutch islands. In time, they formed a small but influential commercial community, despite the persecution of the post-independence caudillo governments. Today, there are only, at most, half a dozen Jews still living in Coro.

The cemetery was founded by Joseph Curiel (1796-1886), a rich Jewish merchant who met Bolívar in Angostura and offered him Jewish help in the cause of independence. His tomb is one of the most elaborate ones, while the grave of his 10-year-old daughter, dated 1832, is the oldest tomb in the cemetery. The Curiel family name occurs the most frequently in the cemetery.

If the cemetery is locked (as it usually is) go to the house diagonally opposite and ask for Pedro Roberto García who takes care of the cemetery. He works, so the best time to find him at home is after 5.30 pm.

North-east of the town is the **Médanos de Coro**, Venezuela's mini-Sahara, with sand dunes rising up to 40 metres. It was declared a national park in 1974. To get there from the city centre, take the city bus marked 'Carabobo' from Calle Falcón and get off

past the huge Monumento a la Federación. Then walk north for 10 minutes along a wide avenida to another public sculpture, Monumento a la Madre. A few paces north and there is nothing but sand. No permit is necessary to enter the park.

About 4.5 km west of the Monumento a la Federación, on the road to La Vela de Coro, is the **Jardín Xerófilo**. Beautiful and well-kept, this xerophytic botanical garden is definitely worth a trip. It's officially open from 8.30 to 11.30 am and 2 to 3.30 pm except Mondays, but the door-keeper lives on the premises and will probably let you in at other reasonable times of the day. To get to the garden, take the La Vela bus from Calle Falcón, anywhere east of Avenida Manaure.

Places to Stay

There are four budget hotels in the historic sector of the city. In ascending order of standard and price, they are: *Martín*, *Roma*, *Colonial* and *Capri*. They are convenient for sightseeing, and all offer simple doubles with fan and bath for about US$6 to US$8. The first two hotels are fairly basic while the last two also have air-conditioned doubles for around US$12. They are all within a couple of hundred metres of each other.

Hotel Venezia (☎ 511844), Avenida Manaure, is a better central option which offers more comfort and facilities, including TV, for US$12/22/28 for singles/doubles/triples.

Hotel Miranda Cumberland (☎ 516732), on Avenida Josefa Camejo, opposite the airport, is the best place to stay in town, with all the amenities and prices to match.

Places to Eat

There are not many restaurants or snack-bars in the city centre. Only recently, new outlets serving fast food have begun to open to fill the gap. One example is the unpretentious *Pizzería La Barra del Jacal* on Avenida Manaure, with good, inexpensive pizzas served until late.

The recently opened *Restaurant Casavieja* on Calle Zamora has reasonably priced food plus a tasty menú ejecutivo at lunch times. *La Tasca Española*, behind the cathedral, has a cheaper but less pleasant menú (though the à la carte dishes are not that cheap).

Near the airport, *Don Camilo* on Avenida Miranda does the honours and does them well. In the airport terminal itself is a good, reasonably priced restaurant (1st floor) serving meals until 4 pm.

Il Ristorante Da Vincenzo Pastas, opposite Hotel Miranda Cumberland, is one of the best restaurants in the city centre. As its name suggests, it specialises in Italian food.

Getting There & Away

Air The airport is just a five-minute walk north of the city centre. Avensa has daily flights to Caracas (US$44) and to Barquisimeto (US$32); for other domestic destinations you have to change at either of the two. You can also use Las Piedras airport, near Punto Fijo on the Paraguaná Peninsula, which is busier, but it's about 90 km from Coro. From Las Piedras, Avensa has daily flights to Aruba and Curaçao (see the Punto Fijo section for details).

From Coro airport, a small local carrier, Aero Falcón (☎ 517884), flies light planes to Aruba (US$120 return, US$140 on weekends), Curaçao (US$100 return, US$120 on weekends), and Bonaire (US$140 return, US$160 on weekends), ie if they collect a minimum of three passengers. The one-way tickets on these routes cost half the price of return fares. You can charter Aero Falcón planes to take you on other routes as well.

Bus The bus station is on Avenida Los Médanos, about two km east of the city centre, and is easily accessible by frequent city transport. Half a dozen buses run daily to Caracas (US$8.50, seven hours) and even more buses go to Maracaibo (US$5, four hours). There are two direct buses a day to Mérida (US$13.50, 12 hours) and one to San Cristóbal (US$14.75, 13 hours); all these buses go via Maracaibo. Buses to Punto Fijo run every half an hour (US$1.50, 1¼ hours). There are also a few buses a day to Adícora

on the eastern coast of Península de Paraguaná.

Boat Coro isn't on the coast. Its port, La Vela de Coro, is 12 km north-east of the city. At the time of writing there were no ferries from La Vela to Curaçao. Neither were there ferries from Punto Fijo to Aruba.

Ferrys del Caribe, the carrier which used to run these ferries, has apparently closed the business altogether. Their main office in Coro, Avenida Independencia, two blocks east of Avenida Los Médanos, has also been closed. Check for news when you get there.

Península de Paraguaná

Shaped vaguely like a human head, the Península de Paraguaná is intriguing in other ways. Its geography, history and culture are quite different from the mainland. Administratively, it's a part of Falcón state.

Once an island, a sandbar known as the Istmo de Médanos was gradually built up by wind and waves, and it continues to expand. The isthmus, together with off-shore areas, has been declared the Parque Nacional Médanos de Coro. It's a semi-desert area cut through by a freeway providing access to the peninsula. The most desert-like and spectacular area is at the base of the isthmus, just north of Coro.

Stretching some 60 km from north to south and about 50 km from east to west, covering an area of about 2500 km, Paraguaná is Venezuela's largest peninsula. It's mostly flat except for an unusual mountain, the Cerro Santa Ana (830 metres), which juts out from the middle of the peninsula. The lowland vegetation is xerophytic, featuring a number of columnar tree cactus. Only in the upper reaches of the Cerro is the plantlife lusher, including a variety of rainforest species.

The climate is dry, with a period of light rain extending from October to December. On average, there are only 40 rainy days per

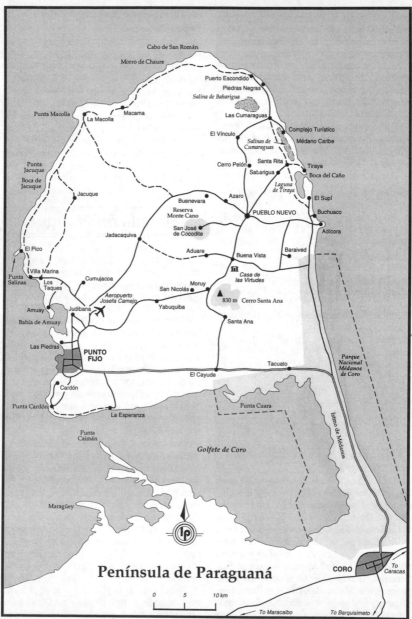

Península de Paraguaná

year. There are no permanent rivers on the peninsula.

The original inhabitants of Paraguaná were the Amuay, Guaranao and Caquetío Indians, all belonging to the Arawak linguistic family. Today these people are extinct. In 1499 Alonso de Ojeda landed at Cabo San Román on the northern tip of the peninsula. Since Dutch settlement in the 1630s on the neighbouring islands of Curaçao, Aruba and Bonaire, there has been a steady mix of the Spanish, Dutch and indigenous cultural influences. Given the considerable isolation from the main province, a distinctive local culture has evolved.

The region was never densely populated, the lack of fresh water effectively hindering development. Water was just about the most precious item on the peninsula. Today, fresh water is piped from the mainland to the whole of the peninsula.

Things began to change with the oil boom. In the 1920s an oil terminal was built in Punto Fijo, to ship oil from Lago Maracaibo overseas. Refineries were added in the 1940s and Punto Fijo boomed, becoming the largest urban centre on the peninsula, and it's still growing rapidly. The area around the city is dominated by the oil industry and criss-crossed by multi-lane highways.

The rest of the peninsula, however, hasn't rushed into progress and modernity. It's still dotted with small, old towns with their colonial churches. These are one of the biggest attractions of the peninsula. Nature reserves, created to protect the most valuable areas, are another highlight. There are also heaps of beaches on Paraguaná.

There's quite a good network of paved roads on the peninsula, except in the north-western, almost uninhabited part. Public transport is pretty regular between the larger localities, including Punto Fijo, Santa Ana, Moruy, Pueblo Nuevo and Adícora. Following the section on Punto Fijo, other points of tourist interest have been grouped into general headings dedicated to colonial towns, natural reserves and beaches. Depending on what your preference is, plan your route and itinerary accordingly.

PUNTO FIJO

The settlement of Punto Fijo only appeared on maps in 1925, following the construction of an oil terminal serving Lago Maracaibo. The building of two refineries, in Amuay and Punta Cardón, boosted the development of the young town. Today it's an industrial city of about 100,000 inhabitants, swiftly approaching the size of Coro. In some aspects Punto Fijo has already overshadowed the traditional capital. Its airport, in Las Piedras, is far busier than the one in Coro, as is trade and the way of life in general.

For tourists, Punto Fijo is of marginal interest and you can give it a miss without feeling deprived. It is, however, the only city on the peninsula and the major transportation hub. It has a range of hotels and restaurants – which are pretty scarce elsewhere on Paraguaná – so you may need to treat the city as a dormitory from where you can explore the western part of the peninsula. You may also have to stay the night in Punto Fijo if you are en route to or back from the Netherlands Antilles. Finally, if you need to rent a car to get comfortably around the region, Punto Fijo is a better place to do it than Coro.

The city centre is concentrated along two north-south streets, Avenida Bolívar and Avenida Colombia. It's in this area that most of the hotels, restaurants, banks and bus company offices are located. Plaza Bolívar is several blocks east of the centre but isn't worth a visit.

Information
Money Useful banks include Banco Unión on Calle Arismendi (cash), Banco Consolidado on the corner of Calle Falcón and Avenida Bolivia (American Express travellers' cheques and credit cards) and Banco de Venezuela on the corner of Avenida Bolivia and Calle Comercio (occasionally cash, Visa and MasterCard).

Car Rental There are a number of car rental companies in town, most of which have their offices at the airport. The Auto Amuay is possibly the largest local operator and definitely the cheapest. They can give you a

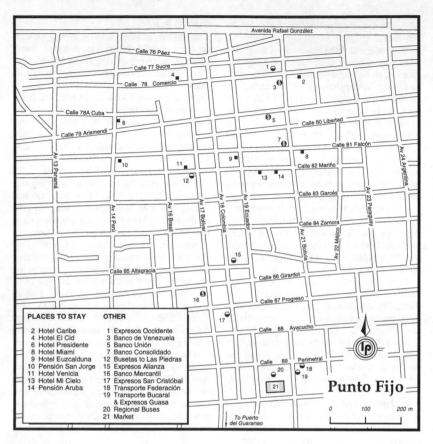

PLACES TO STAY
2 Hotel Caribe
4 Hotel El Cid
6 Hotel Presidente
8 Hotel Miami
9 Hotel Euzcalduna
10 Pensión San Jorge
11 Hotel Venicia
13 Hotel Mi Cielo
14 Pensión Aruba

OTHER
1 Expresos Occidente
3 Banco de Venezuela
5 Banco Unión
7 Banco Consolidado
12 Busetas to Las Piedras
15 Expresos Alianza
16 Banco Mercantil
17 Expresos San Cristóbal
18 Transporte Federación
19 Transporte Bucaral
    & Expresos Guasa
20 Regional Buses
21 Market

Punto Fijo

0   100   200 m

To Puerto
del Guaranao

Chevette for about US$28 a day or a 4WD Toyota for US$75, both with 200 km free mileage. A 25% discount is given if you are renting the car for seven days or more. They have their main office (☎ 463970) on the corner of Avenida Ollarvides and Calle 10, and an outlet at the airport (☎ 461497).

Places to Stay

There are quite a lot of them, but book early as they often tend to fill up with oil workers, business people, seamen etc.

Pensión Aruba, Calle Mariño No 19-138, is about the cheapest in town – US$2.50 per person – but also one of the most basic. Slightly better is *Hotel Mi Cielo*, 50 metres west on the same street (Calle Mariño No 19-24), which has singles/doubles without bath for US$3.50/5.50 and rooms with bath for marginally more.

Hotel Euzcalduna (☎ 451534), Avenida Ecuador No 18-160, is a good budget option. It has rooms from singles to quadruples without bath for US$4/5.50/7.50/9, and matrimoniales/triples with private bath for US$6.50/9.

The well-kept *Hotel Miami* (☎ 458535), Calle Falcón No 21-96, is the cheapest hotel with air-conditioned rooms, for US$8/9/10/12. It also has singles/doubles with fan, for US$6/7.

Five blocks west, on the corner of Calle Falcón and Avenida Perú, is the small, family-run *Pensión San Jorge*, which offers air-conditioned doubles for US$12.

Hotel Venicia (☎ 455743), on the corner of Calle Mariño and Avenida Bolívar, is the cheapest mid-priced option, with singles or doubles for US$14 and triples for US$16. Rooms are air-conditioned and have TV. Marginally more expensive and slightly better is *Hotel Caribe* (☎ 450421), Calle Comercio No 21-112.

Hotel El Cid (☎ 455245), on the corner of Calle Comercio and Avenida Bolívar, and *Hotel Presidente* (☎ 458964), on the corner of Avenida Perú and Calle Cuba, both have comfortable air-conditioned singles/doubles/triples for around US$18/25/30.

Getting There & Away

Air Punto Fijo's airport is in Las Piedras (and is so indicated in the air schedules), several km north-east of the city. Local busetas to the airport depart from the corner of Calle Mariño and Avenida Bolívar.

Avensa and Aeropostal have flights to Caracas (US$51 and US$47, respectively). Avensa also services other domestic destinations, including Maracaibo (US$35).

Avensa has daily flights to Aruba (US$59 one way, US$66 14-day return), and Curaçao (US$89 one way, US$130 14-day return).

Bus Punto Fijo has no central bus terminal; several bus companies have their own offices scattered throughout the city centre. Expresos Occidente have their terminal on Calle Comercio near the corner of Avenida Bolivia; Expresos Alianza are on the corner of Calle Altagracia and Avenida Colombia; and Expresos San Cristóbal's buses depart from Avenida Colombia near the corner of Calle Progreso. They all service long-distance routes, including Caracas (US$10.25, 8½ hours), Maracay (US$8.25, seven hours), Valencia (US$7.25, six hours), Maracaibo (US$6.75, 5½ hours), Mérida

(US$15.25, 14 hours) and San Cristóbal (US$16.50, 14 hours). Most of these buses depart in the afternoon or evening.

Regional buses depart from the market area, around the corner of Calle Peninsular and Avenida Ecuador. Buses to Coro (via a good 82-km freeway) run every half an hour or less, until about 6 pm (US$1.50, 1¼ hours). As far as exploring the peninsula goes, the most useful are buses to Pueblo Nuevo via the freeway, Santa Ana and Moruy, and busetas to Pueblo Nuevo via Judibana and Moruy. Both depart half-hourly from the market. Also from the same area, Transporte Bucaral and Expresos Guasa have several buses a day to Maracaibo and Cabimas, and Transporte Federación runs buses to Barquisimeto.

Boat Punto Fijo's port, Puerto del Guaranao, is about two km south of the city centre. The Punto Fijo-Aruba ferries no longer operate.

COLONIAL TOWNS

The earliest towns on the peninsula emerged not on the coast but inland, at the foot of the Cerro Santa Ana, as that was the only source of fresh water. They still preserve some of their old houses, but what is of particular interest is their churches. The most beautiful colonial churches are in Moruy, Santa Ana, Jadacaquiva and Baraived. The most interesting altar retable is without a doubt in the church of Santa Ana.

Another notable leftover from the colonial past is the number of large mansions scattered around the region, outside the towns. These were once the farmhouses of the *hatos*, large country estates. Most of them were built in the late 18th century – the period when there was intensive trade with the Netherlands Antilles – and therefore reflect the Dutch-Caribbean architectural style. The Casa de las Virtudes is possibly the best example of these mansions (see the Buena Vista section).

Pueblo Nuevo

Home to about 12,000 inhabitants, Pueblo Nuevo is the largest town on the inland portion of Paraguaná. There are still some fine colonial houses dotting the central streets. The church, dating from 1758, was remodelled in the present century. Its interior has been equipped with modern fittings, thus it has largely lost its old-time charm.

Pueblo Nuevo is apparently the only inland town with accommodation. There are two or three family homes that run informal posadas. The most reliable one is just north of the church. If they can't accommodate you, they will direct you to one of the other places. There are several restaurants in town serving inexpensive, unsophisticated meals.

Pueblo Nuevo is the usual starting point for people visiting the Monte Cano reserve which is run by Bioma. The Bioma office (☎ 81048) is a couple of blocks north-west of Plaza Bolívar, near the corner of Avenida Arévalo González and Calle Páez. It's open Monday to Friday from 8 am to noon and 2 to 6 pm.

It's relatively easy to get around the region. Buses to Punto Fijo via Santa Ana run every half an hour. There are also half-hourly busetas to Punto Fijo via Moruy and Judibana. The frequency of por puestos to Adícora depends on the demand.

Jadacaquiva
Jadacaquiva, a village 24 km west of Pueblo Nuevo, is noted for its church. This small and modest building, dating from 1749, has preserved its original retable, a fine, popular piece of art. Beneath it is a painting depicting the port of Willenstad on Curaçao. Next to the church stands a charming *campanario*, a bell tower arch supported by two columns.

Buses to Jadacaquiva depart from the front of the hospital of Pueblo Nuevo, three blocks west of Plaza Bolívar.

Buena Vista
Nine km south of Pueblo Nuevo, Buena Vista is just an ordinary, small town, not worth stopping in. However, it is worth stopping 1.5 km south of the town to see the **Casa de las Virtudes**, the best known and probably the finest old country mansion on the peninsula. The house is private and you

cannot enter; but you can see the exterior, with its characteristic Dutch-style chimney and barred windows. The house is just to the east, off the road, visible as you pass by.

Moruy
Moruy, seven km south-west of Buena Vista, is a small village worth your attention for two reasons: it's the most convenient starting point for a trip to the top of Cerro Santa Ana (see the Nature Reserves section), and it has one of the nicest colonial churches on the peninsula. Built around 1760, the church has recently been repainted and is very attractive. For photographers, the sunlight strikes its cream-coloured façade in the afternoon. The woman who lives in the white house with green barred windows, near the south-eastern corner of the church, has the keys and will probably let you in so you can see some of the old saints' images.

The village is also noted for manufacturing *silletas paraguaneras*, chairs made from cactus wood. Only the trunk of a mature cactus can be used for furniture, and – as is commonly known – the cactus grows painfully slowly. Therefore, no matter how beautiful the chairs are, the activity is creating increasing ecological havoc in the area.

There's nowhere to stay overnight in the village and not much to choose from as far as lunch goes, let alone a dinner. Busetas or/and buses run regularly to Punto Fijo, Pueblo Nuevo and Santa Ana.

Santa Ana
Set at the southern foot of the Cerro, Santa Ana is the oldest town on Paraguaná and its ancient capital. It's reputed to have existed since the 1540s when it was a Caquetío Indian settlement. The church was originally built in the 16th century – thus, it was the first church on the peninsula – and extended and remodelled at the end of the 17th century. The unusual bell tower was added around 1750. Since then the church has hardly changed and it remains one of the prettiest country churches in Venezuela. More than that, it also has one of the most

amazing retables you are likely to encounter in Venezuela.

Dating from the mid-18th century, the retable is a curious piece of popular art which features charmingly naive elements, suggesting that it was made locally. Note the decoration above the three niches of saints, on both sides of the image of St George and the Dragon. On the top is a lovely painting of the patron saint, Santa Ana. The decorative motifs on the wall around the retable were repainted in the 1960s with somewhat shocking colours, giving the whole a still more unusual air.

Except for mass on Sunday at 9 am and the occasional cleaning, the church stays locked. The priest in the Casa Parroquial, on the northern side of Plaza Bolívar, may or may not open it up for you. If you are a photographer, the best sunlight strikes the church's façade in the late afternoon.

If you plan on hiking up to Cerro Santa Ana, it's worth popping into the Inparques office, which is 100 metres north of the church, opposite Restaurant El Cují. The friendly Gloria Tovar, who runs the office, will give you all the necessary information.

There are several basic places to eat in town but nowhere to stay for the night. Buses pass by on the main road every half an hour or so, heading north to Pueblo Nuevo and south to Punto Fijo.

Adícora

The small town of Adícora (population 4500), on the eastern coast of the peninsula, is popular for its beach. Few holidaymakers are attracted by the fact that the town also has quite a bit of old architecture, particularly the picturesque Dutch-Caribbean houses.

Founded on a small headland jutting into the sea, Adícora was used in the 18th century by the Compañía Guipuzcoana as one of their trading bases, which turned it into a prosperous town. Strolling around the streets, you'll still find a dozen or so fine, brightly coloured houses from that time, characterised by their barred windows with pedestals and decorated caps.

Adícora has a choice of hotels – probably more so than any other town on the peninsula, Punto Fijo excluded – which are usually packed out with beach enthusiasts on the weekends. Most of them charge around US$15 for a room which will sleep two to three people. The price is negotiable at some places on weekdays, when there are usually no tourists.

Posada La Carantoña, installed in one of the fine old houses in the town's centre, one block back from the beach, is a pleasant place to stay. Possibly the best choice, however, is *Hotel Montecano* (☎ 88174), half a km from the waterfront along the road towards Pueblo Nuevo. Run by an Italian-Venezuelan couple, it's a very friendly place and has its own restaurant. It's the most popular hotel with foreign travellers. If it's full (as it often is), you have *Hotel Casa Blanca* just 200 metres away, but it's not much compared with the Montecano.

The majority of restaurants have gathered along the beach and most of them are only open on the weekends.

Adícora is linked to Coro by several daily buses, the last of which departs at around 4 pm.

NATURE RESERVES

Although a good part of Paraguaná is just a vast plain covered with semi-desert plant species – the most noticeable of which is the *cardón*, a columnar cactus tree – there are some areas that have quite a distinctive vegetation, or are interesting for other reasons. Most of these small enclaves are today nature reserves, worth visiting if you are wandering around the peninsula.

Cerro Santa Ana

This mountain, rising up from the plains just north of the town of Santa Ana, is probably the most interesting nature reserve and certainly the most visible: you can see it from almost any point on the peninsula. The Cerro actually has three peaks; the highest, reaching 830 metres, is the westernmost, and is dramatic from almost every angle. The summit provides spectacular views over the peninsula and beyond. The mountain along with the surrounding area (19 sq km altogether) has been declared a monumento natural and it is under the control of Inparques.

The vegetation is stratified according to altitude, with xerophytic species at the foot of the mountain and species typical of humid climates at altitudes above 500 metres in a sort of cloudforest. The latter is the most interesting area, where you can even find orchids and bromeliads.

There are two ways of getting to the top. The main route begins from Moruy and heads eastwards along an unpaved road to the camping area (a 20-minute walk to this point). From there, a proper trail heads to the highest peak (a 2½-hour walk). The path is well marked and regularly used so it's impossible to get lost.

Another starting point is the town of Santa Ana from where a rough road heads north to another camping site (a 30-minute walk). The trail which begins there leads to the lowest, eastern peak of the Cerro, then continues up westwards along the crest to the main peak. This path is not used as frequently and is fainter, but even if you lose the trail at some point, you'll always find it again. The total walking time from Santa Ana to the top is about three to four hours.

It's best to go up one way and come back by another. The peak is windy and frequently shrouded in cloud. Occasionally it rains in the upper reaches, especially between September and January, the wet months. Take a sweater and waterproof gear, just in case.

So far, access is unrestricted but Inparques intends to introduce permits, a register of walkers, and, most likely, some limitations on the number of tourists in order to prevent excessive damage to the habitat. They also plan on providing a guide service and building sanitary facilities at their camping grounds. Contact their office in Santa Ana for details (see the Santa Ana section).

Monte Cano

Monte Cano is one of the biological reserves run by Bioma (Fundación Venezolana para la Conservación de la Diversidad Biológica). The foundation was created in 1986 and today has several reserves in the states of Falcón, Mérida and Apure.

Monte Cano lies about 15 km north of Cerro Santa Ana and encompasses 16 sq km. Its research station is in San José de Cocodite, which is accessible by a side road branching off to the west from Pueblo Nuevo-Buena Vista road two km south of Pueblo Nuevo.

The reserve protects the only remaining lowland forest on the peninsula. Surprisingly enough, this small area features 62% of the plant species of Falcón state, including such curiosities as the *barba de palo* (also called *barba de viejo*), a kind of tillandsia. This epiphytic plant that forms spectacular, transparent curtains of foliage is typical of humid areas, but appears here in a semi-arid region.

The reserve is open to visitors Wednesday to Sunday. Arrive early to avoid the heat of the day. Once in the station, the guides will take you around a part of the reserve. They can also show you videos on the subject. Plan to spend up to four hours for the visit. The entrance fee is US$1.20.

There's no public transport to the station. Contact the Bioma office in Pueblo Nuevo (see the Pueblo Nuevo section) for information and help. The station doesn't offer accommodation or food but it's possible to camp.

Lagunas & Salinas

About 10 km north of Adícora is the **Laguna de Tiraya** connected with the sea by **Boca de Caño**. This is the area where flamingos feed, from November to January, but you can be pretty sure of finding smaller or larger numbers of them almost all year round.

Getting to the lagoon is not that straightforward, as there is no public transport. Walking is one option, hitching is another, though the traffic is mainly on weekends, at other times it's pretty sporadic.

From Adícora, take the road to El Supí and turn to the left onto a dirt road that branches off to the west four km north of Adícora. This road leads to Santa Rita, and skirts the lagoon. The flamingos may be quite close to shore or off in the distance, on the opposite, eastern side of the lagoon.

Several km further north, between Santa Rita and Las Cumaraguas, are the **Salinas de Cumaraguas**, where salt is mined using rudimentary methods.

A few km north-west of Las Cumaraguas are the **Salinas de Bajarigua**, which are also feeding grounds for flamingos; at times they attract an even larger colony of them than Laguna Tiraya. There's public transport on a paved road from Las Cumaraguas to Pueblo Nuevo via El Vínculo.

All in all, this is a pleasant, somewhat adventurous one-day trip but be prepared for the heat and don't forget to take a hat. If you have more time or your own transport, you can explore the region further north as far as **Cabo de San Román**, the northernmost point of Venezuela.

BEACHES

The beaches on Paraguaná are not particularly wonderful if one compares them to those of Morrocoy or Henri Pittier, but they do exist. They usually lack shade, as coconut palms are a rare sight here. Like all other beaches in Venezuela, they are quiet on weekdays, and swamped by people on the weekends.

The beaches on the eastern coast stretch almost all the way from Adícora to Piedras Negras. **Adícora** is probably the most popular beach resort, followed by **El Supí** and **Buchuaco**. **Tiraya** is less frequented by holidaymakers, as it's harder to get there.

Several km north of Tiraya is the **Complejo Turístico Médano Caribe**, the best tourist complex on the peninsula, offering accommodation, food, swimming pools and, obviously, the beach. You can stay in their expensive hotel, or just come for the day (entrance fee US$3) and use their facilities. There's no public transport to the complex.

On the west coast, the popular beaches are **Amuay**, **Villa Marina** and **El Pico**, all serviced by local transport from Punto Fijo.

Lara & Yaracuy States

BARQUISIMETO

With its population of about 700,000, Barquisimeto is Venezuela's fourth largest city, after Caracas, Maracaibo and Valencia. It's the capital of Lara state and an important commercial, industrial and transport centre. Set at an altitude of 550 metres, the city has a warm, relatively dry climate with a mean temperature of 24°C.

Initially founded in 1552 on the Río Buría, Barquisimeto was moved three times before it was eventually established at its present-day location in 1563. Its growth was slow, as the Indian tribes in the region were particularly fierce in defending their territory. The 1812 earthquake demolished most of the town.

Like almost every large city in Venezuela, the rush to modernise in recent decades has been intensive and indiscriminate and consequently a death sentence was handed to many of the Spanish structures which had somehow managed to survive the earthquake.

Today Barquisimeto is a predominantly modern city dotted with a number of shady parks and plazas. However, neither its modern aspect nor its scarce old relics justify a special trip to the city. Tourist attractions are few and of rather modest interest. On the other hand, there are some interesting places around Barquisimeto, for which the city may be a jumping-off point.

Information

Tourist Office Dirección de Turismo (☎ 537544) is in Edificio Fundalara on Avenida Libertador opposite La Televisora Niños Cantores. It's over two km north-east of the centre, beyond Parque Bararida.

Inparques The Inparques office (☎ 545065, 542366) is located on Avenida Libertador opposite the Complejo Ferial. Contact them for information about Terepaima and Yacambú, two national parks near Barquisimeto.

Money Most of the major banks are on Avenida 20 (the main commercial street in the centre) and – nice surprise – most are useful. Cash can be exchanged in Banco Unión, Banco Latino, Banco Construcción, Banco de Venezuela and Banco Federal. Banks which service credit cards include Banco Unión (Visa and MasterCard), Banco Maracaibo (Visa), Banco Construcción (Visa), Banco de Venezuela (Visa and MasterCard), Banco Mercantil (Visa and MasterCard) and Banco Consolidado (American Express). The Banco Consolidado changes American Express travellers' cheques. Turisol (☎ 518634, 518734) is in Edificio Hotel Hevelin, Planta Baja, Local 1, Avenida Vargas between Carreras 21 and 22.

Things to See
The **Plaza Bolívar**, the original centre of the city, adorned with yet another replica of the Bolívar statue in Caracas, is now lined with modern edifices except for the **Iglesia de la Concepción** on the southern side of the square. This was Barquisimeto's first cathedral, but it was destroyed in the earthquake of 1812 and reconstructed 30 years later in an altered style.

A few steps south of the church is the **Museo de Barquisimeto**, located in a large building with a rectangular courtyard and a chapel in the middle. It was erected in 1918 as a hospital and performed this function until 1954. It was then used for various purposes until 1977, when authorities decided to demolish it to make way for modern buildings. Thanks to public protests it was restored and turned into a museum which now features temporary exhibitions. It's open Tuesday to Friday from 9 am to noon and 3 to 6 pm, Saturday to Sunday from 10 am to 5 pm.

Plaza Lara, two blocks east of Plaza Bolívar, is apparently the only area in the city with a noticeably old-style appearance. Some of the buildings lining the square have been restored to their original colonial style. One of them, on the eastern side of the plaza, is now the **Centro Histórico Larense** and it displays archaeological and art collections.

The **Iglesia de San Francisco**, on the southern side of the plaza, was built in 1865 and did the honours as the second cathedral, until the modern **Catedral** was constructed in the 1960s on the corner of Avenida Venezuela (Carrera 26) and Avenida Simón Rodríguez (Calle 29). Quite an innovative design, the curving parabolic roof has, unfortunately, already blackened considerably. The cathedral is only open for mass (several times on Sunday, at 6 pm on weekdays) so plan accordingly if you want to see its centrally located high altar.

Possibly the most interesting park in the city is the **Parque Bararida** on the northeastern outskirts of the centre, which has botanical and zoological gardens.

Places to Stay
There are half a dozen undistinguished budget hotels on the northern side of the bus terminal, including *El Terminal*, *El Peregrino*, *Santa Lucía* and *Santa María*. If you need something better in the bus terminal area, the closest decent place, *Hotel Villa Lara* (☎ 461621, 463141), is on the corner of Avenida Rómulo Gallegos and Carrera 21, two blocks south of the terminal. Expect to pay US$15/22/28 for couple/double/triple in comfortable air-conditioned rooms with bath, hot water and TV.

In the city centre, one of the cheapest is the simple *Pensión España*, Calle 30 No 21-80. A double room without bath should cost around US$4, though the manager may ask for more once he sees your gringo face. For slightly more you can have private bath and air-conditioning in the basic *Hotel La Giralda*, Avenida 20 between Calles 36 and 37.

Hotel del Centro (☎ 314524, 315346) on Avenida 20 near the corner of Calle 26 is the cheapest hotel in the vicinity of Plaza Bolívar and probably the best value for your money. Clean and spacious doubles/triples with fan and bath cost US$8/9 while air-conditioned doubles/triples/quadruples go for US$9/10/11.

Hotel Lido (☎ 315568, 315279) at Carrera 16 No 26-92, one block west of Plaza

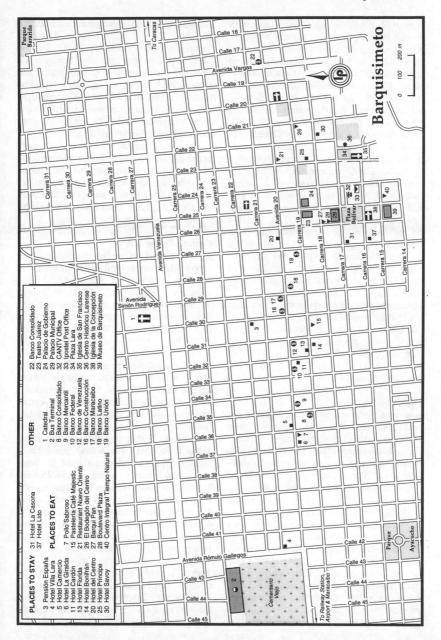

PLACES TO STAY

3   Pensión España
4   Hotel Villa Lara
5   Hotel Camercio
6   Hotel La Giralda
11 Hotel Cardón
13 Hotel Florida
14 Hotel Bonifrán
20 Hotel del Centro
25 Hotel Príncipe
30 Hotel Savoy
31 Hotel La Casona
37 Hotel Lido

PLACES TO EAT

7   Pollo Sabroso
15 Pastelería Café Majestic
21 Restaurant Nuevo Oriente
26 El Bodegón del Centro
27 Barqui Pan
28 Boulevard Plaza
40 Centro Integral Tiempo Natural

OTHER

1   Catedral
2   Bus Terminal
8   Banco Consolidado
9   Banco Mercantil
10 Banco Federal
12 Banco de Venezuela
16 Banco Construcción
17 Banco Maracaibo
18 Banco Latino
19 Banco Unión
22 Banco Consolidado
23 Teatro Juárez
24 Palacio de Gobierno
29 Palacio Municipal
32 CANTV Office
33 Ipostel Post Office
34 Plaza Lara
35 Iglesia de San Francisco
36 Centro Histórico Larense
38 Iglesia de la Concepción
39 Museo de Barquisimeto

Barquisimeto

Bolívar, is a small, good place to stay with air-conditioning and TV. Rooms with one double bed cost US$9, and with two beds US$17. Similar in price and standards, and apparently run by the same management, is *Hotel Savoy* (☎ 315134) on Carrera 18 between Calles 21 and 22. One more place, offering pretty much the same standards, is the *Hotel La Casona* (☎ 315311, 317151), on the corner of Carrera 17 and Calle 27.

There is a range of reasonably-priced hotels on Avenida 20 and Carrera 19 between Calles 30 and 36, including *Hotel Comercio* (☎ 328520) on Avenida 20 near the corner of Calle 36 (US$9/12 single/double with fan, add US$2 for air-conditioning); *Hotel Cardón* (☎ 329963) on Calle 32 off Avenida 20 (US$8/14/19 single/double/triple with air-conditioning and TV); and the best of the lot, *Hotel Florida* (☎ 329804) on Carrera 19 between Calles 31 and 32 (US$12/16/19 single/double/triple with air-conditioning and TV).

Among the best hotels in the city centre are *Hotel Bonifrán* (☎ 320302, 322434) on the corner of Carrera 19 and Calle 31 (US$31/40/45 single/double/triple), and the marginally more expensive *Hotel Príncipe* (☎ 312111, 312544) on Calle 23 between Carreras 18 and 19.

Places to Eat

A row of basic restaurants on Carrera 24, next to the bus terminal, will keep you going if you're waiting for a bus.

One of the cheapest places to eat in the city centre (open until about 9 pm) is the Chinese *Restaurant Nuevo Oriente* on Avenida 20 near the corner of Calle 23, which also serves grilled chicken. Another place for chicken is the *Pollo Sabroso* on the corner of Avenida 20 and Calle 36. The *Hotel La Casona* runs an inexpensive restaurant and the food is OK. *Boulevard Plaza* on Calle 26, one block north of Plaza Bolívar, is essentially a place for snacks, juices etc, but serves a good menu ejecutivo at lunch times.

Reputedly the best central place for an inexpensive vegetarian lunch (from noon to 2 pm only) is the *Centro Integral Tiempo Natural* on Carrera 15 between Calles 24 and 25.

Barqui Pan, corner of Calle 26 and Carrera 18, is possibly the best central panadería and, unusually enough, it has tables outside – a good place for a breakfast or just a cup of coffee. *Pastelería Café Majestic*, Carrera 19 between Calles 30 and 31, is an alternative if you want to have your pastries and coffee at the table.

There are not many up-market restaurants in the city centre and most of these are to be found in the eastern part of the centre, towards Avenida Vargas and beyond. *El Bodegón del Centro*, corner of Carrera 19 and Calle 21, has a good choice of seafood, though it is a bit pricey.

Getting There & Away

Air The airport is four km south-west of the centre. There are several departures a day to Caracas (US$44 with Aeropostal, US$47 with Avensa), two to San Antonio del Táchira (US$45 with Aeropostal, US$53 with Avensa), and one to each of Coro (US$32), Maracaibo (US$40) and Mérida (US$52).

Bus Barquisimeto is a genuine transport hub, with roads (and accordingly buses) leading in all directions. The bus terminal is on the north-western outskirts of the centre and buses go there frequently from the city centre. There are regular connections to Caracas (US$6.50, 5½ hours) and Maracaibo (US$6.50, five hours). Two buses nightly depart to Mérida (US$8.75, eight hours) and to San Cristóbal (US$9.25, nine hours). Transporte Federación runs buses to Coro every other hour (US$7, seven hours). There are also buses to Valera (US$4.25), Trujillo (US$4), Guanare (US$3.25) and Barinas (US$5). Buses within the region run frequently.

Train The only passenger railway in the country links Barquisimeto with Puerto Cabello, via Chivacoa and Morón. Neither the train itself (diesel-powered) nor the route is a particular attraction but the ride costs next to nothing: US$0.30 for the whole stretch.

Trains depart daily from both ends at 6 am and 4 pm and there's an additional departure at 10 am on weekends and holidays. The ride takes 3½ hours. The train stops at a dozen or so intermediate stations.

The railway station is on the north-western outskirts of Barquisimeto. There is no urban transport to the station. Go to El Obelisco and walk north for 10 minutes to the station.

CHIVACOA

Chivacoa, an ordinary town about 60 km east of Barquisimeto on the road to Valencia, is the jumping-off point for the holy mountain of María Lionza, where a mysterious cult is practised.

One of the most astonishing quasi-religious phenomena on the continent, the Cult of María Lionza is a strange amalgam of pre-Hispanic indigenous creeds, African voodoo and Christian practices. It involves magic, witchcraft, esoteric rites and trance rituals.

The origins of the cult are obscure and there isn't much information, except for sensational news stories. So far, there hasn't been much done in terms of serious studies of the cult. What is clear, however, is that the cult attracts more and more followers every day and spiritual centres proliferate in cities throughout the country. The 'guides', or intermediaries, who run these centres, claim to be able to communicate with deities and spirits, heal the sick, read the future and the like. In search of new inspirations – or in order to give more colour and mystery to the cult – some guides adopt ideas and rites from occult cults from other parts of the world such as India, Japan and the Philippines. Consequently, the cult vocabulary is dotted with a plethora of exotic terms like 'karma', 'reincarnation', 'yoga', 'transmigration of souls' etc. These practices only make the María Lionza cult even more confusing, obscure and difficult to investigate.

The cult is pantheistic and involves a constellation of deities, spirits and other personalities with very diverse origins, the number of which is growing year by year. On the top of the hierarchy stands María Lionza, a female deity, usually portrayed as a beautiful woman riding a tapir. La Reina, or Queen – as she is commonly referred to – is followed by countless divinities: historical or legendary personages, saints, powers of nature etc, usually grouped into *cortes* or courts. The list of the most popular deities includes Cacique Guaicaipuro, Negro Primero, Virgen de Coromoto, Negro Felipe and Dr José Gregorio Hernández. For many followers, Hernández is the second in importance after the Reina. See La Candelaria section in the Caracas chapter for more about him.

Although the María Lionza cult is practised throughout Venezuela, its most sacred area and the centre for pilgrimages is the mountain range stretching east-west, several km south of Chivacoa. Devotees come here to practice their rites all year round, mostly on weekends. The biggest celebrations, drawing in thousands of faithful, are held on 12 October, El Día de la Raza (Discovery of America), and during the Semana Santa, or the Holy Week. Inparques has declared the mountain a monumento natural, supposedly to protect the region rather than for any religious reasons.

Several sanctuaries have emerged along the northern foothill of the range, where pilgrims flock before heading up the mountain. The most important of these are Sorte, the earliest and traditional spiritual base for believers, and Quiballo (or Quivayo) which is larger and more tolerant of sporadic visits from tourists. Both have their own Altar Mayor where the initial celebrations are performed before the group and its medium head off to the shrine of their choice, one of any number that are scattered all over the forest. It's at these shrines that the proper rites are performed, and they may last the whole night or longer, and usually include a trance seance.

You'll get your first taste of the cult in Chivacoa. The most characteristic feature of this otherwise undistinguished town is its unusual number of *perfumerías*, shops which sell everything imaginable that is related to the cult. Here you'll find an extensive collection of books and brochures dealing with magic, witchcraft, reading the future and the like, cigars and candles (indispensable ritual accessories), and an unbelievable choice of essences, perfumes, lotions etc. Here you can also familiarise yourself with the cult's pantheon, as every shop has a complete stock of plaster figures of the deities in every size and colour.

The next step is to go to one of the sanctuaries at the foot of the mountain. If you just want to kill your curiosity go to Quiballo which is the largest (so it has the most frequent transport) and it's the most accustomed to casual visitors.

Quiballo is just a collection of several dozen shabby shacks which are either perfumerías or overpriced places to eat. The Altar Mayor is set on the bank of the river. It boasts a bizarre collection of figures which you'll already have seen in Chivacoa – portraits of Bolívar, various Indian caciques, and numerous images of María Lionza herself. Candles are always lit and the faithful sit in front and smoke cigars. The Inparques office is 30 metres from the altar.

From the altar a path goes over the bridge to the other bank of the river (in which the faithful perform ritual ablutions) and then up to the top of the mountain. All the way along the path are *portales* (literally 'gates') which are shrines dedicated to particular deities or spirits. On the top itself, there are Las Tres Casitas (the Three Little Houses) of Cacique Guaicaipuro, Reina María Lionza and Negro Felipe. A sketch map of the route and portales is posted on the side of the Altar Mayor. Technically, the trip to the top takes three hours, but...

Followers of the cult point out that the trip to the top is full of drawbacks. At each portal you have to ask the respective spirit for 'permission' to pass by. This is done by smoking cigars, lighting candles and presenting offerings. Permission may or may not be granted. One of the devotees commented that he had tried several times on

various occasions and hadn't succeeded. Those who continue on without a permit may be punished by the spirits. Some, so local stories claim, have never returned.

Inparques has a far more rational standpoint. They don't recommend the trip to the summit because of the muddy paths, snakes and because you might get lost in the maze of side paths.

There's one more drawback to this hike. Like any place that attracts crowds of people, it attracts thieves and robbers. Some robberies on the mountain have been reported. Try not to venture too far on your own and keep your wits about you. The question of how much or how little you are going to comply with the spirits' wishes is up to you.

Wandering around, especially on weekends, you may come across a group of faithful practising their rituals. Keep away unless you're invited or unless you are with a guide who will introduce you.

Reading

There's not much literature about the cult, and most of what does exist focuses on selected aspects, mainly trance practices, without giving the whole picture. Possibly the best is *María Lionza, Mito y Culto Venezolano* by Angelina Pollak-Eltz (Universidad Católica Andrés Bello, Caracas, 1985). Written by someone who spent over 25 years studying the cult, the book is a compendium of information about the cult's origin, doctrines, ceremonies and deities. It's hard to get this book except in some good bookshops in Caracas.

Places to Stay

Chivacoa has a choice of places to stay, including *Hotel Abruzzese*, Avenida 9 between Calles 10 and 11, *Hotel Venezia*, corner of Calle 12 and Avenida 9, and *Hotel Leonardo*, corner of Calle 11 and Avenida 9. All are reasonably priced and within a couple of blocks of Plaza Bolívar. There are no hotels in either Sorte or Quiballo, but you can camp in the forest, as many pilgrims do.

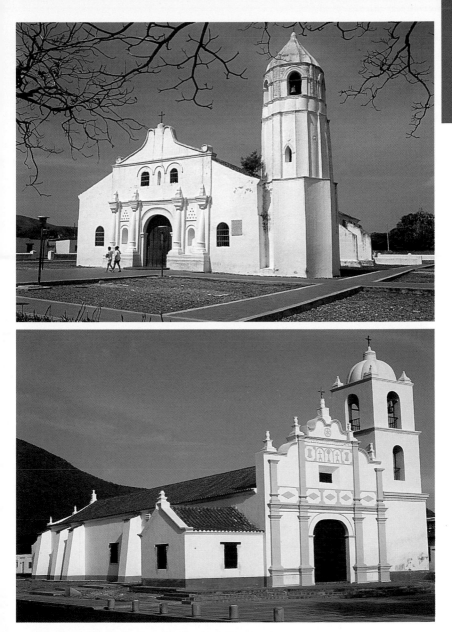

Top: Church in Santa Ana, Península de Paraguana
Bottom: Church in Moruy, Península de Paraguana

Top Left: Old street, Maracaibo
Top Right: Capilla del Calvario, Carora
Bottom: Image of María Lionza, Quiballo

Getting There & Away

There are plenty of buses between Barquisimeto and Valencia, and between Barquisimeto and San Felipe, and all will put you down on the main road on the northern outskirts of Chivacoa, a 10-minute walk to Plaza Bolívar.

There are also buses from Barquisimeto to Chivacoa (marked 'Chivacoa Directo') which will deposit you at the Plaza Bolívar next to the church. They run frequently, cost US$1, and the ride takes a little less than one hour.

Jeeps to Quiballo depart when full from Plaza Bolívar (US$0.80, 20 minutes). They run frequently on weekends but there may be only a few departures on weekdays. Jeeps to Sorte (US$0.70, 15 minutes), are even less frequent. The jeeps travel four km south on a good paved road to a large ceiba in the middle of the road, then turn right onto a rough road and continue on through sugarcane plantations for another four km to Quiballo. The road to Sorte branches off to the left one km past the ceiba.

EL TOCUYO

The town of Nuestra Señora de la Pura y Limpia Concepción del Tocuyo was founded in 1545 in a verdant valley of the Río Tocuyo. Two years later it became the capital of the province of Venezuela, after the authorities moved here from Coro, following the revocation of the contract with the Welsers and the departure of the Germans. El Tocuyo remained the capital until 1577 (when the capital was transferred to Caracas), and over that time it evolved into a graceful colonial town. Despite its political downgrading, the town continued to grow, taking advantage of its fertile soil, which was ideal for growing sugarcane and a variety of vegetables. Over the centuries, seven imposing churches and a number of spacious mansions were built.

Unfortunately, a serious earthquake in 1950 damaged a good number of the buildings. The job was completed by Coronel Marcos Pérez Jiménez, Venezuela's dictator of the time. On his orders, the structures were demolished and a new town was built on the site.

Today, El Tocuyo is just an ordinary town of some 45,000 people. The only important monument related to colonial times is the **Iglesia de Nuestra Señora de la Concepción**, two blocks west of Plaza Bolívar. It shared the fate of most other buildings and was bulldozed (despite the fact that it could have been repaired), and was later reconstructed.

The church's exterior is noted for its exceptional bell tower and fine façade. Inside, the splendid retable from the 1760s (which fortunately survived the earthquake) takes up the whole wall behind the high altar. Like almost all altarpieces of the period, it was carved entirely out of wood but, unusually, it was not painted or gilded, and is the only one of its kind in the country. Look around the interior and you'll see other relics from the colonial past, among them the original pulpit.

The most attractive place to stay (although it's not that cheap) is the *Posada Colonial* (☎ 62403, 62405), on the corner of Avenida Fraternidad and Carrera 8. For something cheaper, try the *Florida* (☎ 61112) or *Nazaret* (☎ 62434), both on Avenida Fraternidad.

Buses between Barquisimeto and El Tocuyo run at least every half an hour (US$1, 1½ hours).

QUIBOR

If you decide to take a day trip from Barquisimeto to El Tocuyo, it's worth stopping off midway in Quibor. This old town, 75 years younger than El Tocuyo, has preserved much more of its colonial fabric, and has some interesting old buildings, including the 17th-century **Ermita de Nuestra Señora de Altagracia**, a fortress-like church on the northern edge of the town.

Another attraction in the town is the museum of the **Centro Antropológico** which features some pre-Hispanic pottery which was excavated a few decades ago at the old Indian cemetery beneath the Plaza Bolívar.

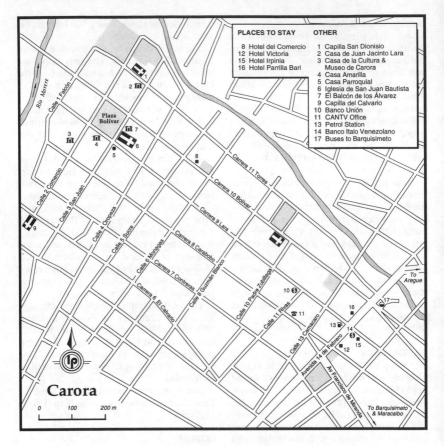

PLACES TO STAY	OTHER
8 Hotel del Comercio	1 Capilla San Dionisio
12 Hotel Victoria	2 Casa de Juan Jacinto Lara
15 Hotel Irpinia	3 Casa de la Cultura &
16 Hotel Parrilla Bari	Museo de Carora
	4 Casa Amarilla
	5 Casa Parroquial
	6 Iglesia de San Juan Bautista
	7 El Balcón de los Álvarez
	9 Capilla del Calvario
	10 Banco Unión
	11 CANTV Office
	13 Petrol Station
	14 Banco Italo Venezolano
	17 Buses to Barquisimeto

Carora

0   100   200 m

CARORA

About 100 km west of Barquisimeto, on the road to Maracaibo, lies Carora, the second largest town in the state, now approaching 90,000 inhabitants. Founded in 1569 on the banks of the Río Morere, the town has experienced several serious floods, the last one in 1973. Despite considerable damage, Carora has preserved a good deal of its colonial architecture. The historic centre has recently been extensively restored, and it's well worth a visit.

The town's main thoroughfares are Avenida Francisco de Miranda and Avenida 14 de Febrero. It's here that most of the shops, offices, hotels and restaurants are located. The historic sector is about one km to the north-west, close to the river. The town is small enough to get around it on foot, and there are micros linking its old and new sectors.

Information

Money The Banco Unión is on the corner of Carrera 9 (Lara) and Calle 11 (Rivas), while the Banco Consolidado is on Avenida Francisco de Miranda, a 10-minute walk south from Avenida 14 de Febrero.

Things to See

The old part of the town, around Plaza Bolívar, is neat, well kept and colonial in style, though not all the buildings date from that period. The more interesting houses have been clearly labelled. Have a look at **Casa Amarilla**, the oldest surviving house in town (mid-17th-century), now a public library; **El Balcón de los Álvarez**, a house from the 18th century where Bolívar stayed in 1821; and **Casa de la Cultura** which houses the modest **Museo de Carora** with its archaeological collection.

The town's churches are particularly beautiful. The **Iglesia de San Juan Bautista** on Plaza Bolívar was built in the middle of the 17th century and the exterior is original. It's open early in the morning and late afternoon, and someone from the Casa Parroquial, just across the street from the church, may open it for you at other times.

The **Capilla del Calvario**, three blocks south-west of Plaza Bolívar, has one of the most amazing façades in Venezuela, an extraordinary example of local Baroque. The third church, the **Capilla San Dionisio**, one block north-east of Plaza Bolívar, is in the final stage of restoration.

Places to Stay & Eat

There are three hotels on Avenida 14 de Febrero, all located within two blocks of the setting-down stop for buses arriving from Barquisimeto. The cheapest is *Hotel Victoria*, on the corner of Carrera 8 (Carabobo). It's rather basic but has a certain charm thanks to two huge mango trees growing in its tiny patio. Be careful as the fruits tend to fall unexpectedly. Doubles with bath and fan cost around US$6.

If you need air-conditioning go to *Hotel Parrilla Bari*, where doubles go for US$10. You can eat in the hotel's restaurant. The best of the lot is *Hotel Irpinia* (☎ 32362, 32322), behind the Banco Italo Venezolano. Comfortable singles/doubles with bath and air-conditioning cost US$14/16. There are several restaurants on and around Avenida 14 de Febrero.

There are no hotels in the historic quarter.

The closest is the basic *Hotel del Comercio*, Carrera 10 (Bolívar) No 5-47. Rooms with a double bed and fan/air-conditioning cost US$5/6. Be warned: the hotel's cervecería (bar) likes to play music at full volume until late.

Getting There & Away

Carora lies a couple of km off the Barquisimeto-Maracaibo road and long-distance buses don't call there. There are two buses (US$1.20) and about 10 busetas (US$1.70) a day between Barquisimeto and Carora. The trip takes 1½ hours on a good autopista across arid, hilly countryside. In Carora, buses park on the corner of Avenida 14 de Febrero and Carrera 10 (Bolívar).

Zulia State

MARACAIBO

Although the region was explored as early as 1499 and Maracaibo was founded in 1574, the town only really began to grow in the 18th century as the result of trade with the Netherlands Antilles. The republicans' naval victory over the Spanish fleet, fought on Lago Maracaibo on 24 July 1823, brought the town some political importance. It was not, however, until the 1920s that the oil boom took off and the city developed into Venezuela's oil capital, with nearly three-quarters of the nation's output coming from beneath the lake.

With a population of about 1.2 million people, Maracaibo is today the country's largest urban centre after Caracas, and it's a predominantly modern, prosperous city. It's the capital of Zulia, Venezuela's richest state, and it's also an important port. Its climate is hot and humid, with an average temperature of 29°C. The region around the city preserves some of its original culture and way of life. The Guajiros to the north and the Yukpa (also known as the Motilones) to the west are amongst the most traditional Indian groups in the country. Maracaibo is probably the only city in Venezuela where you can still see

Indians in their native dress, particularly the Guajiro women in their traditional *mantas*, or colourful long loose dresses, their *alpargatas*, or sandals with giant pompoms, and sometimes with their faces painted with a dark pigment.

Maracaibo has no 'must see' attractions in the city. However, you may need to stop here on the way to the Colombian coast, or you may just want to catch a glimpse of what an oil capital is really like. Like any city of its size, Maracaibo offers both minor sights and tourist facilities, and you may even find it interesting and agreeable, despite the unbearable heat. Maracuchos, as local inhabitants are called, have a more regional outlook than other Venezuelans, with certain separatist tendencies emerging amongst some local government circles and influential groups. They feel that the state produces the country's money but the rest of the country spends it.

With more time, you can explore the surrounding region which offers a range of contrasting attractions, from a community living in houses built on stilts on Sinamaica Lagoon to forests of oil derricks on Lago Maracaibo (see the Around Maracaibo section).

Information

Tourist Office The Corpozulia tourist office (☎ 921811, 921840, 921835) is in the high, modern Edificio Corpozulia on Avenida Bella Vista between Calles 83 and 84. It's about two km north of the city centre; the Bella Vista por puestos from Plaza Bolívar will take you there. The office is open Monday to Friday from 8.30 am to 4.30 pm, though it's better to avoid the period between noon and 1 pm as the staff take their lunch break then. It's worth visiting them if you plan on exploring the city and the region in more detail, as the staff are knowledgeable, and they'll give you a city map which is almost unobtainable elsewhere.

Inparques The Inparques office (☎ 919481) is in Parque Paseo El Lago, Avenida El Milagro.

Money Most main banks are just south of Plaza Bolívar, and they are marked on the map. The Banco Mercantil and Banco de Venezuela change cash while the Banco Consolidado exchanges American Express travellers' cheques. The Banco Unión and the Banco de Venezuela pay advances on Visa and MasterCard.

Turisol (☎ 921833, 921861, 922365) is in Edificio La Guajira, Torre Norte, Planta Baja, Locales 2 and 3, Avenida Bella Vista, corner of Calle 67 (Cecilio Acosta).

Things to See

If you are caught in Maracaibo en route, you probably won't go far beyond the downtown area, the oldest part of the city. Most of the tourist sights are here, a short walk apart. The axis of this sector is the **Paseo de las Ciencias**, a seven-block-long and one-block wide green belt made after demolishing old buildings and establishing a park on the site. This controversial plan was executed in 1973 and it effectively cut the heart out of the old town. The only structure left behind is the **Iglesia de Santa Bárbara** in the middle of the Paseo. The park itself has been dotted with fountains which were once illuminated at night, and embellished with modern works by contemporary artists, including one by Jesús Soto. Unfortunately, none of the fountains works any more and the sculptures are gradually being vandalised.

Beyond the western end of the Paseo stands the **Basílica de Chiquinquirá**, with its opulent, although somewhat hotch-potch interior decoration. The most venerated image is the Virgin of Chiquinquirá, affectionately referred to as La Chinita, which is in the high altar. Legend has it that the image of the Virgin, painted on a small wooden board, was found in 1709 by a humble campesina on the shore of Lago Maracaibo and it began to glow after she brought it home. It was then taken to the church and miracles started to happen. In 1942 the Virgin was crowned as the patron saint of Zulia state.

The image of the Virgin is accompanied by San Andrés and San Antonio. The image is hardly recognisable from a distance. You

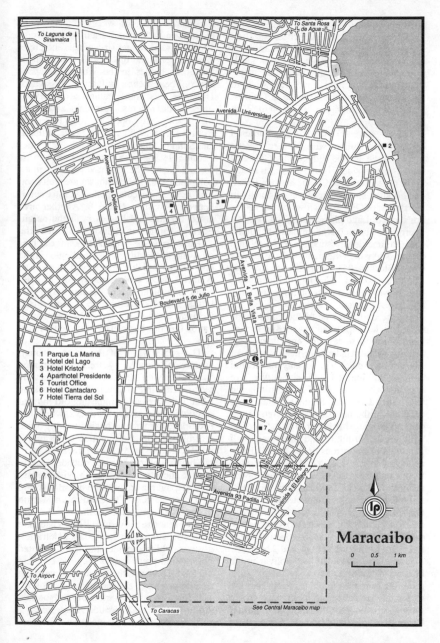

To Laguna de
Sinamaica

To Santa Rosa
de Agua

Avenida   Universidad

Avenida 15 Las Delicias

Avenida 4 Bella Vista

Boulevard 5 de Julio

1 Parque La Marina
2 Hotel del Lago
3 Hotel Kristof
4 Aparthotel Presidente
5 Tourist Office
6 Hotel Cantaclaro
7 Hotel Tierra del Sol

Avenida 93 Padilla

Avenida 2 El Milagro

To Airport

To Caracas

See Central Maracaibo map

Maracaibo

0   0.5   1 km

must get close to it – special access is provided for this purpose. You can then appreciate the crown of the Virgen, made of gold and encrusted with precious stones. Pilgrims flock here all year round but the major celebrations are held for a full week in November, during the Feria de la Chinita, and culminate with a procession on the 18th of that month.

The eastern end of the Paseo is bordered by the **Plaza Bolívar** with the hero's statue in the middle and the 19th-century **Catedral** on the eastern side. The most revered image in the cathedral is the Cristo Negro or Cristo de Gibraltar, so called as it was originally in the church of Gibraltar, a town on the southern shore of Lago Maracaibo. The town was overrun and burnt by Indians in 1600 but the Christ miraculously survived, even though the cross to which the statue was nailed was burnt. Blackened by smoke, Cristo Negro is also known, like La Chinita, for his miraculous powers and attracts pilgrims from the region and beyond.

On the northern side of the plaza is the **Casa de la Capitulación**, also known as Casa Morales, built at the end of the 18th century as the residence of the governor of Maracaibo. Today it's the only residential colonial building left in the city. It was here that on 3 August 1823 the act of capitulation was signed by the Spanish, who were defeated in the naval battle of Lago Maracaibo. The house has been restored, fitted out with period furniture and decorated with paintings of the heroes of the War of Independence. It can be visited Monday to Friday from 8 am to 5 pm. The large building under restoration, across the street from the Casa, is the **Teatro Baralt**, inaugurated in 1883. On the southern side of the plaza is the **Museo de Artes Gráficas**, which stages temporary exhibitions of modern art. It's open Monday to Friday from 8 am to noon and 2 to 6 pm.

One block north of Plaza Bolívar is the **Museo Arquidiocesano**, featuring religious art from the region. It's open Tuesday to Sunday from 9 am to 6 pm. Next to the museum is the **Templo Bautismal Rafael Urdaneta**, open daily from 9 am to 6 pm.

A short walk north-west will take you to the **Museo Urdaneta**. Born in Maracaibo in 1788, General Rafael Urdaneta is the city's greatest hero, and distinguished himself in numerous battles in the War of Independence. The museum, built on the site where Urdaneta was born, features a variety of objects, documents, paintings and other memorabilia. It's open Tuesday to Friday from 9 am to noon and 2 to 5 pm, Saturday and Sunday from 10 am to 1 pm.

Calle 94 has been partly restored to its former glory. The brightly painted, multi coloured façades of the houses are well kept. The most spectacular part of the street is between Avenidas 6 and 8. Another area noted for fine old houses is in the neighbourhood around the Iglesia de Santa Lucía.

The **Capilla de Santa Ana**, on the corner of Avenida El Milagro and Calle 94, is the only chapel which has preserved some of its colonial decoration, namely the retable, Mudéjar vault and pulpit. Today, the Capilla is the lateral chapel of the church in the Hospital Central. It's currently under renovation but may be open by the time you read this.

The sector south of the Paseo is busy, chaotic and dirty. Many streets are occupied by vendors with their stalls which makes the old town feel like a market. The most striking sight in the area is the imposing **old market building**, overlooking the docks, which has been closed as a market but is currently being refurbished with the intention of turning it into the Centro de Arte de Maracaibo.

There's not much to see outside the city centre. The city stretches north, with modern districts, but the architecture doesn't live up to that of Caracas. The **Parque La Marina** on the lakeshore, at the confluence of Avenida El Milagro and Avenida Bella Vista, five km north of the centre, is noted for **El Mirador**, a tower which provides the most elevated observation point overlooking the city and the lake. However, the lift stopped working several years ago and the tower has closed.

A few km further north is **Santa Rosa de Agua**, once a small lakeside village, today a suburb within the city boundaries. There are some *palafitos* or houses built on stilts on the shore, which might be worth a visit if you don't plan on a trip to the Laguna de Sinamaica (see the Around Maracaibo section). Perhaps it was in Santa Rosa that in 1499 the Spaniards first saw these houses and gave Venezuela its name. A bust of Amerigo Vespucci, who supposedly took part in the expedition, stands on the plaza near the waterfront.

On the northern outskirts of Maracaibo, on the road to Sinamaica, is the **Planetario Simón Bolívar**, open Tuesday to Saturday from 8 am to 4 pm, Sunday from 8 am to 6 pm. It's probably best to visit the planetarium on the way to or from Sinamaica, rather than making a special trip.

The **Jardín Botánico**, located on the south-western outskirts of the city, at the intersection of the motorway to La Chinita Airport and the Carretera de Palito Blanco, is probably not worth the journey, even though some leaflets describe it as one of the best in the country.

Places to Stay

Budget accommodation is shabby and often full of oil workers. Many cheapies rent rooms by the hour. If you don't mind this, it's best to start looking behind the cathedral where there are several cheap hotels. The *Carabobo*, *Santa Ana*, *Coruña* and *Aurora No 2* are all rather unattractive places but most have rooms with private baths and the last two have several air-conditioned rooms. Expect to pay around US$4/7/9 for a single/double/triple with fan and about US$3 more for a room with air-conditioning.

Appreciably better is the *Hotel Caribe* on Avenida 7 near the corner of Avenida Padilla. Singles/doubles/triples with air-conditioning and bath go for US$9/10/12.

The *Hotel Victoria*, overlooking Plaza Baralt and the old market building, is the most romantic choice in the city centre. It has clean spacious rooms with bath and air-conditioning which cost US$10/11 for a single/double. Make sure to choose a room with a balcony and a good view over the plaza before booking in.

There are no posh hotels in the city centre; they all opted to base themselves in the more elegant, new districts, mainly in the northern part of the city.

One of the cheapest and closest to the centre is *Hotel Tierra del Sol* (☎ 230521), Avenida Bella Vista No 87-125. This new, small hotel offers singles/doubles for about US$30/40. More expensive but better is *Hotel Cantaclaro* (☎ 222944), two blocks north, on Calle 86A.

There are several classier hotels in the city, among them the four-star *Hotel Kristof* (☎ 72911) at Avenida 8 No 68-48, and the *Aparthotel Presidente* (☎ 83133) at Avenida 11 No 68-50 which is of a similar standard.

Possibly the best place to stay in Maracaibo, and also the most expensive, is the large lakeside *Hotel del Lago* (☎ 912022) on Avenida El Milagro.

Places to Eat

There are a lot of cheap eateries in the city centre, particularly between Calles 96 and 100. They serve set meals and dishes a la carta for about US$2, but the quality of the food mirrors the price. Most of these places do most of their business during the lunch hours, then either close or only serve soft drinks and the like. After 6 pm or so it's difficult to find a budget place to eat except for a rash of street stalls around the corner of Avenida Libertador and Avenida 12. One of the few cheap outlets which keeps going until 9 pm is *Restaurant Friulana*, Calle 95 No 3-06, next door to Hotel Coruña. Its white tiles make it look a bit like a hospital or a public toilet but the portions are large and the food OK.

The best eating establishment in the downtown area is *Restaurant El Zaguán*, on the corner of Calle 94 and Avenida 6. The place consists of a restaurant serving good comida criolla at reasonable prices, a bar, and an open-air café shaded by a beautiful old ceiba. The place is open until 11 pm but closed on Mondays.

There are very few panaderías in the city centre and almost none serve expresso coffee, a sad exception among Venezuelan cities.

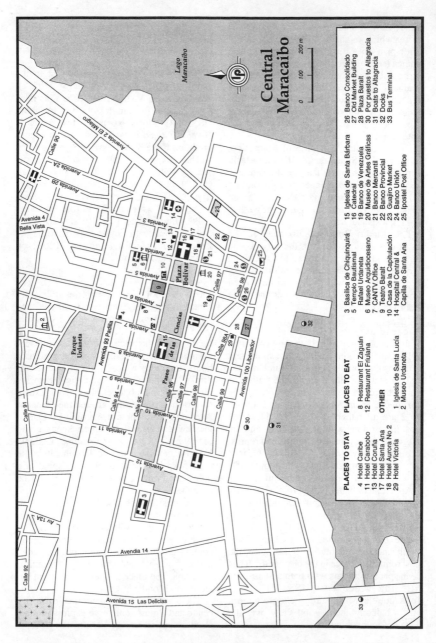

Central Maracaibo

Lago Maracaibo

0   100   200 m

PLACES TO STAY

4   Hotel Caribe
11 Hotel Carabobo
13 Hotel Coruña
17 Hotel Santa Ana
18 Hotel Aurora No 2
29 Hotel Victoria

PLACES TO EAT

8   Restaurant El Zaguán
12 Restaurant Fruiana

OTHER

1   Iglesia de Santa Lucía
2   Museo Urdaneta
3   Basílica de Chiquinquirá
5   Templo Bautismal
    Rafael Urdaneta
6   Museo Arquidiocesano
7   CANTV Office
9   Teatro Baralt
10 Casa de la Capitulación
14 Hospital Central &
    Capilla de Santa Ana
15 Iglesia de Santa Bárbara
16 Catedral
19 Banco de Venezuela
20 Museo de Artes Gráficas
21 Banco Mercantil
22 Banco Provincial
23 Guajiro Market
24 Banco Unión
25 Ipostel Post Office
26 Banco Consolidado
27 Old Market Building
28 Plaza Baralt
30 Por puestos to Altagracia
31 Boats to Altagracia
32 Docks
33 Bus Terminal

Like the hotels, the cream of the restaurants have gathered in the northern sector of the city. Many of them are concentrated around Boulevard 5 de Julio (Calle 77), one of the main commercial areas of new Maracaibo. To name a few: *Mi Vaquita*, corner of Calle 76 and Avenida 3H; *La Hacienda*, corner of Calle 77 and Avenida 3H; *Casa Vieja*, Calle 72 between Avenidas 3E and 3F; and *Pepe*, corner of Calle 72 and Avenida 3H. It's not easy to find somewhere cheap to eat in this area.

Entertainment

Maracaibo's major annual event is the Feria de la Chinita, which springs to life around 10 November and goes on until the coronation of the Virgen on 18 November. This one-week-long festival includes, apart from religious celebrations, plenty of cultural and popular events such as bullfights, toros coleados (a sort of rodeo), street parades and masquerades, and obviously music, above all the gaita, the typical local rhythm.

Gaita came to Venezuela with Spanish priests but some scholars claim that its origins are even earlier and that it has Persian roots. It is sung and accompanied by a band using a variety of typical instruments such as the *cuatro*, *maracas*, *furruco* and *charrasca*. Lyrics are mostly either religious or political and are largely improvised.

The gaita is particularly popular during the Christmas period, but the season often extends from October to January. With less frequency, it can be heard in other months as well. During the Feria de la Chinita, the best time to listen to the gaita is on the eve of 18 November when groups gather in front of the Basílica for the Serenata para la Virgen.

There are several night spots in Maracaibo which present gaita bands, either regularly or from time to time. Check, for example, Palacio de la Gaita on Calle 77 between Avenidas 12 and 13; Casablanca on the corner of Calle 67 and Avenida 3G; or El Solar de Pancho on Avenida 4 between Calles 69 and 70. Have a look in *Panorama*, Maracaibo's major daily paper, for what's going on in the city.

Things to Buy

Maracaibo is possibly the best place to buy Guajiro Indian crafts, amongst the most characteristic being their hammocks and mantas. There are several Guajiro markets in town; a good, centrally-located market is on the corner of Avenida El Milagro and Calle 96. Also check what's on offer at the Turismo del Trópico handicraft shop at Avenida El Milagro No 93-25, which sells Guajiro and other Indian groups' crafts.

Getting There & Away

Air The airport is about 12 km south-west of the city centre. There's no public transport; a taxi will cost about US$8.

There are plenty of flights to the main cities in the country, including more than a dozen flights daily to Caracas serviced by Avensa (US$62) and Aeropostal (US$59). Avensa has daily flights to Mérida (US$44), Las Piedras (US$35), San Antonio del Táchira (US$49), Valencia (US$59) and Barquisimeto (US$40).

Maracaibo is the hometown of Zuliana de Aviación, which operates daily international flights to Miami (US$155), Medellín (US$75) and Bogotá (US$75), and domestic flights to Caracas (US$41) and Porlamar on Isla de Margarita (US$57). Their office (☎ 514775, 514778, 514147) is in Edificio Cosmar, Local 2, Calle 78 No 20-109.

Bus The bus station is about one km south-west of the city centre. Frequent local transport links the terminal to the centre and other districts.

Several buses a day run to Coro (US$5, four hours), and to Caracas (US$13, 11 hours). There are three night buses to Mérida (US$8.50, nine hours); they go via the Pan-American Highway along the northern base of the Cordillera. There are no direct buses on the Trans-Andean mountain road via El Águila. You must go to Valera (buses every half an hour, US$4, four hours) and change there for another one (three buses a day, US$4, five hours). Por puestos (shared taxis) also operate on this route; they are faster but cost about 70% more than the bus. Four or five buses depart nightly for San Cristóbal (US$8, eight hours).

To Maicao in Colombia, there are both buses (US$4.50, four hours) and shared taxis (US$5.75, three hours) operating regularly from about 5 am to 3 pm. All passport formalities are done in Paraguachón on the border. If you come this way from Colombia, expect a thorough search of your luggage by Venezuelan officials.

Maicao is widely and justifiably known as a lawless town and is far from safe – stay there as briefly as possible. Buses from Maicao to Santa Marta are operated by several companies and depart frequently (US$7, four hours).

AROUND MARACAIBO

Maracaibo sits on the strait linking Lago Maracaibo to Golfo de Venezuela. The lake, at 12,870 km, is the largest on the continent. More than that, it is also the richest: enormous deposits of oil discovered in the 1910s underneath the lake's bed have made Venezuela the wealthiest country in South America.

Although oil is the most obvious feature of the Maracaibo region, there's much more to see around the city. The region boasts a variety of attractions, some of which are detailed below.

Puente Rafael Urdaneta

Named after the greatest local hero, the Rafael Urdaneta Bridge spans the neck of Lago Maracaibo just south of the city. It was built in 1963 to provide a short cut to the centre of the country and, at 8679 metres, is perhaps the longest prestressed concrete bridge in the world. A great achievement of local engineers, the bridge is the pride of Maracuchos and appears in every local tourist brochure.

You'll cross the bridge if arriving in Maracaibo from anywhere in the east or south-east. There's a panoramic view of Maracaibo from the bridge and vice versa.

Altagracia

Altagracia is a town facing Maracaibo from the opposite side of the strait. Founded in colonial times, the town has preserved some of its old architecture, particularly the charming, typical houses, recently painted in much the same style as those in Maracaibo. The most interesting area is around Plaza Miranda, the square just one short block up from the lakefront. A stroll about the town, together with a pleasant boat trip from Maracaibo, justifies a half-day trip from the city.

Getting There & Away Boats from Maracaibo to Altagracia depart every half an hour until 6 pm or so from the wharf off Avenida Libertador. The trip takes 20 minutes and costs US$0.80. In Altagracia, the boats anchor at the pier one block below Plaza Miranda.

There are also por puestos which leave when full from next to either wharf. The ride (via the Rafael Urdaneta Bridge) takes 45 minutes and costs US$1.20.

Boats are definitely a more pleasant means of transport but sometimes break down, leaving por puestos as the only option.

Ciénaga de los Olivitos

Ciénaga de los Olivitos, about 20 km northeast of Altagracia, is reputedly the main oasis for flamingos in Venezuela. These lovely birds live there (mainly on the edge of Bahía de Tablazo) all year round, though some of them fly away temporarily to other regions, such as the Península de la Guajira and the Península de Paraguaná. The mangroves growing on the Ciénaga are home to many other bird species as well.

Getting There & Away The Ciénaga is not easy to get to as it is not accessible by road. Either talk to the taxi drivers in Altagracia, some of whom have some idea of where the nearest flamingo viewing point is (about US$15 for the round trip with waiting included), or ask the fishermen in Guarico (port of Altagracia) or (better) Sabaneta, who might take you across the Bahía de Tablazo to the Ciénaga. Alternatively, take a bus or por puesto from Altagracia to Quisiro, get off several km before arriving at Quisiro (make sure that the driver knows where to put you down) and walk north-west to the Ciénaga.

Castillo de San Carlos de la Barra

This fort lies about 30 km due north of
Maracaibo, on the eastern tip of Isla de San
Carlos. It was built in the second half of the
17th century to protect the entrance to the
lake against pirates. Even though the mouth
was largely protected by a sandbar, there were
many marauders eager to cross over and sack
Maracaibo. The fort was in Spanish hands
until the naval battle of Lago Maracaibo in
1823, and after their defeat it passed to the
republicans. In 1903 the fort was bombarded
by a fleet of warships sent by Germany, Italy
and Great Britain to blockade Venezuelan

ports after the country failed to pay its
foreign debts. During the dictatorship of
Juan Vicente Gómez, the fort served as a jail
for political prisoners, after which it was used
as an arms depot. Finally declared a national
monument, it was extensively restorated in
the late 1980s to become a tourist attraction.
The work is still going on, but may be complete by the time you read this.

Castillo de San Carlos is similar to the
forts in Cumaná and those on the Isla de
Maragarita. It's built on a four-pointed star
plan with circular watchtowers on each
corner and a square courtyard in the middle.

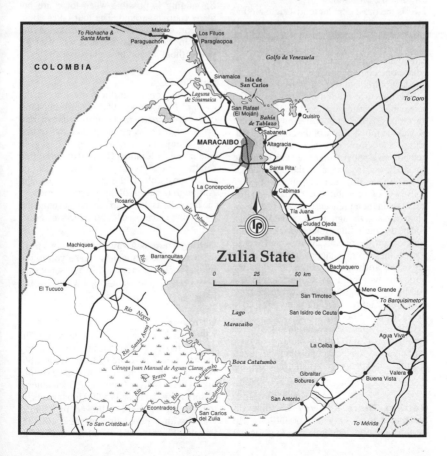

Getting There & Away The fort is accessible by water only, the town of San Rafael (El Moján) being the usual starting point. San Rafael, about 40 km north of Maracaibo, is serviced by a number of buses from the city's terminal. To continue on to the fort you'll need to hire a launch at the town's pier. San Rafael is a fairly undistinguished town except for a huge, somewhat macabre bust of Bolívar in the middle of the central plaza that looks as though his head is separated from his body.

Laguna de Sinamaica

This is the most popular tourist sight around Maracaibo. The lagoon is noted for several hamlets whose inhabitants live in palafitos, or houses built on piles on or off the lake. Sinamaica is famous nationwide as the place where one can see roughly what Alonso de Ojeda would have seen in 1499.

The boat trip around the lagoon and the side caños, passing scattered palafitos along the shores, is the attraction. However, don't expect too much. Some of the houses are still traditionally built of *estera*, a sort of mat made from a papyrus-like reed that grows in the shallows. If you ignore the TV antennas – sticking out from the roof of almost every house – they probably don't look much different from their predecessors 500 years ago. Many houses, though, have adopted modern materials, including timber, brick and tin, which spoil the overall impression. Electric power-lines over the lagoon don't add to the sense of authenticity either. A Parador Turístico was built by Corpozulia in the middle of the lagoon, and has a restaurant, craft shop and toilets. This is an obligatory stop for every boat trip.

Originally the lagoon was inhabited by the Paraujano (or Añú) Indians but they are now extinct; today the local population, estimated at some 2300 people, consists almost exclusively of mestizos.

Getting There & Away Laguna de Sinamaica is an easy half or full-day trip from Maracaibo. First you have to get to the town of Sinamaica, 60 km north of Maracaibo, 19 km past San Rafael. Take a bus to Guane or Los Filuos, whichever departs first, from the Maracaibo bus terminal. The trip to Sinamaica takes up to two hours and costs US$0.80. Get off one block past the main square (just behind the police station). From there, por puestos do the five-km run on a paved road to Puerto Cuervito, which is on the edge of the lagoon (US$0.20, 10 minutes). In Puerto, a fleet of pleasure boats is waiting all day long to take tourists around the lagoon. A boat normally takes six passengers and costs about US$15 (per boat). Bargaining is possible when there are not many tourists around. The tour takes about an hour, but longer if you feel like having lunch in the Parador (the boat will wait for you without any additional charge).

Los Filuos

Los Filuos, on the northern outskirts of the town of Paraguaipoa, 95 km north of Maracaibo, is where a large Guajiro Indian market is held on Monday morning. By dawn of that day, Guajiros from all over the region (including Colombian Guajira) come here to sell their products and buy supplies. It's one of the most colourful markets in Venezuela. Although it runs until the afternoon, most of the business is done early in the morning and by 11 am or so most of the shoppers are gone.

Getting There & Away The Filuos bus from the Maracaibo terminal will take you to the market for US$1 in two to 2½ hours, but start very early if you want to get a feel for the place.

Oil Towns

Although Maracaibo is considered the oil capital, most oil drilling is undertaken along the north-eastern shore of Lago Maracaibo. Here is where genuine oil towns have sprung up, all the way from Cabimas to Bachaquero. Cabimas, with about 175,000 inhabitants, is the largest of them, followed by Ciudad Ojeda with a population of some 100,000 people. There's little to attract tourists in these towns. What is interesting is the forest of old off-shore oil derricks which spread along the shore for some 50 km or more. There's a number of good viewpoints for these derricks; amongst others the waterfronts of Tía Juana and Lagunillas. Although the Corpozulia tourist office states that you can take photos if you wish, the local Guardia Nacional may have a different idea, so take your pictures discreetly. The most impressive photos are to be had at sunset.

Getting There & Away There are plenty of buses from Maracaibo to Ciudad Ojeda and many continue further on to Bachaquero. Oil derricks are visible from the highway on several stretches, so if you want to get a closer look, just get off the bus. Alternatively, ask a local taxi driver to take you to the best viewpoints.

Río Catatumbo

There are plenty of rivers emptying into Lago Maracaibo, but the Río Catatumbo is exceptional. A unique electrical phenomenon occurs near its mouth: almost uninterrupted lightning. It's bright but silent. The phenomenon, referred to as Faro de Maracaibo (Maracaibo Beam) or Relámpago de Catatumbo (Catatumbo Lightning), can be observed at night from all over the region, from hundreds of km away. It's visible, for example, from Maracaibo and San Cristóbal. Travelling by night on the Maracaibo-San Cristóbal or San Cristóbal-Valera roads, you'll get a glimpse of it, weather permitting. Obviously, the closer to the mouth of Río Catatumbo you get to, the more impressive the spectacle. Towns on the western and southern shores of Lake Maracaibo (such as Barranquitas, San Antonio, Bobures or Gibraltar) are good observation points.

The Andes

The highest mountains in Venezuela are to be found in the Andes. The northern end of the great Andean chain runs north-south for the whole length of the Pacific coast of the continent. In Venezuela, the Andes extend from the Táchira depression, near the Colombian border, north-east to Trujillo state. This end of the range is some 400 km long and about 70 to 100 km wide.

Strictly speaking, this range continues on further to the north-east (past another depression in the Barquisimeto region) to the Caribbean coast, and then further east along the coast, almost up to the Orinoco Delta. However, the coastal section is not commonly regarded as the Andes, but is referred to as the Cordillera de la Costa.

There's another Andes range in Venezuela, which runs northward along the Colombian-Venezuelan border. This range is not normally regarded as part of the Andes; it is called the Serranía de Perijá.

The state of Mérida is in the centre of the Venezuelan Andes. The mountains here are not a single ridge, as they sometimes appear on general maps, but two roughly parallel chains separated by a verdant mountain valley. The southern chain culminates with the Sierra Nevada de Mérida, crowned by a series of snowcapped peaks. The country's highest summits are here, including Pico Bolívar (5007 metres), Pico Humboldt (4942 metres) and Pico Bompland (4883 metres). All this area has been declared Parque Nacional Sierra Nevada. The northern chain, the Sierra de la Culata, directly opposite the Sierra Nevada, reaches 4730 metres, and is also a national park. In the deep valley between the two Sierras sits the city of Mérida, the region's major urban centre and the country's mountain capital. The Andes continue on into the neighbouring states of Táchira and Trujillo, and merge into single ridges, which gradually descend to the lowlands.

The mountains are dotted with small

towns whose inhabitants continue the old traditions of their predecessors, the roots of which go back to the Timote-Cuica Indians, the most advanced pre-Hispanic culture of Venezuela. The land seems to be more actively cultivated here than elsewhere in the country, and the local campesinos seem to work harder than their lowland counterparts.

The Andes are popular hiking territory, offering everything from lush tropical rainforests to permanent snow. The *páramos* are particularly interesting. These are a kind of open highland moor which starts at about 3300 metres and stretches up almost to the snowline. Their most curious plant is the *frailejón* (espeletia), found only in highland areas of Venezuela, Colombia and Ecuador. There are about 300 species of espeletia, of which approximately 20% can be found in Venezuela. They are particularly amazing when in bloom, from November to December.

The Venezuelan Andes has a dry season from December to April. Then comes a period in May and June noted for changeable weather with sunshine but also frequent rain (or snow at high altitudes). It can be followed by a short, relatively dry period, usually from late June to late July (which some consider a second dry season) before a long, really wet

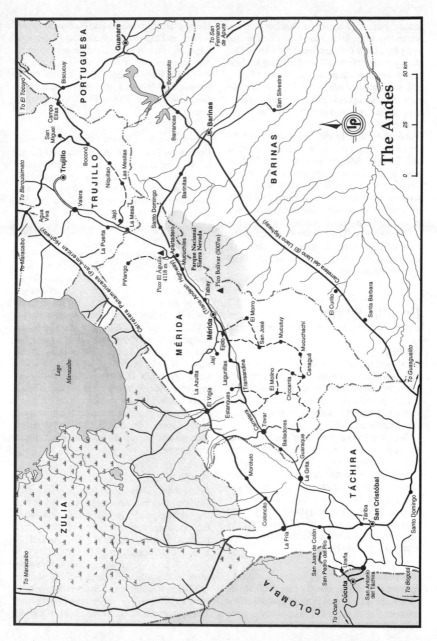

The Andes

season begins. August to October are the wettest months; hiking can be miserable and you probably won't get to see the views. The snowy period (June to October) may be dangerous for mountaineers.

The amount of rain varies locally. Trujillo state, for example, is drier; the rainy season here begins later and ends earlier than in the southern Andes.

Administratively, the Venezuelan Andes are covered by three states: Táchira, Mérida and Trujillo. Mérida state has the highest mountains and the best tourist infrastructure, consequently it has the greatest number of visitors, both local and foreign. Trujillo is still undiscovered with hidden colonial gems and splendid mountain scenery. Táchira has the biggest city, San Cristóbal (which is the least interesting of the three state capitals), and beautiful, unexplored mountains in its four national parks.

Trujillo State

VALERA

With its 130,000 inhabitants, Valera is the largest city in the state; it's almost three times more populous than the capital, Trujillo. It lies at an altitude of 540 metres, and has a pretty hot climate, with an average annual temperature of 25°C.

Founded in 1820, Valera's growth was boosted by the construction of the Trans-Andean Highway, completed in the 1920s. It is now an important regional commercial centre, which has good road connections to Maracaibo, Barquisimeto, Guanare and Mérida. It is likely to be a stopover if you are travelling around the region. However, the city is an unremarkable place and there's not much to see or do here.

Information
Tourist Office The tourist office (*módulo de información turística*) is on Avenida Bolívar between Calles 10 and 11. The office is open daily from 9 am to noon and 2 to 5 pm.

Money The two useful banks, Banco Unión (cash) and Banco Consolidado (American Express travellers' cheques), are both on Avenida Bolívar. Banco de Venezuela, on Plaza Bolívar, accepts Visa credit cards. Other banks marked on the map may occasionally handle some foreign exchange operations.

Tours Casanova Tours (☎ 57718), Centro Comercial Edivica, Calle 8, near the corner of Avenida Bolívar, organises tours around the region. They offer a choice of *circuitos turísticos* (tourist circuit), which includes some of the interesting natural and cultural sights in the Trujillo state.

Places to Stay
One of the cheapest places is the very basic *Pensión Colonial* (no sign on the door), Avenida 13 between Calles 8 and 9. Its matrimoniales cost US$5. A better budget bet is *Hotel Central* (☎ 53697), on Plaza Bolívar, which has doubles with bath for US$7. Doubles in the large, undistinguished and noisy *Hotel Primavera*, on the corner of Avenida Bolívar and Calle 6, cost much the same. *Hotel Marcelino*, one block south along Avenida Bolívar, offers a slightly higher standard, although it too is noisy. It costs US$9/13 for a single/double.

The best place in town is the three-star *Hotel Camino Real* (☎ 53795), on Avenida Independencia, on the eastern edge of the city centre.

Places to Eat
Restaurant Trieste, corner of Avenida Bolívar and Calle 8, is recommended. It's on the 1st floor, with a large terrace overlooking the Avenida, and offers reasonably priced pizzas, spaghetti and steaks. For chicken, go three blocks north along Avenida Bolívar to *Pollo Sabroso La Plata*. There are several more restaurants on Avenida Bolívar, including *Tasca-Restaurant El Boulevard*, which is more expensive. For vegetarians, *Restaurant El Vegetariano*, Calle 11 No 11-21, is a good, budget place.

Getting There & Away

Air The airport is about four km north-east of the city centre. There are two flights a day to Caracas with Avensa (US$54) and one with Aeropostal (US$50).

Bus The bus terminal is about 1.5 km northeast of the centre. To get there, take the city bus marked Plata 3 Terminal.

There are several buses a day to Caracas (US$10.75, 9½ hours), and all pass through Barquisimeto (US$4.25, four hours), Valencia (US$7.75, seven hours) and Maracay

(US$8.75, eight hours). Buses to Maracaibo depart every half an hour (US$4, five hours).

Empresa de Transporte Barinas has three buses a day to Mérida. The first of these departs at 8 am. There is another bus which departs at 11 am and the final bus leaves for Mérida at 1 pm (US$4, five hours). The buses travel along the spectacular Trans-Andean Highway, and reach 4007 metres, which is the highest road pass in Venezuela. For the best views, choose a seat on the left-hand side of the bus. Carritos to Trujillo depart every five to 10 minutes (US$0.60, 50 minutes).

For transport to Jajó, refer to the Jajó section.

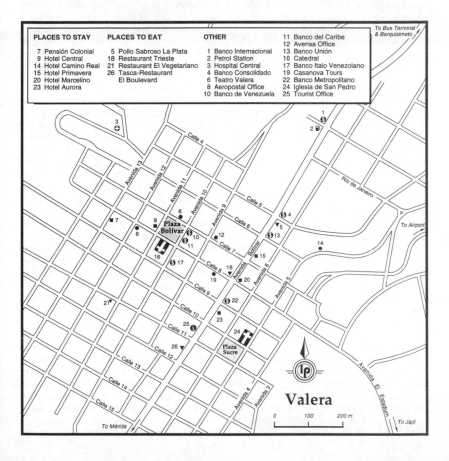

PLACES TO STAY	PLACES TO EAT	OTHER	
7 Pensión Colonial	5 Pollo Sabroso La Plata	1 Banco Internacional	11 Banco del Caribe
9 Hotel Central	18 Restaurant Trieste	2 Petrol Station	12 Avensa Office
14 Hotel Camino Real	21 Restaurant El Vegetariano	3 Hospital Central	13 Banco Unión
15 Hotel Primavera	26 Tasca-Restaurant	4 Banco Consolidado	16 Catedral
20 Hotel Marcelino	El Boulevard	6 Teatro Valera	17 Banco Italo Venezolano
23 Hotel Aurora		8 Aeropostal Office	19 Casanova Tours
		10 Banco de Venezuela	22 Banco Metropolitano
			24 Iglesia de San Pedro
			25 Tourist Office

TRUJILLO

Trujillo is only 35 km from Valera along the recently built autopista, but it seems a world apart with its fine setting, agreeable climate, some colonial architecture and the unhurried air of days gone by. Trujillo can be a quick escape from Valera.

Trujillo was the first town to be founded in the Andes, in 1557, but the continuous hostility of the local Indian group, the Cuicas, led to its being moved from place to place several times. Reputedly, seven different locations were tried before the town, 'the portable city', was eventually and permanently established in 1570 at the site where it now stands..

The ultimate location, in a long, narrow valley, El Valle de los Cedros, determined the unusual and inconvenient layout of the town. It's only two blocks wide, but extends for a few km up the mountain gorge. Although new suburbs have spread along the Río Castán, at the foot of the old sector, Trujillo continues to be a small town with its total population remaining below the 50,000 mark. Traditionally it functions as the state's capital. Its height of around 800 metres keeps the mean temperature at 22°C.

Information

Tourist Office The tourist office (☎ 34411) is not in Trujillo, but in La Plazuela, a small colonial town three km north of Trujillo on the Valera autopista. It's open Monday to Friday from 8 am to noon and 2 to 5.30 pm.

Money There aren't many options for changing money in Trujillo, except for Banco Unión which will probably change cash, and Banco de Venezuela which may accept Visa credit cards.

Things to See

The old part of the town stretches along two east-west streets, Avenida 1 Independencia and Avenida 2 Bolívar, running parallel to each other and one block apart.

Bordered by these streets, at the eastern, lower end of the sector, is **Plaza Bolívar**, the historical heart of the town and still the nucleus of the city's life today. The **Catedral**, completed in 1662, has a lovely white-washed façade, but its refurbished interior is disappointing. There's almost nothing left of the colonial fittings, except for the stone baptismal font.

There are still some graceful old buildings on or just off the plaza, including the house next to the cathedral and the Casa Hogar Monseñor Carrillo. The finest in this area is the carefully restored, fair-sized mansion on the corner just north of the plaza. Built in 1598-1617 as the Convento Regina Angelorum, it's now the public library.

There are more surviving colonial houses west of the plaza, on both Avenida Independencia and Avenida Bolívar. Perhaps the best approach to sightseeing is to take either of the two streets uphill and return back down by the other one. They merge 10 blocks further up to become Avenida Carmona, but the best architecture is within a few blocks of the plaza.

The **Centro de Historia**, Avenida Independencia 5-29, is the most important place to call at. This restored colonial house has been converted into a museum of the history of Trujillo. The museum exhibits include old maps, armour, period furniture, pre-Columbian pottery and even a fully equipped kitchen with a beautiful old stove. It was in this house that, on 15 June 1813, Bolívar signed his controversial *Decreto de Guerra a Muerte*, or War to the Death, under which all royalists captured were to be summarily executed. The table on which the proclamation was signed and the bed in which Bolívar slept are part of the exhibition. The museum is open Monday to Friday from 9 am to noon and 2 to 5 pm, Saturday and Sunday from 9 am to noon.

There are a couple of tourist sights outside the city. The **Monumento a la Virgen de la Paz** was erected in 1983 on the top of the mountain overlooking Trujillo, several km to the west of the city. The 46-metre-high, 1200-tonne statue of the Virgen stands on the 1603-metre top of the Cerro Peña de la Virgen. From several miradores (viewpoints), accessible by staircase, one can

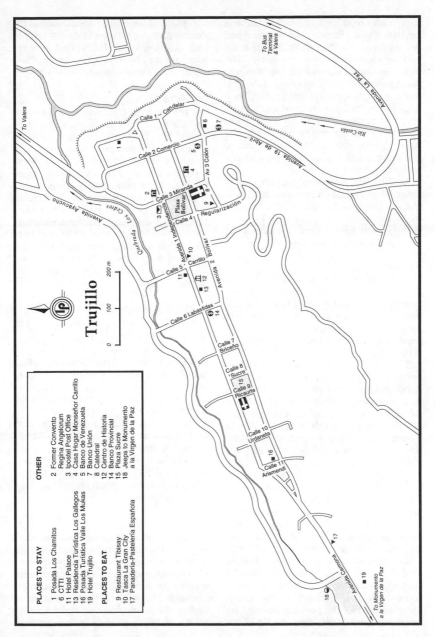

Trujillo

0   100   200 m

PLACES TO STAY

1 Posada Los Chamitos
6 CTTI
11 Hotel Palace
13 Residencia Turística Los Gallegos
16 Posada Turística Valle Los Mukas
19 Hotel Trujillo

PLACES TO EAT

9 Restaurant Tibisay
10 Tasca La Gran City
17 Panadería-Pastelería Española

OTHER

2 Former Convento
Regina Angelorum
3 Ipostel Post Office
4 Casa Hogar Monseñor Carrillo
5 Banco de Venezuela
7 Banco Unión
8 Catedral
12 Centro de Historia
14 Banco Provincial
15 Plaza Sucre
18 Jeeps to Monumento
a la Virgen de la Paz

enjoy views over much of Trujillo state and beyond. On a clear day, the snowcapped peaks of the Sierra Nevada de Mérida and a part of Lago Maracaibo are visible. The monument is open daily from 8 am to 5 pm. Jeeps go there from the upper end of the city, next to the park opposite Hotel Trujillo. They depart when they have collected four passengers and charge US$0.60 per head either way. If you feel like going there on foot, it'll be a 2½-hour walk up. In the rainy season, it's best to start early, as later on the Virgen is usually shrouded by clouds.

La Plazuela, a small colonial town three km north of Trujillo on the Valera autopista, has recently been restored, more or less, to its former form. The place now looks as though it was built yesterday. In one of the renovated houses is the tourist office.

Places to Stay
Probably the cheapest place is the *Posada Los Chamitos* (☎ 32898), Calle Candelaria, two blocks downhill from Plaza Bolívar. It's actually a private house, whose owner rents out a few of the upper-floor rooms, for US$6 per double bed (a couple will fit). The posada is often full.

The *Hotel Palace*, on Avenida Independencia, opposite the Centro de Historia, happily offers you the choice between matrimoniales/doubles/triples with bath for US$8/9/11, and serves inexpensive meals. About 50 metres uphill is the *Residencia Turística Los Gallegos* which has the same prices as the Palace but slightly better standards.

The *CTTI*, or Complejo Turístico Trujillo Internacional* (☎ 31478, 31224), corner of Avenida Colón and Avenida 19 de Abril, is a styleless, modern building that houses a hotel, restaurant and disco (to attract the tours and organised excursions visiting the city). Singles/matrimoniales cost US$11/15.

The best in town is the *Hotel Trujillo* (☎ 33576, 33646), on Avenida Carmona at the upper end of the city. It has good double rooms (US$30), a restaurant, bar and a swimming pool. The pool can be used by nonguests from 9 am to 4 pm, for US$2.50.

A place which is due to open soon is the *Posada Turística Valle los Mukas* (☎ 33184), Calle Arismendi 1-43. It is located in an old house and may be an attractive option. Their restaurant is already open.

Places to Eat
One of the cheapest places in town is *Restaurant Tibisay*, behind the cathedral. It can be entered from both Calle Regularización and Avenida Colón. Straightforward, very cheap meals are served until about 8 pm. More expensive but nonetheless reasonably priced meals are to be had in *Hotel Palace*.

Tasca La Gran City, Avenida Independencia, is open until midnight and has a large menu, with meals costing somewhere between US$3 and US$5. The similarly priced *Valle los Mukas* specialises in typical food, and has good trout. One of the best (and most expensive) places is the restaurant of the *Hotel Trujillo*.

Getting There & Away
Air The city has no airport and uses the one in Valera, 30 km from Trujillo.

Bus The bus terminal is on Avenida La Paz, east of the city, beyond Río Castán. It's quite close as the crow flies, but the road follows the side of the valley. City minibuses link the terminal to the centre.

The terminal is rather quiet, and the only really frequent connection is with Valera (US$0.60, 50 minutes). There are a few buses to Caracas (US$10.75, 9½ hours) and to Boconó (US$1.75, two hours). Most of the villages and towns in the region are serviced by por-puesto jeeps.

BOCONÓ
Boconó, 95 km along a spectacular, winding mountain road from Trujillo, is an old town of 40,000 people. It sits at an altitude of about 1225 metres, and thus enjoys a pleasant temperature of around 20°C. The favourable climate and fertile soil of the region contributed to the development of agriculture. A variety of crops, including coffee, potatoes,

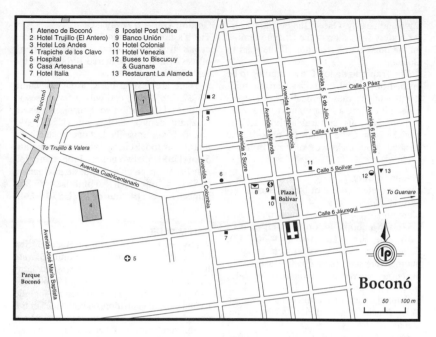

1 Ateneo de Boconó
2 Hotel Trujillo (El Antero)
3 Hotel Los Andes
4 Trapiche de los Clavo
5 Hospital
6 Casa Artesanal
7 Hotel Italia
8 Ipostel Post Office
9 Banco Unión
10 Hotel Colonial
11 Hotel Venezia
12 Buses to Biscucuy & Guanare
13 Restaurant La Alameda

Boconó

0   50   100 m

chickpeas and other vegetables, are cultivated in the surrounding hills.

Boconó was founded as early as 1560 on
one of Trujillo's previous sites. Some of
those early inhabitants of Trujillo decided to
remain and take their lives into their hands.
Isolated for centuries from the outside world,
Boconó grew painfully slowly and remained
largely self-sufficient. It wasn't until the
1930s that the Trujillo-Boconó road was
constructed, and this linked the town to the
state capital and areas beyond.

Today easily accessible by paved road,
Boconó still maintains a sense of isolation,
though tourism has recently begun to
increase. Agriculture apart, the town has
developed into a regional craft centre,
specialising mostly in weaving and pottery.
There are no great attractions in town, but the
place is pleasant enough to look around.
Furthermore, Boconó is a jumping-off point
for San Miguel, famous for its colonial
church (see the following section).

Information

Tourist Office There is no tourist office as
such, but the Alcaldía on Plaza Bolívar may
be able to give you some information.

Money It's better to come with local currency, as Banco Unión, on the north-western
corner of the Plaza Bolívar, may not be
helpful with currency transactions.

Things to See

The **Ateneo de Boconó**, Calle 3 Páez, a
hundred metres below Avenida 1 Colombia,
runs changing art and craft exhibitions and
has a craft workshop which can be visited
(Monday to Friday from 8 am to noon and 2
to 5.30 pm). The **Casa Artesanal**, Calle
Bolívar No 1-30, 1½ blocks downhill from
Plaza Bolívar, is another place where you can
see local crafts. It's open Monday to Friday
from 9 am to noon and 2 to 5 pm, Saturday
from 9 am to noon.

There are several home workshops in the

town and nearby. One of the best known is the pottery workshop of the Briceño family, on the outskirts of Boconó, off the road to Guanare.

The **Trapiche de los Clavo** is going to be opened in the 19th-century sugarcane mill. It will contain a museum dealing with sugarcane and coffee, a library and a workshop, and run various cultural activities. The trapiche is on Calle 6 Jáuregui opposite the hospital, four blocks west of Plaza Bolívar.

Places to Stay

There's quite a choice of budget accommodation. *Hotel Italia* (☎ 52204), Calle 6 Jáuregui No 1-40, is very simple but cheap: US$6 for a couple in a room with its own bath. The *Hotel Los Andes* (☎ 561542), Calle 3 Páez No 1-08, costs much the same, but there are only shared baths. Just around the corner, at Avenida 1 Colombia No 2-47, is *Hotel Trujillo* (☎ 561326), which is perhaps the best of the three and costs the same. It may appear under its new name, *Hotel El Antero*.

Hotel Colonial (☎ 52750), Avenida 3 Miranda No 5-28, is right on Plaza Bolívar. It doesn't offer much more than the Trujillo or Italia, but is dearer (supposedly because of its location): US$7/9 a single/double with bath.

Hotel Venezia (☎ 52778), just off the plaza, Calle 5 Bolívar No 4-39, is marginally better but perhaps overpriced, at US$13 for a double with private bath.

Hotel Vega del Río (☎ 57927) and *Hotel Campestre La Colina* (☎ 52695), both on the north-western outskirts of Boconó, on the road to Trujillo past the bridge, are appreciably better than those listed above, and have their own restaurants.

Places to Eat

Hotel Italia serves inexpensive meals, as does *Hotel Colonial*. There's a number of budget restaurants in the central streets. *Restaurant La Alameda*, Avenida 6 Ricaurte, corner of Calle 5 Bolívar, is one of the better places to eat in town, and it is not expensive.

Getting There & Away

There's no bus terminal in Boconó; buses depart from and arrive at bus company offices which are scattered throughout the central sector of town.

There are several buses a day to Valera (US$2, 2½ hours) and only a few buses to Trujillo (US$1.75, two hours). Buses to Guanare depart until 3 pm (US$2, 3½ hours). If you miss the last one, take a half-hourly bus to Biscucuy, which operate until 5 pm (US$1.50, two hours). From there you may be able to catch a por puesto to Guanare (US$1.25, one hour). Minibuses to San Miguel run every hour or so (US$0.50, 40 minutes).

SAN MIGUEL

A tiny town 27 km north of Boconó, San Miguel is well known for its colonial church. It's an austere, squat, white-washed construction, reputedly built around 1760. The unusual features of the structure include roofed external corridors on both sides of the church and a Latin cross floor plan layout, a design rarely used in Venezuela. However, the highlight is inside: the church has just about the most beautiful folksy retable in the country.

The retable, dating from the time of the church's construction, is a striking, colourful composition, notable for its naive style. In the central niche, above the tabernacle, is the statue of San Miguel (St Michael), the patron saint of the church and the town. The sword in one of his hands is supposed to guard the gates of heaven, whereas the scales in the other hand are to weigh the souls of the dead. Eight other niches – each one occupied by a winged archangel – are distributed symmetrically on two tiers, while the whole remaining surface of the retable is painted with decorative motifs in bright colours, mostly in red, green and yellow.

There are several good statues of saints in the transept and on either side of the decorative arch leading to the presbytery. The statue of the blind Santa Lucía holding her eyes on a plate is particularly interesting. Side retables in the transept are also worth a look.

The church is open daily except Wednesday from 9.30 am to noon and 2 to 5 pm. Mass is at noon on Sunday.

About one km outside San Miguel, on the only road to the town, is the cemetery. Some of the curiously shaped tombstones have been painted with extremely bright colours.

The town's main event is the Romería de los Pastores y Payasos (Feast of Shepherds and Clowns), which is celebrated annually from 4 to 7 January.

Places to Stay & Eat
The *Hostería San Miguel*, the state-owned hotel built during the good years to promote tourism, is the only place to stay. It's pleasant, comfortable, reasonably priced and has its own restaurant. The Hostería is on the opposite side of the plaza from the church.

Getting There & Away
San Miguel lies four km off the Boconó-Trujillo road. The narrow, paved side road to the town branches off 23 km out from Boconó.

San Miguel only has a public transport link with Boconó. Minibuses run between the two towns every hour or so (US$0.50, 40 minutes). In San Miguel, they stop at the plaza in front of the church.

JAJÓ
The road from Valera to Mérida, the central part of the Trans-Andean Highway, is truly spectacular. It winds almost 3500 metres up to the Paso El Águila at 4007 metres (the highest road pass in Venezuela), before dropping 2400 metres down to Mérida. There are several old mountain towns on the road, and others tucked away in the side valleys and on the hillslopes. Of these, Jajó, 48 km south of Valera, is one of the best examples.

Founded in 1611 by Sancho Briceño Graterol amidst the verdant mountains, in the most remote of places, Jajó never grew large or famous. Although paved roads now link the town with both Valera and Mérida, Jajó is still a tiny, sleepy place, and as such it's possibly the finest small colonial town in Trujillo state.

Its prettiest part is around Plaza Bolívar and, particularly, Calle Real which runs northward from the square. If you walk up this street for a hundred metres, you'll get to the **Museo Casa Colonial**, whose collection resembles the contents of a charming antique shop.

Places to Stay & Eat
Jajó has three hotels and all are pleasant. The cheapest is *La Pensión de Jajó*, on the southern side of Plaza Bolívar. It has no sign but you can recognise it by its balcony. Installed in an old house with a patio, there are only a few rooms, all with one double and one single bed and private bath with hot water. A room costs US$9 regardless of the number of people – up to three. La Señora can provide home-cooked meals if you wish, but let her know in advance.

On the western side of the plaza is the *Hotel Turístico Jajó*, the only modern building on the square, which spoils the appearance of the plaza. It's comfortable but doesn't have the charm of the Pensión, and costs US$11 for a single or couple, US$13 for triple and US$14 for a quadruple. The hotel has its own restaurant which serves good trout.

The friendly *Posada Turística Marisabel*, Calle Páez (the northern continuation of Calle Real), a hundred metres north of the square, has good and clean (though dark) rooms, which cost much the same as those in the Hotel. It also has its own restaurant.

One more place to eat is *Restaurant El Balcón de la Abuela*, on Avenida Bolívar, a hundred metres east of the plaza.

Getting There & Away
The usual point of departure for Jajó is Valera. There are hourly buses between Valera and Jajó (US$1, 1½ hours) which operate until 4 or 5 pm. They don't go by the Valera-Mérida Trans-Andean Highway through La Puerta, but along a shorter, eastern road. These buses don't depart from the Valera bus terminal, but from the Plaza San Pedro, Avenida El Estadium, south-east of the city centre.

If you want to get to Jajó from Mérida,

take the morning bus to Valera, get off next to the petrol station at the turnoff to Jajó and try to hitch the remaining 11-km stretch to Jajó. It's fairly easy, though there are not many vehicles using this road.

Mérida State

MÉRIDA

Mérida is one of Venezuela's most popular destinations among foreign travellers. It has an unhurried, friendly atmosphere, plenty of tourist facilities, the famous teleférico and beautiful mountains all around, with the country's highest point, Pico Bolívar, just 12 km south-east as the crow flies. Home to the large Universidad de los Andes (the second oldest university in the country, founded in 1785), the city has a sizeable academic community, which gives it a cultured and bohemian air.

La Ciudad de Santiago de los Caballeros de Mérida was founded in 1558 by Juan Rodríguez Suárez from Pamplona, in Nueva Granada (now Colombia). It's interesting to note that most early towns in the region, including San Cristóbal and Barinas, were founded by expeditions sent from Pamplona, an important political and religious centre of the day, and that they remained under Colombian jurisdiction for a long time after. It was not until 1777 that Mérida (as well as San Cristóbal) became a part of Venezuela. The long association with Colombia can still be felt today, and it is noticeable in the people, culture and language.

Rodríguez Suárez was not authorised to found Mérida. Normally, in order to found a new city in the colony, Spanish approval was necessary. Consequently, Suárez was hunted down and taken to Bogotá where he was placed on trial. As one might expect, there could be only one verdict for such a serious crime – the death sentence – but Rodríguez Suárez miraculously escaped and fled to Trujillo, Venezuela, where he was granted political asylum, reputedly the first case of its kind in the New World.

The foundation affair was fixed up later, after Juan de Maldonado, again from Pamplona, was sent in 1560 with all the paperwork in order, and Mérida was legally founded. However, almost every official source prefers to cite the Rodríguez Suárez adventure as the city's foundation.

Separated by high mountains from both Colombia and Venezuela, Mérida didn't expand rapidly during colonial times. The 1812 earthquake devastated most of the urban fabric, and further hindered development. Two years later, the ruined town gave a warm welcome to Bolívar who passed through, leading his troops on to Caracas. In 1820, Mérida saw Bolívar again, this time on his march to Colombia.

The isolation that had retarded Mérida's progress for centuries, suddenly proved to be its ally. During the federation wars in the mid-19th century, when Venezuela was plunged into full-blown civil war, the city's isolation attracted refugees, and the population began to grow. It was not however until the 1920s that access roads were constructed and later paved. This smoothed the way for Mérida's development. Mérida's transition from a town into a city really only took place over the last few decades.

Mérida sits on a flat *meseta*, a terrace which stretches for a dozen km between two parallel rivers, and the edges of town drop abruptly to the riverbanks. Having filled the meseta as densely as possible, Mérida is now expanding beyond it, and is approaching some 220,000 inhabitants.

Although generally considered by Venezuelans as a 'cold' city (at 1625 metres, it's the highest state capital in the country), Mérida enjoys a pleasant, mild climate, with an average temperature of 19°C. The tourist season is at its peak here around Christmas, Carnaval and Easter, and from late July to early September.

Information
Tourist Office The Cormetur (Corporación Merideña de Turismo) has its main office (☎ 526972) at the junction of Avenidas 1 and 2, a five-minute walk north of Plaza Sucre.

The office is open Monday to Friday from 8 am to noon and 2 to 6 pm, and you'll probably get city maps and good information there. Cormetur also operates several outlets throughout the city, including those at the airport (☎ 639330) and the bus terminal (☎ 633952).

Inparques The Inparques office (☎ 631473, 633189, 631407) is on Avenida Urdaneta, corner of Calle 51, near the airport. You won't actually need it, as trekking permits are issued by the Inparques outlet next to the teleférico, and the maps of the Sierra they sell can also be bought in the Posada Las Heroínas, Calle 24 No 8-95 (Parque Las Heroínas).

Tours, Guides & Maps All you are likely to need is conveniently located in Parque Las Heroínas. There, you'll find two good mountain-tour operators: firstly Yana Pacha Tours (☎ 526910), Calle 24 No 8-97, and secondly Guamanchi Expeditions (☎ 522080), in the Mercado Artesanal, Local 4. Both are run by experienced climbers who either go with you up the mountains or send you there with other well-qualified climbers, who are friends of theirs. They are the cream of Mérida's *montañistas*. If you arrange a mountain expedition with full-service agents in the city centre, they are likely to call one of the above-listed operators and contract a

guide, charging you far more for the service. Both Yana Pacha and Guamanchi offer a guide service only, or can provide you with all the mountaineering equipment you need if you don't have your own gear.

Tom Evenou, the owner of the Posada Las Heroínas (☎ 522665), next door to Yana Pacha, organises tours to the astronomical observatory (see the Around Mérida section). He's also a good contact person for independent local guides and guides for other regions such as Los Llanos and the Amazon. Tom also sells a variety of maps of the region, country and continent, including good Bradt-published maps.

La Casa del Turista, a handicraft shop on Avenida 3 just off Plaza Bolívar, sells a choice of regional guidebooks and maps.

Money Major banks are near Plaza Bolívar, and most of them handle some foreign exchange operations. Almost all banks marked on the map should change cash; the Banco Italo Venezolano and Banco Barinas will probably change travellers' cheques, whereas Banco Maracaibo and Banco Unión service credit card holders. The Banco Consolidado is a short walk north-west along Calle 26 and, as elsewhere, deals with American Express travellers' cheques and credit cards. Turisol (☎ 631085, 632431) is in Centro Comercial Las Tapias, Planta Baja, Locales 5 and 6, Avenida Andrés Bello.

Things to See

The city centre is quite pleasant for leisurely strolls, though there is not much in the way of colonial architecture or outstanding tourist attractions. Plaza Bolívar is the city's heart, but it's not a colonial square. Work on the **Catedral** was begun in 1800, based on plans of the 17th-century cathedral of Toledo in Spain, but was not completed until 1958, and probably only then because the work speeded up over the final stage to meet the celebration for the 400th anniversary of the city's foundation. Not surprisingly, the end result is different from the initial design.

Next to the cathedral, in the Palacio Arzobispal, is the **Museo Arquidiocesano**, with a collection of religious art, open Thursday to Saturday from 9 am to noon. Note the bell, cast in 909, thought to be the second oldest surviving bell in the world. Opposite the museum, across the square, is the **Casa de la Cultura** which provides space for various temporary exhibitions. It's open Monday to Friday from 8 am to noon and 2 to 6 pm, Saturday and Sunday from 10 am to 5 pm.

The Universidad de los Andes building, just off the plaza, houses the **Museo Arqueológico**, open Tuesday to Friday from 3 to 6 pm, Saturday and Sunday from 4 to 8 pm. A small but interesting collection, supported by extensive background information on boards (in Spanish only), gives an insight into the pre-Hispanic times of the region.

Three blocks north-east of the plaza is the recently restored **Casa de los Gobernadores**. Inside, you can see several amazing ceramic models of important city buildings, all made by a noted local artist, Eduardo Fuentes. He has a shop in the Mercado Artesanal, in the Parque Las Heroínas, where you can buy some of his more modest works.

The modern **Biblioteca Bolivariana** features an exhibition related to Bolívar. The showpiece of the collection is a sword made in Peru in 1825 and presented to El Libertador after his victory at Junín. The sheath is made entirely of gold, and encrusted with 1380 precious stones, including diamonds and emeralds.

Two blocks north-east, the **Museo de Arte Colonial** has a small and rather uninspiring collection of mostly sacred art. It's open Tuesday to Friday from 9 am to noon and 3 to 6 pm, Saturday and Sunday from 10 am to 5 pm.

Five blocks north-east, at the end of Avenida 4, you'll find the small **Parque de las Cinco Repúblicas**, boasting the oldest monument to Bolívar, dating from 1842.

Outside the city centre, the **Museo de Arte Moderno**, in Parque Beethoven, at the northern end of the city, has a small but fine collection of contemporary works by national artists. It's open Tuesday to Friday from 9 am to noon and 3 to 6 pm, Saturday and Sunday from 10 am to 5 pm.

Also in the northern sector of the city, but closer to the centre, is the **Parque La Isla** once noted for its variety of orchids. More interesting than the orchids – which are unkempt – is the recently opened **Museo de Apicultura**, which deals with various aspects of beekeeping. Some four km south west of the centre, on Avenida Andrés Bello, the **Jardín Acuario** has an exhibition devoted to the traditional culture of the region.

Teleférico

The highlight of a visit to Mérida used to undoubtedly be the teleférico, the world's highest and longest cable car, constructed in 1958 by a French company. It runs for 12.6 km from Mérida up to the top of Pico Espejo at 4765 metres, covering the 3188-metre climb in four stages. It has five stations: Barinitas (1577 metres), Montaña (2436 metres), Aguada (3452 metres), Loma Redonda (4045 metres) and Pico Espejo (4765 metres). Unfortunately, the whole cable car has been out of order since late 1993 and no date has been set yet for the reopening.

Places to Stay

Mérida has heaps of hotels and most of them offer good value for money. There's an array of places called posadas, which are small,

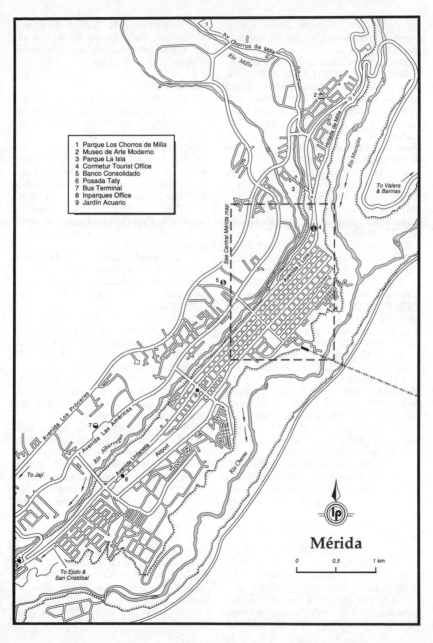

1 Parque Los Chorros de Milla
2 Museo de Arte Moderno
3 Parque La Isla
4 Cormetur Tourist Office
5 Banco Consolidado
6 Posada Taty
7 Bus Terminal
8 Inparques Office
9 Jardín Acuario

Av Chorros de Milla
Río Milla

Holanda de Milla

Río Mucujún

To Valera
& Barinas

See Central Mérida map

Avenida 2 Lora

Avenida Los Próceres

Avenida Las Américas

Río Albarregas

Airport

Avenida Urdaneta

Río Chama

To Jají

To Ejido &
San Cristóbal

Mérida

0   0.5   1 km

family-run guest houses, often with a friendly atmosphere. These are usually good places to stay in.

The cheapest place in the city centre is *Hotel Italia* (☎ 525737), Calle 19 No 2-55. It has small, simple singles/doubles without bath for US$3/5 and doubles/triples with bath for US$6/8. There are several other cheapies in the same area, including *Hotel Budapest* (☎ 526728), *Hotel Las Nieves* and *Hotel Los Frailejones* (☎ 526661), but none of them is as cheap as the Italia.

One place worth special recommendation is the *Posada Las Heroínas* (☎ 522665) in Parque Las Heroínas, run by Tom Evenou, a polyglot Swiss, and his wife. You pay US$4/5 per person in rooms without/with bath. The hotel is often full.

You have more chance of finding a vacancy in the *Residencia Araure* (☎ 525103), Calle 16 No 3-34, which is clean and pleasant and charges US$4 per head for doubles or triples without bath. *Residencias San Pedro* (☎ 522735), Calle 19 No 6-36, offers much the same for US$5 per person.

Other recommended places include *Posada Luz Caraballo* (☎ 525441), Avenida 2 No 13-80 (US$5 per person); the Spanish-run *Hotel Español* (☎ 529235), Avenida 2 No 15-48 (spotlessly clean doubles for US$11); and the German-owned *Posada Alemania* (☎ 524067), Avenida 2 near the corner of Calle 18 (US$10/13 a single/double).

The very agreeable *Posada Turística Marianela* (☎ 526907), Calle 16 No 4-33, has doubles/quadruples without bath for US$13/25, including breakfast. It's run by an extremely friendly English-speaking woman. Her sister runs the equally pleasant *Posada Taty*, on Avenida Urdaneta near the airport.

The *Hotel Santiago de los Caballeros* (☎ 523223), Avenida 3 No 24-19, has good singles/doubles/triples with bath for US$7/10/15. The *Hotel Luxemburgo* (☎ 526865), Calle 24 No 6-37, offers lower standards for slightly more – it has seen better days.

Should you need more comfort, there's a good supply of up-market hotels, including the *Hotel Chama* (☎ 524851), Calle 29 near the corner of Avenida 4, and *Hotel Mintoy* (☎ 520340), Calle 25 No 8-130, just off Parque Las Heroínas. Both have comfortable doubles for around US$28.

Places to Eat

If you are used to unpretentious, low-budget dining, Mérida is for you – it's probably the cheapest place to eat in Venezuela. Plenty of restaurants serve set meals for, at most, US$1.50, including *La Chipilina*, on the corner of Avenida 3 and Calle 19, *El Portón Andino*, on the corner of Avenida 4 and Calle 19, *Los Corales*, on the corner of Avenida 4 and Calle 16, and *Pulcritud*, at Calle 19 No 5-80 (they also have good typical Colombian buñuelos). Slightly better and not much more expensive is *Alfredo's*, on the corner of Avenida 4 and Calle 19.

For cheap vegie meals, try *Madre Tierra*, at Parque Las Heroínas, *La Gran Fraternidad Universal*, on Avenida 4 near the corner of Calle 18, and *El Tinajero*, on Calle 29 near Avenida 4.

El Tatuy, at Parque Las Heroínas, has inexpensive typical food. *Cheo's Pizzería*, in the Hotel El Parque, at Parque Las Heroínas, does some of the best pizzas in town, while *La Guanábana*, Calle 25 No 6-26, is a good if ordinary-looking place for batidos and merengadas. *Onde Jaime*, Avenida 5 No 23-15, is the place to go for typical Colombian food at reasonable prices.

During the fishing season, June to September, many restaurants serve trout, which is usually fresh and tasty, as it comes from the nearby rivers and lakes. Ask for the trucha al ajillo, one of the local specialties.

Café París, Calle 23 off Plaza Bolívar, has tables outside and is a popular rendezvous, for both locals and foreigners. If you want a really good coffee, however, go to *Cafetín Santa Rosa*, on Avenida 4 opposite Banco de Venezuela. For an evening beer in a good atmosphere, try *Birosca Carioca*, Calle 24 No 2-04, which is one of the popular nightspots in the city centre. Good cakes are served in *Tía Nicota*, a cosy place in the Centro Comercial Galerías 1890, at Avenida 3 No 25-42.

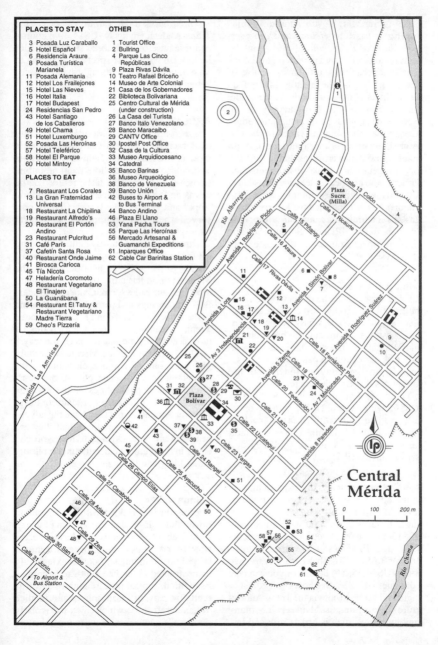

PLACES TO STAY

3 Posada Luz Caraballo
5 Hotel Español
6 Residencia Araure
8 Posada Turística Marianela
11 Posada Alemania
12 Hotel Los Frailejones
15 Hotel Las Nieves
16 Hotel Italia
17 Hotel Budapest
24 Residencias San Pedro
43 Hotel Santiago de los Caballeros
49 Hotel Chama
51 Hotel Luxemburgo
52 Posada Las Heroínas
57 Hotel Teleférico
58 Hotel El Parque
60 Hotel Mintoy

PLACES TO EAT

7 Restaurant Los Corales
13 La Gran Fraternidad Universal
18 Restaurant La Chipilina
19 Restaurant Alfredo's
20 Restaurant El Portón Andino
23 Restaurant Pulcritud
31 Café París
37 Cafetín Santa Rosa
40 Restaurant Onde Jaime
41 Birosca Carioca
45 Tía Nicota
47 Heladería Coromoto
48 Restaurant Vegetariano El Tinajero
50 La Guanábana
54 Restaurant El Tatuy & Restaurant Vegetariano Madre Tierra
59 Cheo's Pizzería

OTHER

1 Tourist Office
2 Bullring
4 Parque Las Cinco Repúblicas
9 Plaza Rivas Dávila
10 Teatro Rafael Briceño
14 Museo de Arte Colonial
21 Casa de los Gobernadores
22 Biblioteca Bolivariana
25 Centro Cultural de Mérida (under construction)
26 La Casa del Turista
27 Banco Italo Venezolano
28 Banco Maracaibo
29 CANTV Office
30 Ipostel Post Office
32 Casa de la Cultura
33 Museo Arquidiocesano
34 Catedral
35 Banco Barinas
36 Museo Arqueológico
38 Banco de Venezuela
39 Banco Unión
42 Buses to Airport & to Bus Terminal
44 Banco Andino
46 Plaza El Llano
53 Yana Pacha Tours
55 Parque Las Heroínas
56 Mercado Artesanal & Guamanchi Expeditions
61 Inparques Office
62 Cable Car Barinitas Station

Central Mérida

Being in Mérida you shouldn't miss paying a visit to *Heladería Coromoto*, Avenida 3 No 28-75, which is just about the most famous ice-cream parlour on the continent (it appears in the Guinness Book of Records). Run by the friendly Manuel da Silva Oliveira (more familiarly, Manolo), the place offers around 110 flavours on an average day, but has 550 flavours altogether. Among the more unusual varieties you can try are Polar beer, shrimp, trout, chicken with spaghetti or, if you are a vegetarian, just ask for 'el vegetariano'. Strike up a conversation with Manolo and he will let you try his latest sophisticated achievements. Ask him whether he has concocted the Lonely Planet flavour (which may appear under the Spanish name, 'Planeta Solitario'). The place is open from 2 to 10 pm, except Mondays.

Getting There & Away

Air The airport is on the meseta, right inside the city, two km south-west of Plaza Bolívar. Frequent urban busetas pass by the airport. The runway is short, and the proximity of high mountains doesn't make landing an easy task, especially in bad weather. Consequently, in the rainy season flights are sometimes diverted elsewhere.

There are five flights daily to Caracas (US$65 with Avensa, US$61 with Aeropostal), and one flight with Avensa to each of San Antonio del Táchira (US$33), Maracaibo (US$44), Valencia (US$69) and Barquisimeto (US$52).

Bus The bus terminal is three km south-west of the city centre and serviced by frequent public transport. Half a dozen buses a day run to Caracas (US$14.00 standard service, US$15.50 deluxe, 11 hours), and three buses to Maracaibo (US$7.75, nine hours). Busetas to San Cristóbal depart every two hours (US$4.25, 5½ hours), or you can take a por puesto (US$6, five hours); all go via El Vigía and La Fría (not via the Trans-Andean route). Por puestos also service many regional routes, such as Apartaderos and Jají.

Three buses a day run to Valera via the Trans-Andean Highway (US$4, five hours), and five buses go to Barinas (US$3.50, four hours). Both roads are spectacular. Going to Valera, take a seat on the right-hand side for better views.

AROUND MÉRIDA

The region surrounding Mérida offers plenty of attractions, and you can easily spend a week or two here. Some sights are accessible by road, so you can explore them on public transport. This particularly refers to the towns and villages which dot the mountain slopes and valleys. Many of them have preserved their old architecture and rural atmosphere from the past.

Other attractions, mostly natural ones, are off the road, and walking is the only way of getting to them. If you plan on hiking, the Mérida region has a lot to offer. Rocky hill tops, verdant valleys, mountain lakes, waterfalls, hot springs and páramos are just some of the attractions. You don't necessarily need a tent, as many routes are one-day walks, or have accommodation facilities on the way.

The Sierra Nevada de Mérida is the only mountain range in Venezuela suitable for mountaineers. The Venezuelan Andes don't offer as many possibilities or the extreme conditions of Colombia, Ecuador, Peru, Chile or Argentina, but they have the advantage of being easier to climb, and they are beautiful anyway. Other activities you can enjoy in the region include mountain biking, paragliding and fishing.

Things to See

The region is sprinkled with old mountain towns and villages, the best-known of which is **Jají**, about 38 km west of Mérida, accessible by por puestos from the bus terminal (US$0.60, 50 minutes). Jají was extensively reconstructed in the late 1960s to become a manicured, typical pueblo andino, and it is pretty touristy. Its Plaza Bolívar has a choice of handicraft shops which enjoy particularly good trade on weekends, when most visitors come. There are two pleasant posadas in the village.

Eight km before Jají, beside the road, is the **Chorrera de los González**, a series of five waterfalls. You can stop here to have a bathe in the falls' ponds, or just to have a look. You can climb three of the waterfalls by taking side paths.

For a more authentic pueblo, try **Mucuchíes**, a 400-year-old town, about 48 km north-east of Mérida. Several km further down the road is **San Rafael**, noted for an amazing small, stone chapel built by a local artist, Juan Félix Sánchez. This is his second chapel; the first, equally beautiful, was constructed two decades ago in the remote hamlet of **El Tisure**, a five-hour walk from San Rafael (there is no access road).

North of San Rafael, at an altitude of about 3600 metres, you will find the **Centro de Investigaciones de Astronomía**, an astronomical observatory which can be visited on some days and evenings of the week (call their Mérida office, ☎ 712780, for details). It's best to go there in the evening so you can look at the stars. The place is off the main road and accessible by a rough track only, and there is no public transport. The owner of Posada Las Heroínas in Mérida runs Saturday evening tours for about US$12 per person (the price includes the US$2 entrance fee to the observatory).

There are a number of *termales* (hot springs) in the region, of which the **Aguas Calientes**, a few km from Ejido (13 km south-west of Mérida), are probably the best known; they have facilities. Carros marked Aguas Calientes go there from Mérida, corner of Calle 26 and Avenida 5.

Possibly the best undeveloped springs are near Tabay, a town 15 km north-east of Mérida, serviced by frequent carros. Once in Tabay, continue along the main road to the end of the town, and take the side road which branches off just before the cemetery and heads uphill. It's about a 45-minute walk to the springs.

There are two open-air museums/amusement parks, **Los Aleros** and **La Venezuela de Antier**, in the vicinity of Mérida. They have become favourite attractions for Venezuelan tourists, though they may look somewhat pretentious (particularly the Venezuela de Antier) for some foreign travellers.

The first, Los Aleros, on the road to Mucuchíes, shortly past Tabay, was opened in 1984. It's a model of a typical Andean village from the 1930s, brought to life with period events, crafts and food. It's open daily from 9 am to 4 pm; admission is US$3.50.

La Venezuela de Antier was opened quite recently. Here, the same entrepreneur, Romer Alexis Montilla, has created a sort of Venezuela in a capsule, by reproducing its landmarks and recreating the country's traditions. Accordingly, you'll find the Plaza Bolívar of Caracas, the Puente Urdaneta of Maracaibo and the oldest monument to Bolívar from Mérida. You'll see Amazonian Indians, Guajiro women in their traditional dresses, and even General Juan Vicente Gómez appears in his uniform. The old trapiche serves sugarcane juice for guests, and cockfights are usually held at weekends. There's also a collection of old cars. The park is several km from Mérida on the Jají road. The entrance fee is US$7.

Mountaineering

Possibly the most popular peak to climb is Venezuela's highest point, **Pico Bolívar** (5007 metres). Given the country's mania for Bolívar monuments, it probably shouldn't come as a surprise that a bust of the hero has been placed on the summit.

The climb is not technically difficult, but you shouldn't do it without a guide unless you have mountaineering experience. Until the last stretch of the teleférico to Pico Espejo reopens, your usual starting point will be Loma Redonda, from where a four-hour walk will take you up to Pico Espejo. There's a simple refuge there, used by trekkers to stay in overnight before the early morning climb to Bolívar's bust. When the last stage of the cable car is again in operation, the trip will be able to be done in one day.

Other peaks can also be scaled without much difficulty; of these, **Pico Humboldt** (4942 metres) is possibly the most attractive goal. There's not much here in the way of mountaineering, but the hike itself is marvellous.

The starting point for the walk is La Mucuy, accessible by road from Mérida. Take a carro to Tabay, from the corner of Calle 19 and Avenida 4. From Tabay's Plaza Bolívar, por puesto jeeps go to La Mucuy; Inparques has its post here.

A three to four-hour walk will take you up to the small Laguna La Coromoto; in another two hours you can reach the Laguna Verde, the largest lake in the area. If it's still not too late, walk for another hour to the Laguna El Suero, where you will find a poor, dilapidated refuge. You are now at an altitude of about 4200 metres, almost at the foot of the glacier. It gets freezing at night, so have plenty of warm clothes.

Pico Humboldt is a two to three-hour ascent, depending on the weather. You reach the snowline at about 4600 to 4700 metres. Further up, crampons are recommended, and keep an eye out for crevices.

Back at Laguna El Suero, you can return the same way to La Mucuy or continue to Pico Espejo (4765 metres). After an initial 500-metre ascent from the Laguna, the trail to Pico Espejo (four hours) goes for most of the way at roughly the same altitude, nearly 4700 metres. You then can 'do' Pico Bolívar, before descending to Loma Redonda and returning by the teleférico. The total return trip will take from three to five days, or even longer, depending on how many peaks you climb and, of course, the weather conditions.

The mountain-tour operators in Mérida, Yana Pacha and Guamanchi, can provide full equipment and guides for these treks. They will give you information on these and other hikes in the area, even if you don't employ their services.

Hiking

If you are not up to scaling the peaks, there's an easy and popular hike from Loma Redonda to **Los Nevados**, a charming mountain pueblo set at an altitude of about 2700 metres (accommodation and food available). It's a 14.5-km trip, (four hours' walk) which includes a short ascent to a pass, Alto de la Cruz, followed by a gentle walk downhill. You can hire mules in Loma Redonda for this trip (US$4 per mule, plus US$4 for the *arriero*). From Los Nevados, you can walk back the same way (six hours), or take one of the sporadic jeeps to Mérida along a very rough track (63 km, US$12, five hours). Most hikers, however, prefer to continue walking for seven hours (21 km) downhill to the village of El Morro (rooms and meals available), from where jeeps run pretty regularly to Mérida.

Another interesting area for hiking is in the north-eastern end of the Sierra Nevada park. For example, take a morning bus to Valera and get off at Venezuela's highest road pass (4007 metres), next to **Pico El Águila** (4118 metres), which is about 60 km from Mérida. Bolívar marched this way on one of his campaigns and, predictably, a monument to the hero has been erected on the pass.

There's a roadside restaurant at the pass where you can have a hot chocolate before setting off. You can sometimes spot condors here which have recently been reintroduced from abroad. Locals with mules are waiting opposite the restaurant to take you to **Laguna Mucubají**, five km due south, but it's better to walk there, to get a closer look at the splendid páramo, filled with frailejones. The walk, downhill all the way, will bring you to the Barinas road. The laguna, just off the road, is the largest in the Sierra Nevada park but not particularly beautiful in itself. It's well worth walking for one hour up the reforested pine slope to **Laguna Negra**, a small but beautiful mountain lake whose water is amazingly dark. About 1½ hours' walk further uphill is another fine lake, **Laguna Los Patos**.

If you want to camp, get a permit from Inparques at Laguna Mucubají. Their office is open from 8 am to 6 pm, and the staff can provide information on other sights in the area. There are two hotels by the road near the lake.

A trail from Laguna Mucubají goes seven km south to the top of **Pico Mucuñuque**

Top: Chapel built by Juan Félix Sánchez, San Rafael, the Andes
Bottom: Heladería Coromoto (ice-cream parlour), Mérida

Top Left: Cerro de Santa Ana, Península de Paraguana
Top Right: Frailejón, typical plant of the Páramos, the Andes
Bottom Left: Médanos de Coro
Bottom Right: Los Llanos landscape

(4672 metres), the highest peak in this range, which is known as the Serranía de Santo Domingo. The round trip will take you a good part of the day. It's a rather difficult hike, as the trail is not clear in the upper reaches and you have to ascend 1425 metres from the laguna. Ask for detailed instructions at the Inparques post.

Mountain Biking

Still a relatively new form of outdoor activity, mountain bike riding in the Andes is nonetheless becoming popular, and there are already a few travel agencies in Mérida which provide bikes and other equipment. One of the most popular routes is a trip to the remote mountain villages south of Mérida, accessible by rough roads only. The loop usually includes the villages of San José, Mucutuy, Mucuchachí, Canaguá, Chocanta, El Molino, Capurí, Guaraque and, last but not least ,Tovar. Inquire at the agencies listed in the Mérida section. Also contact Chucho Faría, at the Inparques office at the teleférico station, who is one of the pioneers of cycling in the region. He organises trips, providing all necessary gear. His home telephone number is ☎ 636491.

Fishing

Anglers may be interested in trout fishing. The most popular spots are Laguna Mucubají and Laguna La Victoria, and, to a lesser extent, Laguna Negra and Laguna Los Patos. The fishing season runs from July to September. You need a permit from the Ministerio de Agricultura y Cría (☎ 632981), Avenida Urdaneta, near the airport in Mérida. The permit costs next to nothing and allows for angling in the national park.

Fishing equipment can be hired in the Posada Las Heroínas in Mérida (US$2.50 per day) or, if you plan on serious angling, buy your own gear in Mérida.

Paragliding

Paragliding is the newest craze in the region, and one can occasionally see gliders circling over Mérida valley, then landing at the airport in the city. Several operators in Mérida have tandem gliders: they include Guamanchi Expeditions; Yana Pacha Tours (see the Mérida section for addresses for both of them); Marcelito, in La Fresa, at the end of Calle 26; and Leopoldo, in Escuela Leonardo da Vinci (☎ 527554). The usual price for a tandem flight is US$50. Marcelito also conducts paragliding courses, and rents gliders for US$50 a day.

Places to Stay & Eat

There's no shortage of accommodation along the Trans-Andean Highway. Almost every sizeable village on the road has a couple of posadas, and there's a satisfactory number of roadside restaurants.

The most charming place to stay in the region is probably the *Hotel Los Frailes*, midway between Apartaderos and Santo Domingo, on the Barinas road. Installed in an old monastery, it costs around US$50 for a double and has a good restaurant. Across the road, the *Hotel Paso Real* is almost just as pleasant at US$30 a double.

The recently built *Castillo San Ignacio* (☎ 81021) in Mucuchíes is a quite different place to splurge. It's a sort of brick castle which looks as though it was transported from medieval Europe, unusually exotic in the Andean setting. Rooms for two to four persons go for somewhere between US$40 and US$50, and there's an atmospheric restaurant downstairs.

Táchira State

SAN CRISTÓBAL

The capital of Táchira state, some 40 km east of the Colombian border, San Cristóbal is today a thriving city of nearly 300,000 inhabitants. Spread over a mountain slope at an altitude of about 800 metres, the city has an attractive location and agreeable climate, with an average temperature of 21°C. However, San Cristóbal has little to offer tourists and it is just a place to pass through rather than being a place to stop.

Founded in 1561 by Juan de Maldonado, the town grew slowly, and three centuries after its birth it was still not much more than an obscure settlement. This is why the city has almost no colonial architecture.

For more than the first 200 years of its life, San Cristóbal was ruled from Nueva Granada (today Colombia). In 1777, with the rest of Táchira, it came under Venezuelan administration. Even then, though, because of the lack of roads to Caracas, the town was linked more to Colombia than to Venezuela. It wasn't until 1925 that the winding Trans-Andean Highway reached San Cristóbal from Mérida, and it was not until the 1950s that the Pan-American Highway was completed, providing a fast, lowland link with the centre of the country.

San Cristóbal is an almost unavoidable transit point if you come from or you're going to Cúcuta in Colombia. But if you arrive late you may need to stay overnight in the city.

Information

Tourist Office The Oficina de Turismo (☎ 59710) is in the Complejo Ferial (Fair Complex), in Pueblo Nuevo district, north of the city centre. They have a stand (*módulo*) (☎ 449171) in the Centro Cívico, just south of Plaza Bolívar.

The Andes – San Cristóbal 227

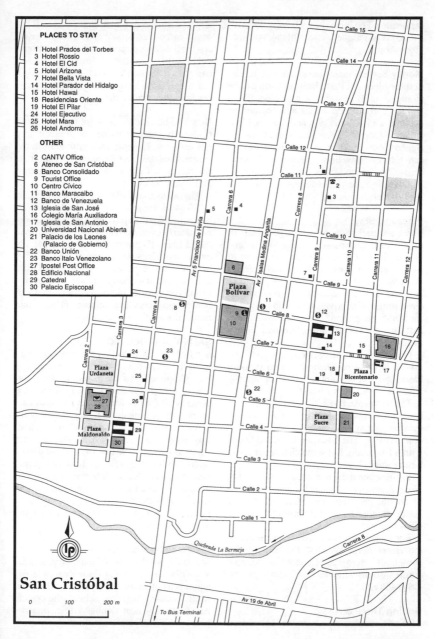

PLACES TO STAY

1 Hotel Prados del Torbes
3 Hotel Rossio
4 Hotel El Cid
5 Hotel Arizona
7 Hotel Bella Vista
14 Hotel Parador del Hidalgo
15 Hotel Hawai
18 Residencias Oriente
19 Hotel El Pilar
24 Hotel Ejecutivo
25 Hotel Mara
26 Hotel Andorra

OTHER

2 CANTV Office
6 Ateneo de San Cristóbal
8 Banco Consolidado
9 Tourist Office
10 Centro Cívico
11 Banco Maracaibo
12 Banco de Venezuela
13 Iglesia de San José
16 Colegio María Auxiliadora
17 Iglesia de San Antonio
20 Universidad Nacional Abierta
21 Palacio de los Leones
   (Palacio de Gobierno)
22 Banco Unión
23 Banco Italo Venezolano
27 Ipostel Post Office
28 Edificio Nacional
29 Catedral
30 Palacio Episcopal

San Cristóbal

0   100   200 m

Inparques The Inparques office (☎ 465216, 27763) is in Parque Metropolitano, Avenida 19 de Abril.

Money Several major banks are within two or three blocks of Plaza Bolívar. Cash can be changed at Banco Maracaibo (on Plaza Bolívar), Banco de Venezuela (corner of Calle 8 and Carrera 9), and Banco Consolidado (corner of Avenida 5 and Calle 8). Banco Consolidado also deals with American Express travellers' cheques and credit cards. The Banco Unión (corner of Avenida 7 and Calle 5) services MasterCard and Visa card holders.

Places to Stay

There are perhaps a dozen budget hotels in the city centre but most double as love hotels. One of the few which doesn't rent rooms to passionate couples is the friendly *Hotel Parador del Hidalgo* (☎ 432839), Calle 7 No 9-35. It's simple and lacks style but has clean rooms with private baths and hot water, for US$5 per person. The hotel has its own restaurant serving unpretentious cheap meals.

One block east, up the steps, at Calle 7 No 10-43, is the *Hotel Hawai*, which is more basic and not so innocent, but cheaper – US$8 for a double with bath.

The *Hotel Andorra*, Carrera 4 No 4-67, near the cathedral, is one of the cheapest options in the city centre, US$7/10 for a double/triple. The hotel, set in an old house with a fine patio, has some charm but fairly basic rooms.

In the same area, at Calle 6 No 3-25, the *Hotel Ejecutivo* (☎ 446298) is also located in an old building, and offers marginally better standards, with doubles/triples for US$8/11.

For something considerably better, go to the *Hotel Bella Vista* (☎ 437866), on the corner of Carrera 9 and Calle 9. Comfortable singles/doubles/triples with bath go for US$14/20/25.

Getting There & Away

Air San Cristóbal has no airport. The closest airports are at Santo Domingo, about 40 km south-east of San Cristóbal (formally considered as the city's airport), and at San Antonio del Táchira, on the Colombian border, roughly the same distance from San Cristóbal. Both have flights to Caracas and several other main cities.

Bus The bus station is about two km south of the city centre, serviced by frequent city bus services. To get to the terminal from the centre, take the 'La Concordia' buseta from the corner of Calle 8 and Carrera 9, next to San José Church.

There are about 10 buses daily to Caracas (US$14 ordinary, US$15.50 deluxe, 13 hours). Most depart in the late afternoon/early evening for an overnight trip via the El Llano Highway. Busetas go to Mérida every two hours until 6 pm (US$4.25, 5½ hours). There are also por puestos for US$6 and they are marginally quicker. Por puestos to San Antonio del Táchira on the Colombian border run every few minutes (US$1, one hour); it's a quite spectacular road.

SAN PEDRO DEL RÍO

San Pedro del Río is a tiny town tucked away from the main roads, about 40 km north of San Cristóbal. It's clean, well cared for, lethargic and colonial looking. There are perhaps altogether four calles and four carreras, all cobblestoned, and lined with meticulously restored and white-washed, single-storey houses. There are no particular sights as such, but the town as a whole makes up for this by being a fine architectural piece, and an oasis of peace – a perfect place if you need a rest in an old-time atmosphere. The small **El Pequeño Museo**, on the main square, has some objects related to the town's history.

Places to Stay & Eat

The only hotel is the *Posada Turística La Vieja Ecuela* (☎ 93664), Calle Real No 3-61, and it is as pleasant and inviting as the town itself. Located in an old school, the posada has spotlessly neat doubles/triples/quadruples for US$11/15/18.

There are four or five restaurants, the best of which is probably *El Balcón*, near the Posada, located in the only two-storey colonial house in town. They have some regional specialties, including good mondongo, a kind of tripe stew. Should you feel like having a drink, ask for the calentado (a sort of cane brandy with honey, cloves and often other condiments) or for leche de burra (a local liquor with egg). The *Antojitos Andinos*, near the main plaza, serves cheap set meals.

Getting There & Away

San Pedro del Río lies five km off the San Cristóbal-La Fría road. From San Cristóbal, take the half-hourly bus to San Juan de Colón and get off at the alcabala (US$0.80, one hour) a few km before reaching San Juan, where the road to San Pedro branches off. From there, catch the half-hourly bus to San Pedro (US$0.20, 10 minutes) which comes through from San Juan.

If you are coming from the north (as you will be if coming from Mérida or Maracaibo), stop in San Juan de Colón and take the bus to San Pedro (US$0.25, 15 minutes); it departs every half an hour from just near the main plaza.

SAN ANTONIO DEL TÁCHIRA

San Antonio is a border town with some 50,000 people, living off trade with unloved, neighbouring Colombia. The centre is tightly packed with shops, though avalanches of Colombian consumers seem to be a thing of the past. Now, Venezuelans go to Cúcuta in search of bargains. For travellers, San Antonio is a place to pass through quickly, stopping only for passport formalities. Move your watch one hour forward when crossing from Colombia to Venezuela, and one hour backward if you enter Colombia from Venezuela.

Information

Tourist Office There's no tourist office in town, but travel agents will solve your transport problems. There are three agencies on the town's main thoroughfare, La Avenida (Carrera 4): Viajes Turismo San Antonio (☎ 77730), Carrera 4 No 6-31; Viajes Turismo Uribante (☎ 78050), Carrera 4 No 5-59; and Turismo Internacional (☎ 78778), corner of Avenida 4 and Calle 4. All three will book and sell air tickets for flights within Venezuela (but not for Colombian domestic flights).

Money There are more than half a dozen banks in San Antonio, but none of them changes cash. Only Banco Consolidado, on Plaza Bolívar, accepts American Express travellers' cheques and credit cards, and Banco Unión, on Calle 4, off the plaza, deals with Visa card holders.

There are plenty of casas de cambio in the centre, particularly around La Avenida. They all change dollars, bolívares and Colombian pesos in any direction. None of the casas changes travellers' cheques.

Immigration The DIEX office is on Carrera 9 between Calles 6 and 7, and is theoretically open daily from 6 am to 8 pm, although they use to close earlier. You have to get an exit or entry stamp in your passport here.

Your don't need a visa to enter Colombia (unless you are a Chinese citizen), but you must get an entry stamp from DAS (the Colombian immigration authorities). The DAS office is just behind the frontier (open Monday to Saturday 7 am to 7 pm, on Sunday until 6 pm), on your right, past the bridge over the Río Táchira, the actual border. It's only a few hundred metres from San Antonio, but it's best to walk over the bridge, as some cases of robbery have been reported. The favourite scam seems to be that someone 'accidentally' bumps into you, throwing you off balance, while your backpack is ripped off you and thrown over the bridge, and accomplices below take care of it from there. Instead of walking, take a bus or a colectivo (that's what por puestos are called in Colombia) which will let you down in front of DAS.

There's another DAS office in Cúcuta, in San Rafael suburb, Avenida 1 No 28-57

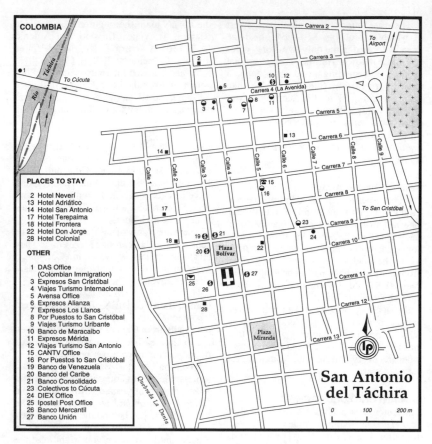

PLACES TO STAY

2 Hotel Neverí
13 Hotel Adriático
14 Hotel San Antonio
17 Hotel Terepaima
18 Hotel Frontera
22 Hotel Don Jorge
28 Hotel Colonial

OTHER

1 DAS Office
  (Colombian Immigration)
3 Expresos San Cristóbal
4 Viajes Turismo Internacional
5 Avensa Office
6 Expresos Alianza
7 Expresos Los Llanos
8 Por Puestos to San Cristóbal
9 Viajes Turismo Uribante
10 Banco de Maracaibo
11 Expresos Mérida
12 Viajes Turismo San Antonio
15 CANTV Office
16 Por Puestos to San Cristóbal
19 Banco de Venezuela
20 Banco del Caribe
21 Banco Consolidado
23 Colectivos to Cúcuta
24 DIEX Office
25 Ipostel Post Office
26 Banco Mercantil
27 Banco Unión

San Antonio del Táchira

0   100   200 m

(open daily from 6 am to noon and 2 to 8 pm). There's also a DAS office at Cúcuta airport, but they will only give you an entry stamp if you fly out of Cúcuta.

Places to Stay

Hotel Frontera, Calle 2 No 8-70, is possibly the cheapest in town (US$4 a double) but basic. The best budget bet is *Hotel Colonial* (☎ 713123), Carrera 11 No 2-52, which has good clean double rooms with fan and private bath for US$7. The *Hotel San Antonio* (☎ 711023), corner of Carrera 6 and Calle 2, costs much the same as the Colonial

but is not as good. Yet another budget option, the *Hotel Terepaima* (☎ 711763), Carrera 8 No 1-37, charges US$4 per person and has a cheap restaurant.

The cheapest air-conditioned rooms are in the *Hotel Neverí* (☎ 714632), Carrera 3 No 3-13, one block from the border crossing. Singles/doubles/triples/quadruples cost US$10/12/14/15.

The two best hotels in town are *Hotel Don Jorge* (☎ 711932), Calle 5 No 9-20 (US$18/21/24 a single/double/triple), and the *Hotel Adriático* (☎ 715757), Calle 6, corner of Carrera 6 (US$18/24/30).

Getting There & Away

Air The airport is close to San Antonio, and serviced by frequent por puestos. There are four flights daily to Caracas (US$70 with Avensa, US$66 with Aeropostal) and one to Mérida (US$33) and Maracaibo (US$49).

There are no direct flights to Colombia. Cross the border to Cúcuta, from where there are domestic flights to all major Colombian cities, including Bogotá, Medellín and Cartagena. The airport is five km from Cúcuta's centre.

Bus San Antonio has no central bus terminal; each company has its own office. They are close to each other on or just off La Avenida. Four companies – Expresos Mérida, Expresos Los Llanos, Expresos Alianza and Expresos San Cristóbal – operate buses to Caracas, with a total of seven buses daily. All depart in the late afternoon or early evening and all go via El Llano Highway; they reach their destination in about 14 hours. The ordinary fare is US$15. Los Llanos and Mérida also have air-conditioned buses for US$16.50.

There are no direct buses to Mérida; go to San Cristóbal and change. Por puestos to San Cristóbal leave frequently from Calle 5 (US$1, one hour).

To/From Colombia Buses and shared taxis (colectivos) run frequently to Cúcuta, about 12 km from San Antonio. Catch buses (US$0.30) on Calle 6 or La Avenida, and colectivos (US$0.50) on Calle 6 near the corner of Carrera 9. Both go to the Cúcuta bus terminal, passing through the city centre on their way. You can pay in bolívares or pesos.

The Cúcuta terminal is dirty, busy and dangerous – one of the poorest in Colombia. Watch your belongings closely. You may be approached by well-dressed English-speaking gentlemen who will offer to buy a bus ticket for you. Ignore them – they are conmen. Buy your ticket directly from the bus office.

There are frequent buses to Bucaramanga (US$8, six hours). At least a dozen air-conditioned buses run daily to Bogotá (US$23, 16 hours).

If you plan on staying in Cúcuta, don't go all the way to the terminal, but get off in the centre.

Los Llanos

Occupying the entire central part of Venezuela, roughly a third of the national territory, Los Llanos (literally 'the plains') are billiard-table-flat, low-lying savannas. They extend south-westwards, well into Colombia, taking up almost as vast an area of the neighbouring country as they do in Venezuela. An accumulation of sand, clay and mud deposited by rivers over millions of years, these eerie expanses lack any distinguishing features. They are mostly grassy plains, with ribbons of forest along the creeks and rivers, and scattered woodlands here and there.

Rivers are numerous, and in the wet season voluminous; the main ones are the Apure, Meta, Arauca and Capanaparo – all of which are left-bank tributaries of the Orinoco, which itself is the south-eastern border of the Llanos.

The climate is extreme in both the rainy and dry seasons. The former (referred to as *invierno*), which lasts from May to November, is characterised by frequent and intense rains. The rivers overflow, turning much of the land into shallow lagoons. Humboldt, who was here in this season, compared the Llanos to 'an ocean covered with seaweed'. In December, the rains stop and the rivers return to their normal courses, steadily getting narrower as the dry season (called *verano*) progresses. The sun beats down on the parched soil and winds blow the dust around.

The Llanos are sparsely populated. Except for San Fernando de Apure, in the heart of the region, all significant urban centres developed in the more hospitable environment at the northern outskirts of the plains. Roads are few, but the state, in an attempt to open up the plains, has built a few access roads. San Fernando de Apure is accessible by paved roads from Maracay/Caracas in the north, and Barinas/Guanare in the west. The road from San Fernando southwards to Puerto Páez, on the Colombian frontier, is partly surfaced. Other than these, all-season

roads are few and far between, and much of the transport, particularly during the wet season, is confined to rivers.

The inhabitants of the plains, the *llaneros*, are tough and resistant people, used to the hard life. Not without reason, Bolívar employed them in his army to fight against the Spaniards, with great success.

As the soil is not all that fertile, the people of the plains have dedicated themselves to cattle raising, and the region is Venezuela's major meat producer. It also produces dairy products and agricultural crops and provides the country with river fish. Since the discovery of large oil reserves in Anzoátegui state and smaller ones in Barinas state, the Llanos have become increasingly important economically. Oil from both fields is pipelined north to the coast and from there shipped overseas.

This doesn't make the Llanos sound like an alluring tourist destination, and in many ways they are not. The difficult access, uninviting climate and monotonous landscape are the main factors that deter tourists from coming and exploring the plains; in fact it's Venezuela's least visited region.

However, this is only half the picture. Surprisingly the Llanos are Venezuela's greatest repository of wildlife, especially birds, who live here permanently or gather seasonally to breed and feed. About 350 bird species have been recorded in the region, which accounts for nearly 30% of all bird species found in Venezuela. The majority of these birds are water birds, and the group includes ibis, herons, cormorants, egrets, jacanas, gallinules and darters, to name just a few. The *corocoro*, or scarlet ibis *(Eudocimus ruber)*, noted for their bright orange-red plumage, are perhaps the most spectacular (they come here only for the dry season).

There are more than 50 species of mammal, the most characteristic of the region being the *chigüire*, or capybara *(Hydrochoerus hydrochaeris)*. This is the world's largest rodent. It grows to about 60 kg, has a guinea-pig face and bear-like coat. It's equally at home on land and in water, and feeds mainly on aquatic plants. It's the most visible mammal in Los Llanos, apart from ubiquitous zebu (local cattle) herds and it is often seen in families, two adults and several young, or in large groups.

Other mammals to be found in the Llanos include armadillos, peccaries, opossums, tapirs, ocelots and the occasional jaguar. Two particularly interesting aquatic mammals are *toninas*, or freshwater dolphins *(Inia geoffrensis)*, and *manatí*, or manatee *(Trichechus manatus)*, which inhabit the larger tributaries of the Orinoco. Both, particularly the latter, are endangered species.

Also threatened with extinction is the largest American crocodile, the *caimán del Orinoco*, or the Orinoco cayman *(Crocodylus intermedius)*. This huge reptile, up to eight metres from head to tail, once lived in safety, but it has been decimated by ranchers who kill it for its skin. Far more numerous is the *baba*, or the spectacled cayman *(Caiman crocodylus)*, the smallest of the family of local crocodiles which grows to about two to three metres in length.

The llaneros have developed a distinctive culture and folklore of their own, which has close affinities to that of the Colombian Llanos. One of their favourite pastimes is the sport known as *toros coleados*, a sort of rodeo. Its aim is to bring down a bull by grabbing its tail whilst riding a galloping horse. Today, toros coleados can be seen in other parts of the country, usually accompanying local festivals, but in Los Llanos they are more authentic and spontaneous.

Music is an integral part of Llanos life, more so than in other regions. The main llanero musical form is *joropo*, which has its origins in flamenco, although it has changed considerably over the centuries. It's sung and accompanied by *harpa llanera* (a sort of local harp), *maracas* (gourd rattles), and *cuatro* (a small, four-stringed guitar). The harp came over from Spain during the colonial period, but it was not until the beginning of the present century that it made its way into joropo music. By that time it had evolved into quite a different instrument: it's now smaller and less elaborate than its European parent. The cuatro is also of European origin (and it also gradually changed); only the maracas is a native American instrument.

Joropo has two major forms, *golpes* and *pasajes*, which include a variety of rhythms such as *pajarillo*, *zumba que zumba*, *quirpa* etc. Generally speaking, pasajes are slower

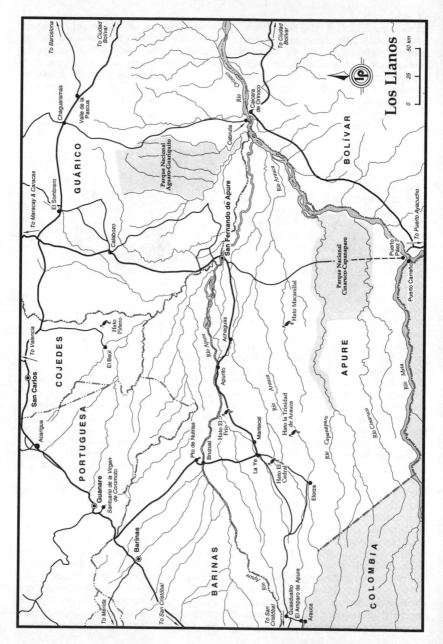

and gentler than golpes. The harp, normally associated with lyrical salon music, finds a different form of expression in joropo. Reflecting the hard life of the llaneros, the harp sounds clear and sharp, at times even wild.

Although you'll hear joropo music all over Venezuela (it's the national music), it's at its best and most original in the Llanos. Every second inhabitant of the plains sings or plays one of the instruments, and every village has at least one joropo ensemble. Joropo is typical to Venezuela and, to a lesser extent, Colombia, and is almost unknown beyond the borders of these two countries. It may take some time to become accustomed to it, but with time, you are likely to fall in love with it.

The wildlife, joropo and the llaneros' lifestyle in general, are all worth experiencing if you have the time and you want something different to the usual tourist sights.

In administrative terms, the Llanos comprises the states of Barinas, Apure, Portuguesa, Cojedes and Guárico. Often the southern parts of Anzoátegui and Monagas are also regarded as the Llanos (they are called Llanos Orientales, or Eastern Llanos). The Llanos are at their best down south, in Apure state, which is generally referred to as the Llano Bajo (Lower Llano).

Two large national parks, Cinaruco-Capanaparo (also known as Santos Luzardo) and Aguaro-Guariquito, have been established in Los Llanos to protect important wildlife habitats. A third park, Río Apure, is planned for the near future.

GUANARE

The capital of Portuguesa state, set on the northern edge of Los Llanos, Guanare is a 400-year-old city which today has about 130,000 people. The city is not inspiring and there is not much to see. Yet Guanare is a major destination for Venezuelans; local sources estimate that the city witnesses some half a million visitors annually. This is because Guanare is Venezuela's spiritual capital; it boasts the Nuestra Señora de Coromoto, the country's patron saint.

Founded in 1591 by Juan Fernández de León, La Ciudad del Espíritu Santo del Valle de San Juan del Guanaguanare is one of the few towns in Venezuela whose original act of foundation document is still kept in Sevilla, Spain. Like most early towns, Guanare's development was precarious and hindered by Indian groups inhabiting the region. Things began to change on 8 September 1652, when the Virgen de Coromoto miraculously appeared before an Indian cacique on the Río Guanaguanare, near the town (see the box). As with all miracles, the place became a destination for pilgrims in search of help with their problems, expecting to be healed of their diseases and forgiven of their sins.

A fair-sized church was built for the Virgin, and the town steadily developed around the cult. A serious earthquake in 1782 ruined most of the buildings, the church included. By that time, the town's population had already reached 13,000. However, partly because of the earthquake and partly because of the War of Independence, the population was halved by 1817.

Nonetheless, the miraculous powers of the Virgin continued to draw in the faithful in increasing numbers. The coronation of the Virgin as the patron saint of Venezuela, in 1949, contributed to even larger floods of pilgrims. Its religious status apart, Guanare has also developed into an important regional centre for cattle raising.

Most pilgrims flock to the city in time for 8 September, the anniversary of the Virgin's appearance. There may also be crowds of believers on 2 February, the anniversary of the day when the image of the Virgin was moved from the actual site of the apparition to the city. Guanare is also noted for its Mascarada, the three-day-long, colourful Carnaval celebration, which culminates in a parade of carrozas (floats).

Things to See

The most important monument in the city is the **Basílica de la Virgen de Coromoto**, on Plaza Bolívar. The church was constructed in the 1720s, but the 1782 earthquake almost completely destroyed it. The image of the Virgen, which had been kept inside, was saved and temporarily guarded in the chapel of the hospital, while the church was reconstructed in a different style, the work being completed in 1807.

Inside the church, the showpiece is the large, three-tier main retable, an excellent piece of colonial Baroque art made by Pantaleón José Quiñones de Lara in 1739. It later took 16 months for Romualdo Antonio Vélez to gild it.

In front of the retable stands the 3.4-metre-high, elaborate *sagrario* (tabernacle), made entirely of silver in 1756. On its upper tier, invisible behind the doors, is a *custodia* (monstrance) of 1738, where the image of the Virgin was kept for two centuries until 1949 when it was taken back to the site of the apparition.

At the head of the right-hand aisle is a statue of the Virgen de Coromoto. Climb a few steps to the feet of the Virgin, to have a look through a magnifying glass at a photo of the original image. Another statue of the Virgin is at the opposite end of the same aisle. Note the number of votive offerings and commemorative plaques distributed along the aisle.

A painting on the dome over the high altar depicts the legend of the Virgen de Coromoto. The stained glass windows were commissioned in Munich, Germany.

If you need more statues of the Virgin, there's a **Monumento de Nuestra Señora de Coromoto**, erected in 1928, seven blocks east of Plaza Bolívar along Carrera 5.

The **Convento de San Francisco**, corner of Carrera 3 and Calle 17, constructed in the mid-18th century, was another important religious building during colonial times, but neither the convent nor the adjoining church any longer serves its original purpose. In 1825 the convent was turned into a college, the first institution of its kind in Venezuela.

Virgen de Coromoto

The Virgen de Coromoto allegedly appeared on 8 September 1652 to the Cacique of the Cospes Indians. The miraculous apparition took place on the bank of a river, some 20 km south of Guanare. As legend has it, the Virgin not only appeared, but also talked to the Indian chief in his own language, convincing him to have holy water poured over his head so that he would be able to enter heaven. More than that, the Virgin left the Cacique an image of herself, radiating with rays of brilliant light.

Astonished and confused, the chief ignored the advice and fled into the mountains. As soon as he entered the woods, however, he was bitten by a venomous snake. Only then, moments before his death, did he ask to be baptised, telling his tribe to do likewise.

On 2 February 1654, the Spanish brought the image to Guanare, and placed it in a small sanctuary. Meanwhile, a cross was placed at the site where the Virgin appeared. News of the miracle spread throughout the region and beyond, and both places began to attract believers. Miracles began to multiply...

As its fame spread far and wide, the town set about building a church to provide a more decent shelter for the image. The image itself is tiny: it's an oval painting, measuring 22 by 27 mm, made on papyrus-like paper. Today its colours have almost totally washed out.

In 1942, the Virgen de Coromoto was declared patron saint of Venezuela, and solemnly crowned by Pope Pius XII in 1949. A year later a statue of the Virgin and an open-air chapel were erected at the site of the apparition, and now a huge church is also being built there. ∎

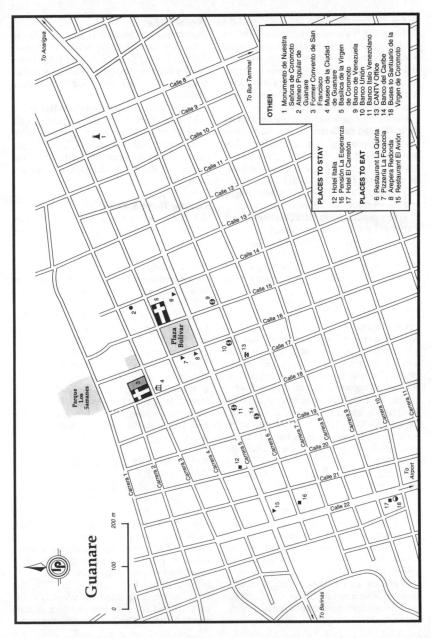

Guanare

OTHER

1 Monumento de Nuestra
   Señora de Coromoto
2 Ateneo Popular de
   Guanare
3 Former Convento de San
   Francisco
4 Museo de la Ciudad
   de Guanare
5 Basílica de la Virgen
   de Coromoto
9 Banco de Venezuela
10 Banco Unión
11 Banco Italo Venezolano
13 CANTV Office
14 Banco del Caribe
18 Buses to Santuario de la
   Virgen de Coromoto

PLACES TO STAY

12 Hotel Italia
16 Pensión La Esperanza
17 Hotel El Carretón

PLACES TO EAT

6 Restaurant La Quinta
7 Pizzería La Focaccia
8 Arepera Redonda
15 Restaurant El Avión

Today, the building houses the offices of the Universidad Nacional Experimental de los Llanos. You can enter its spacious courtyard which has preserved much of the old style and charm. The church, too, has a beautiful façade, but its interior has had its decoration removed and is now used for university meetings and symposiums.

Directly opposite the church is the **Museo de la Ciudad de Guanare**, installed in one of the few remaining colonial buildings. The museum presents a small collection related to the town's history. The **Ateneo Popular de Guanare**, Calle 14 No 3-16, also occupies an old house recalling Spanish times, and stages some cultural activities.

Three blocks north of Plaza Bolívar is **Parque Los Samanes**, named after a species of the spreading trees which grow in the park. You'll find the first impressive specimen in front of the entrance. It's thought that Bolívar's troops camped here in 1813.

Places to Stay

Given Guanare's large number of visitors, it's surprising to find that accommodation seems to be pretty tight. There were a few budget places in the vicinity of Plaza Bolívar but they all appeared to have closed down.

One of the cheapest places in the city, though truly basic, is the *Hotel El Carretón*, Calle 22 No 9-22. There are no private baths, but there are plenty of mosquitoes. If you are hard up, this may be an option, at US$5 for a double bed.

Slightly better is *Pensión La Esperanza*, Carrera 6 near the corner of Calle 22, but it is often full. It costs US$7 for a double.

The best value for money in town is the central *Hotel Italia*, Calle 20, near the corner of Carrera 5. Run by a friendly Italian, the hotel offers good air-conditioned singles/doubles/triples with private bath and TV for US$9/11/13.

There are two relatively decent motels, *Motel Portuguesa* and *Motel Los Cortijos*, both on the north-eastern outskirts of the city, on the road to Acarigua.

Places to Eat

Restaurant El Carretón is like the hotel in which it is located: cheap and basic. *Restaurant El Avión*, Carrera 5 No 21-43, looks shabby but it is open until midnight, sometimes longer, and has good inexpensive chicken.

Pizzería La Focaccia, on Plaza Bolívar, is a pleasant place with tables outside, open until 10.30 pm. It serves a variety of reasonably priced pizzas, spaghetti, hamburgers, juices etc. On the same side of the plaza, the *Arepera Redonda* does arepas and does them well.

Getting There & Away

Air The airport is two km south of the city centre. CAVE has one flight a day to Caracas (US$45).

Bus The bus terminal is three km south-east of the centre, and it's serviced by frequent local transport.

Guanare sits on the El Llano Highway, so there is regular traffic heading west to San Cristóbal (US$7.50, 6½ hours) and east to Valencia (US$5, 4½ hours). Most eastbound buses continue on to Caracas (US$8, seven hours). There are several departures a day to Barquisimeto (US$3.25, three hours). Buses to Barinas depart frequently (US$1.75, 1½ hours). If you are heading to Mérida, go to Barinas and change. A few buses daily run to San Fernando de Apure (US$8.50, eight hours).

SANTUARIO DE LA VIRGEN DE COROMOTO

This is the place where the Virgen de Coromoto appeared in 1652. However, since the holy image of the Virgin moved to Guanare, that city has become the shrine, and does the honours as Venezuela's spiritual capital. The site of the apparition was for centuries isolated, had nothing more than a cross, and was not often visited.

Now things are changing. In 1980, the construction of a huge church was commenced and the concrete structure is now nearly finished. The Templo Votivo – as it is called ¬ is monumental, strikingly modern and truly impressive. Most of the beautiful stained glass windows have already been installed. It's certainly worth a visit.

Getting There & Away
The Santuario is 25 km south of Guanare: 10 km by the main road towards Barinas plus 15 km by the side (but paved) road branching off to the south. Small buses, operated by Línea Los Cospes, depart regularly from Calle 22 No 9-26, next door to the Hotel El Carretón (US$0.30, 45 minutes). They will deposit you right at the church's entrance.

BARINAS
Barinas was founded in 1576 by Spanish conquerors from Pamplona in Nueva Granada. At the beginning of the 17th century, tobacco gave the town an economic base and overseas fame. Barinas was the only region in the province allowed by the Crown to grow tobacco. Crops such as sugar-cane, bananas and cacao were subsequently introduced to the region, as was cattle raising. By the end of the 18th century, Barinas was the second largest town in Venezuela, after Caracas.

The War of Independence and the civil wars which plagued Venezuela during the 19th century seriously affected the town's and the state's development, and many inhabitants fled, mostly to the Andes. In that period a lot of colonial architecture was lost, either destroyed during the struggles or abandoned.

Once the civil wars ended, a steady revival began. Agriculture and cattle raising were joined by a short-lived timber industry, which took advantage of extensive tropical forest in the western part of the state, indiscriminately and rapidly logging it until it was almost completely destroyed. Meanwhile, oil was discovered in the region, 50 km south of Barinas, and it is now pipelined to the coast near Morón.

Today Barinas is the capital of the state of the same name and a city of some 180,000 inhabitants. It remains the centre of a vast agricultural and ranching region. The climate is hot and damp, with an average temperature of 27°C and frequent rains from May through to November. There's not much to see or do in the city, and accordingly, few travellers bother to stop here.

Information
Tourist Office Barinas has a well-organised tourist information service. The main office (☎ 27091) is on Avenida Marqués del Pumar, half a block back from Plaza Bolívar, and is open Monday to Friday from 8 am to noon and 2 to 5 pm. There are also three *módulos de información turística* (open daily), at the airport, bus terminal and in the Parque Los Mangos which is on Avenida Cuatricentenaria. They distribute free city maps and brochures on the city and the state.

Money Major banks are scattered between Calle Cruz Paredes and Plaza Bolívar (see the map). As always, Banco Consolidado and Banco Unión are the most reliable.

Things to See
The focus of tourist interest is, as almost anywhere else in Venezuela, the Plaza Bolívar. There are still a few surviving colonial buildings which form the border of this two-block-long square.

The **Catedral** dates from the 1770s, but the bell tower, added in the present century, is unremarkable, and doesn't match up to the handsome façade. The church's interior has been finely renovated, but there are no important colonial remnants left.

Opposite the cathedral, across the plaza, is the large **Palacio del Marqués**, which occupies one entire side of the square. Commissioned by the Marqués de las Riberas de Boconó y Masparro as his private residence, and constructed at the end of the 18th century, the palace reflected the owner's wealth and the town's prosperity at the time. The palace was partly ruined during the Wars of Federation in the mid-19th century, but was restored to its previous state in the 1940s. It now houses the municipal council and the police station.

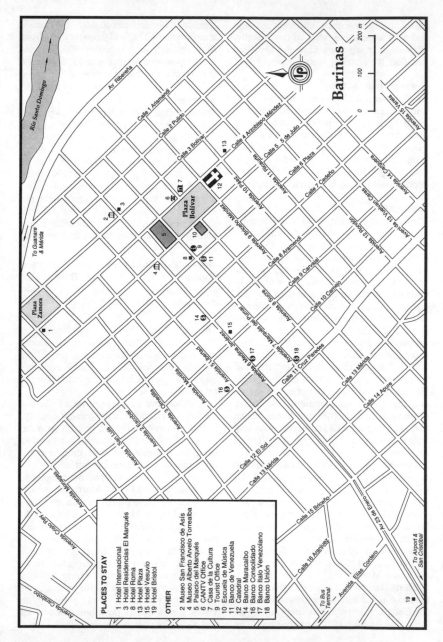

Barinas

Río Santo Domingo

To Guanare
& Mérida

Av Ribereña

Calle 1 Arismendi

Calle 2 Pulido

Calle 3 Bolívar

Calle 4 Arzobispo Méndez

Calle 5 5 de Julio

Calle 6 Plaza

Calle 7 Cedeño

Plaza
Bolívar

Avenida 11 Briceño

Avenida 10 Páez

Avenida 9 Bolívar

Avenida 8 Briceño Méndez

Avenida 7 Marqués del Pumar

Avenida 6 Medina Jiménez

Avenida 5 Libertad

Avenida 4 Montilla

Avenida 3 Ortecilla

Avenida 2 Socorro

Avenida 1 San Luis

Plaza
Zamora

Calle 8 Arzamendi

Calle 9 Carvajal

Calle 10 Camejo

Calle 11 Cruz Paredes

Calle 12 El Sol

Calle 13 Mérida

Calle 13 Mérida

Calle 14 Apure

Avenida 15 Varela

Avenida 14 Carúpana

Avenida 13 Vuelvan Caras

Avenida 12 Rondón

Calle 15 Briceño

Calle 16 Araniyes

Avenida Elías Cordero

Av 23 de Enero

To Bus
Terminal

To Airport &
San Cristóbal

Avenida Morreras

Avenida Cristo Rey

Avenida Carabobo

200 m

100

0

PLACES TO STAY

1   Hotel Internacional
3   Hotel Residencias El Marqués
8   Hotel Roma
13 Hotel Plaza
15 Hotel Vesuvio
19 Hotel Bristol

OTHER

2   Museo San Francisco de Asis
4   Museo Alberto Arvelo Torrealba
5   Palacio del Marqués
6   CANTV Office
7   Casa de la Cultura
9   Tourist Office
10 Escuela de Música
11 Banco de Venezuela
12 Catedral
14 Banco Maracaibo
16 Banco Consolidado
17 Banco Italo Venezolano
18 Banco Unión

On the northern side of the plaza is the **Casa de la Cultura**, built during the final decades of the 18th century as the town hall and jail. José Antonio Páez was imprisoned here, but managed to escape, liberating 115 of his fellow prisoners on the way. The house did the honours as the town jail until 1966. Today it's a cultural centre, running art exhibitions and various cultural events. The finely restored house on the southern side of the square, which is now the **Escuela de Música**, was originally the masonic lodge.

The city has two museums. The **Museo Alberto Arvelo Torrealba** (named after a noted local poet), corner of Calle 5 de Julio and Avenida Medina Jiménez, presents some aspects of the life and culture of the llaneros. It's open Tuesday to Saturday from 9 am to noon and 3 to 6 pm, Sunday from 9 am to noon. The **Museo San Francisco de Asís**, Avenida Medina Jiménez No 2-89, has a collection of colonial (mostly religious) objects.

The city's **Jardín Botánico** is located on the campus of the Universidad Nacional Experimental de los Llanos, three km south-west of the centre, on the road to San Cristóbal.

Places to Stay

If you are in Barinas for one or two nights only, it's probably best to look for a budget room around the bus terminal. There are half a dozen inexpensive hotels on the street that forms the western border of the terminal. Among them, you'll find the *Motel San Marino* (☎ 22351) is one of the cheapest and possibly the best value for money. Doubles with private bath and fan/air-conditioning cost US$4.50/6.50.

In the city centre, the cheapest (but also the simplest) is *Hotel Vesuvio* (☎ 24294), Avenida Medina Jiménez No 8-38. Doubles with bath and fan go for US$6; add a dollar for air-conditioning.

There are three inexpensive hotels near Plaza Bolívar: *Hotel Residencias El Marqués* (☎ 26576), Avenida Medina Jiménez No 2-88; *Hotel Plaza* (☎ 24918), Calle Arzobispo Méndez No 10-20; and the *Hotel Roma*

(☎ 24624), Avenida Marqués del Pumar, corner of Calle Plaza. All three offer much the same for similar prices: about US$8.50 for air-conditioned doubles with bath. The Roma also has cheaper rooms with fan, whereas El Marqués has air-conditioned triples with bath for US$9.

There's a choice of three-star hotels in town. Of these, the closest to Plaza Bolívar is *Hotel Internacional* (☎ 23303), Calle Arzobispo Méndez, facing Plaza Zamora. Others, including *Hotel Bristol* (☎ 20911), *Hotel Turístico Varyná* (☎ 22033) and *Hotel Valle Hondo* (☎ 23677), are all on Avenida 23 de Enero, south-west of the old centre, near the airport. They are all comfortable and provide decent standards and facilities like TV and hot water, and each has its own restaurant and bar.

Places to Eat

The cheapest restaurants are in the bus terminal area. The vicinity around Plaza Bolívar doesn't have much to choose from,

José Antonio Páez in plainsman wear,
Fritz George Melbye (1867)

except for a few fast food outlets. Avenida Marqués del Pumar is the main commercial street and there are some restaurants along it. Several better restaurants can be found on Avenida 23 de Enero.

Getting There & Away

Air The airport is 1.5 km south-west of Plaza Bolívar. Avensa has two flights a day to Caracas (US$59).

Bus The bus terminal is two km west of Plaza Bolívar, and it's serviced by local transport.

Barinas has regular bus services west to San Cristóbal (US$6, five hours), and east to Caracas (US$9.75, 8½ hours), and all points in between such as Guanare (US$1.75, 1½ hours), Valencia (US$6.50, six hours) and Maracay (US$7.50, seven hours). Transporte Barinas has five departures a day to Mérida (US$3.50, four hours). Expresos Los Llanos and Expresos Zamora operate buses south-east into Los Llanos, with a total of half a dozen departures a day to San Fernando de Apure (US$8, 7½ hours).

SAN FERNANDO DE APURE

The capital of Apure state, San Fernando de Apure is the largest city of the Lower Llano and the only city of any size for a couple of hundred miles around. Sitting on the southern bank of Río Apure, in the very heart of Los Llanos, it has a population of 90,000, and it is an important regional trading centre for most of the Río Apure basin. Cattle raising and, to a lesser extent, farming are the two major activities in the region, and crops and livestock are funnelled through San Fernando and trucked north to the central states like Distrito Federal, Miranda, Aragua and Carabobo.

San Fernando was born as a missionary outpost at the end of the colonial era and its development was for a long time hindered by its isolation. It wasn't until the road from Calabozo was extended south to the Río Apure, that the town began to grow more swiftly. Today the city also has good road links with western states like Barinas, Mérida and Táchira.

San Fernando is certainly not a tourist attraction in itself and has little to keep you in the city. On the other hand, the vast region all around boasts some of the best of what the Llanos have to offer. San Fernando is a jumping-off point for the majority of hatos (refer to the following section).

Information

Tourist Office There doesn't seem to be one in town but you probably won't need much information about the city anyway. What you are likely to need is information about the region, essentially the hatos. Go to Agencia de Viajes y Turismo Doña Bárbara (☎ 25003, fax 27902), Edificio Hotel La Torraca, Piso Bajo, Paseo Libertador. They run their own Campamento Doña Bárbara in the Hato La Trinidad de Apure (for which they can book and arrange transport) and have information about other hatos in the region, including El Frío and El Cedral, both on the way to La Trinidad.

Money For such a small, tucked away town, there is a surprising number of useful banks. Cash can be exchanged in Banco Unión, Banco Consolidado, Banco Principal and Banco Italo Venezolano. American Express travellers' cheques are changed by all these banks except Banco Unión which, however, accepts Visa and MasterCard. Visa and MasterCard can also be cashed in Banco Provincial.

Things to See

If you have some time to kill, walk along Paseo Libertador, the city's main thoroughfare. At its northern end is a circular square with a large fountain adorned by concrete alligators. Beside the square is the **Monumento a Pedro Camejo**, one of the most famous lancers to have fought under General José Antonio Páez in Bolívar's army. Camejo, who died in the Battle of Carabobo, is commonly known as Negro Primero, as he

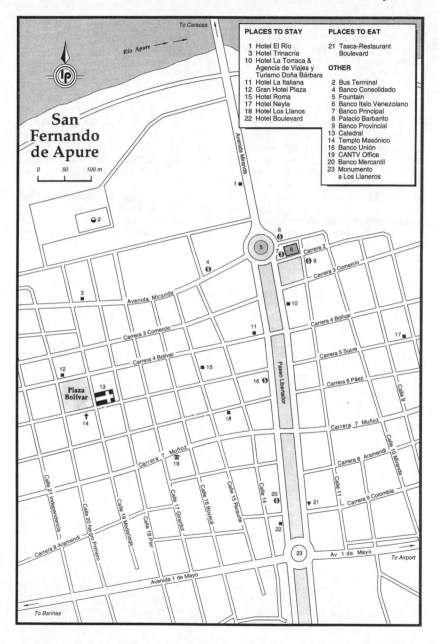

San Fernando de Apure

0   50   100 m

Río Apure

To Caracas

To Barinas

To Airport

Plaza Bolívar

Paseo Libertador

Avenida Miranda

Avenida Miranda

Carrera 3 Comercio

Carrera 4 Bolívar

Carrera 7 Muñoz

Carrera 8 Aramendi

Avenida 1 de Mayo

Carrera 2

Carrera 3 Comercio

Carrera 4 Bolívar

Carrera 5 Sucre

Carrera 6 Páez

Carrera 7 Muñoz

Carrera 8 Aramendi

Carrera 9 Colombia

Av 1 de Mayo

Calle 21 Independencia

Calle 20 Negro Primero

Calle 19 Madariaga

Calle 18 Píar

Calle 17 Girardot

Calle 16 Boyacá

Calle 15 Ricaurte

Calle 14

Calle 11

Calle 10 Miranda

Calle 9

PLACES TO STAY

1 Hotel El Río
3 Hotel Trinacría
10 Hotel La Torraca &
   Agencia de Viajes y
   Turismo Doña Bárbara
11 Hotel La Italiana
12 Gran Hotel Plaza
15 Hotel Roma
17 Hotel Neyla
18 Hotel Los Llanos
22 Hotel Boulevard

PLACES TO EAT

21 Tasca-Restaurant
   Boulevard

OTHER

2 Bus Terminal
4 Banco Consolidado
5 Fountain
6 Banco Italo Venezolano
7 Banco Principal
8 Palacio Barbarito
9 Banco Provincial
13 Catedral
14 Templo Masónico
16 Banco Unión
19 CANTV Office
20 Banco Mercantil
23 Monumento
   a Los Llaneros

was the first Black who distinguished himself in the War of Independence.

Just east of the fountain is **Palacio Barbarito**, possibly the most interesting architectural relic surviving in the city. It was built by Italian merchants at the turn of the century. At that time the Río Apure used to pass just a few metres from the palace pier, and boats came directly from Europe, up the Orinoco and Apure. Most of the trade was related to egret feathers and cayman leathers, and was initially very profitable. Later on the business deteriorated and the Italians sold the palace and left. It then passed through the hands of various owners who divided and subdivided it repeatedly, so that much of the original internal design has been lost.

A part of the upper floor is today occupied by Fundación Rómulo Gallegos, which displays a small collection of pre-Hispanic pottery which was found in the region. Remains of the frescoes on the ceiling (painted by artists brought from Italy) can still be seen.

Eight blocks south, along Paseo Libertador, is a large **Monumento a Los Llaneros**, dedicated to the tough and brave people who made up the backbone of Bolívar's army.

The **Plaza Bolívar**, six blocks west of Paseo Libertador, boasts a modern cathedral and an old masonic lodge (both of minor interest), and is pleasantly shaded with trees.

Places to Stay

One of the cheapest places in town is *Hotel Neyla* (☎ 23347), Carrera Sucre, four blocks east of Paseo Libertador. It costs US$4/5/6 for a single/double/triple with bath and fan, which is not bad for that price.

Hotel La Italiana (☎ 21658), Carrera Bolívar No 59, is a more central alternative but poorer: it only has shared baths, and rooms cost a dollar more than those at the Neyla.

If you need air-conditioning, the cheapest option is *Hotel Roma* (☎ 23652), Calle Ricaurte No 4, but it only has matrimoniales (US$7 for a room with bath) and is pretty basic. For something better, try either *Hotel El Río* (☎ 23454), Avenida Miranda, close to the bus terminal, or *Hotel Los Llanos* (☎ 22703), Carrera Páez No 118. Both offer air-conditioned doubles with bath and TV for US$10. You can expect much the same at the *Hotel Boulevard* (☎ 23230), Paseo Libertador, but you'll pay a little more.

Hotel La Torraca (☎ 22777), on Paseo Libertador, is a good central option, with fairly decent singles/doubles/triples for US$11/12/13. However, before booking in, check *Hotel Trinacría* (☎ 23578), Avenida Miranda, which has large airy singles/doubles with TV (some with fridge as well) for US$13/15.

The best in town is the *Gran Hotel Plaza* (☎ 21504), on Plaza Bolívar. Comfortable air-conditioned rooms with two or three beds, cost around US$30. Choose one of the upper-floor rooms which looks over the plaza.

Places to Eat

None of the better hotels has its own restaurant, so one must rely on independent establishments scattered mostly around the central area, between Plaza Bolívar and Paseo Libertador. There are not many of them but there are enough to choose from for lunch or dinner. As you might expect, the carne llanera, the local beef, appears on every menu, as does fish from the local rivers.

Getting There & Away

Air The airport is about three km east of the city centre; a taxi there shouldn't cost more than US$3. San Fernando is a regular stopover for flights between Caracas and Puerto Ayacucho. Avensa and Aeropostal both have one flight a day in each direction. The airfare to Caracas is US$47 with either carrier; to Puerto Ayacucho it's US$35 with Aeropostal, but US$41 with Avensa.

Bus The bus terminal is on the northern outskirts of the city, near the river. You can either walk (five minutes to Plaza Bolívar) or take a taxi (US$1).

There are only two or three buses a day directly to Caracas (US$7.75, eight hours), but about 10 buses run to Maracay (US$6, 6½ hours), so you can simply go to Maracay and change. Five or six buses a day depart to Barinas (US$8, 7½ hours) and one of them continues on to San Cristóbal (US$14, 12½ hours).

Two or three buses a day (all in the morning) set off for an interesting ride south to Puerto Ayacucho (US$10,25, eight hours), via Puerto Páez. The road is in part unpaved, and the trip includes a few ferry crossings, the longest one being across the Orinoco. The route is unpassable for part of the rainy season.

Boat Despite its location on a large river, the Río Apure, (which was once the region's transport lifeline), San Fernando has no regular passenger boat service, either up or downstream.

HATOS

Most of Los Llanos is divided into large ranches known as hatos. They are principally dedicated to cattle raising – as they have been for a century or more – but some of them have recently turned to ecotourism. They have built lodges equipped with reasonable facilities, which they call *campamentos*, and will show guests the local wildlife. Some hatos dealing with tourists have taken a serious approach to environmental issues, introducing the protection of wildlife within their ranches, installing research stations, contributing to ecological funds and the like.

So far there are perhaps a dozen campamentos, and it's here that the overwhelming majority of foreign visitors to Los Llanos end up. The most popular of the hatos are listed here. The approximate location of the campamentos has been marked on the Los Llanos map.

Almost all the campamentos offer packages, which have to be booked and paid for beforehand. Packages are usually three-day/two-night visits, unless you want to stay longer (but rarely shorter), and cost somewhere between US$80 and US$150 per person a day. The package includes full board and one or two excursions each day.

It's these excursions that essentially justify the whole tour. They are like safaris, in a jeep or boat. There's usually one trip in the morning and another one in the afternoon, the best times to observe the wildlife and the more pleasant periods of the day, avoiding the unbearable midday heat. There will be more boat trips in the rainy period and more jeep rides in the dry season. Whichever means of transport is used, however, you are taken into wilderness areas, where animals, mostly birds, are plentiful and easy to see. Amongst the mammals and reptiles, capybaras and caymans are particularly common. Refer to the introduction to this chapter for more information about the local fauna.

Most hatos offer pretty much the same services, and the fauna is similar across the region. For example, El Frío, El Cedral and La Trinidad are located relatively close to each other, so you can expect similar wildlife habitats in each of them. All three have had enthusiastic comments from previous travellers and all are recommended. You may consider other factors such as the price and facilities (eg El Cedral has a tiny swimming pool and air-conditioning), but otherwise there is no great difference between the ranches.

Generally speaking, the dry season is considered as the peak season (in some hatos this is reflected by the higher tour prices). This is a good time to come, as you can at least expect good weather. Another bonus is that

Capybara *(chigüire)*

there are usually more options to choose from, as a greater area is accessible by land.

The wildlife, however, is equally abundant in both the rainy and dry seasons (probably even more numerous in the rainy period). The main difference is that in the dry season, most animals flock to scarce sources of water, which makes them easy to watch. In the wet season, on the other hand, when most of the land is half-flooded, animals are virtually everywhere. When I was in El Frío in the rainy season, our jeep had to stop frequently on the causeway between two lagoons, as large capybara families were sunning themselves on this one relatively dry piece of land, and caymans crossed the track from one lagoon to the other. Birds were everywhere.

If you go in the dry season, take a hat, sunglasses and sunscreen. In the wet season, make sure to have wet weather gear. Whenever you come, don't forget a torch, good binoculars and plenty of film. Mosquito repellent is essential during the rainy season, but it is also very useful in the dry period.

As many campamentos require advance booking and pre-payment, plan ahead. Tours to most hatos can (or must) be arranged in Caracas. Refer to the Tour section of the Caracas chapter for relevant tour operators. If you want to arrange a tour from Mérida, contact the Posada Las Heroínas. Its owner has contacts with independent guides who run three-day/two-night tours to the Llanos for about US$150.

Otherwise, you can explore Los Llanos on your own. The Barinas-San Fernando road cuts through an interesting part of the plains and it is serviced by regular transport (about six buses a day in either direction). The portion of the road between Bruzual and Apurito is perhaps the most spectacular as far as animal watching is concerned. Plenty of birds can be seen from the road itself if you go by bus. There is a choice of simple accommodation in Bruzual and Mantecal, either of which can serve as jumping-off points for excursions around the area. You can also try the Mantecal-Guasdualito road, which then continues on to San Cristóbal.

Buses and other traffic on this road, however, are not so regular. The best time for bird-watching is shortly after dawn.

Hato El Frío

Occupying about 800 sq km, Hato El Frío lies on both sides of the Mantecal-San Fernando road, and has around 44,000 head of cattle. Its campamento is located two km north of the road, 187 km west of San Fernando (42 km east of Mantecal). It has a lodge with 10 double rooms (with the capacity for 20 guests, currently being extended to 30), a pleasant dining house and a biological station where they breed caymans.

There are three boats and four jeeps which take visitors for two four-hour excursions, at 8 am and 3.30 pm. There's a choice of about 10 excursions in verano and five in invierno. Tours can be conducted in Spanish, English or Italian. The campamento is administered by Carlos Lasso and run by a friendly Spanish couple, Ana and Ramón. It's estimated that about 20,000 chigüires and 25,000 babas live in the hato.

So far, El Frío seems to be pretty tolerant of individual travellers, and will probably accept you if you turn up unexpectedly, if they have vacancies. The price per day per person is US$90. They are about to open an office in Achaguas, 89 km towards San Fernando, to deal with the stream of visitors. For the time being, you can book through Epsilon in Caracas. If you get to San Fernando without booking, check with Doña Bárbara travel agency for news.

El Frío is easily accessible by public transport; the San Fernando-Mantecal buses will put you down at the main gate, a 20-minute walk to the campamento. There's an airstrip nearby.

Hato El Cedral

About 70 km south-west by paved road from El Frío, one gets to Hato El Cedral. This one covers around 560 sq km and has around 20,000 head of cattle. The campamento is seven km west off the road. It provides comfortable lodging in cabañas, which are equipped with air-conditioning and private baths with hot water, and there is a tiny swimming pool.

They have half a dozen different excursions, by boat or specially prepared minibus, but their trips seem to be shorter than El Frío's. About 200 bird species have been recorded on the ranch (much the same as in El Frío), and 14,000 capybaras, not to mention the numerous representatives of other species.

El Cedral is quite rigorous about tours, which have to be booked beforehand from Caracas (through Turven). If you come without a booking, you are likely to be turned away. The price in the peak season (15 November to 15 April) is US$120 per person a day in a double room, and US$155 in a single room. In the off season, it's US$80 and US$115, respectively. This price doesn't include transport to/from the hato. It can be arranged for an extra fee, when you book your package; the return trip from San Fernando airport to El Cedral costs US$25.

Hato La Trinidad de Arauca

Better known by the name of its campamento, Doña Bárbara, this hato is pretty close to El Cedral, but it's accessible via a roundabout route through Elorza. In the dry season, the campamento can be reached by road, but in the wet season, the only access is by river (two hours from Elorza).

With 360 sq km, La Trinidad is smaller, but has as equally a rich and diversified wildlife as El Frío and El Cedral, except for capybaras, which are not so numerous here. Its campamento is pleasant and well organised, and is one of the few which offer horseback excursions. Bookings can be made in Caracas or through Doña Bárbara travel agency in San Fernando. The price is US$104 per person a day.

The campamento was named after Rómulo Gallego's classic novel, for which the hato provided the setting and principal character. The grave of Francisca Vásquez de Carrillo (the real name of the owner of the hato, on whom Doña Bárbara was based) is in the hato, as is a replica of her house, a modest, thatched adobe structure, with some old objects inside. Today the campamento is run by the friendly Estrada family.

Hato Macanillal

Owned by Francisco Freites, Hato Macanillal is located in the fork of the Río Cuanaviche and the Río Cuanavichito, some 50 km south of Achaguas as the crow flies. Encompassing 320 sq km, the hato has over 10,000 head of cattle. Following the recent construction of the Campamento de Aventura Los Indios, the ranch has joined the ranks of tourist operators.

The campamento is modern and purpose-built. It has simple but comfortable rooms with bath and fan, a dining room, bar, two small, round swimming pools (one for adults, the other one for kids), its own airstrip and specially adapted pick-up trucks for safaris.

The three-day/two-night package includes accommodation, full board and three excursions, one on each day, into the surrounding countryside. The programme appears to be more relaxed than in other hatos, supposedly in order to be suitable for Venezuelan families with children. The organisers say they can provide German and English-speaking guides. Packages normally have to be booked and bought from the Caracas office of the owner. If you happen to be in San Fernando without one, contact Flavio Freites (☎ 26946).

The cost in the peak season (15 December to 31 May) is US$120 per person a day, not including transport there – this can be provided at an extra cost. In the dry season, the campamento is accessible from San Fernando by road/dirt track; pick-up trucks (taking up to 10 passengers) will charge US$120 for a return trip. In the rainy season, access is by a combination of road/river transport. Alternatively, the campamento offers light planes which will take you in 25 minutes from/to San Fernando (US$340 return for four passengers).

Hato Piñero

The best-known ranch in the Llano Alto (Upper Llano), the Hato Piñero is located in Cojedes state, close to the east of the town of

El Baúl. It's easily accessible by road from anywhere in the central states. If starting from Caracas, you go to Valencia, from where it's about 210 km south.

Given its location, the Piñero has a somewhat different spectrum of wildlife to that of the hatos in Llano Bajo. The topography of this ranch (about 800 sq km) is more diverse, and forests cover part of the hato. The wet season comes later (in late May or early June) and ends earlier (in September). Although capybaras and caymans are not so ubiquitous here, there is a variety of other animals, including ocelots, monkeys, anteaters, agoutis, foxes, tapirs and iguanas. This is largely the effect of hunting and deforestation bans, which were introduced as early as the 1950s.

There are tourist facilities for about 20 guests, and packages can be booked in Caracas. Like other hatos, they offer full board and excursions, and cost between US$100 and US$120, depending on the season.

The North-East

Venezuela's north-east is of interest to travellers primarily for outdoor activities; this is the place to go sailing, walking, snorkelling, and sunbathing. The coast is at its best here, particularly Mochima National Park. Another of the region's highlights is the Guácharo Cave.

It was here that the Spaniards first arrived and settled, but there's not much from the colonial period left, except in some parts of the towns of Barcelona and Cumaná, and some old churches and forts scattered over the region.

Administratively, the north-east region includes Sucre state and the northern parts of Anzoátegui and Monagas, plus Nueva Esparta, which comprises the islands of Margarita, Coche and Cubagua.

Anzoátegui, Sucre & Monagas States

Most of the cultural and historic attractions are close to the coast as it was essentially the coastal region that was conquered and inhabited by the Spanish. There are also many natural beauties here, such as the coast itself and the extension of the mountain range known as the Cordillera de la Costa. The major points of interest have been ordered in this section from west to east, as if you were travelling eastwards from Caracas.

CLARINES & PÍRITU

There are several colonial churches in small towns throughout the northern part of Anzoátegui state. Among them, those in Clarines and Píritu have been restored and are the most interesting. Both towns are on the Caracas-Barcelona highway.

Clarines, founded in 1694, lies about one km south of the highway. Its church, Iglesia de San Antonio, is located at the upper end of the old town. Built in the 1750s, the church is a massive, squat construction laid out on a Latin cross floor plan, and is one of only a few examples of its kind in Venezuela. The austere façade is bordered by square twin towers. Perhaps the most unusual features of the structure are the two external arcades running between the towers and the transepts on both sides of the church.

The single-nave interior is topped with a wooden cupola and is refreshingly well-balanced in proportion and decoration. Over the high altar is a three-tier main retable from around 1760. It is placed against the wall, which still bears its original painting depicting a curtain. The church is open from approximately 9.30 to 11.30 am and 3 to 6 pm.

Píritu lies 16 km east of Clarines, just north of the highway (but the access road branches off from the highway two km before the town and rejoins it two km beyond it). The town was founded in 1656, and about half a century later the church, the Iglesia de Nuestra Señora de la Concepción, was built. It also looks a bit like a fortress, though the structure's design is quite different: there's only one bell tower, no transept and no arcades. The church is spectacularly sited on a hill.

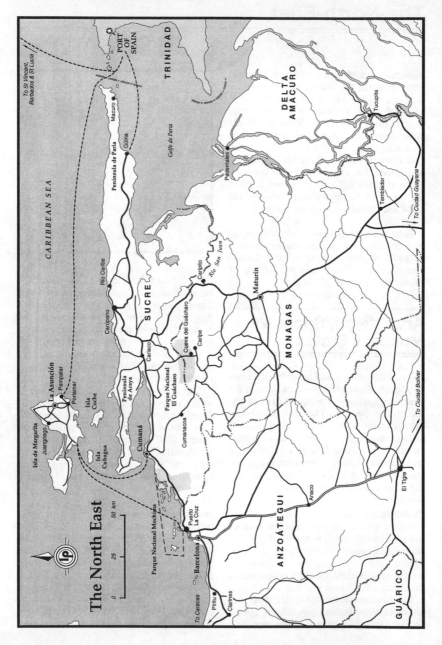

This is a three-nave church, and it boasts quite a number of remarkable colonial altarpieces. The main retable and the two side retables date from about 1745 and, like most of the others, are richly gilded. Note the painted decoration of the vault in the presbytery.

Getting There & Away
As both towns are just off the Caracas-Barcelona road, access is easy and the transport frequent. Apart from the long-distance buses running between these two cities, there are regional two-hourly buses from Barcelona to both Píritu and Clarines.

BARCELONA
Barcelona was founded in 1671 by a group of Catalans and named after their mother town in Spain. It is gradually merging with its dynamic young neighbour, Puerto La Cruz. Barcelona has 270,000 people and it is the capital of Anzoátegui state.

It's a pleasant enough place with several plazas in the centre and some relatively well-preserved colonial architecture. The old town has been in large part restored and white-washed throughout. This gives it a pleasant appearance, even though the houses are a mish-mash dating from different periods. The city hasn't rushed into modernity and the air of old times is still noticeable within the historical sector.

Information
Tourist Office Barcelona has two tourist offices. The Dirección de Turismo is just off Plaza Boyacá and is open Monday to Friday from 8 am to noon and 2 to 5.30 pm. At the time of writing it was planning to relocate to the Edificio de la Gobernación, on Avenida 5 de Julio.

The Coranztur (☎ 777110) is on Plaza Rolando and is open Monday to Friday from 8 am to 3 pm.

Money There are only a few banks in central Barcelona; you'd be well advised to have sufficient bolívares before coming here, or you may need to go to Puerto La Cruz to change money. The Banco Mercantil, on Plaza Bolívar, might advance you cash on Visa and MasterCard, while Banco Unión changes cash (but not travellers' cheques) and services Visa card holders.

Things to See
The historic centre of the city is **Plaza Boyacá**, with the statue of General José Antonio Anzoátegui, a Barcelona-born hero of the War of Independence, in its centre. On the western side of the tree-shaded square stands the **Catedral**, built a century after the town's foundation. The most venerated object in the church is the glass reliquary in a chapel off the left aisle, where the embalmed remains of the Italian martyr San Celestino are kept. The neoclassical main retable dates from the beginning of the 19th century, but the images of saints were made in modern times.

On the southern side of the plaza is the **Museo de Anzoátegui**. Located in the carefully restored, oldest surviving building in town (from 1671), the museum features a variety of objects related to Barcelona's

Colonial religious statue

PLACES TO STAY

2 Hotel Neverí
5 Hotel Nacional
18 Hotel Cultura
19 Hospedaje Bella Venezia
21 Hotel Barcelona
22 Hotel Canarias
23 Hotel Madrid
26 Hotel Plaza

PLACES TO EAT

13 Lunchería Doña Arepa
17 Restaurant Las 4 Esquinas
20 Arepera 5 de Julio
25 Restaurant Boyacá
31 Tasca La Burra de la Fortuna
32 Mercado Municipal La Aduana

OTHER

1 Edificio de la Gobernación
3 Banco Mercantil
4 Casa Fuerte
6 Teatro Cajigal
7 Iglesia del Carmen
8 Gunda Arte Popular
9 Centro Teatral Teófilo Leal
10 Ateneo de Barcelona
11 CANTV Office
12 Iposтел Post Office
14 Coranztur Tourist Office
15 Dirección de Turismo
16 Banco de Venezuela
24 Catedral
27 Museo de Anzoátegui
28 Petrol Station
29 Galería de Arte
30 Banco Unión
33 Bus Terminal

Barcelona

0   100   200 m

history. Note the curious collection of religious statues equipped with movable limbs; only their faces, hands and feet have been properly finished. They were dressed in robes according to the occasion and their pose adjusted to the situation. The museum is open Tuesday to Sunday from 8 am to noon and 2 to 5 pm. There's usually a guide in the museum who can explain the collection (in Spanish only).

An extension to the museum is housed in the **Ateneo de Barcelona**, two blocks east. On the 1st floor of this colonial building is a small but quite representative collection of modern Venezuelan paintings (most dating from the 1940s and 1950s). All the works once belonged to Miguel Otero Silva, a well-known novelist; after his death the paintings were donated to the state. The museum is open Monday to Friday from 8 am to noon and 2 to 5 pm, Saturday and Sunday from 9 am to noon and 2 to 5 pm. The Ateneo also presents temporary exhibitions on the ground floor and conducts various cultural activities. There's a handicraft shop attached, but a far larger selection of crafts is offered by **Gunda Arte Popular**, a shop on Calle Bolívar.

The **Plaza Rolando** is lined by younger buildings, among which the two most worthy of a look are the **Iglesia del Carmen** and the **Teatro Cajigal**, both dating from the 1890s. The latter is an enchanting, small theatre which seats 300 people. It stages theatre performances and musical concerts; the security guards can let you in during the day.

There are a few more plazas further to the north-west, including Plaza Miranda and Plaza Bolívar, just one block apart. The western side of the latter is occupied by the **Casa Fuerte**, once a Franciscan hospice, destroyed by the royalists in a heavy attack in 1817. Over 1500 people, both defenders and the civilians who took refuge here, lost their life in the massacre which followed. The surviving parts of the walls have been left in ruins as a memorial.

The Palacio Legislativo, two blocks south of Plaza Boyacá, has the **Galería de Arte** featuring temporary exhibitions.

Places to Stay

Hospedaje Bella Venezia, on Calle Freites, is one of the cheapest places in town (US$5.50 for a couple), but it's basic and only has shared baths. Marginally more expensive is the *Hotel Nacional* (☎ 771243), on Calle Zamora; it has an agreement with the Corpoven oil company to rent its rooms to them, so it's almost always full. Rooms (singles or doubles) cost US$6.

One of the viable budget alternatives is *Hotel Cultura*, on the corner of Calle Freites and Avenida 5 de Julio. Simple singles or doubles with shared bath cost US$8.

Probably the most pleasant budget place is *Hotel Plaza* (☎ 772843), on Plaza Boyacá. It's in a nice colonial house with a patio, and has rooms of different standards and prices. Doubles without bath cost US$7.50, and they are possibly the best bet: they are spacious and overlook the plaza and the cathedral. There are also some air-conditioned doubles for around US$10. A stone's throw away, at the back of the cathedral, is the less attractive *Hotel Madrid*, costing US$5 per head.

The *Hotel Canarias* (☎ 771034), on Calle Bolívar near the corner of Avenida 5 de Julio,

offers a better standard. Again, it's a colonial house with a patio and spotlessly clean rooms, all with private bath. Singles/doubles with fan go for US$6.50/9.50, while doubles/triples with air-conditioning cost US$14/19. Diagonally opposite is the *Hotel Barcelona* (☎ 771087), where air-conditioned doubles cost around US$20.

More pleasant and slightly cheaper is *Hotel Neverí* (☎ 772376), on Avenida Miranda. Air-conditioned singles/doubles cost US$13/19. The *Hotel Oriana* (☎ 764953), on Calle Caracas, five blocks west of the Plaza Bolívar, is possibly the best of all, and costs much the same as the Hotel Barcelona.

Places to Eat

A cheap place to eat is the market, the *Mercado Municipal La Aduana*, next to the bus terminal. Avenida 5 de Julio is lined with restaurants, snack luncherías, fuentes de soda and street food vendors. Just to name a couple, *Arepera 5 de Julio* serves arepas and cheap typical meals, whereas *La Burra de la Fortuna* is one of the better tascas in the city centre. There are also several places to eat on Avenida Miranda. In the old town, budget eateries include the *Restaurant Boyacá*, on Plaza Boyacá, *Lunchería Doña Arepa*, on Calle Bolívar, and *Las 4 Esquinas*, on the corner of Calle Freites and Calle Maturín.

Getting There & Away

Air The airport is two km south of the city centre and is accessible by urban transport. There are a few flights daily to Porlamar on Isla de Margarita (US$28 with Aeropostal, US$29 with Avensa), and a dozen flights to Caracas (US$42 with Aeropostal, US$46 with Avensa). Avensa has one direct flight a day to Ciudad Guayana (US$47) and Valencia (US$59).

Bus The bus terminal is about one km south of the city centre, next to the market. To get there, take a buseta going south along Avenida 5 de Julio, or walk (15 minutes).

There are regular departures to Caracas (US$6.50, 4½ hours) and Cumaná (US$2, two hours). Many Cumaná buses continue east up to Carúpano (US$4.50, four hours). Several buses daily (approximately every two hours) run south to Ciudad Bolívar (US$5.25, four hours), then continue on to Ciudad Guayana (US$7.25, 5½ hours).

To Puerto La Cruz, catch a city bus from Avenida 5 de Julio (US$0.20). They go by either of two routes, Avenida Intercomunal or Vía Alterna. Either will put you down in the centre of Puerto La Cruz, one block from Plaza Bolívar.

PUERTO LA CRUZ

Puerto La Cruz is a young but dynamic and expanding city which has rapidly become one of Venezuela's most important ports. Until the 1930s, it was no more than an obscure village, but after rich oil deposits were discovered in the region to the south it boomed. The port of Guanta was built east of town, and it is continuously being enlarged to cope with the increasing amount of oil piped from the oil wells and shipped abroad.

The city has become touristy, far more so than its colonial neighbour, Barcelona. It has an attractive 10-block-long waterfront boulevard, Paseo Colón, lined with hotels, bars and restaurants. It comes alive in the evening, and plenty of craft stalls, which open at that time, add local colour. A large tourist complex, the Complejo Turístico El Morro, is being built on the waterfront five km west of the city centre. Apart from these attractions, however, the city doesn't have much to offer tourists: a block or two back from the beach and it's just an ordinary place.

Puerto La Cruz is the major gateway to Isla de Margarita for holiday-makers from Caracas. The city is also a jumping-off point for the beautiful Parque Nacional Mochima, which stretches just north and east of the city.

Information
Tourist Office The Coranztur tourist office is midway along the Paseo Colón, and is open daily from 8 am to 8 pm.

Money Major banks are a few blocks northeast of Plaza Bolívar (they are located on the map). The most useful banks are the Banco

Unión (cash, Visa, MasterCard), the Banco de Venezuela (cash, Visa, MasterCard), and the Banco Consolidado (American Express travellers' cheques and credit cards). Next door to Banco Consolidado is Turisol (☎ 668859, 668806, 668952, fax 669910).

There are also several casas de cambio, most of which are on Paseo Colón and in the neighbouring streets.

Tours A score of travel agents have mushroomed in the city, taking advantage of the tourist dollar. Many can be found on Paseo Colón: some have their own self-contained offices, while others nestle in handicraft shops, hotels, etc. They offer tours to anywhere in the country, from the Gran Sabana to the Andes, but it's far cheaper to arrange one from the local centre (Santa Elena de Uairén and Mérida, respectively). Isla de Margarita is another of their destinations but, once again, it will work out cheaper to make arrangements in Porlamar.

It is, however, worth giving some thought to regional tours, principally to Parque Nacional Mochima. Agents offer trips in speed boats, and some have sailing boats if you want to take it at a more leisurely pace. One-day tours are standard, but longer trips can be arranged if you wish. Tours usually include snorkelling (equipment provided), but may also include fishing, scuba diving, water sports and the like.

Complejo Turístico El Morro
As one of the most ambitious urban projects to be carried out in the country, the Complejo has been planned as a sort of modern residential/tourist complex. Set on a coastal stretch of land, roughly in the form of a one by two-km rectangle, the Complejo is to be a model district, designed in its entirety and built from scratch. The area has already been criss-crossed by a maze of canals, on the banks of which a city of apartment blocks and houses is being built. Many of the inhabitants will have direct access to the waterfront and their own piers and slipways. The city is to be equipped with commercial centres, hotels, parks, gardens and golf courses.

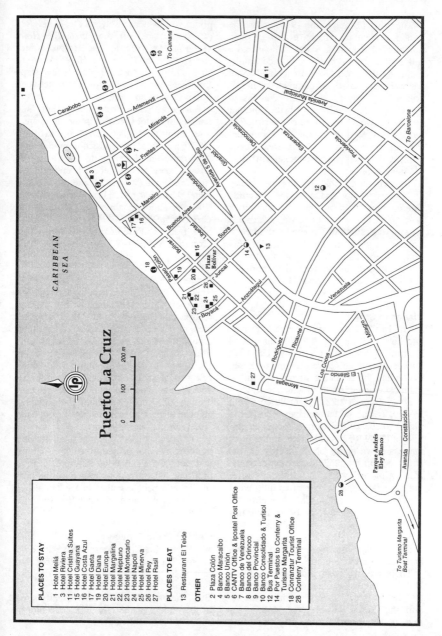

Puerto La Cruz

CARIBBEAN
SEA

PLACES TO STAY
1 Hotel Meliá
3 Hotel Riviera
11 Hotel Cristina Suites
15 Hotel Guayana
16 Hotel Costa Azul
17 Hotel Gaeta
19 Hotel Diana
20 Hotel Europa
21 Hotel Margelina
22 Hotel Neptuno
23 Hotel Montecarlo
24 Hotel Napoli
25 Hotel Minerva
26 Hotel Rey
27 Hotel Rasil

PLACES TO EAT
13 Restaurant El Teide

OTHER
2 Plaza Colón
4 Banco Maracaibo
5 Banco Unión
7 CANTV Office & Ipostel Post Office
8 Banco de Venezuela
9 Banco del Orinoco
10 Banco Consolidado & Turisol
12 Banco Provincial
14 Por Puestos to Conferry &
   Turismo Margarita
   Bus Terminal
18 Conranztur Tourist Office
28 Conferry Terminal

To Cumaná
To Barcelona
To Turismo Margarita
Boat Terminal

Parque Andrés
Eloy Blanco

The project began in the 1970s and some of the residential areas have already been inhabited. The marina, yacht harbour and a few of the planned chain of seaside hotels, including the Hotel Doral Beach and Mare Mares Resort, have been completed. There's still a long way to go before the design becomes reality. It will probably take another decade or two, as the speed of construction work has slowed down recently. Nonetheless, it's worth seeing what has already been built, especially if you are interested in urban planning or architecture.

To get to the Complejo from either Puerto La Cruz or Barcelona, take the 'Avenida Intercomunal' bus and get off one block north of the Cruzero de Lechería, at the place where five 20-storey residential towers, known as the Conjunto Residencial Vistamar, loom. From there, por puestos go north, skirting the western, then northern side of the Complejo, and take you to the marina.

Places to Stay

Puerto La Cruz is an expensive place to stay, and hotels fill up fast. It's difficult to find anything reasonable for below US$10 a double. Most hotels have gathered on Paseo Colón and the adjoining streets, and this is the most enjoyable area in which to stay.

Hotel Diana (☎ 22326), at Paseo Colón No 99, is one of the cheapest acceptable places to stay. It has various rooms, beginning at US$9 for a double. In a similar price range are two places on Calle Boyacá, the Hotel Napoli (☎ 22526) and next door the Hotel Minerva (☎ 23672). Both only offer matrimoniales and they are often full. Avoid the Hotel Costa Azul on Calle Maneiro – to describe it as 'basic' would be to flatter this scruffy, dirty place. Its only advantage is the price: US$4/6.50 for singles/doubles without bath (with fan) and US$7/9 with bath and air-conditioning.

There are two good places on the Plaza Bolívar: the very small Hotel Guayana (☎ 21056), for US$12/15 a double/triple, and the Hotel Europa (☎ 664688), for marginally more. At roughly the same price, you also can stay in the Hotel Rey (☎ 686810) just off the plaza, the Hotel Margelina (☎ 687545), the Hotel Montecarlo (☎ 685677) or the Hotel Neptuno (☎ 691738). The last three are a few steps from each other on Paseo Colón, between Calles Boyacá and Juncal.

Further up the price scale, there's a number of options located in the same area, for example the Hotel Gaeta (☎ 691816), for US$36 a double. Top-end accommodation is well represented in Puerto La Cruz; the poshest hotels on the waterfront are the four-star Hotel Rasil (☎ 672422) and the five-star Hotel Meliá (☎ 691311), both expensive. Cheaper, although almost as good, is the Cristina Suites (☎ 674712), a few blocks back from the Paseo Colón. Its suites cost around US$50/60/70 for one/two/three persons.

Places to Eat

There are lots of places to eat in the city, and if you are up to it financially you can eat really well. The waterfront is the up-market area, so if you are after budget eating, shop around the streets back from the water. One of the cheapest places serving tasty meals is Restaurant El Teide (no sign on the door), next to a farmacia, on Avenida 5 de Julio No 153. An unpretentious main course will cost around US$1.50. For about the cheapest chicken in town go to Mister Pollo, opposite Hotel Europa, on Calle Sucre.

The cream of the city's restaurants and trendy bars have gathered on Paseo Colón and along Calle Carabobo. This area is alive until late, when fresh breezes cool the heat of day and people gather in the numerous open-air establishments which look over the beach.

Getting There & Away

Air Puerto La Cruz doesn't have its own airport. The nearest is in Barcelona (see that section for details).

Bus The bus terminal is conveniently sited in the middle of the city, just three blocks south of Plaza Bolívar.

Left & Right: Santuario de la Virgen de Coromoto, near Guanare
Bottom: The high altar of the church in San Miguel

Top Left: Salinas de Araya
Top Right: Saint, Museo de Anzoátegui, Barcelona
Bottom Left: Parque Nacional Mochima
Bottom Right: Santa Inés church, Cumaná

Frequent buses run to Caracas (US$6.50, five hours), and in the opposite direction, to Cumaná (US$1.75, 1½ hours); some buses continue east to Carúpano (US$4.25, 3½ hours), or even to Güiria (US$7, 5½ hours). If you go eastwards (to Cumaná or further on), grab a seat on the left side of the bus: there are some spectacular views over the islands of Parque Nacional Mochima.

There are half a dozen buses travelling daily to Ciudad Guayana (US$7.50, six hours), and all go via Ciudad Bolívar (US$5.50, 4½ hours); Expresos Caribe operates this route.

To Barcelona, you take the urban bus from Avenida 5 de Julio. They go either by Avenida Intercomunal or Vía Alterna. Both will deposit you in Barcelona's centre in 45 minutes to one hour, depending on the traffic.

Boat Puerto La Cruz is the major departure point for Isla de Margarita. There are two boats daily by Turismo Margarita and eight ferries by Conferry. In the off season, count on half that number. The passenger fare with either carrier is US$6.50 (1st class) and US$5 (2nd class). Turismo Margarita takes some 2½ hours, while Conferry takes twice that long. They have separate terminals, one km from each other, both west of the city centre. Por puestos run frequently to both ferry terminals from the corner of Avenida 5 de Julio and Calle Juncal. Ferry tickets can only be bought two hours before the scheduled time of departure, at the respective terminal. Take this trip during the daytime: it's a spectacular journey between the islands of the Parque Nacional Mochima.

PARQUE NACIONAL MOCHIMA

Occupying an area of 950 sq km, the Parque Nacional Mochima covers the offshore belt of the Caribbean coast between Puerto La Cruz and Cumaná, including a wealth of islands and islets, plus a strip of the hilly coast noted for its deep bays and white sandy beaches.

The main groups of islands include, from west to east, Las Borrachas, Las Chimanas and Las Caracas. Closer to the mainland and easier to reach are Isla de Plata and Isla Monos. Some of the islands are hilly with rocky cliffs and are quite spectacular. Many islands are surrounded by coral reefs and they offer excellent snorkelling and scuba diving. The waters are warm and usually calm, and they abound in marine life. The weather is fine for most of the year, with moderate rainfall mainly between July and October.

With its fine beach and coral reefs, the **Isla de Plata** is the most popular island among tourists. It's about 10 km east of Puerto La Cruz and accessible by boat from the pier near Pamatacualito, the eastern suburb of the port of Guanta which is serviced by por puestos from Puerto La Cruz. Boats run regularly during weekends (but not on weekdays), taking 10 minutes to get to the island. There are food and drink stalls on the island but no fresh water. Boats can also be rented for longer trips to other islands, such as **Isla Monos**, which is good for snorkelling.

The Puerto La Cruz-Cumaná road, in parts, skirts the seafront, so you'll glimpse some terrific views, particularly between El Chaparro and Santa Fe. There are several beaches off the road, possibly the best being **Playa Arapito**, some 23 km from Puerto La Cruz, and **Playa Colorada**, four km further east.

About 20 km further along this road, a side road branches off to the north and goes five km to the village of **Mochima**. Mochima sits in the deep Bahía Mochima, and is a good jumping-off point if you want to explore the park. From the wharf, boats can take you out to the islands or put you down on one of several isolated mainland beaches such as Playa Blanca or Playa Cautaro, which are inaccessible by road. Accommodation and food are available in the village.

The ferry between Puerto La Cruz and Isla Margarita sails between some of the park's islands, providing good views on either side. Tours organised from Puerto La Cruz are another way of visiting the area.

Finally, for a sweeping, panoramic view of the park, complete with its islands, bays and beaches, go to **Los Altos**, a village some

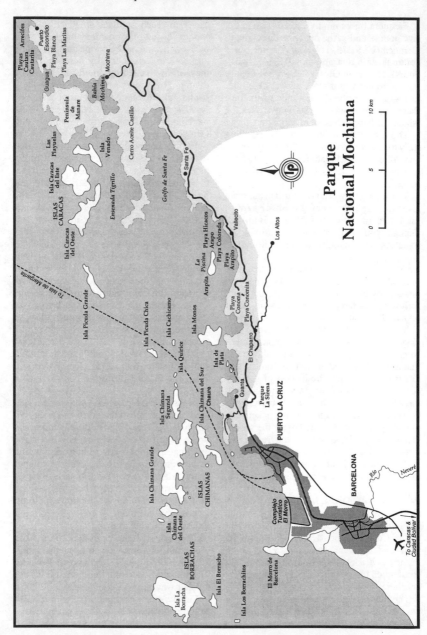

Parque
Nacional Mochima

25 km east of Puerto La Cruz. Los Altos is at an altitude of about 900 metres and is only three km from the seashore, giving it fabulous views. It is surrounded by fresh green highlands, sprinkled with coffee and cacao haciendas which can be visited (eg Hacienda El Mirador). Jeeps to Los Altos depart from Puerto La Cruz bus terminal, regularly in the morning but not so in the afternoon. The trip takes 45 minutes and costs US$0.70. You can stay overnight in the pleasant and reasonably priced Posada del Paraíso.

CUMANÁ

The capital of Sucre state, Cumaná is a city of some 250,000 inhabitants and an important port for sardine fishing and canning. Founded by the Spaniards in 1521, Cumaná takes pride in being the oldest surviving town on South America's mainland. There's not much in the way of centuries-old architecture, however; three earthquakes (in 1684, 1765 and 1929) reduced the town each time to a pile of rubble, and its colonial character largely disappeared in the subsequent reconstructions.

Cumaná is noted more for its attractive environs than for the city itself. There are some beaches nearby, the closest being Playa San Luis, on the south-western outskirts of the city; frequent busetas go there from the centre. Cumaná is one of the two gateways to Isla de Margarita (the other one being Puerto La Cruz), and it is a convenient jumping-off point for the Cueva del Guácharo (see that section).

Information

Tourist Office The Dirección de Turismo is on Calle Sucre, close to the Santa Inés Church. The office is open Monday to Friday from 8 am to noon and 2.30 to 5.30 pm. There's also a tourist stand at the airport.

Inparques The Inparques office (☎ 311570) is on Boulevard La Margariteña, Parque Guaiquerí, Avenida Arismendi.

Money Major banks are on Avenida Mariño and Avenida Bermúdez, and most of them will change cash dollars. Travellers' cheques can be changed in the Banco Unión and Banco Consolidado, the latter being a long way from the centre, on the corner of Avenida Bermúdez and Avenida Arístides Rojas. The Banco Unión seems to be one of the few to service credit card holders.

Things to See

Some streets around the **Santa Inés Church** retain some of their former appearance. The church itself dates from 1929, and only a few objects from an earlier time decorate its interior: note the 16th-century statue of the patron saint over the high altar. The **Catedral**, on Plaza Blanco, is also relatively young, and has a hotchpotch of altarpieces in its largely timbered interior.

Perhaps the best-restored colonial structure in town is the **Castillo de San Antonio de la Eminencia**, overlooking the city from a hill just south-east of the centre. Originally constructed in 1659, on a four-pointed star plan, it suffered pirate attacks and earthquakes but the coral rock walls survived in a pretty good shape. The fort commands good views over the city and the bay; go there for sunset.

The city has three museums. The **Casa Natal de Andrés Eloy Blanco** is the house where this poet, who is considered one of Venezuela's most extraordinary literary talents, was born in 1896. It's open Monday to Friday from 9 am to noon and 3 to 8 pm, Saturday and Sunday 3 to 8 pm. The **Museo Gran Mariscal de Ayacucho** is dedicated to the Cumaná-born hero of the War of Independence, General Antonio José de Sucre, best remembered for liberating Peru and Bolivia. It's open Monday to Friday from 9 am to noon and 3 to 6 pm, Saturday and Sunday from 4 to 9 pm. The **Museo del Mar** is at the old airport, a couple of km south-west of the city centre. None of these museums is particularly inspiring.

There are two very pleasant parks in the centre, the **Parque Ayacucho** and **Parque Guaiquerí**, and several tree-shaded plazas.

Places to Stay

The city has over 30 hotels and there's generally no problem finding somewhere to stay. Almost all the budget places are conveniently located in the city centre, within a couple of blocks of Plaza Bolívar. All hotels listed below have rooms with private bath and either fans or air-conditioning.

The cheapest in town (US$5 for a double) seems to be the *Hospedaje La Gloria* (☎ 661284), on Calle Sucre, but only a miracle can get you a room there. Most rooms are rented for long periods and some guests seem to live there for years. Marginally more expensive are the *Hotel Vesuvio* (☎ 26941), the *Hotel Cumaná* (☎ 24766) and the *Hotel Italia* (☎ 663678), all on Calle Sucre, but they, too, can be often full.

The cheapest viable option is possibly *Hospedaje Lucila*, on Calle Bolívar, in the same area. It's clean and quiet, though there will probably be some loving couples passing through from time to time. Doubles with bath and fan cost US$7.

Inexpensive options with air-conditioning include *Hotel Astoria* (☎ 662708), Calle Sucre, and *Hotel América* (☎ 22605), Calle América. The former costs US$7/9/10 for

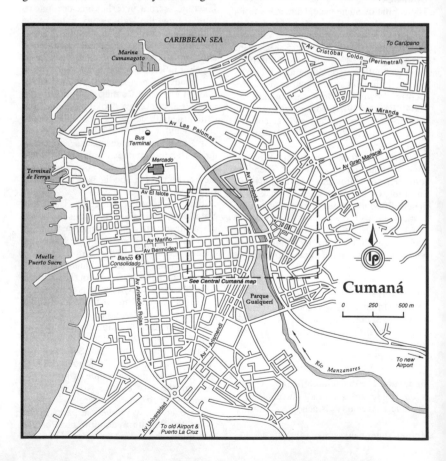

Cumaná

singles/doubles/triples; the latter is slightly more expensive but a bit better.

There are several inexpensive hotels just west across the river from Plaza Miranda. In ascending order of price they are *Hotel Dos Mil* (☎ 24809) at US$9/11 a single/double, *Hotel Master* (☎ 663884) at US$10/14/18 a single/double/triple, *Hotel Turismo Guaiquerí* (☎ 310821) at US$18 a double, *Hotel Regina* (☎ 23442) at US$20 a double, and *Hotel Mariño* (☎ 22663) at US$23 a double. The Regina is possibly the best choice of the lot.

Up-market hotels are away from the centre, mainly on Avenida Perimetral and Avenida Universidad, both near the waterfront. The best place to stay in town is the four-star *Hotel Los Bordones* (☎ 653644), at the end of Avenida Universidad, near the beach but a long way from the centre.

Places to Eat

About the cheapest central place for a soup and a main course is the *Restaurant París* on Plaza Miranda, but the food is nothing special. The cheapest grilled chicken is served in *Pollo a la Brasa*, on Plaza Bolívar (half a chicken for US$2.50) but, again, the price represents the value. Other inexpensive options include the two areperas, *19 de Abril* (the better of the two) and *El Punto Criollo*, and the open-air parrilla on Plaza Ribero.

A considerably better choice for a lunch or dinner is the *Restaurant Polo Norte* or, still better but more expensive, the *Restaurant El Colmao*.

Two panaderías on Plaza Blanco, *Super Katty* and *La Catedral*, offer a variety of cakes and pastries plus good coffee.

The *Fuente de Soda Jardín Sport*, on Plaza Bolívar, is an open-air bar open until 1 am and popular with local beer fans. This is the place to have a beer or ten if you want to follow the local male style, accompanied by typical music from the jukebox. At the same time, you can learn the peculiar way of serving beer which is common in down-to-earth drinkeries in Venezuela and Colombia. Waiters leave the empty bottles on the table in order to calculate the final bill after the drinking session is over. If the bottles don't fit on the table, a beer box is provided and put beside it to make room for the following rounds. There may be a lot of boxes around in the late evening.

Getting There & Away

Air The old airport, two km south-west of the city centre, has been closed down, and a new one opened about four km south-east of the city. Aeropostal, Avensa and Aereotuy service Cumaná, with three direct flights daily to Caracas (US$47) and one to Porlamar on Isla de Margarita (US$28).

Bus The bus terminal is 1½ km north-west of the city centre and it's linked by frequent urban buses.

There is a regular bus service to Caracas operated by a number of companies (US$8.25, 6½ hours). All buses go through Puerto La Cruz (US$1.75, 1½ hours) and Barcelona (US$2, two hours). Half a dozen buses depart daily for Ciudad Bolívar (US$7.25, six hours) and continue on to Ciudad Guayana (US$8.75, 7½ hours). Three or four buses go daily to Güiria (US$5.50, 4½ hours). For Cueva del Guácharo, take the Caripe bus (two daily, at 7 am and noon, US$3, 3½ hours). There are also por puestos (US$5.50).

Boat All ferries and boats to Isla de Margarita depart from the wharf next to the mouth of Río Manzanares and arrive on the island at Punta de Piedras. There is no urban bus service from the city centre to the ferry docks but por puestos go there from the door of the Hotel Dos Mil (US$0.20).

Conferry runs large ferries which take up to 60 cars and 1000 passengers, daily at 7 am and 4 pm. The passenger fare is US$4.50 and the trip takes three to four hours.

Naviarca sails the same route for the same price, daily at noon and 10 pm, but it's not as reliable a carrier. The schedule is, as they say, 'flexible'.

Finally, there's Turismo Margarita, which runs a 400-seat boat, *Gran Cacique*, daily at 7.30 am and 1.30 pm (on Friday at 7 am, 1 and 6 pm). The boat takes only people, not

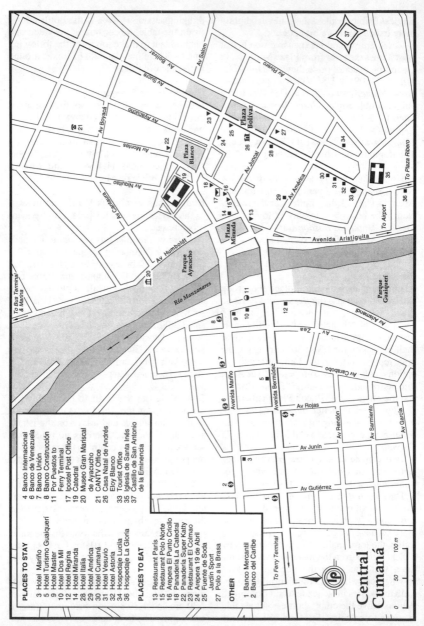

PLACES TO STAY

3 Hotel Mariño
5 Hotel Turismo Guaiqueri
9 Hotel Master
10 Hotel Dos Mil
12 Hotel Regina
14 Hotel Miranda
28 Hotel Italia
29 Hotel América
30 Hotel Cumaná
31 Hotel Vesuvio
32 Hotel Astoria
34 Hospedaje Lucila
36 Hospedaje La Gloria

PLACES TO EAT

13 Restaurant París
15 Restaurant Polo Norte
16 Arepera El Punto Criollo
18 Panadería La Catedral
23 Panadería Super Katty
24 Restaurant El Colmao
25 Arepera 19 de Abril
27 Pollo a la Brasa

OTHER

1 Banco Mercantil
2 Banco del Caribe
4 Banco Internacional
6 Banco de Venezuela
7 Banco Unión
8 Banco Construcción
11 Por Puestos to
   Ferry Terminal
17 Ipostel Post Office
19 Catedral
20 Museo Gran Mariscal
   de Ayacucho
21 CANTV Office
26 Casa Natal de Andrés
   Eloy Blanco
33 Tourist Office
35 Iglesia de Santa Inés
37 Castillo de San Antonio
   de la Eminencia

Central
Cumaná

To Ferry Terminal

0   50   100 m

cars, for US$5.50 1st class, and US$4.50 2nd class. The trip takes two hours.

Naviarca operates ferries to Araya, on the Península de Araya, theoretically at 6 and 9 am and 1 and 4 pm, Monday to Friday, and at 9 am on Saturday and Sunday, but they are even less reliable than those to Margarita Island. It's better to go directly to the Muelle Puerto Sucre (about one km to the south from ferry docks), from where boats to Araya run approximately every two hours until about 4 pm (US$0.75, one hour).

The area around the ferry docks and Puerto Sucre is not famous for its safety, so use a por puesto instead of walking.

If you are coming in on a yacht, note that Cumaná has just about the best marina in the country, and possibly the cheapest. Purpose-built, well-organised and dotted with facilities, the Marina Cumanagoto (☎ 311423) is a good place to visit if you are en route to somewhere else or if you just want somewhere to anchor your vessel before you head off on an overland trip around the country. Daily rates are US$9 for boats up to 40 feet long, US$11 for those between 40 and 60 feet, and US$15 if they are longer. There are various discounts (up to 40%) for leaving the boat for a longer period.

If you are looking for a lift on a boat around the Caribbean, it's worth coming here and trying your luck. The marina is a 10-minute-walk from the bus terminal.

PENÍNSULA DE ARAYA
This 70-km-long and 10-km-wide peninsula stretches east-west along the mainland's coast, with its tip lying due north of Cumaná. Punta Arenas, on the peninsula's end, is just five km from Cumaná as the crow flies, but it's some 180 km by road. The peninsula is hilly, arid and infertile. Its eastern half is higher and more rugged, with the highest peak reaching 596 metres. The population is small and lives in a handful of villages on the coast, mostly on the northern side, along which the only peninsular road runs. Sandwiched between the peninsula and the mainland is Golfo de Cariaco, a quiet, deep, intensely blue body of water.

The Spaniards first landed on the peninsula in 1499. After the unexpected discovery of fabulous pearl fisheries around the islands of Cubagua and Coche, Pedro Alonso Niño and Cristóbal de la Guerra sailed down to the western tip of the peninsula to find another, quite different treasure – extensive salinas, or saltpans. These salt beds were and still are Venezuela's largest salt deposits.

At that time, salt was increasingly sought after in Europe, as an indispensable means for the preservation of food, mainly fish. The Dutch, who, by then, already had a well-developed fishing industry but only a scarce supply of salt, were the first to realise the value of the Spanish discovery. They soon began to take advantage of it.

Meanwhile, the Spaniards, who had some salt reserves at home, foolishly concentrated on the pearl harvesting of Cubagua and Coche Islands. As soon as the pearl beds were wiped out, however, which happened around the mid-16th century, they turned to the saltpans.

During the second half of the 16th century, the salinas of Araya were furtively exploited, mostly by the Dutch and English, and the Spanish could do nothing about it. Various battles were fought by the Spaniards in defence of their treasured possession, but the indiscriminate plundering of the salt continued. To prevent further attempts to steal the salt, the Crown eventually set about building a fortress.

After carefully selecting the location, work on the fort began in 1618 and took almost 50 years to be completed. Progress was interrupted by pirates and storms, and hindered by the extreme heat. The heat was so bad that most of the work had to be carried out at night. The fortress ended up being the most costly Spanish project to be realised in the New World up to that time. Yet it was also the most powerful and magnificent. Equipped with 45 cannons and defended by a 250-man garrison, La Real Fortaleza de Santiago de León de Araya successfully repelled all attempts to take it.

A turning point in the fort's history came in 1726 with a hurricane. The storm not only

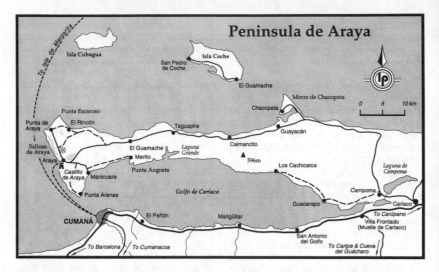

damaged the structure but, more importantly, produced a tide which broke over the salt lagoon, flooding it and turning it into a gulf. Salt could no longer be exploited.

With the salt gone, the fort lost its role and the Spanish decided to abandon the peninsula. Before leaving, however, they decided to blow up the fortress, to prevent it falling into foreign hands. Despite using all the available gunpowder, the structure largely resisted the efforts to destroy it. Damaged but not ruined, the mighty bulwarks still proudly crown the waterfront cliff.

Meanwhile, as the years passed, the salinas slowly returned to their old state, and mining was gradually reintroduced. Today they provide a good part of the salt produced by Venezuela.

Araya

The fort and the salinas are the peninsula's two major attractions. They are both in the town of Araya on the western end of the peninsula. Incidentally, Araya is the easiest point to get to on the peninsula.

Araya is the largest settlement on the peninsula and the major destination for ferries and boats from Cumaná. The town sits in a bay, Bahía de Araya, with its muelle (wharf) in the middle. Half a km to the south looms the massive ruin of the fortress, while to the north the salinas spread outwards.

The **Salinas de Araya** is where most of Venezuela's salt comes from. The salt mining is operated by ENSAL, a government company, which has built installations on the seafront and which produces half a million tons of salt per year. The salt works can be visited and it's one of the most unusual sights you'll see in the area.

Before you can visit the salinas you have to go to the Gerencia, or the company's main office, to get a permit. The office is at the northern end of the town, in what was previously the Hotel Araya. It's right behind the installation complex, but you won't be allowed to pass through direct, so you have to take a roundabout inland way. You can walk there (a 15-minute walk from the ferry landing), or try to wave down any of the ENSAL pick-up trucks, which run around the town providing transport for the workers; they frequently call at the Gerencia.

The Gerencia will find you a guide to show you around the complex. It may take some time to organise, however, as company employees (who double as guides) may not be immediately available. The tour itself takes somewhere between two and three hours. The tour is free; you don't have to pay for the permit or the guide.

There are three areas to visit: the salinas naturales (which they call 'Unidad 1'), salinas artificiales (Unidad 2) and the main complex of buildings where the salt is sorted, packed and stored. The salinas naturales, about one km east of town, is an intriguingly pink salt lagoon, from which the salt is dragged to the shore by specially constructed boats and then put into piles for drying. You'll be shown the rudimentary-looking machinery and may even be taken for a short ride on the lagoon.

The salinas artificiales, some two km north of the town, near the sea shore, is an array of rectangular pools which are filled in with salt water and left to dry out. Thanks to the intense strength of the sun, the water evaporates leaving behind pure salt. The salt is then dragged out, the pool refilled, and the whole process starts again. What is particularly amazing here is the unbelievable pink of the water. Since pools are in different stages of evaporation, there's an incredible variety of tones, ranging from creamy pink to deep purple. Here you'll also visit a laboratory where you will be shown the artemia, a kind of microscopic saltwater shrimp, which is responsible for the water colouration.

A mirador (lookout) has been built on the hill to the east of the salinas, and this provides a panoramic view over the whole chessboard of pools. It's not on the tour route but you can go there afterwards; it's on the road to Punta de Araya, two km north of Araya.

The third area to be visited is the complex where the salt is sorted and packed. Unless you want to see the archaic, noisy machinery, operating without any safety measures – Chaplin's *Modern Times* comes to mind – this is, perhaps, the least interesting sight.

The installations close at 2 pm, so start early to allow sufficient time for a guide to be found for you and for the leisurely tour to be completed by noon, time for lunch, which paralyses all other activities. Be prepared for baking heat: a hat or other head protection is a must. It's wise to carry a large bottle of water or other drink.

The **Castillo de Araya** – as the fort is commonly referred to – stands on the cliffs at the southern end of the bay, a 10-minute walk along the beach from the wharf. It's ruined, but, despite the damage, the mighty walls still overlook the bay and give a good impression of what the fort once looked like. You can wander freely around the place, as there's no gate.

Places to Stay There are three or four simple posadas in town, two of which are within a few hundred metres of the wharf, on the road to the salinas naturales.

Getting There & Away There are ferries and boats to Cumaná. In theory, the ferry is scheduled to sail four times a day (once on weekends), but sometimes a day will pass without there being a single departure. Boats are more reliable, and go to Cumaná every two hours or so, until 4 or 5 pm (US$0.75, one hour). Upon arrival at Araya, check the schedule of the boats back to Cumaná and keep in mind that the last boat may depart earlier than scheduled, or sometimes not at all.

Although there's a paved road to Cariaco (95 km), there's not much travelling along it. Infrequent por puestos go to El Guamache and sometimes on to Caimancito or Guayacán (from where occasional por puestos run to Cariaco). There are almost no por puestos that run all the way from Araya to Cariaco. You can try hitching but the traffic is minimal. It dies completely after 3 or 4 pm.

Around the Peninsula

Given the scarcity of roads and public transport, you are likely to limit your visit to Araya, making it a fabulous one-day trip out of Cumaná. If you have more time to spend, you may like to go to the sleepy fishing village of Punta Arenas, 10 km south of Araya. It has a good beach and two posadas. Another nearby village, Manicuare, is known for its pottery, which has been produced here since time immemorial, but there's nowhere to stay for the night. Infrequent por puestos go from Araya to both Punta Arenas and Manicuare.

The peninsula has some attractive natural areas and quite a varied wildlife, including lizards, snakes and a diversity of birds. The lagoon near Chacopata is favoured by pink flamingos. A particularly spectacular region, noted for its cliffs, stretches along the rugged coastline east of Chacopata. The Cariaco-Chacopata road skirts some of the coast and provides dramatic views.

For any off-the-road walks on the peninsula, wear sturdy shoes, not so much for the snakes but to protect feet against cacti, an important component of the local flora. Don't forget that there's almost no shade on the peninsula, so a hat, water, sunglasses, suncream and the like are essential.

CARIPE

Caripe is a pleasant, easy-going small town noted for its agreeable climate, its coffee and orange plantations and its proximity to Cueva del Guácharo, Venezuela's most magnificent cave.

The town is clean and prosperous-looking, with elegant villas and manicured gardens. The place is quite touristy, and on weekends it's full of people escaping the tropical humidity, which dominates most of the region. The town is no more than two parallel streets, around which most activities and services are centred.

Information

The Top Trekking Travel Tours (☎ 51843), the local travel agency, will give you information about walks in the area and, if you wish, will put together a tour according to your interests, providing transport and camping equipment. Their office is in the Cabañas Pueblo Pequeño, a couple of km west of town, but they plan on opening another office in the town. One of the owners, Alexander, speaks fluent German while another one, Pablo, speaks English.

Banco Unión and Banco del Orinoco change travellers' cheques but not cash. Banco Unión and Banco de Venezuela may service credit card holders.

Things to See & Do

Save for a fine colonial high altar in the modern parish church there's nothing special to see in town, but the hilly surroundings are beautiful and pleasant for walks. The No 1 attraction is obviously the Cueva del Guácharo, 10 km from the town (see the following section). There are also two nice waterfalls, **Salto La Payla** near the cave and the 80-metre **Salto El Chorrerón**, an hour's walk from the village of Sabana de Piedra.

El Mirador, the highest hill (1100 metres) just to the north of the town, commands an excellent view over the whole Valle del Caripe. It's a 45-minute walk from town, or you can go there by road.

For those on a more leisurely schedule, there are a couple of balnearios (natural pools with facilities), the nearest being **La Poza de Lorenzo**, in the village of Teresén. The village also has a vivero (nursery) with a variety of orchids (they flower in May, and sometimes in November). There's another vivero in La Frontera close to Caripe.

Numerous longer trips are possible, including the hike to the highest peak in the region, **Cerro Negro**.

Places to Stay

Caripe is becoming increasingly popular with tourists, and there is a score of places to stay in and around the town. Hotel prices tend to rise on weekends.

The cheapest in town (US$7 a double) is the simple but acceptable *Hotel Caripe*, followed by the similar *Hotel San Francisco* (US$8 a double). Appreciably better are the *Hotel Venezia* (US$10 a double) and the *Mini Hotel Familiar Nicola* (US$12 a double). The *Hotel Samán* costs twice that, although it's not twice as comfortable.

If you are in a large party, it may work out cheaper to take a cabaña; there are several of them on the road between Caripe and the village of El Guácharo.

Camping is possible next to the reception building at the entrance to Cueva del Guácharo (after 5 pm), and on the soccer field in Caripe (ask the Guardia for permission). You can also camp not far out of town.

Places to Eat

Most of the better hotels and cabañas have their own restaurants. The cheapest place for a meal is the restaurant in the *Hotel Caripe*, whereas the best food in town seems to be served in *Hotel Venezia*.

Getting There & Away

There's no bus terminal in town. Buses and por puestos park on Calle Monagas in the centre. There's an evening bus direct to Caracas via Maturín (US$12.50, 11 hours), and two buses to Cumaná, at 6 am and at noon (US$3, 3½ hours). They pass the Cueva del Guácharo on the way. There are also infrequent por puestos to Cumaná (most reliable in the morning).

CUEVA DEL GUÁCHARO

The Guácharo Cave, 10 km from Caripe on the road towards the coast, is Venezuela's longest, largest and most magnificent cave. It was known to the local Indians long before Columbus crossed the Atlantic, and it was later explored by Europeans. The most eminent explorer, Alexander von Humboldt, penetrated 472 metres into the cave in September 1799, and it was he who was the first to classify its most unusual inhabitant, the guácharo.

The guácharo, or oilbird *(Steatornis caripensis)*, is a nocturnal, frugivorous (fruit-eating) bird, the only one of its kind in the world. It inhabits caves in various tropical parts of the Americas, living in total darkness and leaving the cave only at night for food, principally the fruit of some species of palms. The guácharo has a sort of radar-location system similar to that of bats, which enables it to get around. The adult bird is about 60 cm long, with a wingspan of a metre.

In Venezuela, the guácharo has been seen in over 40 caves; the biggest colony, estimated at about 15,000 birds, is here, in the Guácharo Cave. They inhabit only the first chamber of the cave, the 750-metre-long Humboldt's Hall.

In order to protect the habitat where the bird feeds, a large wooded area around the cave has been declared the Parque Nacional El Guácharo (the cave itself is the Monumento Natural Cueva del Guácharo).

The guácharo apart, the cave offers a variety of amazing formations (stalactites, stalagmites, columns and the like) and a rich and complex flora and fauna. Many speleologists agree that this is one of the most complete cave ecosystems to be found anywhere in the world.

The cave is open daily from 8 am to 4 pm and all visits are guided in groups of up to 10 people; the tour takes about an hour. A 1½-km portion of the total 10½-km length of the cave is visited, though occasionally in August the water can rise, limiting sightseeing to half a km. You have to leave backpacks and bags by the ticket office, but cameras with flashes are permitted in the cave beyond the area where the guácharo live. The ticket costs US$0.70 (US$0.40 for students).

You can camp near the cave (but only after closing time); if you do so, you'll see hundreds of birds pouring out of the cave mouth at around 7 pm and returning about 4 am. A 35-metre-high waterfall, Salto La Payla, is a 25-minute walk from the cave.

Guácharo *(Steatornis caripensis)*

CARÚPANO

East of Cumaná, Carúpano is the last city of any size on Venezuela's Caribbean coast. It's approaching 100,000 inhabitants and is an active port for cacao which is cultivated in the region before it's shipped overseas. The city has an airport where large jets land, and it is linked by paved roads with Cumaná to the west and Ciudad Guayana to the south. Despite its regular chessboard layout, suggesting its colonial origins, the town is rather unremarkable and has no significant attractions in itself. Carúpano is centred around Plaza Colón. Plaza Bolívar is stranded in a far south-western suburb.

This rather quiet place springs to life for four days (Saturday to Tuesday) before Ash Wednesday, when the Carnaval is held. There are dances, parades and a lot of music and rum. It's worth visiting during Carnaval if you happen to be wandering around somewhere in the region. At other times, the town is just a transit or overnight stop on the route to a more exciting destination.

Information

Money All major banks are located around Plaza Colón. The most reliable is the Banco Consolidado which changes cash and travellers' cheques and which services Visa and MasterCard holders. Banco Unión, Banco del Caribe and Banco del Orinoco can be useful for credit card holders but not really for anyone else.

Places to Stay

There are not many hotels in the town. If you come by bus for just an overnight stay, the cheapest bet is the *Pensión Raúl Leoni* close to the bus terminal. It's a clean, safe and quiet place even though all its bathrooms are shared. The hotel charges US$4 per person. Next to the Pensión is the *Residencias Virgen del Valle*, but it's more basic and more expensive.

For the cheapest rooms with private bath and fan, go to *Residencias Ecuador* on Avenida Independencia. Ample doubles/triples cost US$8/10. Inexpensive places offering rooms with air-conditioning include the *Hotel Bologna* (☎ 311241), at Avenida Independencia 47,

and *Hotel María Victoria* (☎ 311170), on Avenida Perimetral, at the north-east end of the town near the port. Doubles in either of these will cost around US$11.

If you are after comfort try the two central hotels: the *Hotel San Francisco* (☎ 311074), at Avenida Juncal 87A, and the *Hotel Lilma* (☎ 311341), at Avenida Independencia 161. Both have air-conditioned doubles/triples with bath, costing around US$18/22. Alternatively, try the *Hotel El Yunque*, which faces the sea from Avenida Perimetral, about a km west of the market.

The best in town is *Hotel Victoria* (☎ 311554), on Avenida Perimetral, a 10-minute walk east of the bus terminal. Singles/doubles cost US$25/32.

Places to Eat

There are plenty of eateries throughout the city but not much to choose from for a great meal. In the centre, the best reasonably priced food is supposedly in the restaurants belonging to the *Hotel San Francisco* and the *Hotel Lilma*. The *Hotel Victoria* has an even better restaurant but it's more expensive. The *Yong Shing*, on Avenida Libertad 82, does cheap Chinese food.

The *Pastelería Challa* has good cheese and ham pasteles and coffee, though there are no tables for you to sit down and eat. *La Juma de Mipai*, on Plaza Colón, is the place for an evening beer or a stronger drink.

The market is, as elsewhere, one of the cheapest options for unsophisticated local dishes, and the one in Carúpano is quite large.

Getting There & Away

Air The airport is 1½ km west of the city centre. Avensa has one flight a day to Porlamar on Isla de Margarita (US$28), and three flights to Caracas (US$49). Aeropostal flies to Caracas once a day (US$49).

Bus The bus terminal is a short walking distance north of the centre, on the Avenida Perimetral. Buses to Caracas go regularly throughout the day (US$10.75, 8½ hours). Frequent buses leave for Cumaná (US$2.50, two hours). There are four buses to Güiria

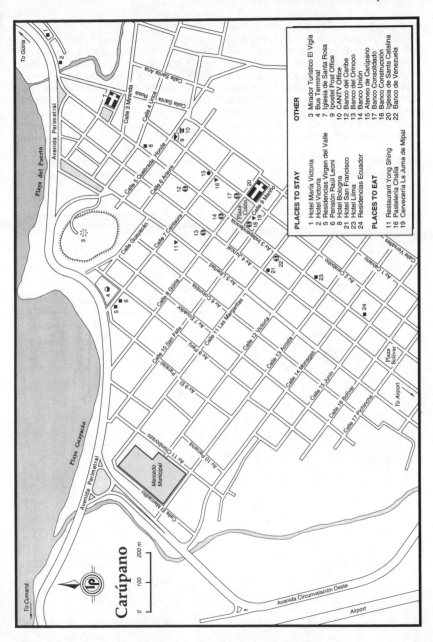

Carúpano

0   100   200 m

PLACES TO STAY
1   Hotel María Victoria
2   Hotel Victoria
5   Residencias Virgen del Valle
6   Pensión Raúl Leoni
8   Hotel Bologna
21 Hotel San Francisco
23 Hotel Llima
24 Residencias Ecuador

PLACES TO EAT
11 Restaurant Yong Shing
16 Pastelería Challa
19 Cervecería La Juma de Mipai

OTHER
3   Mirador Turístico El Vigía
4   Bus Terminal
7   Iglesia de Santa Rosa
9   Ipostel Post Office
10 CANTV Office
12 Banco del Caribe
13 Banco del Orinoco
14 Banco Unión
15 Ateneo de Carúpano
17 Banco Consolidado
18 Banco Construcción
20 Iglesia de Santa Catalina
22 Banco de Venezuela

(US$3, 2½ hours), all coming through from Caracas; por puestos go to Güiria regularly from both the bus terminal and Plaza Colón (US$4.25, two hours). Three morning buses go to Ciudad Guayana, (US$7.50, seven hours).

For Cueva del Guácharo, take the Caracas/Cumaná bus, get off by the petrol station at Muelle de Cariaco (US$1.50, one hour), and catch one of the two buses coming through from Cumaná to Caripe (passing through about 8 am and 1 pm) which will drop you down at the cave (US$1.75, 2½ hours); or hitch, though the traffic is sporadic.

GÜIRIA

Güiria is the easternmost point on Venezuela's coast that you can reach by road, after a 275-km ride from Cumaná. Home to some 20,000 people, Güiria is the largest town on the Península de Paria and an important fishing port. The town itself is rather an ordinary place with no tourist attractions. The region around it, however, is attractive and worth exploring, particularly the Parque Nacional Península de Paria, a mountainous landscape covered with lush cloudforest, stretching along the northern coast. Near the

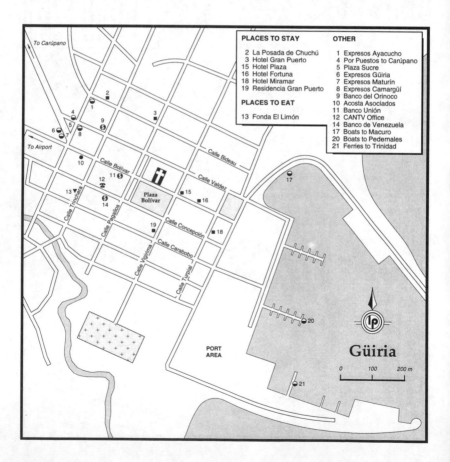

PLACES TO STAY

2 La Posada de Chuchú
3 Hotel Gran Puerto
15 Hotel Plaza
16 Hotel Fortuna
18 Hotel Miramar
19 Residencia Gran Puerto

PLACES TO EAT

13 Fonda El Limón

OTHER

1 Expresos Ayacucho
4 Por Puestos to Carúpano
5 Plaza Sucre
6 Expresos Güiria
7 Expresos Maturín
8 Expresos Camargüí
9 Banco del Orinoco
10 Acosta Asociados
11 Banco Unión
12 CANTV Office
14 Banco de Venezuela
17 Boats to Macuro
20 Boats to Pedernales
21 Ferries to Trinidad

To Carúpano

To Airport

Calle Bideau

Calle Bolívar

Calle Valdez

Calle Trinchera

Calle Pagallos

Calle Vigirima

Plaza Bolívar

Calle Concepción

Calle Carabobo

Calle Turpial

PORT AREA

Güiria

0   100   200 m

eastern tip of the peninsula is the small town of Macuro (accessible only by water), the only place on South America's mainland where Columbus set foot, in August 1498, having come from Trinidad.

Güiria has a ferry connection with Trinidad and other islands of the Lesser Antilles, and it is a possible starting point for a trip to the Orinoco Delta.

Information

Money Banco de Venezuela and Banco del Orinoco change cash and travellers' cheques. Neither bank will accept notes of less than US$50. Banco de Venezuela and Banco Unión may give advances on Visa and MasterCard.

Tours The Acosta Asociados (☎ 81679, 81233), Calle Bolívar 31, offers a variety of tours and other travel services. They sell tickets for the ferry to Trinidad and arrange all the necessary formalities.

Places to Stay & Eat

At the low-budget end, the best place to stay is the *Hotel Plaza*, on the corner of Plaza Bolívar. It costs US$7 for a double with a bath and fan, and it has its own restaurant, the best inexpensive eatery in town.

For a similar price, you can have a double in the *Hotel Fortuna*, on Calle Bolívar, 50 metres from the plaza, or in the *Hotel Miramar*, on Calle Turpial, a little bit further towards the port.

The *Residencia Gran Puerto* (☎ 81085), on Calle Vigirima, close to the central square, has good singles/doubles with bath and fan for US$9/10, and also a few air-conditioned doubles for US$14. Its sibling, the *Hotel Gran Puerto* (☎ 81343), on Calle Pegallos near Calle Bideau, offers marginally better standards for US$12/15. The best in town is *La Posada de Chuchú* (☎ 81266), Calle Bideau 35, which has doubles/triples for US$20/25, and its own restaurant which is in keeping with the standard of the hotel. Another place for tasty food is the *Fonda El Limón* on Calle Trinchera.

Getting There & Away

Air The airport is a 15-minute walk west of the town's centre. There are Avensa flights on light planes to Porlamar on Isla de Margarita, on Monday, Wednesday and Friday (US$35). These flights continue on to Caracas on large jets (US$72 from Güiria).

Bus Several bus companies have their offices around the triangular Plaza Sucre, two blocks from Plaza Bolívar; Expresos Ayacucho is one block north. There are three or four buses to Caracas (US$13.75, 11 to 12 hours). They all go via Cumaná, Puerto La Cruz and Barcelona. From the same square frequent por puestos run to Carúpano (US$4.25, two hours).

Boat Windward Lines operate a ferry on the Güiria-Trinidad-St Vincent-Barbados-St Lucia route. The whole loop takes a week, as the ferry spends several hours in each port. The Güiria-Trinidad portion takes seven hours. From Güiria, the ferry leaves on Wednesdays at 11 pm; from Trinidad to Güiria, it departs on Tuesdays at 5 pm. Theoretically, the ferry calls in at Güiria every second Wednesday, on alternate Wednesdays it goes to Pampatar on Isla de Margarita. In practice, however, this is not always the case. Check by phone beforehand for the nearest arrival.

Deck fares (in US$) from Güiria are:

To	One-way	Return
Trinidad (Port of Spain)	40	60
St Vincent (Kingstown)	83	138
Barbados (Bridgetown)	89	148
St Lucia (Castries)	95	158

Cabins cost about US$10 per bed per night. Acosta Asociados (see Tours), the Venezuelan representative of the Windward Lines, provides information and sells tickets. The ferry docks at the far southern end of the port, a 15-minute walk from the town's centre. The passport formalities are conducted on board before departure or upon arrival.

There are also irregular boats to Port of Spain; they depart when they have enough passengers, and charge about US$60 per head.

Peñeros (open fishing boats) leave from the northern end of the Güiria port to Macuro, every morning without fixed schedule. They charge US$2.50 and the trip takes 1½ to two hours. In Macuro ask for Doña Guillermina or Doña Beatriz, who run two simple posadas (US$4 per person) and who can also provide meals. There's a path from Macuro to Uquire, on the northern coast (a six-hour walk); you can hire a boat to take you there, but it's expensive.

Irregular fishing and cargo boats (one or two per week) go to Pedernales, at the northernmost mouth of the Orinoco Delta. The trip takes four to five hours and the fare is largely negotiable; you shouldn't pay more than US$8 per person.

From Pedernales, there are boats south to Tucupita, which usually call in at the small Warao Indian settlements.

Isla de Margarita

With an area of about 920 sq km, Isla de Margarita is Venezuela's largest island. It is 67 km from east to west and 32 km from north to south. It lies some 40 km off the mainland, due north of Cumaná. It is composed of what were once two neighbouring islands which are now linked by a narrow, crescent-shaped sandbank, La Restinga, which was gradually built by waves. In time, a mangrove ecosystem developed south of the isthmus, and it is now a national park.

The eastern part of Margarita is larger and more fertile, and contains 95% of the island's total population of 300,000. All the major towns are here, connected by quite a developed array of roads. The western part, known as the Península de Macanao, is arid and scarcely populated, with its 15,000 people living in a dozen or so villages located mostly along the coast. Both sections of the island are hilly; their highest peaks approaching 1000 metres.

Isla de Margarita is known nationwide for two reasons. Firstly, its beaches draw people to the island. Actually, Margarita is the No 1

destination for Venezuelan holiday-makers seeking white sand, surfing, snorkelling and scuba diving.

The island's other magnet is shopping. Margarita is a duty-free zone, so the prices of consumer goods are lower than on the mainland, though in many cases there's no significant difference. Despite that, local shops are packed with bargain seekers, who return home with large bags and sacks full of goods.

The tourist infrastructure has developed over the past decade, and Margarita now has a collection of posh hotels comparable only to those in Caracas. Peak periods for Venezuelan tourists include Christmas, Easter and the August vacation.

The climate is typical of the Caribbean: average temperatures range between 25°C and 28°C, and the heat is agreeably cooled down by evening breezes. The rainy season goes from November to January, with rain falling mostly during the night.

Administratively, Isla de Margarita and the two small islands of Cubagua and Coche make up the state of Nueva Esparta. Although the largest city on the island is Porlamar, the small sleepy town of La Asunción has traditionally done the honours as the state capital.

Information

Tourist Office There are three tourist boards on the island, operating independently and issuing their own publications. The government-run Dirección de Turismo is based in the Centro Artesanal Los Robles, in Los Robles, midway between Porlamar and Pampatar. The private corporation Cámara de Turismo has its main office in Porlamar and a stand at the airport. The third, the Fondene (Fondo para el Desarrollo del Estado de Nueva Esparta), operates from Pampatar and has several outlets throughout the island. See those sections for more information.

Getting There & Away

Air Margarita's airport is at the southern part of the island, 20 km south-west of Porlamar, reached by frequent por puestos and

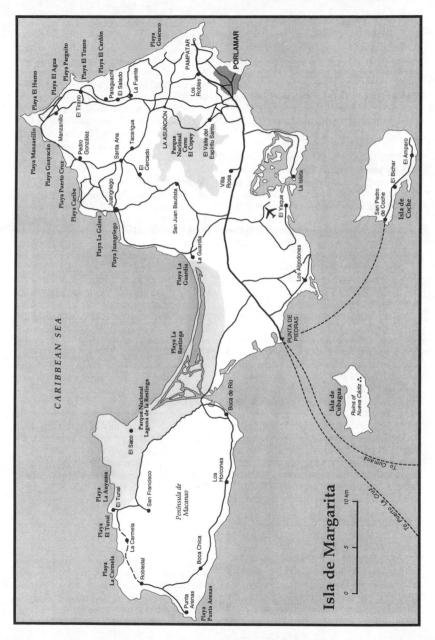

Isla de Margarita

minibuses (US$0.50). Taxis on this route will cost about US$7.

The airport is quite busy, with plenty of domestic and some international flights. There are flights to most major cities throughout the country, including a dozen flights a day to Caracas (US$47 with Aeropostal, US$51 with Avensa). Light planes go three times per week to Güiria (US$35).

Boat All ferries to/from Venezuela's mainland anchor in Punta de Piedras, 29 km west of Porlamar. There are frequent micros and por puestos (US$0.75 for either) between the ferry docks and Porlamar. Margarita has ferry links with Cumaná and Puerto La Cruz on the mainland. The Pampatar-Carúpano service was discontinued after the ferry broke down.

Three companies service Margarita: Conferry, Naviarca and Turismo Margarita. All carriers operate the Cumaná route, theoretically twice daily. The *Gran Cacique*, a hydrofoil belonging to Turismo Margarita, carries passengers only, and the trip takes two hours; the other two operators run car/passenger ferries which need three to four hours to cover the route. The passenger fare with any of the three is US$5.50 in 1st class and US$4.50 in 2nd class. Cars are shipped for US$9, jeeps for US$11 and motorbikes for US$4.

Conferry and Turismo Margarita cover the Puerto La Cruz route. The former has, in theory, eight departures daily and the trip takes five hours; the latter has two boats a day which run the distance in 2½ hours. Passenger fare with both carriers is US$6.50 in 1st class and US$5 in 2nd class; Conferry charges US$14 for cars, US$16 for jeeps and US$4 for motorbikes. Conferry also goes once a day from Punta de Piedras to Isla de Coche (US$1, one hour).

Tickets can only be bought on the day of the journey, an hour before the planned departure time. The service is not very reliable, with boats usually departing later than scheduled, but sometimes earlier. In the off season, there are fewer boats than listed.

Turismo Margarita is perhaps the most reliable operator.

There's an international ferry service between Pampatar and Trinidad, operated by Windward Lines. The ferry is supposed to arrive at Pampatar every other Wednesday in the morning, and depart for Trinidad the same day in the afternoon. The one-way deck fare is US$50 (US$75 return). The ferry then continues to St Vincent, Barbados and St Lucia. Refer to the Güiria section for further details.

Getting Around

There's frequent public transport in the main, eastern part of the island, so getting around this section is quite easy. There's no regular transport on Macanao. Infrequent por puestos go as far as Boca de Pozo along the southern shore, and up to San Francisco via the northern road.

If you are in a group of three or four, or if money is not a problem, a car may be an interesting proposition. There are a dozen car rental companies at the airport and most have another office in Porlamar. The rental prices in the off season may be attractive: as low as US$30 per day for a small car. Scooters and bicycles can also be hired at several places in Porlamar.

PORLAMAR

Porlamar is the largest urban centre on the island and will probably be your first destination when coming from the mainland. It's a modern, bustling city of 80,000 or so inhabitants, replete with shopping centres, hotels and restaurants. Tree-shaded Plaza Bolívar is the historic centre of the city, but Porlamar has progressively expanded eastward; a forest of high-rises has been built there over the past decade and it is getting thicker and more extensive year by year.

Porlamar is not a place for sightseeing, other than wandering around trendy stores packed with imported goods from everywhere. The most elegant and expensive shopping areas are on and around Avenida Santiago Mariño and Avenida 4 de Mayo. The two central pedestrian malls, Boulevard

Guevara and, to a lesser extent, Boulevard Gómez, south of Plaza Bolívar, trade mostly in clothing and their prices are more affordable.

One of the few real tourist sights is the **Museo de Arte Contemporáneo Francisco Narváez**, in a large modern building on the corner of Calle Igualdad and Calle Díaz. On the ground floor, on permanent display, is the collection of sculptures and paintings by this noted Margarita-born artist (1905-82), while the salons on the upper floor are used for temporary exhibitions. The museum is open from 9 am to noon and 2 to 6 pm, except Mondays.

A small but colourful **market** is held in the morning on the waterfront at the southern end of Boulevard Gómez. As might be expected, there are plenty of fish, including sharks.

Information
Tourist Office The Cámara de Turismo is on Avenida Santiago Mariño, next to Calle Hernández, and is open Monday to Friday from 8 am to noon and 2 to 6 pm. Fondene operates two information stands in Porlamar: near the corner of Avenida Santiago Mariño and Avenida 4 de Mayo, and on Boulevard Guevara, close to the corner of Calle Maneiro. They don't seem to be open regularly in the off season.

Pick up a copy of the bilingual Spanish/English newspaper *La Isla*, which is distributed free in some of the up-market hotels, travel agencies, tourist offices etc. Don't miss getting hold of *Mira!*, a well-written English-language monthly paper full of practical details and interesting background information about the island and the whole country. It, too, can be obtained free from a range of tourist establishments, but if you can't find it, contact the publisher in Porlamar, Avenida Santiago Mariño 14-97 (corner of Calle Tubores), Edificio Carcaleo Suites, Apartamento 2-A (☎ 613351).

Inparques The Inparques office is in Quinta Bayzarak, Calle Paralela.

Money Many of Porlamar's banks handle some foreign exchange operations. Their locations are given on the map. At the time of writing, cash was changed by Banco Principal, Banco Comercial Amazonas, Banco Construcción and Banco Mercantil. Travellers' cheques were exchanged by Banco Consolidado, Banco Principal and Banco Mercantil among others. Banks dealing with Visa and MasterCard include Banco de Venezuela, Banco Mercantil and Banco Unión.

There are several casas de cambio, most of which are located in the area of Avenida Santiago Mariño. Many stores will also exchange cash, at a rate which is about 1% to 2% lower than banks. Credit cards are widely accepted for payment in shops, up-market hotels and restaurants.

Turisol (☎ 610056, 610302, 610442, fax 610480) is in Centro Comercial People, Local 9, Calle Hernández, corner of Avenida 4 de Mayo.

Places to Stay
Porlamar has loads of hotels for every budget. As a general rule, the price and standard rise from west to east. Accordingly, there are no fancy places to stay west of Plaza Bolívar, but cheapies in this area are plentiful. On the other hand, looking for a budget room around Avenida Santiago Mariño is a waste of time.

There are a score of budget hotels within a few blocks to the south-west of Plaza Bolívar. Among them, one of the best cheap bets is the friendly *Hotel España* (☎ 612479), Calle Mariño No 6-35, near the waterfront. It has a variety of simple rooms, and a restaurant serving inexpensive, tasty meals. Expect to pay about US$5/7 for a single/double with bath, a dollar less for a room without private bath.

Other good budget options in the area include the *Hotel OM-21* (☎ 632367), on Calle San Nicolás, *Hotel Plaza* (☎ 630395), on Calle Velásquez, and *Hotel San Miguel* (☎ 630395), a few steps from the Hotel Plaza. All three have singles/doubles/triples/quadruples with bath for US$6/7/8/9, which works out quite well for a larger party. The *Hotel Caroní*, sandwiched between the Hotel Plaza and Hotel San Miguel, offers pretty much the same for marginally less. One of the cheapest in the area, the *Residencia El Paraíso*, has basic doubles with bath for US$5.

There are more cheapies in the vicinity of the market near the seafront. Here, possibly the cheapest acceptable place is *Hotel Coromoto* (☎ 635240), on Calle Maneiro. It has rooms with baths, capable of accommodating from one to five people. They cost US$4/5/6/7.50/8.50 respectively.

For inexpensive air-conditioned rooms, try *Hotel Central* (☎ 614757), conveniently located on Boulevard Gómez. Doubles/triples go for US$10/13. Better still is the friendly *Hotel Torino* (☎ 610734), Calle Mariño, which has singles/doubles with air-conditioning, TV and fridge, for US$10/14.

There are several mid-priced hotels a couple of blocks east of Plaza Bolívar, including *La Ópera*, *Evang*, *Porlamar* and *Canadá*. There are more hotels nearby, so have a look around.

In the eastern, modern part of the city, hotel prices begin at around US$20 a double. That is what you'll pay at the *Hotel Internacional* (☎ 618912), on Avenida 4 de Mayo. More appealing is the quiet *Gran Avenida Hotel* (☎ 619143), on Calle Cedeño

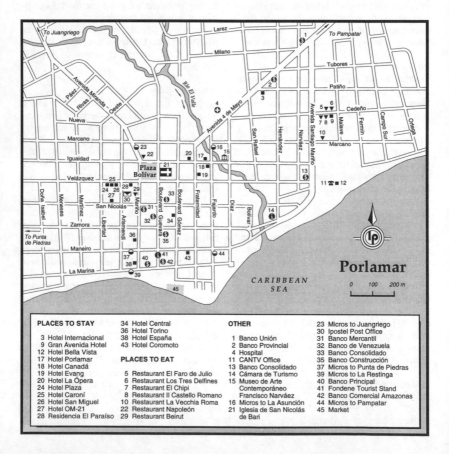

PLACES TO STAY

3 Hotel Internacional
9 Gran Avenida Hotel
12 Hotel Bella Vista
17 Hotel Porlamar
18 Hotel Canadá
19 Hotel Evang
20 Hotel La Ópera
24 Hotel Plaza
25 Hotel Caroní
26 Hotel San Miguel
27 Hotel OM-21
28 Residencia El Paraíso
34 Hotel Central
36 Hotel Torino
38 Hotel España
43 Hotel Coromoto

PLACES TO EAT

5 Restaurant El Faro de Julio
6 Restaurant Los Tres Delfines
7 Restaurant El Chipi
8 Restaurant Il Castello Romano
10 Restaurant La Vecchia Roma
22 Restaurant Napoleón
29 Restaurant Beirut

OTHER

1 Banco Unión
2 Banco Provincial
4 Hospital
11 CANTV Office
13 Banco Consolidado
14 Cámara de Turismo
15 Museo de Arte Contemporáneo Francisco Narváez
16 Micros to La Asunción
21 Iglesia de San Nicolás de Bari
23 Micros to Juangriego
30 Ipostel Post Office
31 Banco Mercantil
32 Banco de Venezuela
33 Banco Consolidado
35 Banco Construcción
37 Micros to Punta de Piedras
39 Micros to La Restinga
40 Banco Principal
41 Fondene Tourist Stand
42 Banco Comercial Amazonas
44 Micros to Pampatar
45 Market

which is close to several good eateries. Air-conditioned doubles with TV cost US$25.

For something considerably better, go to the four-star, high-rise *Hotel Bella Vista* (☎ 618264), which offers all facilities including a swimming pool and a nightclub, for US$85 a double.

Places to Eat

If you want a budget meal look for it in this old centre. The best inexpensive food in this area seems to be served in the *Restaurant España*, in the hotel of the same name. A couple of blocks north along the same street, the *Restaurant Beirut* has reasonably priced Lebanese food. The *Restaurant Napoleón*, on the corner of Plaza Bolívar, serves cheap pseudo-Italian food.

Like hotels, most of the finer restaurants are in the eastern sector, so if you are after a well-appointed place with atmosphere and a selection of quality food, go for a stroll there. On Calle Cedeño alone, just west of Avenida Santiago Mariño, there are half a dozen good restaurants including *El Chipi* (international menu), *Il Castello Romano* (Italian food), *Los Tres Delfines* (Cantonese cuisine) and *El Faro de Julio* (seafood). One block south, on Calle Marcano, is *La Vecchia Roma*, probably the best and most authentic Italian restaurant in town.

Getting There & Away

There's frequent transport to most of the island, operated by small buses locally called micros. They leave from different points of the city centre; the departure point for some of the main tourist destinations have been indicated on the map.

PAMPATAR

Pampatar, 10 km north-east of Porlamar, is today a town of some 8000 people. It was perhaps the first settlement on Margarita, founded in the 1530s, and within 50 years it grew into the largest shipping centre in what is now Venezuela. Its fort, the **Castillo de San Carlos de Borromeo** was built in the 1660s on the site of the previous stronghold which had been destroyed by pirates. It is the best preserved and restored construction of its type on the island. It's a classic example of fort architecture, similar to many others on the island and to that in Cumaná. Its partly roofed patio is, however, a later addition. In several rooms surrounding it, there is an exhibition of paintings and coats of arms, but they are of little interest. The fort is right in the centre of the town, on the waterfront. It can be visited daily from 9 am to noon and 2 to 5 pm.

Opposite the fort is the **parish church**, dating from the mid-18th century. A sober white-washed construction, it's noted for its crucifix, Cristo del Buen Viaje, over the high altar. The legend has it that the ship which carried the crucifix from Spain to Santo Domingo called en route at Pampatar, but despite repeated efforts it couldn't depart until the Christ image had been unloaded. It has been left in Pampatar since and is much venerated by local fishermen.

A hundred metres east of the church is a neoclassical building from 1864, known as **Casa de la Aduana**. It's now home to Fondene (see 'Information' below) which holds temporary exhibitions on the ground floor.

The fishing port, which extends along the beach for a km east of the fort, has plenty of old-world charm, with rustic boats anchored in the bay or on the shore, and fishermen repairing nets on the beach. The cape at the far eastern end of the bay is topped with another fort, the **Fortín de la Caranta**. It's completely ruined but commands better views than the Castillo.

Information

Tourist Office Pampatar is the headquarters of the Fondene tourist office (☎ 622342, 622494). It's in the Casa de la Aduana and is open Monday to Friday from 8 am to noon and 1 to 4.30 pm. They have good information about the island and sell maps. Fondene operates information stands in Porlamar, Juangriego and at the airport.

Places to Stay & Eat

Pampatar is a place to visit en route rather than to stay in; not many foreigners stay in town. The beach is more suitable for watching fishing activities than for sunbathing or swimming, as the water is pretty polluted.

Most places are aparthoteles, offering mini-apartments including a kitchen complete with pots and pans.

At the bottom end, there are the *Aparthotel Don Juan* (☎ 623609), with very small rooms (US$16 for two or three people), and *Casitas Vacacionales Trimar* (☎ 621657), costing US$20 for up to five people. Both hotels are on Calle Almirante Brion, opposite each other; the Trimar faces the beach and has possibly the best reasonably priced restaurant in town. There are many other open-air eateries along the beach.

Better places to stay for not much more are on Calle El Cristo, a five-minute walk east, and include *Los Chalets de la Caranta* (☎ 621214), with its own restaurant, and *Aparthotel Pampatar* (☎ 621935).

There's a choice of top-end hotels in or around the town, including the five-star *Flamingo Beach* (☎ 624750) and the *Margarita Hilton* (☎ 615822).

Getting There & Away
Buses between Porlamar and Pampatar run every five minutes (US$0.15, 20 minutes).

LA ASUNCIÓN
La Asunción, set in a fertile valley in the inland portion of the island, is the official capital of the Nueva Esparta state, even though it's far smaller than Porlamar. It's distinguished by its lush vegetation and its tranquillity. There's virtually no duty-free commerce here, and hotels and restaurants are scarce.

Built in the second half of the 16th century, the **Catedral** on Plaza Bolívar is just about the oldest colonial church in the country. It's noted for its austere, simple form, with a delicate Renaissance portal on the façade and two more doorways on the side walls.

On the northern side of the plaza is the **Museo Nueva Cádiz**, named after the first Spanish town in South America. Nueva Cádiz was established around 1500 (but officially founded in 1519) on Isla Cubagua,

south of Margarita. The town was completely destroyed by the 1541 earthquake and all traces of it disappeared with time until a 1950 excavation uncovered its foundations, some architectural details and various other objects. The museum displays some photos of the excavation work, plus a small, haphazard collection of exhibits, including two huge anchors recovered from shipwrecks.

Equally modest is the **Museo Casa Natal de Juan Bautista Arismendi**, dedicated to a hero of the independence struggles, one block off the plaza. On the plaza itself, opposite the cathedral, is the **Casa de la Cultura**, which has an exhibition of copies of pre-Columbian pottery from various regions of the country.

Just outside the town, a 10-minute walk up the hill, is the **Castillo de Santa Rosa**, one of numerous forts built on the island to protect it from pirate attacks. Apart from the view of the town, there is some old armour on display.

Getting There & Away
Micros from Porlamar will put you down on the tree-shaded Plaza Bolívar of La Asunción. After having a look around, you can either return to Porlamar or continue on to Juangriego – there is frequent transport to either destination. If you are going to the latter, you can stop in Santa Ana to see its church which is similar to the La Asunción cathedral but two centuries younger. By the way, try to visit El Cercado, a nearby village where typical Venezuelan pottery is made.

JUANGRIEGO
Set on the edge of a fine bay in the northern part of Margarita, Juangriego is a swiftly growing town of 10,000 inhabitants. Having covered the waterfront the town is now spreading inland. A series of large concrete edifices of rather disappointing appearance have been constructed and more are to come. The town has caught duty-free fever, and nowadays shops and consumers crowd the centre. Nevertheless, the beach, with its rustic fishing boats and visiting yachts, is an

enjoyable place to hang around. On the far horizon, the peaks of Macanao are visible, and they are particularly spectacular when the sun sets behind them.

The **Fortín de la Galera**, the fort crowning the hill just north of town, is today not much more than a ring of stone walls with a terrace and a refreshment stand on the top. It provides a good view of the sunset, at which time it's packed with tourists, although a similarly attractive view can be enjoyed from the beach in town.

North of town, as far as the northernmost point of the island, are half a dozen beaches. Some are developed while others are isolated and still almost virgin. The first, **Playa La Galera**, is just north of the fort. It's lined with restaurants, but it is unpleasant because of the stink from the contaminated lagoon just behind it.

The paved road continues two km north to **Playa Caribe**. This beach is wide, long, clean and still relatively solitary, although perhaps not for long, as a large tourist complex is being built. There are a few restaurants here. The next beach, **Playa La Boquita**, is probably the most deserted in the whole area, but has no shade at all.

Information

Tours There are some local operators organising tours to isolated beaches in the far northern end of the island and to the Archipiélago Los Frailes, north-east of Margarita. The seven-hour tour to Los Frailes including snorkelling and fishing (equipment provided) will cost around US$45 per person. Information is available at the El Búho restaurant or you can call Gerardo (☎ 54205).

Places to Stay & Eat

Juangriego is increasingly catering to tourism; it already has about 15 hotels and even more restaurants (there are a few banks in which to change your dollars and travellers' cheques).

Roughly in the middle of the Juangriego beach is a white house operating as the *Hotel Nuevo Juangriego*. Choose a room facing the bay (double with bath for US$9), and you

will get a perfect snap of the sunset from your window. Downstairs is the restaurant, with some umbrella-shaded tables outside on a terrace and others right on the beach, serving slightly overpriced food.

Hotel El Fortín, a few hundred metres north along the beach, offers better standards for the same price, and has equally excellent views of the sunset, although there are only three rooms facing the bay. Its restaurant, and *El Búho*, next door, are more pleasant places to eat than the Hotel Nuevo Juangriego. *El Viejo Muelle*, a few paces away, is another romantic place for a beer at sunset, although, again, the prices seem to be a bit inflated.

Other accommodation options include the *Hotel Gran Sol*, on the waterfront promenade (US$15 a double) and the *Hotel Digida* a hundred metres inland (US$12 a double). There are several other hotels in the same area.

You'll find several cheap, basic places to eat further off the beach, such as *Don Arepón*, on the corner of Calle Guevara and Calle Marcano, close to Hotel Digida.

Getting There & Away

Frequent micros run between Porlamar and Juangriego (US$0.40).

PARQUE NACIONAL LAGUNA DE LA RESTINGA

Laguna de la Restinga is one of two national parks on the island (the other one is Cerro El Copey, near La Asunción). The park contains a lagoon which has an extensive mangrove area at its western end. This is a favourite habitat for a variety of birds including pelicans, cormorants and scarlet ibis.

Busetas from the waterfront in Porlamar go regularly to La Restinga (US$0.80) and will deposit you at the entrance to the wharf. From there, five-seater motor boats will take you for a round trip (US$9 per boat) along a maze of *caños* (natural channels) that cut through thick mangroves. The excursion includes a stop on a fine shell beach on the sand bank, where you can grab a good fried fish in one of the open-air restaurants before returning.

BEACHES

Isla de Margarita has 167 km of shoreline endowed with some 50 beaches big enough to deserve a name, not to mention smaller sections of sandy coast. Many beaches have been developed and have a range of services such as restaurants and bars, and deckchairs and sunshades for hire. Although the island is no longer a deserted paradise, you can still find a relatively quiet strip of sand.

On the whole, Margarita's beaches have little shade, and some are virtually barren. The beaches on the northern and eastern coasts are better than those skirting the southern shore of the island.

If you are after a well-developed beach, go to the trendy Playa El Agua, where you can rub shoulders with some of the beautiful and arty people of Venezuela. Other popular destinations include Playa Guacuco and Playa Manzanillo. Perhaps Margarita's finest beach is Playa Puerto Cruz, which apparently has the widest, whitest stretch of sand and still isn't over-developed. If you want to escape from people, head for the northern coast of Macanao, which is the wildest part of the island. In the main, eastern section of Margarita, one of the most deserted beaches is Playa La Boquita (see the Juangriego section for more information).

You can camp on the beach if you wish, but use common sense and be cautious. Don't leave your tent unattended.

Guayana

Guayana is the part of Venezuela that lies south and east of Río Orinoco. The Orinoco Delta is usually included in this region. In administrative terms, Guayana covers the states of Bolívar, Amazonas, and Delta Amacuro. The region sprawls over exactly half of the country's area; yet it holds only 1.2 million people, which is scarcely 6% of the nation's population. Three-quarters of that population is concentrated in the only two important cities of the region, Ciudad Bolívar and Ciudad Guayana, while the rest are scattered over a vast area without any significant urban centres.

Guayana is home to the majority of Venezuela's Indian groups. Though the most numerous group, the Guajiro, live in Zulia state, all the other main communities, including the Warao, Pemón, Yanomami and Piaroa, inhabit Guayana. They constitute about 10% of the total population of the region.

The region is rich in natural resources, with extensive deposits of iron ore and bauxites (from which aluminium is made), and two particular treasures – gold and diamonds.

Almost all these riches are in Bolívar state. The Lower Orinoco is the most industrialised area of Guayana; Ciudad Guayana has become Venezuela's major centre of heavy industry.

The region is also noted for its natural beauty, with the vast Orinoco Delta, mysterious tepuis (massive table mountains), wild Amazon jungle, and sweeping savannas. Guayana has seven national parks (about 20% of the region's area), including Venezuela's three largest nature reserves (Parima-Tapirapecó, Canaima and Serranía La Neblina).

Most of the region is little explored and some areas have hardly been penetrated. Roads are few and far between, so most transport is by jeep, boat or light plane. None of these operate on any regular basis, only according to demand. Accordingly, exploring the region on one's own is not easy, except for the more developed areas. Any travel further afield involves a charter flight, and that's not cheap.

Organised tourism (read 'tours') is relatively new to Guayana, although it has developed considerably over the past decade, cutting further and further into the wilderness. However, it's not cheap either.

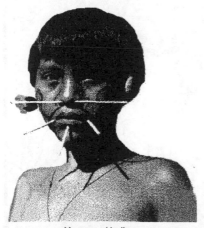

Yanomami indian

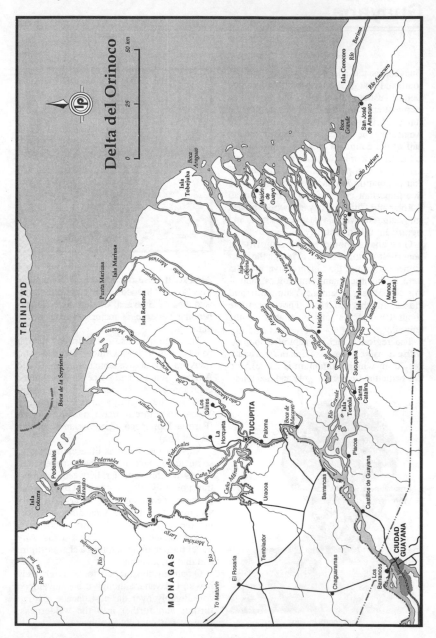

Delta del Orinoco

Delta del Orinoco

The second largest delta on the continent (after the Amazon), the Orinoco Delta covers an area of about 25,000 sq km. The river reaches a width of 20 km and splits into about 40 major *caños* (channels) which carry the waters down into the Atlantic. Their *bocas* (mouths) are distributed along some 360 km of the coast. The southernmost channel, Río Grande, is the main one and is used by ocean-going vessels sailing upriver to Ciudad Guayana.

The delta formed over the millennia as sediments were brought down by the river and accumulated. The process continues, so the delta is slowly extending out into the ocean. In the course of the last century alone, about 900 sq km of new land appeared. The delta consists of a maze of islands separated by caños. The land is largely covered by mixed forests, which include a variety of palms, of which the *moriche* is the most typical of the region. It has traditionally been the basic food of the locals. A good part of the banks of the channels close to the sea are lined by mangroves.

The delta is inhabited by the Warao (or Guarao) Indians, the second largest indigenous group in Venezuela (after the Guajiro), numbering about 24,000 people. They live along the caños, constructing their *palafitos* (houses on stilts) on the riverbanks and live mostly off fishing. There lives are integrally linked with water, even the name of the tribe indicates this ('wa' in the local language means 'canoe', 'arao' means 'people').

Many of the Waraos still use their native language (classified as independent, or not belonging to any of the major language families); only half the Indian population speaks Spanish. Two-thirds of the indigenous population live in the eastern part of the delta, between Caño Mariusa and Río Grande, distributed across about 250 tiny communities.

The Waraos are skilful craftspeople. They are noted for their basketry and woodcarvings, especially *curiaras* (dugouts) and animal figures carved from balsawood. Their *chinchorros* (hammocks), made from the fibre of the moriche palm, are also widely known.

The climate of the delta is hot and humid. The average annual temperature is around 26°C and remains at this level for most of the year. However, the temperature variation between day and night is considerable at times. The annual rainfall is relatively high, exceeding 2000 mm in many areas, and, in general, the closer you get to the coast the more it rains. The driest period is from January to March; the remaining part of the year is wet or very wet.

This rainfall pattern doesn't exactly correspond with the water level of the Orinoco, which essentially depends on the climate in the upper reaches of the river and its major tributaries. The lowest water level is usually in March, while from August to September the water level is highest. In that time, parts of the delta become marshy or flooded.

Curiously enough, the state is not named after the Orinoco, but after Río Amacuro, a small river which runs along a part of the Guyana border and empties into Boca Grande, the main mouth of the Orinoco. Tucupita is the state capital and its largest town. This is the major point of departure for organised tours to the delta, and the place to arrange a tour. However, the nondescript town of Barrancas (not to be confused with Los Barrancos, opposite San Félix) is the delta's busiest port, from which non-tourist boats run through to most delta destinations, particularly towards Lower Delta, to the east and north-east.

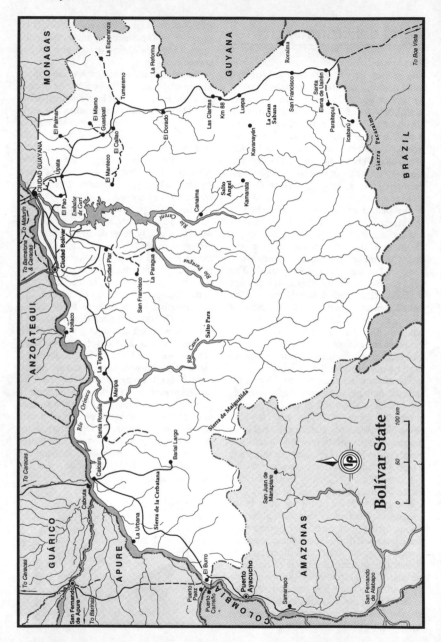

TUCUPITA

The capital of the state, Tucupita is a hot river town of about 60,000 people. It sits on the banks of the Caño Mánamo, the westernmost channel of the delta, which flows northwards some 110 km before emptying into Golfo de Paria near the town of Pedernales. Caño Mánamo has been blocked by a dyke which is 20 km south of Tucupita. The dyke was built in the 1960s as part of a flood-control programme which aimed to secure land in the northern delta for farming and stock raising. The only access road to the delta runs across the top of the dyke and this provides Tucupita with an overland link to the rest of the country.

Tucupita was born in the 1920s as one of a chain of Capuchin missions that were founded in the delta to convert the Indians. This opened up the region for both governmental activities and criollo colonists. The missions established social programmes which focused on providing Indians with education and health services. Other missions scattered throughout the region include the Araguaimujo, Nabasanuka and Guayo.

Tucupita is essentially a base for exploring the delta rather than an attraction in itself. Although you may find it pleasant enough strolling around the central streets or along the riverbank esplanade, Paseo Mánamo, there are no special sights in town.

Information

Money Only Banco de Venezuela is likely to change your cash and travellers' cheques, while Banco Unión might possibly provide advance payments on Visa credit cards.

Tours There are at least four tour operators in town and all focus on trips into the delta.

The cheapest is the young Orinoco Tours, Calle Mariño 13, called the 'pirata' by the other operators. They organise one/two/three-day tours which head in the direction of Pedernales, to the north of the delta, and charge about US$35 per day per person, all inclusive, or US$30 if you prefer to take your own food. A minimum of two persons is required. They don't have their own campamento, instead they provide casual accommodation

in hammocks in one of the Indian settlements or simply set up camp on a riverbank.

Delta Surs (☎ 22434), Calle Mariño, has a longer history and better reputation. They offer three or four-day tours to their campamento at Misión de Guayo. This is possibly a more interesting area, as far as nature and the more numerous Indian population is concerned. Five people are needed for a tour, which will cost about US$75 per person per day, all inclusive.

Tucupita Expeditions (☎ 22496), Calle Bolívar, is probably the only local operator with bilingual guides, but a tour with them will cost at least US$85 per day. They have a campamento in Guamal, north-west of Tucupita, and run excursions which last up to five days. A minimum of three or four persons is usually required.

Mánamo Tours (☎ 22190), at Plaza Bolívar, wasn't running tours at the time of writing, but planned to resume trips to the eastern part of the delta (like Delta Surs) by 1994.

There are also independent guides who hang around the central streets looking for tourists, and often call at hotels. Their tours are cheaper, though you never actually know what you'll get for that money: it can sometimes be a fascinating trip, even better than those with reputable operators, but sometimes not. Clarify the length of time, places to be visited, food and lodging details, and have a look at the boat and its engine before you commit yourself. After you and your guide agree on a price, don't pay everything up-front, but only the money necessary for pre-departure expenses (gasoline, food). Insist on a substantial part being paid on your return.

Things to See

The oldest building in town is the **Iglesia de San José de Tucupita**, the Capuchin mission church built in 1930. It served as a parish church until the monumental **Catedral de la Divina Pastora** was recently completed after nearly three decades of painstaking work.

Several km south of Tucupita, in Paloma, is the **Casa Indígena**, a house built for Indians

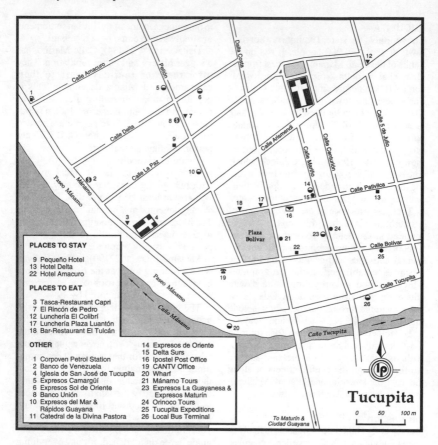

PLACES TO STAY

9 Pequeño Hotel
13 Hotel Delta
22 Hotel Amacuro

PLACES TO EAT

3 Tasca-Restaurant Capri
7 El Rincón de Pedro
12 Lunchería El Colibrí
17 Lunchería Plaza Luantón
18 Bar-Restaurant El Tulcán

OTHER

1 Corpoven Petrol Station
2 Banco de Venezuela
4 Iglesia de San José de Tucupita
5 Expresos Camargüí
6 Expresos Sol de Oriente
8 Banco Unión
10 Expresos del Mar &
     Rápidos Guayana
11 Catedral de la Divina Pastora
14 Expresos de Oriente
15 Delta Surs
16 Ipostel Post Office
19 CANTV Office
20 Wharf
21 Mánamo Tours
23 Expresos La Guayanesa &
     Expresos Maturín
24 Orinoco Tours
25 Tucupita Expeditions
26 Local Bus Terminal

To Maturín &
Ciudad Guayana

Tucupita

0   50   100 m

to provide them with accomodation while in Tucupita for supplies and for selling their crafts. Good chinchorros (typical hammocks) and baskets can usually be bought here.

Places to Stay

Accommodation is scarce in Tucupita. There are apparently only three or four hotels in the town centre and one or two more outside the central area. None of them is anything special.

The cheapest, Pequeño Hotel (☎ 21388), is on Calle La Paz. It has doubles with bath and fan/noisy air-conditioning for US$9/10.

The Hotel Delta (☎ 21219), Calle Pativilca,

has marginally better doubles with fan/ slightly quieter air-conditioning for US$11/15. The third of the central options, the Hotel Amacuro (☎ 21057) on Calle Bolívar, just around the corner from Plaza Bolívar, is the best of the lot. Air-conditioned rooms cost much the same as those at the Delta.

Places to Eat

There's a range of simple places to eat in town. Among cheapies, *El Rincón de Pedro*, opposite Banco Unión, serves inexpensive chicken, while the *Lunchería El Colibrí* has typical food. *Tasca-Restaurant Capri*, on

Calle Mánamo, is better but more expensive. For a good coffee, go to the *Lunchería Plaza Luantón*, on Plaza Bolívar, which also serves a choice of snacks.

Getting There & Away

Air The airport (currently closed for upgrading) is several km north of town. It's accessible by local transport – the San Rafael carrito goes there from the town's centre and the ride takes 10 minutes. Avensa used to have flights to Porlamar and Caracas, which may have been re-introduced by the time you read this.

Bus There is no central bus terminal; each of the seven bus companies servicing Tucupita has its own office from which their buses leave. All are in the town centre and are marked on the map.

There are four buses to Caracas (US$13.75, 11 hours), one each by Expresos Camargüí, Expresos Sol de Oriente, Expresos de Oriente and Rápidos Guayana. Camargüí may sell tickets at discount prices, some 10% lower than that of the other companies. All these buses go via Maturín.

Expresos La Guayanesa operate buses to Ciudad Guayana (US$3.75, three hours), or you can take a por puesto from Plaza Bolívar (US$4.50, 2½ hours). These trips include a ferry ride across the Orinoco from Los Barrancos to San Félix (no extra charge).

Boat There are no regular passenger services around the delta. You can try arranging a river trip with fishermen at the wharf at the southern end of Paseo Mánamo, or you can try looking around for a boat at Casa Indígena. Another place to check out is the Puerto de Volcán, the port beside the dyke, 20 km south of Tucupita.

Most boats to the eastern part of the delta (Curiapo, Misión de Guayo, Misión Araguaimujo, San José de Amacuro etc) depart from Barrancas, not Tucupita, so if you plan on any travel on your own in that direction, start shopping around in the port of Barrancas. There are also sporadic boats from Barrancas to Georgetown in Guyana.

The Lower Orinoco

The Lower Orinoco is the industrial heart of Guayana. This is the most densely populated area of the region, and the only one which has a road network to speak of. Here are Guayana's only two cities, Ciudad Bolívar and Ciudad Guayana, both of which sit on the right bank of the Orinoco, in Bolívar state (Venezuela's largest state, occupying over a quarter of the country's territory).

While Ciudad Bolívar is an important historic city with character and charm, Ciudad Guayana is not much more than a vast urban sprawl dotted with industrial installations. Either of the two cities makes a convenient starting point for exploring Bolívar state, especially its most attractive south-eastern part, which includes Salto Angel, the Gran Sabana and Roraima. The state is bisected by an excellent and spectacular highway, which runs from Ciudad Guayana south to Santa Elena de Uairén on the Brazilian border.

CIUDAD BOLÍVAR

Ciudad Bolívar is a hot city set on the southern bank of the Orinoco, about 420 km upstream from the Atlantic. Founded in 1764 on a rocky elevation at the river's narrowest point, the town was appropriately named Angostura (literally 'narrows'), and remained for a long time a sleepy river port hundreds of miles from any important centres of population. Then, suddenly and unexpectedly, Angostura became the place where much of the country's (and the continent's) history was forged.

It was here that Bolívar came in 1817, soon after the town had been liberated from Spanish control, and set up the base for the military operations that led to what proved to be the final stage of the War of Independence. The town was made the provisional capital of the country which had yet to be liberated. It was in Angostura that the British Legionnaires joined Bolívar before they set off for the battle of Boyacá that secured the independence of Colombia. Finally, it was here that the Angostura Congress convened in 1819 and gave birth to Gran Colombia, a unified republic comprising Venezuela, Colombia and Ecuador. In honour of El Libertador, in 1846 the town was renamed Ciudad Bolívar.

Today, Ciudad Bolívar is the capital of Venezuela's largest state, Bolívar, and a fair-sized city of some 270,000 inhabitants. It has retained the flavour of an old river town and still conserves some of the architecture dating from its 50-year-long colonial era.

Information

Tourist Office The tourist office (☎ 26491) is in a pavilion next to the airport terminal, and is open Monday to Friday from 8.30 am to noon and 2 to 5.30 pm.

Money There are four useful banks on or near Paseo Orinoco: Banco Italo Venezolano and Banco International change cash and travellers' cheques; Banco de Venezuela accepts Visa and MasterCard; and Banco Unión handles all these operations. Moneychangers flock around the entrance of Gran Hotel Bolívar and change dollars for 2% less than banks.

Should you need a bank near the airport, Banco Consolidado is on the corner of Avenida Aeropuerto and Avenida Andrés Bello, 100 metres from the airport terminal.

Inparques The Inparques office (☎ 27022, 27723) is in the CVG building (Edificio de la CVG), on Avenida Germania (corner of Avenida Andrés Bello). You might need them to get a permit for the Canaima National Park if you want to camp in Canaima.

Tours to Salto Angel Ciudad Bolívar is the main gateway to Salto Angel, as almost all flights to the waterfall either originate from the city or pass through it. Trips to the falls are the staple of all tour operators and small regional airlines. Most are in the airport terminal, so start shopping around there.

Tour operators offer one-day return trips to the falls on light (usually five-seater) planes. The tour includes a flight over Salto Angel, lunch and a short boat excursion to other nearby falls (usually to Salto El Sapo). Tours depart from Ciudad Bolívar around 7 to 8 am and return at 4 to 5 pm. The price is US$130 to US$140. Two-day trips are also available with some operators (about US$200, all inclusive). Turi Express (☎ 24097) has been recommended by some travellers.

All these trips operate on a charter basis, with a five-person minimum (or you pay for the empty seats). Most operators won't accept credit cards, or will charge 5% to 10% more if you pay with a credit card.

These tours can also be arranged (for much the same price) directly with some of the airlines (all of which have their offices in the terminal). There are at least half a dozen of them, including Aero Servicios Caicara, Transmandú, Rutaca, Aerobol and Serami. The first three seem to be more reliable than the others.

They also offer no-frills trips to Salto Angel (without lunch or side excursions), for around US$100. The usual scenario is as follows. You depart in the morning, heading towards Canaima. If the pilot expects the sky over Salto Angel to be clear, he flies directly to the waterfall and puts you down at Canaima, picking you up later in the afternoon after he has completed his scheduled flights for that day. If the pilot predicts bad weather, he flies you directly to Canaima and tries again in the afternoon after he's finished his rounds.

These airlines can also fly you just to Canaima without going over Salto Angel. The fare is US$35 either way. They are not exactly regular flights, but one or another carrier usually manages to collect a sufficient number of passengers for take-off.

Read How to Plan the Trip in the Salto Angel section before you decide which tours to take.

Other Tours Other tours out of Ciudad Bolívar include trips to the Gran Sabana (which can be organised much more cheaply from Santa Elena de Uairén) and Roraima. The latter is best done on your own; agents in Ciudad Bolívar will ask least US$350 per

Top: Parque Cachamay, Ciudad Guayana
Bottom: Hacha Falls, Canaima

Top Left: Salto el Sapo, Canaima
Top Right: Hacha Falls, Canaima
Bottom Left: Quebrada de Jaspe, La Gran Sabana
Bottom Right: Salto Aponguao, La Gran Sabana

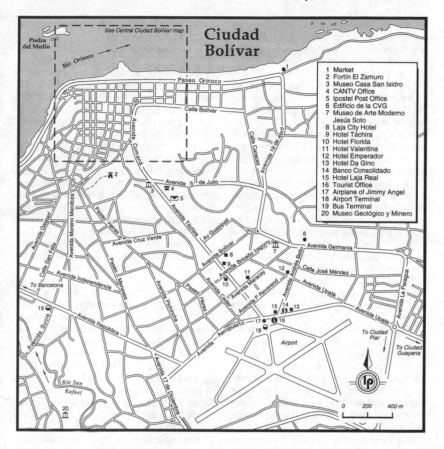

Ciudad Bolívar

1 Market
2 Fortín El Zamuro
3 Museo Casa San Isidro
4 CANTV Office
5 Ipostel Post Office
6 Edificio de la CVG
7 Museo de Arte Moderno Jesús Soto
8 Laja City Hotel
9 Hotel Táchira
10 Hotel Florida
11 Hotel Valentina
12 Hotel Emperador
13 Hotel Da Gino
14 Banco Consolidado
15 Hotel Laja Real
16 Tourist Office
17 Airplane of Jimmy Angel
18 Airport Terminal
19 Bus Terminal
20 Museo Geológico y Minero

person for this trip. If you are interested, contact Rosario Enrique Zambrano of Neckar Tour in Gran Hotel Bolívar, who is possibly the cheapest operator running this tour. He also organises more adventurous trips (such as a 13-day trip to the top of Auyantepui, US$70 a day). He is going to open his own agency soon.

Pop into Hotel Italia which has a board with ads for trips offered by independent guides (eg a boat trip from Ciudad Bolívar to Puerto Ayacucho, US$75, two days, all inclusive). The Hotel Italia restaurant is the main rendezvous for guides and tourists, so

it's a good place for information about guides and for the comments of travellers who've just returned.

Things to See

Stroll along **Paseo Orinoco**, an attractive waterfront boulevard lined with arcaded houses, some of which date back to Bolívar's days. Midway along the Paseo is the **Mirador Angostura**, a rocky headland that juts out into the river at its narrowest point. If you happen to be here in August, when the water is at its highest, you may have the river just below your feet. This is also the time to watch fishermen with their typical *atarrayas*, fishing for the delicious *zapaora*, which appear only during this short period. In March, by contrast, the water level may well be 15 or more metres below.

The Mirador commands good views up and down the Orinoco. Five km upriver you'll see a suspension bridge, **Puente de Angostura**, constructed in 1967; it's the only bridge across the Orinoco for the entire length of its course. It's 1678 metres long, and its central, highest section is over 50 metres above the river.

Close to the lookout, on the corner of the Paseo and Calle Igualdad, is the **Museo Etnográfico** which features the crafts of Indian tribes from Venezuela's south. Two blocks west along the Paseo, you'll come across the **Museo de Ciudad Bolívar**, housed in the Casa del Correo del Orinoco. It was here that the republic's first newspaper was printed in 1818, and you can see the original press on which it was done, along with other objects related to the town's history.

Walk south up the hill to the historic heart of the city, **Plaza Bolívar**. Apart from the usual monument to El Libertador in the middle, there are five allegorical statues on the square which personify the five countries Bolívar liberated. To the east looms the massive **Catedral**, begun right after the town's foundation but successfully completed only 80 years later. Half of the western side of the plaza is taken up by the **Casa del Congreso de Angostura**, built in the 1770s and serving as the venue for the lengthy debates of the 1819 Angostura Congress before it eventually agreed on creating Gran Colombia. You can have a look around inside the house.

Three blocks south of Plaza Bolívar is the pleasantly shaded **Plaza Miranda**. A large building on its eastern side was constructed in 1870 as a hospital, but it never served that purpose. In 1892, it was turned into barracks and served the army until 1954, only to become a police station afterwards. Eventually, after an extensive refurbishing, it reopened in 1992 as the **Centro de las Artes**, which stages temporary exhibitions (open Tuesday to Friday from 9.30 am to 5.30 pm, Saturday and Sunday from 10 am to 5 pm). Ask the attendants to let you upstairs to the mirador on the roof, from where one gets a good view of the **Fortín El Zamuro**, crowning the top of the highest hill in the city, half a km south of the Centro. The fort is open to visitors and provides fine views over the old town.

Beyond the fort, on the corner of Avenida Táchira and Avenida 5 de Julio, is the **Museo Casa San Isidro**, installed in a beautiful colonial house which once belonged to a hacienda which, in turn, once stretched as far as the airport, although it's now little more than a garden. Bolívar stayed here for 29 days during the Angostura Congress. The house interior has retained its original 18th-century style. It can be visited Tuesday to Saturday from 9 am to noon and 2.30 to 5 pm, Sunday from 9 am to noon.

Go one km south on Avenida Táchira and take Avenida Briceño Iragorry to the left, which will lead you to the **Museo de Arte Moderno Jesús Soto**. The museum has an amazing collection of works by this famous kinetic artist (who was born in Ciudad Bolívar in 1923), as well as works by other national and international artists. The museum is open Tuesday to Friday from 9.30 am to 5.30 pm, Saturday and Sunday from 10 am to 5 pm.

In front of the airport terminal, a 10-minute walk from the museum, stands the legendary **Airplane of Jimmie Angel** (read more about him in the Salto Angel section). This is the original plane, which has been removed from the top of Auyantepui and restored in Maracay. The engine is a replica; the original is in Maracay.

In the south-western suburb of the city is the small **Museo Geológico y Minero**, which introduces Guayana's mines, mining techniques, machinery etc.

Places to Stay

The most pleasant area to stay in is the bustling and atmospheric Paseo Orinoco and, fortunately, most budget hotels are gathered on or just off this boulevard. All hotels listed have fans in the rooms (or air-conditioning where indicated).

One of the cheapest in town is *Hotel Boyacá*, Calle Babilonia, costing US$4 for a double, but it's basic and does some of its trade on an hourly basis.

A more decent double room without bath can be had for US$5 in *Hotel Ritz* (☎ 23886), Calle Libertad 3, or *Hotel Delicias* (☎ 20215), Calle Venezuela 6. The former also has air-conditioned rooms with bath for US$9; the latter is located in an old, increas-ingly dilapidated house, but has some charm (choose a large room upstairs).

For cheap rooms with private bath near the riverfront, try *Hotel Unión* (☎ 23374), Calle Urica 11, or *Hotel Caracas* (☎ 26089), Paseo Orinoco 82. Both have singles/doubles for US$5/6. The Unión provides slightly better standards but the Caracas has a large terrace overlooking the Paseo, where one can sit over a bottle of beer enjoying the evening breeze.

If price is more important than location, go to *Hotel Roma*, on Avenida Cumaná five

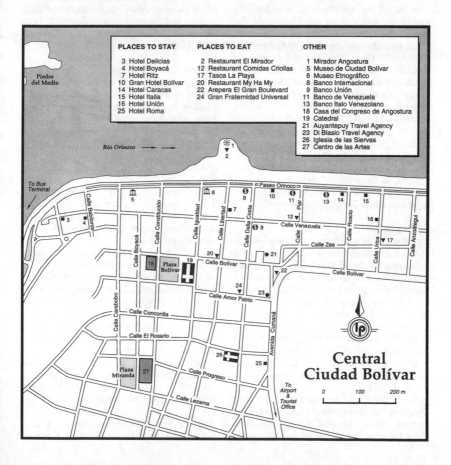

PLACES TO STAY	PLACES TO EAT	OTHER
3 Hotel Delicias	2 Restaurant El Mirador	1 Mirador Angostura
4 Hotel Boyacá	12 Restaurant Comidas Criollas	5 Museo de Ciudad Bolívar
7 Hotel Ritz	17 Tasca La Playa	6 Museo Etnográfico
10 Gran Hotel Bolívar	20 Restaurant My Ha My	8 Banco Internacional
14 Hotel Caracas	22 Arepera El Gran Boulevard	9 Banco Unión
15 Hotel Italia	24 Gran Fraternidad Universal	11 Banco de Venezuela
16 Hotel Unión		13 Banco Italo Venezolano
25 Hotel Roma		18 Casa del Congreso de Angostura
		19 Catedral
		21 Auyantepuy Travel Agency
		23 Di Blasio Travel Agency
		26 Iglesia de las Siervas
		27 Centro de las Artes

Central Ciudad Bolívar

blocks south of the riverbank, which has singles/doubles with bath for US$4/5. The rooms are dark but otherwise OK.

Hotel Italia (☎ 20015), Paseo Orinoco 131, is perhaps the most popular among foreigners. It has singles/doubles with bath and fan for US$6/8 and rooms with air-conditioning for US$8/10. There's a good, cheap restaurant attached.

The best place to stay on the Paseo is the old-style *Gran Hotel Bolívar* (☎ 20101), where comfortable, air-conditioned singles/doubles/triples cost US$18/22/26; you can eat in one of the two hotel restaurants.

Most of the middle-price and top-end hotels are away from the river, near the airport. You may need them if you plan to catch an early morning flight to Canaima.

Hotel Da Gino (☎ 26634) and *Hotel Laja Real* (☎ 27911) are both 100 metres east of the airport terminal. The former costs US$18/20/25 for a single/double/triple, whereas the latter is about the best hotel in town and charges US$35/40 for a single/double.

Two blocks north of the airport, on Avenida Maracay, is the small, quiet and good *Hotel Valentina* (☎ 22145), for US$20/24/28 a single/double/triple. Cheaper options in the area (in ascending order of price) include *Hotel Florida*, *Hotel Emperador* and *Hotel Táchira*.

Places to Eat

Perhaps the best inexpensive option in the area of Paseo Orinoco is the restaurant belonging to the *Hotel Italia*. Two blocks south is *La Playa*, one of the few central tascas, but it's more expensive than the Italia.

The cheapest typical food is probably to be found at the market, at the far eastern end of Paseo Orinoco. The *Comidas Criollas*, on Calle Piar, is a shabby-looking eatery but has tasty, cheap typical food. Two blocks to the south is *El Gran Boulevard*, the best central arepera where you can get arepas with a score of fillings.

In the old town, one block downhill from the cathedral, the *My Ha My* is a simple place serving cheap pseudo-Chinese food. The *Gran Fraternidad Universal*, on Calle Amor

Patrio, has good, cheap vegetarian meals, at lunch time only. Get there just after noon, as they run out of food quickly.

Don't forget the two restaurants in *Gran Hotel Bolívar*, which have some Italian dishes in their menu at affordable prices. The service, however, leaves a bit to be desired. Check whether the *El Mirador* open-air restaurant has reopened, which may be a good up-market proposition.

Things to Buy

Ciudad Bolívar is a good place to buy gold jewellery. Most of the gold shops nestle in two passageways off Paseo Orinoco: Pasaje Bolívar and Pasaje Trivigno/Guayana, both within the block between Calle Piar and Calle Dalla Costa.

Getting There & Away

Air The airport is two km south-east of the riverfront and is linked to the city centre by frequent busetas. Busetas marked Ruta 1 going eastbound along Paseo Orinoco will take you there.

There are three flights daily to Caracas with Avensa (US$58), and one with Aeropostal (US$54). Aeropostal flies once a day to Barcelona (US$35).

Aereotuy has a daily morning flight to Santa Elena de Uairén (US$60). These flights are on 19-seater light planes and usually have a few stopovers en route, which vary from day to day.

Avensa has one flight a day to Canaima (US$45), but will probably only sell tickets on the day of the flight (they want to fill up their package excursions, which are more profitable). Two travel agents in the city centre, Di Blasio (☎ 21931) at Avenida Cumaná 6, and Auyantepuy (☎ 20748) on Boulevard Bolívar, may sell Avensa tickets to Canaima in advance.

Several small, local carriers operate flights to regional destinations (including Canaima), mostly on a charter basis. See the Tours section for further details.

Bus The bus terminal is on the junction of Avenida República and Avenida Sucre, about two km south of the centre. To get there, take the westbound buseta marked 'Terminal' from Paseo Orinoco. Busetas heading to further southern suburbs will also drop you at the bus terminal.

More than 15 buses a day run to Caracas (US$11 ordinary, US$12.25 deluxe, eight to nine hours). Most of them depart in the evening and travel overnight. A number of buses run to Barcelona (US$5.25, four hours) and Puerto La Cruz (US$5.50, 4½ hours). To Ciudad Guayana, buses depart every 15 minutes or so (US$2, 1½ hours).

Línea Orinoco and Transmundial operate buses to Santa Elena de Uairén (US$11.50). Both companies have one 'Especial' and one 'Regional' bus, so there are four buses a day altogether. The 'Especial' buses travel overnight and are quicker (11 hours), but if you want to catch some glimpses of the Gran Sabana scenery take either of the morning 'Regional' buses. They call in at towns en route and the trip may take up to 14 hours. Additionally, there's the express bus coming through from Caracas, which reaches Santa Elena in less than 10 hours (US$13).

At least six buses a day go to Puerto Ayacucho (US$10.75, 10 hours) along a new, fully paved road (which still hasn't been marked on the majority of local maps).

Six buses a day depart for Ciudad Piar (US$2, two hours) and four buses go as far south as La Paragua (US$4.25, 4½ hours). There are also por puestos to both Ciudad Piar (US$3.50, 1½ hours) and La Paragua (US$6, 3½ hours).

Boat There is no regular passenger boat service, in either direction.

CIUDAD GUAYANA

Set on the southern bank of the Orinoco at its confluence with the Río Caroní, Ciudad Guayana is a somewhat strange city. It was officially founded in 1961 to serve as an industrial centre for the region, and took into its metropolitan boundaries two quite different urban components: the old town of San Félix on the eastern side of the Caroní, and the new-born Puerto Ordaz on the opposite bank.

Ciudad Guayana is Venezuela's fastest growing city. At the time of its foundation the total population of the area was about 40,000. Thirty years later, the two parts have virtually merged together into a 20-km-long urban sprawl populated by some 600,000 people.

Two bridges across the Caroní have been built to link the two sections, and another two are planned for the future. Despite its unified name, people persistently refer to it as either San Félix or Puerto Ordaz, depending on which part they are talking about.

San Félix was founded in the 16th century but don't let this date confuse you – there's nothing old about the town, apart perhaps from the chessboard layout on which it was planned. The town's centre is today a busy, dirty commercial sector with nondescript architecture. It's essentially a workers' suburb.

Puerto Ordaz is quite a different story: it's modern, well planned, and has a good infrastructure of roads, supermarkets, and services. The centre is quite clean and pleasant, and it's here that the cream of restaurants and trendy shops are located. It's basically the executive zone, as you can easily tell from the people, their cars and the general atmosphere. On the whole, though, Puerto Ordaz lacks the soul characteristic of older cities that have evolved in a natural way over the centuries.

The city was named after Diego de Ordaz, the first Spanish explorer who, in 1531-32, sailed up the Orinoco to the Raudales de Atures near what is now Puerto Ayacucho. He was searching for gold, as it was thought that the Orinoco was a gateway to the mythical land of El Dorado. Gold was found only in the middle of the 19th century, in the region around El Callao. This is today the main area for gold mining. It's estimated that the total gold reserves of Guayana are about 8000 tonnes.

Puerto Ordaz is the seat of the CVG, or Corporación Venezolana de Guayana. This is the regional government body founded in

1960 to run and integrate industrial development of the region with ecological protection and conservation.

Save for two beautiful waterfalls, there's not much to see or do in the city. It is a transit point on the way between Caracas/Ciudad Bolívar and the Gran Sabana/Brazil, and all buses pass through, so you don't even have to get off. On the other hand, like any city of that size, Ciudad Guayana has well-established tourist facilities, so you can eat and sleep well, change money easily, arrange a tour or buy any provisions you need for further travel, and while you're there you can see the waterfalls.

Busetas run constantly between the two sections, and most of them call in at the bus terminal in San Félix on the way. The airport is at the western end of Puerto Ordaz.

Information
Tourist Office The tourist office is at the airport. Alternatively, you can call in for information at any of the travel agencies in the centre of Puerto Ordaz (see 'Tours' below).

Money As elsewhere, changing money is a bit of a trial-and-error affair and may involve some tramping around. Most of the central banks are marked on the Puerto Ordaz and San Félix maps.

At the time of writing, Banco Consolidado, Banco Unión, Banco de Venezuela and Banco del Caribe changed cash and travellers' cheques. Banco Unión gives cash advances on Visa and MasterCard. MasterCard is also handled by Banco Mercantil.

Tours There are a dozen tour operators – virtually all in Puerto Ordaz – of which the ones with perhaps the best reputation are Anaconda Tours (☎ 223130) on Avenida Las Américas, Selva Tours (☎ 225537) on Calle Caura, Keyla Tours (☎ 229195) on Avenida Monseñor Zabaleta and Happy Tour (☎ 227748) in the Hotel Intercontinental Guayana.

Their staple offer is the four to five-day tour around the Gran Sabana, including

visits to most of the waterfalls. This tour will cost around US$80 to US$90 per person a day. It's far cheaper to go by bus to Santa Elena and arrange the tour there (see the Santa Elena de Uairén section for details).

Another tour offered by agents is the three to four-day trip by boat around the Orinoco Delta, including calls at Warao Indian settlements. This, too, is an expensive proposition, with prices around US$80 to US$90 per day per person. Read the Tucupita section to find out how to do this trip more cheaply.

Quite recently, a tour to Salto Pará, in the middle course of the Río Caura (south-west of Ciudad Bolívar), has begun to appear on agents' lists (eg Keyla Tours). These spectacular waterfalls are reached by boat from the village of Maripa (on the Ciudad Bolívar-Caicara road), after a 200-km trip up the Río Caura. Given a minimum of four persons, the four to five-day tour will cost US$80 to US$100 a day per head.

Amongst the shorter and cheaper options are city tours (not very inspiring and perhaps not worth doing) and the half-day trip to the Castillos de Guayana, 38 km east of Ciudad Guayana (US$23 per person).

The CVG office is the place to call in at for information about tours to the city's industrial establishments, including the steel mill and aluminium plants. They will also have updated information about visiting Represa de Guri and Cerro Bolívar (refer to those sections). The headquarters of the CVG are in Edificio CVG, Calle Cuchiveros, in the Alta Vista district (Puerto Ordaz).

Things to See
The city's No 1 attraction is the **Parque Cachamay**, a pleasant riverside park, a 15-minute walk south from the centre of Puerto Ordaz. It's here that the Río Caroní picks up speed, turning into a series of rapids and eventually into a spectacular 200-metre-wide line of waterfalls. Adjoining the park, to the south-west, is the **Parque Loefling**, where there's a small zoo, with some animals in cages and others wandering freely around. The park was named after a Swedish botanist, Peter Loefling (1729-56), who came to

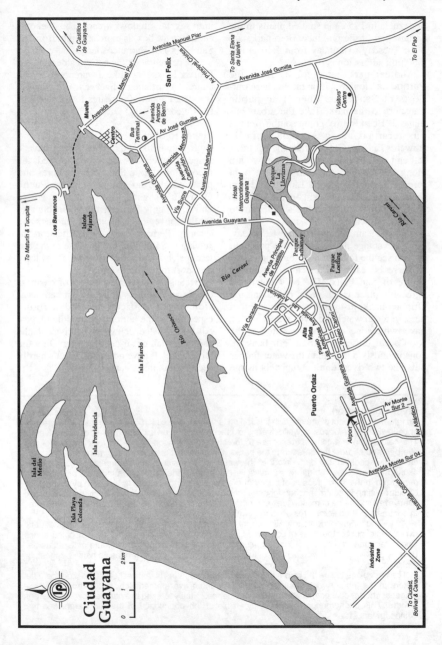

Venezuela in 1754 and studied plants in the eastern part of the province. Both parks are open Tuesday to Sunday from 5.30 am to 6.30 pm; admission is free.

Another park noted for its falls, the **Parque La Llovizna**, is on the southern outskirts of San Félix. There's no public transport to the park. Take the urban bus marked 'Buen Retiro' going south from the bus terminal along Avenida Gumilla (towards El Pao). Get off when the bus turns left and continue walking south for two km along the Avenida and then take the right turnoff marked 'Salto La Llovizna'. From there it's another two km to the visitors' centre. From there, a free bus-shuttle runs to the park, which is on an island, every hour or so, from 9 am to 3 pm Tuesday to Sunday. Several vantage points within the park will let you see the falls from various angles.

There is really not much to see in the centre of San Félix. The only quiet and agreeable place is the green belt along the Orinoco bank, just off Plaza Bolívar. From here, you can watch the river, whose waters have two distinct colours: the waters of the Río Caroní, closer to the San Félix bank are conspicuously darker than the water further out. The two rivers don't completely merge until several km downstream. The phenomenon (see the box) is more apparent from the San Félix-Los Barrancos ferry.

The cathedral on the eastern side of Plaza Bolívar looks more like a warehouse than a church. A particularly lively and dirty market is located about 100 metres to the north of the Catedral.

Places to Stay

Both San Félix and Puerto Ordaz have a range of hotels. As might be expected, the accommodation in San Félix is poorer but, paradoxically, no cheaper than in Puerto Ordaz. It's a good idea to stay in Puerto Ordaz, not only for the better value, but also for the convenience, nicer surroundings and security. Perhaps the only justification for staying in San Félix is to be close to the bus terminal, but you can easily get there by local transport from Puerto Ordaz.

Because of the large number of business people and workers in the city, it can occasionally be difficult to find a room, especially in the bottom and middle ranges. All hotels listed below have private baths and either fan or air-conditioning. Only the top-end hotels have hot water, but it's hardly necessary in that steamy climate.

River Colouration

An interesting aspect of the rivers in this region is their colour, which can range from light-greyish or yellowish (*ríos blancos*, or white rivers), to dark coffee or even ink (*ríos negros*, or black rivers). The colouration is a complex response to the chemical components of the rock and soil of the riverbed and shores, the flora along the banks, the climate, the season, and many other factors. Generally speaking, the dark colour of the water is the result of scarce organic decomposition caused by the poor nutriments in the soils (such as in the Amazon rainforest), or the acids generated in the slow process of decay of organic substances which is hindered by the lack of calcium (which is common when igneous rock prevails in a region). Interestingly enough, black rivers are almost free of mosquitoes and other insects, and caymans are virtually unknown there. In contrast, all these creatures abound in white rivers.

As for the Orinoco tributaries, Río Caroní, Río Atabapo and Río Sipapo are examples of dark rivers, while most of the rivers of Los Llanos (eg Río Apure or Río Arauca) have a light colouration. Understandably, the colour of the Orinoco itself largely depends on the colours of its affluents. Broadly speaking, the lower its course, the lighter the colour. Río Negro, as its name suggest, is a black river.

The best place to see the colour difference of any two rivers is, naturally, their confluence. The waters of the tributary don't usually mix with the main river immediately, but gradually, over a longer or shorter distance, down from the confluence, initially forming two parallel flows of different colours. This phenomenon is particularly visible at the confluence of the Río Caroní and the Orinoco rivers. ∎

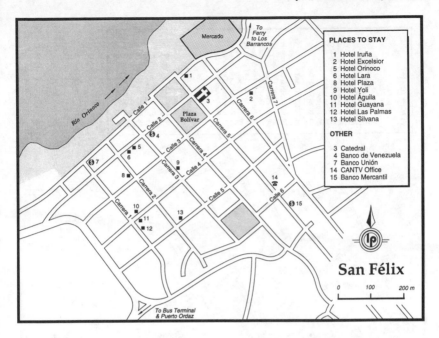

PLACES TO STAY
1 Hotel Iruña
2 Hotel Excelsior
5 Hotel Orinoco
6 Hotel Lara
8 Hotel Plaza
9 Hotel Yoli
10 Hotel Águila
11 Hotel Guayana
12 Hotel Las Palmas
13 Hotel Silvana

OTHER
3 Catedral
4 Banco de Venezuela
7 Banco Unión
14 CANTV Office
15 Banco Mercantil

San Félix

0   100   200 m

San Félix There are about a dozen hotels in the town centre, of which the overwhelming majority operate exclusively or partly as sex hotels. There are probably only three hotels which don't let in passing couples. The cheapest of them is the *Hotel Yoli* (☎ 41423), on Carrera 3, which has very rundown doubles for US$10 that shouldn't really cost half that price. The *Hotel Excelsior*, on Calle 3, is marginally better but not worth the US$10/14 for a single/double it charges. Perhaps the best choice is the Hotel Águila (☎ 44291), on Calle 4, which costs US$11/14 for a single/double.

Most of the other places marked on the map are shabby sex hotels which may accept you for the night if you turn up in the evening. Avoid the sleazy Hotel Guayana.

Puerto Ordaz The main hotel area is in the centre, around Avenida Principal de Castillito. Supposedly the cheapest in town is the *Residencias Montecarlo*, at US$4 for a double, but it is full most of the time. The *Hotel Roma* (☎ 223780), next door, is a much more reliable choice and it is quite acceptable for its price – US$6 for a double. Round the corner, the *Residencias 101* offers a similar price and standard, as does the *Residencias Santa Cruz* in the same area. All the above double as love hotels.

A better double room, for around US$10, can be found at the *Hotel Habana Cuba* (☎ 224904) on Avenida Las Américas, or at the *Hotel Carlos* (☎ 225557) on Calle Urbana. For a few dollars more, you can stay in the really quite good *Hotel La Guayana* (☎ 227375) on Avenida Las Américas, the *Hotel Saint Georges* (☎ 220088) on Carrera Aripao, or, the best of the lot, the *Hotel Tepuy* (☎ 220120) on Carrera Upata.

The *Hotel Embajador* (☎ 225511), on the corner of Avenida Principal de Castillito and Calle Urbana, is a good and comfortable central place to stay, for US$25/30 a single/double.

Possibly the best in the city centre is the

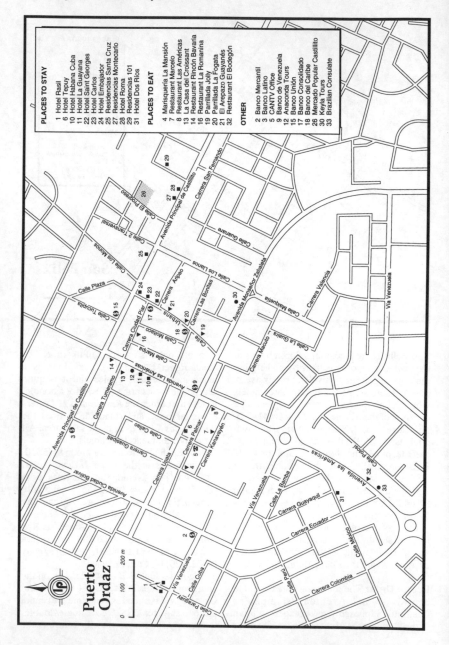

Puerto Ordaz

PLACES TO STAY
1 Hotel Rasil
6 Hotel Tepuy
10 Hotel Habana Cuba
11 Hotel La Guayana
22 Hotel Saint Georges
23 Hotel Carlos
24 Hotel Embajador
25 Residencias Santa Cruz
27 Residencias Montecarlo
28 Hotel Roma
29 Residencias 101
31 Hotel Dos Ríos

PLACES TO EAT
4 Marisquería La Mansión
7 Restaurant Marcelo
8 Restaurant Las Américas
13 La Casa del Croissant
14 Restaurant Rincón Bavaria
16 Restaurant La Romanina
19 Parrillada Jolly
20 Parrillada La Fogata
21 El Arepazo Guayanés
32 Restaurant El Bodegón

OTHER
2 Banco Mercantil
3 Banco Latino
5 CANTV Office
9 Banco de Venezuela
12 Anaconda Tours
15 Banco Unión
17 Banco Consolidado
18 Banco del Caribe
26 Mercado Popular Castillito
30 Keyla Tours
33 Brazilian Consulate

huge *Hotel Rasil* (☎ 222688), at US$40/44/48 for a single/double/triple. Its older section, in a smaller building on the other side of Calle Paraguay, is maybe half that price. The *Hotel Intercontinental Guayana* (☎ 222244) is the best hotel in town but it's out of the centre, on the bank of the Caroní River.

Hotel Dos Ríos (☎ 220679), on the corner of Calle México and Carrera Guayaquil, is a fair way from the centre and not worth the walk. It's unkempt and overpriced, at US$20/24 for a single/double.

Places to Eat
There are lots of restaurants in both San Félix and Puerto Ordaz and you can eat quite well if you wish. All the up-market establishments are in Puerto Ordaz and this is a much more pleasant area for dining. San Félix abounds in rather ordinary eateries and, like the hotels there, the food is no cheaper than in Puerto Ordaz – not worth a trip unless you happen to be staying there. On Sunday, many restaurants close, especially in Puerto Ordaz.

In Puerto Ordaz, the bottom end of the gastronomic scene is represented by the street stalls along Avenida Principal de Castillito and Calle Los Llanos, around the budget hotels area. There are several chicken outlets there, where half a chicken with yuca and salad can be bought for less than US$3 and makes a filling meal. You can also find cheap meals at the Mercado Popular Castillito, in the same area. *El Arepazo Guayanés*, on Calle Urbana, is a popular place serving arepas filled with everything from cheese to seafood, for US$1 each. Up the same street are two parrilladas, *La Fogata* and *Jolly*, with good Argentine-style steaks. *Las Américas*, on Avenida Las Américas, serves the same for a little less.

There are several restaurants on Carrera Ciudad Piar and its continuation, Carrera Tumeremo, of which *La Romanina* is possibly the best place for both Italian food and steaks. Opposite is the *Mario*, a cheaper Italian outfit but not as good as La Romanina. Just around the corner, on Avenida Las Américas, is a good German restaurant, *Rincón Bavaria*.

Carrera Upata and its surroundings is another area packed with restaurants. Just walk around and take your pick. For seafood, places worth a mention include *La Mansión* on Carrera Palmar and *El Bodegón* on Avenida Las Américas.

La Casa del Croissant, on Carrera Tumeremo, is a small café which is good for breakfast; it serves a variety of pastries plus delicious coffee.

Getting There & Away
Air The airport is at the western end of Puerto Ordaz, on the road to Ciudad Bolívar. Urban busetas don't call directly at the airport, but they pass by it within reasonable walking distance.

Aeropostal only has direct flights to Caracas (US$59, five flights daily) from where you can get connections to elsewhere in the country. Avensa has direct flights to Caracas (US$62), Barcelona (US$47) and Porlamar (US$44) with connections to other destinations.

Keep in mind that the city's airport appears in all national schedules as Puerto Ordaz, not Ciudad Guayana.

Bus The bus terminal is in San Félix, on Avenida Gumilla, about one km south of the centre. Plenty of local busetas pass by the terminal on their way between Puerto Ordaz and San Félix.

Buses to Ciudad Bolívar depart every 15 minutes or so (US$2, 1½ hours). There are regular departures to Caracas (US$13, 10 hours).

Four buses daily, with Transporte Mundial (Transmundial) and Línea Orinoco, go to Santa Elena de Uairén (US$10, nine to 12 hours); all these buses come through from Ciudad Bolívar. Expresos Maturín has buses travelling north to the coast, to Carúpano (US$7, 6½ hours) and Güiria (US$9.50, nine hours); these trips involve a ferry ride across the Orinoco from San Félix to Los Barrancos.

Buses to Tucupita are scarce, but por puestos go there regularly (US$4.50, 2½ hours). For Castillos de Guayana, take an urban buseta to El Mirador in San Félix, from where por puestos go to the forts (US$1.25).

If you are looking for a bus to Ciudad Guayana, look out for San Félix – this is how the city is listed in all bus schedules throughout the country.

CASTILLOS DE GUAYANA

About 38 km east of San Félix, two old forts sit on the hilly right bank of the Orinoco, overlooking the river. They were built to protect Santo Tomás, the first Spanish settlement founded on the riverbank in 1595.

The older fort, the **Castillo de San Francisco** (named after the monastery of San Francisco de Asís which stood on the site before the fort was built) dates from the 1670s. As pirate raids continued unabated, a second fort, the **Castillo de San Diego de Alcalá**, went up in 1747 on a nearby, higher hill. However, this didn't provide adequate protection either. The settlement was eventually moved upriver in 1762, and refounded two years later as Santo Tomás de la Guayana de Angostura (today Ciudad Bolívar). The forts were abandoned. At the end of the 19th century, the forts were remodelled and used to control the river traffic, which they did until 1943. In the 1970s, they were restored to their original condition and became tourist attractions. The higher fort commands excellent views over the Orinoco and beyond.

Getting There & Away

The forts are accessible by road from San Félix. Por puestos take you there from the place known as El Mirador, at the eastern end of San Félix, which can be reached by city buses. The ride to the forts costs US$1.25 and takes 1¼ hours.

Alternatively, take a tour. Several travel agencies (Anaconda Tours, amongst others) operate half-day tours to the Castillos, for around US$23 per person.

REPRESA DE GURI

Due south of Ciudad Guayana is a large lake, Embalse de Guri. This is the reservoir of the second largest hydroelectric project in the world (the recently completed Itaipú on the frontier of Brazil and Paraguay is the largest).

The Represa Raúl Leoni – as it is officially named, though commonly referred to as Represa de Guri (Guri Dam) – was built in the lower course of the Río Caroní, about 100 km upstream from its inlet into the Orinoco. The work was carried out in stages, from 1963 to 1986. Eight million cubic metres of concrete were used to build a gigantic 1304-metre-long dam, which is 162 metres high at its highest point. Covering an area of about 4250 sq km, the reservoir created by the dam is Venezuela's largest lake after Lago Maracaibo. It now abounds in fish, mainly *pavón* (peacock bass) and its equally ferocious cousin, the *payara*. The lake has become increasingly popular as a sport-fishing destination.

With a potential of 10 million kilowatts, the complex satisfies over half of the country's electricity demand. The Guri Dam provides power not only for the giant industrial plants of the region, but also supplies electricity to central Venezuela, Caracas included.

The dam and some of the installations can be visited. The Electrificación del Caroní (EDELCA), the state company which operates the dam, runs free tours, daily at 9 and 10.30 am and 2 and 3.30 pm.

From the visitors' centre, you are taken in their bus for a one-hour trip around the complex. Although they don't actually show you much of the installations, you do get to realise how enormous the project is.

The tour includes a stopover at a lookout, from where you get a good general view of the dam and of a large kinetic sculpture by Alejandro Otero. You are then shown one of the units of the powerhouse, embellished with a geometrical decoration by Carlos Cruz Díez. Finally they take you to the Plaza del Sol y la Luna, noted for a huge dial showing months, hours and minutes.

Places to Stay & Eat

There's a good *Hotel Guri* in the Guri compound, where a double room costs around US$30. The hotel has its own restaurant and a pool.

Getting There & Away

This is a bit complicated, as there's no public transport to the dam. The entrance to the complex is at the north-western end of the Embalse de Guri, about 78 km by road from Puerto Ordaz. The first 60 km of this route goes along the Ciudad Guayana-Ciudad Piar highway, and this portion can be done by bus – take the bus to Ciudad Piar from the San Félix bus terminal, and get off at 'desvío a Guri' (the Guri turn-off). From this point, you still have 18 km to the alcabala at the entrance to the Guri complex. No public buses go along this road but EDELCA vehicles run regularly to the dam (as do visitors in their cars) and someone is likely to give you a ride. At the alcabala, you will be given a permit; the visitors' centre is five km further inside the compound, so again you have to rely on someone's vehicle.

Tours to Guri Dam (usually combined with a visit to Cerro Bolívar) are available from a few travel agents in Ciudad Guayana. Expect to pay US$60 to US$80 for this tour.

CERRO BOLÍVAR

Jutting 600 metres out of the surrounding plains, some 100 km south of Ciudad Bolívar, Cerro Bolívar is a huge, oval, iron mountain, 11-km-long and three-km-wide. The mountain has intrigued explorers since the early days of the Spanish conquest. Around the mid-18th century, Capuchin missionaries set up the first forges here, but it actually was not until 1947 that US geologists confirmed the unusually high grade of the ore (up to 60% pure iron in some parts), which led the way for large-scale exploitation. Since then, the ore has been systematically stripped from the mountain by men and machines, and now the Cerro is terraced all around. The ore is then loaded onto rail cars and transported to the steel mill at Puerto Ordaz.

About 10 km south-west of the Cerro is Ciudad Piar, a town founded in the 1950s to provide the operational and administrative centre for the mining company (Ferrominera) and accommodation for the workers. Today, it's a town of 20,000 inhabitants. The Ferrominera administration building is at the western end of the town, at the entrance to the mine's restricted area. This is where you get a permit to visit the mine.

Getting There & Away

Ciudad Piar is accessible by buses from both Ciudad Bolívar (US$2, two hours) and Ciudad Guayana (US$2.50, 2½ hours).

If you fly from Ciudad Bolívar to Canaima (for Salto Angel), you'll get a bird's-eye view of the Cerro, as planes normally pass over it.

Salto Angel

Commonly known to the English-speaking world as Angel Falls, Salto Angel is the world's highest waterfall. Its total height is 979 metres, recorded by a National Geographic Society expedition after accurate measurements in 1949. It also has the world's greatest uninterrupted drop – 807 metres, which is 16 times the height of Niagara Falls. The waterfall has become Venezuela's No 1 promotional landmark, and you'll find its photo in just about every tourist brochure.

Salto Angel spills from the Auyantepui (meaning 'Mountain of the God of Evil' in the Pemón language), the largest (but not the highest) of the tepuis, with a surface of about 700 sq km. The waterfall drops from the tepui into what is known as Cañón del Diablo (Devil's Canyon).

The fall is not named, as one might expect, after a divine creature, but after an American bush pilot, Jimmie Angel (1899-1956), who landed on the boggy top of the tepui in 1937 in his four-seater airplane, in search of gold. The plane stuck in the marshy surface and Angel couldn't take off again. He, his wife and two companions walked through rough terrain to the edge of the plateau, then descended over a km of almost vertical cliff to return to civilisation after an 11-day odyssey.

Salto Angel is in the heart of Bolívar state, a distant wilderness, isolated from the

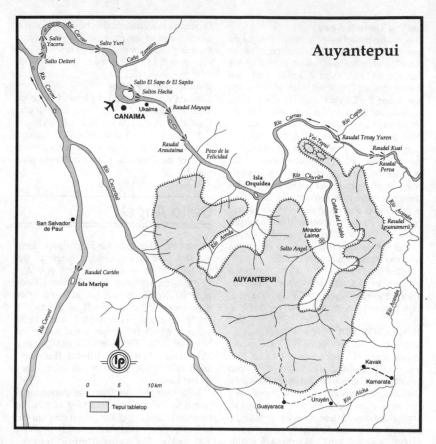

Auyantepui

Tepui tabletop

outside world. The village of Canaima, about 50 km north-west of Salto Angel, has become a gateway for the falls. Canaima doesn't have any overland link to the rest of the country (except for a couple of adventurous, seasonal trails) but it does have an airport, the region's only decent airport.

A visit to Salto Angel is normally undertaken in two stages, with Canaima as the stepping-stone. First you fly into Canaima, from where you take a light plane or boat (only in the rainy season) to the falls. No walking trails go all the way from Canaima to the falls.

CANAIMA

Originally a small Pemón Indian settlement, Canaima has become an important point on the tourist map after the Campamento Canaima, a large tourist resort, and the airport, capable of receiving large jets, were built here. Today, it's a village of some 1000 people.

Without a doubt, Canaima's location is spectacular. It sits on a peaceful, wide stretch of the Río Carrao, known as Laguna Canaima, just below the point where the river becomes a chain of seven magnificent falls, Saltos Hacha (in the dry period, there may only be three of them). The rose-coloured lagoon is bordered by a pink beach. The falls, too, have conspicuously coloured water, ranging from yellowish to brownish tones, which vaguely remind one of beer or tea. The colouring of these (as well as of other rivers and falls in the region) is caused by the *tanino*, or tannin, a solid compound found in some local trees and plants, especially in the Brommetia tree.

The Campamento is right on the bank of the romantic lagoon. The airport is a five-minute walk to the north-west. The Indian village stretches south of the Campamento.

Canaima is a hive of tour business activity, with half a dozen tour operators and their planes, boats and jeeps. They offer a range of excursions not only to Salto Angel but also to other nearby falls, Indian villages and whatever other interesting sights they have discovered in the area.

Information

Money Campamento Canaima changes cash dollars (but not travellers' cheques) at a rate which is about 3% lower than the bank rate. Some tour operators may accept payment for their services in US dollars. Tomás of Bernal Tours can (but not always) change your cheques at the same rate as what the Campamento pays for cash. In any case, it's best to come with a sufficient amount of bolívares.

When to Go The dry season normally lasts from December to April; rains tend to begin in late May or early June and continue well into September. They gradually ease in November and stop in December. Understandably, the season determines the volume of Salto Angel (and other waterfalls). At times in the dry season, it can be pretty faint – just a thin ribbon of water fading into mist halfway down its drop. In the rainy months, on the other hand, it's often voluminous and spectacular. The waterfall is at its most impressive after heavy rains, which occur frequently in August and September. Unfortunately, this is precisely the period when it is hardest to see, as it's often covered by clouds. In general, the best time of the day as

far as the waterfall's visibility is concerned is somewhere between 10 am and 1 pm.

The rainy season is certainly a better time to come to admire Salto Angel and other falls, though, of course, it's more risky. Canaima's peak season normally runs from July to September.

What to Bring Bring waterproof gear, swimsuit, insect repellent and plenty of film. A hat or other head protection from sun and rain is a wise idea. If you plan on boat excursions, make sure to have a plastic sheet or bag to protect your backpack. A tent or hammock (preferably with a mosquito net) will save you having to spend money at Canaima's hotels, while food brought from the outside will save you money on restaurants. Also, with your own camping equipment and food, you may be able to take a transport-only boat trip to Salto Angel, which is a considerable saving.

How to Plan the Trip If money is not a problem, the Avensa packages come in handy – they are a comfortable and easy solution. If, however, you want to cut the costs down as much as possible and at the same time get the most out of your trip, the following guidelines may be helpful.

The first thing to decide is whether to take the tour from Ciudad Bolívar or to go to Canaima and shop around there. Both options have pros and cons.

The cheapest way to get to Salto Angel is to take a no-frills one-day trip with one of the small airlines in Ciudad Bolívar (see 'Tours to Salto Angel' in the Ciudad Bolívar section). However, in the rainy season you may end up not seeing the waterfall. The airlines offering these trips are essentially commercial passenger carriers who fly people (mainly miners and their families) between the scattered towns and villages, on a more or less regular schedule.

Flying around Salto Angel is for them only a part of their activity, and not necessarily the major one. The pilots will fly you there, but according to their schedule, ie on the way to Canaima in the morning or on the way back to Ciudad Bolívar in the afternoon. If the waterfall happens to be visible you are lucky; if not, you've paid for nothing.

It's probably better, though more expensive, to fly to Canaima, and to arrange a flight over Salto Angel from there with local operators. The planes in Canaima are specifically there to fly over the waterfall, so they'll usually wait until the best chance of seeing the falls arrives.

This alternative also means that you can take a boat trip to the waterfall. This is a memorable experience – every bit as fascinating as the flight – which allows you to see the waterfall from a different perspective, and, more importantly, to enjoy it at a more leisurely pace. It's better to take a two-day trip (or at least 1½ days) than a one-day excursion. Note that Salto Angel faces east, so the best time to take photos of it is in the morning. To keep costs down, camping equipment would be a good idea, as well as food brought in from Ciudad Bolívar.

Tours Obviously, Salto Angel is the main attraction, and focus of tour operators. As there are no trails to the waterfall, you have two options – plane or boat.

Salto Angel by Plane Excursiones Canaima operate five-seater Cessnas which take tourists on a 45-minute flight over the waterfall. The pilots fly two or three times back and forth over the face of the falls, circle the top of the tepui and then return. If there are four or five people for the flight, the price is US$40 per person. Excursiones Canaima's planes can also be chartered for specific purposes (eg, filming which requires the removal of the plane's doors), and for flights to other destinations.

Servivensa, which flies the guests of Campamento Canaima to Salto Angel, uses 22-seater DC-3s. These planes – which probably remember WWII – have been remodelled by the enlarging the windows to provide better views. They can take you to the falls, if there are vacancies, for US$32 per person.

Various light planes which come to Canaima (mostly from Ciudad Bolívar) can sometimes be contracted for a flight to the falls.

Salto Angel by Boat Motorised canoes only operate in the rainy season, usually June to November, when the water level is sufficiently high. The boats depart from Ucaima, above Hacha Falls, and go up the Carrao and Churún rivers to Isla Ratoncito at the foot of Salto Angel. From there, you walk for one hour up to Mirador Laime, the outcrop in front of the falls.

The return trip can be done in one day, but it's better to go for two, to give yourself more time for seeing the falls.

All Canaima-based tour operators offer boat trips to the falls, with accommodation and food provided. A minimum of five to six persons is usually required (boats have a capacity of 10 passengers), but some operators may be satisfied with just four. Transport-only trips can also be arranged. See the following Tour Operators section for details.

Children below six years of age are not allowed to take part in boat excursions.

Tour Operators Following is a list of local tour operators and their prime destinations. All but Bernal Tours have desks at the airport and wait for incoming flights. The prices given below are the approximate costs of the tour per person, as advertised by the operators. Treat them as guidelines only, as the eventual price depends on a number of conditions and circumstances, and it is usually a matter of negotiation.

Canaima Tours
They are probably the most expensive operator and apparently the only one which won't negotiate a price. Their one-day boat trip to Salto Angel costs US$90, while a three-day trip goes for US$170 (all inclusive, minimum of six persons). They also offer a four-hour excursion to Salto El Sapo and Raudal Mayupa (US$25), and a three-hour trip to Salto Yuri (US$25).
Excursiones Churum Vená
Their one-day boat trip to Salto Angel costs US$75 (all inclusive), or US$55 (transport only). They are the only operator offering return trips to Kamarata by Río Carrao and Río Acanán, with a

Kamarata by Río Carrao and Río Acanán, with a side trip to Salto Angel, and to Cueva de Kavak (seven days, all inclusive, minimum of six persons, US$250). Their shorter excursions include Salto El Sapo (two hours, US$11), Salto Yuri and Isla Orquídea. They also run a hotel (see Places to Stay).

Tiuna Tours
Their 1½-day boat trip to Salto Angel can be bought for US$75, while a three-day excursion costs US$120 (all inclusive, minimum of six persons). Apparently they are the only operator which offers excursions to the south and west of Canaima, by the Cucurital and Caroní rivers, with visits to Indian settlements in the area; these are combined jeep/boat trips. They also have trips to Salto El Sapo (US$11, minimum of three persons).

Excursiones Canaima
Run by Hermanos Jiménez, their boat excursions to Salto Angel (all inclusive) cost: US$65 for one day, US$90 for two days, US$130 for three days. A 1½-day trip (transport only) is offered for US$45, with a minimum of four persons. Their short boat excursion include Raudal Mayupa (half day), Isla Orquídea (full day) and Salto Yuri (half day). They are the only operator (apart from Servivensa) offering air trips to Salto Angel (US$40, minimum of four persons). They also run a hotel (see Places to Stay).

Kamaracoto Tours
One of the cheapest operators, they can take you on a 1½-day trip to Salto Angel for US$45 (transport only), or for a three-day, all-inclusive tour for US$110. A number of shorter excursions can be arranged with them as well.

Bernal Tours
Run by Tomás Bernal Pérez from his home on the island (see Places to Stay), his three-day boat trip to Salto Angel is offered for US$140 (all inclusive) and other excursions can be arranged according to your interests. His prices seem to be largely negotiable.

Places to Stay & Eat

Canaima's main lodging/eating venue is the *Campamento Canaima*, operated by Hortuvensa (Hoteles y Turismo Avensa). The camp consists of about 100 palm-thatched cabañas, with comfortable rooms with bath and hot water. The camp has its own restaurant, bar and fuente de soda. The cabañas, scattered along the lagoon bank, are built in the typical local style; the restaurant is good and offers an excellent view over the Hacha Falls; the fuente de soda is right on the beach. The only nuisance is the price.

Hortuvensa only rents out their cabañas as part of a package. The package includes accommodation, full board, a short boat trip around the lagoon, a flight over Salto Angel in their DC-3 (weather permitting) and a complimentary drink on arrival. Two kinds of packages are available: a two-day/one-night stay for US$290, and a three-day/ two-night stay for US$570. Note that the packages don't include the flight into and out of Canaima, so keep US$100 in reserve (see Getting There & Away for figures). Also keep in mind that if you don't see the falls because of bad weather, Hortuvensa won't give you any money back; it's just your bad luck.

If you are interested anyway, packages can be bought from any Avensa office throughout the country, and from most travel agencies. The Hortuvensa main office is in Caracas, Torre El Chorro, Piso 13, Avenida Universidad, Esquina El Chorro (☎ 564-0098, fax 564-7936). In the peak season, book these packages in advance.

The camp's restaurant, bar and fuente de soda are open for non-guests but it's expensive: breakfast costs US$4, lunch – US$9 and dinner – US$11. On a more pleasant note, there's a large coffee maker in the restaurant and apparently the coffee is free.

Some potential travellers to Canaima are put off by the apparent monopoly of the camp. However, there are cheaper options for both accommodation and food.

Excursiones Churum Vená, a local tour operators, runs a six-room hotel, where a double room costs US$32, or they can set you up in one of their hammocks for US$6. If you have your own hammock, you can string it up under their roof (and use their facilities) for US$3. The hotel can provide meals (breakfast for US$3, lunch and dinner for US$6 either).

Excursiones Canaima, another local tour organiser, has also put up a small hotel. Offering slightly better standards, their prices are: US$28 per person in a double room, US$5 a hammock, US$4 breakfast, US$7 lunch or dinner.

Tomás of Bernal Tours lives on the island on Laguna Canaima, opposite the Campamento Canaima, in a dilapidated if charming house. He has several hammocks equipped with mosquito nets, which he rents out to guests for US$5. He can cook for you or you can use the kitchen if you have your food. Facilities are very simple, but there are some advantages in staying here. First, you save on the tour to Salto El Sapo and Salto El Sapito, as they are an easy 15-minute walk from Tomás's home. You have a good, pink beach in front of Saltos Hacha with an excellent view over the falls. And right next to the house is the tomb of Anatol (a Russian, the previous owner of the house), topped by an 'onion' typical of Russian Orthodox churches – which is an additional, if morbid attraction. Finally, you can escape from the other tourists, although this can be inconvenient if you want to arrange a flight to Salto Angel or another tour.

Tomás doesn't wait at the airport for incoming flights (as all other tour operators do), but you'll probably find him in the fuente de soda, his favourite place to sit over a bottle of beer. From there, he will take you in his boat to his home.

If you have your own tent, you can camp free in Canaima. Don't forget to get a permit to Canaima National Park from the Inparques office in Caracas (also available in Ciudad Bolívar). The usual place to camp is on the beach next to the Guardia Nacional post, a hundred metres beyond Campamento Canaima. You may be able to arrange with the Guardia to leave your stuff in the post while you are away.

There are a few shops in the village (two of which, Tienda Creaciones Karina and Kiosko Bony, are close to the church) and they sell basic supplies such as bread, canned fish, biscuits etc, but the prices are rather high. If you plan on self-catering, it's best to bring your own food with you to Canaima.

Other Excursions The most frequently visited waterfall in the area after Salto Angel is **Salto El Sapo**. You can't get to the falls on foot (as it's on the other side of the Río Carrao), so you'll have to take a boat excursion. It's a 10-minute (or less) boat trip plus a short walk.

Salto El Sapo is beautiful and unusual in that you can walk under it. Be prepared to get drenched by the waterfall in the rainy season, so take a swimsuit. A few-minutes' walk from El Sapo is **Salto El Sapito**, another attractive waterfall which is normally included in the same excursion.

On the small island between El Sapo and El Sapito is La Cueva (actually an overhanging rock), the previous 'home' of Tomás who lived here for 10 years, before he moved to Anatol's house. It was Tomás who traced the trail under Salto El Sapo.

Other popular destinations include **Salto Yuri** (a jeep plus boat trip), **Raudal Mayupa** and **Isla Orquídea**. Refer to the following section for further information.

Getting There & Away

Avensa has one flight a day on jets from Caracas (departing at 10.15 am) to Canaima (arriving at noon), via Ciudad Bolívar. If you buy either of their packages, they will sell you a discount ticket for US$80 return. Otherwise they will ask for their normal fare of US$75 one way (US$150 return). From Ciudad Bolívar, their official one-way fare to Canaima is US$45, but they may not want to sell tickets in advance if you don't buy the package (or more precisely, they can sell an open ticket without a confirmed OK booking), hoping to fill up their flights with the package passengers. These flights don't pass over Salto Angel; only occasionally pilots will make a detour to please the tourists, but it will just be a short glimpse.

Several small regional carriers fly from Ciudad Bolívar to Canaima on a semi-regular or charter basis. They can either fly you only as far as Canaima (US$35 one way) or they can include a flight over Salto Angel as a part of the ticket. Refer to 'Tours to Salto Angel' in the Ciudad Bolívar section for details.

KAMARATA

Kamarata is a Pemón village at the southeastern foot of Auyantepui. It's slowly beginning to be used by some of the more adventurous travellers as an alternative jumping-off point for Salto Angel. Boat trips to the waterfall can be arranged with locals, in the rainy season only. The boats go down the Acanán and Carrao rivers, then up the Churún to Isla Ratoncito. The prices of these trips are comparable to those out of Canaima.

Kamarata is also a starting point for a trip (or rather, an expedition) to the top of Auyantepui. Guides for this long hike (10 days at least) can be contracted in the village. The trail leads through Kavak (a two-hour walk) to Guayaraca, from where it approaches the foot of the tepui before snaking one km up, following roughly the same route Jimmie Angel used for his descent in 1937.

Both Kamarata and Kavak have airstrips where Aereotuy planes land once or twice a week from Ciudad Bolívar and Santa Elena de Uairén (about US$45 to/from either).

La Gran Sabana

A rolling grassy highland set in Venezuela's far south-eastern corner, La Gran Sabana is vast, wild, beautiful, empty and silent. In geographical terms, it's the upland region lying in the basin of the upper Caroní River at an elevation of over 800 metres. Its area is put at some 35,000 sq km. Correctly speaking, La Gran Sabana doesn't include the Kamarata Valley and the Sabanas of Urimán and Canaima.

The only town in the region is Santa Elena de Uairén (see that section), close to the Brazilian frontier. The remaining part of the sparse population, mostly Pemón Indians, the traditional inhabitants of this land, live in scattered villages and hamlets. It's estimated that there are about 15,000 Indians living in some 270 settlements.

Until recently, the Gran Sabana was virtually inaccessible by land. It wasn't until 1973 that an unsurfaced road between El Dorado and Santa Elena was completed, and it was not until 1990 that the last stretch of this road

was paved. Today, it's one of the best highways in the country, and one of the most spectacular. The entire length of the road is signposted with kilometre marks, telling you how far you are from El Dorado. The El Dorado fork is 'km 0' and Santa Elena is 'km 319'. These are a great help and are often included in tourist publications to help you determine the location of various sights.

Undoubtedly, the most striking natural feature of the Gran Sabana are the tepuis which dominate the skyline. Tepui (also spelled tepuy; plural, tepuyes) is the Pemón Indian word for 'mountain', and it has been adopted as the term to identify this specific type of mesa. There are over a hundred such plateaux. They dot the vast region from the Colombian border in the west up into Guyana and Brazil in the east. Their major concentration, though, is in the Gran Sabana.

The term 'tepui' is only used in the Pemón linguistic area, ie in the Gran Sabana and its neighbourhood. Elsewhere, the table mountains are called either cerros or montes.

Geologically, these sandstone mesas are the remnants of a thick layer of Pre-Cambrian sediments (some two billion years old) which gradually eroded leaving behind only the most resistant rock 'islands'. Effectively isolated over millions of years from each other and from the eroded lower level, the tops of tepuis saw the independent evolution of flora and fauna. Many species have preserved features of their remote ancestors, and outside tepuis can only be seen in fossilised remains.

Every tepui has a characteristic plant life, different from any of its neighbours. Scientific explorations show that roughly half of a total of some 2000 plant species found on top of the tepuis are endemic, that is, they grow only there. This is about the highest percentage of endemic flora found anywhere in the world. Yet, only a handful of tepuis have been researched, and there are still many virtually untouched by human foot.

The best-known of all the tepuis is Roraima, one of the few that can be climbed (see the respective section), although the trip will take at least five days.

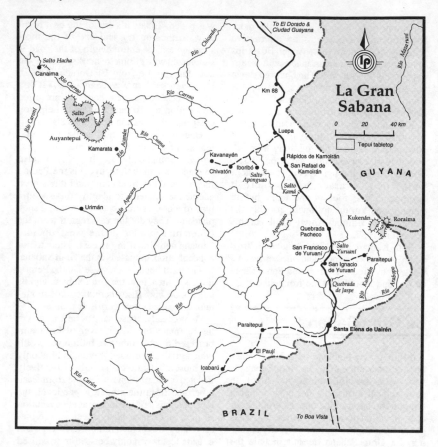

It's worth mentioning here another geological curiosity of south-eastern Venezuela (although outside the Gran Sabana): the simas. These are huge, holes in the forested highlands. They have vertical walls and flat bottoms – one might say they are a mirror image of tepuis. They were explored for the first time in 1974, and are unique. Only a few of them, so far, have been found, the largest of which is about 350 metres in diameter and 350 metres deep. They are all in the Parque Nacional Jaua-Sarisariñama, some 400 km west of La Gran Sabana. The region is only accessible by helicopter.

There are many other sights in La Gran Sabana that are easier to visit; some of them are conveniently located on the main road. Particularly amazing are the many waterfalls. A few of the best examples are detailed in the following sections.

Getting around the Sabana is not all that easy, as public transport only operates along the highway and it is infrequent (four buses a day in either direction). Given time, you can visit the sights on the main road by a combination of hitching and taking buses. Heading towards Kavanayén, however, may prove difficult, as there are no buses on this road and traffic is sporadic. A comfortable solution is a tour from Santa Elena (see that section for details).

Whichever way you choose to explore the region, bring plenty of good insect repellent. The Sabana is infested by a kind of a gnat known as *jején*, commonly (and justifiably) called *la plaga*, or the plague. They are ubiquitous and voracious, especially so in the morning and late afternoon. Their bites itch for days.

SALTO APONGUAO

Salto Aponguao, also known by its Indian name of Chinak-Merú (merú means 'waterfall' in the Pemón language), is one of the most impressive and photogenic waterfalls in the Gran Sabana. However, it's not all that easy to get to on one's own. The waterfall is off the highway, 30 km along an unpaved road towards Kavanayén plus another 10 km southward to the Indian hamlet of Iboribó. The villagers offer rustic lodging in hammocks in their huts, and can also cook you simple meals.

One of the locals will take you in a *curiara* (a dugout canoe) to the other side of the Río Aponguao (US$0.75 return per person), from where it's a half-hour walk to the Salto. You can also go all the way to the waterfall by boat (US$3 return per person if there's a minimum of four passengers). One more option is to go to the falls by boat and return on foot, but it won't be any cheaper than the return boat trip.

The Salto is about 105 metres high, and even in the driest season it's pretty spectacular. In the wet season, it can be a wall of water nearly 100 metres wide. There's a well-marked path leading downhill to the foot of the falls where you can bathe and swim in one of the natural pools. Here is the place to take pictures of the Salto; sunlight strikes the falls from mid-morning until early afternoon. There's an idyllic place for camping some 200 metres down from the falls with an excellent view of it.

Getting There & Away

See the Kavanayén section for information.

KAVANAYÉN

Lost in the middle of the Gran Sabana, some 60 km west of the highway along a rough road, is the Indian village of Kavanayén. Here is where the Capuchins established their mission half a century ago and erected a massive stone building for this purpose. They also must have taken good care of the locals: almost all houses in the village are well-built stone constructions – a striking contrast to the humble, thatched adobe dwellings you'll see elsewhere in the region.

Another curiosity of the village is its spectacular location. Set on the top of a small mesa, the village is surrounded by tepuis, and one can appreciate at least half a dozen of these mountains, including the unique cone-shaped Wei Tepui, or Mountain of the Sun.

A rough, dusty track leads from the village to the Karuai-Merú 20 km away, which is a fine waterfall at the base of Ptari Tepui. The road is so bad the trip may take up to 1½ hours. Otherwise, it's a five-hour walk each way; it's worth doing this trip for the fabulous scenery along the way.

Places to Stay & Eat

The mission will give you a bed for around US$2 in one of several dormitories. There's a restaurant in the village which serves unsophisticated but cheap and filling meals.

There are also accommodation facilities (US$20 for four persons) and food available in Chivatón, 17 km before Kavanayén. The place is frequently used by tours as an overnight stop, but for individual travellers it's not convenient.

Getting There & Away

The road leading to Kavanayén is almost traffic-free, so it may take a long time to hitch. Quicker options are either tours (but not all tours include Kavanayén in their routes) or taxis. The nearest place where you can be sure of hiring a taxi is Km 88. Count on roughly US$50 for a one-way trip to Kavanayén (up to four people) and US$60 to US$80 for the return journey, depending on how long you are going to spend in the village. In the wet season, not many taxi drivers are eager to go to Kavanayén, as the last 10-km stretch is tortuous, with all kinds of potholes, and sometimes the road is only passable with a 4WD. It's well worth including Salto Aponguao in the trip to Kavanayén, for some US$20 to US$30 more. Taxis from Km 88 to the waterfall and back (without visiting Kavanayén) shouldn't cost more than US$40 return.

If you plan on staying overnight in Kavanayén you will need to look for transport back to the main road. A few locals have jeeps and may take you back to Luepa for about US$40, or you can wait until a delivery truck appears.

SALTO KAMÁ
Salto Kamá, or Kamá-Merú, is a 50-metre-high, lovely waterfall, just 200 metres west of km 202. Don't miss a walk down the right (northern) bank to its base. For photographers, sunlight strikes the falls from mid-morning through to mid-afternoon.

Places to Stay & Eat
There's a small house beside the waterfall, where a bed costs US$4. Next to the house is a camping area, US$2 per tent, or you can pitch your tent anywhere else for free. Basic meals are served for around US$3.

At km 172, in Rápidos de Kamoirán, is a restaurant and a hotel, which is one of the favourite overnight stops for tours around the Gran Sabana.

Getting There & Away
If you're travelling on your own, just stay on the road and flag down anything that is heading in your direction. Keep an eye on the parked cars belonging to tourists visiting the falls.

QUEBRADA PACHECO
Also known as Arapán-Merú, this is a handsome multi-step cascade, just one hundred metres to the east of the road at km 237. It's much nicer up close than you'd think from looking at it from the road. The best light for photos is in the afternoon.

There are some tourist facilities, including lodging in hammocks in a typical hut (US$6 per person) and meals (US$3), or you can camp free nearby.

SALTO YURUANÍ
Ten km south of the Pacheco, at km 247, you pass over a bridge across the Yuruaní River. From the bridge you'll see the waterfall which is about one km to the east, with the Yuruaní Tepui in the background. The way to the falls is along the southern bank of the river. It's a wonderful mini-Niagara, about seven-metres-high and 100-metres-wide, with an amazing water colouration reminiscent of beer. The best sunlight strikes the falls in the afternoon. There's an excellent place for camping next to the falls but bring a lot of insect repellent: this waterfall is notorious for the jejenes.

RORAIMA
Straddling the borders of Venezuela, Guyana and Brazil, Roraima is one of the largest tepuis (about 280 sq km) and one of the highest (the mean altitude of this plateau is around 2700 metres and it peaks at 2810 metres). It was the first of the tepuis to be climbed, in 1884, and since then it has been much explored by botanists. Interestingly, although Roraima is a classic example of a tepui and it lies within the Pemón linguistic area, it is not called a 'tepui' but a 'monte' – nobody knows why.

Roraima is the easiest mountain to ascend, and increasingly popular with travellers. Perhaps 100 people trek to the top every month in the dry season, about 80% of whom are foreigners.

To start with, you need a minimum of five days, camping equipment and food. Be prepared for a hard walk and some discomfort, including plenty of rain and la plaga. Still you'll be rewarded by perhaps the most unusual and memorable experience, you are able to have in the country. The hike itself is fascinating and the top of the mesa is a dream.

The usual starting point for the trip is the small village of San Francisco de Yuruaní,

69 km north of Santa Elena on the main road. There's a small Hospedaje Minina in a white roadside house at the northern end of the village. A few basic eateries, including Restaurant Roraima at the central junction, will keep you going.

First you need to get to the hamlet of Paraitepui, the only gateway to Roraima, about 25 km east of San Francisco. You can either hire a jeep in San Francisco (US$50, regardless of the number of passengers, up to about 10), or you can walk. The road to Paraitepui branches off the highway one km south of the village. The unpaved but not bad road turns midway into a dusty 4WD track. It's a hot, steady seven-hour walk, mostly uphill, to Paraitepui (in reverse, back to San Francisco, it's six hours).

The road is not difficult to follow, except for one point (some five hours' walk from San Francisco), where it divides. The road which goes straight ahead leads to the hamlet of Chirimatá, while the Paraitepui road proper (which you should follow), branches off sharply to the right. Don't worry too much if you miss this turn-off; there's a path from Chirimatá to Paraitepui.

You may be lucky enough to hitch a jeep ride on this road, but the traffic is sporadic and drivers are likely to charge you for the ride (a far more reasonable fare than the jeep rental in San Francisco).

Paraitepui is a shabby, nondescript Indian village of about 270 people, which has largely lost its identity because of the tourists or, more precisely, because of the tourists' money. Heaps of empty beer cans at the entrance to the village show how the money is spent.

Upon arrival, you will invariably be greeted by one of the village headmen, who will show you the list of guides (apparently every adult male in the village is a guide) and inform you on their prices. Guides charge US$25 a day per group. Porters, should you need one, charge US$30 per day and can carry up to about 17 kg. Although you don't really need a guide to follow the track up to the tepui, the village headmen won't let you pass through without one. Since the village

has virtually monopolised access to Roraima, the prices of guides and porters may go up; don't be surprised if they are higher than listed above. Guides can also be hired in San Francisco, for around the same price.

There are no hotels in the village, but you can camp on the central square, near the school, in one of the two thatched shelters (US$2 per person). Overpriced hot meals are available in the house next to the school. A few shops in the village sell basic food (canned fish, biscuits, packet soups) at exorbitant prices.

Once you have your guide, you can set off for Roraima. The trip to the top takes two days (the total walking time is about 12 hours up and 10 hours down). There are several good places to camp (with water) on the way, so you have some flexibility in choosing where to stay, depending on how fast or slow you walk. The most popular camp sites are on the Río Tek (four hours from Paraitepui), on the Río Kukenán (30 minutes further on), and the so-called *campamento base* (base camp) at the foot of Roraima (three hours uphill from the Río Kukenán). The steep and tough four-hour ascent from the base camp to the top is the most spectacular part of the hike.

Once you reach the top, you walk for some 15 minutes to the place known as El Hotel, one of the few good sites for camping. It's actually a patch of sand large enough for, at most, four small tents, and it's partly protected by an overhanging rock. There's another, smaller 'hotel' 10 minutes' walk further on.

The scenery all around is a moonscape, evocative of science-fiction movies: impressive blackened rocks of every imaginable shape, gorges, creeks, pink beaches and gardens filled with flowering plants you will never have seen before. Frequent and constantly changing mists and fogs add mystery to the landscape.

It's here that the guide finally comes in handy, as it's very easy to get lost in this labyrinth. Plan on staying at least one full day on the top, but it's better to allow two or three days. Ask your guide to take you to the Pozo Azul, a curious, round pool in a deep rocky hole. It's about a three-hour walk one way from El Hotel. On the way, you'll pass the amazingly lush Valle Arabopo. Beyond the pool is the Valle de los Cristales and the Laberinto, both well worth a trip.

Recently, the Kukenán (also spelled Kukenam or Cuquenán), the neighbouring tepui to Roraima, has started to become a new challenge for trekkers. There's a trail to the top which branches off the Roraima path, past the Río Tek. Total walking time to the top is around four hours longer than what it takes to get to the top of Roraima, and the climbing is more difficult. A rope is necessary to lift up backpacks on one particularly steep portion of the climb.

When to Go
The dry season in the region runs from December to April, but the tops of the tepuis are affected by the Atlantic winds all year round, hence they are characterised by heavy rainfall and changeable weather. Bright sunshine or heavy rain are possible at any time.

What to Bring
A good tent, preferably with a flysheet, is a must. It gets bitterly cold at night on the top, so bring a good sleeping bag and warm clothes. You also need reliable raingear, sturdy shoes, a cooking stove, plus the usual hiking equipment. Bring enough food to share with your guide. Buy all food provisions in Ciudad Bolívar, Ciudad Guayana or Santa Elena depending on where you set off from. Don't count much on shopping in San Francisco, let alone in Paraitepui.

There's no plaga on the top, but you will have plenty of these nasty biting gnats on the way, so take an effective insect repellent. Don't forget a good supply of films. A macro lens is recommended for photographing the small plants. Make sure to bring along plastic bags, to take ALL your garbage back with you to civilisation.

Getting There & Away
San Francisco de Yuruaní is on the Ciudad Guayana-Santa Elena highway, and about four buses a day run in either direction. There are also por puestos between Santa Elena and San Francisco.

If you came from the north (Ciudad Bolívar or Ciudad Guayana) and plan on walking to Paraitepui, you may consider taking either of the two night buses which reach San Francisco at about 4.30 and 5.30 am, respectively. Ask the driver to set you down one km past the village, where the road to Paraitepui branches off. Start walking straight away (it's easy to follow the initial part of this road at night) to avoid having to walk in the heat of day.

QUEBRADA DE JASPE
Between San Francisco and Santa Elena, at km 273, is yet another Gran Sabana waterfall. This one is small and faint, but what is truly amazing is the intense orange-red colour of pure jasper rock over which the creek flows. The Quebrada is 200 metres to the east of the highway, hidden in a stretch of woodland.

SANTA ELENA DE UAIRÉN
Founded in 1922, Santa Elena began to develop in the 1930s when diamonds were discovered in the region of Icabarú, some 100 km to the west. However, isolated from the centre of the country by the lack of roads, it remained a small village. The second development push came with the opening of the highway from El Dorado.

Today, it's a pleasant, easy-going border town of 10,000 people, with an agreeable, if damp, climate, and a Brazilian air, thanks to the significant number of residents from over the frontier. The Carnaval here has a distinctly Brazilian feel, with samba rhythms and a parade of carrozas. Small as it is, Santa Elena is the 'capital' of the Gran Sabana and the biggest town before you reach El Dorado, 320 km to the north.

Information
Tourist Office There's no tourist office in town. Travel agencies are the place to go to if you need information about the region.

Money The only bank, Banco Guayana, changes neither cash nor travellers' cheques. Various establishments, including shops, travel agencies and hotels, may change cash (at a rate which is about 3% lower than the bank rate) and occasionally travellers' cheques (paying about 10% less). La Boutique Zapatería is one of the most reliable places to change both cash and cheques, and offers the best rate in town. The next best is, perhaps, Anaconda Tours. Gold and diamond buyers (look out for boards reading 'Compro Oro y Diamantes') might also be interested in buying some of your dollars but not cheques.

If you are heading north into Venezuela, keep in mind that the next place you may be able to change money is El Dorado, though it's better to count on banks in either Ciudad Guayana or Ciudad Bolívar.

Brazilian Consulate The consulate is at the north-eastern end of town, close to the bus terminal. It's open Monday to Friday from 8 am until noon. It's a good idea to get your visa elsewhere, as this consulate doesn't seem to be very efficient.

Immigration The DIEX office is behind the consulate and is open Monday to Friday from 8 am to noon and 2 to 5 pm, Saturday and Sunday 8 to 10 am and 2 to 4 pm. Be sure to have your passport stamped here before leaving or upon arrival in Venezuela. Brazilian passport formalities are done at the border itself.

Tours The tour business has developed a great deal in Santa Elena and there are already half a dozen tour operators with their own offices (see the map for location) and still more without an office but with jeeps. Their standard tour is a one or two-day trip around the Gran Sabana, with visits to the most interesting sights. They can bring you back to Santa Elena, or drop you on the road at the northernmost point of the tour, if you plan on continuing northwards. Count on roughly US$35 a day per person if you are in a group of four, and slightly less in a larger party. Shop around, as prices and routes vary, and you may find an agent who has already collected some tourists and can take some more.

Some operators offer tours to El Paují and the surrounding region, west of Santa Elena. Agents can also take you to Paraitepui, the starting point for the Roraima trek, for around US$90 for a trip (and will charge another US$90 if you want them to pick you up at a prearranged date and take you back). It works out cheaper to go by bus or por puesto to San Francisco, and hire a jeep there (US$50) or walk.

Places to Stay

There's no shortage of accommodation in Santa Elena, and it's easy to find a room, except perhaps mid-August when the town celebrates the feast of its patron saint. The town's water supply is problematic, so check whether your hotel has water tanks. Few hotels in Santa Elena have single rooms; obviously, you can be accommodated in a double room but you'll have to pay the double room price. All the hotels listed have rooms with fan and private bath.

The *Hotel José Gregorio*, next to the bus terminal, is one of the cheapest in town, US$7.50 a double, and has its own restaurant. A few paces further on is the more pleasant *Hotel La Nona*, at US$10 for a double.

In the town's central area, the bottom end of the price scale is represented by the *Hotel Luz* (single/double/triple for US$6.50/ 7.50/ 9), the more basic *Hotel Yarima* (the same price), and the good, clean *Hotel Las Tres Naciones* (double/triple for US$7.50/9).

Before you book into any of them, check out Alfonso Tours; the friendly couple who run it were going to open a mini-hospedaje and keep the prices lower than any other hotel. They are possibly the only tour operator that organises trips to the mines.

Hospedaje Turístico Uairén is simple but clean and pleasant, and costs US$7.50/10 for a single/double. The *Hotel Paraytepuy*, in the heart of the town, charges US$9 for a double, but it's perhaps better to stay in the *Hotel Victoria Plaza*, next door, for a dollar more.

Santa Elena de Uairén

0   100   200 m

To Airport, El Paují
& Boa Vista (Brazil)

To Caracas

PLACES TO STAY
5   Hotel José Gregorio
6   Hotel La Nona
8   Hotel Panayma
13 Hotel Victoria Plaza
14 Hotel Paraytepuy
20 Hospedaje Turístico Uairén
27 Hotel Yarima
28 Hotel Luz
29 Hotel Frontera
30 Hotel Las Tres Naciones
33 Hotel Lucerna

PLACES TO EAT
7   Restaurant El Miura
9   Restaurant La Estancia
10 Panadería La Tremenda
19 Restaurant Tropicalia
21 Panadería Santa Elena
22 Restaurant La Churuata
24 Restaurant Don Carleone
25 Tasca de Carlitos
26 Restaurant La Dorada

OTHER
1   DIEX Office
2   Brazilian Consulate
3   Petrol Station
4   Bus Terminal
11 Anaconda Tours
12 Happy Tour
15 La Boutique Zapatería
    (Money Exchange)
16 Adventure Tour Khasen
17 Banco Guayana
18 Ipostel Post Office
23 CANTV Office
31 Alfonso Tours
32 Tao Excursiones
34 Hospital

The best in town is the *Hotel Frontera*, noted for its attractive patio. Rooms are rather small but have TV; doubles go for US$14.

Places to Eat
La Churuata is an agreeable, open-air restaurant, one of the cheapest in town. At lunch time, they have a tasty, filling menú del día (a set meal consisting of a soup and a main course) for US$2.50 – come early, as it runs out fast. *La Dorada* is one place for cheap chicken; a quarter of chicken with rice and potatoes costs US$2.

Tasca de Carlitos and *Tropicalia* serve inexpensive Brazilian food. The latter also has cheap spaghetti. *Don Carleone* is yet another place with good food. They also have a choice of tempting tortas (cakes).

El Miura is more expensive but worth it. La Estancia just down the road is better.

Panadería Santa Elena opens at 6 am and is one place for an early breakfast, while *Panadería La Tremenda* has great coffee.

Getting There & Away
Air The airport is about five km south of town, off the road to the frontier. There's no

The only air connection is to Ciudad Bolívar, once daily by Aereotuy (US$60). This flight is on a light plane and calls at small towns (including Kamarata and Kavak which may be back door starting points for Angel Falls); the route varies from day to day. Anaconda Tours will book and sell tickets.

Bus The bus terminal is at the north-eastern end of town. There are four buses daily to Ciudad Bolívar (US$11.50, 11 to 14 hours), and one air-conditioned evening bus direct to Caracas (US$28.50, 16 hours). All these buses go via Ciudad Guayana.

Jeeps to El Paují depart early in the morning (US$7.50, three hours). Por puestos to San Francisco de Yuruaní run irregularly until the afternoon.

To/From Brazil There's one morning bus to Boa Vista, Brazil, scheduled at 8.30 am (US$13, five to six hours). The road is unpaved, so after heavy rains the trip may take longer. Arrive early at the bus terminal, buy your ticket, then go to the DIEX office a hundred metres away to get your exit stamp in your passport. Better still, go to the terminal the day before, and as soon as you have the bus ticket in hand (though it doesn't necessarily mean that the bus will depart as scheduled), go and get your exit stamp at DIEX. Be wary of fellow passengers and officials who board the bus. Thefts have been reported by travellers, particularly during the searches along the road.

The border, locally known as La Línea, is about 15 km south of Santa Elena. The bus calls in at the Brazilian border immigration post for passport formalities.

Amazonas

Venezuela's southernmost state, Amazonas, has an area of 175,000 sq km, or approximately a fifth of the national territory; yet, it has, at most, 1% of the country's population. Despite its name, most of the territory lies within the Orinoco drainage basin, while the Amazon basin takes up only the south-western portion of the state. The two basins are linked by the most unusual river, or more precisely channel, the Brazo Casiquiare, which sends a portion of the waters of the Orinoco to the Río Negro and down to the Amazon. The strangeness of the phenomenon consists in the fact that the route down to the Atlantic via the Amazon is over twice as long as that via the Orinoco.

The region is mainly thick tropical rainforest criss-crossed by rivers and sparsely populated by a mosaic of Indian groups. The total Indian population is estimated at 40,000, half of what it was in 1925. The three main Indian groups, Yanomami, Piaroa and Guajibo (Guahibo), make up about three-quarters of the whole indigenous population, while the remaining quarter is composed of Yekuana (Maquiritare), Curripaco, Guarekena, Piapoco, Baniva and a number of smaller communities. Approximately 20 Indian languages are used in the region.

In contrast to the central Amazon basin, the Venezuelan Amazonas is quite diverse topographically, its most noticeable feature being the tepuis. Though not as numerous and perhaps not as 'classical' as those in the Gran Sabana, they do give the green carpet of the land a distinctive and spectacular appearance.

The best known of the Amazonas tepuis is Cerro Autana, about 80 km south of Puerto Ayacucho. It is the sacred mountain of the Piaroa Indians, who consider it the birthplace of the universe. The tepui is reminiscent of a gigantic tree trunk which looms some 700 metres above the surrounding plains. There's a unique cave about 200 metres below its peak, which cuts right through the Cerro.

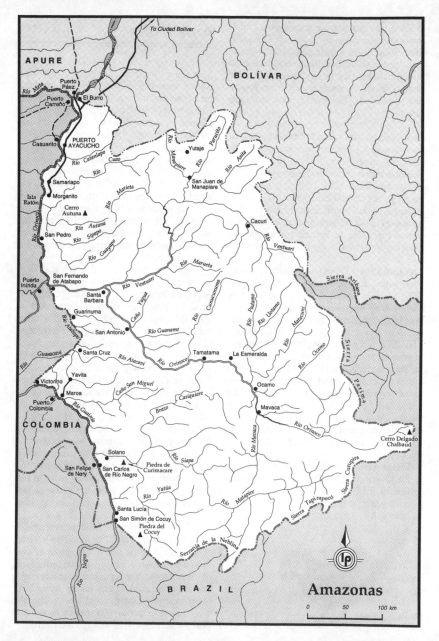

Amazonas

At the far southern end of the region, along the border with Brazil, is the Serranía de la Neblina, or Misty Mountain, hardly ever explored and virtually unknown. It's another tepui, but different to many others because it has a canyon running through its middle which is considered to be one of the world's deepest. It's also thought that La Neblina has the richest endemic plant life of any tepui. Finally, at 3014 metres, it's the tallest mesa, and the highest mountain on the continent east of the Andean chain.

Puerto Ayacucho, at the north-western tip of Amazonas, is the only town of significance, and it is the main gateway to and supply centre for the entire state. It's also the chief transport hub, from where a couple of small regional airlines fly in light planes to the major settlements in the region. As there are no roads, transport is by river or air. There's virtually no regular passenger boat service on any stretch of any river, which makes travel on one's own difficult, if not next to impossible. Tour operators in Puerto Ayacucho have swiftly filled this gap and can take you just about anywhere – at a price, of course.

The climate is not uniform throughout the region. At the northern edge, there's a distinct dry season which goes from December to April. April is the hottest month. The rest of the year is marked by frequent heavy rains. Going southwards, the dry season becomes shorter and not so dry, and eventually disappears. Accordingly, the southern part of the Amazonas is wet all year round.

PUERTO AYACUCHO

Set halfway along the Orinoco, Puerto Ayacucho is the only town of any size in the region and the capital of Amazonas. It was founded in 1924, together with another port, Samariapo, 63 km upriver; the two ports have been linked by road to each other, to bypass a stretch of the Orinoco which is unnavigable because of a series of rapids. The road served as an overland bridge to enable cargo to be shipped from the upper Amazonas down along the Orinoco.

For a long time, and particularly during the oil boom, Amazonas was a forgotten

territory and the two ports were little more than obscure villages. The link between them was the only paved road in the whole region; the only connection to the rest of the country was by rough track. Only in the late 1980s, when this track was surfaced, did Puerto Ayacucho start to grow dramatically, becoming a town of some 60,000 inhabitants. Paradoxically, its port, which was responsible for the town's birth and initial growth, has lost much of its importance, as most cargo is now trucked by road.

Puerto Ayacucho is the main gateway to the Venezuelan Amazon and has swiftly gained a reputation as a tourist centre. There's a range of hotels and restaurants, and several travel agents can take you up the Orinoco and its tributaries, deep into the jungle. Puerto Ayacucho is also a transit point on the way to Colombia and Brazil (see Getting There & Away in this section).

Information
Tourist Office The tourist office is in the Gobernación building, on Plaza Bolívar; the entrance is from Avenida Río Negro. The office is open Monday to Friday from 8 am to noon and 2 to 5.30 pm.

Inparques The office (☎ 21647) is in MARNR, Avenida Los Lirios, on the way to the airport.

Money Banco de Venezuela and Banco Unión change cash but not travellers' cheques. They both have daily limits on the amount of foreign currency they can change, so get there early. The latter gives cash advances to Visa card holders.

The Hotel Orinoco may change your dollars and travellers' cheques, apparently at any time of the day, at a rate 3% lower than that given by the banks.

Immigration The DIEX office, Avenida Aguerrevere, is open Monday to Friday from 8 am to noon and 2 to 6 pm, though it doesn't seem to keep strictly to these hours. Get your passport stamped here when leaving/entering Venezuela.

Tours The tour business has flourished over the past few years, and there are already more than half a dozen operators with their own offices, and a number of guides offering their services on the street. Tour agents have some standard tours, but most of them can structure a tour to suit your interests and time.

One of the most popular tours is a two to three-day trip up the Sipapo and Autana rivers to the foot of Cerro Autana. Expect to pay US$40 to US$60 per person a day, all inclusive.

A longer and more adventurous proposition is the so-called Ruta Humboldt, following the route of the grand explorer. The trip goes along the Orinoco, Casiquiare and Guainía up to Maroa. From there the boat is transported overland to Yavita, and you then return down the Atabapo and Orinoco back to Puerto Ayacucho. This is a fascinating trip but takes six to 10 days and is expensive.

Some guides operating from the street offer a trip to the Yanomami tribe in the far south-eastern part of the Amazonas. However, these excursions, theoretically at least, are to a restricted area requiring special permits.

Probably the best tour operator in town is Autana Aventura (☎ 21369), at Avenida Amazonas 91. Friendly and knowledgeable, they are not the cheapest but they are professional and responsible.

Tobogán Tours (☎ 21700), at Avenida Río Negro 44, was the first agency to open in Puerto Ayacucho. They now focus on easy, mostly one-day tours, though they can also organise something more adventurous on demand. Their prices are rather high.

Check Turismo Yutajé (☎ 21664), Monte Bello 31, to see what's on offer; they can even take you to Manaus. They run a hotel for those who take part in their tours.

Warely Expeditions (☎ 21445), on Avenida Aguerrevere, is one of the youngest and cheapest operators. So far, we haven't received any comments about their services.

The Campamento Calypso run by a Swiss is a countryside resort providing accommodation, food and a camping ground. They also organise tours and can, for example,

arrange helicopter flights over the Cerro Autana. The camp is outside the city and there's no public transport there; a taxi will take you there for US$5.

The Aguas Bravas (☎ 21541), on Avenida Orinoco, offers rafting over the Atures rapids. They run two trips a day (about three hours long), at US$30.

Things to See

Puerto Ayacucho is hot, but it is pleasantly shaded by luxuriant mango trees and has some interesting sights. The **Museo Etnológico**, on Avenida Río Negro, gives an insight into the culture of the main Indian groups of the region, including the Piaroa, Guajibo, Yekuana and Yanomami. It's a good selection with interesting background information, in Spanish only. The museum is open Tuesday to Friday from 8.30 to 11 am and 2.30 to 6 pm, Saturday from 9 am to noon and 3.30 to 7 pm, Sunday from 9 am to 1 pm. The entrance fee is US$0.50, half that price for students.

Right opposite the museum, the **Mercado Indígena** is held every Thursday and Friday morning (and sometimes Saturday and Sunday as well), and here you can see and buy Indian crafts made for tourists.

The **Cerro Perico**, just south-west of the town's centre, provides good views over the Orinoco and the town. Another hill, Cerro El Zamuro, commonly known as **El Mirador**, is 1.5 km south of the centre and overlooks the Raudales Atures, the spectacular rapids that block river navigation (the other rapids, the Raudales Maipures, are near Samariapo). Both are far more impressive in the rainy season, when the water level is high. The difference between the water level in the dry and rainy periods can surpass 15 metres.

There are some attractions around Puerto Ayacucho. The **Parque Tobogán de la Selva** is a large, steep, smooth rock with water running over it – a sort of natural toboggan. It's 30 km south of town along the Samariapo road and six km off to the east. There's no transport directly to the park. You can either take a por puesto to Samariapo, get off at the turn-off and walk the remaining

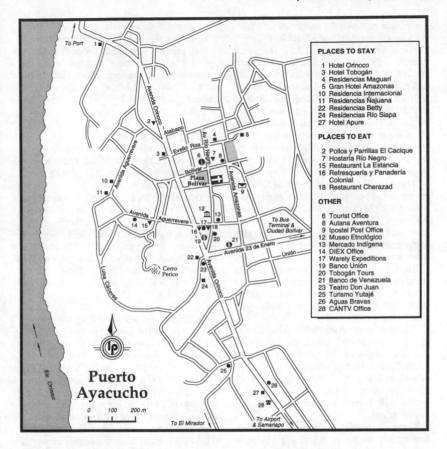

PLACES TO STAY

1 Hotel Orinoco
3 Hotel Tobogán
4 Residencias Maguarí
5 Gran Hotel Amazonas
10 Residencia Internacional
11 Residencias Ñajuana
22 Residencias Betty
24 Residencias Río Siapa
27 Hotel Apure

PLACES TO EAT

2 Pollos y Parrillas El Cacique
7 Hostaría Río Negro
15 Restaurant La Estancia
16 Refresquería y Panadería Colonial
18 Restaurant Cherazad

OTHER

6 Tourist Office
8 Autana Aventura
9 Ipostel Post Office
12 Museo Etnológico
13 Mercado Indígena
14 DIEX Office
17 Warely Expeditions
19 Banco Unión
20 Tobogán Tours
21 Banco de Venezuela
23 Teatro Don Juan
25 Turismo Yutajé
26 Aguas Bravas
28 CANTV Office

Puerto Ayacucho

0   100   200 m

To El Mirador

To Airport & Samariapo

distance, or negotiate a taxi in Puerto Ayacucho. At weekends, it's quite easy to hitch, as the rock is one of the favourite places of local people who, unfortunately, leave it increasingly littered.

Another popular weekend place among locals is the **Pozo Azul**, a small pond with a beautiful blue tint to its water. It's 30 km north of town, just off the road.

Less frequented by locals, but perhaps more interesting, is the **Cerro Pintado**, a large rock with pre-Columbian petroglyphs carved high above the ground in a virtually inaccessible place. The Cerro is 17 km south

of town and a few km off the main road to the left. Try to arrange the trip with someone who knows the place. The best time to see the carvings is either early in the morning or late in the afternoon.

Places to Stay

The town has a dozen hotels, some of which have already become popular with foreign travellers. All those listed have private baths, and fan or air-conditioning.

The best budget choice seems to be the *Residencia Internacional* (☎ 21242) which is at Avenida Aguerrevere 18. It's simple but clean, safe and friendly and costs US$5/6/8 for a single/matrimoniales/double.

For a similar price, you can stay in the more central *Residencias Maguarí* (☎ 21120), Calle Evelio Roa 35, but it's unkempt and not as good as the Internacional. Other inexpensive hotels (US$8 to US$10 for a double) include the *Residencias Ñajuana*, close to the Internacional (favourite place among bus drivers, so often full); the very small and simple *Residencias Betty*; and the better *Hotel Tobogán* (☎ 21320) on Avenida Orinoco.

The *Residencias Río Siapa* (☎ 21138) will give you the best value for your money. It is a good and pleasant place with friendly management. Rooms cost US$11/13/16 for matrimoniales/double/triple. There's no sign at the entrance, so when walking down the street keep your eyes open.

The *Gran Hotel Amazonas* (☎ 21155) was perhaps the best hotel in town when built but its good ol' days have passed. Singles/doubles/triples with noisy air-conditioning cost US$15/17/19.

The best places to stay in town include the *Hotel Orinoco* (☎ 21285), on the north-western fringes of the town near the port (US$25/32 a double/triple), and the brand-new *Hotel Apure* (☎ 21516), Avenida Orinoco 28, at the southern end of town (US$36 a double). Both have comfortable air-conditioned rooms.

There are several resort camps and cabañas outside the town, but unless you have your own transport, they are not convenient.

Places to Eat

A good number of the gastronomic establishments are located along Avenida Orinoco, the town's main thoroughfare. *Refresquería y Panadería Colonial*, on the corner of Avenida Orinoco and Avenida Aguerrevere, has good tortillas con jamón, though the service could be quicker. Probably the cheapest chicken in town is served in *Pollos y Parrillas El Cacique* in the market area on Avenida Orinoco.

La Estancia, on Avenida Aguerrevere, has possibly the best food in town and is not that expensive. Alternatively, try *Hostaría Río Negro*, Avenida Río Negro off Plaza Bolívar, which serves some Italian food. Yet another good choice is the *Cherazad*, near the museum, which has some Arab dishes in the menu. Close to El Mirador, in the southern suburb, is the *Montegrí*, which does good parrillas.

Getting There & Away

Air The airport is six km south-east of the town's centre; taxis cost US$4. There are two flights daily to Caracas (US$61); both go via San Fernando de Apure.

Two small local carriers, Aguaysa and Wayumi, operate flights within the Amazonas. There are daily flights to San Fernando de Atabapo (US$25), twice weekly flights to San Juan de Manapiare (US$35), and one flight a week (usually on Saturday) to San Carlos de Río Negro (US$55). Other, smaller localities are serviced irregularly, depending on the demand.

Bus The bus terminal is a long way east of the centre, on the outskirts of town. To get there, take the city bus from Avenida 23 de Enero or Avenida Orinoco.

Two buses run daily to Caracas via Caicara (US$18.50, 16 hours). Buses to Ciudad Bolívar depart regularly throughout the day (US$10.75, 10 hours). In the dry season, there are a few direct buses to San Fernando de Apure via Puerto Páez (US$10.25, eight hours), a couple of which continue on to Maracay and Valencia.

Carritos to Samariapo depart from Avenida Orinoco, next to Teatro Don Juan (US$1.75, 1½ hours).

Boat There are no passenger boat services down the Orinoco, and cargo boats are infrequent.

To/From Colombia The nearest Colombian town, Puerto Carreño, is at the confluence of the Meta and Orinoco rivers, and is accessible in two ways.

You can take a boat from the Puerto Ayacucho wharf (at the north-eastern end of

Top Left: Tabletop of Roraima
Top Right: Windcarved rocks, Roraima
Bottom: Jaguar

Endemic plants of Roraima

town) across the Orinoco to Casuarito, a Colombian village. The boat makes the crossing regularly. From Casuarito, the *voladora* (speed boat) departs at 4 pm to Puerto Carreño (US$6, one hour); in the opposite direction, the voladora leaves Puerto Carreño at 6 am.

Alternatively, get to El Burro (about 80 km north of Puerto Ayacucho) by bus, por puesto or by hitching. Take a ferry across the Orinoco to Puerto Páez. Get the exit stamp in your passport from DIEX, if you haven't done it in Puerto Ayacucho. Boats between Puerto Páez and Puerto Carreño run regularly between 6 am and 6 pm.

Puerto Carreño is a long, one-street town which has an airport, six or so hotels (*La Vorágine*, near the Venezuelan Consulate, is the best budget bet), and a number of places to eat. Go to the DAS office (Colombian immigration), one block west of the main square, to get the entry stamp in your passport. A number of shops will change bolívares over to pesos.

There are three flights per week to Bogotá (US$80). Buses operate only in the dry season, from mid-December to mid-March approximately. They depart once a week, on Saturday at 3 am, for the two-day journey along a rough road to Villavicencio (US$48). Villavicencio is four hours by bus from Bogotá.

To/From Brazil Take the Saturday flight from Puerto Ayacucho to San Carlos de Río Negro, from where irregular boats will take you to San Simón de Cocuy, on the frontier. Take a bus to São Gabriel (Brazil) and search there for cargo boats down the Río Negro to Manaus.

Glossary

For food and drink terms see the Food & Drink section in the Facts for the Visitor chapter.

abasto – grocery store.

acure – a hare-sized rodent, species of agouti.

AD – Acción Democrática, or Democratic Action Party; populist party, created in 1941 by Rómulo Betancourt and until recently one of the two leading political parties.

adeco – a member or follower of the Acción Democrática party.

adobe – sun-dried brick made of mud and straw, used in traditional rural constructions.

alcabala – a police checkpost on the road.

alcarabán – stone curlew, large shore birds.

andino – inhabitant of the Andes.

apamate – *Tabebuia rosea*, a large tree with pink flowers.

araguaney – *Tabebuia chrysantha*, the trumpet tree, a large tree with yellow flowers (Venezuela's national tree).

atarraya – a kind of traditional, circular fishing net, which is widely used on the coast and rivers.

ateneo – culture centre.

autopista – freeway.

baba – a species of small crocodile.

balneario – seaside or river bathing place with facilities.

Baré – also referred to as Bale, an Indian group living in southern Amazonas.

barrio – a low-income suburb.

bolo – informal, short term for bolívar (currency).

bonche – party (informal).

bongo – large dugout canoe; traditionally hand-hewn, today usually equipped with outboard motor.

boro – acuatic plant whose leaves look like small balloons; its flowers are mauve or white; capybaras' favourite dish.

broma – literally joke; a problem, or an object or entity that need not be precisely named (informal).

bucare – *Erythrina poeppigiana*, a large tree with red flowers; often provides shade to coffee or cacao plantations; its branches house orchids and bromeliads.

buhonero – street vendor.

buseta – small bus.

cabaña – cabin, found mostly on the coast or in the mountains.

cachicamo – armadillo.

caimán – American crocodile, similar to alligators but with a more heavily armoured belly.

caminata – trekking.

campesino – rural dweller, usually of modest economic means; a peasant.

canoa – a dugout canoe.

CANTV – state telephone company.

caño – channel.

carabobeño – inhabitant of Carabobo state, particularly Valencia.

Caracazo – the violent street riots of 27-29 February 1989 in Caracas, resulted in some 300 dead.

caraqueño – person born and/or residing in Caracas.

cardón – columnar type of cactus, typical of Península de Paraguaná.

cascabel – rattlesnake.

caserío – hamlet.

catire – a person of light complexion.

caudillo – term referring to military dictators governing Venezuela from 1830 to 1958.

Causa R – the Causa Radical, a left-wing political party founded by unionists in opposition to the traditional parties.

cédula - the national identity card

ceiba – a common tree of the tropics; can reach a huge size.

cogollos – the top ranks of two traditional political parties.

cola – literally 'tail'; also used in the sense of 'lift' as in *dar una cola* (to give a lift), *pedir una cola* (to ask for a lift); useful expressions when hitchhiking.

colibrí – hummingbird.

cónchale – informal tag word; used on its own or added to the beginning of a sentence to emphasise emotional involvement.

conuco – a cultivated piece of land.

coño – similar meaning to *cónchale* but stronger and can be rude (informal).

Copei – Partido Social Cristiano, or Social Christian Party, founded by Rafael Caldera in 1946 in opposition to the leftist AD party; initially conservative and catholic-oriented, since the 1970s it has gradually moved leftward to become the essentially populist party; for the last three decades, until the 1993 election, Copei and AD almost monopolised the popular vote.

copeyano – a member of the Copei party.

corrida – bullfight.

criollo – Creole, a person of European blood but born in the Americas.

cuadra – city block.

cuatro – a sort of small four-stringed guitar, used in *joropo* music.

cuñado – literally 'brother-in-law'; mate, friend (informal).

curiara – a small dugout canoe.

chalana – river ferry for people and often vehicles as well.

chaguaramo – popular term for royal palm.

chama/o – girl/boy; young person.

chapaletas – fins, flippers (rubber paddle-like devices used for swimming, snorkelling etc).

chévere – good, fine (informal).

chigüire – capybara.

chimó – tobacco tar used by people in the Amazon, the Andes and other regions. A ball of chimó is placed under the tongue or between the gum and cheek until it dissolves. A 'nicotine candy'.

chinchorro – a hammock woven of cotton threads or palm fibre like a fishing net; used by many Indian groups.

chiripa – a crawling insect; also used to describe a small newly born political party.

chirrinchi – alcoholic beverage made by Guajiro Indians.

churuata – a typical palm-thatched circular Indian hut.

danta – tapir.

denuncia – an official report/statement to the police.

DIEX – Dirección Nacional de Identificación y Extranjería (Venezuelan immigration authorities).

(El) Norte - popular term for the USA.

E'ñepá – see *Panare*.

esquina – street corner.

estacionamiento vigilado – guarded car park.

farmacia – pharmacy.

flamenco – flamingo.

flor de mayo – a species of orchid and Venezuela's national plant.

fortín – a small fort.

fósforos – matches.

frailejón – a species of plant typical of the *páramo*.

fuerte – fort.

fundo – country estate.

furruco – musical instrument consisting of a drum and a wooden stick piercing the drumhead; the sound is produced by simultaneously moving the stick up and down and striking the drumhead; used in popular music of some regions.

gaita – popular music played in Zulia state.

garza – heron.

gavilán – sparrow hawk.

gringo – any White foreigner, not only those from *El Norte*.

guacamayo – macaw.

guácharo – oilbird, a species of nocturnal bird living in caves.

Guajibo – or Guahibo (Hiwi in the native language); an Indian group living in parts of the Llanos and Amazonas along the frontier with Colombia.

Guajiro – often referred to by their native name of Wayú, Venezuela's most numerous Indian group, living in Zulia state (Venezuela) and Península de la Guajira (Colombia).

guarupa – jacaranda, a tall tropical tree with lavender-blue blossoms.

hacienda – a country estate, often of large size.
hato – large cattle ranch, typical of Los Llanos.
Hiwi – see Guajibo.
hospedaje – cheap hotel.

invierno – literally 'winter' but refers to the rainy season.
Ipostel – name of the state company operating a network of post offices.

jején – a species of small biting flies which infest the Gran Sabana and, to a lesser extent, some other regions.
jíbaro – drug dealer (informal).
joropo – typical music of Los Llanos, today widespread throughout the country; considered Venezuelan national rhythm.

lapa – a species of agouti, a rabbit-sized rodent whose brown skin is dotted with white spots.
lechero – literally a 'milk truck', but popularly used to describe any means of transport which is slow or stops a lot, eg a flight with several stopovers.
libre – taxi.
liqui liqui – Venezuelan national costume, typical of most of the Caribbean; a white or beige suit worn by men, usually accompanied by white hat and shoes.
loro – parrot.

llanero – a man of Los Llanos.
Llanos – literally plains; Venezuela's vast central region.

malandro – scoundrel, villain.
manatí – manatee; a cetaceous herbivore living in calm rivers; can reach five metres in length.
mapanare – a venomous snake common in Venezuela.
Maquiritare – see *Yekuana*.
maracas – gourd rattles; an indispensable accompanying instrument of the *joropo*.
maracucho – person from Maracaibo, often

extended to mean anyone from the Zulia state.
margariteño – person from the Isla de Margarita.
médanos – sand dunes near Coro.
merú – Pemón Indian word for waterfall.
mesonera/o – waitress, waiter.
mestizo – a person of mixed European-Indian blood.
mirador – lookout, viewpoint.
monedero – public telephone operated by coins.
mono – monkey.
moriche – a palm common in the Llanos and the Orinoco Delta; used by Warao Indians for construction, food, handicrafts etc.
morocho – person of dark complexion; usually a mix of Black and White ancestry.
morphos – large, electric-blue butterflies common in Venezuela.
morrocoy – tortoise, typical to the Llanos and Guayana.
mosquitero – mosquito net.
mulato – a person of mixed European-Black blood.
musiú – old-fashioned term for foreigner with strong accent; derived from the French 'monsieur'.

nevado – a snow-capped peak.

orquídea – orchid.
oso hormiguero – anteater.

palafito – a house built on stilts over the water; a typical Warao dwelling (Orinoco Delta), also found in Zulia state, especially in the Laguna de Sinamaica.
palos – drinks (informal).
pana – mate (informal).
Panare – known by their native-language name of *E'ñepá*, an Indian group living in Bolívar and Amazon states.
paño – small towel, the one you'll get in cheap hotels.
parada – bus stop.
páramo – highland moors above about 3300 metres, typical of Venezuela, Colombia and Ecuador.
parapente – paraglider.

pardo – mulatto; person of mixed European-African descent.

paují – a black bird which inhabits cloud-forest in the north and west of Venezuela.

pelícano – pelican.

Pemón – Indian group inhabiting La Gran Sabana and neighbouring areas.

peñero – open fishing boat made from wood.

pereza – sloth.

Piaroa – originally called Wóthuha, an Indian group living in Amazonas state.

por puesto – a popular means of transport, most often a shared taxi.

posada – a small, usually family-run hotel.

primo – literally 'cousin'; mate, brother (informal).

propina – tip.

Pumé – see *Yaruro*.

puri-puri – small biting flies, also called *jején* in some regions.

quinta – a house with a garden.

ranchería – Indian hamlet.

ranchos – shabby dwellings built of waste materials by the poor on public or private land around big cities; collectively referred to as shantytowns, particularly extensive in Caracas; they occur throughout South America, though in each country have different names, such as *tugurios* in Colombia, *favelas* in Brazil, *villas de miseria* in Argentina, *cantegriles* in Uruguay, *barriadas* in Peru and *callampas* in Chile.

raudal – rapids.

real – pronounced 'ree-al', an informal term for the bolívar (currency).

redoma – roundabout (circular road junction).

residencias – cheap hotel or, more often, apartment building.

rústico – jeep.

salinas – seaside saltpans or shallow lagoons used for the extraction of salt.

salsa – a type of Caribbean dance music of Cuban origin, evolved and matured in Puerto Rico from where it conquered the whole Caribbean basin and surrounding countries.

servicio ejecutivo – a modern, air-conditioned bus service.

shabono – a large circular house used by the Yanomami Indians.

SIDA – AIDS.

sifrino – yuppie (informal).

soroche – altitude sickness.

tapara – cup-like vessel made from a hollowed-out pumpkin cut in half, traditionally used in some rural areas for drinking, washing etc.

tarjetero – public telephone operated exclusively by phone cards.

tasca – a Spanish-style tavern which also serves food.

telenovela – soap opera.

tepui – also spelled tepuy, a flat-topped sandstone mountain with vertical flanks; derived from Pemón Indian word for mountain.

terminal de pasajeros – bus terminal.

tigre – jaguar.

tonina – fresh-water dolphin.

toros coleados – a form of rodeo practised in Los Llanos; the aim is for the horse-rider to bring down the bull by pulling the latter's tail.

trapiche – traditional sugarcane mill.

tucán – toucan.

turpial – the national bird.

urbanización – suburb.

vallenato – typical Colombian music, widespread in Venezuela's north-west.

vaquero – cowboy of the Llanos.

vená – Pemón Indian word for high waterfall.

verano – literally 'summer' but used in the sense of dry season.

Warao – Indian group living in the Orinoco Delta.

Wayú – see *Guajiro*.

Wóthuha – see *Piaroa*.

yagrumo – a tree with large palmate silver-coloured leaves.

Yanomami – Indian group living in the Venezuelan and Brazilian Amazon.

Yaruro – known by their native-language name of Pumé, an Indian group living in Apure state (Venezuela) and Arauca and Casanare states (Colombia).

Yekuana – also referred to as Maquiritare, an Indian group inhabiting parts of Amazonas and Bolívar states.

yoppo – hallucinogenic powder inhaled through the nostrils using a long pipe; used by Yanomami shamans.

zamuro – vulture.

Index

MAPS

TEXT

327

LONELY PLANET TV SERIES & VIDEOS

Lonely Planet travel guides have been brought to life on television screens around the world. Like our guides, the programmes are based on the joy of independent travel, and look honestly at some of the most exciting, picturesque and frustrating places in the world. Each show is presented by one of three travellers from Australia, England or the USA and combines an innovative mixture of video, Super-8 film, atmospheric soundscapes and original music.

Videos of each episode – containing additional footage not shown on television – are available from good book and video shops, but the availability of individual videos varies with regional screening schedules.

Video destinations include:
Alaska; Australia (Southeast); Brazil; Ecuador & the Galapagos Islands; Indonesia; Israel & the Sinai Desert; Japan; La Ruta Maya (Yucatan, Guatemala & Belize); Morocco; North India (Varanasi to the Himalaya); Pacific Islands; Vietnam; Zimbabwe, Botswana & Namibia.

Coming in 1996:
The Arctic (Norway & Finland); Baja California; Chile & Easter Island; China (Southeast); Costa Rica; East Africa (Tanzania & Zanzibar); Great Barrier Reef (Australia); Jamaica; Papua New Guinea; the Rockies (USA); Syria & Jordan; Turkey.

The Lonely Planet television series is produced by:
Pilot Productions
Duke of Sussex Studios
44 Uxbridge St
London W8 7TG
United Kingdom

Lonely Planet videos are distributed by:
IVN Communications Inc
2246 Camino Ramon, San Ramon
California 94583, USA

107 Power Road, Chiswick
London W4 5PL, UK

For further information on both the television series and the availability of individual videos please contact Lonely Planet.

PLANET TALK
Lonely Planet's FREE quarterly newsletter

We love hearing from you and think you'd like to hear from us.

When...is the right time to see reindeer in Finland?
Where...can you hear the best palm-wine music in Ghana?
How...do you get from Asunción to Areguá by steam train?
What...is the best way to see India?

For the answer to these and many other questions read PLANET TALK.

Every issue is packed with up-to-date travel news and advice including:

- *a letter from Lonely Planet founders Tony and Maureen Wheeler*
- *travel diary from a Lonely Planet author - find out what it's really like out on the road*
- *feature article on an important and topical travel issue*
- *a selection of recent letters from our readers*
- *the latest travel news from all over the world*
- *details on Lonely Planet's new and forthcoming releases*

To join our mailing list contact any Lonely Planet office.

Also available: Lonely Planet T-shirts. 100% heavyweight cotton (S, M, L, XL)

LONELY PLANET PUBLICATIONS
Australia: PO Box 617, Hawthorn 3122, Victoria
tel: (03) 9819 1877 fax: (03) 9819 6459 e-mail: talk2us@lonelyplanet.com.au

USA: Embarcadero West, 155 Filbert St, Suite 251, Oakland, CA 94607
tel: (510) 893 8555 TOLL FREE: 800 275-8555 fax: (510) 893 8563
e-mail: info@lonelyplanet.com

UK: 10 Barley Mow Passage, Chiswick, London W4 4PH
tel: (0181) 742 3161 fax: (0181) 742 2772 e-mail: 100413.3551@compuserve.com

France: 71 bis rue du Cardinal Lemoine – 75005 Paris
tel: 1 44 32 06 20 fax: 1 46 34 72 55 e-mail: 100560.415@compuserve.com

World Wide Web: http://www.lonelyplanet.com/

Guides to the Americas

Alaska – a travel survival kit
Jim DuFresne has travelled extensively through Alaska by foot, road, rail, barge and kayak, and tells how to make the most of one of the world's great wilderness areas.

Argentina, Uruguay & Paraguay – a travel survival kit
This guide gives independent travellers all the essential information on three of South America's lesser-known countries. Discover some of South America's most spectacular natural attractions in Argentina; friendly people and beautiful handicrafts in Paraguay; and Uruguay's wonderful beaches.

Backpacking in Alaska
This practical guide to hiking in Alaska has everything you need to know to safely experience the Alaskan wilderness on foot. It covers the most outstanding trails from Ketchikan in the Southeast to Fairbanks near the Arctic Circle – including half-day hikes, and challenging week-long treks.

Baja California – a travel survival kit
For centuries, Mexico's Baja peninsula – with its beautiful coastline, raucous border towns and crumbling Spanish missions – has been a land of escapes and escapades. This book describes how and where to escape in Baja.

Bolivia – a travel survival kit
From lonely villages in the Andes to ancient ruined cities and the spectacular city of La Paz, Bolivia is a magnificent blend of everything that inspires travellers. Discover safe and intriguing travel options in this comprehensive guide.

Brazil – a travel survival kit
From the mad passion of Carnival to the Amazon – home of the richest ecosystem on earth – Brazil is a country of mythical proportions. This guide has all the essential travel information.

Canada – a travel survival kit
This comprehensive guidebook has all the facts on the USA's huge neighbour – the Rocky Mountains, Niagara Falls, ultramodern Toronto, remote villages in Nova Scotia, and much more.

Central America on a shoestring
Practical information on travel in Belize, Guatemala, Costa Rica, Honduras, El Salvador, Nicaragua and Panama. A team of experienced Lonely Planet authors reveals the secrets of this culturally rich, geographically diverse and breathtakingly beautiful region.

Chile & Easter Island – a travel survival kit
Travel in Chile is easy and safe, with possibilities as varied as the countryside. This guide also gives detailed coverage of Chile's Pacific outpost, mysterious Easter Island.

Colombia – a travel survival kit
Colombia is a land of myths – from the ancient legends of El Dorado to the modern tales of Gabriel Garcia Marquez. The reality is beauty and violence, wealth and poverty, tradition and change. This guide shows how to travel independently and safely in this exotic country.

Costa Rica – a travel survival kit
Sun-drenched beaches, steamy jungles, smoking volcanoes, rugged mountains and dazzling birds and animals – Costa Rica has it all.

Eastern Caribbean – a travel survival kit
Powdery white sands, clear turquoise waters, lush jungle rainforest, balmy weather and a laid back pace, make the islands of the Eastern Caibbean an ideal destination for divers, hikers and sun-lovers. This guide will help you to decide which islands to visit to suit your interests and includes details on inter-island travel.

Ecuador & the Galápagos Islands – a travel survival kit
Ecuador offers a wide variety of travel experiences, from the high cordilleras to the Amazon plains – and 600 miles west, the fascinating Galápagos Islands. Everything you need to know about travelling around this enchanting country.

Guatemala, Belize & Yucatán: La Ruta Maya – a travel survival kit
Climb a volcano, explore the colourful highland villages or laze your time away on coral islands and Caribbean beaches. The lands of the Maya offer a fascinating journey into the past which will enhance appreciation of their dynamic contemporary cultures. An award winning guide to this exotic fregion.

Hawaii – a travel survival kit
Share in the delights of this island paradise – and avoid its high prices – both on and off the beaten track. Full details on Hawaii's best-known attractions, plus plenty of uncrowded sights and activities.

Honolulu – city guide
Honolulu offers an intriguing variety of attractions and experiences. Whatever your interests, this comprehensive guidebook is packed with insider tips and practical information.

Mexico – a travel survival kit
A unique blend of Indian and Spanish culture, fascinating history, and hospitable people, make Mexico a travellers' paradise.

Pacific Northwest USA – a travel survival kit
Explore the secrets of the Northwest with this indispensable guide – from island hopping through the San Juans and rafting the Snake River to hiking the Olympic Peninsula and discovering Seattle's best microbrews.

Peru – a travel survival kit
The lost city of Machu Picchu, the Andean altiplano and the magnificent Amazon rainforests are just some of Peru's many attractions. All the travel facts you'll need can be found in this comprehensive guide.

Rocky Mountain States USA – a travel survival kit
Whether you plan to ski Aspen, hike Yellowstone or hang out in sleepy ghost towns, this indispensable guide is full of down-to-earth advice for every budget.

South America on a shoestring
This practical guide provides concise information for budget travellers and covers South America from the Darien Gap to Tierra del Fuego.

Southwest USA – a travel survival kit
Raft through the Grand Canyon in Arizona, explore ancient ruins and modern pueblos of New Mexico and ski some of the world's best slopes in Utah. This guide leads you straight to the sights, salsa and saguaros of the American Southwest.

Trekking in the Patagonian Andes
The first detailed guide to this region gives complete information on 28 walks, and lists a number of other possibilities extending from the Araucanía and Lake District regions of Argentina and Chile to the remote icy tip of South America in Tierra del Fuego.

Also available:
Brazilian phrasebook, **Latin American Spanish** phrasebook, **Quechua** phrasebook and **USA** phrasebook.

Lonely Planet Guidebooks

Lonely Planet guidebooks cover every accessible part of Asia as well as Australia, the Pacific, South America, Africa, the Middle East, Europe and parts of North America. There are seven series: *travel survival kits*, covering a country for a range of budgets; *shoestring guides* with compact information for low-budget travel in a major region; *walking guides*; *city guides*, *phrasebooks, audio packs* and *travel atlases*.

EUROPE

Austria • Baltic States & Kaliningrad • Baltics States phrasebook • Britain • Central Europe on a shoestring • Central Europe phrasebook • Czech & Slovak Republics • Dublin city guide • Eastern Europe on a shoestring • Eastern Europe phrasebook • Finland • France • Greece • Greek phrasebook • Hungary • Iceland, Greenland & the Faroe Islands • Ireland • Italy • Mediterranean Europe on a shoestring • Mediterranean Europe phrasebook • Poland • Prague city guide • Russia, Ukraine & Belarus • Russian phrasebook • Scandinavian & Baltic Europe on a shoestring • Scandinavian Europe phrasebook • Slovenia • St Petersburg city guide • Switzerland • Trekking in Greece • Trekking in Spain • Vienna city guide • Western Europe on a shoestring • Western Europe phrasebook

NORTH AMERICA & MEXICO

Alaska • Backpacking in Alaska •

Baja California • Canada • Hawaii • Honolulu city guide • Los Angeles city guide • Mexico • Pacific Northwest USA • Rocky Mountain States • San Francisco city guide •

CENTRAL AMERICA & THE CARIBBEAN

Central America on a shoestring • Costa Rica • Eastern Caribbean • Guatemala, Belize & Yucatán: La Ruta Maya

SOUTH AMERICA

Argentina, Uruguay & Paraguay • Bolivia • Brazil • Brazilian phrasebook • Chile & Easter Island • Colombia • Ecuador & the Galápagos Islands • Latin American Spanish phrasebook • Peru • Quechua phrasebook • Rio de Janeiro city guide • South America on a shoestring • Trekking in the Patagonian Andes • Venezuela

AFRICA

Africa on a shoestring • Cape Town city guide • Central Africa • East Africa • Trekking in East Africa • Kenya • Swahili phrasebook • Morocco • Arabic (Moroccan) phrasebook • North Africa • South Africa, Lesotho & Swaziland • West Africa • Zimbabwe, Botswana & Namibia • Zimbabwe, Botswana & Namibia travel atlas